W9-BDN-106

MAKING CONNECTIONS: Foundations for Algebra
Course 2, Version 3.0

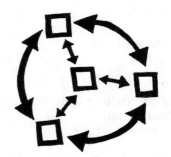

Managing Editors / Authors

Leslie Dietiker (Both Texts)
Michigan State University
East Lansing, MI

Evra Baldinger (Course 1)
Phillip and Sala Burton Academic High School
San Francisco, CA

Barbara Shreve (Course 2)
San Lorenzo High School
San Lorenzo, CA

Contributing Authors

Elizabeth Baker
Zane Middle School
Eureka, CA

Tara Bianchi
American Canyon Middle School
American Canyon, CA

Bev Brockhoff
Glen Edwards Middle School
Lincoln, CA

Mark Coté
Beaver Lake Middle School
Issaquah, WA

Suzanne Cisco Cox
Turner Middle School
Berthoud, CO

Kathleen Davies
Rincon Valley Middle School
Santa Rosa, CA

Josea Eggink
El Colegio Charter School
Minneapolis, MN

William Funkhouser
Zane Middle School
Eureka, CA

Brian Hoey
CPM Educational Program
Sacramento, CA

Janet Hollister
La Cumbre Jr. High School
Santa Barbara, CA

Carol Jancsi
CPM Mentor Teacher
Cardiff by the Sea, CA

Rakesh Khanna
Hotmath, Inc.
Berkeley, CA

Judy Kysh, Ph.D.
San Francisco State University
San Francisco, CA

Bruce Melhorn
Whatcom Middle School
Bellingham, WA

Chris Mikles
Post Falls Middle School
Post Falls, ID

Misty Nikula
Whatcom Day Academy
Bellingham, WA

Bob Petersen
CPM Educational Program
Sacramento, CA

Tom Sallee, Ph.D.
Department of Mathematics
University of California, Davis

Lorna Thomas Vázquez
Math Consultant
Neillsville, WI

Stephanie Whitney
Illinois Institute of Technology
Chicago, IL

Program Directors

Leslie Dietiker
Michigan State University
East Lansing, MI

Brian Hoey
CPM Educational Program
Sacramento, CA

Judy Kysh, Ph.D.
Departments of Education and Mathematics
San Francisco State University, CA

Tom Sallee, Ph.D.
Department of Mathematics
University of California, Davis

Puzzle Investigator Problems

Ethan Baldinger
Sonoma State University
Rohnert Park, CA

Susan Baskin
Math Consultant
Oakland, CA

Leslie Dietiker
Michigan State University
East Lansing, MI

Parent Guide

Brian Hoey
Sacramento, CA

Bob Petersen
Sacramento, CA

Extra Practice Materials

Bob Petersen
Sacramento, CA

Based on the Skill Builder materials created for Foundations for Algebra (2003), created by:

Heidi Ackley
Bev Brockhoff
Scott Coyner
Brian Hoey
Robert Petersen
Kristie Sallee

Steve Ackley
Ellen Cafferata
Sara Effenbeck
Judy Kysh
Edwin Reed
Tom Sallee

Elizabeth Baker
Elizabeth Coyner
William Funkhouser
Kris Petersen
Stacy Rocklein
Howard Webb

Assessment Manager

Karen Wootten
Director of Assessment
Odenton, MD

Assessment Assistants

Elizabeth Baker
Zane Middle School
Eureka, CA

William Funkhouser
Zane Middle School
Eureka, CA

Illustration

Jonathan Weast
Sacramento, CA

Cover Art

Kevin Coffey
San Francisco, CA

Technical Managers

Sarah Maile
Sacramento, CA

Aubrie Maze
Sebastopol, CA

Technical Assistants

Robert Ainsworth
Jason Cho
Matthew Donahue
Jerry Luo
Atlanta Parrott
Rachel Smith

Bethany Armstrong
Hannah Coyner
Bethany Firch
Eli Marable
Anna Poehlmann
Alex Yu

Rebecca Bobell
Carmen de la Cruz
Michael Li
James McCardle
John Ramos

1 2 3 4 5 6   16 15 14 13 12 11 10

Printed in the United States of America

Version 3.0

ISBN-13: 978-1-60328-040-2

A Note to Students:

Welcome to a new year of math! In this course, you will learn to use new models and methods to think about problems as well as solve them. You will be developing powerful mathematical tools and learning new ways of thinking about and investigating situations. You will be making connections, discovering relationships, figuring out what strategies can be used to solve problems, and explaining your thinking. Learning to think in these ways and communicate about your thinking is useful in mathematical contexts, other subjects in school, and situations outside the classroom. The mathematics you have learned in the past will be valuable for learning in this course, and will prepare you for future courses.

In meeting the challenges of this course, you will not be learning alone. You will cooperate with other students as a member of a study team. Being a part of a team means speaking up and interacting with other people. You will explain your ideas, listen to what others have to say, and ask questions if there is something you do not understand. In this course, a single problem can often be solved several ways. You will see problems in different ways than your teammates do. Each of you has something to contribute while you work on the lessons in this course.

Together, your team will complete problems and activities that will help you discover mathematical ideas and develop solution methods. Your teacher will support you as you work, but will not take away your opportunity to think and investigate for yourself. Each topic will be revisited many times and will connect to other topics. If something is not clear to you the first time you work on it, you will have more chances to build your understanding as the course continues.

Learning math this way has an advantage: as long as you actively participate, make sure everyone in your study team is involved, and ask good questions, you will find yourself understanding mathematics at a deeper level than ever before. By the end of this course, you will have a powerful set of mathematical tools to use to solve new problems. With your teammates you will meet mathematical challenges you would not have known how to approach before.

In addition to the support provided by your teacher and your study team, CPM has also created online resources to help you, including help with homework, a parent guide, and extra practice. You will find these resources and more at www.cpm.org.

We wish you well and are confident that you will enjoy this next year of learning!

Sincerely,

The CPM Team

Making Connections: Foundations for Algebra
Course 2
Student Edition
Version 3.0

Chapter 6 Graphing and Solving Equations

Chapter 7 Slopes and Rates of Change

Probability and Portions

CHAPTER 1   Probability and Portions

Welcome to math class! This chapter will introduce you to many of the big ideas that you will explore and the ways that you will work during this course. You will apply your current mathematical knowledge to solve problems, some of which you will solve again later in the course using new tools.

This chapter will also introduce you to the five Ways of Thinking that are threaded throughout this course. They are **generalizing** (finding ways to describe all members of a group), **reasoning and justifying** (explaining, verifying, and communicating your ideas), **reversing your thinking** (creating and solving problems "backwards and forward"), **choosing a strategy** (deciding what the most useful tools are for solving a problem), and **visualizing** (creating and using visual representations).

Guiding Questions

Think about these questions throughout this chapter:

How can I represent this?

How can I organize my work?

How can the number be rewritten?

Are the numbers equal?

Later in the chapter, you will focus on finding **probability**, a way of measuring the chance that something will happen. You will also look carefully at relationships between fractions, decimals, and percents to rewrite numbers in different forms and to compare them to each other.

In this chapter, you will learn new ways to:

> ➤ Find out how likely it is that a specific event will occur.

> ➤ Calculate the probabilities of two separate events to decide which is more likely to happen.

> ➤ Rewrite numbers in different forms in order to compare them.

> ➤ Determine whether a fraction can be rewritten as a repeating decimal.

Chapter Outline

Section 1.1   This section will introduce you to many of the big ideas of the course. Each problem will require your study team to work together using several problem solving strategies and the five Ways of Thinking.

Section 1.2   You will learn to find the probability of a specific event. You will learn strategies for rewriting portions as fractions, decimals, or percents and for adding and subtracting portions.

Section 1.3   In this section, you will look at numbers represented as fractions and as decimals, and will investigate the question, "What makes some decimals repeat?"

1.1.1 What do they have in common?

· ·

Finding Shared and Unique Characteristics

Have you ever tried to learn how to play a new game just by watching others play it? Chances are you were watching for patterns in the game such as what each player did to earn points or what actions earned penalties. If you were watching a game of soccer, you might figure out that kicking the ball into the goal earned the team a point. You might also notice that the goalie is the only player allowed to use his or her hands on the field. Describing those patterns could help you describe some of the rules of the game. This type of observation is also called **generalizing**. When you make an observation about what a set of objects or actions have in common, like the actions that will *always* allow you to score a point, you are making a **generalization**.

Today you will be working in a team with the goal of making **generalizations** about characteristics of various sets of objects. As you work, keep the following questions in mind:

What do the items have in common?

What makes the items different?

What are other characteristics that could describe the groups or sets?

1-1.   MATH STARS

What do you have in common with your teammates? What makes you unique? Today you will work with your teammates to discover some characteristics that you share and some that make each person in your team different.

Your task: Get a copy of the Lesson 1.1.1A Resource Page and scissors. Fold the resource page along the dotted lines and then cut along the solid lines. Unfold the cutout and glue it onto a piece of paper. Write each team member's name on a star.

- As a team, brainstorm something that all of you have in common that the rest of the class does not already know.

- List your team's common attribute on the paper in the center of the four stars.

- Find ways that each person in the team is unique from the others (things that are true about that person only), and write those things on the individual's star.

To help you work together today, each team member has a specific job, assigned by your first name (or by your last name if two individuals have the same first name).

Team Roles

Resource Manager: If your first name comes first alphabetically:

- Make sure your team has a Lesson 1.1.1A Resource Page, scissors, a glue stick, and colored paper.

- Ask the teacher when the *entire* team has a question. *"No one has an idea? Should I ask the teacher?"*

- Make sure your team cleans up by delegating tasks. You could say, *"I will put away the _____ while you _____ ."*

Facilitator: If your first name comes second alphabetically:

- Start the team's discussion of similarities and differences by asking, *"What might we have in common?"*

- Keep everyone discussing each part together by asking questions such as,
  "Does anyone have ideas for what makes us each unique (different)?" and *"What else might we have in common?"*

Recorder/Reporter: If your first name comes third alphabetically:

- When your team is called on, share your team's ideas and **reasons** with the class.

- Help the team agree on an idea: *"Do we agree that this would not be obvious to the rest of the class?"*

Task Manager: If your first name comes fourth alphabetically:

- Remind the team to stay on task and not to talk to students in other teams. You can suggest, *"Let's move on to the next part of the problem."*

  Listen for **reasons** and ask your teammates to **justify** their thinking. *"Why do you think that?"* or *"Would this be obvious to the rest of the class?"*

1-2.   WHAT DO THEY HAVE IN COMMON?

In mathematics it is sometimes useful to make **general** statements about sets of objects. In this problem you will be given a set of cards with mathematical objects on them. With your team:

- Determine what each set has in common.

- Record what is written on the cards on your paper.

- Add two new examples that would belong in the set on your paper.

- Describe in words what it is they have in common.

When you are finished with a set of cards, call the teacher to your team. Explain your **generalization** to the teacher and get another set of cards.

1-3.   **Mathography:** A mathography is a lot like your life history, except that it is focused on the mathematics in your life.

   a.   Write a letter about yourself to your teacher. The letter will help your teacher get to know you as an individual. The letter should talk about these three general topics: you, you as a student, and you as a math student.

   Remember to use complete sentences and make sure that it is neat enough to be read easily. Start the letter with "Dear...." Make sure you sign your letter. This assignment should take 15 to 20 minutes to complete. Parts (b), (c), and (d) have suggestions for what to write about each of the three topics.

   b.   **You:** Introduce yourself using the name you like to be called. Describe your hobbies, talents, and interests. State your goals or dreams. What are you proud of? What else would you like to share?

Problem continues on next page. →

1-3.   Problem continued from previous page.

    c.   **You as a Student:** State the importance of school in your life. Describe yourself as a student. What kinds of classroom activities do you do best? What kinds of activities do you find frustrating? Explain which subject(s) is/are your favorites. Tell why you like it (them). How often do you finish in-class assignments? How faithfully do you do your homework?

    d.   **You as a Math Student:** Describe your most memorable moment in math and explain why you remember it. State your favorite math topic. Name your least favorite. Explain how you feel about math this year.

1-4.   Decide what the shapes below have in common. Write your answer in a complete sentence. Then draw two more shapes that belong to the same set.

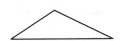

1-5.   According to the diagrams below, how long is each unknown piece?

a.

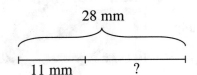

b.

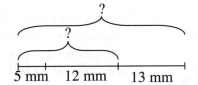

Making Connections: Course 2

1.1.2 How does it change?

· ·

Perimeter and Area Relationships

Many ancient cities were constructed inside great walls in order to protect and defend the city. The city of Carcassonne, France, still exists and has a double wall around it. The length of the inner wall around the city measures about 1245 meters and the land inside the walls is approximately 105,400 square meters.

When measuring shapes it is sometimes important to look at the space the shape covers, while other times it can be important to look at the length of the boundary around a shape. In this lesson you will be using toothpicks and tiles to measure attributes of various shapes, and to complete a challenge with your team. For example, when describing the shape above there are several things you could say, including, *"There are 11 tiles,"* *"It takes 14 toothpicks to surround the shape,"* or *"It takes three more toothpicks to surround the figure than tiles to fill it."*

1-6.   TOOTHPICKS AND TILES

Cruz, Sophia, and Savanna are using toothpicks and tiles to describe the attributes of the shapes below. Cruz made a pattern and gave the girls the number of tiles, and Sophia and Savanna each tried to be the first to see who could call out how many toothpicks, or units of length, were on the outside.

a.   Cruz made the tile pattern shown at right and said, "There are six tiles." Savanna quickly said, "There are ten toothpicks." Copy the tile pattern on your paper and show where Savanna counted the 10 toothpicks. **Justify** your answer with words, numbers, or pictures.

b.   Cruz put down the pattern as shown at right, but he ran out of toothpicks. How would you describe this shape using toothpicks and tiles?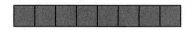

c.   Get a set of tiles from your teacher and work with your team to:

   • Make a pattern so that there are four more toothpicks than tiles.

   • Draw your tile pattern on your paper

   • Label the number of toothpicks and tiles on your drawing.

   Is there more than one answer?

1-7.   When you are working with your team to solve "Toothpicks and Tiles" puzzles, as well as other problems in this course, it will be important to work effectively with other people. Effective math conversations are a valuable part of the learning process throughout this course. Choose a member of your team to read aloud these Collaborative Learning Expectations:

COLLABORATIVE LEARNING EXPECTATIONS

Working with other students allows you to develop new ways of thinking about mathematics, helps you learn to communicate about math, and helps you understand ideas better by having to explain your thinking to others. The following expectations will help you get the most out of working together.

T   Together, work to answer questions.

E   Explain and give **reasons**.

A   Ask questions and share ideas.

M   Members of your team are your first resource.

S   Smarter together than apart.

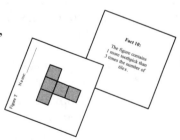

1-8.   TEAM CHALLENGE: TOOTHPICKS AND TILES

Today you and your team members will work together to participate in the "Toothpicks and Tiles" challenge. You each will have one card that shows a tile shape and there will be a fifth card to share as a team. Any extra cards should go in the center of your workspace so that everyone can see them.

Your task: As a team, do the following:

- Each team member should write his or her name on one of the shape cards.

- Place any extra shape cards and all of the fact cards face up in the middle of the table so that everyone can see them.

- Work together to match each tile shape with one fact statement so that each fact has *only one* shape and each shape has *only one* fact.

- If you want to change the shape that matches a fact card, you *must* convince the person whose name is on the card of the shape you want to change. He or she is the only person who can touch that shape card.

- Once everyone in your team is convinced that each fact is paired with one shape, call your teacher over. Be prepared to **justify** your choices!

Making Connections: Course 2

1-9. Does changing the number of toothpicks always change the number of tiles? Think about this question as you look at the following tile shape.

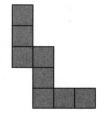

a. Write a fact statement that includes information about the number of tiles and toothpicks that would describe the tile shape at right.

b. How can you add a tile to the shape in part (a) but not change the number of toothpicks? **Justify** your response.

1-10. The **perimeter** of a design is the length of the boundary around the outside of the design (the toothpicks). The number of squares needed to fill the design (the tiles) is called the **area**.

a. Use these words to write a fact statement with your team describing the toothpicks and tiles in the tile pattern at right.

b. For your fact statement in part (a), build and draw a different shape that could also be described by the fact. Label the figure with the area (tiles) and perimeter (toothpicks).

METHODS AND MEANINGS

Perimeter and Area

The **perimeter** of a shape is the total length of the boundary (around the shape) that encloses the interior (inside) region on a flat surface. In the game, "Toothpicks and Tiles," the number of tile side lengths (toothpicks) is the same as the **perimeter** of the shape. See the examples at right.

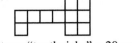

Perimeter = "toothpicks" = 20 units

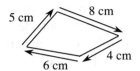

Perimeter = 5 + 8 + 4 + 6 + = 23 cm

The **area** is a measure of the number of square units needed to cover a region on a flat surface. In the game, the **area** is equal to the number of "tiles" in the shape.

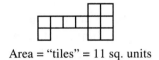

Area = "tiles" = 11 sq. units

A **rectangle** is a quadrilateral (four sides) with four right angles. The opposite sides are equal in length. Two sides that come together (meet) at a right angle are referred to as the length and width or base and height. The area of a rectangle is found by multiplying the lengths of the base and height.

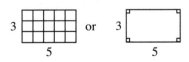

Area = $5 \cdot 3 = 15$ square units

1-11.   Janelle wants to challenge you to a "Toothpick and Tiles" game (described in problem 1-8). Using exactly four tiles, solve her challenges below. **Justify** your answers with pictures and labels.

   a.   Find a tile pattern where the number of toothpicks is exactly double the number of tiles.

   b.   Find a tile pattern where the number of toothpicks is more than double the number of tiles.

1-12.   In this lesson, you looked at the number of tiles and number of toothpicks used to form shapes made of square tiles as you played the "Toothpick and Tiles" game. The math words that also describe the number of tiles and toothpicks are *area* and *perimeter*. Read the Math Notes box for this lesson to review how area and perimeter are related to tiles and toothpicks, then answer the questions below.

   a.   Find the area and perimeter of the figure at right.

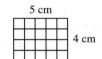

   b.   Find the area and perimeter of the rectangle below right.

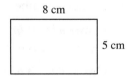

   c.   Now design your own shape with 5 square tiles. Record the perimeter and the area.

1-13.   How long is the unknown piece?

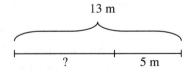

1-14.   Copy the number line below onto your paper. Place a point on the number line and label the point for each of the following numbers: −4 , 3, 0.5, −3.5, 0, 1, −2, 5.

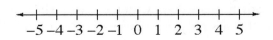

1.1.3 What is my number?

Finding Unknowns

Today you will think about how to find a mystery number based on information given to you as part of a game. You will practice mental math computations and investigate ways to represent the situation as you try to solve the problem. When you solve these puzzles, you might need to **reverse your thinking**. **Reversing** is an important way of thinking mathematically. It means solving problems both backwards and forwards. As you work with your team, ask the following questions:

How can I represent it?

What is the best approach for this problem?

Have I found all of the answers?

1-15.   GUESS MY NUMBER

Today you will play the "Guess My Number" game. You will need a pencil and a piece of paper. Your teacher has thought of a number and will tell you some information about it. Your task is to figure out what your teacher's number is. (You can use your paper if it helps.) Then explain why you think it is the mystery number.

Game #1: *When I triple my number and add five, I get eleven. What is my number?*

Game #2: *When I add two to my number and then multiply it by five, I get thirty. What is my number?*

Game #3: *When I take half of my number and add two, I get twenty-four. What is my number?*

Game #4: *When I double my number and add eight I get my number plus twelve. What is my number?*

Game #5: *When I double my number, add four, and then subtract my number and subtract three, I get my number plus one. What is my number?*

1-16.   Make up your own Guess My Number games with your team and be ready to share them with the class. Make at least one game that has only one answer and one that works for all numbers. Can you create a game that works for no numbers?

METHODS AND MEANINGS

Mean

To understand a set of data, you often need to be able to describe the approximate "center" of that data. One way to do this is to find the **mean** of the data set, which is also called the **arithmetic average**.

To find the mean of a set of data, add the values of the data elements (numbers) and then divide by the number of items of data. The mean is a useful way to describe the data when the set of data does not contain **outliers**, that is, numbers that are much smaller or much larger than most of the other data in the set.

Suppose the following data set represents the number of home runs hit by the best seven players on a major league baseball team:

16, 26, 21, 9, 13, 15, and 9.

The mean is $\frac{16+26+21+9+13+15+9}{7} = \frac{109}{7} \approx 15.57$.

This number shows that a typical player among the best seven home run hitters on the team hits about 15 or 16 home runs each season.

1-17.   Thu wants to play "Guess My Number." She states, *"When I triple my number and add 5, I get 26. What is my number?"* What is her number? Show how you know.

1-18.   One of the subjects that you will study in this course is how to describe a set of data. One of the ways that you may have seen before is finding an **average** (also called a **mean**). Review what an average is, as well as how to find it, in the Math Notes box for this lesson. Then find the average (mean) for each set of data below.

   a.   Jane's quiz scores: 82, 64, 73, 91, 85

   b.   The number of cats your teammates have as pets: 0, 1, 3, 2

   c.   The number of minutes Pam talked on the phone: 35, 40, 12, 16, 25, 10

1-19.   Find the perimeter of each polygon below. Note that the markings on part (e) show that all sides are the same length. Show your work.

a.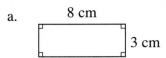

8 cm

3 cm

b.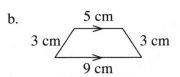

5 cm

3 cm   3 cm

9 cm

c.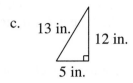

13 in.

12 in.

5 in.

d.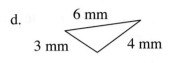

6 mm

3 mm   4 mm

e.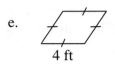

4 ft

f.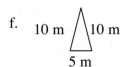

10 m   10 m

5 m

1-20.   For each shape drawn in problem 1-19, choose one of the labels below that best describes that shape. Be as specific as you can. Look in the glossary of this book for more information if you do not remember what one of the words describes.

right triangle   scalene triangle   obtuse triangle

isosceles triangle   rhombus   rectangle

square   trapezoid   hexagon

1-21.   Use the bar graph at right to answer the following questions.

a.   How many people attended the fair on Tuesday?

b.   Which day had the largest attendance?

c.   What was the total attendance for the week?

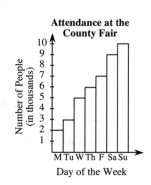

Attendance at the County Fair

Number of People (in thousands)

M Tu W Th F Sa Su
Day of the Week

1.1.4 How can I organize information?

Representing Data

Perhaps the most famous frog jumping contest takes place each May in Calaveras County, California. For more than 80 years, contestants have been entering large bullfrogs that measure at least 4 inches long in a contest to see which frog can move the farthest in three hops. Each year people travel from around the country (and sometimes the world) to see the frogs jump. Scientists have come to the fair to study the frogs.

In this lesson, you will ask questions and analyze data about some of the frogs in the contest. As you work, you will need to **choose a strategy** for organizing the information that will show patterns. As a team, you will need to share ideas about how to represent the data and work together to describe it as completely as you can.

1-22. JUMPING FROG JUBILEE

When it is time to compete in the Jumping Frog Jubilee, the frog is put on a starting pad. The frog hops three times, and then the distance is measured from the center of the starting pad to the end of the third hop to get the official jump length.

The chart below shows data about the 8th place frogs in 2008 and 2009. Your teacher will show you a chart of data with the best eight frogs from each of those years. *Before* you look at the rest of the data, think about what else you could learn about the frogs and their jumps from the numerical data.

a. With your team, brainstorm questions that you could use the numbers (data) to answer. For example, you might ask, *"What was the longest jump?"* Use the bullet points below to help your team come up with as many questions as you can (at least four).

Frog name	Jump length (inches)	Year
Dr. Frog	185.25	2009
Delbert Sr.	216.5	2008

- What could the numbers tell us about all of the frogs as a group?
- What could the numbers tell us about the frogs in just 2008 or just 2009?
- What could we ask to compare frogs from 2008 to frogs from 2009?
- What could we ask to compare individual frogs?

Problem continues on next page. →

1-22.   *Problem continued from previous page.*

      b.   As a class, discuss the different questions each study team wrote. Then, look over the data from the contest found on the Lesson 1.1.4A Resource Page. Decide which questions you can answer using the data and which you cannot.

      c.   With your team, choose two of the class questions to answer.

- Choose one that requires using all of the numbers to answer the question.

- Choose one that can be answered using just some of the data.

Think carefully about how to organize the data in order to find the answer. Write your conclusions in complete sentences.

1-23.   Different ways of presenting data can tell you different things. For example, some of your questions might have been easy to answer with an organized table of data. However, other questions can be easier to answer if the data is arranged in a different way, such as in the **histogram** below.

      a.   Look carefully at the graph. Use it to try to answer the questions below. If you cannot answer a question, explain why not.

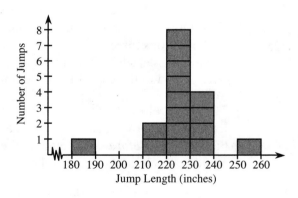

- Between which two numbers on the graph were most of the jump lengths?

- What was the median jump length?

- What was the mean (average) jump length?

      b.   What other statements can you make for this graph?

1-24.   In the book, *If You Hopped Like a Frog*, written by David M. Schwartz and illustrated by James Warhola, the author shares that when he was a child, he wondered how far he could hop if he hopped like a frog. In his letter to the reader at the front of his book, he wrote, "I imagined soaring through the air with grace and ease, landing gently on my big, springy legs. How far could I hop?"

   a.   Obviously, people and frogs are different sizes and have different jumping abilities. But imagine if you had the hopping muscles of a bullfrog but were still the same size you are now: how far could you hop? With your team:

   - Estimate how far *you* might be able to jump if you were a giant frog. (Think about how the information from problem 1-22 could help you.)

   - **Justify** your estimate.

   - Use pictures and/or words to help explain your thinking.

   b.   The book assumes that a 3-inch frog can jump about 60 inches in one hop. Does this estimate seem **reasonable** when looking at the data from problem 1-22? Why or why not?

1-25.   **Additional Challenge:** With your team, take measurements to predict how far you could jump if you were a bullfrog competing in the contest. Discuss what extra information you will need to make your prediction and how you will get it. Use words and/or pictures with labels to explain your process.

Methods and Meanings

Median and Mode

The mean is a useful way to find the center when data values are close together or are evenly spaced. Two other tools, **median** and **mode**, locate the approximate "center" of a set of data in different ways.

The **median** is the middle number in a set of data <u>arranged numerically</u>. If there are an even number of values, the median is the mean of the two middle numbers. The median is more accurate than the mean as a way to find the center when there are outliers in the data set.

The **mode** is the value in the data set that occurs more often than any other value. Data sets may have more than one mode, and some do not have any mode. The mode is useful when the data are not numeric, such as showing a "most popular" choice.

Example: Suppose the following data set represents the number of home runs hit by the best seven players on a major league baseball team:

16, 26, 21, 9, 13, 15, and 9.

The median is 15, since, when arranged in order (9, 9, 13, 15, 16, 21, 26), the middle number is 15.

The mode is 9, since it occurs twice and no other number appears more than once.

Mean, median, and mode are called **measures of central tendency** because they each describe the "center" of a set of data, but in different ways.

1-26.   In the Math Notes box for this lesson, read and review the information about median and mode. Use that information to decide what the median and mode are for Andy's test scores: 76, 84, 93, 67, 82, 87, and 76.

1-27.   Copy the number patterns below and write the next four numbers in the sequence. Assume the pattern continues as shown. Describe the pattern in words.

   a.   2, 7, 12, 17, 22, ___, ___, ___, ___

   b.   1, 4, 9, 16, 25, ___, ___, ___, ___

   c.   1, 1, 2, 3, 5, 8, ___, ___, ___, ___

1-28.   Audrey made the histogram at right to show her recent bowling scores.

   a.   How many games did she play in total?

   b.   Between what two values did most of her scores fall?

   c.   What portion of her scores fell between 130 and 140?

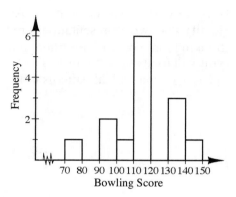

1-29.   The graph at right shows how far Ben is from home during a typical school day. Use the graph to answer the questions. Write your answers in complete sentences.

   a.   What was Ben doing between 7:00 a.m. and 8:00 a.m.?

   b.   What do you think Ben was doing between 9 a.m. and 2:30 p.m.?

   c.   What time did Ben leave to return to his starting point?

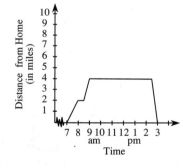

1-30.   As you can tell from the examples of the number lines below, not all number lines change by one unit from mark to mark. Copy these number lines onto your paper and fill in the missing numbers.

   a.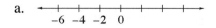

   b.

   c.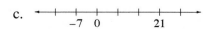

   d.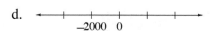

Investigating Number Patterns

In the past, you may have looked at number patterns to answer questions or to find the next part of a sequence, but have you ever considered the beauty of mathematics in those patterns? Today you are going to investigate number patterns and learn about equivalent ways to write the same number. As a team, you will share your **reasoning** and work to **justify** that two representations are the same. **Reasoning and justifying** is a way of thinking that you will use often in this course. When you are **reasoning and justifying**, you will focus on what makes a statement convincing or how you can explain your ideas. As you look at patterns today, ask your team:

What can we predict about the next number in the pattern?

How can we **justify** our answer?

1-31.   Use a calculator to calculate the value of each expression below.

   a. $1 \cdot 8 + 1$

   b. $12 \cdot 8 + 2$

   c. $123 \cdot 8 + 3$

   d. $1234 \cdot 8 + 4$

   e.   What patterns do you see? Discuss them with your team. Be sure that when your team agrees on something, it is recorded on each person's paper.

   f.   Use patterns you found to *predict* the next three expressions and their solutions. Do not calculate the answers yet. Instead, what do you think they will be?

   g.   Use your calculator to check the solution for each expression you wrote in part (f). Were your predictions correct? If not, look at the pattern again and figure out how it is changing.

1-32. Sometimes patterns are not created with addition and multiplication, but with the numbers themselves. For example, when the fractions in the sequence below are changed to decimals, an interesting pattern develops.

$$\frac{1}{9}, \frac{2}{9}, \frac{3}{9}, \text{ and } \frac{4}{9}$$

a. Use your calculator to change each of the fractions above to a decimal. Write each fraction and its equivalent decimal on your paper.

b. Decimals like 0.3333... and the others you found in part (a) are called **repeating decimals** because the digits continue infinitely. Instead of using "..." to show that the numbers repeat, mathematicians write a bar over the digits that repeat, like this: $0.\overline{3}$. It is standard to write the repeating digits just once. For example, $0.2222... = 0.\overline{2}$.

List the next five fractions in the sequence $\frac{1}{9}, \frac{2}{9}, \frac{3}{9},$ and $\frac{4}{9}$. Predict how they will look rewritten as decimals.

c. Find the decimal equivalents of the five fractions you wrote in part (b) using your calculator. Do they match your predictions? Are there any that are different?

1-33. Are 0.999..., $0.\overline{9}$, and 1 equal? How do you know? Discuss this with the class and **justify** your response. Help others understand what you mean as you explain your thinking. A visual demonstration is available at www.cpm.org/students/technology.

1-34. Decimal numbers that have only a finite number of digits such as 2.173 and 0.04 are called **terminating decimals**. Some fractions can be written as terminating decimals, such as the examples below.

$$\frac{1}{2} = 0.5 \qquad \frac{3}{4} = 0.75$$

Do the decimal equivalents of the numbers below terminate or repeat? Be ready to **justify** your answer.

a. 0.125

b. $0.\overline{6}$

c. $\frac{5}{6}$

d. 4

e. $\frac{2}{5}$

f. -0.33

1-35.   Representing numbers in multiple
ways can help to show what those
numbers mean. In problem 1-32, you
saw that the fraction $\frac{9}{9}$ (or 1) can be
represented as the decimal $0.\overline{9}$, and it
can also be represented geometrically
with a diagram. Portions can also be
represented in words, such as "nine-
ninths," and as **percents**, which are
portions of 100. The diagram at right
is called the "Portions Web."

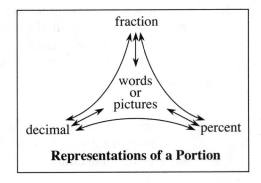

Draw each of the portions webs below on your paper and complete them for the
given fractions. In each part, determine if the decimal representation is
terminating or repeating.

a. $\frac{2}{3}$ b. $\frac{5}{4}$

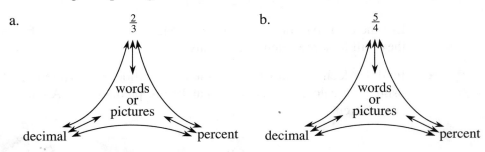

METHODS AND MEANINGS

Representations of Portions

MATH NOTES

The portions web diagram at right
illustrates that fractions, decimals, and
percents are different ways to represent a
portion of a number. Portions can also
be represented in words, such as "four-
fifths" or "seven-fourths" or diagrams
such as those shown below.

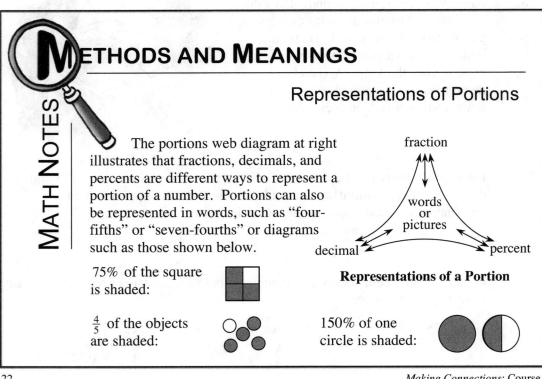

Representations of a Portion

75% of the square
is shaded:

$\frac{4}{5}$ of the objects
are shaded:

150% of one
circle is shaded:

1-36.   Copy the rows of equations below and write what you *predict* will be the next five rows in the sequence, if the numbers continue to change in the same way.

$1 \cdot 9 + 2 = 11$

$12 \cdot 9 + 3 = 111$

$123 \cdot 9 + 4 = 1111$

$1234 \cdot 9 + 5 = 11111$

a.   What patterns do you see? Write your answer in complete sentences.

b.   Use a calculator to discover if your predictions were correct. If they were not correct, look at the pattern again and figure out how it is changing.

1-37.   Look at the representations shown in the Math Notes box for "Representations of Portions." Copy the diagrams below and write a fraction and a percent for the shaded portion of each one.

a.   b.   c.

1-38.   Represent each of these fractions with a diagram and with words.

a. $\frac{2}{3}$ b. $1\frac{1}{8}$ c. $\frac{6}{9}$

1-39.   Jack has four tiles and wants to find out how many different shapes he can make with them.

a.   Sketch all of the arrangements that Jack could make with his tiles so that all of the tiles touch at least one other tile completely along a side. Assume that no tiles can overlap. How many arrangements are there?

b.   For each diagram that you drew in part (a), find the area (the "tiles") and the perimeter (the "toothpicks"). What do you notice?

1-40.   Find the mean, median, and mode for the lengths of the jumping frogs' bodies shown below (the lengths are in centimeters).

20.3, 12.5, 7.6, 13.9, 9.2, 21.7, 7.6, 17.5, 15.6, 14.1

1.2.1 How likely is it?

Exploring Probability

Every day we have to make decisions, many of them based on what we think will lead to the best result for each situation. You may pick a certain time to call your friend because she is more likely to answer. You might decide to do extra chores to improve the chance that you will be allowed to go to the movies this weekend. If you are deciding whether to enter a raffle, you may weigh the cost of the ticket against the chances that you would have of winning the prize. When you base decisions on your instincts about what will happen, you are using your sense of how likely an outcome will be. In this section, you will learn about ways to analyze the **probability** of an outcome using mathematics.

1-41. Make a number line on your paper. Place the letter (a, b, c, ...) from each statement below in a position on the line that corresponds to the probability (that is, likelihood) of the event happening. Part (a) is done as an example.

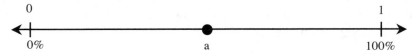

a. It will rain today. (The weather station states there is a 50% chance of rain.)

b. A space alien will walk into class now.

c. You will learn something new in math class this week.

d. Someday, a member of your class will be elected president of the United States.

e. You will eat some vegetables for dinner today.

1-42. THE GIANT SPIN

At a carnival, the most popular game is the Giant Spin, where players spin a giant wheel divided into 24 sections that are labeled with the numbers $-2, -1, 0, 1, 3$. The number that the spinner lands on determines whether a player will win a prize. The winning number and the prize change every day. Get a copy of the Lesson 1.2.1 Resource Page and look at the Giant Spin spinner.

Problem continues on next page. →

Making Connections: Course 2

1-42.   *Problem continued from previous page.*

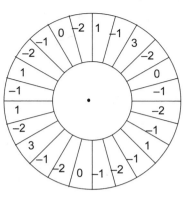

a.   Based on a quick look at the wheel, can you predict on which number the spinner will land most often? Where will it land least often?

b.   On Mondays, a player will win a stuffed animal if the spinner lands on a "0" space and a free ride on the roller coaster if it lands on a "1" space. Work with your team to find the **probability** of winning each kind of prize.

   •   Read the Math Notes box about probability at the end of this lesson.

   •   Use that information and the spinner to find the probability that the spinner lands on "1," written P(1), and then the probability that it lands on "0," or P(0).

   •   Determine the probability that a player will not win a prize.

c.   On Tuesdays, the rules change. Players win if they do *not* spin −1. Find P(not −1) and explain how it is related to P(−1).

d.   On Wednesdays, a player will win a gift certificate if she spins −1 or 3. During this time, what is the probability of winning, P(−1 or 3)?

e.   The carnival owner wants to set up the wheel so that on Fridays, players have a 50% chance of winning. Work with your team to find the number (or numbers) the owner could choose as the winning spin. Is there more than one choice the owner could make? Be prepared to share your **reasoning** with the class.

1-43.   If you played the Giant Spin 50 times, about how many times do you think the spinner would land on either a −1 or 1? Discuss this as a team, then write down a prediction.

a.   Use the Lesson 1.2.1 Resource Page and a bobby pin to make the Giant Spin spinner. Work with your team to spin the wheel 50 times. Record the outcome of each spin.

   •   How many times did your team spin a 1?

   •   How many times did your team spin a −1?

b.   How did your results compare to your predictions? If they were different, why do you think that happened? Explain your **reasoning**.

1-44.   Lila is making a spinner game for her cousins to
play. She has divided it into 8 equal sections, and
has labeled each one with a symbol. When the
spinner lands on a flower (✿), her cousins will
win a prize.

a.   What is P(★)?

b.   What is P(not ♦)?

c.   What is P(✿)?

d.   If Lila's cousins spin 100 times, about how many times would you expect them to
spin a heart (♥)?

1-45.   **Additional Challenge:** Lila's sister wants to increase the chances that her
cousins will spin a flower when they play Lila's game. *"I wonder how I should
change the spinner to help people spin the flower (✿)?"* she asked. Analyze
each of her ideas below.

a.   What will happen to the chances of spinning a flower if Lila's sister
changes all of the heart (♥) spaces to flowers (✿)? Find P(✿) for this new
spinner.

b.   What would happen to the chance of spinning a flower (✿) if the number of
spaces with each symbol is doubled, so that there are 16 equal spaces on the
wheel? How does this answer compare to the probability of spinning a
flower that you found in problem 1-44?

c.   What would happen to the chances of spinning a flower (✿) if Lila's sister
makes a new wheel, and doubles only the number of flower spaces?
(Assume all the spaces on the new wheel are still equal to each other in
size.) Find P(✿) for this new wheel.

d.   Look at your answers for parts (a) through (c). Answer each question
below and explain your **reasoning**.

   •   Which changes to the wheel changed the probability of landing on a
   flower (✿) space, and which did not?

   •   How would you change the original spinner if you wanted to increase a
   player's chances of spinning a heart (♥)?

Methods and Meanings

Probability

The **probability** of an event is the likelihood or chance that the event will occur. An **event** is the desired outcome (sometimes called favorable outcome) from among all possible outcomes. If all outcomes are equally likely, we can calculate the probability of an event, written **P(event)**, as:

$$P(\text{event}) = \frac{\text{number of outcomes in the event}}{\text{total number of possible outcomes}} .$$

For a standard number cube like the ones shown here, P(2) means the probability of rolling a 2 (the event). To calculate the probability, first figure out how many possible outcomes there are. Since there are six faces on the number cube, the number of possible outcomes is 6. Of the six faces, only one of the faces has a 2 on it. Thus, to find the probability of rolling a 2, you would write:

$$P(2) = \frac{\text{number of ways to roll 2}}{\text{number of possible outcomes}} = \frac{1}{6} \text{ or } 0.1\overline{6} \text{ or approximately } 16.7\%.$$

Probabilities may be written as fractions, decimals, or percents. An event that is guaranteed to happen has a probability of 1, or 100%. An event that has no chance of happening has a probability of 0, or 0%. Events that "might happen" have probabilities between 0 and 1 or 0% and 100%. In general, the more likely an event is to happen, the greater its probability.

Examples:

The probability of pulling a king out of a standard deck of cards, P(king), is $\frac{4}{52} = \frac{1}{13}$, since there are 4 kings and 52 cards.

The probability of getting tails when you flip a coin, P(tails), is $\frac{1}{2}$.

The probability of landing on a number less than 5 on a spinner with nine equal regions numbered 1 to 9, P(less than five), is $\frac{4}{9}$.

1-46.   Copy the number line below and place the following probabilities on it:

a.   A $\frac{1}{4}$ chance that you will be the team member who gets supplies tomorrow.

b.   A 25% chance of snow tomorrow.

c.   A 0.8 probability of eating vegetables with dinner.

d.   P(blue marble) $= \frac{5}{8}$.

e.   A 0.01 probability that it will be 85° on Saturday.

1-47.   A standard deck of playing cards has four suits (symbols) in two colors: diamonds and hearts are red; clubs and spades are black. Each suit has 13 cards: an ace, the numbers two through ten, a jack, a queen, and a king.

a.   What is P(black)?   b.   What is P(ace)?   c.   What is P(club)?

d.   If you drew a card from the deck and then replaced it, and repeated this 100 times, about how many times would you expect to draw a face card (king, queen, or jack)?

1-48.   FRACTIONS AND PERCENTS

Marianna represented several percents as portions of 100 in the pictures below.

i.   *ii.*   *iii.*

a.   Write the percent represented in each picture.

b.   Write the portion represented in each picture as a fraction in at least two different ways.

1-49.   Simplify the expressions in parts (a) through (f). Then answer the questions in part (g) using complete sentences.

   a. $13 \cdot 1$

   b. $1 \cdot 5.5$

   c. $6 \cdot \frac{1}{2}$

   d. $12 \cdot 2$

   e. $4 \cdot \frac{3}{3}$

   f. $14 \cdot \frac{1}{7}$

   g.   Use these examples to answer the following questions:

   - What happens when you multiply a number by one?

   - What happens when you multiply a positive number by a positive number less than one?

   - What happens when you multiply a positive number by a number greater than one?

1.2.2   How accurately can I predict it?

Comparing Experimental and Theoretical Probabilities

Sometimes an event is guaranteed to happen (for example, rolling a number less than 7 with a standard number cube), so it is called a **certainty**. Other times, an event is an **impossibility** (for example, rolling a 10 with a standard number cube), and so it has 0 (or no) chance of happening. For an event that will happen sometimes, you saw in Lesson 1.2.1 how math can help to predict how often it will happen. In life, however, results are often less exact than we might expect. In this lesson, you will explore the difference between mathematical predictions and real-world outcomes.

1-50.   COIN FLIP EXPERIMENT

   When a coin is flipped, there are two possible outcomes: heads or tails. A fair coin is one where heads and tails are equally likely outcomes of a flip.

   a.   What is the probability that you will flip heads when you flip a fair coin?

   b.   If you flip the same coin 30 times, how many times do you think you should flip heads? Write a prediction.

Problem continues on next page →

1-50.   *Problem continued from previous page.*

    c.   What will really happen? To find out, your teacher will assign you and a partner a number of flips and give you a Lesson 1.2.2 Resource Page to match that number of flips. With your partner, flip a coin and:

- Record the outcome (heads, H, or tails, T) on the chart.

- Keep flipping until you have data for each row of the chart (or charts) on your resource page.

        How many times did you flip heads? Was the result what you expected?

    d.   Your prediction in part (a) is called a **theoretical probability** because it is calculated based on analyzing the possible outcomes in the situation (heads and tails) and the desired outcome (heads). The results you got in part (c), written as a probability, are called an **experimental probability**. It is called experimental because it is based on data you collected in your experiment.

        Write the experimental probability for your coin flipping results from part (c) and record your probability with the results from other pairs of students as directed by your teacher.

1-51.   People often make statements about probability when they talk about future events. For example, weather forecasters often describe "the chance of rain tomorrow" as they announce their forecasts. Another example is the likelihood that you will be allowed to go to the mall this weekend. For each of the problems below, decide whether the situation is describing a theoretical or experimental probability. Be prepared to explain your **reasoning**.

    a.   The probability I can come to your house is 100% because the last twelve times I asked my dad if I could, he said yes.

    b.   The likelihood of rolling a 4 on a standard number cube is $\frac{1}{6}$ because there is only one side with a 4 and there are six sides.

    c.   The probability of winning the state lottery is said to be $\frac{1}{1000000}$ because only one combination of one million possible combinations will be selected.

    d.   Based on my last 60 times batting in softball, I have a $\frac{4}{5}$ chance of striking out.

    e.   There is a 0% probability that it will snow today in Fiji because snow has never been recorded there.

1-52.   Look at the class results for the Coin Flip Experiment (problem 1-50).

   a.   Did all teams get the same experimental probability?

   b.   Which team flipped the highest proportion of heads? How can you compare the different results?

1-53.   After 25 flips in the Coin Flip Experiment (problem 1-50), Lorraine and her partner recorded 14 heads ($\frac{14}{25}$ heads).

   a.   Is this more than, less than, or equal to 50%, the theoretical probability of flipping heads? Talk with your partner about how you know.

   b.   Percentages are one way to compare different portions of the total. If you have not already done so, work with your partner to calculate what percentage of Lorraine's flips were heads. Be prepared to share your **strategy** for finding the percentage with the class.

1-54.   DaMarr wrote his experimental probability of flipping heads as the fraction $\frac{7}{20}$. He wants to rewrite $\frac{7}{20}$ as a percent. To do that, he knows he needs to rewrite it as a portion of 100. He started by drawing the picture at right to represent $\frac{7}{20}$:

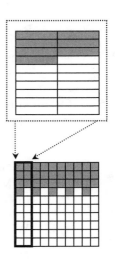

   a.   As he looked at his picture, DaMarr realized that he could adjust his drawing to show 100 parts instead of 20. DaMarr then drew a new diagram below his original picture. How many of the 100 parts are shaded? Explain your **reasoning**.

   b.   Explain how DaMarr can use his new picture to write $\frac{7}{20}$ as a percent.

   c.   Use a similar **strategy** to rewrite $\frac{3}{10}$ as a percent. Show your steps.

New diagram

1-55.   Randy was playing "Double Heads" where he would flip two coins at a time. He recorded the number of times he flipped two heads at the same time. He flipped the coins 50 times and there were 20 times when both coins landed heads up, which he recorded as $\frac{20}{50}$.

Note: This stoplight icon will appear periodically throughout the text. Problems with this icon display common errors that can be made. Be sure not to make the same mistakes yourself!

   a.   How does $\frac{20}{50}$ compare to 50%?

   b.   Randy claims, "$\frac{20}{50}$ is equivalent to $\frac{70}{100}$ *because if I add 50 to the denominator to get 100 and add 50 to the numerator to get 70, the fraction becomes $\frac{70}{100}$.*" Explain to Randy why $\frac{20}{50}$ and $\frac{70}{100}$ are not equivalent portions.

1-56.   Three students invented a game in which they flip coins for a minute then determine who flipped the highest percentage of heads. After their first round, each of them thinks that they won the game. Below is what they reported:

   •   "I think I won," said Maria, "Of my flips $\frac{12}{25}$ were heads."

   •   Autymn said, "I flipped my coin 40 times and had a total of 18 heads. Since both of my numbers are larger than yours, I must have won."

   •   Kumar reported, "I recorded 44% of my flips as heads."

Help the students determine their percentage of heads. **Justify** your answer.

1-57.   Did your experimental probability of flipping heads in the Coin Flip Experiment (problem 1-50) exactly match the theoretical probability of 50%, or $\frac{1}{2}$? Was it close?

   a.   Change the results from each team in problem 1-50 to percents using DaMarr's **strategy** from problem 1-54. Add your results to your paper and the class data.

   b.   Which result was closest to 50%? Which result was the most surprising?

   c.   Combine all of the results for the number of flips and the number of heads to get a total number of flips and a total number of heads for the class.

      •   What percent of the flips landed heads?

      •   How does the experimental probability for the class compare to your own results?

      •   How does it compare to the theoretical probability?

METHODS AND MEANINGS

Probability: Vocabulary and Definitions

Outcome: Any possible or actual result or consequence of the action(s) considered, such as rolling a five on a standard number cube or getting heads when flipping a coin.

Event: A desired (or successful) outcome or group of desired (successful) outcomes from an experiment, such as rolling an even number on a standard number cube.

Sample Space: All the possible outcomes of a situation. For example, the sample space for flipping a coin is H and T; rolling a standard number cube has six possible outcomes: 1, 2, 3, 4, 5, and 6.

Theoretical Probability: A calculated probability based on the possible outcomes when each outcome has the same chance of occurring.

$$\text{Theoretical Probability} = \frac{\text{number of successful outcomes (events)}}{\text{total number of possible outcomes}}$$

By "successful" we usually mean desired or specified outcome (event), such as rolling a five on a standard number cube ($\frac{1}{6}$), pulling a king from a deck of cards ($\frac{4}{52} = \frac{1}{13}$), or flipping a coin and getting heads ($\frac{1}{2}$).

Experimental Probability: The probability based on data collected in experiments.

$$\text{Experimental Probability} = \frac{\text{number of successful outcomes in the experiment}}{\text{total number of outcomes in the experiment}}$$

Impossibility: An event that has a probability of zero; that is, an event that cannot occur, such as rolling a seven on a standard number cube.

Certainty: An event that has a probability of one or 100%; that is, an event that will definitely occur, such as rolling a number between one and six on a standard number cube.

1-58.   For each situation below, write the indicated probability.

   a.   A coin is flipped 80 times. It lands "tails" 47 times. Based on this data, what is the experimental probability that the coin will land on heads?

   b.   A bag contains purple and orange marbles. Samantha randomly takes out one marble, and then returns it to the bag. She does this 18 times, and 12 of those times an orange marble is pulled out. For her experiment, what is the probability that she will pull out a green marble?

   c.   Sarina pulls a playing card from a standard deck and then replaces it. She does this 30 times, and 40% of the time it is hearts. Based on these results, what is the probability that she will *not* pull a heart out of the deck?

1-59.   Write four different fractions that are equal to 1. Use your calculator to check that you are correct.

1-60.   Elizabeth wants to challenge you to a "Toothpicks and Tiles" game. Using exactly 6 tiles, solve her challenges below. **Justify** your answers with pictures and labels.

   a.   Find a pattern where the number of toothpicks is more than double the number of tiles.

   b.   Find a pattern where the number of toothpicks is 4 more than the number of tiles.

1-61.   Kayla has a 14-foot rope. She cut it into three parts. Two of the pieces are the same length and the third piece is 2 feet long.

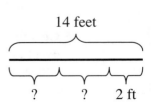

   a.   Copy Kayla's diagram at right onto your paper.

   b.   How long were each of the two equal pieces?

1-62.   Rewrite each fraction as a percent and each percent as a fraction. Show your thinking with pictures or labeled calculations.

a. $\frac{2}{5}$ b.   45%   c.   120%   d. $\frac{21}{40}$

1-63.   Locate the coordinates of the three highlighted points on the graph of the triangle below and write them as ordered pairs (x, y).

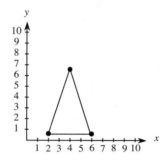

1-64.   Lulu is playing "Toothpicks and Tiles" from Lesson 1.1.2. She has arranged 10 tiles as shown at right. She wants to rearrange them so that the number of toothpicks is still equal. Draw one possible arrangement of the tiles.

1-65.   Find a pattern in each number sequence below. Then use your pattern to generate the next five numbers in the sequence. Explain the pattern.

a.   2, 5, 3, 6, 4, ____, ____, ____, ____, ____

b.   100, 99, 97, 94, 90, ____, ____, ____, ____, ____

1-66.   Alice said, "*I am thinking of a number. If you triple my number and subtract 11, you get my number plus 33. What's my number?*" Find Alice's number. Show how you know your answer is correct.

1.2.3 How can I represent it?

Rewriting Fractions

When probabilities and portions are expressed as fractions, they can sometimes be difficult to compare. For example, is a $\frac{2}{5}$ probability of winning a game greater than a $\frac{3}{7}$ probability?

Earlier, you used different ways to represent a portion to help figure out if $0.\overline{9}$ is equal to 1. In this lesson, you will develop **strategies** for rewriting fractions in different forms in order to compare different portions.

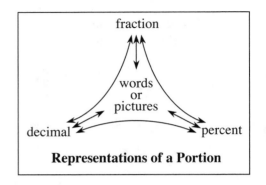

Representations of a Portion

1-67.   FRACTION TO PERCENT

Lila wants to rewrite $\frac{10}{25}$ as a percentage. She decided to represent $\frac{10}{25}$ first in a picture.

a.   How many sets of 25 will she need to make 100?

b.   How many sets of shaded squares will she need? How many shaded squares is that in total?

c.   Lila drew the picture below, and then wrote the equation to the right to represent her work with the shapes:

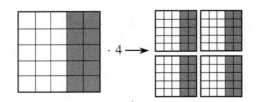

When Lila multiplies the number of shaded squares by 4 and the number of total squares by 4, did the amount of shading compared to the total squares change? Explain how you know.

Making Connections: Course 2

1-68.   Multiplying any number by one does not change the value of the number; this is
called the **Identity Property of Multiplication**. When the numerator (top
number) and denominator (bottom number) of a fraction are multiplied by the
same number, some people like to say the fraction is multiplied by a **Giant
One**. For example:

$$\frac{10}{25} \cdot \frac{4}{4} = \frac{40}{100}$$

a.   Why is the fraction $\frac{4}{4}$ called a Giant One?

b.   Use a Giant One to rewrite each fraction by multiplying each expression
below.

   i. $\frac{9}{25} \cdot \frac{6}{6}$ ii. $\frac{6}{15} \cdot \frac{3}{3}$

c.   What if you do not know which numbers to use in a Giant One? Copy and
complete each problem below on your paper.

   i. $\frac{5}{7} \cdot \boxed{} = \frac{40}{}$ ii. $\frac{5}{7} \cdot \boxed{} = \frac{}{70}$

1-69.   Use the Giant One to rewrite each fraction as a part of 100. Then write the
equivalent percentage.

a. $\frac{3}{4} \cdot \boxed{} = \frac{}{100}$ b. $\frac{42}{200} \cdot \boxed{} = \frac{}{100}$ c. $\frac{7}{16} \cdot \boxed{} = \frac{}{100}$

d.   How do you decide which number to use in the Giant One?

1-70.   Deanna is trying to compare $\frac{3}{7}$ to $\frac{2}{5}$. She started by representing $\frac{3}{7}$ in a
picture, then she divided the picture into five horizontal rows to rewrite the
portion as $\frac{15}{35}$. Here is her work so far:

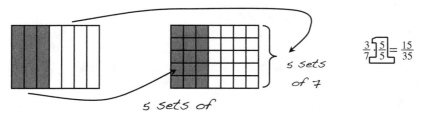

5 sets of

5 sets
of 7

$$\frac{3}{7} \cdot \frac{5}{5} = \frac{15}{35}$$

a.   Rewrite $\frac{2}{5}$ as a portion of 35. Is $\frac{2}{5}$ bigger or smaller than $\frac{3}{7}$?

b.   Why does rewriting the fractions make it easier to compare the two
fractions?

c.   Why did Deanna choose 35 for her new denominator? Could she have
chosen a different number?

1-71.   FAMILIES OF FRACTIONS

Using a Giant One, any fraction can be rewritten as a different fraction that represents the same portion of a whole. Fractions that are equal but are written in different ways are called **equivalent fractions**.

Make three new fractions that are equivalent to each fraction below.

a. $\frac{7}{12}$ b. $\frac{3}{10}$ c. $\frac{9}{27}$

1-72.   Adele, Karla, and Lisa are reading the same book, and they have each read a different number of pages.

Adele has read $\frac{5}{8}$ of the book.

Karla has read $\frac{12}{16}$ of the book.

Lisa has read $\frac{13}{24}$ of the book.

Help them decide who has the most left to read.

a.   What denominator could they use to compare the portions they have read?

b.   Which girl has the largest part left to read? **Justify** your ideas.

c.   How many pages could the book have? Be ready to explain your answer.

1-73.   Which of the events below is most likely to happen? **Justify** your answer by rewriting the portion in a different form. In each case, show your thinking with pictures or labeled calculations.

a.   A $\frac{4}{5}$ chance of the teacher assigning homework today.

b.   A 78% chance of a thunderstorm tomorrow.

c.   A $\frac{7}{10}$ probability of picking a green marble.

1-74.   LEARNING LOG

In this course, you will often be asked to reflect on your
learning in a Learning Log. Writing about your
understanding will help you pull together ideas, develop
new ways to describe mathematical ideas, and recognize
gaps in your understanding. Your teacher will tell you
where your Learning Log entries should go.

For your first entry, think about which methods you have for comparing two
probabilities to decide which is greater. In your Learning Log, create an
example and explain two different **strategies** for comparing them. Title this
entry "Comparing Probabilities," and label it with today's date.

Ⓜ️ETHODS AND MEANINGS

MATH NOTES

Additive and Multiplicative Identities

If any number or expression is multiplied by the number "one,"
the number or expression does not change. The number "one" is called
the **multiplicative identity**. So, for any number x:

$$1 \cdot x = x \cdot 1 = x$$

One way the multiplicative identity is used is to
create equivalent fractions using a Giant One.

$$\frac{2}{3} \cdot \left[\frac{2}{2}\right] = \frac{4}{6}$$

By multiplying a fraction by a fraction equivalent to one, a new
equivalent fraction is created.

The number "zero" is the **additive identity** since adding zero does not
change the value or expression.

1-75. In problem 1-67, Lila rewrote $\frac{10}{25}$ as $\frac{40}{100}$ and represented it with the picture at right. Tony thinks this fraction is also equal to $\frac{2}{5}$.

a. Is Tony correct? Use the picture or calculations to explain your **reasoning**. Write your answer in complete sentences.

b. How could Tony write an equivalent (equal) fraction using tenths? That is, what fraction in the form $\frac{?}{10}$ can represent the diagram above?

1-76. Zaria wants you to solve this puzzle: "*I am thinking of a number. If you divide my number by two and subtract 4, you will get 2. What is my number?*" Show how you know your answer is correct.

1-77. Marissa is drawing coins from a bag that contains 5 pennies, 4 nickels, 5 dimes, and 2 quarters.

a. What is the probability that she will draw a nickel?

b. If one penny, two dimes, and one quarter are added to the bag, what is the new probability that she will draw a nickel?

c. In which situation is it more likely that she will draw a nickel?

1-78. Rewrite each fraction below as an equivalent fraction and as a percent.

a. $\frac{5}{20}$

b. $\frac{9}{25}$

c. $\frac{9}{6}$

1-79. Rewrite each expression as a single fraction.

a. $\frac{3}{8} + \frac{1}{8}$

b. $\frac{4}{5} + \frac{3}{5}$

c. $\frac{6}{7} - \frac{2}{7}$

1.2.4 What if there are multiple outcomes?

Compound Probability and Fraction Addition

So far in this section, you have worked with probabilities where there is one specific outcome that is desired. Today you will investigate probabilities of **compound events**, that is, events with combinations of outcomes. Think about these questions as you work with your study team:

How is this probability related to the probability of a single event?

How can probabilities be combined?

Does this answer make sense?

1-80. A bag holds 40 marbles, and each marble is either yellow or green. If you reach into the bag and randomly pull out a marble, you have an 80% chance of pulling out a yellow marble.

a. How many of the marbles are green? Show how you know.

b. How could you add or remove marbles in the original bag to change the probability of drawing a green marble to 50%?

c. **Additional Challenge:** Design a new bag of marbles that contains at least 50 marbles that are yellow, green, or red. How many of each color should you put in the bag to create a 25% probability of drawing red? Is there more than one possible way?

1-81.   Thomas helps around the house by doing one chore after school. Each day Thomas and his aunt use the spinner at right to decide which chore he will do. Here is what Thomas knows:

- The sections on the spinner for "rake leaves" and "do laundry" are the same size.

- The sections for "clean bathroom" and "vacuum" are equal in size and together make up half the spinner.

a.   What is the probability that Thomas will spin "do laundry"?

b.   Thomas hates to clean the bathroom. When he spins the spinner, what is the probability that it will not point to "clean bathroom"? Explain how you found this answer.

1-82.   Thomas' aunt hopes that he will spin "clean bedroom" or "rake leaves" today.

a.   What is P(clean bedroom)? What is P(rake leaves)?

b.   Spinning either chore would make Thomas' aunt happy. With your study team, discuss the questions below and record your team's answers. Be sure to **justify** your conclusions.

- What is the probability that he will spin either one of the chores?

- How can you write the two outcomes as a single probability?

1-83.   Ms. Nguyen lets her students borrow pens and pencils on days when they have a quiz. She has a paper bag with hundreds of wooden pencils, mechanical pencils, and blue pens in it.

Stuart forgot his pencil, and it is quiz day! Ms. Nguyen tells him that one out of every three students who reaches into the bag pulls out a wooden pencil. Two out of every five students pull out a mechanical pencil. The rest of the students pull out a blue pen.

a.   If Stuart reaches into the bag without looking, is it more likely that he will choose a wooden pencil or a mechanical pencil? **Justify** your thinking.

b.   How can you describe the probability that Stuart will pull out some kind of pencil by using the probabilities that you already know? Consider what you know about adding and subtracting fractions and see if you already have a **strategy** to write this probability as a single number.

Making Connections: Course 2

1-84. Felicia was trying to find the probability that she would pull a pencil out of Ms. Nguyen's bag from problem 1-83. *"I think I need to combine the probability that I will get a wooden pencil with the probability that I will get a mechanical pencil,"* she said. She set up this expression and drew a picture:

$\frac{1}{3} + \frac{2}{5}$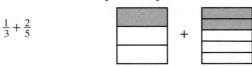

a. Felicia wondered if she could add the parts. Is the sum $\frac{3}{8}$? Why or why not?

b. Discuss with your team how Felicia could change the way she writes each fraction so that she can add them easily. Be ready to explain your **reasoning**. Then, find the sum.

1-85. Justin is working on a new problem: $\frac{1}{3} + \frac{1}{2}$. He drew the picture below to represent the problem:

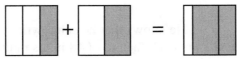

a. Could you name Justin's sum as a single fraction? Would he be correct to name it $\frac{2}{3}$?

b. Kermit sees Justin's work, and says, *"You need to make all of the pieces the same size before you try to write the sum. You can use a Giant One to rewrite $\frac{1}{3}$ and $\frac{1}{2}$ each as sixths."* He writes:

$$\frac{1}{3} \cdot \boxed{} = \frac{\ }{6} \qquad \frac{1}{2} \cdot \boxed{} = \frac{\ }{6}$$

Finish Kermit's work to rewrite each fraction so that its denominator is six.

c. What is the sum of the new fractions? Fix Justin's picture or draw a new diagram to explain why your answer makes sense.

d. Discuss with your team why Kermit might have chosen to rewrite each fraction as sixths. Could he have used a different number? Be ready to share your thinking.

1-86.   Before we can write the sum of two fractions, they must be rewritten so that both wholes have an equal number of parts. In other words, they must be rewritten to have a **common denominator**. Three students were adding the fractions $\frac{1}{4} + \frac{5}{12}$ below, and they each found a different common denominator:

Lily: $\frac{1}{4} + \frac{5}{12}$ Armando: $\frac{1}{4} + \frac{5}{12}$ Josue: $\frac{1}{4} + \frac{5}{12}$

$\frac{12}{48} + \frac{20}{48}$ $\frac{3}{12} + \frac{5}{12}$ $\frac{6}{24} + \frac{10}{24}$

$\frac{32}{48}$ $\frac{8}{12}$ $\frac{16}{24}$

a.   Who is correct? Can any number be a common denominator? Explain your **reasoning**.

b.   Which of their common denominators is easiest to work with? Why?

c.   Find at least three different common denominators you could use to add $\frac{3}{10} + \frac{1}{5}$.

1-87.   Vu needs to add $\frac{3}{8} + \frac{5}{6}$. He knows that he can rewrite each fraction as a portion of 48 because 6 and 8 are each factors of 48 in his multiplication table. *"Is there a smaller number that could work as a common denominator?"* he wonders.

a.   Where can you look in the multiplication table to see if 6 and 8 are each factors of a number less than 48?

b.   Use the multiplication table on the Lesson 1.2.4 Resource Page to find other number(s) you could use as a common denominator to add $\frac{3}{8}$ and $\frac{5}{6}$.

c.   If Vu's next problem is to add $\frac{5}{4} + \frac{7}{10}$, use the multiplication table to find the smallest number you could use as a common denominator, called the **lowest common denominator**. Then, find the sum.

	1	2	3	4	5	6	7	8	9	10
1	1	2	3	4	5	6	7	8	9	10
2	2	4	6	8	10	12	14	16	18	20
3	3	6	9	12	15	18	21	24	27	30
4	4	8	12	16	20	24	28	32	36	40
5	5	10	15	20	25	30	35	40	45	50
6	6	12	18	24	30	36	42	(48)	54	60
7	7	14	21	28	35	42	49	56	63	70
8	8	16	24	32	40	(48)	56	64	72	80
9	9	18	27	36	45	54	63	72	81	90
10	10	20	30	40	50	60	70	80	90	100

1-88.   One study team is trying to find the sum $\frac{5}{6} + \frac{3}{4} + \frac{1}{5}$.

a.   They first tried to use 24 as a common denominator. Why does 24 not work as a common denominator?

b.   Find a common denominator for this problem and explain how you found it.

c.   With your study team, describe how factors and multiples can help you to find a common denominator.

1-89.   With your team, find each sum. You may want to use the multiplication table to help you find common denominators.

a. $\frac{1}{4} + \frac{3}{5}$ b. $\frac{2}{7} + \frac{2}{3}$ c. $\frac{5}{8} + \frac{1}{2}$ d. $\frac{2}{3} + \frac{1}{2} + \frac{1}{6}$

1-90.   THE POWER OF PRIME NUMBERS

Additional Challenge: Prime numbers are numbers that have exactly two factors, namely, one and themselves. Said another way, prime numbers can only be divided evenly by themselves and one (except for 1, which is not prime). Every number that is not prime can be rewritten as a product of **prime factors**. For example, $20 = 2 \cdot 2 \cdot 5$ or $36 = 2 \cdot 2 \cdot 3 \cdot 3$. Prime factors can be used to build common denominators for fractions.

a.   What are the prime factors of each denominator in the sum $\frac{5}{6} + \frac{3}{4} + \frac{1}{5}$ (from problem 1-88)?

b.   What are the prime factors of the common denominator you found in part (b) of problem 1-88?

c.   What do the lists of factors you made in parts (a) and (b) have in common?

d.   How could the prime factors of each denominator in a pair of fractions help you find a common denominator for those fractions? Explain your thinking.

METHODS AND MEANINGS

Equivalent Fractions

Fractions that are equal, but written in different forms, are called **equivalent fractions**. Rewriting a fraction in an equivalent form is useful when you want to compare two fractions or when you want to combine portions that are divided into different size pieces.

A Giant One is a useful tool to create an equivalent fraction. To rewrite a fraction in a different form, multiply the original fraction by a fraction equivalent to 1. For example:

$$\frac{2}{3} \cdot \boxed{\frac{4}{4}} = \frac{2 \cdot 4}{3 \cdot 4} = \frac{8}{12}$$

A picture can also demonstrate that these two fractions are equivalent:

 =

Review & Preview

1-91.   What is the probability of getting blue or green on a spinner that is $\frac{3}{10}$ green and $\frac{1}{5}$ blue? Show your work.

1-92.   The value of a decimal becomes clearer when the place value is spoken or written as the number it names. For example, 0.1 makes more sense if it is read as "one-tenth" rather than "zero point one."

   a.   Write the following numbers in words so that the place value can be identified.

   0.4   1.3   0.56   2.008

   b.   Now **reverse your thinking**. Write the decimals that go with the following words.

   thirty-five hundredths   three and two-tenths   six-hundredths

Making Connections: Course 2

1-93.   For each part below, find a Giant One that will multiply the fraction on the left side of the equation to create the equivalent fraction on the right side of the equation. Then complete any other missing information.

a. $\frac{5}{6} \cdot \boxed{} = \frac{15}{}$

b. $\frac{}{3} \cdot \boxed{} = \frac{4}{6}$

c. $\frac{}{2} \cdot \boxed{} = \frac{8}{16}$

d. $\frac{}{4} \cdot \boxed{} = \frac{6}{24}$

1-94.   How many different rectangles can you draw with an area (number of "tiles") of 28? What is the perimeter (number of "toothpicks") of each one? Show your work.

1-95.   Fareed wants to add $\frac{1}{4} + \frac{5}{8}$.

a.   Add the fractions by using a Giant One to create a common denominator.

b.   How can factors help you find a common denominator?

1-96.   Marisa and Mario were visiting the carnival when they noticed a few number relationships. They made them into brainteasers for you.

a.   If three-tenths of the visitors were adults and there were 100 visitors, how many visitors were adults?

b.   Five-eighths of the prizes at the Giant Spin were dolls. If there were 64 prizes, how many prizes were not dolls?

1-97.   Order these numbers from least to greatest.

$$\frac{1}{2} \quad 1.1 \quad \frac{5}{3} \quad 2 \quad 0 \quad 0.4 \quad -2 \quad \frac{5}{8}$$

1-98.   Here are the lengths (in inches) of snakes in a reptile display at the zoo: 10, 31, 36, 36, 38, 42, 47, 48, 49, 52. Find the mean, median, and mode of the lengths.

1-99.   Find each sum.

a. $\frac{3}{5} + \frac{1}{3}$

b. $\frac{5}{7} + \frac{1}{2}$

c. $\frac{1}{6} + \frac{2}{8}$

1.2.5 What part is missing?

Subtracting Fractions

In this section, you have calculated probabilities for single events and combinations of events. You have also compared those probabilities to decide which outcomes are most likely. In this lesson, you will work with your study team to apply your knowledge of fractions to represent and calculate probabilities of a variety of events. As you work today, ask each other these questions to focus your discussion:

How can probabilities be combined?

How can the answer be rewritten in a different form?

1-100.   Eustice is adding fractions. Here is her work:

$$\tfrac{1}{2} + \tfrac{2}{4} = \tfrac{3}{6}$$

a.   How do you think Eustice got her answer? Does her answer make sense? Discuss Eustice's work with your team, and then explain your **reasoning** on your paper with diagrams and words.

b.   Help Eustice find the correct answer.

1-101.   Lindsay has a paper bag full of Fruiti Tutti Chews in three different fruit flavors. She says, *"If you reach into the bag, you have a $\tfrac{1}{3}$ chance of pulling out a Killer Kiwi. There is a $\tfrac{3}{5}$ chance that you will get Crazy Coconut."* If you reach into the bag:

a.   What is P(coconut or kiwi)?

b.   Does there have to be another flavor in the bag? How can you tell? If so, assuming that there is only one other flavor, what is the probability of getting that flavor?

c.   How many candies might Lindsay have in the bag? Is there more than one possibility? Assume that all candies in the bag are whole candies.

1-102.   Lyle asked for a challenge problem, and his teacher gave him this one:

There is a $\frac{2}{7}$ chance of drawing a red marble out of a bag of marbles. If the probability of drawing a red or a blue marble is $\frac{2}{3}$, what is the probability of drawing a blue marble?

When Lyle's teammates saw the challenge he was working on, they each had a different idea for how he should start.

- Mayra suggested that he start by rewriting $\frac{2}{3}$ and $\frac{2}{7}$ so that they have a common denominator.

- Kenessa disagreed. *"You want to set up a subtraction problem,"* she said. She wrote the expression $\frac{2}{3} - \frac{2}{7}$ to show the number Lyle needs to find.

- Darren had a different idea. *"The probability that you would draw either red or blue is the same as the probability of drawing red added to the probability of drawing blue,"* he said. He wrote this expression:

$$\tfrac{2}{7} + ? = \tfrac{2}{3}$$

a.   Which way would you suggest Lyle start working to find P(blue)?

- Discuss your ideas with your study team.

- Write a clear explanation of which method you recommend and why.

- Include your ideas about whether the other **strategies** will solve the problem and why you did not choose them.

b.   What is the probability of drawing a blue marble? Explain your **reasoning**.

1-103.   Louise is playing a game, but the spinner is incomplete. Each section of the spinner is labeled with the probability of spinning it. What fraction is missing?

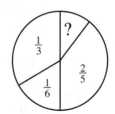

1-104.   What math operations can you use to show your **reasoning** in problems 1-102 and 1-103? Discuss your **strategies** with your study team. Try to find more than one way to explain how you found each missing piece.

1-105. Charles found a spinner his teacher was making. He knew that if he put his problem-solving skills to use, he would be able to figure out the missing piece and finish the spinner for his teacher.

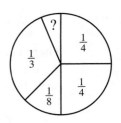

a. Write an expression for the problem Charles needs to solve. Is there more than one way to do this?

b. Find the solution.

1-106. Work with your study team to invent two new spinners with missing parts, like the spinners in problems 1-103 and 1-105. Then,

- Find the missing piece on your own paper.

- On a new sheet of paper, draw and label your spinner.

- Trade problems with another study team and find the missing parts of their spinners while they find yours.

1-107. LEARNING LOG

In your Learning Log, describe the process you use to add or subtract fractions when the fractions have different denominators. Create an example and show your solution with pictures and number expressions. Then, answer the questions:

- How do you rewrite the fractions to represent pieces that are the same size?

- How do you identify what common denominator to use?

Label this entry "Adding Fractions with Unlike Denominators," and include today's date.

METHODS AND MEANINGS

MATH NOTES

Scaling a Graph

The numbers on the axes of a graph show the **scaling** of the axes. The difference between consecutive markings tells the size of the **interval**. When you scale each axis you must use equal intervals to represent the data accurately. For example, an interval of 5 creates a scale numbered $-15, -10, -5, 0, 5, 10, 15$, etc. Unequal intervals distort the relationship in the data.

Notice on the graph at right that 80 marks the end of the *fourth* interval from zero. If you divide 80 years by 4 you can see the length of an interval on this graph is 20.

$$80 \div 4 = 20$$

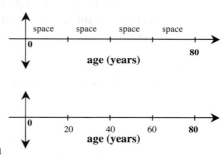

The second graph at right has each interval labeled. We call labeling the graph "scaling the axis."

1-108.   Rewrite each fraction in at least 2 different ways.

a. $\frac{6}{9}$ b. $\frac{11}{12}$ c. $\frac{3}{8}$ d. $\frac{10}{7}$

1-109.   Jonathan measured two cups of flour into a bowl on the counter. Then he spilled part of it, and now there is only $\frac{3}{8}$ cup left. How much did he spill?

1-110.   Mario is trying to explain to Marissa how to add fractions. He has written the work at right.

   a.   Why did Mario start by rewriting the fractions using a Giant One? Why did he choose 20 as his new denominator?

$\frac{1}{4} + \frac{2}{5}$

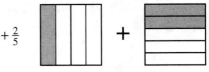

   b.   Finish the problem. Explain each step you would take, and why.

Step 1: $\frac{1}{4} \cdot \boxed{\frac{5}{5}} = \frac{5}{20}$ $\frac{2}{5} \cdot \boxed{\frac{4}{4}} = \frac{8}{20}$

1-111.   Maggie is making a recipe that produces 18 muffins.

   a.   There are 12 people in Maggie's book club. If the muffins are divided evenly among each person, how much will each person get? Explain your thinking.

   b.   If Maggie wanted to divide the muffins evenly between the 36 students in her class, how much muffin would each person get? Explain your thinking.

1-112.   Read the Math Notes box about scaling axes in this lesson. Then copy these incomplete axes on your paper and write the missing numbers on each one.

a.
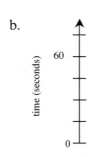

b.

c.
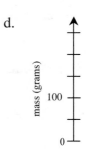

d.

1.3.1 When do decimals repeat?

Fraction to Decimal Conversions

In Sections 1.1 and 1.2, you explored different representations of portions (parts) of wholes. You looked at portions represented as fractions and as decimals, and went back and forth between the representations. Some pieces look very similar when represented as fractions, but their decimal representations can appear different. Why does this happen? In this lesson, you will work with your team to determine what makes some decimals terminate (end) and some repeat.

1-113.   Compare the portions in each picture below:

Portion A: 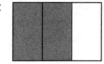   Portion B: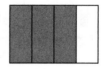

a.   Represent each portion as a fraction and as a decimal.

b.   The pictures and fractions for each representation are similar, but the decimals look very different. With your team, discuss how the two decimals look different and why they might look this way. Be ready to share your ideas.

1-114.   In Lesson 1.1.5 you rewrote fractions like
$\frac{1}{9}$ as decimals by dividing on your
calculator. Looking at how division works
can help explain why fractions that look
similar can look so different as decimals.

$$\frac{1}{9} = 1 \div 9 = 0.999... = 0.\overline{9}$$

Imagine that you have 13 cheese sticks that you need to divide evenly among 5
people. You can write this as 13 cheese sticks ÷ 5 people or $\frac{13}{5}$ or $5\overline{)13}$. The
problem is represented with the pictures and symbols below.

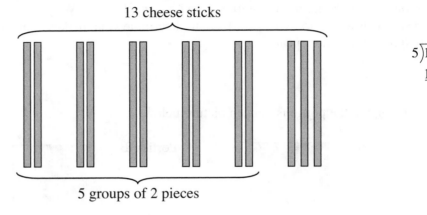

13 cheese sticks

5 groups of 2 pieces

a.   Talk with your team about how this diagram represents beginning to divide
13 by 5, or $\frac{13}{5}$. Why are there five groups of two pieces?

b.   What does the 2 above the division symbol represent? What does the 10
represent?

c.   Where are the three leftover pieces shown in the symbols?

d.   To share the three leftover pieces between the 5 people, divide them up into
tenths. Add a decimal point in the dividend to show that the three wholes
are being rewritten as thirty tenths (3.0), as shown below:

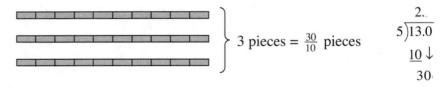

3 pieces = $\frac{30}{10}$ pieces

How many tenths will each person get? Where is this written in the
division problem?

e.   How much cheese will each person receive? Write your answer as a
fraction and as a decimal.

1-115. Set up your own division problem to rewrite $\frac{3}{4}$ as a decimal *without a calculator* using the Lesson 1.3.1 Resource Page. Show your work on the diagram and in symbols.

a. Are there enough whole pieces (each bold line represents one piece) to put some in each of four groups? Explain.

b. Divide each of the whole pieces into tenths and then divide these into four groups. How many tenths are left over?

c. If you divide each tenth that is left over into 10 pieces again, what fraction of the original is each new piece? How many are there? You may need to **visualize** these pieces instead of drawing them.

d. How many of these new smaller pieces will be in each of the four groups? How many will be left over?

e. How can you tell that the decimal has terminated (ended)?

1-116. To see why $\frac{2}{3}$ does not terminate, use the Lesson 1.3.1 Resource Page to rewrite it as a decimal *without a calculator*.

a. As you divide, what happens to the remainders?

b. How is the process of dividing $\frac{2}{3}$ the same as dividing $\frac{3}{4}$, and how is it different? Why does one decimal terminate, but the other does not?

1-117.   Katrina works at the Fraction Factory. Her job is to sort
         all of the customer orders into two groups: terminating
         decimals and repeating decimals.

    a.   Katrina's boss wants her to write $\frac{20}{33}$ as a decimal
         without using a calculator. Katrina's work so far is
         shown at right. What results did she get each time
         she subtracted?

    b.   Will the decimal for $\frac{20}{33}$ terminate or repeat? How
         do you know? How far should Katrina continue
         with her division to be sure?

```
        0.60
33 ) 20.000
      19 8 ↓
         2 0
           0
         2 0 0
```

1-118.   Represent $\frac{1}{7}$ as a decimal. When does it repeat?
         How do you know?

1-119.   THE ROLE OF THE DENOMINATOR

         Additional Challenge: Both $\frac{1}{3}$ and $\frac{2}{3}$ can be rewritten as repeating decimals
         ($0.\overline{3}$ and $0.\overline{6}$). Does the number in the denominator cause the fraction to repeat?
         For example, will every fraction with a denominator of 15 be equivalent to a
         repeating decimal? (Ignore fractions that are equal to whole numbers, like
         $\frac{15}{15} = 1$ or $\frac{45}{15} = 3$.)

    a.   With your team, try to find a fraction with 15 in the denominator that does
         not repeat (and is not equal to a whole number). Are you able to find one?
         More than one?

    b.   Why do some numbers with a denominator of 15 repeat and others do not?
         Discuss this with your team. Write down an idea, and test it.

METHODS AND MEANINGS

Fraction ⇔ Decimal ⇔ Percent

The **Portions Web** diagram at right illustrates that fractions, decimals, and percents are different ways to represent a portion of a number. Portions can also be represented in words, such as "four-fifths" or "twelve-fifteenths" or with diagrams.

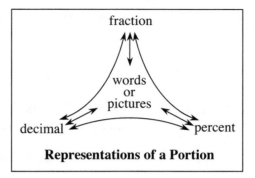

Representations of a Portion

The examples below show how to convert from one form to another.

Decimal to percent:
Multiply the decimal by 100.

$$(0.34)(100) = 34\%$$

Percent to decimal:
Divide the percent by 100.

$$78.6\% = 78.6 \div 100 = 0.786$$

Fraction to percent:
Set up an equivalent fraction using 100 as the denominator. The numerator is the percent.

$$\frac{4}{5} \cdot \boxed{\frac{20}{20}} = \frac{80}{100} = 80\%$$

Percent to Fraction:
Use 100 as the denominator. Use the digits in the percent as the numerator. Simplify as needed.

$$22\% = \frac{22}{100} \cdot \boxed{\frac{1/2}{1/2}} = \frac{11}{50}$$

Decimal to fraction:
Use the digits as the numerator. Use the decimal place value as the denominator. Simplify as needed.

Fraction to decimal:
Divide the numerator by the denominator.

1-120.   How many tenths are in one whole? How many hundredths?

1-121.   Convert the following fractions to decimals. Show your work.

a. $\frac{2}{5}$ b. $\frac{3}{8}$ c. $\frac{30}{20}$

1-122.   Mario ordered a pizza for dinner. When it arrived, Mario quickly ate $\frac{1}{8}$ of the pizza. While Mario was getting napkins, his pet poodle ate $\frac{1}{3}$ of the pizza.

a.   Draw a model of the pizza that shows the portion that has been eaten.

b.   Write a numerical expression to show the fraction of the pizza that is left.

c.   About what percent of the pizza is left?

1-123.   Nicole has a machine that will produce a number from 1 through 50 when she pushes a button. If she pushes the button, what is:

a.   P(multiple of 10)?   b.   P(not 100)?

c.   P(not a multiple of 4)?   d.   P(one-digit number)?

1-124.   Lyle and his study team are designing spinners.

a.   If one-half of the sections on a spinner are green and there are 14 sections, how many are green?

b.   If three-fourths of the sections on a different spinner have stripes and there are 24 sections, how many sections have stripes?

1-125.   Copy the rows of equations at right onto your paper. If the numbers in the equations continue to change in the same way as the pattern shows, write the next five rows of equations in the sequence.

$$9 \cdot 9 + 7 = 88$$
$$98 \cdot 9 + 6 = 888$$
$$987 \cdot 9 + 5 = 8888$$
$$9876 \cdot 9 + 4 = 88888$$

1.3.2 How can I rewrite a decimal?

Rewriting Decimals as Fractions

In Lesson 1.3.1, you worked with different fractions and found ways to rewrite those fractions as repeating and terminating decimals. In this lesson, you will **reverse your thinking** and instead represent decimals as fractions.

As you work with your team today, ask each other these questions to focus your discussion:

How else can I describe the portion?

How many pieces are in the whole?

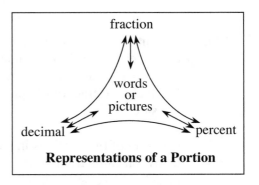

Representations of a Portion

1-126. Complete the portions web for each number below. An example for $\frac{2}{3}$ is shown at right.

a. $\frac{7}{10}$ b. 0.75

c. Three-fifths   d. $\frac{5}{8}$

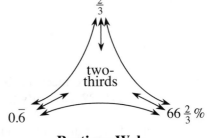

Portions Web

e. With your team, explain how you rewrote 0.75 as a fraction in part (b). Is there more than one way? Be as specific as possible.

1-127. Since 0.7 is described in words as "seven tenths," it is not a surprise that the equivalent fraction is $\frac{7}{10}$. Obtain a set of decimal cards from your teacher or use the list below to complete the following tasks:

- Use the names of fractions (like "twenty-three hundredths") to rewrite each terminating decimal as a fraction. First try to use what you know about place value to write the fraction.

- Check that the fraction is equal to the decimal with your calculator.

a. 0.19   b. 0.391   c. 0.001

d. 0.019   e. 0.3   f. 0.524

1-128. Jerome works at the Fraction Factory in the department that changes decimals into fractions. He has just received an order to rewrite $0.\overline{73}$ as a fraction. He started to rewrite it as $\frac{73}{100}$, but he is not sure that he is correct. Is $\frac{73}{100}$ equal to $0.\overline{73}$? Be ready to **justify** your answer.

1-129. Katrina is now responsible for finding the decimal equivalent for each of the numbers below. She thinks these fractions have something to do with the decimals and fractions in problem 1-127, but she is not sure.

Get a set of the fractions in parts (a) through (f) below on cards from your teacher, and use your calculator to change each fraction into a decimal. Add the decimal information to the card. Can you find a pattern?

a. $\frac{19}{99}$ b. $\frac{391}{999}$ c. $\frac{3}{9}$

d. $\frac{1}{999}$ e. $\frac{524}{999}$ f. $\frac{19}{999}$

g. What connections do these fractions have with those you found in problem 1-127? Be ready to share your observations with the class.

h. Use your pattern to predict the fraction equivalent for $0.\overline{24}$. Then test your guess with a calculator.

i. Use your pattern to predict the decimal equivalent for $\frac{65}{99}$. Check your answer with your calculator.

1-130.   REWRITING REPEATING DECIMALS AS FRACTIONS

Jerome wants to figure out why his pattern from
problem 1-129 works. He noticed that he could
eliminate the repeating digits by subtracting, as he did
in the work at right. This gave him an idea. *"What if I
multiply by something before I subtract, so that I'm left
with more than zero?"* he wondered. He wrote:

$$0.\overline{73} = 0.737373....$$
$$-0.\overline{73} = 0.737373....$$
$$0 = 0$$

$$10(0.\overline{73}) = 7.373737...$$
$$- (0.\overline{73}) = 0.737373...$$

*"The repeating decimals do not make zero in this problem. But if I multiply by
100 instead, I think it will work!"* He tried again:

$$100(0.\overline{73}) = 73.737373...$$
$$- 0.\overline{73} = 0.737373....$$
$$99(0.\overline{73}) = 73.0$$

a.   Discuss Jerome's work with your team. How did he get 99 sets of $0.\overline{73}$?
What happened to the repeating decimals when he subtracted?

b.   *"I know that 99 sets of $0.\overline{73}$ are equal to 73 from my equation,"* Jerome
said. *"So to find what just one set of $0.\overline{73}$ is equal to, I will need to divide
73 into 99 equal parts."* Represent Jerome's idea as a fraction.

c.   Use Jerome's **strategy** to rewrite $0.\overline{85}$ as a fraction. Be prepared to explain
your **reasoning**.

1-131.   DESIGN A DECIMAL DEPARTMENT

Congratulations! Because of your new skills rewriting fractions and decimals, you have been put in charge of the Designer Decimals Department of the Fraction Factory. People write to your department and order their favorite fractions rewritten as beautiful decimals.

Recently, your department has received some strange orders. Review each order below and decide if you can complete it. If possible, find the new fraction or decimal. If not, write to the customer explaining why their order cannot be completed.

Order 1:   "Please send me $0.4\overline{3}$ written as a fraction."

Order 2:   "I'd like a terminating decimal to represent $\frac{44}{99}$."

Order 3:   "Could you send me 0.208 as two different fractions, one with 125 in the denominator and one with 3000 in the denominator?"

1-132.   **Additional Challenge:**
A strange order has arrived in the Designer Decimals Department, asking for a new kind of decimal to be written as a fraction. The order is reprinted at right. With your team, rewrite the decimal as an equivalent fraction or explain why you cannot.

Please send me the decimal 0.01001000100001... rewritten as a fraction.

Review & Preview

1-133.   Which of the following fractions are repeating decimals and which are terminating? Show how you made your decisions.

a. $\frac{2}{15}$ b. $\frac{11}{20}$ c. $\frac{17}{40}$ d. $\frac{1}{12}$

1-134.   Copy the Portions Webs below and fill in the missing parts.

a.

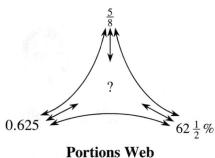

Portions Web

b.

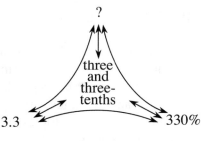

Portions Web

1-135.   Find the perimeter and area of the given shape.

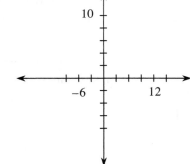

1-136.   Copy the graphs below onto your paper. Then complete the scale by labeling the remaining tick marks.

a.

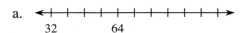

b.

c.

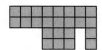

1-137.   About three out of every 25 Americans live in California. About three out of every 50 Americans live in New York, and about two out of every 25 Americans live in Texas.

a.   Which state has the largest population?

b.   Which state has the smallest population?

c.   About what percentage of Americans do *not* live in California, New York, or Texas?

Chapter 1 Closure   What have I learned?

Reflection and Synthesis

The activities below offer you a chance to reflect about what you have learned during this chapter. As you work, look for concepts that you feel very comfortable with, ideas that you would like to learn more about, and topics you need more help with. Look for connections between ideas as well as connections with material you learned previously.

①   SUMMARIZING MY UNDERSTANDING

This section gives you an opportunity to show what you know about certain math topics or ideas.

Fraction, Decimal, Percent Pamphlet

You have been using fractions, decimals, and percents to write probabilities and portions, and to compare different numbers. You have seen that rewriting numbers in different forms can make it easier to compare them (for example, rewriting fractions with common denominators or percents can make it easier to decide which is greater). Now you will create a pamphlet explaining to others how fractions, decimals, and percents are related to each other and how to rewrite them in the other forms.

Set up the pamphlet: Follow your teacher's directions for folding a piece of paper to make a pamphlet. Your teacher may give you a Chapter 1 Closure GO Resource Page (pictured at right) to use. (GO is short for Graphic Organizer.)

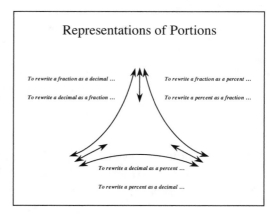

Examples to show what you know: Your teacher will help you choose one fraction, one decimal, and one percent for your explanations. Review how to rewrite numbers using your Toolkit, textbook and other classroom resources. Then, write each example number in each of the other representations. Use words, pictures, and color to show connections between the representations.

Explain your thinking: Write a **general** explanation for how to change from one representation to another.

WHAT HAVE I LEARNED?

Working the problems in this section will help you to evaluate which types of problems you feel comfortable with and which ones you need more help with. This section will appear at the end of every chapter to help you check your understanding.

Solve each problem as completely as you can. The table at the end of this closure section has answers to these problems. It also tells you where you can find additional help and practice on problems like them.

CL 1-138. Make three new fractions that are equivalent to $\frac{6}{24}$. Show your work.

CL 1-139. Aiden is drawing coins from a bag containing 6 pennies, 3 nickels, 4 dimes, and 2 quarters. What is the probability that he will draw a penny?

CL 1-140. Tuan is playing a game, but the spinner is incomplete. If the numbers in the sections of the spinner represent the probabilities of spinning each section, help him figure out the fraction for the missing section of the spinner.

CL 1-141. Complete each portion web.

a.

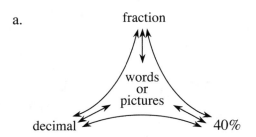

b.

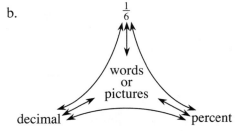

c.

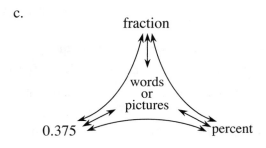

CL 1-142. Add $\frac{1}{6} + \frac{1}{2}$. Show all of your steps.

CL 1-143. Find the perimeter and area of each figure below.

a.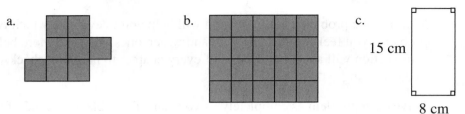

b.

c. 15 cm 8 cm

d. Sketch at least one way to rearrange the tiles in part (a) so that the shape has a larger perimeter.

CL 1-144. Cheryl's parents and her older brother all have cell phones. Cheryl would like her own phone, so she surveyed her friends to see how many cell phones were in each of their homes. Here are her results: 3, 1, 7, 1, 1, 4, 2, 5, 3, 2, 6, 4, 1, 2, 3. Find the mean, median, and mode for the data. Can Cheryl use the results of her survey to convince her parents that she should have a cell phone?

CL 1-145. Kimberly is playing "Guess My Number." Her clue is, *"When I triple my number and subtract 7, I get 83."* Find Kimberly's number and explain how you know your answer is correct.

CL 1-146. For each of the problems above, do the following:
- Draw a bar or number line that represents 0 to 10.

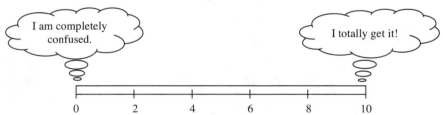

- Color or shade in a portion of the bar that represents your level of understanding and comfort with completing that problem on your own.

If any of your bars are less than a 5, choose *one* of those problems and complete one of the following tasks:
- Write two questions that you would like to ask about that problem.
- Brainstorm two things that you DO know about that type of problem.

If all of your bars are a 5 or above, choose *one* of those problems and do one of these tasks:
- Write two questions you might ask or hints you might give to a student who was stuck on the problem.
- Make a new problem that is similar and more challenging than that problem and solve it.

③   WHAT TOOLS CAN I USE?

You have several tools and references available to help support your learning – your teacher, your study team, your math book, and your Toolkit, to name only a few. At the end of each chapter you will have an opportunity to review your Toolkit for completeness as well as to revise or update it to better reflect your current understanding of big ideas.

The main elements of your Toolkit should be your Learning Log, Math Notes, and the vocabulary used in this chapter. Math words that are new to this chapter appear in bold in the text. Refer to the lists provided below and follow your teacher's instructions to revise your Toolkit, which will help make it a useful reference for you as you complete this chapter and prepare to begin the next one.

Learning Log Entries

- Lesson 1.2.3 – Comparing Probabilities
- Lesson 1.2.5 – Adding Fractions with Unlike Denominators

Math Notes

- Lesson 1.1.2 – Perimeter and Area
- Lesson 1.1.3 – Mean
- Lesson 1.1.4 – Median and Mode
- Lesson 1.1.5 – Representations of Portions
- Lesson 1.2.1 – Probability
- Lesson 1.2.2 – Probability: Vocabulary and Definitions
- Lesson 1.2.3 – Additive and Multiplicative Identities
- Lesson 1.2.4 – Equivalent Fractions
- Lesson 1.2.5 – Scaling a Graph
- Lesson 1.3.1 – Fraction $\leftrightarrow$ Decimal $\leftrightarrow$ Percent

Mathematical Vocabulary

The following is a list of vocabulary found in this chapter. Make sure that you are familiar with the terms below and know what they mean. For words you do not know, refer to the glossary or index. You might also want to add these words to your Toolkit for a way to reference them in the future.

area	equivalent fractions	experimental probability
histogram	mean	median
mode	outcome	percent
perimeter	prime number	probability
repeating decimal	terminating decimal	theoretical probability

Process Words

These words describe problem solving strategies and processes that you have been involved in as you worked in Chapter 1. Make sure you know what each of these words means. If you are not sure, you can talk with your teacher or other students or look through your book for problems in which you were asked to do these things.

brainstorm	choose a strategy	describe
generalize	justify	predict
reason and justify	represent	reverse your thinking
visualize		

Answers and Support for Closure Activity #2
What Have I Learned?

Problem	Solution	Need Help?	More Practice
CL 1-138.	Possible answers include: $\frac{1}{4}$, $\frac{2}{8}$, $\frac{3}{12}$, $\frac{4}{16}$, $\frac{8}{32}$, $\frac{12}{48}$	Lessons 1.2.2 and 1.2.3	Problems 1-67, 1-70, 1-93, and 1-108
CL 1-139.	$\frac{6}{15}$ or $\frac{2}{5}$	Lesson 1.2.1 Math Notes boxes in Lessons 1.2.1 and 1.2.2	Problems 1-44, 1-47, 1-58, 1-80, and 1-83
CL 1-140.	$\frac{3}{10}$	Lessons 1.2.4 and 1.2.5 Math Notes box in Lesson1.2.4 Learning Log (problem 1-107)	Problems 1-81, 1-82, 1-103, 1-105, and 1-122
CL 1-141.	a. Two fifths, 0.4, 40% b. One sixth, $0.1\bar{6}$, 16.67% c. Three eighths, 0.375, 37.5%	Lessons 1.1.5, 1.2.3, 1.3.1, and 1.3.2 Math Notes box in Lesson 1.3.1	Problems 1-35, 1-37, 1-38, 1-48, 1-62, 1-78, 1-92, 1-121, 1-126, and 1-134
CL 1-142.	$\frac{8}{12}$, $\frac{4}{6}$, or $\frac{2}{3}$	Lesson 1.2.4 Math Notes boxes in Lessons 1.2.3 and 1.2.4 Learning Log (problem 1-107)	Problems 1-84 through 1-89, 1-100, and 1-110

Problem	Solution	Need Help?	More Practice
CL 1-143.	a. Perimeter: 14 units Area: 8 square units b. Perimeter: 18 units Area: 20 square units c. Perimeter: 46 cm Area: 120 cm d. Possible arrangement: 	Lesson 1.1.2 Math Notes box in Lesson 1.1.2	Problems 1-10, 1-12, 1-19, 1-39, and 1-135
CL 1-144.	Mean 3, median 3, mode 1; Cheryl probably cannot use her data to convince her parents because none is 4 or more.	Lessons 1.1.3 and 1.1.4 Math Notes boxes in Lessons 1.1.3 and 1.1.4	Problems 1-18, 1-26, 1-40, and 1-98
CL 1-145.	Kimberly's number is 30. $30 \cdot 3 - 7 = 83$	Lesson 1.1.3	Problems 1-15, 1-16, 1-17, 1-66, and 1-76,

Puzzle Investigator Problems

Dear Students,

Puzzle Investigator Problems (PIs) present you with an opportunity to investigate complex, interesting problems over several days. Their purpose is to focus on the process of solving complex problems. **You will be evaluated on your ability to show, explain, and justify your work and thoughts**. Save **all** of your work, including what does not work, in order to write about the processes you used to reach your answer.

Completion of a PI problem includes four parts:

- **Problem Statement:** State the problem clearly in your own words so that anyone reading your paper will understand the problem you intend to solve.

- **Process and Solutions:** Describe in detail your thinking and **reasoning** as you work from start to finish. Explain your solution and how you know it is correct. Add diagrams when it helps your explanation. Include what you do that does not work and changes you make along the way. If you do not complete this problem, describe what you <u>do</u> know and where and why you are stuck.

- **Reflection:** Reflect about your learning and your reaction to the problem. What mathematics did you learn from it? What did you learn about your math problem solving **strategies**? Is this problem similar to any other problems you have done before? If yes, how?

- **Attached work:** Include <u>all</u> your work and notes. Your scratch work is important because it is a record of your thinking. Do not throw anything away.

PI-1.   SQUARES GALORE

How many squares do you see at right? Can you identify more than 4 squares? How can we know when we have found all the squares? The puzzles below will help you investigate these questions.

a.   How many squares can you find on an 8×8 checkerboard, like the one shown at right? (By the way, there are more than 65 squares.) Organize your work so that you can find patterns that help you to determine how many 1×1 squares, 2×2 squares, and so on, that you can find.

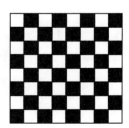

Problem continues on next page. →

PI-1.   *Problem continued from previous page.*

b.   Use your patterns from part (a) to figure out how many squares would be in a design made with square tiles if it is 30 tiles wide and 30 tiles long. Can you do this without drawing a diagram?

c.   Is there a square made up of square tiles (like the checkerboard) that has only 75 squares overall? What about one that has 120 squares overall? If it is possible, show the square design and explain how you found it. If it is not possible, explain why that design cannot exist.

PI-2.   TOOTHPICK CHALLENGES

This challenge will require you to **visualize** new shapes that can be made from the toothpick designs below. Keep in mind that for no puzzle should you have toothpicks that overlap or "cross" each other. To help you solve the challenges below, you may want to get toothpicks and use them to build models.

a.   The design at right is made with 16 toothpicks.

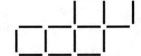

i.   Move only 2 toothpicks so that the result has only 4 congruent (identical) squares.

ii. Starting with the original design, move 2 toothpicks so that the design has a total of 6 squares. Note: The squares do not need to have the same area.

iii. Starting with the original design, which 2 toothpicks could you move so that 5 squares of the same size remain? Is there more than one way to do this?

b.   This time, 9 toothpicks are used to make 4 equilateral triangles at right.

i.   Move only 2 toothpicks so that the result has only 3 equilateral triangles.

ii. Starting with the original design, move only 5 toothpicks so that the result has 3 equilateral triangles.

Making Connections: Course 2

CHAPTER 2
Transformations and Area

While you may not think about how you move objects in daily life, such movements involve changing directions, much like placing a piece in a jigsaw puzzle. In Sections 2.1 and 2.2 you will investigate different kinds of motion on a number line and on a graph. You will begin by describing how a point moves on a number line using addition and subtraction of integers. You will also learn how to give directions to slide, flip, turn, and stretch flat shapes on a coordinate grid and show where the shapes will be after a series of moves.

Section 2.3 focuses on the question, *"How can we use what we know about the area of basic shapes to find the area of complex shapes?"* As you develop new **strategies** for finding the area of shapes, you will be able to solve new problems involving areas of a park.

In this chapter, you will learn how to:

➤ Connect addition and subtraction of integers to movement along a number line.

➤ Transform shapes by flipping, turning, and sliding them on a coordinate grid.

➤ Describe movement on a graph using coordinates and expressions.

➤ Find the area of shapes, including rectangles, triangles, parallelograms, and trapezoids.

➤ Break complex shapes into smaller pieces in order to find area.

Guiding Questions

Think about these questions throughout this chapter:

How can I visualize it?

How can I describe the motion?

How can I transform it?

How can I break it into smaller pieces?

How can I rearrange the shape?

Chapter Outline

Section 2.1 You will describe motion on a number line using integers and will learn how addition and subtraction can help you predict the starting or ending point of a series of moves.

Section 2.2 You will use a technology tool to move a shape on a coordinate grid using slides, flips, and turns, and will use integers to describe those moves.

Section 2.3 You will find the area of different shapes such as parallelograms, triangles, and trapezoids by rearranging them into rectangles.

Making Connections: Course 2

2.1.1 How does it move?

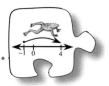

Adding Positive and Negative Numbers

In Chapter 1, you learned about the famous frog-jumping contest that takes place each spring in Calaveras County, California. In the contest, the final measure represents the distance the frog moves away from a starting pad after three separate hops. The three hops can be different lengths and go in different directions.

In this section you will solve problems that involve distances and directions with diagrams and numbers.

2-1.   GETTING THERE

Elliott has been watching Dr. Frog take practice jumps all day. The frog keeps landing 15 feet from the starting pad after making three hops. Answer the questions below to consider ways that the frog can travel 15 feet in three hops.

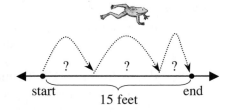

- How many combinations of hops can you find to move Dr. Frog 15 feet from where he started? Show your work with pictures, words, numbers, or symbols.

- Can the frog move 15 feet in three equal hops?

- If two of the frog's hops are 10 feet long, how could you describe the third hop? Is there more than one possibility?

2-2.   Elliott is so interested in the frogs that he is developing a video game about them. In his game frogs start on a number line like the one below. The frogs can hop to the left and to the right.

One game starts with the frog sitting at the number 3 on the number line. Use your Lesson 2.1.1 Resource Page to help you answer Elliott's challenges below.

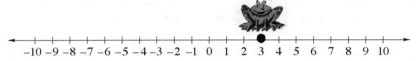

a.   If the frog hops to the right 4 units, to the left 7 units, and then to the right 6 units, where will the frog end up?

b.   If the frog makes three hops to the right and lands on 10, list the lengths of two possible combinations of hops that will get it from 3 to 10.

c.   Could the frog land on a positive number if it makes three hops to the left? Use an example to show your thinking.

d.   **Additional Challenge:** The frog made two hops of the same length to the right and then hopped 6 units to the left. If the frog ended up at 11 on the number line, how long were the first two hops?

2-3.   While designing his videogame, Elliott decided to replace some of his long sentences describing hops with symbols. For example, to represent where the frog traveled and landed in part (a) of problem 2-2, he wrote:

$$3 + 4 + (-7) + 6$$

a.   How does Elliott's expression represent the words in part (a) of problem 2-2? Where did the 3 come from? Why is one number negative?

b.   If another set of hops was represented by $5 + (-10) + 2 + 1$, describe the frog's movements. Where did the frog start, and where did it end up?

c.   One game used the expression $-5 + 7$. Where does the frog start? Where does it end up?

d.   Another game had a frog start at 12, hop 5 units to the left, 6 units to the right, and 9 units to the left. Write an expression to represent the frog's motion on the number line. Where did the frog end up?

Making Connections: Course 2

2-4.   Another frog starts at –3 and hops four times.
        Its hops are listed at right.

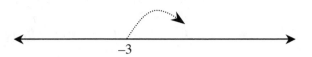

Hop Lengths
Right 2 units
Left 7 units
Right 10 units
Left 3 units

a.   Is it possible for the frog to finish at 2 on the
     number line? Explain.

b.   If you have not done so already, write an expression (sum) for the frog's
     movements. Where does the frog end up?

c.   Will the frog land in a different place if it makes its hops in a different
     order? In other words, does it matter which hop the frog takes first,
     second, etc.?

d.   Kamille says that for the frog to end up at –1, she can ignore the last three
     hops in the list. She says she only needs to move the frog to the right
     2 units. Is she correct? Why?

2-5.   When adding, the order in which the numbers are added does not matter. That
        means that you will get the same answer if you add $2+5$ or if you add $5+2$.
        This property is called the **Commutative Property of Addition**. Read the
        Math Notes box for this lesson and answer the questions below.

a.   Why does $2+5=5+2$? Use your number line to explain.

b.   Does the Commutative Property work with negative numbers? Use a
     number line to verify that $-3+10=10+(-3)$.

c.   Use the Commutative Property to rewrite the expression $6+4+(-3)$ in two
     different ways. Use a number line to show that they all have the same
     value.

2-6.   In part (d) of problem 2-4, Kamille noticed that she could group some of the numbers together first before finding the entire sum. When she grouped the last three hops, she actually calculated the expression $-3 + 2 + (-7 + 10 + (-3))$.

She wonders, *"When adding, will grouping the terms in different ways affect the sum?"*

a.   The expressions below use the same numbers that are grouped differently. Find the sums. Use a number line if it will help. Do you get the same answers?

i. $5 + (4 + (-1))$ ii. $(5 + 4) + (-1)$

b.   In an addition problem, the numbers that are added can be grouped together in different ways and the sums will be the same. This is called the **Associative Property of Addition**. The Math Notes box for this lesson has information about this property.

Show that $(-2 + 6) + 9 = -2 + (6 + 9)$.

MᴇᴛHODS AND Mᴇᴀɴɪɴɢꜱ

<small>MATH NOTES</small>

Commutative and Associative Properties of Addition

When two numbers are combined together using addition, changing the order in which they are added does not matte, so $5 + 7 = 7 + 5$. This fact is known as the **Commutative Property of Addition**. This result is generalized using variables as:

$$a + b = b + a$$

Note that subtraction does not satisfy the Commutative Property of Addition since $7 - 5 \neq 5 - 7$.

The **Associative Property of Addition** states that changing the grouping of the numbers does not change the result of the addition. The answer to the problem $(7 + 5) + 9$ is the same as $7 + (5 + 9)$. This is generalized using variables as:

$$(a + b) + c = a + (b + c)$$

Note that subtraction is not associative since $(7 - 5) - 1 \neq 7 - (5 - 1)$.

$$2 - 1 \neq 7 - 4$$

2-7. Lucas' frog is sitting at –2 on the number line.

    a. His frog hops 4 units to the right, 6 units to the left, and then 10 more units to the right. Write an expression (sum) to represent his frog's movement.

    b. Where does the frog land?

2-8. Nathan wants you to solve this puzzle: *"I am thinking of a number. If you divide my number by three and add –3, you will get 4. What is my number?"* Show all of your work.

2-9. Simplify the following expressions.

    a. $\frac{2}{3} - \frac{1}{6}$ b. $\frac{7}{10} - \frac{1}{5}$ c. $\frac{1}{2} - \frac{3}{4}$

2-10. One of the topics you will review in Chapter 2 is reading graphs. Look at the graph at right. This graph shows positive and negative values on both axes and it divides the plane into four parts, or quadrants. It is called a **four-quadrant** graph.

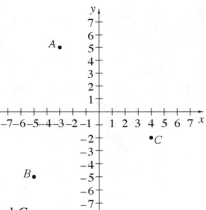

    a. The coordinates (the x- and y-values) for point A are $(-3, 5)$. Explain how these numbers tell you the position of point A using the graph.

    b. Name the coordinates (x, y) for points B and C.

    c. If Samantha moved point A 9 units down and 6 units to the right, at what point would she end up?

2-11. Rewrite the following fractions as decimals and decide if they are terminating or repeating decimals. Show your work and explain how you made your decision.

    a. $\frac{7}{8}$ b. $\frac{2}{9}$ c. $\frac{4}{7}$ d. $\frac{11}{22}$

2-12. Copy the sequences and fill in the missing numbers. Explain the pattern in words.

    a. 5, 14, 23, 32, 41, ___, ___, ___

    b. 3, 6, 12, 24, 48, ___, ___, ___

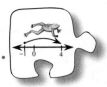

2.1.2 How can I record it?

Adding and Subtracting Integers

Mathematical symbols and expressions are like shorthand. Instead of writing "The sum of positive four and positive seven and negative two," we can write $4 + 7 + (-2)$. These symbols give information about how the numbers are related and can also be used to describe real-life situations.

In this lesson you will use movement on a number line to make sense of expressions involving addition and subtraction.

2-13.   Before you find each sum below, predict whether the answer will be positive, negative, or zero. Then draw a number line on your paper and use it to find the sum. Be ready to share your **strategy**.

  a. $-2 + (-9)$ b. $5 + (-5)$ c. $4 + (-7)$ d. $-6 + 2$

2-14.   Emre is looking at the expression $4 + (-7)$, which his teammate wrote to represent starting at 4 and moving seven units to the left. *"I can also show addition with + and – symbols."* He made the diagram below.

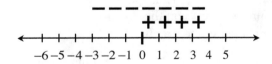

  a.   Why do you think Emre placed four + symbols where he did?

  b.   What do the – symbols represent?

  c.   How does Emre's diagram show that the sum is −3?

  d.   Use the idea of frog hopping to explain why the tiles at right add up to zero.

$$- - - -$$
$$+ + + +$$

Making Connections: Course 2

2-15.   Emre's diagram for $-5+9+(-1)$ is shown below.

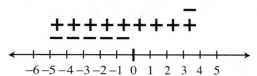

a.   Copy his diagram on your paper and describe the motion it represents in words.

b.   Circle any "**zeros**" (+ and – symbols that add up to zero). What is left?

c.   What is the sum of $-5+9+(-1)$?

d.   What if the + and – symbols are not on the number line? What if Emre organized the symbols in separate rows, like those shown at right? Does the sum change?

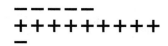

2-16.   Your teacher will give you tiles to represent + and – symbols to use to build expressions. For each part below:

- Build the expressions with tiles and find the sum.

- **Visualize** the frog hopping on a number line to confirm your answer.

- Record your work by drawing the + and – symbols and circling zeros.

a. $6+(-5)+2$ b. $-8+8+(-2)$ c. $-7+(-2)$

2-17.   What if you do not have enough tiles and your number line is not long enough? Without using tiles, add the numbers in each part below. Explain your **strategy**.

a. $32+(-38)$ b. $-150+(-50)$ c. $-41+28$

2-18.   SUBTRACTION

What is the connection between adding negative numbers and subtraction? Use + and – tiles from your teacher to answer the questions below.

a.   Build $8+(-2)$ with tiles. Draw a picture on your paper. What is the sum?

b.   How could you use the tiles to simplify $8-2$? Talk about this with your team and find the answer. Draw a picture to show your **strategy**.

c.   Compare your answers to parts (a) and (b) above. Explain why they give the same answer.

d.   How could you use a number line to figure out $8-2$? Draw a number line on your paper. Be ready to share your ideas with the class.

2-19.   For each part below, simplify the expression using tiles or a number line. If one **strategy** does not work, try a different **strategy**. Be sure to draw a diagram to show your work.

   a. $9 - 8$ b. $7 - 11$ c. $-5 - (-2)$ d. $0 - 6$

2-20.   MAKING CONNECTIONS

One way to use + and – tiles to show that
$-5 - (-2) = -3$ is shown at right.

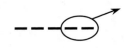

   a.   Now think about this problem on a number line. How could you start at –5 and make one "hop" to end up on –3? Which direction do you move? How far do you travel?

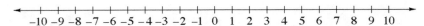

   b.   The symbol "–" can be read aloud as *subtract* or *negative*. But sometimes it makes more sense to translate it as *opposite*. For example, $-5 - (-2)$ can be read as, "Start at –5 and move the *opposite* direction of -2, so move the opposite direction of 'to the left 2'."

        Use this idea to help you figure out $4 - (-6)$ on a number line.

   c.   Now use + and – tiles to simplify $-10 - (-6)$. Draw a diagram to show this on your paper.

   d.   How can you use a number line to simplify $-10 - (-6)$? Show how you get your final answer on a number line.

2-21.   Lani is stuck. She wants to use + and – tiles to simplify $7 - (-2)$. She has 7 + tiles. *"I don't have any negative tiles to take away!"*

   a.   Her friend, Carla, told her to try using the tiles at right. Explain why she can use the tiles at right to represent 7.

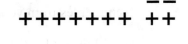

   b.   Use Carla's idea to simplify $7 - (-2)$.

   c.   Did subtracting a negative number make the answer larger or smaller? Explain.

Making Connections: Course 2

2-22.   Find the missing value in each number sentence below.

   a. $-5 + 3 + (-7) =$ ___

   b. $4 - 2 - (-3) =$ ___

   c. $15 + (-30) =$ ___

   d. $8 +$ ___ $= 0$

   e. $-3 - 4 = -2 +$ ___

   f. $-10 -$ ___ $= 15$

   g. $-22 + 40 =$ ___

   h. $25 - 75 + (-10) =$ ___

   i. $16 + 5 + (-30) - (-5) =$ ___

2-23.   Olivia drew number line diagrams to help her solve several integer problems. For each of the problems below, compare her picture to the expression and answer these questions:

   •   How does her number line represent the problem?

   •   How is her picture helpful for evaluating the expression? That is, why did she stop at zero in parts (a), (b), and (c)?

   •   What other expression(s) could you write to represent her picture?

   a. $5 + (-6)$

   b. $3 - 5$

   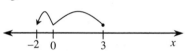

   c. $-7 + 9$

   d. $8 + (-6)$

2-24.   Write two different expressions to represent each picture below.

   a.

   b.

   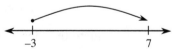

2-25.   LEARNING LOG

   The symbol for minus ("$-$") can be translated into words as *subtract*, *take away*, *negative*, or *opposite*. In your Learning Log, explain how you think of this symbol when adding and subtracting on a number line. Explain how you think of it when you use $+$ and $-$ tiles. Give examples. Label this entry "Meanings for $-$" and today's date.

2-26.   Find the missing value in each number sentence.

a. $4 + (-3) + 3 - 1 =$ ____   b. $-2 - (-4) + 4 =$ ____   c. $5 -$ ___ $= 7$

2-27.   Find the measure indicated in each question below.

a.   Find the perimeter.

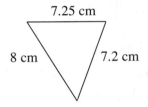

7.25 cm

8 cm   7.2 cm

b.   Find the area.

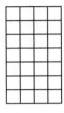

c.   Find the area and perimeter
     of the rectangle at right.

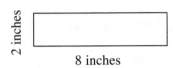

2 inches

8 inches

2-28.   Marguerite wants to convince her parents to raise her monthly allowance. She
        decided to take a quick poll of her five best friends to see what they receive for
        their allowance. Here are the results:

Friend	Allowance
Kari	no allowance
Wanda	$25
Gary	$100
Donna	$20
Jorge	$20

a.   Calculate the mean, median, and mode for her friends' allowances.

b.   Her current allowance is $30.00. Which measure of central tendency
     should she use to get her allowance increased? Why?

2-29.   Look at the two units of measure at right.

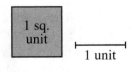

1 sq.
unit

1 unit

a.   Which of them would you use to measure the top
     surface of your desk? Explain your thinking.

b.   What part(s) of your desk could you measure using the linear unit? Draw a
     picture and show how that unit could be used.

2-30.   In parts (a) and (b) below, copy the number lines and use them to show the
         solution to the problems.

         a. 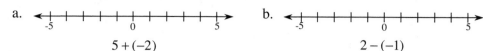   b.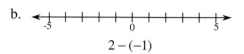

              $5 + (-2)$ $2 - (-1)$

         c.   Show $-3 + 4 + (-1)$ on a number line.

         d.   Rachel said that $-4 + (-3)$ will be positive because two negatives always
              give a positive. Draw the problem on a number line, then explain whether
              you agree or disagree with Rachel.

2-31.   State which direction you should move on a number line from -5 in each
         expression below. Then simplify each expression.

         a. $-5 + (-4)$ b. $-5 - 8$ c. $-5 - (-6)$

2-32.   One of the topics you will soon review in
         Section 2.2 is graphing shapes. The graph at
         right is called a **first quadrant graph**. It uses
         two number lines that only show positive
         numbers and zero.

         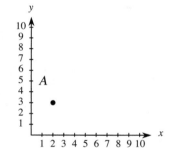

         a.   Carefully copy the **axes** (the number lines)
              and point A on a piece of graph paper.

         b.   Plot the points listed below. Then connect
              them in the order given. Point A is given
              for you.

              A $(2, 3)$, B $(3, 7)$, C $(7, 7)$, D $(8, 3)$ Then connect D to A.

         c.   What is the name of the shape that you drew?

2-33.   Evan's uncle gave him money for his birthday.

         a.   Evan plans to put half of the money in his savings account, spend $\frac{1}{5}$ of the
              money on bubble gum to share with his friends, and buy comic books with
              the money he has left. What portion of the money will he spend on comic
              books?

         b.   Evan uses some of his comic book money to buy a magazine for $4. If
              Evan's uncle gave him $30, what fraction of this money did he spend on the
              magazine?

2-34. Look carefully at the key at right. Which of the keys below could you create by spinning (rotating) the original key? Which keys could you create by flipping (reflecting) the original key?

original

a. 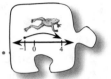 b. c. d.

2.1.3 How can I predict the result?

More Integer Operations

So far in this chapter, you have made connections between moving left and right on a number line and integer expressions. Today you will use a technology tool to check your understanding and describe patterns in your results. By the end of this lesson, you should be prepared to answer these target questions:

How can I decide if the frog will hop to the right or to the left?

Why does subtracting a negative number make the original number greater?

How can I tell if the answer will be positive or negative?

2-35. HOP TO IT

You have learned about how adding and subtracting **integers** (positive and negative whole numbers and zero) moves points on a number line. Today you will practice adding and subtracting integers using a game called "Hop To It" that is available at www.cpm.org/students/technology. After you have played for awhile, think about the following questions and be ready to share your responses with the class. You should be able to **justify** your answers.

a. When you add two negative numbers, will you get a negative or positive answer? Why does this happen?

b. If you add a positive number to a negative number, will you get a negative or positive answer? Why does this happen?

c. When you subtract a negative number, is your answer greater than or less than the number you started with? Why does this happen?

Making Connections: Course 2

2-36.   Simplify each expression. **Visualize** the movement of a frog on a number line and its landing point. You may want to use the number lines on the Lesson 2.1.1 Resource Page to help you.

   a. $-1 + 2$ b. $-5 + 3$ c. $-2 - (-4)$

   d. $6 - (-3)$ e. $8 - 9$ f. $6 + (-7)$

   g. $4 - (-4)$ h. $3 + (-3)$ i. $-4 - 3$

   j. $20 + (-18)$ k. $20 - (-18)$ l. $-30 - (-22)$

2-37.   Predict whether each answer below will be positive or negative. You may want to **visualize** a number line or + and – tiles. Then find the answer to check your prediction.

   a. $5 - 10$ b. $2 + (-8)$ c. $-5 - (-6)$ d. $15 + (-4)$

2-38.   **Additional Challenge:** Given the hop lengths –8, –5, 2, –3, and –1, can a frog start at 4 on a number line and end up on –2? You do not need to use all of the hop lengths. Can you find more than one way to do this?

2-39.   LEARNING LOG

   In your Learning Log, answer the target questions from the beginning of this lesson. The questions are reprinted for you below. Title this entry, "Subtraction of Integers," and include today's date.

   How can I decide if the frog will hop to the right or to the left?

   Why does subtracting a negative number make the original number greater?

   How can I tell if your answer will be positive or negative?

2-40. Simplify the following expressions. Show your work.

   a. $8 - (-10)$ b. $-6 - 9$ c. $8 - 3 + (-4)$ d. $0 - (-3)$

   e. $15 - 20$ f. $-9 + 14$ g. $11 + (-7)$ h. $5 - 9$

2-41. Solve the number puzzles below.

   a. If I add 9 to my number, I get 6. What is my number?

   b. If I start at –5 on a number line and end up at –8, what direction did I move? How many units did I move?

   c. If I moved to the right 8 and moved to the left 8, what can you tell me about my ending position?

2-42. John has a bag of marbles that contains 12 red marbles, 20 green marbles, and 17 blue marbles.

   a. If John pulls one marble out of the bag, what is the probability that it will not be red, that is, P(not red)?

   b. What is the probability that he will draw a purple marble, that is, P(purple)?

2-43. Copy and complete each of the Portions Webs below.

   a.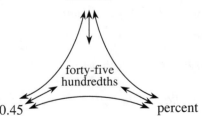

   b.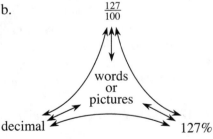

2-44. Find the missing lengths in the problems below. Assume each line segment is subdivided into equal segments. Show your work.

   a.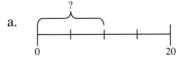

   b.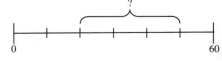

88   *Making Connections*: Course 2

2.2.1   How can I move a shape on a grid?

Rigid Transformations

How can you describe the movement of a figure on a flat surface when it is not moving in a straight line? For example, when you need to move a loose puzzle piece into the puzzle (as shown at right), how can you describe the way its position changes?

Today you will explore mathematical ways of sliding, turning, and flipping an object without changing its size or shape in order to solve challenges. These movements are called **rigid transformations**.

2-45.   KEY IN THE LOCK PUZZLES

Use the transformation buttons (shown at right) with the technology tool "Key-Lock Transformations," to move the key to the keyhole to unlock the door. (The game is available at www.cpm.org/students/technology.)

Slide

Turn

Flip

You will need to tell the computer about how you want the key to move. For example, how far to the left or right and how far up or down do you want the key to slide? Which direction do you want your key to flip?

Your task: For each puzzle, move the key to the keyhole. Remember that to unlock the door, the key must fit exactly into the keyhole and not be upside down! Your key will also not be able to move through walls.

Be sure to record your moves on the Lesson 2.2.1 Resource Page.

Discussion Points

In what direction does the key need to move?

How can we get the key to fit the keyhole?

What information do we need to give the computer so that it moves the key into the lock?

M ETHODS AND MEANINGS

Adding & Subtracting Integers

Integers are positive and negative whole numbers and zero. One way that integers can be combined is by **adding**, which can be thought of as walking on a number line. If you walk one step left, and then one step back to the right, you end up in the same place as you started. This is represented on the number line as $-1 + 1 = 0$. A number and its opposite, like 5 and -5, are called **additive inverses**, and their sum in zero (0).

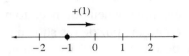

To **add integers** on a number line, mark the position of the first integer, and then move in the direction of the second integer the number of units indicated. Positive numbers indicate movement to the right, while negative numbers indicate movement to the left. Study the examples below:

Example 1: $-5 + (2)$

Example 2: $-6 + (-2)$

One method for **subtracting integers** is to use a number line as you did with addition, except that instead of moving in the direction indicated by the second integer, you must move in the opposite direction to "**undo**" that motion. For example, adding -3 would indicate moving to the left on the number line, so **subtracting** -3 would undo that motion, and mean moving to the right on the number line.

Example: $3 - (-3) = 3 + 3$

Example: $-2 - 5 = -2 + (-5) = -7$

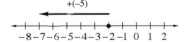

2-46.   Finding patterns is an important problem solving skill used in mathematics. You will use the patterns in Diamond Problems to solve other problems later in the course. Can you discover a pattern for the numbers in each of the four diamonds below?

Copy the Diamond Problems below and use the pattern you discovered to complete each of them.

a.   b.   c.   d.

2-47.   Describe what moves you could use to create the transformation of the original image shown at right.

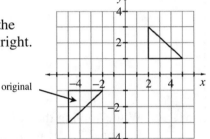

2-48.   Simplify each expression.

a. $-32 + 10 - (-2)$

b. $17 + (-50) - 5$ c. $-5 - (-8) - 1$

2-49.   Lisa and Nicole are playing a new version of Toothpicks and Tiles. Instead of showing Nicole a shape so that she has to find the number of toothpicks and the number of tiles, Lisa describes the shape and Nicole has to build it out of tiles.

Lisa says, *"My shape has 14 tiles and 16 toothpicks."*

a.   Draw a shape that matches Lisa's description. **Justify** your answer.

b.   Is there more than one shape that matches this description? If so, sketch a second shape.

2-50.   Thu has a bag with 7 green marbles, 5 blue marbles, and 4 red marbles. For each part below, if the marble selected in replaced before the next marble is drawn, what is the probability that she will draw:

a.   A red marble?   b.   A red or a green marble?   c.   An orange marble?

2.2.2   How can I move a shape on a grid?

Rigid Transformations on a Coordinate Grid

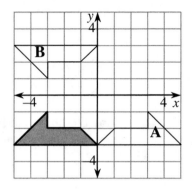

Have you ever had trouble giving directions?
Sometimes describing where something is or how it
moved is difficult. For this reason, people often use
coordinate grids, like the one show at right, to help
describe directions by using words like "left" and
"down." They can also help you measure distances.

Today you will work with your team to describe
movement on a grid. You will also look at ways to
describe where an object is on the grid before and after
a transformation. As you work, use the questions
below to help start math discussions.

Is there a different way to get the same result?

Did we give enough information?

How can we describe the position?

2-51.   While solving the key challenge in
Lesson 2.2.1, Rowan made more than
one move to change his key from point
A to point B and from point C to point
D, as shown on the graph at right. Both
of these keys are shown as triangles on
the Lesson 2.2.2 Resource Page.

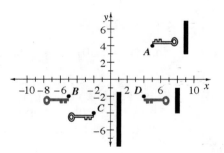

Your task: With your team, describe how Rowan could have moved each key
from the starting position to the ending position using slides (also called
translations), turns (also called **rotations**), and/or flips (also called
reflections).

- Make sure you provide enough detail to describe the moves completely.

- Try to find more than one way he could have moved each key.

- Be ready to **justify** your ideas with the class.

2-52.   **WHERE DOES IT LAND?**

Felicia found a copy of a puzzle like the one in problem 2-45, but the lock is missing. All she has are the starting points and the moves to unlock the lock. This time her key is shaped like a triangle.

The points are at A(-5, 0), B(-5, 3), and C(-1, 0).

Step 1:   Translate 4 units to the right and 2 units up.

Step 2:   Reflect across the x-axis.

Step 3:   Rotate counter-clockwise 90° about point (3, -2).

Help Felicia find out where the lock is by following her steps. The following questions are designed to help you.

a.   With your team, set up your own coordinate grid on graph paper. The questions below will help. Refer to the Math Notes box at the end of this lesson if your team needs more information about how to set up the graph.

   •   How many **quadrants** (regions) should the graph have? Should it be an "L" graph with only the first quadrant? Or a "T" graph with four quadrants?

   •   How can the **x-axis** (which is horizontal ↔) and **y-axis** (which is vertical ↕) be labeled so we can remember which one is which?

   •   How should the axes be **scaled?** How many units should you use for each side length of a grid square?

b.   Plot triangle *ABC* to represent the key.

c.   Follow Step 1 to translate the triangle. Name the new location of each **vertex**, or corner, of the triangle in the form (x, y).

d.   Complete Step 2. Sketch the triangle in its new position and label the coordinates of each vertex.

e.   Where does her triangle end up? Complete Step 3 on the graph and label the coordinates of each vertex.

2-53.   Could Felicia's team have used different steps to "unlock" her puzzle in
          problem 2-52? In other words, could she use different moves and still have the
          key end up in the same final position?

          •   If it is possible, list a new set of steps that would move her key from the
              same starting location to the same final position.

          •   If it is not possible, explain why not.

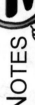

METHODS AND MEANINGS

MATH NOTES

Graphing Points on an *xy*-Coordinate Grid

Coordinate axes on a flat surface are formed by drawing
vertical and horizontal number lines. The **origin** is the point where the
two number lines cross, which is 0 on each axis.

Numerical data can be
graphed on a flat surface
using **points**. Points on the
graph are identified by two
numbers in an **ordered pair**
written as (x, y). The first
number is the **x-coordinate** of
the point and the second
number is the **y-coordinate**.

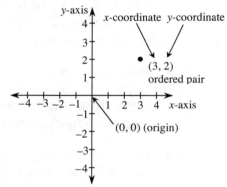

To locate the point $(3, 2)$ on an *xy*-graph, go three units from the origin
to the right to mark 3 on the horizontal axis and then, from that point, go
2 units up. To locate the point $(-2, -4)$, go 2 units from the origin to the
left to the mark -2 on the horizontal axes and then 4 units down.

Review & Preview

2-54.   Copy these incomplete axes. Label the missing numbers on each number line.

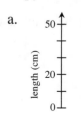

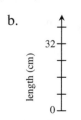

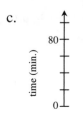

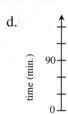

Making Connections: Course 2

2-55.   On graph paper draw a coordinate grid with x- and y-axes. Graph shapes A, B, and C as described below.

   a.   Shape A is a triangle with vertices $(1, 1)$, $(3, 3)$, and $(2, 4)$.

   b.   Shape B is a square with vertices $(2, -1)$, $(4, -1)$, $(2, -3)$, and $(4, -3)$.

   c.   Shape C is a rectangle with vertices $(-3, 1)$, $(-3, 4)$, $(-1, 4)$, and $(-1, 1)$.

2-56.   On the same grid you used in problem 2-55, slide triangle A four units right and three units up to create triangle D. Write the coordinates of the new vertices.

2-57.   Copy and complete each of the Diamond Problems below. The pattern used in the Diamond Problems is shown at right.

   a.   b.   c.   d.

2-58.   After a pizza party, Julia has parts of five pizzas left over. The shaded areas represent the slices that were not eaten. If each pizza was originally cut up into 12 pieces:

pizza A   pizza B   pizza C   pizza D   pizza E

   a.   What fraction of pizza A is left?

   b.   If all of the pieces were put together, how many whole pizzas could she make? How many extra pieces would she have?

   c.   Julia wants to write the amount of pizza left over as a single fraction. How could she do this?

Describing Transformations

In Lesson 2.1.2, you used numbers and symbols to describe how a frog moved on a number line. These expressions described the starting place, the motion, and the point where the frog landed. Today, you will write similar expressions to describe transformations on a grid.

2-59.   Rosa changed the position of quadrilateral *ABCD* to that of quadrilateral *WXYZ*. "*How did the coordinates of the points change?*" she wondered.

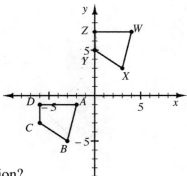

   a.   Describe how Rosa transformed *ABCD*. Was the shape translated (slid), rotated (turned), or reflected (flipped)? Explain how you know.

   b.   How far did *ABCD* move? In which direction?

   c.   Point *B* became point *X*. What are the coordinates of points *B* and *X*? Name them using (x, y) notation.

   d.   How did the *x*-coordinate of point *B* change? How did its *y*-coordinate change? For each coordinate, write an expression using addition to show the change.

   e.   **Visualize** translating *WXYZ* 10 units to the right and 12 units up. Where will point *X* end up? *Without counting on the graph*, work with your team to find the new coordinates of point *Y*. Write expressions using addition to show the change.

2-60.   Rosa translated a different shape on a grid. Use the clues below to figure out how her shape was moved.

   a.   The point $(4, 7)$ was translated to $(32, -2)$. Without graphing, describe how the shape moved on the grid.

   b.   Another point on her original shape was $(-16, 9)$. After the translation, where did this point end up? For each coordinate, write an expression using addition to show the change.

2-61.   Rowan transformed triangle *DEF* at right to get
         triangle *QRS*.

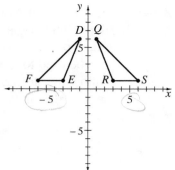

   a.   Describe how Rowan transformed the
         triangle. Was the shape translated, rotated,
         or reflected? Explain how you know.

   b.   Rowan noticed that the *y*-coordinates of the
         points did not change. What happened to the
         x-coordinates? Compare the *x*-coordinate of
         point *D* with the *x*-coordinate of point *Q*. Do
         the same with points *E* and *R* and with
         points *F* and *S*. What do you notice?

   c.   Can you describe the change to all of the *x*-coordinates with addition like
         you did in problems 2-59 and 2-60? If not, what other operation could you
         use? Explain.

2-62.   What if Rowan reflected triangle *DEF* from problem 2-61 across the *x*-axis (the
         horizontal axis)? What would happen to the coordinates?

   a.   First **visualize** how the triangle will reflect across the *x*-axis.

   b.   Neatly set up a four-quadrant graph on graph paper and plot triangle *DEF*
         from problem 2-61.

   c.   Reflect triangle *DEF* across the *x*-axis to get triangle *KLM*.

   d.   Compare the coordinates of point *D* with point *K*, point *E* with point *L*, and
         point *F* with point *M*. What do you notice? How can you use
         multiplication to describe this change?

2-63.   In problem 2-61, Rowan noticed that multiplying the *x*-coordinates by –1
         reflects the shape across the *y*-axis.

   a.   Test this **strategy** on a triangle formed by the points *A*(–3, 5), *B*(1, 2), and
         C(0, 8). Before you graph, multiply each *x*-coordinate by –1. What are the
         new points?

   b.   Graph your original and new triangle on a new set of axes. Did your
         triangle get reflected across the *y*-axis?

2-64. Stella used three steps to move the key on the graph at right from *A* to *B*. On your graph paper, draw the key at *A*. (A triangle can be used to represent the key.) Then follow the steps Stella wrote below. What was her last move?

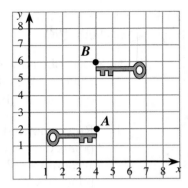

1. Slide the key to the right 3 units and up 6 units.

2. Reflect the key across the line x = 4.

3. ???

2-65. **Additional Challenge:** Is there a way to use translations to create a reflection or a rotation? Can reflections be used to move a shape in the same way as a rotation? To investigate these questions, begin by making a graph like the one below:

a. Reflect (flip) the triangle across the *x*-axis. Then, reflect the new triangle over the *y*-axis.

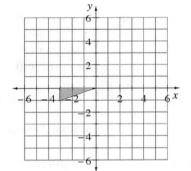

b. Rotate the original triangle 180° around the point $(0,0)$. What you notice?

c. Is there a way to use more than one reflection step so that at the end, the triangle looks like it was translated (slid)? If so, describe the combination of moves you would use.

2-66. LEARNING LOG

In your Learning Log, describe what the words *translate*, *rotate*, and *reflect* mean in your own words. For each word, demonstrate the movement with a diagram. Title this entry "Rigid Transformations" and include today's date.

Making Connections: Course 2

METHODS AND MEANINGS

MATH NOTES

Rigid Transformations

Rigid transformations are ways to move an object while not changing its shape or size, namely: translations (slides), reflections (flips), and rotations (turns). Each movement is described below.

A **translation** slides an object horizontally (side-to-side), vertically (up or down), or both. To translate an object, you must describe which direction you will move it, and how far it will slide. In the example at right, triangle A is translated 4 units to the right and 3 units up.

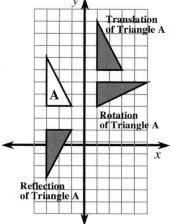

A **reflection** flips an object across a line (called a **line of reflection**). To reflect an object, you must describe the line the object will flip across. In the example at right, triangle A is reflected across the x-axis.

A **rotation** turns an object about a point. To rotate an object, you must choose a point, direction, and angle of rotation. In the example above, triangle A is rotated 90° clockwise (↻) about the origin $(0,0)$.

2-67.   Erin started with one corner of a figure located at $(-4, 5)$ and translated it to end at $(6, 8)$. To find out how far the shape moved horizontally, she decided to find the difference between the two x-coordinates. She wrote: $6 - (-4)$.

a.   When Erin simplified $6 - (-4)$ she got 2 as her answer. Is this correct? If not, what is the correct simplification?

b.   Write another expression to find out how far the shape moved vertically ($\updownarrow$). Simplify both expressions and describe the translation.

c.   Describe each of the translations below.

   i. $(3, -2) \rightarrow (5, -9)$ ii. $(-1, 4) \rightarrow (6, -2)$

   iii. $(0, 0) \rightarrow (-4, -7)$ iv. $(-2, -9) \rightarrow (2, 9)$

2-68.   On grid paper, set up *x*- and *y*-axes for a four quadrant graph. Then draw a triangle with vertices at $(1, 1)$, $(5, 1)$, and $(6, 3)$. Label this triangle T.

    a.   Translate (slide) the triangle left 3 units and down 4 units. Label this triangle A and list the vertices.

    b.   Reflect triangle T across the *y*-axis. Label this triangle B and list the vertices.

    c.   Are triangles T, A, and B congruent (that is, do they have the same shape and size)? Explain.

2-69.   Draw an example of each of the following shapes. Refer to the glossary in the back of the book if you need help.

    a.   rectangle   b.   square   c.   parallelogram

    d.   trapezoid   e.   scalene triangle   f.   right triangle

2-70.   Copy each expression below and simplify it. Be sure to show the steps you use to get the answer.

    a. $\frac{11}{12} - \frac{7}{12}$ b. $\frac{1}{2} + \frac{1}{8} + \frac{3}{4}$ c. $\frac{3}{4} - \frac{1}{6}$

2-71.   Erica is making a quilt like the one shown at right. She is going to give each square to a different person to decorate before she sews them together.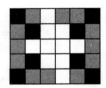

    a.   If she gives people squares at random, what is the probability that she will give her mother a gray square?

    b.   What is the probability that she will give her brother a gray or a black square to decorate?

    c.   What is the area of the white region? What is the perimeter of the white region?

2.2.4 What if I multiply?

Multiplication and Dilation

When an object is translated, rotated or reflected, it stays the same size and shape even though it moves. For this reason, they are called **rigid transformations**. In this lesson you will explore a new transformation that changes how the object looks. As you work today, ask these questions in your team:

What parts of the shape are changing? What parts stay the same?

What happens when we multiply by a negative number?

2-72.   PREPARING FOR THE CONTEST

Milo's frog is ready for the frog-jumping contest. If the frog hops three times to the right, and each hop is 5 feet long, then Milo records the jump as $(3)(5) = 15$. This means that the frog ends up 15 feet from its starting position (0 on a number line).

a.   What if each hop is to the left 5 feet? How could Milo change his equation to show this? Discuss this with your team and describe a way to change his equation.

b.   What if the frog hops twice and each hop is 8 feet to the left? Where does the frog end up? How should Milo record the hops?

c.   Milo recorded one set of hops as $(-4)(-2) = 8$. His sister complained, *"Didn't the frog hop to the left?"*

Milo answered, *"No, he did the opposite."* What did he mean? How this is shown in his equation?

2-73.   Describe how Milo's frog hopped based on the expressions below. Assume the frog starts at zero on the number line each time, and that all measurements are in feet. For each part, describe in words how the frog hopped (how far, how many times, and in what direction)? Also find the product, that is, the place the frog lands.

a. $(6)(4)$ b. $(-3)(-7)$ c. $(5)(-1)$ d. $(-1)(5)$

e.   Explain what happens when you multiply a positive number by a negative number. What happens when you multiply a negative number by a negative number?

2-74.   When all of the *x*- or *y*-coordinates of each vertex of a shape are changed by adding or subtracting the same numbers, the shape translates (slides) to a new position on the coordinate grid.

How does the shape change when the *x*- and *y*-coordinates are doubled? Use the directions below to help you answer this question.

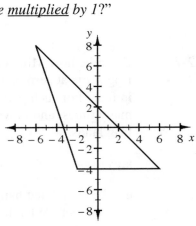

a.   Plot the following points on graph paper: $(2,1)$, $(3,1)$, $(5,5)$, $(2,5)$. Connect the points to make a quadrilateral.

b.   Without graphing, predict how you think the figure would change if the *x*- and *y*-coordinates were multiplied by two and then plotted.

c.   Test your prediction by doubling the coordinates from part (a) and plotting them on your graph paper. Was your prediction correct?

d.   With your team members look at the figure you just graphed. Transforming a graphed shape by multiplying each coordinate by the same number is called a **dilation**. With your team, discuss how this figure compares to the original. Be specific!

2-75.   INVESTIGATING DILATIONS

The students in Ms. Stanley's class were studying what happens to the graph of a shape when each coordinate is multiplied by the same number. They came up with the following questions:

- *"What happens when each coordinate is <u>multiplied</u> by one-half?"*

- *"What changes when the coordinates are <u>multiplied</u> by 1?"*

- *"What happens when the coordinates are all <u>multiplied</u> by –1?"*

a.   Use the shape at right to investigate the questions above. Use graph paper to make the dilations.

b.   How did the figure change in each of the investigations? Explain what your team learned about the three questions you investigated.

Making Connections: Course 2

2-76.   In problem 2-75, you investigated questions about multiplying coordinates that
         were posed by other students.

   a.   With your team, write a different question about the effect of multiplying
         the coordinates of a shape on a grid. This question might start, *"What
         happens when you multiply..."*

   b.   On graph paper, investigate your question by multiplying the coordinates of
         the shape in problem 2-75 as you described in your question.

   c.   What happened? Write a **conjecture** — that is, an educated guess based on
         the evidence in the last two problems — to answer your question.

METHODS AND **M**EANINGS

MATH NOTES

Mixed Numbers and Fractions Greater Than One

The number $4\frac{1}{3}$ is called a **mixed number** because it is
composed of a whole number, 4, and a fraction, $\frac{1}{3}$.

The number $\frac{13}{3}$ is a called a **fraction greater than one** because the
numerator is larger than the denominator and so its value is greater than
one. (Sometimes such fractions are called *improper fractions* but this is
just an historical term. There is nothing wrong with the fraction itself.)
The fraction $\frac{13}{3}$ is equal to the mixed number $4\frac{1}{3}$.

Whether to write a number as a mixed number or a fraction greater than
one depends on what arithmetic operation(s) you are performing. For
some arithmetic operations — especially multiplication and division —
you will usually want to use fractions greater than one.

2-77. Louis is dilating triangle *ABC* at right. He multiplied each *x*-coordinate and *y*-coordinate of triangle *ABC* by −2.

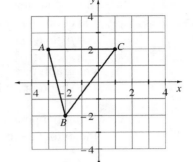

    a. What are the new coordinates of the points?

    b. Graph Louis' new triangle.

    c. Describe how triangle *ABC* changed.

2-78. Linh has a bag of beads that contains 10 glass beads, 7 metal beads, 15 plastic beads, and 3 clay beads. For each part below, if the bead selected is replaced before the next draw, what is the probability that she will pull out a:

    a. Metal bead?   b. Bead that is not plastic?

    c. Glass or plastic bead?

2-79. Gracie loves to talk on the phone, but her parents try to limit the amount of time she talks. They decided to keep a record of the time she spends on the phone each day. For the past nine days the data was: 120, 60, 0, 30, 15, 0, 0, 10, and 20.

    a. Find the mean, median, and mode for the information.

    b. Which of the three measures in part (a) might give Gracie's parents the most accurate information about her phone use? Why do you think so?

2-80. If the line segment at right is subdivided into equal parts, what is the length of the marked portion of the line?

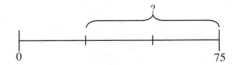

2-81. Read the Math Notes box for this lesson. Then, rewrite each number below as a single fraction greater than one.

    a. $1\frac{1}{11}$ b. $3\frac{2}{5}$ c. $2\frac{4}{15}$

Extension Activity What can I create?

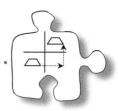

Using Rigid Transformations

In the last several lessons you have described translations using coordinates, and developed **strategies** for determining where an object started when you know how it was translated and its final position. In this lesson, you will continue to practice transforming objects on a coordinate grid by translating (sliding), rotating (turning), and reflecting (flipping). As you work, **visualize** what each object will look like after the transformation and use the graph to check your prediction.

2-82.   BECOMING AN ARTIST

Have you ever seen directions for drawing a cartoon figure such as a face? Usually these directions start by helping you to put some basic shapes together to form an outline. Then they give you ideas for how to finish the drawing. An example showing how you could draw a dinosaur is at right.

Your task: Obtain Extension Activity Resource Page A from your teacher. On it, you will find shapes A, B, and C provided. Follow the directions below to create a design. Whenever one of the shapes is mentioned below, start with the original shape on the left side of the paper. The final result of each step is part of the outline of the design.

Once you have finished following all of the directions, describe the picture that is formed. Then use the outline to create a cartoon drawing complete with color and other details.

- Draw a rectangle with vertices $(5,0)$, $(9,0)$, $(9,8)$, and $(5,8)$.

- Translate circle A so that its center is at $(7,6)$. Describe how the shape moved.

- Rotate (turn) triangle C 180° clockwise about the point $(-6,3)$. Record the coordinates of the new vertices. Then add 15 to each x-coordinate and graph the final result. What transformation does "adding 15" represent?

- Reflect (flip) triangle B across the y-axis.

Problem continues on next page. →

2-82.   *Problem continued from previous page.*

   • A new shape, triangle D, has vertices at $(-7, 13)$, $(-8, 11)$ and $(-6, 11)$. Translate triangle D so that its top vertex is at $(7, 4)$.

   • Translate triangle C to the right 11 units. Then reflect the result across the horizontal ($\leftrightarrow$) line that goes through $y = 3$.

   • Translate circle A so that the *x*-coordinates increase by 13 units and the *y*-coordinates increase by 11 units.

2-83.   CREATE A DESIGN

   Now create your own design using basic shapes A through F on the Extension Activity Resource Page C. Write complete directions at the bottom of your resource page (such as those in problem 2-82) for creating your design. Make sure you provide all the necessary information.

2-84.   **Additional Challenge:**
   Visualize a pattern of squares covering a coordinate grid as show at right. What transformations could you make that would move the whole pattern so that the squares and lines in the pattern line up exactly over other squares and lines?

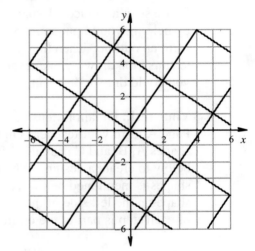

2-85.   Sketch the graph at right on your paper.

   a.   Write directions to translate the original triangle to make the new triangle.

   b.   What are the coordinates of the vertices (corners) of the new shape?

   c.   On your graph, reflect the original triangle over the *y*-axis. What are the coordinates of the new triangle?

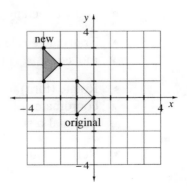

2-86.   Copy each Portions Web below and fill in the missing parts.

a.

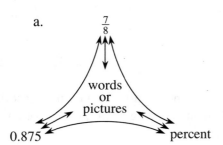

b.

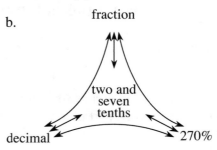

2-87.   Copy and complete each of the Diamond Problems below.
The pattern used in the Diamond Problems is shown at right.

a.

b.

c.

d.

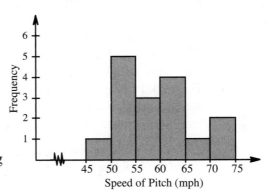

2-88.   Craig is practicing his baseball
pitching. He kept track of the
speed of each of his throws
yesterday, and made the
histogram at right.

a.   Can you tell the speed of
Craig's fastest pitch? Explain.

b.   Between what speeds does Craig
usually pitch?

c.   Based on this data, what is the probability that Craig will pitch the ball
between 70 and 75 miles per hour?

2-89.   How many different rectangles can you draw with an area of 16 square units?
What is the perimeter of each one? Show your work.

2.3.1 How big is the part?

Multiplication of Fractions

You often only need part of something. You might need part of a gallon of gasoline to fill the tank of a scooter, part of a can of paint to finish covering a wall, or part of a piece of paper to complete an assignment.

But what happens when you need a part of a part? Cooks, construction workers, and city planners often need to find part of something that is already a part of something else.

As you work with your team to find parts of parts, be sure to draw diagrams and clearly label all of the pieces in them so that you know what they represent. Think about the following questions:

How can I represent it?

What does each part represent in the situation?

2-90.   PLANNING FOR THE PARK

The city council is trying to decide how to budget for mowing the city park shown in the diagram at right. The park is all grass except for an activity area, picnic area, and basketball court.

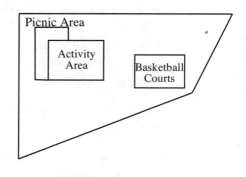

a.   What information does the council need in order to make its decision?

b.   Can you determine how much grass will need to be mowed? Why or why not?

c.   In this section, you will develop new tools that will help you find the area of irregular shapes with portions removed, like this park. At this point, what do you know about finding the area of shapes? Individually reflect about what you know.

2-91.   SKATE PARK

Someone has given our community money for a
new activity area in the city park that will include
a skate park with a pyramid. The City Council
wants to build the activity area soon, but there are
some limits to the actual design. According to the
donor, $\frac{3}{4}$ of the activity area must be used for the
skate park, and $\frac{1}{3}$ of the skating section should be
reserved for a pyramid.

   a.   Use a whole index card to represent the entire activity area. How can you
        show the $\frac{3}{4}$ portion that will be the skate park? How can you show that $\frac{1}{3}$
        of the skate park region will be a pyramid?

   b.   Determine what fraction of the activity area should be reserved for the
        pyramid.

   c.   Label all parts of the diagram and be prepared to share your thinking with
        the class.

2-92.   In the Skate Park problem (2-91), you drew a diagram to represent the situation
         in the activity area. The index card represented the whole activity area.

   a.   To create her diagram, Dalia divided her index card into four equal
        columns. Then, she divided the card into three equal rows in the other
        direction and drew lines across the card. Copy her diagram onto your
        paper, then:

        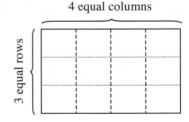

        • Color the fraction *of the activity
          area (card)* that represents the
          skate park with one color.

        • Color the fraction *of the skating
          section* that will be the pyramid
          with a new color.

        • Determine what fraction of the activity
          area will be covered by the pyramid.

   b.   The fraction of the skate park that is reserved for a pyramid can be
        represented by the multiplication problem $\frac{1}{3} \cdot \frac{3}{4}$. With your team, discuss
        and decide how this expression is related to the diagram you drew using the
        index card in problem 2-91 or to Dalia's diagram. Record your conclusions
        on your paper.

   c.   What is a way to multiply $\frac{1}{3} \cdot \frac{3}{4}$? Does this **strategy** give you the answer
        you found in part (b) of problem 2-91?

2-93.   GREATEST GREENSPACE

The mayor of your city has just announced
he will give an award of $1500 to the
neighborhood that can build the largest new
park. As part of the city planning team, you
are in charge of looking at the applications
and choosing the winner.

The two neighborhoods with the best
applications are West Vale and Cozy
Corner. West Vale will build a park that
measures $\frac{3}{5}$ mile by $\frac{1}{2}$ mile. Cozy Corner
has an open space for a park that measures
$\frac{1}{3}$ mile by $\frac{4}{5}$ miles.

a.   Without calculating, predict which park you
     think will be bigger. Why do you think so?

b.   Will either park have an area more than one square mile? Will either have
     an area less than $\frac{1}{2}$ square mile? How do you know?

c.   How can the West Vale Park (that will be $\frac{3}{5}$
     mile by $\frac{1}{2}$ mile) be represented in this 1 square
     mile diagram? Copy the diagram and work
     with your team to represent this park as a
     portion of 1 square mile.

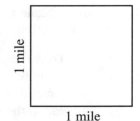

d.   What would the area of the West Vale Park be?
     Use your diagram to help you.

e.   Draw the Cozy Corner Park as a portion of 1 square mile and find its area.

f.   Which park is larger? **Justify** your answer.

2-94.   The mayor is donating land to build a new park that is $\frac{2}{3}$ mile on one side by
        $2\frac{1}{2}$ miles on the other.

a.   Draw a picture to represent the park. Label each side length.

b.   Divide the shape into smaller pieces and find the area of each piece.

c.   What will be the total area of the new park (in square miles)?

Making Connections: Course 2

2-95.   A number, such as $2\frac{1}{2}$, which is composed of a whole number and a fraction, is called a **mixed number** because it has two whole units and $\frac{1}{2}$ of another whole.

    a.   How many halves are in $2\frac{1}{2}$?

    b.   How can you rewrite the fraction $2\frac{1}{2}$ as a single fraction (greater than one) so you can use it in a multiplication problem?

    c.   Write and solve a multiplication problem to represent the park in problem 2-94. Show all work and include a diagram.

2-96.   Erik is painting the fence at the park. With the first can of paint he covered an area that measures $\frac{2}{5}$ the length of the fence and $\frac{1}{2}$ the distance from the top of the fence to the ground.

    a.   What portion of the fence surface area has he covered? Be ready to explain your team's **strategy** for finding the area through pictures and equations.

    b.   How many more cans of paint will he need to finish the job? Show how you found your answer.

    c.   If the full area that Erik will paint is 1400 square feet, how many square feet has he painted so far?

2-97.   Zac is making cookies, but he does not have enough flour to make a full recipe. The full recipe calls for $\frac{2}{3}$ cup of brown sugar.

If Zac is making $\frac{3}{5}$ of the full recipe, how much brown sugar should he use?

    a.   Represent the $\frac{2}{3}$ cup of brown sugar with a diagram.

    b.   Represent the portion of brown sugar that Zac needs if he makes only $\frac{3}{5}$ of the recipe.

    c.   What math operation should Zac use to find the amount of brown sugar he needs? Write an expression and find a solution.

2-98.   Simplify the following fraction expressions. Show all of your work.

   a. $\frac{3}{4} + \frac{2}{3}$ b. $\frac{7}{8} - \frac{1}{4}$ c. $\frac{3}{5} \cdot \frac{1}{3}$ d. $\frac{4}{7} \cdot \frac{2}{3}$

2-99.   What is the length of the marked portion of each line segment? Copy the segment onto your paper before finding the missing length. Assume the entire line segment is subdivided into equal sections.

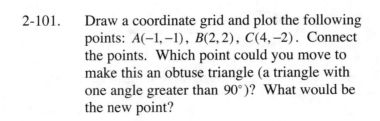

2-100.   On Saturday, Stella worked for two hours helping her mother around the house. She spent $\frac{1}{3}$ of her time doing laundry, $\frac{1}{4}$ of her time cleaning, and the rest of her time working in the yard. How much of her time was spent in the yard? Show all your work. Use a diagram if it would help.

2-101.   Draw a coordinate grid and plot the following points: $A(-1,-1)$, $B(2,2)$, $C(4,-2)$. Connect the points. Which point could you move to make this an obtuse triangle (a triangle with one angle greater than 90°)? What would be the new point?

2.3.2 What if it's not a rectangle?

Decomposing and Recomposing Area

In previous classes you have had experience with finding the area of squares and other rectangles, but what about finding the area of irregular shapes? Landscape designers, floor tilers, and others often have to deal with areas that are made of several shapes combined into one. As you work on the problems in this lesson, you will need to **visualize** the new shapes, and predict what they will look like after they are changed.

As you work through this section, it will be important to describe how you **see** different shapes and to organize your work to show your thinking. Ask each other these questions to get discussions started in your study team:

What other shapes can we **see** in this figure?

Where should we break this shape apart? How should we rearrange the pieces?

Will the area change?

2-102. RECTANGLE PUZZLE

Corey and Morgan were given two shape puzzles and asked to find the area of each one. They know how to find the area of a rectangle, but they have never worked with these shapes.

Corey and Morgan would like to rearrange each figure to make it into a single rectangle. Using a Lesson 2.3.2 Resource Page, help them decide how to cut each shape into pieces that they can put back together as *one* rectangle.

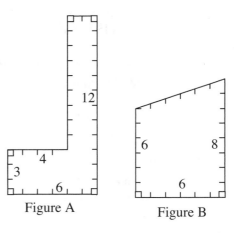

Figure A   Figure B

- On your own, **visualize** and **strategize** how to cut each shape into pieces that will make a rectangle.

- Discuss and decide on one **strategy** to try with your team.

- Cut and rearrange each shape into a rectangle to test your **strategy**.

2-103.   Find the area of Figures A and B from
          problem 2-102. Does it matter if you
          use the original or rearranged shape?
          Be sure to show your calculations.

2-104.   Find the area of each of the pieces that
          you made when you cut up the original
          Figure A. How does the sum of these
          areas compare to the area of the larger
          rectangle you found for Figure A in
          problem 2-103? Why?

2-105.   Compare each of the rearranged rectangles
          that your team made with the rectangles of
          other teams in your class.

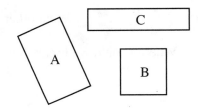

    a.   To talk about rectangles, it is useful to
          have words to name the different sides.
          What are some of the words you have
          used to name the sides of a rectangle?

    b.   The words "length" and "width" are only used to describe rectangles and
          not used for other shapes that you will study. This book will use the words
          base and **height** instead. Often the bottom side is called the base when a
          rectangle is shown in a horizontal position, like rectangle C above, but
          "base" can actually refer to any side of the rectangle. Once the base is
          chosen, the height is either side that is perpendicular (at a right angle) to it.
          Read the Math Notes box in this lesson for more examples.

    c.   Are all of the rectangles your class created for the figures from problem
          2-102 the same? Use the words *base* and *height* to discuss similarities and
          differences between the rectangles.

    d.   Do all of the rearranged rectangles for each figure have the same area?
          Why or why not?

2-106.   LEARNING LOG

          In your Learning Log, explain why rearranging a shape
          might be a good **strategy** to find the area of an unusual
          shape. Title this entry "Rearranging Shapes to Find
          Area" and include today's date.

2-107. **Additional Challenge:** How can rectangles help you find the area of the irregular shapes below? Talk about what rectangles you **see** in the shapes and how the areas of those rectangles can help you find the total area. All angles are right angles.

a.   Find the shaded area.

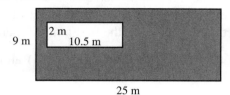

b.

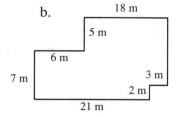

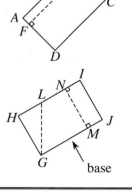

METHODS AND MEANINGS

MATH NOTES

Base and Height of Rectangles

Any side of a rectangle can be chosen as its **base**. Then the **height** is either of the two sides that intersect (meet) the base at one of its endpoints. Note that the height may also be any segment that is perpendicular to (each end forms a 90° angle with) both the base and the side opposite (across from) the base.

In the first rectangle at right, side $\overline{BC}$ is labeled as the base. Either side, $\overline{AB}$ or $\overline{DC}$, is a height, as is segment $\overline{FE}$.

In the second rectangle, side $\overline{GJ}$ is labeled as the base. Either side, $\overline{HG}$ or $\overline{IJ}$, is a height, as is segment $\overline{MN}$. Segment $\overline{GL}$ is not a height, because it is not perpendicular to side $\overline{HI}$.

2-108.   Use the following directions to create a mystery letter! On a piece of graph paper, use a ruler to draw a four-quadrant graph. Scale each axis from 6 to –6. Plot these points and connect them in order to create a rectangle: $(2,1)$, $(2,4)$, $(3,4)$, $(3,1)$. Be sure to connect the last point to the first point. Then:

   a.   Rotate the rectangle $90°$ clockwise (↻) about the point $(2,1)$ and draw the rotated rectangle.

   b.   Reflect the new rectangle over the line $y = 2$ and draw the reflected rectangle.

   c.   Name the letter of the alphabet that your graph resembles.

2-109.   Copy and complete the Portions Web at right.

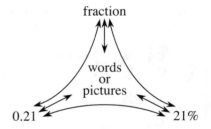

2-110.   For each shape drawn below, choose one of the names on the list above them that best describes that shape. Be as specific as you can. If you do not remember what one of the shape names means, you might want to look in the glossary of this book for more information.

right triangle	scalene triangle	obtuse triangle
equilateral triangle	parallelogram	rectangle
rhombus	trapezoid	acute triangle

   a. 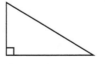   b.    c. 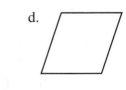   d.

2-111.   Melissa collected the date for all of her friends' birthdays. The histogram shows what she found out. Make a list of the months when her friends' birthdays occur and how many birthdays there are in each month.

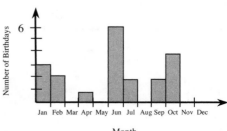

2-112.   Bianca is trying to find the area of this
          rectangle. She already measured one side as
          10 cm. Which other length(s) could she
          measure to use in her area calculation?
          Explain your **reasoning**.

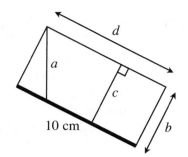

2.3.3   Can I make a rectangle?

Area of Parallelograms

In Lesson 2.3.2, you worked with your study team to rearrange two irregular shapes into
rectangles in order to find their areas more easily. Today will use a technology tool
(available at www.cpm.org/students/technology) to investigate the question: *Can all
shapes be rearranged to make rectangles?* As you work, **visualize** what each shape will
look like cut into pieces and how those pieces could fit back together to make a rectangle.
Ask yourself these questions while you investigate:

> How can I break this shape apart?

> How can I rearrange the pieces of the shape to make a new shape?

2-113.   CHANGE IT UP

          What kinds of shapes can be rearranged to make rectangles? If one complete
          rectangle is not possible, can any shape be divided into a few different
          rectangles?

          Using the technology tool Area Decomposer
          (available at www.cpm.org/students/technology)
          and the Lesson 2.3.3A Resource Page provided by
          your teacher, figure out which shapes can be
          changed into rectangles. If you find a way to
          rearrange the shape on the computer, record your
          work on the resource page by:

          •   Drawing lines on the original shape to show
              the cuts you made.

          •   Drawing the rectangle made out of the cut pieces.

          •   Finding the area of the shape.

2-114.   REARRANGING CHALLENGE — PARALLELOGRAMS

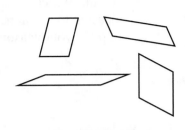

The shapes at right are each an example of a
parallelogram, that is, a quadrilateral with two
pairs of opposite parallel sides. With your
partner, decide if there is a **strategy** for cutting
and rearranging *any* parallelogram that will
always change it into a rectangle. To start, set
the technology tool to show you a parallelogram
like one of those shown at right.

While one person controls the computer, the other (or
others) should show on the Lesson 2.3.3C Resource
Page how the parallelogram was cut and rearranged.
Remember that everyone should share ideas about
how to try to cut and rearrange the shape. Make sure
that each person has an opportunity to control the
computer during the investigation.

a.   How can you cut and rearrange the parallelogram so that you end up with a
      rectangle? Draw your cuts on the original figure, then draw what the final
      rectangle looks like. Use arrows to show where the pieces move.

b.   Will this cutting **strategy** work for any parallelogram? Show the cuts that
      you would make, and use arrows to show where the pieces would move, on
      a new sketch of a different parallelogram. Use your picture to explain a
      general strategy.

2-115.   AREA OF A PARALLELOGRAM

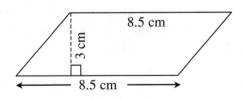

Lydia encountered the following
parallelogram on her homework
assignment. The problem asked her to
find the area of the shape.

Lydia decided to cut and rearrange the shape to make a rectangle (like she did in
problem 2-114). However, she was not sure what the measurements of that
rectangle would be.

a.   With your team, figure out what the base and height of Lydia's new
      rectangle will be. Which side did you use for the height? How do you
      know which side is the height? Draw a diagram to show how you know.

b.   What is the area of the parallelogram? Show your work.

Problem continues on next page. →

Making Connections: Course 2

2-115.   *Problem continued from previous page.*

c.   What about other parallelograms? For example, the parallelogram at right has lengths marked b, c, and h.

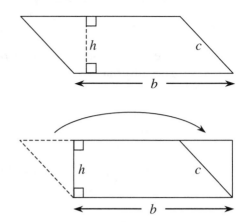

What will be the base of the new rectangle? What will be its height? Talk with your team about the difference between the parts labeled h and c.

d.   How would you find the area of the rectangle? Which lengths would you use? Why?

e.   What is the area of the parallelogram? That is, if A represents the area of the parallelogram, use the variables in the picture to write a formula for calculating the area of any parallelogram.

METHODS AND MEANINGS

MATH NOTES

Parallelogram Vocabulary

Two lines in a plane (a flat surface) are **parallel** if they never meet no matter how far they extend. The distance between the parallel lines is always the same. The marks " >> " indicate that the two lines are parallel.

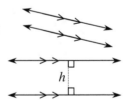

The **distance** between two parallel lines or segments is the length of a line segment that is **perpendicular** (its ends form right angles) to both parallel lines or segments. In the diagram at right, h is the distance between the two parallel lines. It is also called the **perpendicular distance**.

A **parallelogram** is a quadrilateral (a four-sided figure) with two pairs of parallel sides. Any side of a parallelogram can be used as a base. The height (h) is perpendicular to one of the pairs of parallel bases (b), as in the example at right.

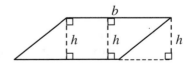

2-116. Use any of your new **strategies** to find the area of the parallelograms below. The information in the Math Notes Box may help.

a.

20 in.
25 in.
20 in.

b.

8 mm
10 mm
10 mm

2-117. Camille had a very fun birthday party with lots of friends and family attending. The party lasted for three hours. If $\frac{3}{8}$ of the time was spent playing games, 50% of the time was spent eating, and the remainder of the time was spent opening presents, draw a diagram and make calculations to show the amount of time spent opening presents.

2-118. Copy and complete each of the Diamond Problems below. The pattern used in the Diamond Problems is shown at right.

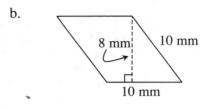
xy
x y
$x+y$

a.
−8   −6

b.
−96
12

c.
0.3
0.5

d.
−20
−1

2-119. Copy each expression and then simplify it without a calculator. Be sure to show all steps.

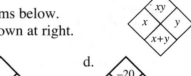

a. $7\frac{5}{8} + 2\frac{9}{16}$

b. $2\frac{7}{8} + 6\frac{1}{6}$

c. $8 - 6\frac{2}{5}$

2-120. Insert whole numbers from 0 to 9 (each digit may only be used once and 6 and 8 are already used) in the blanks below to make the largest number possible. Then repeat the process to make the smallest number possible. Record each answer using numbers and words.

___ 8. ___ 6 ___

2.3.4 What if I add to the shape?

Area of Triangles

So far in this chapter you found the area of different shapes by dividing them into smaller pieces and then putting the pieces back together to make rectangles. In this lesson you will look at **strategies** for making shapes larger in order to find their areas. As you work today, consider these questions:

How can I make a rectangle?

How are the areas related?

Which lengths help me find the area?

2-121.   AREA CHALLENGE — TRIANGLES

Think about how you might find the area of the obtuse triangle shown at right.

a.   Can you cut and rearrange this shape to make a rectangle?

b.   What if you had two copies of this triangle? What shapes could you make by putting the copies together? To find out:

- Get a set of triangles from the Lesson 2.3.4A Resource Page.

- Carefully cut out the obtuse triangle by cutting along the sides of the figure.

- Find the person in your team who has a triangle that matches yours in size and shape. This person will be your partner.

- Work with your partner to combine the two triangles into a four-sided shape. Sketch the shapes that you create on your paper.

- Decide if each shape can be easily formed into a rectangle by cutting and rearranging.

c.   What about triangles that are not obtuse? Cut out the other two triangles from the resource page. Work with the same partner to combine the two acute triangles. Sketch your results. Can any of your arrangements be formed into a rectangle?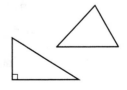

d.   Repeat the process you used in part (c) for the two right triangles.

2-122. Look carefully at the shapes you found in problem 2-121 that can be cut and rearranged into rectangles.

a. What lengths would you need to know to find the area of each rectangle? Where can you find those lengths on the parallelograms before you rearrange them into rectangles? Draw and label them on your sketches.

b. How is the area of each parallelogram related to the area of the two triangles that made it?

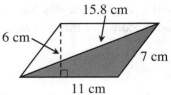

c. Darla created the shape at right out of two triangles and has measured and labeled some of the lengths. Which measurements should she use to find the area of the shaded triangle? What is the area?

d. Where else could you draw the height on Darla's shape?

2-123. Leticia is looking at a triangle (see her figure at right). *"I know how it can be copied and made into a parallelogram, which can then be made into a rectangle,"* she said, *"But when I look at this shaded triangle, I see it inside a rectangle instead."*

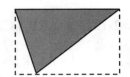

What fraction of the rectangle is this triangle? Work with your team to **justify** your ideas. Be sure to include a labeled diagram as part of your explanation.

2-124. Describe how to find the area of *any* triangle. That is, when a triangle has a base of length b and a height of length h, what expression will calculate the area of the triangle?

2-125. **Additional Challenge:** On graph paper, graph $\triangle ABC$ if A is at $(-2, -3)$, B is at $(-2, 5)$, and C is at $(3, 0)$.

a. What is the length of the base of $\triangle ABC$? Label side AB with its length in grid units.

b. What is the height of $\triangle ABC$? Draw this length on your graph and label it.

c. What is the area of $\triangle ABC$? Show how you get your answer.

d. If you formed a parallelogram using a copy of $\triangle ABC$ with the triangle on your graph, where would the fourth vertex be? Is there more than one possible answer?

2-126.   LEARNING LOG

In your Learning Log, describe how to find the areas of
parallelograms and triangles. This entry does not ask for
simply writing a formula. Instead, for each description:

- Sketch an example shape.

- Show how you found the area.

- Explain how finding the area of each shape is the same and how it is
  different.

Label this entry, "Area of Parallelograms and Triangles" and include today's
date.

METHODS AND **M**EANINGS

Area of a Parallelogram

A parallelogram can be decomposed
and rearranged into a rectangle with the same
base length and height. Since the area of a
shape does not change when it is cut apart and
its pieces are put together in a different
arrangement (a principle called **conservation
of area**), the area of the parallelogram must
equal the product of its base and height.

Therefore, to find the area of a
parallelogram, find the product of the length
of the base (b) and the height (h).

$$A = b \cdot h$$

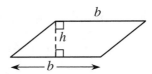

2-127.   Simplify each multiplication problem below.

a. $\frac{5}{8} \cdot \frac{2}{3}$ b. $\frac{3}{4} \cdot \frac{2}{5}$

2-128.   Find the area of each parallelogram. Show all of your work. Use the Math
         Notes box if you need help.

a.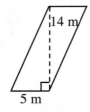
      14 m

      5 m

b.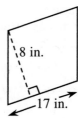
      8 in.

      17 in.

2-129.   Find the area of the following triangles. Show all your work.

a.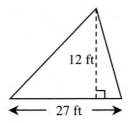
      12 ft

      27 ft

b.
      9 mm

      8.5 mm

2-130.   Simplify the expressions below.

   a. $8 - 13 - (-4)$ b. $4 - (-7) + (-2)$ c. $-7 + 3 - 20$

2-131.   Copy the trapezoid at right on grid paper.

   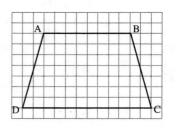

   a.   Find the length of the bottom base (segment
         CD), the length of the top base (segment AB),
         and the distance between the two bases. Use
         grid units.

   b.   Use what you learned about cutting up figures
         to find the area of the trapezoid.

2-132.   Draw a coordinate grid, then plot and connect the following points: $A(-3, 1)$,
         $B(-1, 3)$, $C(4, 2)$, $D(2, 0)$.

   a.   What is the shape you created?

   b.   Reflect the shape across the x-axis. List the coordinates of the new points.

   c.   Multiply each coordinate of the original shape by three. Graph the dilated
         shape. What are the new coordinates of the points?

Making Connections: Course 2

2.3.5 How can I find the area?

Area of Trapezoids

In this chapter, you have used the process of cutting apart and rearranging shapes to help you find their areas. You have also made some shapes larger to help find their area. In this chapter you have developed several different **strategies** for finding the area of shapes. For example, you have found the sum of the areas of multiple smaller parts, rearranged smaller parts into rectangles to find area, and made shapes bigger in order to find their area. In this lesson you will focus on how to **choose a strategy** to find the area of a new shape: a trapezoid. As you work with your team, practice **visualizing** how each shape can be changed or rearranged. Ask each other these questions:

What **strategy** should we **choose**?

Which lengths are important?

2-133. AREA CHALLENGE — TRAPEZOIDS

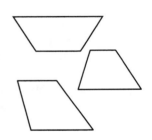

So far in this chapter, you have learned how to find the area of an unfamiliar shape by cutting and rearranging pieces to form a parallelogram or rectangle. Will these **strategies** work to find the area of a **trapezoid** (a shape like the ones at right, with four sides and at least one pair of opposite sides that are parallel)?

To investigate how to find the area of this new shape, get a set of three trapezoids from the Lesson 2.3.5A Resource Page.

Your task: Work with your team to identify at least two ways to rearrange a trapezoid into another shape (or set of shapes) for which you could find the area. Then discuss how you could find the area of each original trapezoid. Use the Discussion Points below to get started.

Discussion Points

How can we cut and rearrange a trapezoid
into another shape for which you can find the area?

What shapes can we make from two congruent (identical) trapezoids?

Which lengths are needed to find the area?

How is the area of each original trapezoid related to the area of the other shapes you created?

2-134. Sheila thinks she can make a trapezoid into a parallelogram (and then a rectangle). She started by folding her trapezoid so that the two parallel sides lined up. She then cut along the fold line (the dashed line in the picture).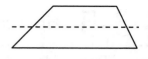

    a.   Fold and cut one of your trapezoids in the way Sheila did. What two new shapes have you created?

    b.   How can Sheila rearrange her two pieces to make one parallelogram? Sketch her shape.

    c.   Locate the base and the height of the parallelogram. Where could she find these lengths on her original trapezoid?

2-135.   AREA OF A TRAPEZOID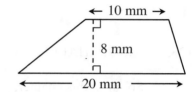

Dejon's homework tonight includes a problem where he has to find the area of the trapezoid at right.

    a.   Draw a copy of Dejon's trapezoid on your paper. Then choose a way to form a parallelogram. Sketch the rearrangement on your paper and label the base and height of the parallelogram.

    b.   Find the lengths on the trapezoid that make the base of the parallelogram. These lengths are called the **bases** of the trapezoid.

    c.   Where can you **see** the height of the parallelogram on the trapezoid? What does it measure?

    d.   Find the area of the new parallelogram or rectangle. How is this area related to the area of the trapezoid? Explain how you found your answer.

    e.   If you have not already done so, find the area of the trapezoid.

2-136.   PARK PROBLEM REVISITED

At the beginning of Section 2.2, your
team looked at problem 2-90, Planning
for the Park. In this park, the city
planners are trying to figure out the size
of the grassy area that they need to mow
so they can determine the mowing costs
for their budget.

Using what your team now knows about
finding the areas of rectangles,
parallelograms, triangles, and trapezoids,
and using the Lesson 2.3.5CB Resource
Page, calculate the area of the park that
will need to be mowed. Assume that all
angles that appear to be right angles are
right angles. If you have time, find two
different ways to find the total area. Be
sure to show all of your work so that you
can explain your **strategies** to other teams.

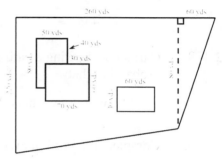

METHODS AND **M**EANINGS

Area of a Triangle

Since two copies of the same triangle
can be put together along a common side to
form a parallelogram with the same base and
height as the triangle, then the area of a triangle
must equal half the area of the parallelogram
with the same base and height.

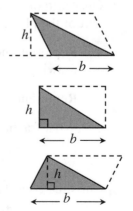

Therefore, if b is the base of a triangle and h is
the height of the triangle, we can think of
triangles as "half parallelograms" and calculate
the area of any triangle:

$$A = \tfrac{1}{2} bh$$

2-137. Use any of your new **strategies** to find the area of the shapes below. The information in the Math Notes boxes may help. Assume the shape in part (a) is a parallelogram, and the shape in part (b) is a trapezoid.

a.

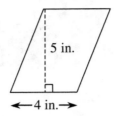

5 in.

←4 in.→

b.

← 6 in.→

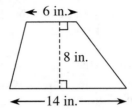

8 in.

←——14 in.——→

2-138. Carmen is drawing a card from a standard deck of playing cards. What is the probability that:

a. She will draw a heart?

b. She will *not* draw a club?

2-139. Complete the Portions Webs below.

a.

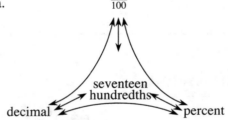

$\frac{17}{100}$

seventeen hundredths

decimal   percent

b.

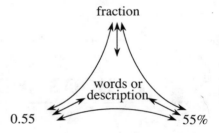

fraction

words or description

0.55   55%

2-140. One-third of a rectangular playground is designed for young children. In that part of the playground, a play structure covers $\frac{2}{5}$ of the children's space.

a. Represent the portion of the playground that is the play structure with a drawing.

b. Represent the problem with multiplication.

c. What fraction of the total playground is the play structure? Show all of your work.

2-141. Christina collected the ages of the players on her softball team. The team ages were: 10, 12, 14, 13, 12, 11, 13, 12, 11, 12, 12, and 13. Christina wants to describe the players' ages in an article for the school newspaper. Since she did not want to list all of the ages, should she use the range or a measure of central tendency (mean, mode, median) to describe them? **Justify** your choice.

2.3.6 How do I calculate it?

Order of Operations

If you know the length of the base and height of a triangle, how do you find its area? Some people **reason** this way: *Since I know that two of the triangles can make a parallelogram, then the area of the triangle must be half the area of the parallelogram. Therefore, it is half the product of the length of the base and the length of the height.*

However, this relationship can also be written as a **rule**, such as $A = \frac{1}{2}bh$, where A represents the area of the triangle, b represents the length of the base, and h represents the height of the triangle.

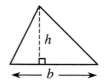

There are many other relationships that can be written with symbols that you may have seen before. Perhaps one of the most famous rules is Einstein's formula $E = mc^2$, relating energy, mass, and the speed of light. Work with your team to use some rules you already know to find a quantity.

2-142.   FUNKY TRAPEZOID RULES

During a discussion in Lesson 2.3.5, some students in Mrs. Cho's class wrote different rules to find the area (A) of the trapezoid at right. Their rules are reprinted below.

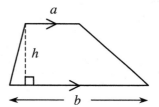

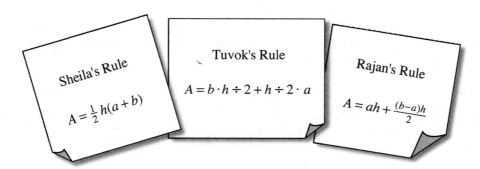

Sheila's Rule

$A = \frac{1}{2}h(a+b)$

Tuvok's Rule

$A = b \cdot h \div 2 + h \div 2 \cdot a$

Rajan's Rule

$A = ah + \frac{(b-a)h}{2}$

a.   Trace the trapezoid on your paper and label its side lengths. Explain how Sheila may have rearranged the trapezoid to build her rule. That is, why did she add the lengths a and b together in her rule? Why did she multiply by $\frac{1}{2}$?

b.   Pick one of the other rules and explain how the student may have built the rule. Use a diagram to show how the trapezoid might have been cut apart and rearranged.

2-143. Your teacher will provide your team with a diagram of a trapezoid with the values of *a*, *b*, and *h* labeled.

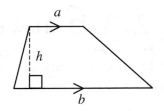

a. Find the area of your team's trapezoid using each rule from problem 2-142. Each person in your team should use each rule to find the area, rather than splitting the work among team members.

b. Do each of the rules give you the same area? If not, use problems 2-144 through 2-147 to help your team find any errors in your work.

Further Guidance

2-144. An expression represents mathematical relationships using numbers, letters, and/or symbols. The rules for simplifying expressions are called the **order of operations**. These rules state that operations like addition and multiplication are performed in a specific order when calculating the value of expressions. Review the Math Notes box for order of operations at the end of this lesson. Then answer the questions below.

a. Axel was solving for the area of a trapezoid using Tuvok's rule. In Axel's trapezoid, $h = 4$, $a = 3$, and $b = 8$. Axel substituted numbers into the equation that he was using and circled the terms. It looked like this:

$$b \cdot h \div 2 \ + \ h \div 2 \cdot a$$
$$8 \cdot 4 \div 2 \ + \ 4 \div 2 \cdot 3$$
$$\boxed{8 \cdot 4 \div 2} + \boxed{4 \div 2 \cdot 3}$$

b. Copy Axel's work on your paper. Evaluate each **term** (part of the expression) in Axel's expression, and then add the terms together to get the area of his trapezoid.

2-145. Copy Tuvok's rule below on your paper and substitute the measures of the trapezoid your teacher gave you into his rule.

$$A = b \cdot h \div 2 + h \div 2 \cdot a$$

a. What **operations** (addition, subtraction, multiplication, or division) are used in Tuvok's rule?

b. Addition and subtraction separate terms. Therefore, Tuvok's rule has two terms. Circle the terms on your paper.

c. Calculate the value of the terms separately and add the results. Remember that multiplication and division are performed in order from left to right.

2-146. Copy Sheila's rule below on your paper and substitute the measures of the trapezoid your teacher gave you into her rule.

$$A = \tfrac{1}{2}h(a+b)$$

a. What operations are being used in Sheila's rule? If any multiplication is not marked, you may want to add a " · " symbol.

b. Is $\tfrac{1}{2}h$ multiplied by a, the sum of a and b, or b? How do you know?

c. One way to show the different quantities within a single term is to circle the separate parts as shown at right.

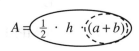

- Find the value of $(a+b)$ for your trapezoid.

- Multiply h by $\tfrac{1}{2}$, then multiply the result by the value of $(a+b)$ to find the area of your trapezoid.

2-147. Copy Rajan's rule (below) on your paper and substitute the measures of the trapezoid that your teacher gave you into his rule:

$$A = ah + \tfrac{(b-a)h}{2}$$

a. In your rule, circle the terms.

b. In the term $\tfrac{(b-a)h}{2}$, there is a group that must be calculated first. What is it?

c. Calculate the area of your trapezoid by following the order of operations.

—————— *Further Guidance* ——————
section ends here.

2-148. Problem 2-142 used three different ways to represent the area of a trapezoid with bases a and b and height h.

Sheila wonders if there are different ways to write some of the other formulas she has developed in the chapter. She checked with her class and found that there were at least two ways that the formula for the area of a triangle was written. They are shown below. Are these formulas the same? How do you know?

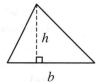

$$A = bh \div 2 \quad \text{and} \quad A = \tfrac{1}{2}bh$$

2-149.   Science, economics, and business are just a few of the fields that often describe relationships with rules (or formulas). For each part below, substitute the given values into the rule, then follow the order of operations to find the value of the remaining variable.

   a.   FALLING OBJECTS

   $h = \frac{1}{2} gt^2$, where h is the height an object falls (in feet), g is gravity (in feet per square seconds), and t is time (in seconds).

   Let $g = 32$ feet/sec^2 and $t = 10$ seconds. Find the height in feet.

   b.   SIMPLE INTEREST

   $I = prt$, where I is the interest, p is the starting value (in dollars), r is the interest rate per year, and t is the number of years the interest is added to the account.

   Let $p = \$50$, $r = 0.085$ per year, and $t = 2$ years. Find the interest earned in dollars.

   c.   CONVERSION FROM CELSIUS TO FAHRENHEIT

   $C = \frac{5(F-32)}{9}$, where C is degrees in Celsius and F is degrees in Fahrenheit.

   Let $F = 212$ degrees. Find the temperature in degrees Celsius.

   d.   **Additional Challenge:** ENERGY OF A MASS

   $E = mc^2$, where E is the amount of energy in an object (in joules), m is its mass (in kilograms), and c is the speed of light (in meters per second).

   Let $m = 2$ kilograms and $c = 300,000,000$ m/s. Find the amount of energy in the object in joules.

2-150.   LEARNING LOG

In your Learning Log, describe how to find the area of trapezoids. For your description, sketch an example shape and include work showing how you found the area. Label this entry, "Area of Trapezoids" and include today's date.

⊕ETHODS AND MEANINGS

Order of Operations

A **numerical term** is a single number, or numbers multiplied together. A **numerical expression** is a combination of numbers and operation symbols such as $+, -, \cdot, \div$. Examples of numerical terms include 4, $3(6-3)$, $\frac{5+4}{2}$, 10^2, and $-\frac{1}{2}(5-9)$.

A numerical expression is a sum or difference. To evaluate an expression:

Example:

1. *Circle* the parentheses or any other grouped numbers, and then circle the terms inside the grouping. See note below.

$$3(6-3\cdot1) + 4\cdot5^2 - \frac{13-3}{2}$$

$$3\!\left(\!6-3\cdot1\!\right) + 4\cdot5^2 - \left(\frac{13-3}{2}\right)$$

$$3\!\left(\!\left(6\right)-\left(3\cdot1\right)\!\right) + 4\cdot5^2 - \left(\frac{13-3}{2}\right)$$

2. *Simplify* each term in the parentheses.

$$3(3) \quad + \quad 4\cdot5^2 \quad - \quad \frac{10}{2}$$

3. *Circle* the terms in the expression.

$$\left(3(3)\right) + \left(4\cdot5^2\right) - \left(\frac{10}{2}\right)$$

4. *Simplify* each term until it is one number by:

$$\left(9\right) + \left(4(25)\right) - \left(5\right)$$

$$9 \quad + \quad 100 \quad - \quad 5$$

   - Evaluating each exponential (e.g., 5^2).

$$109 - 5 = 104$$

   - Multiplying and dividing from left to right.

5. Finally, *combine* terms by adding and subtracting left to right.

Note: In the example above, $\frac{13-3}{2}$ is treated as $\frac{1}{2}(13-3)$, that is, a term with parentheses.

Review & Preview

2-151. Find the area of these trapezoids.

a.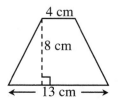
4 cm
8 cm
13 cm

b.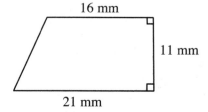
16 mm
11 mm
21 mm

2-152. Simplify each expression. You may want to refer to the Math Notes box for help.

a. $16 - 5(3 - 1)$

b. $31 \cdot 4 + 18 \cdot 6$

c. $3(2^2) - 8 \cdot 1$

d. $4 \cdot 5 - 2^2 + 3(5 - 4)$

2-153. Copy each expression and simplify it. Be sure to show the steps you use to get the answer.

a. $\frac{19}{20} - \frac{1}{4}$

b. $\frac{22}{25} - \frac{7}{10}$

c. $\frac{9}{32} + \frac{7}{8}$

2-154. Graph the points $X(-3, 5)$, $Y(-2, 3)$ and $Z(-1, 4)$. Connect them to make a triangle.

a. Reflect the triangle over the y-axis. What are the new coordinates of point Z?

b. Translate the original triangle down six units and right 3 units. What are the new coordinates of point Y?

c. Dilate the original triangle by multiplying each coordinate by -1. Describe the new shape you create.

2-155. Identify the length of the missing section of each line. Assume that the lines are divided into equal parts.

a.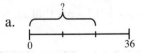

b.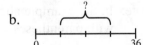

c.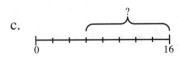

Chapter 2 Closure   What have I learned?

Reflection and Synthesis

The activities below offer you a chance to reflect
about what you have learned during this chapter.
As you work, look for concepts that you feel very
comfortable with, ideas that you would like to learn
more about, and topics you need more help with.
Look for connections between ideas as well as
connections with material you learned previously.

①   SUMMARIZING MY UNDERSTANDING

This section gives you an opportunity to show what you know about certain
math topics or ideas. Your teacher will give you directions for exactly how to
do this and will provide you with instructions about how to summarize your
understanding of transformations and **undoing** transformations. In this activity,
you will use a triangle to review transformations.

Predict and Order: Predict how
each transformation will change
or move the shape. Select an
order for the four
transformations and predict
what the new coordinates of the
vertices will be after each step.

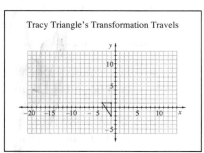

Tracy Triangle's Transformation Travels

Apply Transformations: Follow the transformation steps you described on the
graph. Use color and written descriptions to show how each transformation
alters the shape and its position on the coordinate grid. Check that the
coordinates you predicted were correct.

Tracy Triangle's Transformative Travels	Tracy Triangle's Transformative Travels
Add 5 to each x-coordinate	Multiply each y-coordinate by -1.
Tracy Triangle's Transformative Travels	**Tracy Triangle's Transformative Travels**
Multiply each coordinate by 2	Add -8 and then 3 to each x-coordinate Add 9 and -4 to each y-coordinate

Problem continues on next page. →

① *Problem continued from previous page.*

Undo Transformations: To get the triangle back to the original position, **undo** your transformations. You may choose to **undo** *each* transformation step or to find a new series of steps to return the shape to its original position. Show, using color, symbols, and written descriptions, how each transformation changes the shape's size and position on the coordinate grid.

② WHAT HAVE I LEARNED?

Working the problems in this section will help you to evaluate which types of problems you feel comfortable with and which ones you need more help with.

Solve each problem as completely as you can. The table at the end of this closure section provides answers to these problems. It also tells you where you can find additional help and practice on problems like them.

CL 2-156. The histogram at the right shows the weights of the frogs entered in the Jumping Frog Jubilee.

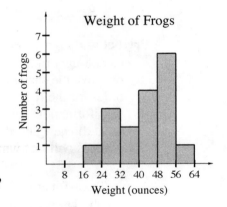

a. How many frogs weigh more than two pounds (32 ounces)?

b. What is the most common weight for the frogs?

c. What is the weight of the largest frog(s)?

CL 2-157. Find the mean, mode, range, and median of the values:

$$8, 13, 6, -1, 10, 0, -3, 5, 7, 1$$

CL 2-158. Copy the graph at right on your paper. You will need a second graph for List II. Complete each list of transformation steps you could use to move triangle B back to where it started at position A, and show each transformation on your graph.

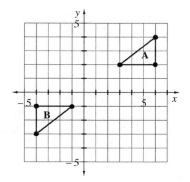

List I	List II
1. Rotate triangle B 180° about point $(-1,-1)$ 2. ?	1. Reflect triangle B across the y-axis 2. ? 3. ?

CL 2-159. Neatly graph the points $(-2,9)$, $(-3,7)$ and $(-5,10)$ on a four-quadrant graph. Connect them to make a triangle. Then, for each transformation described below:

- Write and simplify an expression to find the new coordinates.

- Check your answer on your graph.

a. Slide the triangle right 4 units and down 6 units.

b. Reflect the triangle across the y-axis.

CL 2-160. George is playing a game, but the spinner is incomplete. Help him figure out what fraction is missing.

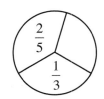

CL 2-161. Multiply $\frac{2}{3} \cdot \frac{1}{2}$. You may want to copy and complete the diagram at right to show your work.

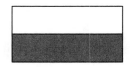

CL 2-162. Mary has a bag of colored tiles. There are 8 red tiles, 7 blue tiles, 9 yellow tiles, and 12 green tiles. If she reaches into the bag, what is the probability of picking a:

a. Yellow tile?   b. Green tile?   c. Purple tile?

CL 2-163. Copy each shape below on your paper, then find its area and perimeter. Show all your work.

a.

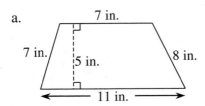

b.

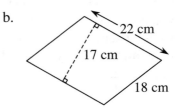

c.

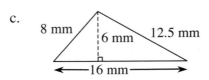

CL 2-164. For each of the problems in this section of closure, do the following:

a.   Draw a bar or number line like the one below that represents 0 to 10.

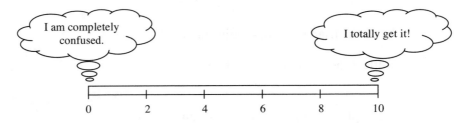

b.   Color or shade in a portion of the bar that represents your current level of understanding and comfort with completing that problem on your own.

c.   If any of your bars are less than a 5, choose *one* of those problems and do one of the following tasks:

  • Write two questions that you would like to ask about that problem.

  • Brainstorm two things that you DO know about that type of problem.

d.   If all of your bars are a 5 or above, choose one of those problems and do one of these tasks:

  • Write two questions you might ask or hints you might give to a student who was stuck on the problem.

  • Make a new problem that is similar and more challenging than that problem and solve it.

Making Connections: Course 2

③   WHAT TOOLS CAN I USE?

You have several tools and references available to help support your learning –
your teacher, your study team, your math book, and your Toolkit, to name only
a few. At the end of each chapter you will have an opportunity to review your
Toolkit for completeness as well as to revise or update it to better reflect your
current understanding of big ideas.

The main elements of your Toolkit should be your Learning Log, Math Notes,
and the vocabulary used in this chapter. Math words that are new to this chapter
appear in bold in the text. Refer to the lists provided below and follow your
teacher's instructions to revise your Toolkit, which will help make it a useful
reference for you as you complete this chapter and prepare to begin the next
one.

Learning Log Entries
- Lesson 2.1.2 – Meanings for –
- Lesson 2.1.3 – Subtraction of Integers
- Lesson 2.2.3 – Rigid Transformations
- Lesson 2.3.2 – Rearranging Shapes to Find Area
- Lesson 2.3.4 – Area of Parallelograms and Triangles
- Lesson 2.3.6 – Area of Trapezoids

Math Notes
- Lesson 2.1.1 – Commutative and Associative Properties of Addition
- Lesson 2.2.1 – Adding and Subtracting Integers
- Lesson 2.2.2 – Graphing Points on an xy-Coordinate Grid
- Lesson 2.2.3 – Rigid Transformations
- Lesson 2.2.4 – Mixed Numbers and Fractions Greater Than One
- Lesson 2.3.2 – Base and Height of Rectangles
- Lesson 2.3.3 – Parallelogram Vocabulary
- Lesson 2.3.4 – Area of a Parallelogram
- Lesson 2.3.5 – Area of a Triangle
- Lesson 2.3.6 – Order of Operations

Mathematical Vocabulary

The following is a list of vocabulary found in this chapter. Some of the words have been seen in the previous chapter. The words in bold are the words new to this chapter. Make sure that you are familiar with the terms below and know what they mean. For the words you do not know, refer to the glossary or index. You might also want to add these words to your Toolkit for a way to reference them in the future.

area	**associative property**	**commutative property**
coordinate grid	**coordinates**	**expression**
integers	**lengths**	**mixed numbers**
origin	**parallelogram**	**quadrant**
quadrilateral	**reflection**	**rigid transformation**
rotation	**term**	**translation**
trapezoid	**triangle**	**vertex**
x-**axis**	*y*-**axis**	

Process Words

The list of words below are problem solving strategies and processes that you have been involved in throughout the course of this chapter. Make sure you know what it means to do each of the following. If you are not sure, look through your book for problems when you were asked to think in the following ways.

brainstorm	choose a strategy	decompose
describe	explain your reasoning	justify
predict	rearrange	reverse your thinking
test your prediction	visualize	

Answers and Support for Closure Activity #2
What Have I Learned?

Problem	Solution	Need Help?	More Practice
CL 2-156.	a. 13 frogs b. between 49 and 56 ounces c. between 57 and 64 ounces	Lesson 1.1.4	Problems 1-23, 1-28, 2-88, and 2-111
CL 2-157.	mean: 4.6 median: 5.5 mode: none range: −3 to 13	Lessons 1.1.3 and 1.1.4 Math Notes boxes in Lessons 1.1.3 and 1.1.4	Problems CL 1-44, 2-28, 2-79, and 2-141
CL 2-158.	List I: 2. Translate (slide) triangle B right 4 units and up 3 units. List II: 2. Reflect triangle B across the *x*-axis. 3. Translate triangle right 2 units and up 1 unit. 	Lessons 2.2.1, 2.2.2, and 2.2.3 Math Notes box in Lesson 2.2.3 Learning Log (problem 2-66)	Problems 2-47, 2-51, 2-52, 2-59 through 2-64, 2-68, 2-85, 2-132, and 2-154
CL 2-159.	a. $x: -2+4=2$, $y: 9-6=3$; $(2,3)$ $x: -3+4=1$, $y: 7-6=1$; $(1,1)$ $x: -5+4=-1$, $y: 10-6=4$; $(-1,4)$ b. *y*-coordinates remain the same. $x: -2\cdot(-1)=2$; $(2,9)$ $x: -3\cdot(-1)=3$; $(3,7)$ $x: -5\cdot(-1)=5$; $(5,10)$ 	Lessons 2.2.1, 2.2.2, and 2.2.3 Math Notes box in Lesson 2.2.3 Learning Log (problem 2-66)	Problems 2-47, 2-51, 2-52, 2-55, 2-59 through 2-64, 2-68, 2-77, 2-85, 2-108, 2-132, and 2-154

Problem	Solution	Need Help?	More Practice
CL 2-160.	$\frac{4}{15}$	Lessons 1.2.4 and 1.2.5 Math Notes box in Lesson 1.2.4 Learning Log (problem 1-107)	Problems CL 1-140, 2-9, 2-98, and 2-153
CL 2-161.	$\frac{2}{6}$ or $\frac{1}{3}$	Lesson 2.3.1	Problems 2-93, 2-94, 2-98, and 2-127
CL 2-162.	a. $\frac{9}{36}$ or $\frac{1}{4}$ b. $\frac{12}{36}$ or $\frac{1}{3}$ c. 0: There are no purple tiles; impossible	Lessons 1.2.1 and 1.2.2 Math Notes boxes in Lessons 1.2.1 and 1.2.2	Problems CL 1-139, 2-42, 2-50, 2-71, 2-78, and 2-138
CL 2-163.	a. 45 square inches, 33 inches b. 60 square cm, 35 cm	Lessons 2.3.2 through 2.3.5 Math Notes boxes in Lessons 2.3.2 through 2.3.5 Learning Log (problems 2-106, 2-126, and 2-150)	Problems 2-102, 2-112, 2-115, 2-116, 2-124, 2-128, 2-129, 2-135, 2-137, and 2-151

Puzzle Investigator Problems

PI-3.   SIERPINSKI TRIANGLES

Fractals are geometric structures developed by repeating a process over and over. A famous example of a fractal is the **Sierpinski Triangle**, shown below. To create this design, start with a triangle, as shown in Figure 1. Then find and connect the midpoints of all of the sides of the triangle, subdividing it into four smaller triangles. Shade all but the central triangle as shown in Figure 1.

Then repeat the process by finding and connecting the midpoints of the shaded triangles of Figure 1. Shade all but the center triangles, as shown in Figure 2. If this process is continued infinitely, the result is the Sierpinski Triangle.

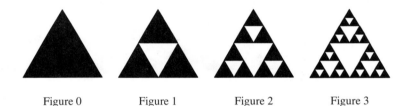

Figure 0   Figure 1   Figure 2   Figure 3

a.   On the PI-3 Resource Page (which can be downloaded at www.cpm.org/students), shade in the next figure in the sequence.

b.   For Figures 1 through 4, write a fraction to represent the amount of the entire triangle that is shaded. As you work, look for patterns. What is happening to the numerator and denominator of the fraction? What is happening to the amount shaded?

c.   Use your pattern to predict what portion of Figure 5 and Figure 6 in the sequence will be shaded.

d.   The shaded portion of Figure 2 could be written as $\left(\frac{3}{4}\right)^2$. Rewrite the other figures in this form. According to this pattern, what should the value of $\left(\frac{3}{4}\right)^0$ to be? Explain why.

e.   Is there any figure that will have less than 10% shaded? If so, use your pattern to explain how you know.

PI-4.   FAIR SHARES?

Three students baked cookies to share the next day and put them on a plate. However, Latisha woke up in the middle of the night and ate one-third of the cookies and went back to sleep. A little while later, Susan woke up, ate one-third of what was left and fell asleep. Then Hieu woke up, ate one-third of what was left, and went back to sleep. When all three students woke up, they discovered 8 cookies were left.

a.   How many cookies did they bake? Drawing diagrams may help.

b.   What if there had been four students instead? Solve the problem again where four students bake cookies and each of them wakes up separately and eats one-fourth of the cookies that are left. This time, assume that at the end, 81 cookies were on the plate. How many cookies did they bake?

c.   For each situation above, compare the original number of cookies to the final number of cookies left. What is their relationship?

Building Expressions

3

CHAPTER 3   Building Expressions

You may have heard the saying, "Mathematics is a universal language." This is sometimes said because mathematics uses symbols (like letters and numbers) to describe mathematical ideas and relationships in **general** ways to understand specific cases. For example, a statement like, "*I am exactly 3 years older than my cousin*," describes a **general** relationship that is true for any specific age of your cousin. To represent **general** relationships like this, you will use variables (like x) and build expressions (like $x + 3$).

Section 3.1 begins building expressions by using a new tool called "algebra tiles." You will use a variable to help you describe the perimeter and area of shapes built with tiles when one dimension is unknown or can represent various lengths.

Guiding Questions

Think about these questions throughout this chapter:

How can I write it?

How can I represent the relationship?

How can I organize my thinking?

Are these representations equivalent?

In Section 3.2, you will use variables to represent a single unknown number in different contexts, such as the balance of your bank account or the number of minutes you spend doing homework. You will learn about the 5-D Process, a **strategy** to organize your thinking that can help you solve problems.

In this chapter, you will learn how to:

➢ Combine like terms and simplify variable expressions.

➢ Use a variable to represent any number.

➢ Substitute a given value for a variable and evaluate an expression.

➢ Solve situational problems using the 5-D Process.

Chapter Outline

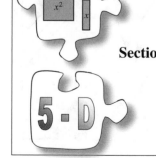

Section 3.1 This section introduces algebra tiles and uses their area and perimeter to develop the skills of building expressions and combining like terms. Variable expressions will be simplified and evaluated for given values.

Section 3.2 This section will introduce the 5-D Process as a problem-solving method. You will learn how to understand a problem by drawing, describing, and defining its elements. You will learn **strategies** that will help you throughout the course and lead to writing and solving equations later in the course.

3.1.1 What is the area?

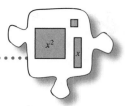

Area of Rectangular Shapes

Mathematics can be used to describe patterns in the world. Scientists use math to describe various aspects of life, including how cells multiply, how objects move through space, and how chemicals react. Often, when scientists try to describe these patterns, they need to describe something that changes or varies. Scientists call those quantities that change **variables**, and represent them using letters and symbols.

In this course you will spend time learning about variables, what they can represent, and how they can serve different purposes. To start, you will use variables to describe the dimensions and area of different shapes and begin to organize those descriptions into **algebraic expressions**.

As you work with your teammates, use the following questions to help focus your team's discussion:

How can we organize groups of things?

What is the area?

Which lengths can vary?

3-1.   Find the area of each rectangle below. Show your work. In part (b), each small square in the interior of the rectangle represents one square unit.

a.
15 cm

25 cm

b.

c.
0.75 m

1.8 m

d. Explain your method for finding the area of a rectangle.

3-2.   AREA OF ALGEBRA TILES

Your teacher will provide your team with a set of
algebra tiles. Remove one of each shape from the
bag and put it on your desk. Trace around each
shape on your paper. Look at the different sides of
the shapes.

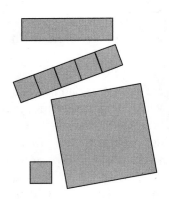

a. With your team, discuss which shapes have the
    same side lengths and which ones have
    different side lengths. Be prepared to share
    your ideas with the class. On your traced
    drawings, color code lengths that are the same.

b. Each type of tile is named for its area. In this course we will say that the
    smallest square has a side length of 1 unit, so its area is 1 square unit. We
    will call this tile "one" or the "unit tile." Can you use the unit tile to find
    the side lengths of the other rectangles? Why or why not?

c. If the side lengths of a tile can be measured
    exactly, then the area of the tile can be
    calculated by multiplying these two lengths
    together. The area is measured in square units.
    For example, the tile at right measures 1 unit by
    5 units, so it has an area of 5 square units.

1

The next tile at right has one side length that is
exactly one unit long. If we cannot give a
numerical value to the other side length, what
can we call it?

1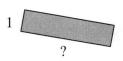
?

d. If we agree to call the unknown length "x," label the side lengths of each of
    the four algebra tiles you traced. Find each area and use it to name each
    tile. Be sure to include the name of the type of units it represents.

3-3.   Jeremy and Josue have each sketched three *x*-tiles on their papers.

Jeremy has labeled each tile with an *x*. *"They are three x-tiles, each with dimensions 1 by x, so the total area is 3x square units,"* he said.

Josue labeled the dimensions, that is, length and width, of each tile. His sketch shows six *x*-lengths.

Jeremy's sketch   Josue's sketch

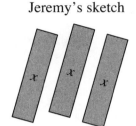

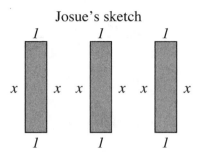

a.   Why do the two sketches each show a different number of *x* labels on the shapes?

b.   When tiles are named by their area, they are named in square units. For example, the *x* by *x* tile (large square) is a shape that measures x^2 square units of area, so we call it an x^2-tile.

What do the six *x*'s on Josue's sketch measure? Are they measures of square units?

3-4.   When a collection of algebra tiles is described with mathematical symbols it is called a **variable expression**. Take out the tiles shown in the picture below and put them on your table.

•   Use mathematical symbols (numbers, variables, and operations) to record the area of this collection of tiles.

•   Write at least three different variable expressions that represent the area of this tile collection.

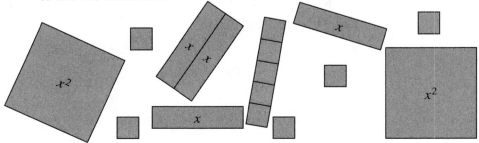

3-5.   Take out the tiles pictured in each collection below, put them on your table, and
        work with your team to find the area as you did in problem 3-4.

a.

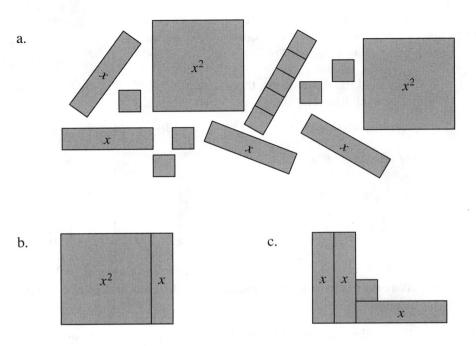

b.   c.

d. Is the area you found in part (a) the same or different from the area of the
    collection in problem 3-4? **Justify** your answer using words, pictures, or
    numbers.

3-6.   Build each collection described below with algebra tiles and use them to help
        you to answer the questions.

a. If a person combined a collection of three x^2-tiles, two x-tiles and five unit
    tiles with one x^2-tile and two x-tiles, how many of each tile would they
    have?

b. If a student started with three x^2-tiles, two x-tiles and five unit tiles and
    removed two x^2-tiles, two x-tiles and three unit tiles, what would remain?

METHODS AND **M**EANINGS

MATH NOTES

Area of Trapezoids

There are multiple ways to divide a trapezoid and rearrange the pieces into a parallelogram with the same area. For example, the trapezoid can be divided parallel to its two bases to create two smaller trapezoids that are each half of the height of the original trapezoid. Those two pieces can be rearranged into a parallelogram, as shown below.

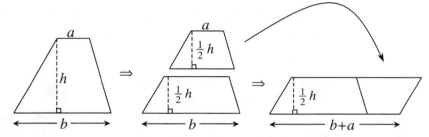

Therefore, to find the **area of a trapezoid**, find the product of half of the height (h) and the sum of the two bases (a and b).

$$A = \tfrac{1}{2}h(a+b)$$

3-7. Sketch the shape made with algebra tiles at right on your paper. Then answer parts (a) and (b) below.

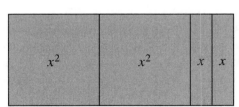

a. Find the area of the shape.

b. If the algebra tiles were rearranged into a different shape, how would the area change?

3-8.   Your team forgot to clean up their algebra tiles and now they are all over your desk.

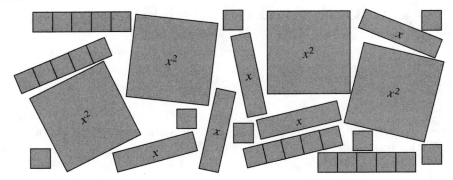

Sort the tiles so that they are in groups that are all the same and write a sentence explaining how many of each type of tile you have.

3-9.   Suppose that a triangle is created on a graph by connecting points A, B, and C below. Marika, Kimiku and Marcus want to move triangle ABC five units to the left and four units down. Write an integer expression to record how the shape moves and find the new coordinates for each vertex.

a. $A(-1, 3)$ b. $B(5, -1)$ c. $C(0, 1)$

3-10.   Find the area and perimeter of the shape at right.

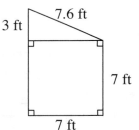

3-11.   Find the area of each square with the given side lengths.

a.
4 cm

4 cm

b.
10 in.

10 in.

c.
12 km

12 km

d.
5 units

5 units

e.   Describe the method you used to find the area of the squares.

Making Connections: Course 2

3.1.2 What is a variable?

Naming Perimeters of Algebra Tiles

How much homework do you have each night? Some nights you may have a lot, while other nights you may have no homework at all. The amount of homework you have varies from day to day. In mathematics we use letters such as x and y, called **variables**, to represent quantities that are not constant.

In Lesson 3.1.1 you used variables to name lengths that could not be precisely measured. Using variables allows you to work with lengths that you do not know exactly. Today you will work with your team to write expressions to represent the perimeters of different shapes using variables. As you work with your teammates, use the following questions to help focus your team's discussion:

Which lengths can vary?

How can we see the perimeter?

How can we organize groups of things?

3-12. TOOTHPICKS AND ALGEBRA TILES

In Chapter 1, you played the game "Toothpicks and Tiles." However, this time, you will play it using algebra tiles!

Work with your team to find the "tiles" (the area) and "toothpicks" (the perimeter) for the following figures.

a.   b.    c.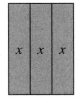

d. What is different about the shape in part (c)?

e. Is the perimeter of the shape in part (c) greater or less than the perimeter of the shape in part (a)? Explain your thinking.

3-13. The perimeter of each algebra tile can be written as an expression using variables and numbers.

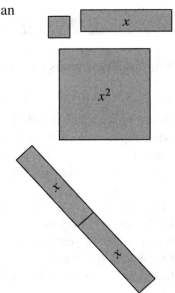

Write at least two different expressions for the perimeter of each tile shown at right.

a. Which way of writing the perimeter seems clearest to you? What information can you get from each expression?

b. Lisa wrote the perimeter of the collection of tiles at right as $2x+1+2x+1$ units, but her teammate Jody wrote it as $4x+2$. How are their expressions different?

c. Which expression represents the perimeter?

3-14. The expressions that you have written to represent area and perimeter are made up of **terms**. A **term** may be a single number, variable, or product of numbers and variables such as $3x$, x^2, 8, $-2xy$, or $6(x-7)$.

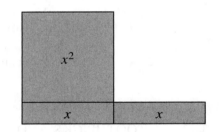

For the shape at right, one way to write the perimeter would be to include each side length in the sum:
$$P = x+x+x+1+x+x+1+x$$

a. How many x lengths are represented in this expression? How many unit lengths?

b. **Combining like terms**, that is, terms that contain the same variable, is a way of simplifying an expression. Rewriting the perimeter of the shape above as $P = 6x+2$ **combines** the separate x-terms as $6x$ and combines the units in the term 2.

If you have not already done so, combine like terms for the perimeter of the different algebra tiles in problem 3-13.

3-15.   Using algebra tiles, on your desk, make the shapes shown below. Trace each shape and label the length of each side on your drawing. With your team, find and record the total perimeter and area for each shape. If possible, write the perimeter in more than one way.

a.

b.

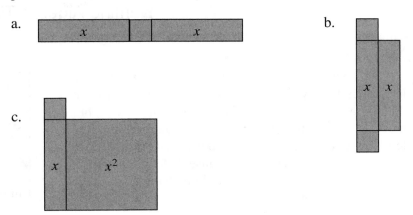

c.

3-16.   In problem 3-15, x is a variable that represents a number. The value of x determines the size of the perimeter and area of the shape.

Using the shapes from the previous problem, sketch and label each shape with the new lengths given below. Rewrite the expressions with numbers and simplify them to determine the perimeter and area of each shape.

a. $x = 6$ units for all three shapes

b. $x = 2$ units for all three shapes

c.   Compare your method for finding perimeter and area with the method your teammates used. Is your method the same as your teammates? If so, is there a different way to find the perimeter and area. Explain the different methods.

3-17.   LEARNING LOG

In your Learning Log, explain what a variable is in your own words. What does it mean for the length of an x-tile to be a variable? What is an expression? Use examples with drawings to illustrate your statements. Title this entry "Variables" and include today's date.

METHODS AND MEANINGS

Naming Algebra Tiles

Algebra tiles help us represent unknown quantities in a concrete way. For example, in contrast to a 1×5 tile that has a length of 5 units, like the one shown at right, an x-tile has an unknown length. We can represent its length with a symbol or letter (like x) that represents a number, called a **variable**. Because its length is not thought to be fixed, the x-tile could be 6 units, or 5 units, or 0.37 units long.

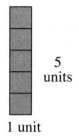

5 units

1 unit

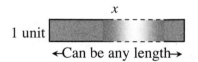

x

1 unit

←Can be any length→

Algebra tiles can be used to build **algebraic expressions**. An algebraic expression is similar to numerical expressions defined in Chapter 2, but its terms include variables. The three main algebra tiles are shown at right. The large square has a side of length x units. Its area is x^2 square units, so it is referred to as an x^2-tile.

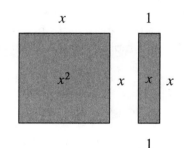

The rectangle has length of x units and width of 1 unit. Its area is x square units, so it is called an x-tile.

The small square has a side of length 1 unit. Its area is 1 square unit, so is called a one or unit tile. Note that the unit tile in this course will not be labeled with its area.

3-18.   Natalie and her little sister, Coco, found an old trunk
         in the attic. They decided to explore the contents of
         the trunk. It had 25 baseball cards, three hats, four
         pair of gloves, five books, two photo albums, one
         pair of boots and two hairbrushes.

         The girls want to organize the objects into two
         groups of things that are alike. Help them sort the
         objects and explain how you created the two groups.

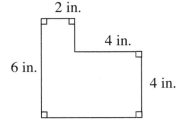

3-19.   Find the perimeter of the figure at right.

3-20.   Copy the diagrams of algebra tiles below on your
         paper. Then find the perimeter of each shape.

a.
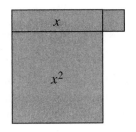

b.
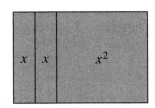

3-21.   Paige traveled to Australia and is making her favorite bread
         recipe. She usually bakes the bread in a 350°F oven. She $C = \frac{5(F-32)}{9}$
         is surprised to learn that the oven temperatures in Australia
         are measured in degrees Celsius. Using the formula at
         right and the order of operations, help Paige determine how
         she should set the oven in degrees Celsius.

3-22.   Simplify the following expressions.

         a. $\frac{2}{5} - \frac{1}{6}$ b. $\frac{3}{7} - \frac{7}{14}$ c. $\frac{5}{8} - \frac{2}{3}$

3-23.   Mr. Hill has a deck of math flashcards that include addition, subtraction, and multiplication problems. Twenty-five cards show addition problems, 30 are subtraction problems, and 45 are multiplication problems.

    a.   What is the probability of drawing a card with an addition or subtraction problem on it?

    b.   If Mr. Hill adds 40 division flashcards to the deck, what will P(division) be?

    c.   In the new deck, which is greater: the probability of drawing an addition or subtraction flashcard, or the probability of drawing a multiplication or division flashcard? **Justify** your conclusion.

3.1.3   How can I rewrite it?

Combining Like Terms

In Lesson 3.1.2, you looked at different ways the perimeter of algebra tiles can be written, and created different expressions to describe the same perimeter. Expressions that represent the same perimeter in different ways are called **equivalent**. Today, you will extend your work with writing and rewriting perimeters to more complex shapes. You will rewrite expressions to determine whether two perimeters are equivalent or different. As you work today, keep these questions in mind:

Are there like terms I can combine?

How can I rearrange it?

How can I see (**visualize**) it?

3-24.   Build each of these shapes using algebra tiles and look carefully at the lengths of the sides:

i.    *ii.*   *iii.*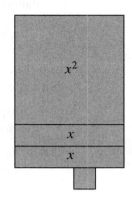

a.   Sketch each figure on your paper and color code the lengths that are the same. Which figures have side lengths that are different than those you have measured before? How are they different?

b.   Label each length on your paper. Discuss with your team how to label the new lengths. Explain your **reasoning**.

c .   Find the perimeter of each figure. Write the perimeter in simplest form by combining the like terms.

3-25.   In any expression, the number that tells you how many of each variable or quantity you have is called a **coefficient**.

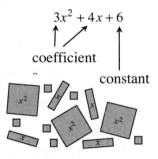

For example, for the expression that describes the collection at right, the coefficient "3" shows that there are three x^2-tiles, and the coefficient "4" shows that there are four x-tiles. The 6 is the **constant**, because it shows the number of units.

Answer each question below for each of the perimeters you found in problem 3-24.

- How many x (or y) lengths are there in the perimeter?
- How do you **see** the coefficient of x (or y) in your expression and in the shape?
- What is the constant in the expression? How do you **see** the constant in the shape?

3-26.　**HOW MANY PERIMETERS?**

Erik cannot keep his hands off the algebra tiles! He has made several different shapes, each one using the same tiles. *"Will every shape I create with these tiles have the same perimeter?"* he wonders.

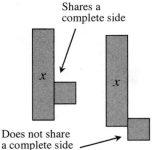

Shares a complete side

Help Erik investigate by making different shapes with your team. Your shapes must follow these rules:

- Shapes must use exactly three tiles: a one tile, an x-tile, and an x^2-tile.

- Tiles must share a complete side. An example of tiles that do, and do not, share complete sides is shown at right.

Does not share a complete side

a.　Rearrange the tiles until each teammate has a shape that follows the rules and has a different perimeter. Discuss why the perimeters are different. Trace each shape, color-code the sides, and label their lengths. Write an expression for the perimeter of each shape and simplify it by combining like terms.

b.　Are other perimeters possible with the same pieces? As you find others:

- Trace the shapes.

- Color-code and label the sides.

- Write the perimeter in simplest form.

Be prepared to share your list of perimeters with the class.

c.　Are there different shapes that have the same perimeter? Why or why not?

3-27.　**Additional Challenge:** Build this shape out of algebra tiles. Then, on grid paper, draw the shape when x is equal to each of the lengths below.

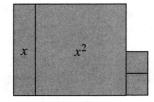

a.　$x = 5$ units　　b.　$x = 3$ units

c.　$x = 2$ units　　d.　$x = 1$ unit

3-28.　LEARNING LOG

In your Learning Log, describe what a "term" is in math. Using algebra tiles, make up an example to explain how to combine like terms. Why is it useful to combine like terms? Title this entry "Combining Like Terms" and include today's date.

Making Connections: Course 2

METHODS AND **M**EANINGS

Combining Like Terms

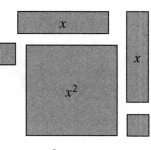

A **term** is an expression that contains a single number (called a **constant**), single variable, or the product of numbers and variables. This course uses tiles to represent variables and constants. Combining tiles that have the same area to write a simpler expression is called **combining like terms**. See the example shown at right.

$$x^2 + 2x + 2$$

More formally, **like terms** are two or more terms that have the same variable(s), with the corresponding variable(s) raised to the same power.

Examples of like terms: $2x^2$ and $-5x^2$, $4ab$ and $3ab$.

Examples that are *not* like terms: 5 and $3x$, $5x$ and $7x^2$, a^2b and ab.

When you are not working with the actual tiles, it helps to **visualize** them in your mind. You can use these images to combine those terms that are the same. Here are two examples:

Example 1: $2x^2 + x + 3 + x^2 + 5x + 2$ is equivalent to $3x^2 + 6x + 5$

Example 2: $3x^2 + 2x + 7 - 2x^2 - x + 7$ is equivalent to $x^2 + x + 14$

When several tiles are pushed together and form a more complicated figure, the area of the new figure is the sum of the areas of the individual pieces, and the perimeter is the sum of the lengths around the outside. Area and perimeter expressions can be **simplified**, or rewritten, by combining like terms.

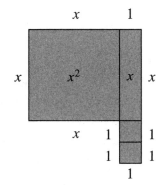

For the figure at right the perimeter is:
$x + 1 + x + 1 + 1 + 1 + 1 + x + x = 4x + 6$ units

3-29. Find the perimeter of each figure made of algebra tiles below.

a. 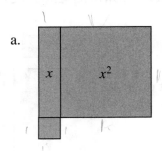   b. 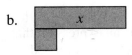   c.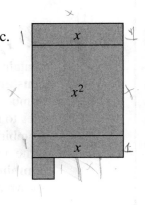

3-30. Copy and simplify each expression.

a. $6 + (-18)$ b. $12 + (-25)$ c. $-9 + (-9)$ d. $-12 + 6 + 15$

3-31. Find the mean, mode, range, and median of the values:

12, 4, –2, 0, 9, –2, 1, 7, 8, 2.

3-32. Sketch the collection of algebra tiles that is described by the following expression. Rewrite the area of the collection by combining like terms.

$$7x + 2x^2 + 3x^2 + 3 + x$$

3-33. Copy and complete the portions web at right by including a picture, decimal, and percent representation of $\frac{9}{20}$.

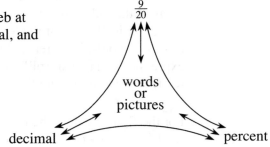

Making Connections: Course 2

3.1.4 What can a variable represent?

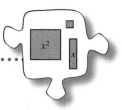

Evaluating Variable Expressions

In the past three lessons, you have learned how to find the perimeter and area of a shape using algebra tiles. Today, you will challenge the class to find the perimeter and area of shapes that you create. As you work, keep in mind these questions:

Which lengths are constant?

Which lengths can change?

3-34.   Use the perimeter expressions you found in problem 3-29 to answer the questions below.

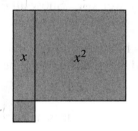   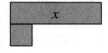   

a.   Determine each perimeter if $x = 5$ units.

b.   Determine each perimeter if $x = 2\frac{1}{2}$ units.

c.   Using a technology tool or grid paper as directed by your teacher, carefully draw each shape with the specified length of x units.

3-35.   SHAPE CHALLENGE

You and your team will choose four algebra tiles that
will be used to build a shape to challenge your
classmates. You may choose whatever tiles you would
like to use as long as you use exactly four tiles.

As a team, decide on the shape you want to make.
Experiment with different shapes until you find one you
think will have a challenging perimeter and area for your
classmates to find. Then, to share your challenge with
the class:

- Build the shape with algebra tiles in the middle of your team so everyone
  can see it.

- Get an index card from your teacher. On one side, neatly draw the shape
  and label each side.

- Write a simplified expression for the perimeter and for the area on the
  same side of the card. This will be the answer key. Show all of your
  steps clearly.

- Turn the card face down so the answer is hidden, put the names of your
  team members on the top of the card, and then put it beside the shape you
  built with your algebra tiles.

Remember, your work needs to be clear enough for your classmates to
understand.

Follow your teacher's directions to complete challenges created by other teams.
As you look at their shapes, sketch them on your paper. Work with your team
to label the sides and find the perimeter and area of each shape. Be sure to
combine like terms to make the expressions as simple as possible.

3-36.   Choose two of the shapes from problem 3-35. Sketch each shape and label it
with its perimeter and area. Do not forget the correct units. It is not necessary
to draw the figures to scale. Rewrite each expression with the values given
below and then evaluate it.

a. $x = 1.5$ units

b. $x = 3\frac{3}{4}$ units

3-37.   LEARNING LOG

In your Learning Log, sketch a complex shape made out of algebra tiles (you might choose one from the Shape Challenge). Explain your **strategies** for finding the area and perimeter of the shape. Use color, arrows, and labels to explain your work. Title this entry "Perimeter and Area Using Algebra Tiles" and include today's date.

METHODS AND MEANINGS

Evaluating Expressions

The word **evaluate** indicates that the value of an expression should be calculated when a variable is replaced by a numerical value.

For example, when you evaluate the expression $x^2 + 4x - 3$ for $x = 5$, the result is:

$$(5)^2 + 4(5) - 3$$
$$25 + 20 - 3$$
$$42$$

Using the expression $3x^2 - 5x + 2$ for $x = 4$, the result is:

$$3(4)^2 - 5(4) + 2$$
$$3(16) - 5(4) + 2$$
$$48 - 20 + 2$$
$$30$$

In each case remember to follow the order of operations.

3-38.   Sketch the algebra tile shape at right on your paper.
         Write an expression for the perimeter of the shape, then
         find the perimeter for each of the given values of x.

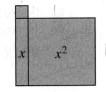

         a. $x = 7$ units   b. $x = 5.5$ units

         c. $x = \frac{7}{3}$ units

3-39.   Copy each expression and simplify it. Show all of your steps.

         a. $1.234 + 0.58 + 5.316$ b. $6.1 - 1.536$ c. $4.8(0.6)$

3-40.   Multiply $\frac{4}{5} \cdot \frac{1}{3}$. You may want to show your thinking with a diagram.

3-41.   On a coordinate grid, graph these points to create a triangle:

$$(-2, 3), \ (3, -2), \ (-2, -2)$$

         a.   What kind of triangle is it?

         b.   Where could you add a fourth point so that when the points are connected
               you will make a rectangle?

         c.   What point can you add to create a trapezoid?

         d.   Translate the original triangle 5 units to the left and 4 units down. Label the
               coordinates of the vertices of the new triangle.

3-42.   Simplify each expression.

         a. $-\frac{4}{5} + \frac{3}{10}$ b. $2\frac{5}{8} - 1\frac{1}{3}$

3.1.5 Are they related?

Perimeter and Area of Algebra Tile Shapes

People often assume that area and perimeter are related. It seems reasonable that if the area of a shape gets bigger (or smaller), then its perimeter should also get bigger (or smaller). But is this always true? In Chapter 1 you learned that the "tiles" could stay the same, but you could increase the "toothpicks" by changing the arrangement of squares. In this lesson you will continue to investigate whether there is a relationship between perimeter and area using algebra tiles.

As you work with your team, it is important that you share your ideas so that you are able to understand many different ways of **seeing** the shapes. Be prepared to **justify** how you are finding perimeters and how you are simplifying the expressions. Ask yourself these questions to help you to explain your **reasoning**:

How can I see the perimeter?

Where am I adding (or covering) length?

How can I rearrange the tiles?

3-43. HOW MANY PERIMETERS?

Obtain a set of algebra tiles from your teacher. For each problem below, use exactly three x-tiles to build a shape with the specified perimeter. Sketch the shapes on your paper, label the sides, and show how you combined like terms. Be prepared to **justify** your answer.

a. $P = 2x + 6$ b. $P = 4x + 2$

c. $P = 6x + 2$

3-44. Look at the shapes you made in problem 3-43. How do the areas of each of the shapes compare? How do the perimeters compare? Explain.

3-45. Build and sketch a shape with an area of $x^2 + x$ square units and a perimeter of $6x$ units.

3-46.   The shapes you made in problem 3-43 each had a different perimeter, but each one used the same algebra tiles. Can you make more than one perimeter with *any* collection of algebra tiles? Assume the tiles share a complete side. Consider the three different sets of tiles listed below:

Collection I: one x^2-tile and one x-tile

Collection II: one x^2-tile and one unit tile

Collection III: two x^2-tiles

a.   With your team, make shapes with each pair of tiles that have different perimeters. Make as many different perimeters as you can. Remember, a perimeter is only different if the expression is different after you combine like terms. Each time you create a new perimeter, write it down and sketch the shape.

b.   When the areas of two shapes are the same, are the perimeters equal? If so, explain why. If not, give an example in which they are not.

3-47.   Build the shape at right in the center of your table, and sketch it on your paper.

a.   Write an expression for the perimeter of the shape.

b.   Where could you add another unit tile to the shape without changing the perimeter? Decide with your team where to put it, then sketch the new shape on your paper. Label the sides and find the perimeter.

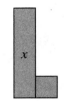

c.   Are the areas of the two shapes the same or different? Explain your **reasoning**.

3-48.   **Additional Challenge:** In the shape at right, one of the x lengths on the x^2-tile is partially covered by three 1-unit lengths. What happens to the perimeter if x has a value less than 3? Investigate this by answering the questions below.

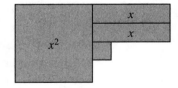

a.   Write an expression for the perimeter and for the area of the shape.

b.   Use your expressions to predict the perimeter and area of the shape when $x = 4$, $x = 3$, $x = 2$, and $x = 1$.

c.   Draw the algebra tile diagram on grid paper to **scale**, using each of the four side lengths. In other words, first draw all of the sides of length x so that they are 4 units long. Then, draw the diagram again and make all of the sides of length x just 3 units long. Do the same for $x = 2$ and $x = 1$.

d.   Use your diagrams to measure the actual area and perimeter of each shape. What do you notice? Can you explain why this happens?

Making Connections: Course 2

3-49.   Evaluate each expression for the given value.

a. $2a - 7$ when $a = 3$ b. $10 + 4m$ when $m = -2$

c. $9 + (-2n)$ when $n = 4$ d. $\frac{x}{2} + 5$ when $x = 6$

3-50.   The Kennedy High School cross-country running team ran the following distances in recent practices:

3.5 miles, 2.5 miles, 4 miles, 3.25 miles, 3 miles, 4 miles, and 6 miles.

Find the mean, median, and mode of the team's distances.

3-51.   Sketch the rectangle at right on your paper. Calculate the perimeter and area for the given x-values.

3 ⬚ (rectangle, width x)

a. $x = 5$ b. $x = 9$ c. $x = 4.6$

3-52.   Where would the point $(11, -18)$ be after each transformation described below? Write an integer expression to find each new coordinate.

a.   Reflect $(11, -18)$ across the x-axis, then reflect that point across the y-axis.

b.   Translate $(11, -18)$ 5 units to the right and 3 units down.

3-53.   Set up a 4-quadrant graph and graph the points below to make the 4-sided shape $PQRS$.

$P(-2, 4)$ $Q(-2, -3)$ $R(2, -2)$ $S(2, 3)$

a.   What shape is $PQRS$?

b.   Find the area of the shape.

3.2.1 How can I draw it?

Describing Relationships Between Quantities

You may not know it, but you use mathematical thinking every day. You think mathematically when you figure out if you can afford items you want to buy, or when you read a graph on a web page. You also think mathematically when you double a recipe or when you estimate how much longer it will take to get somewhere based on how far you still have to go. Math can describe many of the relationships in the world around you.

Building your interpretation skills and developing ways to represent situations will help you solve problems. In this section you will learn new ways to show your thinking when using math to solve problems. As you work today, think about the following questions:

How can I represent this with a diagram?

Who has more? Who has less?

3-54. Sometimes using the same words in a slightly different way can change their meaning. Read and compare the two situations below.

Situation 1	Situation 2
Myra has 15 marbles. This is ten less than Dahlia.	Myra has 15 marbles. Dahlia has ten less than Myra.

a. For each situation, draw a picture to represent the marbles each girl has. What is the difference between the problems?

b. In which problem does Myra have more marbles than Dahlia?

c. How many marbles does Dahlia have in Situation 1 above? How many does she have in Situation 2?

Making Connections: Course 2

3-55. Ellie is building a dollhouse. She has boards that are two different lengths. One long board is 7 inches longer than the total length of three of the short boards.

    a.   Draw a picture showing how the short and long boards are related.

    b.   What are some possible lengths of her boards?

    c.   If one of the long boards is 50 inches long, how long is a short board? Be ready to share your thinking with the class.

3-56. Now read and compare Problems A and B below.

Problem A	Problem B
Dianna has $16. Jairo has twice as much money as Dianna. Who has more money?	Dianna has $16. She has twice as much money as Jairo. Who has more money?

    a.   Represent each problem with a diagram.

    b.   Compare the amount of money Jairo has in part (a) to the amount he has in part (b). Explain how you know in which situation he has more money.

3-57. Now you are going to **reverse** your thinking. Examine the pictures below, then use words to describe the relationship you see in the pictures. Assume the lengths that appear to be equal are equal.

    a.    b.

    c.

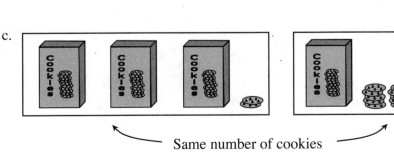

Same number of cookies

3-58.   Richard, Arielle and Kristen just measured how tall they are in feet. Their heights are shown in the bar graph at right.

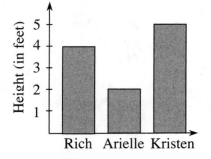

Decide which statements below are true and which statements are false. Rewrite the false statements to make them true.

a.   Richard is one foot shorter than Kristen.

b.   Arielle is twice as tall as Richard.

c.   Kristen is one foot taller than twice Arielle's height.

d.   The sum of the three children's height is 10 feet.

3-59.   **Additional Challenge:** Represent this description with a picture.

Ellen is gluing tiles on the four vertical sides of a rectangular planter box. The longer side of the box is covered by six more than two times as many tiles as the shorter side.

3-60.   Find the area of each figure below.

a.
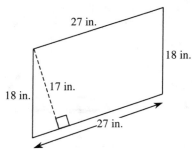

b.
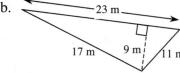

3-61. Find the missing information from the following relationships.

a. Mark has downloaded four times as many songs on his music player as Chloe. If Mark has 440 songs, how many songs does Chloe have?

b. Cici likes to collect shoes, but she only has half the number of pairs of shoes that her friend Aubree has. If Cici has 42 pairs of shoes, how many pairs of shoes does Aubree have?

c. Tito walked three more miles than Danielle. If Danielle walked 2 miles, how far did Tito walk?

3-62. Evaluate the expression $10 - 2x$ for the given x-values.

a. $x = 2$ b. $x = \frac{1}{2}$ c. $x = -2$

3-63. Copy and complete each of the Diamond Problems below. The pattern used in the Diamond Problems is shown at right.

a.
b.
c.
d.

3-64. Complete a Portions Web, described in Lesson 1.1.5, for each number below.

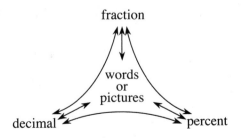

a. 0.25

b. $\frac{3}{4}$

c. $33\frac{1}{3}\%$

3.2.2 How can I organize it?

. . . .

Solving a Word Problem

You have seen that being able to draw diagrams and describe relationships is helpful for solving problems. In this lesson, you will learn another way to organize your thinking as you solve word problems.

3-65.   FENCING THE BASKETBALL COURT

The Parent Club at Post Falls Middle School needs 183 feet of fencing to go around the rectangular outdoor basketball court behind the school gym. They will only need to place a fence on three sides of the court because the wall of the gym will form the fourth side. The length of the court is 32 feet more than the width. One of the shorter sides will be 5 feet shorter than the other one to leave room for a gate.

Your task: Determine how much fencing will be used on each side of the court. Be prepared to **justify** your answer and show all of your work. Be sure that someone who is not on your team can read and understand your work.

Discussion Points

What information do we know in the problem?

What do we need to figure out?

What diagram can we draw to represent this situation?

How did we organize our work?

How can a wrong answer help us revise our thinking?

3-66.   If another team came to look at your paper for problem 3-65, could they understand your work? Why or why not? What else could you do to make it so that someone else could make sense of your work just by looking at it?

3-67.   Daniel, Donald, and Debra decided to organize their thinking in a table using a method they call the 5-D Process. Get a Lesson 3.2.2A Resource Page from your teacher that shows their work. Then answer some of the following questions during the whole class discussion.

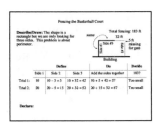

- *"What are the students Describing and Drawing?"*
- *"What is in the Define column?"*
- *"What is the Do column used for?"*
- *"What are they trying to Decide?"*
- *"What might the Declare section be for?"*

3-68.   While one team was working on problem 3-65, they decided to see if a width of 30 feet would use all of the 183 feet of fencing. They figured out that, with a 30-foot width, the length would be 62 feet and the side with the gate would be 25 feet. Only 117 feet of fencing would be used.

What is a logical number that they should try next for the width so that all of the fencing is used? Explain your **reasoning**.

3-69.   Finish problem 3-65 using the 5-D Process. Continue the chart you looked at in problem 3-67 to find the answer.

3-70.   Use the steps of the 5-D Process to organize and solve each of the parts below. The Lesson 3.2.2C Resource Page may help you set up your table. Be sure to show each of the "D" steps clearly in your solution process.

a.   Laura takes very good care of her vehicles. She owns a blue van and a red truck. Although she bought them both new, she has owned the truck for 17 years longer than the van. If the sum of the ages of the vehicles is 41 years, how old is the van and how old is the truck?

b.   Ryan is thinking of a number. When he multiplies this number by 6 and then subtracts 15 from the answer, he ends up with his original number. What number is Ryan thinking of?

3-71. Sketch the algebra tile shape shown at right on your paper. Then:

- Write an expression for the area of the shape.

- Write and simplify an expression for the perimeter of the shape.

- Calculate the area and perimeter of the shape for each value of x.

a. $x = 7$ b. $x = 2.5$ c. $x = 15$

3-72. Copy and simplify each expression.

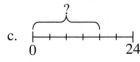

a. $7 \cdot (-2)$ b. $-3 \cdot 10$

c. $4 \cdot (-3)$ d. $-8 \cdot (-6)$

3-73. What fraction of one hour (60 minutes) is represented by the following numbers of minutes? Simplify each fraction whenever possible. A sketch of a clock might help you.

a. 10 minutes   b. 15 minutes   c. 30 minutes   d. 20 minutes

3-74. Write a sentence that describes the relationship in words. For example, "$5, $8" could be $8 is three more than $5.

a. $13, $39   b. 25 feet, 17 feet   c. 38 lbs., 19 lbs.

3-75. Find the missing parts of each number line. Assume that the lines have been split into equal parts.

a. ? 0 42   b. ? 0 64   c. ? 0 24

Strategies for Using the 5-D Process

Math is used to solve challenging problems that apply to daily life. For example, how much fresh water is on the planet? How many area codes (for telephone numbers) are needed in a city? Where should a city build transportation lines such as city bus systems and subways to reduce traffic on the freeways? Mathematics can provide helpful insights for the solutions.

When trying to solve a new and challenging problem, it is useful to have a **strategy**. The 5-D Process that you learned about in Lesson 3.2.2 will often work when you are trying to solve a problem you have not seen before.

In this lesson you will practice using this process to solve more word problems and you will compare the different ways that your classmates use the 5-D Process to help them. Be sure to write your work neatly and be prepared to **justify** your **reasoning**.

As you work using the 5-D Process, consider the following questions:

How can we describe the problem?

How can we decide how to label the columns?

How can we organize the columns?
How can we decide which quantity to start with?
Does it matter which one we choose?

How can we decide which number to try first?

Your team may be asked to present your responses to one or more of the target questions above at the end of this lesson.

3-76.   **A scalene triangle** has three unequal side lengths. The medium-length side is 7 cm longer than the shortest side. The longest side is twice as long as the shortest side. The total perimeter is 39 cm. What are the lengths of the sides of the triangle?

3-77.   Travis and Angela were playing a Guess My Numbers game. Angela told Travis, "I'm thinking of two positive numbers. The difference of my numbers is 4 and the product of my numbers is 96. What are my numbers?" Help Travis find Angela's numbers.

3-78.   The Potter Valley basketball team did not record how many baskets each player made during the last game. Jenny remembers that she made three times as many baskets as Grace. Alexis knows that she made six more baskets than Grace. Joan thinks that she made 4 fewer baskets than Grace. Tammy is sure that she made the same number of baskets as Joan. Altogether the five players made 40 baskets. How many baskets did each player make?

3-79.   Ramon was studying pond life in Doyle Park. In two hours, he counted four more frogs than turtles. The number of crayfish he counted was three more than twice the number of turtles. In total, he counted 54 turtles and crayfish. How many frogs were there?

3-80.   Dawn is trying to find the dimensions of a parallelogram. She knows that the base is one unit less than twice the height of the shape. The area is 91 square units. How long are the base and height?

3-81.   Ms. Pacheco, Mr. Edwards, and Mr. Richards are three math teachers at Turner Middle School. Ms. Pacheco is three years older than Mr. Richards. Mr. Edwards is twice as old as Mr. Richards. The sum of Mr. Richard's age and Mr. Edwards' age is 81. How old is each person?

3-82.   **Additional Challenge:** If one side of a square is increased by 12 feet and the side connected to it is decreased by three feet, a rectangle is formed. The perimeter of the rectangle is 62 feet. How long was the side of the original square?

3-83.   With your team, re-read the focus questions for this lesson, reprinted below:

How can we describe the problem?

How can we decide how to label the columns?

How can we organize the columns?
How can we decide which quantity to start with?
Does it matter which one we choose?

How can we decide which number to test first?

Discuss the **strategies** you use with the 5-D Process as a team. Be prepared to share your ideas with the class.

METHODS AND MEANINGS

Solving Problems with the 5-D Process

The **5-D Process** is an organized method to solve problems. The D's stand for Describe, Define, Do, Decide, and Declare. An example of this work is shown below.

Problem: The base of a rectangle is 13 centimeters longer than the height. If the perimeter is 58 centimeters, find the base and the height of the rectangle.

Describe/Draw: The shape is a rectangle and we are looking at the perimeter.

height

base

Define		Do	Decide
Height (trial)	Base (height + 13)	Perimeter 2(base) + 2(height)	58?
Trial 1: 10	10 + 13 = 23		66 is too high

Use a trial value.

Use the relationships stated in the problem to determine the values of the other quantities (such as base and perimeter).

Decide if the answer is correct. Revise and make another trial until you find the correct answer.

Trial 2: 7	7 + 13 = 20	2(20) + 2(7) = 54	too low
Trial 3: 8	8 + 13 = 21	2(21) + 2(8) = 58	correct

Declare: The base is 21 centimeters and the height is 8 centimeters.

3-84. If the total area of this algebra tile shape is 168 square units, how long is each side? To find out how long the x side must be, copy the diagram and table and answer the questions below.

Describe/Draw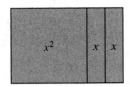

	Define		**Do**	**Decide**
	Side #1	Side #2	(Side one)·(Side	Area = 168?
Trial 1:	10	12		
Trial 2:				

Declare:

a. Describe how the lengths of the two sides are related to each other.

b. Which side of the rectangle does Side #2 represent?

c. Use the 5-D Process to complete the table. Find the length of the two sides of the rectangle.

3-85. Evaluate the expression $5 + (-3x)$ for the given x-values.

a. $x = 3$ b. $x = \frac{1}{3}$ c. $x = -3$

3-86. Troy has a number cube with the numbers 1 through 6 on it. If each side is equally likely to appear when he rolls the cube, find the following probabilities. (Note: When two or more numbers are multiplied, each of the numbers is a factor of the product.)

a. P (rolls a 2)   b. P (rolls an odd number)

c. P (rolls a factor of 6)

Making Connections: Course 2

3-87. Simplify the following expressions using the order of operations.

a. $3(8-4)+4^2-(2+3)$

b. $7 \cdot 4 - 3 \cdot 8 + 2^2 - 6$

c. $7-(-3)+(-4+3)$

d. $-6-4(3 \cdot 2)+5^2$

3-88. Write expressions for the perimeter and the area of this algebra tile shape. Then simplify each expression by combining like terms.

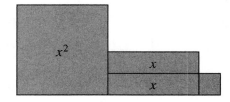

3.2.4 How can I represent it?

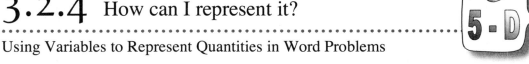

Using Variables to Represent Quantities in Word Problems

In Section 2.1, you used variables to help you describe the perimeter of tiles. In that situation x could be stretched to represent any positive number. Today you will continue to use the 5-D Process as you solve word problems and you will use a variable to represent the unknown value in the problem.

Think of these questions as you work on the problems today:

What is the problem asking?

What is the relationship between the quantities involved?

How can I choose which part of the problem to represent with a variable?

3-89. Thu has one mini-box of Choco-Blasters, and Warren gave her three more pieces. Samara has two mini-boxes of Choco-Blasters and she gave six pieces to Will. Now Thu and Samara have the same number of Choco-Blasters left.

How many Choco-Blasters are in a mini-box? Assuming all mini-boxes of Choco-Blasters have the same number of pieces in them, use the 5-D Process to solve this problem.

3-90. Allen's team was working on a problem but did not have time to finish it. They also did not follow the teacher's directions for showing work in the Define section. Discuss with your team what information you can get from Allen's table below.

Define		Do	Decide
Length	Width	Double each side and add together	Target perimeter = 36?
Trial 1: 3	9	$2(3)+2(9)=24$	Too small
Trial 2: 4	?		

a. Is there enough information in Allen's table to finish the problem? Why or why not?

b. What would you need to know in order to complete Trial 2? Explain your thinking.

3-91. Allen's teammate, Scott, was also working on problem 3-90, but he organized his table differently. As Scott explained his table to Allen, he used the pattern in the first two trials to represent the quantities with a variable, x.

Look at the table below.

a. How is it different from Allen's chart?

b. What does the x in the table represent?

c. Describe the relationship between the length and the width in words.

d. Where did the expression $x+x+(2x+3)+(2x+3)$ come from? Explain your thinking.

Define		Do	Decide
Length	Width	Add all 4 sides together	Target perimeter = 36?
Trial 1: 3	$2(3)+3$	$3+3+9+9=24$	Too small
Trial 2: 6	$2(6)+3$	$6+6+15+15=42$	Too large
x	$2(x)+3$	$x+x+(2x+3)+(2x+3)$	

3-92. Izzy's team used a 5-D table to solve a problem that involved **consecutive integers**, which are integers that follow each other on a number line. The numbers 1, 2, 3, …, 14, 15, 16, …, or –5, –4, –3, ... are all examples of consecutive integers. The table below shows part of their work on the problem.

Copy the chart and finish the problem. Apply Scott's idea from problem 3-91 to add variable summaries in the chart after you find a solution.

	Define			Do	Decide
	1st number	2nd number	3rd number	Add all numbers together	Target sum = 57
Trial 1:	15	$15+1$	$15+2$	$15+16+17=48$	Too small
Trial 2:	20	$20+1$	$20+2$	$20+21+22=63$	Too large

3-93. Meiko saw someone's expressions in the 5-D Process table below and wanted to **reverse** the process. The problem involved a bag of green, red, and blue marbles.

	Define			Do	Decide
	Green	Red	Blue	Total Marbles	Total = 71?
Trial 1:	15				
	x	$x-2$	$2x+5$	$x+(x-2)+(2x+5)$	

a. One of the variable expressions describes how the number of red marbles compares with the number of green marbles. How can you describe this relationship in words?

b. Based on the variable expressions, use words to describe how the number of blue marbles compares with the number of green marbles.

c. How many total marbles are in the bag?

d. If there are 15 green marbles in the bag, how many red and blue marbles are in the bag? Show your work.

3-94.   Camille knew that a triangle had one side with a length of 16 inches and another side was 20 inches. She did not know the length of the third side, but she did know that the perimeter was five times the length of the unknown side. How long is the unknown side?

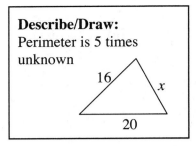

Describe/Draw:
Perimeter is 5 times unknown

Copy the table below and complete the chart. You may add as many rows as you need to solve the problem. Remember to summarize the relationships with a variable line and to complete the Declare sentence.

	Define		Do	Decide
	Unknown Side	Perimeter	Compare sum to perimeter	Same?
Trial 1:	5	5(5)	$\overset{?}{5+16+20=25}$ $41 \neq 25$	No

Declare:

3-95.   Margaret was working on the problem below:

Michael earned four times as much money last summer as his sister Mackenzie. Together they earned $475. How much did each person earn?

The table below shows the first two trials Margaret made. Based on the results, work with your study team to suggest a number she should try next. (You do not need to solve the problem.) Is it **reasonable** for different members of your team to suggest different numbers?

- Are there some numbers that would not be helpful? Explain.

	Define		Do	Decide
	Mackenzie's earnings	Michael's earnings	Add both of their earnings together	Target sum = $475
Trial 1:	$50	4($50)	$50 + $200 = $250	Too small
Trial 2:	$100	4($100)	$100 + $400 = $500	Too large

3-96.   Dawn and Myrna's father has asked them to build a rectangular pen for their dog. They have 74 feet of fencing. They want the length to be one more than twice the width. Use the 5-D Process to help Dawn and Myrna find the dimensions (both length and width) of the pen.

184   *Making Connections*: Course 2

3-97.   **Additional Challenge:** Use the 5-D Process to find three consecutive integers that have a product of 3360.

3-98.   LEARNING LOG

In your Learning Log, describe how you decide which number to use as your first trial in the 5-D Process. Then explain how you use the results of your first trial to choose your next trial number. You may want to include an example from your recent work to help you explain. Title this entry, "Defining and Deciding" and label it with today's date.

METHODS AND **M**EANINGS

Consecutive Integers

MATH NOTES

Consecutive integers are integers that come "one after another" in order (that is, without skipping any of them). For example: 11, 12, and 13 are three consecutive integers. The numbers 10, 12, 14, and 16 are four **consecutive even integers** because in counting up from 10, no even numbers are skipped. Likewise, 15, 17, and 19 are **consecutive odd integers**.

At times in algebra it is necessary to represent a list of consecutive integers. To represent any list in **general** we must use variables, and it is common to let x represent the first integer. See the examples of how to write a list of consecutive integers below:

Three consecutive integers: $x, \ x+1, \ x+2$

Three consecutive odd integers: $x, \ x+2, \ x+4$

Three consecutive even integers: $x, \ x+2, \ x+4$

Note that consecutive even integers and odd integers look alike because both even integers and odd integers are two apart.

3-99.   Think about the mathematical process you use as you solve the following problems. Show your work and your solutions.

    a.   If there are 100 students in a room and 40 of them are boys, how many are girls?

    b.   If there are 17 blue and white stripes on a flag and 9 of them are blue, how many are white?

    c.   If there are 250 pennies and dimes in a box and 130 of them are pennies, how many are dimes.

    d.   Now **generalize**: Imagine you know how many items you have in a collection of two types of things. If you know how many of one of the items you have, how could you find how many of the other item you have?

3-100.   Copy and simplify each expression.

    a. $-2+5$ b. $(-4)\cdot(6)$ c. $4-(-3)$

    d. $10+(-2)-7$ e. $-5-3(2-6)$ f. $(3-3)(10^2-11)$

3-101.   Daisy and Alexandra each have a group of algebra tiles on their desks as described below.

                Daisy has these tiles: $x, x, x^2, 1, x^2, x, x^2$, and x.

                Alexandra has $x^2, x, 1, 1, 1, x, x^2, x$, and 1.

    a.   Sketch each girl's tiles.

    b.   If the girls put their tiles together, how many of each type of tile will they have? Write an expression that represents this sum.

3-102.   Rewrite each percent as a fraction and each fraction as a percent.

    a.   20%   b. $\frac{2}{5}$ c.   75%   d. $\frac{2}{3}$

                                       Making Connections: Course 2

3-103. Manuel used Pattern Blocks to build the shapes below. The block marked "A" is a square, "B" is a trapezoid, "C" is a rhombus (a parallelogram with equal sides) and "D" is a triangle. Find the area of Manuel's shapes.

a.

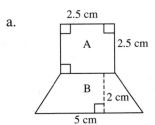

2.5 cm

A 2.5 cm

B 2 cm

5 cm

b.

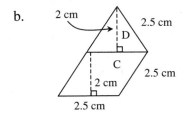

2 cm

D 2.5 cm

C

2 cm 2.5 cm

2.5 cm

$3.2.5$ How can I solve it?

More Word Problem Solving

So far in Section 3.2, you have been using a 5-D Process as a way to organize and solve problems. Today you will continue using this process to solve problems in a variety of situations.

As you work, use the following questions to focus your team's discussion:

What is the problem asking?

What is the relationship between the quantities involved?

How can we decide which part of the problem to represent as x?

What if a different quantity were represented with x?

3-104.   According to many sources, insects are the most diverse group of animals on the planet. The number of species is estimated at between six and ten million and insects are said to represent more than half of all known living organisms and potentially over 90% of the differing life forms on Earth.

The following problems are about insects and other creepy crawly creatures. Use your math skills to find out some fascinating facts about them. Your teacher will assign your team one of the following problems to solve. Be prepared to present your solution, including all steps of your 5-D solving process, to the class.

a.   Many insects migrate (travel) between their summer and winter homes. The Desert locust migrates about 800 miles farther then the Monarch butterfly every spring and the Pink-spotted hawkmoth migrates about 200 miles less than four times the distance of the Monarch butterfly every spring. Laid end to end, the distances traveled by a Monarch butterfly, a Desert locust, and a Pink-spotted hawkmoth is about 12,600 miles every spring. How far does each species travel?

b.   Bees, wasps, and ants all live in colonies that have a queen. The queen of the colony is really the mother of all the insects in the colony. During the spring and summer, many eggs are laid in bee, wasp, and ant colonies all over the world. This is sometimes easy to see when there is a bee, wasp, or ant colony close to your house or school because there will be lots of these insects in the area.

Queen bees lay about double the number of eggs in a day that queen ants lay. Queen wasps lay about 600 fewer eggs a day than queen ants do. An average queen bee, ant, and wasp together lay about 2,600 eggs a day. How many eggs would each type of queen lay in one day?

c.   Flies cannot see much past 24 to 36 inches, but that is not because they do not have lots of lenses in each eye. Dragonflies even have more! In one eye, dragonflies have two thousand more that seven times the number of lenses that houseflies have in one eye. If one housefly eye and one dragonfly eye together have 34,000 lenses, how many lenses do houseflies have in one eye? How many do dragonflies have in one eye?

Problem continues on next page. →

3-104.   *Problem continued from previous page.*

d.   Think you do not have enough room to farm? Think again. You could farm worms under your desk with a commercially available worm farm that measures 16" x 16" x 28". You can buy the worms online. At 1200 worms per pound you could start your own business just like John did. He's not good at keeping his records, however, and needs your help.

John buys his worms from two online stores, Worm Heaven and Wiggles R Us. John remembers that he ordered 1200 more than twice as many worms from Worm Heaven as he did from Wiggles R Us. He also knows he has 18,000 worms. How many worms did he order from each store.

e.   There are many kinds of animals that live in and on our bodies, called parasites. Some of the longest parasites live in our intestines. Two of these parasites are roundworms and tapeworms. Their lengths can be quite different depending on how long they have been living in someone's body!

One of the longest tapeworms ever measured was three feet less than seven times the length of the longest roundworm ever measured. If you laid these two worms end to end, they would measure an amazing 69 feet! How long was the tapeworm and how long was the roundworm?

f.   Did you know that most of the states in this country have official state insects and butterflies? Out of 30 states, the three most common insects are Monarch butterflies, honeybees, and ladybugs. The number of states that have Monarch butterflies as their official insect is one more than the number of states that have ladybugs as their official insect. The number of states that have honeybees as their official insect is three times the number of states with ladybugs as their state insect minus one. How many states have each kind of insect as their state insect?

3-105.   The number of girls at Middle School
         Cyber Summer Camp was six more
         than twice the number of boys. There
         were a total of 156 middle school
         students at the camp. Use the 5-D
         Process to find the number of boys
         and the number of girls at camp.

3-106.   The daily high temperatures in degrees Fahrenheit for the last two weeks in
         Grand Forks, North Dakota were: 7, 1, –3, 0, 4, –1, 2, 5, 7, 7, 3, –2, –4, –5.

         a.   Calculate the mean temperature.

         b.   Calculate the mode of the data.

         c.   Calculate the median temperature.

         d.   Which measure of central tendency do you think best represents the
              weather in Grand Forks? Why?

3-107.   On graph paper, graph the shape that has coordinates $(-2,-1)$, $(1,2)$, and $(-2,3)$.

         a.   Predict the coordinates of the shape after it is translated three units to the
              right and one unit down. Check your prediction on the graph.

         b.   Dilate the original shape by multiplying both the x- and y-coordinates by 2.

         c.   Reflect the original shape over the y-axis. What are the new coordinates?

3-108.   Which expressions are equivalent to the
         perimeter of the shape? How do you know?

         a. $x+3+3x+1$ b. $2x+4+x$

         c. $4x+4$ d. $2x+2+2x+2$

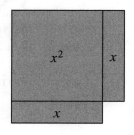

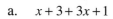

Chapter 3 Closure   What have I learned?

Reflection and Synthesis

The activities below offer you a chance to reflect on
what you have learned during this chapter. As you
work, look for concepts that you feel very comfortable
with, ideas that you would like to learn more about, and
topics you need more help with. Look for connections
between ideas as well as connections with material you
learned previously.

①   SUMMARIZING MY UNDERSTANDING

You have been working with finding
areas and perimeters of triangles,
rectangles, trapezoids, parallelograms,
and shapes created by algebra tiles.
This section gives you an opportunity
to showcase what you know about
area and perimeter. Your teacher will
provide you with instructions about
how to create a "magic book." In this
book you will summarize your
understanding of area and perimeter as
well as show how your understanding
can be used to find areas and perimeters of various shapes.

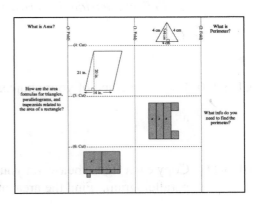

Assemble the Book: Follow your teacher's instructions to create a special
book. It will become clear later why this is called a "magic book."

What are Area and Perimeter? Use your Toolkit, textbook, and other
classroom resources to explain what you know about area. Include an
explanation about how the area formulas for triangles, parallelograms, and
trapezoids are related to the area of a rectangle. Diagrams might be helpful.

In your magic book, also explain what you know about perimeter. Be
specific about the information you need to know about a shape in order to
determine its perimeter.

Area and Perimeter Examples: Follow your teacher's instructions to reveal
the hidden portion of the book. In this region of the book, show how to find
the area and perimeter of the eight shapes in the booklet. Note: It might be
easier to show the connections between the shape, its area, and its perimeter
if you redraw the shape.

Working the problems in this section will help you to evaluate which types of problems you feel comfortable with and which ones you need more help with.

Solve each problem as completely as you can. The table at the end of this closure section has answers to these problems. It also tells you where you can find additional help and practice on problems like them.

CL 3-109. Matt moved Triangle A on the graph at right to match up with Triangle B in three moves. Follow the steps Matt wrote below. What was his final move?

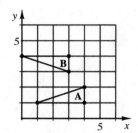

1. *Slide the triangle up 3 units.*

2. *Reflect the triangle across the line y = 4.*

3. *?*

CL 3-110. Using a method of your choice, find the products of the following fractions.

a. $\frac{3}{4} \cdot \frac{1}{4}$ b. $\frac{4}{5} \cdot \frac{4}{3}$

CL 3-111. Copy each figure below on your paper. Assume that the shape in part (a) is a parallelogram. Find the area and perimeter of each shape. Show all your work.

a.

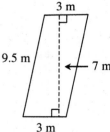

3 m

9.5 m   7 m

3 m

b.

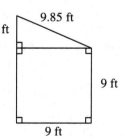

9.85 ft

4 ft

9 ft

9 ft

CL 3-112. Sketch the shape made with algebra tiles at right on your paper. Then answer parts (a) through (c) below.

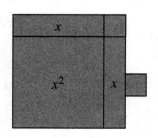

a.   Find the perimeter of the figure.

b.   Find the area of the figure.

c.   If the algebra tiles were rearranged how would the area change?

CL 3-113. Julia has two children who are four years apart in age. Julia is four times older than her youngest child. The sum of the ages of Julia and her children is 76 years. Use the 5-D Process to find the ages of Julia and each of her children.

CL 3-114. Robert found a spinner for a game that was not completely labeled. The spinner is shown at right. Help Robert figure out what fraction of the spinner is missing.

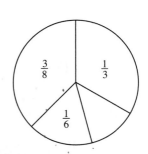

CL 3-115. Evaluate each expression for the given variable.

a. $3a - 7$ when $a = 2$

b. $8 + 5m$ when $m = -2$

c. $13 + (-3n)$ when $n = 4$

d. $\frac{x}{3} + 2$ when $x = 6$

CL 3-116. Copy and simplify each expression.

a. $7(5 - 1) + (-3) - 2^2$

b. $2 \cdot 7 + (-5)(3) - 4$

c. $6 - (-2) + (-5 + 8)$

d. $-2 + 3(3 \cdot 2) - 3^2$

CL 3-117. For each of the problems above, do the following:

    o Draw a bar or number line that represents 0 to 10.

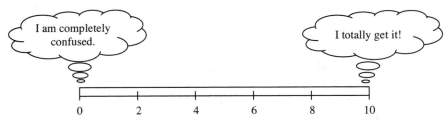

    o Color or shade in a portion of the bar that represents your level of understanding and comfort with completing that problem on your own.

If any of your bars are less than a 5, choose *one* of those problems and do one of the following tasks:

    o Write two questions that you would like to ask about that problem.

    o Brainstorm two things that you DO know about that type of problem.

If all of your bars are a 5 or above, choose one of those problems and do one of these tasks:

    o Write two questions you might ask or hints you might give to a student who was stuck on the problem.

    o Make a new problem that is similar and more challenging than that problem and solve it.

③   WHAT TOOLS CAN I USE?

You have several tools and references available to help support your learning – your teacher, your study team, your math book, and your Toolkit to name only a few. At the end of each chapter you will have an opportunity to review your Toolkit for completeness as well as to revise or update it to better reflect your current understanding of big ideas.

The main elements of your Toolkit should be your Learning Log, Math Notes, and the vocabulary used in this chapter. Math words that are new to this chapter appear in bold in the text. Refer to the lists provided below and follow your teacher's instructions to revise your Toolkit, which will help make it useful for you as you complete this chapter and as you work in future chapters.

Learning Log Entries

- Lesson 3.1.2 – Variables
- Lesson 3.1.3 – Combining Like Terms
- Lesson 3.1.4 – Perimeter and Area Using Algebra Tiles
- Lesson 3.2.4 – Defining and Deciding

Math Notes

- Lesson 3.1.1 – Area of Trapezoids
- Lesson 3.1.2 – Naming Algebra Tiles
- Lesson 3.1.3 – Combining Like Terms
- Lesson 3.1.4 – Evaluating Expressions
- Lesson 3.2.3 – Solving Problems With the 5-D Process
- Lesson 3.2.4 – Consecutive Integers

Mathematical Vocabulary

The following is a list of vocabulary found in this chapter. The words in bold are the words new to this chapter. It is a good idea to make sure that you are familiar with these words and know what they mean. For the words you do not know, refer to the glossary or index. You might also want to add these words to your Toolkit for a way to reference them in the future.

5-D process	**algebraic expression**	**coefficient**
combining like terms	**constant**	**consecutive integers**
equivalent	evaluate	factor
simplified	term	**variable**

Process Words

These words describe problem solving strategies and processes that you have been involved in as you worked in this chapter. Make sure you know what each of these words means. If you are not sure, you can talk with your teacher or other students or look through your book for problems in which you were asked to do these things.

calculate	decide	declare
define	describe	draw
evaluate	illustrate	organize
predict	represent	reverse your thinking
rewrite	simplify	visualize

Answers and Support for Closure Activity #2
What Have I Learned?

Problem	Solution	Need Help?	More Practice
CL 3-109.	Slide the triangle left 1 unit.	Lessons 2.2.1 and 2.2.2 Math Notes box in Lesson 2.2.3 Learning Log (problem 2-66)	Problems CL 2-158, 3-9, 3-52, and 3-107
CL 3-110.	a. $\frac{3}{16}$ b. $\frac{16}{15}$	Lesson 2.3.1	Problems CL 2-161, and 3-40

CL 3-111.	a. Area: 21 square meters
	   Perimeter: 25 meters
	
	b. Area: 99 square feet
	   Perimeter: 40.85 feet
		Lessons 2.3.2 through 2.3.5
		
		Math Notes boxes in Lessons 2.3.2 through 2.3.5
		
		Learning Logs (problems 2-126 and 2-150)
			Problems CL 2-163, 3-10, 3-19, 3-60, and 3-103

CL 3-112.	a. $P = 4x + 6$ units b. $A = x^2 + 2x + 2$ square units c. The area would not change.	Lessons 3.1.1, 3.1.2, 3.1.3, and 3.1.5 Math Notes boxes in Lessons 3.1.2 and 3.1.3 Learning Logs (problems 3-28 and 3-37)	Problems 3-7, 3-13, 3-14, 3-15, 3-20, 3-24, 3-29, 3-38, 3-45, 3-71, 3-88, and 3-108
CL 3-113.	Julia is 48. The children are 12 and 16.	Lessons 3.2.2, 3.2.3, 3.2.4, and 3.2.5 Math Notes box in Lesson 3.2.3 Learning Log (problem 3-98)	Problems 3-67 through 3-70, 3-76 through 3-81, 3-89 through 3-96, 3-104, and 3-105

Problem	Solution	Need Help?	More Practice
CL 3-114.	$\frac{3}{24}$ or $\frac{1}{8}$	Lessons 1.2.4 and 1.2.5 Math Notes box in Lesson 1.2.4 Learning Log (problem 1-107)	Problems CL 1-140, and CL 2-160
CL 3-115.	a. -1 b. -2 c. 1 d. 4	Lesson 3.1.4 Math Notes box in Lesson 3.1.4 Learning Log (problem 3-17)	Problems 3-34, 3-38, 3-49, 3-62, and 3-85
CL 3-116.	a. 21 b. -5 c. 11 d. 7	Lessons 2.1.1, 2.1.2, 2.1.3, and 2.3.6 Math Notes boxes in Lessons 2.2.1 and 2.3.6 Learning Log (problem 2-39)	Problems 2-152, 3-30, 3-72, 3-87, and 3-100

Puzzle Investigator Problems

PI-5.   WEIGHING PUMPKINS

Every year at Half Moon Bay, there is a pumpkin contest to see who has grown the largest pumpkin for that year.

Last year, one pumpkin grower (who was also a mathematician) brought 5 pumpkins to the contest. Instead of weighing them one at a time, he informed the judges, *"When I weighed them two at a time, I got the following weights: 110, 112, 113, 114, 115, 116, 117, 118, 120, and 121 pounds."*

Your task: Find how much each pumpkin weighed.

PI-6.   PASCAL'S TRIANGLE

The number pattern started at right is called **Pascal's Triangle**. While it looks like a simple arrangement of numbers, it has many interesting patterns within it. In this challenge, you will learn more about the hidden patterns of Pascal's Triangle.

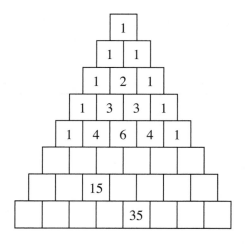

a.   Using the PI-6 Resource Page (which you can download at www.cpm.org/students), use the patterns to complete the missing numbers. Some of the numbers are given so you can check your work.

b.   What is the sum of the 20th row of the triangle? Can you find this without extending the triangle? Explain how you found your answer.

c.   Using a see-through highlighter, color in the squares that contain odd numbers. Describe the pattern that emerges.

d.   Find at least three other patterns in Pascal's Triangle that you have not described so far.

Making Connections: Course 2

Proportional Reasoning and Statistics

4

CHAPTER 4   Proportional Reasoning and Statistics

How often do you need to compare one thing to another? Perhaps you compare prices when you are buying something or you compare heights of the basketball players on the court. In mathematics, comparing one thing to another is an important **strategy** to learn about how they are related. We do it when dealing with ratios, fractions, decimals, percents, and similar figures.

You will begin comparing parts and wholes in Section 4.1. You will use these relationships to find percentages, something that you use in your daily life.

In Section 4.2, you will return to the Calaveras Frog Jumping Contest data and use new analysis tools to compare groups of frogs. You will also look at ways to display and interpret data.

Guiding Questions

Think about these questions throughout this chapter:

What's the relationship?

How can I represent the data?

What is the part?

What is the whole?

Section 4.3 will have you investigate how shapes change using mathematics you already know. You will also determine the unknown length of a side in a figure when given information about the lengths of other sides in the figure and in related figures.

In this chapter, you will learn how to:

➢ Find and use percentages to solve problems.

➢ Use measures of central tendency, histograms, stem-and-leaf plots, and box-and-whisker plots to compare data.

➢ Compare shapes and use similarity to find missing side lengths of polygons, especially triangles.

Chapter Outline

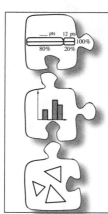

Section 4.1 This section introduces a linear diagram that you will use to represent relationships between parts and the whole to solve problems.

Section 4.2 This section introduces you to multiple ways of representing data, including histograms, stem-and-leaf plots, and box-and-whisker plots. You will compare sets of data using these representations.

Section 4.3 This section will introduce similarity and congruence for polygons.

Making Connections: Course 2

4.1.1   How can I find a percentage?

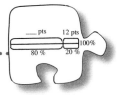

Part-Whole Relationships

Food labels tell you about what is in the food you eat. The nutrition facts label lists the percentages of vitamins and minerals in each serving. But often it does not tell you exactly how much of each vitamin or mineral is in the food or how much you should have each day to be healthy.

If you know how much Vitamin C is in a serving, can you figure out how much is needed in a day? To help you answer questions like that, this section will develop **strategies** that will help you find information about parts and wholes.

Nutrition Facts

Serving Size 1 cup (228g)
Serving Per Container 4

Amount Per Serving

Calories 250	Calories from Fat 110

	% Daily Value*
Total Fat 12g	18%
Saturated Fat 3g	15%
Cholesterol 30mg	10%
Sodium 470mg	20%
Total Carbohydrate 31g	10%
Dietary Fiber 0g	0%
Sugars 5g	
Protein 5g	

Vitamin A	4%
Vitamin C	2%
Calcium	20%
Iron	4%

4-1.   **WHAT ARE YOU EATING?**

The government has created guidelines for how much of various vitamins, minerals, and other substances a person should eat or drink each day to be healthy. These guidelines are then used to create labels (like the one shown above) to inform the public about the nutritional content of food.

According to the sample label above, one serving of Cheesy Mac macaroni and cheese contains 20% of the recommended daily amount of calcium. Doctors recommend a person have a total of 1300 mg calcium each day. How many milligrams of calcium are in one serving of Cheesy Mac?

Your task: With your team, determine how many milligrams of calcium are in one serving of Cheesy Mac macaroni and cheese. Look for more than one way to solve the problem, and be ready to explain all of your **reasoning**.

Discussion Points

What information do we have about the part?

What do we know about the whole?

How could we represent this situation with a number line?

4-2.   To help you represent the situation in problem 4-1, copy the number line below
on your paper.

Recommended Daily Intake of Calcium

0%   100%

a. With your team, decide how to **partition** the line (divide it into equal parts)
so that 20% is shown. Why did you choose to make that number of parts?
Is there another way that you could have divided the line?

b. The recommended daily intake of calcium
is 1300 milligrams. Where should 1300
milligrams be labeled on the number line?
Add this number to your diagram and
justify your decision.

c. Use your diagram to help you decide how
much calcium is in one serving of Cheesy
Mac. Record your thinking.

Further Guidance
section ends here.

4-3.   One way to write a percentage is as a **ratio** (comparison) of parts out of 100.
For example, the ratio $\frac{20}{100}$ represents 20 parts out of 100 total parts.

a. Jill represented the amount of calcium in one serving of Cheesy Mac with
the ratio $\frac{260}{1300}$.

   • What does the 260 represent?

   • What does the 1300 represent?

b. The ratios $\frac{20}{100}$ and $\frac{260}{1300}$ are two different ways to compare the calcium in
one serving to the recommended daily amount. How can you show that the
ratios are equivalent (the same)?

4-4.   One granola bar contains 4 g of dietary fiber. The label says that 4 g is 16% of the daily recommended amount. Louis decided to draw a diagram like the one below to understand this situation.

Recommended Daily Intake of Fiber

0%   100%

a.   Copy the diagram on your paper and add the label for 16%.

b.   How many grams of fiber are recommended each day? How can you show this with equal ratios?

c.   What percent of fiber should Louis get from other foods? Why is this percent equivalent to the ratio $\frac{21 \text{ g}}{25 \text{ g}}$?

d.   What other amounts are missing on the diagram? Add labels for all parts, percents, and the whole.

e.   Chris is eating cookies that contain 12 g of dietary fiber, which he says is 48% of the recommended daily amount. How can you use ratios to check that 12 g is equivalent to 48%?

4-5.   One large carrot contains approximately 6 mg of Vitamin C. The recommended daily intake of Vitamin C is 60 mg. Resa wanted to find out what percentage of her daily Vitamin C she gets from one carrot. She started with a line divided into 10 parts.

Recommended Daily Intake of Vitamin C

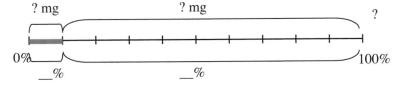

a.   Why do you think she divided the line segment into 10 parts?

b.   Copy the diagram on your paper and fill in the missing labels.

c.   The ratio $\frac{6 \text{ mg}}{60 \text{ mg}}$ represents the portion of Vitamin C in one large carrot. Work with your team to find this ratio in the diagram. Where do you see each amount? What other ratio could you write that would be equal to this?

d.   Use the diagram to help you find and write at least two more ratios on the number line that are equal to each other.

4-6. Resa was mixing blue and red paint to create purple paint. She created the drawing below to show the portions of blue paint to red that she used.

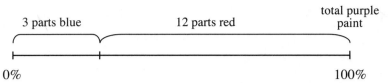

a. What does the picture tell you about the paint mixture? What statements can you make?

b. If you have not stated it yet, what percent of the paint is blue? What percent of the paint is red? **Justify** your answer.

4-7. **Additional Challenge:** Turner Middle School has 110 boys. Fifty-six percent of the students in the school are girls. How many students go to this school?

a. Create a model like Resa's from problem 4-5. Label the percentage of girls, the percentage of boys, and the number of boys on your drawing, as well as 0% and 100%.

b. How many students go to the school? How do you know?

c. How many girls go to the school? Explain your **reasoning**.

4-8. **Additional Challenge:** Regina is making paper flowers as decorations for the fall dance. She has made 40 flowers so far, and she is 16% finished. If she plans to finish making 70% of the flowers tonight, how many more will she need to make? Show your work.

METHODS AND MEANINGS

Equivalent Ratios

A **ratio** is a comparison of two amounts. A ratio can be written in words, as a fraction, or with colon notation. Most often in this course we will write ratios as fractions or state them in words.

For example, if there are 28 students in a math class and 15 of them are girls, we can write the ratio of the number of girls to the number of students in the class as:

15 girls to 28 students $\frac{15 \text{ girls}}{28 \text{ students}}$ 15 girls : 28 students

You used a Giant One to write equivalent fractions in Chapter 1. To rewrite any ratio as an **equivalent ratio**, write it as a fraction and multiply it by a fraction equal to one. For example, you can show that the ratio of girls to students is the same for a larger classroom using a Giant One like this:

$$\frac{5 \text{ girls}}{9 \text{ students}} \cdot \frac{3}{3} = \frac{15 \text{ girls}}{27 \text{ students}}$$

Equivalent fractions (or ratios) can be thought of as families of fractions. There are an infinite number of fractions that are equivalent to a given fraction. You may want to review the basis for using a Giant One — the Multiplicative Identity — in the Math Note in Lesson 1.2.3.

4-9. Find the missing values on the diagram below. Assume that the line is evenly divided.

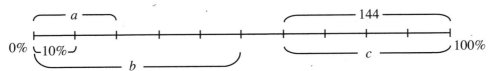

4-10.   A fish tank that holds 80 gallons of water is 55% full.

    a.   Create a drawing like Resa's in problem 4-4 to represent this situation.

    b.   How many gallons are in the tank now? How many more gallons are needed to fill the tank?

4-11.   Fill in the missing numbers in each number sentence.

    a. $\frac{5}{8} \cdot \frac{3}{3} = \frac{?}{?}$ b. $\frac{9}{15} \cdot \frac{?}{?} = \frac{?}{60}$ c. $\frac{7}{20} \cdot \frac{?}{?} = \frac{?}{110}$ d. $\frac{44}{100} \cdot \frac{?}{?} = \frac{?}{60}$

    e.   What **strategies** did you use to find the numbers in the Giant One in parts (b), (c), and (d)?

4-12.   Okie is a western lowland gorilla that lives at the Franklin Park Zoo near Boston, MA. He loves to finger paint and many of his paintings have been sold because their colors are so interesting. One painting was sold for five times the amount of a second, and a third was sold for $1500. If the total sale was for $13,500, how much did the most expensive painting sell for?

    Set up a 5-D Process table and solve the problem. Then represent the relationships using a variable.

4-13.   Simplify the following expressions.

    a. $\frac{2}{3} + \frac{4}{5}$ b. $\left(\frac{4}{5}\right)\left(\frac{2}{3}\right)$ c. $\frac{4}{5} - \left(-\frac{2}{3}\right)$

4-14.   Lucy keeps track of how long it takes her to do the newspaper crossword puzzle each day. Her recent times (in minutes) were:

        8   22   19   12   18   19   10   35   12   19   16   21

    a.   What is the median of her data?

    b.   What is the mode?

4.1.2 What is the percentage of the whole?

Finding and Using Percentages

How are sales advertised in different stores? In a clothing store, items are often marked with signs saying, "20% off" or "40% discount." In a grocery store, sale items are usually listed by price. For example, pasta is marked, "Sale price 50¢," or boxes of cereal are marked "$2.33 each." In the clothing store you are able to see how much the discount is, but the price you will pay is often not stated. On the other hand, sometimes in the grocery story it is not possible to tell the size of the discount. It might only be a small fraction of the original price.

The actual dollar amount of the discount and the percentage comparing it to the whole are important information that help you decide if you are getting a good deal. Today you will create complete information about a sale situation from the information given in a problem.

By the end of this lesson, you will be expected to answer the following target questions:

How can I find a percentage of a whole?

How can I find a percent if you have two parts that make a whole?

How can I find the whole amount if you know the parts?

4-15.   Marisa is always looking for a great deal while shopping. She found a sale rack where all of the jeans are marked 40% off. Her favorite jeans regularly cost $65.

a.   To figure out if she has enough money to buy a pair of jeans, Marisa decides to estimate. She thinks that the jeans will cost approximately $30. Is her estimate reasonable? Explain your thinking.

b.   To find the exact answer, Marisa created the diagram below. How could she add marks to evenly partition the line? Partition the line and calculate the missing values.

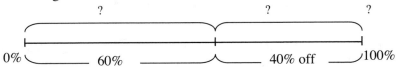

Problem continues on next page. →

4-15.   *Problem continued from previous page.*

    c.   How much money will Marisa save? What is the price she will have to pay?

    d.   Marisa wants to check her answer from part (c). How could she use the amount she saved and the original price to verify that she received a 40% discount?

4-16.   At the same sale, Kirstin sees a shirt that originally cost $50 on sale for just $37.50.

    a.   Estimate the percentage of the discount on the shirt.

    b.   Draw a diagram to represent this situation. Label all the parts.

    c.   What percent is the discount on Kirstin's shirt?

    d.   What is the relationship between the discount, sale price, and the original price? Write a statement that shows the relationship between the sale price, discount, and original price.

4-17.   So far in this section, you have used a linear model to represent percent problems in various contexts.

    a.   Obtain a Lesson 4.1.2 Resource Page (available at www.cpm.org/students) and use the linear models to find parts and wholes when different types of information are provided on the diagrams.

    b.   For each diagram, write at least three statements describing how parts and percentages are related. Some statements are started for you.

4-18.   When Kirstin was about to pay for her clothes, she realized that she had forgotten to include an 8% sales tax.

    a.   The belt Kirstin wants to buy costs $15 and she does not have paper to draw a linear model. To estimate tax, she figured that calculating 10% would be close enough. Explain how Kirstin might find 10% of $15 without a linear model.

    b.   Calculate exactly how much the 8% sales tax will cost Kirstin. What will be the total amount she will have to pay to the store?

METHODS AND MEANINGS

Part to Whole Relationships

MATH NOTES

Percentages, fractions, and decimals are all different ways to represent a portion of a whole or a number. Portion-whole relationships can also be described in words.

We can represent a part to whole relationship with a linear model like the one below. To solve a percentage problem described in words, you must first identify three important quantities: the percent, the whole, and the part of the whole. One of the quantities will be unknown. A diagram can help to organize the information. For example:

There are 220 boys in the 8th grade class. If boys make up 40% of the 8th graders, how many students are in the whole class?

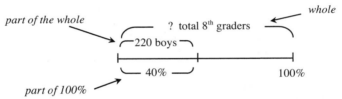

Once the parts have been identified, you can use **reasoning** to extend the part to the whole. For example, if 220 students are 40% of eighth graders, then 10% must be $220 \div 4 = 55$. Then 100% must be $55 \cdot 10 = 550$ students. Another way to solve the problem is to find the ratio of 220 boys to the whole (all students) and compare that ratio to 40% and 100%. This could be written

$$\frac{40}{100} \cdot \boxed{} = \frac{220}{?} \text{, then } \frac{40}{100} \cdot \boxed{\frac{5.5}{5.5}} = \frac{220}{?}$$

so the total number of 8th graders is 550.

To remember how to rewrite decimals or fractions as percents and percents as fractions or decimals, refer to the Math Notes box at the end of Lesson 1.3.1.

4-19. A shade of orange paint is made with 5 parts red paint and 15 parts yellow paint.

a. What percent of the paint is red?

b. What is the simplified ratio of yellow to red paint?

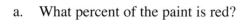

4-20. Janelle earned 90% on a test and got 63 points. How many total points were possible on the test? Draw a diagram to organize your information before solving the problem.

4-21. Use graph paper to solve the following problem.

a. Draw a four-quadrant graph and label each axis. Plot the following ordered pairs: $(-3, 2)$, $(-8, 2)$, $(-10, 8)$, $(-5, 8)$. Connect the points in the order given as you plot them, then connect the fourth point to the first one.

b. Describe the shape on your graph. What is its area?

4-22. Copy and simplify each expression.

a. $7 + (-3)$
b. $(10)(-5)$
c. $-5 + 6$
d. $(-2) \div (-2)$

4-23. When solving a problem about the perimeter of a rectangle using the 5-D Process, Herman built the expression below.

$$\text{Perimeter} = x + x + 4x + 4x \text{ feet}$$

a. Draw a rectangle and label its sides based on Herman's expression.

b. What is the relationship of the base and height of Herman's rectangle? How can you tell?

c. If the perimeter of the rectangle is 60 feet, how long are the base and height of Herman's rectangle? Show how you know.

4.2.1 How can I compare the data?

Measures of Central Tendency

You are exposed to a huge amount of information every day in school, in the news, in advertising, and in other places. It helps to have tools to be able to understand what different data mean. In this section, you will turn your attention to what you can learn (and not learn) from data.

4-24. JUMPING FROG JUBILEE

In Chapter 1 you examined results of the Calaveras County Frog Jumping Contest, and saw that the 2009 competition winner jumped 20.5 inches farther than the 2008 winner. Do you think that the winner in 2009 was a special frog? Or were the frogs in 2009 in general better jumpers than the frogs in 2008?

With your team, brainstorm ways that you could compare the two groups of frogs. Recall some of the measures of central tendency from Chapter 1.

2008		2009	
Frog Name	**Jump Length**	**Frog Name**	**Jump Length**
Skeeter Eater	231.5 in.	For the Sign	252 in.
Warped	230 in.	Alex Frog	236.5 in.
Greg Crome Dome	229 in.	Shakit	231.5 in.
R.G.	227 in.	Six Mile Shooter	226.75 in.
The Well Ain't Dry	221.5 in.	Spare the Air Everyday	223.25 in.
Winner	220.5 in.	Hooper	223.25 in.
7 lb 8 oz. Baby	217 in.	Jenifer's Jumper	222.25 in.
Delbert Sr.	216.5 in.	Dr. Frog	185.25 in.

a. Look at the 2008 and 2009 data above (or on the Lesson 4.2.1 Resource Page). What was the **range** (the span of smallest and largest values) of the jumps in each year? What does this tell you about the frog jumps?

b. What was the typical jump length of the frogs each year? How did you find this value?

c. Were the jumps all about the same, or were some jumps **outliers** (data that is much higher or lower than the others)? Name any outliers and why you think they are outliers.

d. Describe how the frogs jumped in each year as completely as you can. Was one year's frogs a better group of jumpers than the other? How do you know?

4-25.   How can other representations help you analyze the data? Use the Representing Data technology tool (available at www.cpm.org/students/technology) to create histograms of the data from problem 4-24. Set the bin size of each histogram to 10 inches. Then compare the histograms and answer the questions below as a team or class.

a.   How does each histogram organize the data? For example, why is the column between 220 and 230 inches for 2008 four units tall? Why is the 2009 column between 230 and 240 two units tall?

b.   What new statements can you make based on the histograms that you did not see when the data was in a list? Is there information that is easier to see in the histogram?

c.   The technology tool shows the mean and median of the data below the histogram. However, if those were not labeled, is there a way to determine the median or mean from a histogram alone? Explain.

4-26.   How does changing the data affect the mean, median, or mode? Use the 2009 data from problem 4-25. For each of the following changes to the data, predict:

   •   How would the mean of the data change?

   •   How would the median change?

   •   How would the mode change?

Be sure to **justify** your prediction. Only after your team has made a prediction should you calculate or use the technology tool to test your idea. Remember to start with the original 2009 data for each part.

a.   What if the 9th place jump length for 2009 (which was 182 inches) was included in the data?

b.   What if the 8th place jump length for 2009 was 201 inches instead?

c.   What if the 1st place frog was disqualified and only the remaining 7 frogs were included in the data?

4-27. Efren has been keeping data on the Calaveras Frog Jumping Contest for several years. Look carefully at the **stem-and-leaf plot** he made for the top 8 jumpers in 2007, shown at right.

A **stem-and-leaf plot** displays data by ordering it from least to greatest. All of the digits except the last one form the **stem** (in this case, the tens and hundreds places) and the last digit (in this case the ones) forms the **leaf**. The leaf portion is arranged in order from least to greatest.

**2007 Frog Jump Winners
Stem-and-Leaf Plot**

Note: 22 | 1 means 221 inches

stem

```
22 | 1  2  5  8
23 | 4  8
24 | 5
25 | 6
```

leaf

a. What is the **minimum** (smallest) value? What is the **maximum** (largest) value?

b. Are there any outliers in the data?

c. Is it possible to find the **median** of the data in the stem-and-leaf plot? If so, find the median. If not, explain why not.

d. Is it possible to find the **mean** with the stem-and-leaf plot? Calculate it and explain what the mean tells you about the frog jumps in 2007.

e. Create a new stem-and-leaf plot for the 2006 data below. Use your plot to identify the **median** and the **mode**.

2006	
Frog Name	**Jump Length**
Clausenn's Cuzor	235 in.
Whipper	222 in.
Me Me Me Me	212 in.
Haren's Heat	212 in.
Midnight Croaker	209 in.
Alex's Hopper	208 in.
Oh Sweet Sue	205 in.
Humpty Jumpty	204 in.

4-28.   **Additional Challenge:** A visitor to the
frog jumping contest told of another
similar contest he attended. He made the
statements about the frogs in this contest
below. Find a possible set of data that
would satisfy all of his statements.

- The measures of the jumps of the seven frogs were all integers and had a
  median of 14 meters.

- The minimum of the jump data was 11 meters and the maximum was
  15 meters.

- The mode of the jump data was 11 meters.

4-29.   LEARNING LOG

The mean, median, and mode are each different ways of
describing the "center" value of a set of data. You have
been finding mean, median, and mode for different data sets
since Chapter 1. Describe how to find the mean, median, and mode for a set of
data. If a data set includes an outlier, which measure best describes the middle?
Title this entry "Measures of Central Tendency" and include today's date.

4-30.   Mrs. Sakata is correcting math tests. Here are the scores for the first fourteen
tests she has corrected: 62, 65, 93, 51, 55, 12, 79, 85, 55, 72, 78, 83, 91, and 76.
Which score does not seem to fit in this set of data? How will the outlier score
affect the mean of the data? Explain.

4-31.   On graph paper, plot the points $A(2, 4)$, $B(0, 0)$, and $C(6, 2)$ to form
triangle ABC.

a.   Multiply the coordinates of each point by 2 and plot the new points. What
happened to the triangle?

b.   Predict what happens when you multiply each *original point* by $\frac{1}{2}$. Then
multiply the coordinates and plot the new points. Was your prediction
correct?

4-32. Sketch the algebra tile shape shown at right on your paper. Write expressions for the area and perimeter of the shape. Then, calculate the area and perimeter of the shape for each x-value.

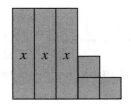

a. $x = 9$ cm

b. $x = 0.5$ cm

c. $x = 15$ cm

4-33. Sophie claims that whenever she increases the perimeter of a rectangle, its area increases.

a. She showed the rectangle at right and said, *"If I make the base twice as long, then the area increases."* Is her statement correct? Draw a diagram of the rectangle she described and explain whether the area is greater or less than the rectangle above.

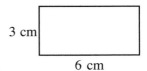

3 cm

6 cm

b. Is her claim about the relationship of area and perimeter correct for all figures? For example, is there any way that she could have a rectangle with a greater perimeter but with the same area? Give examples and explain your **reasoning**.

4-34. Evaluate the expression $2x^2 + x + 6$ for the given values of x below.

a. $x = 3$ b. $x = -2$ c. $x = 0$ d. $x = 5$

4.2.2 How can I represent it?

Multiple Representations of Data

Mark Twain, a famous American writer and humorist (1835–1910), once said, "Get your facts first, and then you can distort them as much as you please. (Facts are stubborn, but statistics are more pliable.)" What do you think he meant? Much of what we learn and interpret about different sets of data is based on how it is presented.

In this lesson you will use several mathematical tools to look at data in different ways. As you work, use these questions to help focus your discussions with your team:

What can we conclude based on this representation?

What cannot be concluded based on this representation?

How are the representations related?

4-35. **GLOBAL WARMING?**

Is the planet getting hotter? Experts look at the temperature of the air and the oceans, the kinds of molecules in the atmosphere, and many other kinds of data to try to determine how the earth is changing. However, sometimes the same data can lead to different conclusions because of how the data is represented.

Your teacher will provide you with some temperature data from November 1, 1975, and November 1, 2000. In all, there is data from 35 cities selected from different parts of the United States. To make sense of this data, you will first need to organize it in a useful way to help some relationship stand out.

a. Your teacher will assign you a city and give you two sticky notes. Label the appropriately colored sticky note with the name of the city on the front and its temperature in 1975 on the back, and label the other sticky note with its city name on the front and temperature in 2000 on the back.

b. Follow the directions of your teacher to place your sticky note on the class histograms. Use the axis at the bottom of the graph to decide into which **bin**, or interval, to place your sticky note.

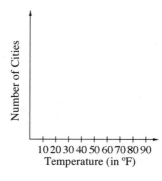

4-36.   Look at the graphs of temperatures the class created. According to these histograms, what can you say about the temperatures on November 1 in 1975 and 2000? Do the graphs show that one date was warmer than the other? Or are the temperatures basically the same? Be prepared to share your **reasoning**.

4-37.   The histograms your class made in problem 4-35 group data together in different **bins**, that is, intervals along the horizontal axis where data is grouped.

a. What are the benefits of a histogram? What are the limitations?

b. Another way to restructure the data is to form a **box-and-whisker plot**, which divides the data into four equal parts, or **quartiles**. To create one, follow the steps below with the class or in your team:

1. With a sticky dot provided by your teacher, plot the 1975 temperature for your city on a number line in front of the class.

```
◄─┤┼┼┼┼┤┼┼┼┤┼┼┼┼┤┼┼┼┤┼┼┼┼┤┼┼┼┤┼┼┼┼┤┼┼┼┤┼┼┼┼┤►
  0  10 20 30 40 50 60 70 80 90
```

2. What is the median temperature for 1975? Place a vertical line segment — about one-half inch long — marking this position above the number line on your resource page.

3. How far does the data extend from the median? That is, what are the minimum and maximum temperatures in 1975? Place vertical line segments marking these positions above the number line on your resource page.

4. The median splits the data into two sets: those that come before it and those that come after it when the data is ordered from least to greatest, like it is on the number line. Find the median of the lower set (called the **lower quartile**). Mark the lower quartile with a vertical line segment above the number line.

5. Look at the temperatures that come after the median in your ordered number line. The median of this portion of data is called the **upper quartile**. Mark the upper quartile with a vertical line segment above the number line.

6. Draw a box that contains all the data points between the lower and upper quartiles. Your graph should be similar to a "box" with "whiskers" like the one shown at right.

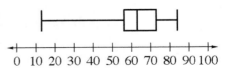

Problem continues on next page. →

4-37.   *Problem continued from previous page.*

    c.   What does the box-and-whisker plot tell you about the temperatures of the cities in 1975 that the histogram did not?

    d.   With your team, create a new box-and-whisker plot of the temperature data for the same cities on November 1, 2000 on your resource page. Be sure to identify each of the values below.

       •   The minimum and maximum data values (endpoints of the whiskers)

       •   The median temperature

       •   The upper and lower quartiles

4-38.   Compare the box-and-whisker plots for 1975 and 2000.

    a.   According to the box-and-whisker plots, how do the temperatures on November 1, 2000 compare to temperatures in 1975?

    b.   Did your observations about the differences or similarities of the temperatures from 1975 and 2000 change based on the box-and-whisker plots? If so, how and why did they change?

4-39.   The box-and-whisker plot at right shows the different grades (in percents) that students in Ms. Drew's class earned on a recent quiz.

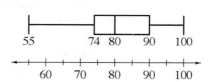

    a.   What was the median score on the quiz? What were the highest and lowest scores?

    b.   Did most students earn a particular score? How do you know?

    c.   If Ms. Drew has 32 students in her class, about how many students earned a grade of 80% or higher? About how many earned more than 90%? Explain how you know.

    d.   Can you tell if the scores between 80% and 90% were closer to 80% or closer to 90%? Explain.

METHODS AND MEANINGS

Histograms and Bar Graphs

Data can be displayed visually in different formats depending on the kind of information collected and the purpose for displaying it. Two of those formats are histograms and bar graphs, which look similar but are used in different ways.

A **bar graph** is used to represent discrete quantities—such as the number of eighth graders in your school or the number of people who are wearing blue jeans today. The height of the bar graph shows the frequency (the number of times something occurs) of the data in each category. The quantities are "discrete" because the categories are separate. For example, in the graph at right, a student is either a seventh or an eighth grader; no one is a 7.64[th] grader. Traditionally, the bars in bar graphs are separated, and each bar has a different label.

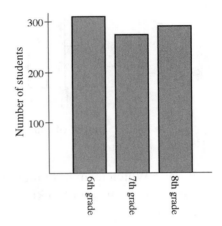

A **histogram**, on the other hand, is a way of representing a collection of data from a continuous set—such people's weight or their distance from home. Each bar represents data in an interval of numbers, called a **bin**. The vertical axis shows the number of pieces of data that fall into a bin (frequency). In the example, the bar on the left shows that there are 3 people in the data set whose weight is from 110 to just below 120 pounds. (Someone who weighs 120 pounds would be counted in the next bin.) For histograms, we label the horizontal axis by the numbers that mark the lower endpoints of each bin.

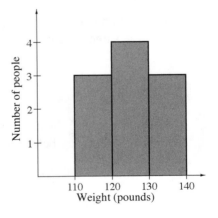

4-40.   Look at the two histograms below. They give you information about the heights of players on two basketball teams, the Tigers and the Panthers. Use the histograms to answer the following questions.

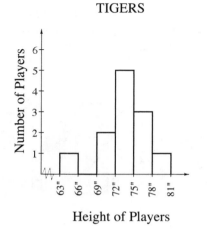
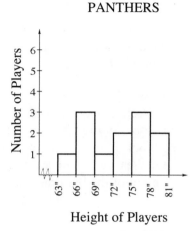

a.   Which team has taller players? Shorter players? Explain your thinking.

b.   Which team has heights that vary more? Explain your thinking.

c.   Which team has more players that are about the same height?

4-41.   Erika is tracking the depth of the water in her local creek. Her first nine measurements are below, in inches:

16 15 13 12 17 14 11 9 11

a.   What is the median of her data?

b.   Erika's next three measurements are 9 inches, 10 inches, and 9 inches. What is the new median?

4-42.   Latisha wants to get at least a B+ in her history class. To do so she needs to have an overall average of at least 86%. So far she has taken three tests and her scores were 90%, 82%, and 81%.

   a.   Use the 5-D Process to help Latisha determine what percent score she needs on the fourth and last test of the grading period to get the overall grade that she wants.

   b.   The teacher decided to make the last test worth twice as much a regular test. How does this change the score that Latisha needs on the last test to get an overall average of 86%? Support your answer with mathematical work. You may choose to use the 5-D Process again.

4-43.   A lemonade recipe calls for using a ratio of 2 cups of lemon juice for every 4 cups of water.

   a.   Draw and label a diagram like the one below to show the percent of lemonade that is water and the percent that is lemon juice.

Old-Fashioned Lemonade

   b.   What is the ratio of lemon juice to total liquid?

   c.   Angel made 10 cups of lemonade. He used 3 cups of lemon juice in his mixture. Did he follow the same recipe? In other words, did he use the same ratio of lemon juice to total liquid?

4-44.   Use your **reasoning** about numbers to answer the following questions.

   a.   If multiplying by $\frac{1}{4}$ makes a positive number smaller, then what does dividing by $\frac{1}{4}$ do to the value of the number? Explain your **reasoning**.

   b.   If multiplying by 1 does not change the value of a number, then what effect does multiplying by $\frac{2}{2}$ have? Explain your **reasoning**.

   c.   If you find 80% of a number, do you expect the answer to be greater or less than the number? What if you find 120%? Explain your **reasoning**.

4-45.   Darnell designed the spinner at right for a
         game. It still has one incomplete section.

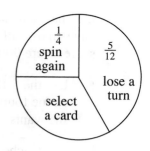

    a.   Help him figure out the probability of selecting
         a card on any turn. Show how you got your
         answer.

    b.   What is the probability that on any turn you will
         not get to spin again?

    c.   Which is more likely: to lose a turn or to select a card? Show how you know.

4-46.   Elin has made 29 note cards for her friends. She plans to send out a total of
         40 cards. What percentage of the cards has she finished? Represent your work
         clearly on your paper.

4-47.   A triangle has a base that is three times longer than its height. It has an area of
         486 sq cm.

         Use the 5-D Process to find the base and height of the triangle. Write a variable
         expression for each column of your chart.

4-48.   Copy and complete each of the Diamond Problems below.
         The pattern used in the Diamond Problems is shown at right.

    a.   b.   c.   d.

4.2.3 What happens when the data changes?

Analyzing Box-and-Whisker Plots

So far in this course, you have considered static (unchanging) sets of data, such as temperatures on a specific date in time or the lengths of leaps of the top performing frog jumpers. However, most of the time, data sets are growing and changing. For example, as you take quizzes or tests in your class, your overall average changes. Similarly, if you decided to track the average temperature on November 1 for each year, then the average you calculate each year would change as you add new pieces of data.

Today, you will explore how each representation changes when the data it describes changes. You will investigate questions like, "What happens if a new piece of data is added?" and "Is there a way to add data without changing the representation?" You can help your study team succeed today by sharing your ideas and your **reasoning** out loud in your team and by working hard to understand other people's ideas.

4-49.   ALDEN'S SODA

Alden created a box-and-whisker plot for the calories in 11 different brands of sodas as shown below.

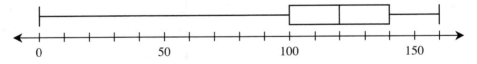

a.   According to this graph, what can you say about the calories of the 11 brands of soda?

b.   This is a list of the calories in the sodas represented in the plot:

   0, 90, 100, 100, 110, 120, 125, 140, 140, 145, 160

   What can you now say about the data (besides the individual values) that you could not say before? Be prepared to **justify** your conclusions.

4-50.   Alden found information about three new sodas. The new sodas have 75, 85, and 105 calories in them.

   a. Predict how adding the three new pieces of data will change the box-and-whisker plot from problem 4-49.

   b. Add the new calories to the data in problem 4-49. What are the new median, minimum, maximum, upper quartile, and lower quartile values? Show how you get your answer.

   c. On graph paper, make a new box-and-whisker plot that includes the additional sodas. Label each of the important points (listed in part (b)).

   d. Compare this box-and-whisker plot to the plot from problem 4-49. How did the first box-and-whisker plot change when you added these three pieces of data?

   e. How could you change the data to make the whiskers longer? Shorter? **Justify** your response.

4-51.   How do box-and-whisker plots help compare data? Think about this question as you compare the data below that shows the ages of the students at three schools.

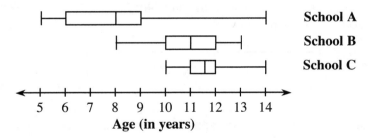

   a. Which school is a K-8 school and how do you know? Does that school have more students in K-2, grades 3-5, or 6-8? Why?

   b. What does the box-and-whisker plot for School C tell you about 11 year-olds at that school?

   c. What statements can you make about School B based on its box-and-whisker plot?

Making Connections: Course 2

4-52. Levi used the box-and-whisker plot below to say, "*Half of the class walked more than 30 laps at the walk-a-thon.*" Levi also knows that his class has more than 20 students.

Number of Laps per Person

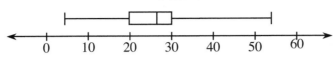

a. Do you agree with him? Explain your **reasoning**. If you do not agree with him, what statement could he say about those who walked more than 30 laps?

b. Levi wants to describe the portion of students who walked between 20 and 30 laps (the box). What statement could he say?

c. How could you alter a single data point and not change the graph? How could you change one data value and only move the median to the right?

4-53. What set of data can you add to any box-and-whisker plot to make one whisker longer, but not change anything else?

4-54. LEARNING LOG

What information can you get from a box-and-whisker plot? Sketch one of the box-and-whisker plots you looked at in this lesson in your Learning Log. Clearly label each number on the plot with the word that describes it. Write one question about the data that you could answer using this plot, and one question about the data that would be impossible to answer. Title this entry, "Box-and-Whisker Plot," and include today's date

4-55. **Additional Challenge:** Find a set of data that has all of these properties:

Mean = 17

Median = 16

Mode = 22

Range = 50

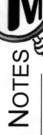

METHODS AND MEANINGS

Quartiles

Quartiles are points that divide a data set into four equal parts (and thus, the use of the prefix "quar" as in "quarter"). One of these points is the median, which you learned about in Chapter 1, since it marks the middle of the data set. In addition, there are two other quartiles in the middle of the lower and upper halves: the **lower quartile** and the **upper quartile**.

Suppose you have the data set: 22, 43, 14, 7, 2, 32, 9, 36, and 12.

To find **quartiles**, the data set must be placed in order from smallest to largest. Then divide the data set into two halves by finding the median of the entire data set. Next find the median of the lower and upper halves of the data set. (Note that if there are an odd number of data values, the median is not included in either half of the data set.) See the example below.

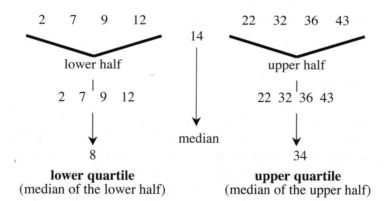

4-56.   Lucy and Marissa each designed a box-and-whisker plot to
          represent this data set:

$$16 \quad 18 \quad 19 \quad 19 \quad 25 \quad 26 \quad 27 \quad 32 \quad 35$$

          Their plots are shown below. Which plot is scaled correctly and why? Explain
          the mistakes in the incorrect plot.

          a.   b.
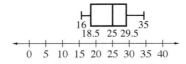

4-57.   Simplify the expressions below.

          a. $7 \cdot 2 + 4 - 2(7 + 3)$ b. $6 \cdot 2 + 3 \cdot 4 - 8$

          c. $3^2 + 5(1 - 3) + 4 \cdot 5 + 1$ d. $(8 - 12) + 10 \cdot 3$

4-58.   Due to differences in gravity, a 100-pound
          person on Earth would weigh about 38 pounds
          on Mars and 17 pounds on the moon.

          a.   What would a 150-pound person on Earth
               weigh on Mars? Explain your **reasoning**
               with words or a diagram.

          b.   What would a 50-pound person on Earth
               weigh on the moon? Explain your
               reasoning with words or a diagram.

          c.   **Additional Challenge:** If an astronaut on the moon weighed about 34
               pounds, what would that astronaut weigh on Mars? Show how you know.

4-59.   Use the 5-D Process to solve the following problem. Write an expression to
          represent each column of your table.

          Yosemite Falls, the highest waterfall in the United States, is actually made up of
          three smaller falls. The Lower Yosemite Falls is 355 feet shorter than the
          Middle Cascades Falls. The Upper Yosemite Falls is 80 feet more than twice
          the Middle Cascades Falls. If the entire set of waterfalls is 2425 feet long, how
          tall is each of the smaller waterfalls?

4-60.   Find the perimeter and area of each algebra tile shape below. Be sure to combine like terms.

a.

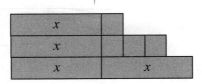

b.

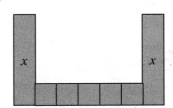

4.2.4   Which representation should I use?

Comparing and Choosing Representations

There are many different representations for displaying data. In this chapter, you have looked at three different representations: histograms, stem-and-leaf plots, and box-and-whisker plots. Today you will compare these representations to decide when one might be a better way to communicate information from a set of data.

4-61.   DATA SET DECISIONS

Ms. Anderson's math class has taken a test and she wants to find a good way to display the data from their test scores so that the students understand them.

- Michaela thinks the best representation is a stem-and-leaf plot because it organizes information quickly.

- Gabe thinks Ms. Anderson should use a histogram because it gives a picture that is easier to look at.

- Geri does not agree. She thinks a box-and-whisker plot shows information that the other two representations do not show.

a.   Discuss with your team which representation Ms. Anderson should use to display the data. On your paper, **justify** your choice.

b.   The test scores for the class are: 78, 62, 91, 51, 55, 93, 76, 82, 65, 85, 79, 83, 55, and 72. On the Lesson 4.2.4 Resource Page, make a stem-and-leaf plot, histogram, and a box-and-whisker plot for this data. Be sure to include a title and labels on all the representations.

Making Connections: Course 2

4-62.   The principal, Mr. Siebers, wants to get information about Ms. Anderson's latest test scores (those listed in problem 4-61). He is interested in the class median, but also wants to know what percentage of students scored lower than a C+ (less than 77 points) on the test.

   a.   What is the median of the class test scores? Which graph makes this the quickest to see?

   b.   What percentage of the students scored lower than a C+? Which graph makes this the easiest to see?

4-63.   Mrs. Smith, another math teacher, also wants to look at Ms. Anderson's test scores. She wants to see information about how many students earned more than 60 points on the test.

   a.   Which representation(s) would show her this information? **Justify** your answer.

   b.   Is your answer to this problem the same as or different from your answer to part (a) of problem 4-62? Why or why not?

4-64.   Ms. Anderson still does not know what kind of representation she should use. She knows that each representation shows different kinds of information. Using the representations that you made in problem 4-61:

   •   List and explain what measures of central tendency or other information will be easily read from each kind of graph listed below.

   •   List the information that will not be easy to obtain. **Justify** your answers.

   a.   Histogram

   b.   Stem-and-leaf plot

   c.   Box-and-whisker plot

Methods and Meanings

Box-and-Whisker Plots

A **box-and-whisker plot** displays a summary of data using the median, quartiles, and extremes of the data. The box contains "the middle half" of the data. The right whisker represents the top 25% of the data and the left whisker represents the bottom 25% of the data. A box-and-whisker plot makes it easy to see where the data are spread out and where they are concentrated. The larger the box, the more the data are spread out.

To construct a box-and-whisker plot using a number line that shows the range of the data, draw vertical line segments above the median, lower quartile and upper quartile. Then connect the lines from the lower and upper quartiles to form a rectangle. Place a vertical line segment above the number line at the highest and lowest data values. Connect the minimum value to the lower quartile and the maximum value to the upper quartile using horizontal segments. For the data set used in the Quartile Math Note, namely, 2, 7, 9, 12, 14, 22, 32, 36, and 43, the box-and-whisker plot is shown below.

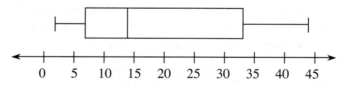

4-65.　Jerome is keeping track of how many books he and his friends have read during the first 100 days of school. Make a stem-and-leaf plot of how many books each person has read to help Jerome present the data to his teacher. The numbers of books are: 12, 17, 10, 24, 18, 31, 17, 21, 20, 14, 30, 9, 25.

　　a.　Make a stem-and-leaf plot of the data.

　　b.　Jerome wants to present the data with a plot that makes it possible to calculate the mean, median, and mode. Can he do this with a stem-and-leaf plot? He is not asking you to calculate them, but he wants you to tell him if it is possible and why.

　　c.　Use the stem-and-leaf plot to describe how the data is spread. That is, is it spread out? Or is it concentrated mostly in a narrow range?

4-66.　Copy and simplify the following expressions by combining like terms. Using algebra tiles may be helpful.

　　a.　$3 + 4x + 2 + 2x + 2x$
　　b.　$8x + 4 - 3 - x$

　　c.　$7x^2 + 3x + 4 + 7x^2 + 3x + 4$
　　d.　$5x + 4 + x + x^2 + 1$

4-67.　Twenty-five percent of the students at Marcus Garvey Middle School bring their lunches from home. 225 students do not bring their lunch. How many students attend the school? Draw and label a diagram to show the number and percent of each group of students.

4-68.　Find three fractions that are equivalent to three-eighths. Explain your method.

4.3.1 How do shapes change?

Dilations and Similar Figures

Have you ever wondered how different mirrors work? Most mirrors show you a reflection that looks just like you. But other mirrors, like those commonly found at carnivals and amusement parks, reflect back a face that is stretched or squished. You may look taller, shorter, fatter or skinnier. These effects can be created on the computer if you put a picture into a photo program. If you do not follow the mathematical principles of proportionality when you enlarge or shrink a photo, you may find that the picture is stretched thin or spread out, and not at all like the original. Today you will look at enlarging and reducing shapes using dilations to explore why a shape changes in certain ways.

4-69.   UNDOING DILATION

In Chapter 2, you looked at dilations and multiplied each of the coordinates of a shape to change its size. How can you undo dilation?

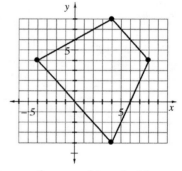

Charlie multiplied each coordinate of the vertices of a shape by 4 to create the dilated shape at right.

a.   If Charlie multiplied to find this shape, what operation would undo his dilation? Why?

b.   On a Lesson 4.3.1A Resource Page, undo the dilation on the graph above. Label the vertices of Charlie's original shape. How does the shape compare to the dilated shape?

Making Connections: Course 2

4-70.   Alana was also working with dilations. She wondered, *"What would happen if I multiplied each coordinate of a shape by $\frac{1}{3}$?"* On the Lesson 4.3.1A Resource Page, graph and connect the points below in order to form her dilated shape.

   $(-1,-1)$ $(-1,1)$ $(1,2)$ $(2,-1)$

   a.   Alana graphed this shape by multiplying each of her original coordinates by $\frac{1}{3}$. What do you think Alana's shape looked like before the dilation? Make a prediction.

   b.   On the same graph, undo the dilation to show Alana's original shape. List the coordinates of the vertices of Alana's original shape.

   c.   What did you do to each coordinate to undo the dilation? How did the shape change?

   d.   Why do you think the shape changed in this way?

4-71.   With your team, look carefully at Alana's dilated and original shapes and describe how the two shapes are related. Use the questions below to help you.

   •   How are the sides of the small and large shape related?

   •   How many of the small sides does it take to measure the **corresponding** (matching) side of the large shape? Is this true for all of the sides?

   •   Compare the four angles of the smaller shape to those of the larger shape. What can you say for sure about one matching pair of these angles? What appears to be true about the other three pairs?

4-72.   **CHANGING SHAPE**

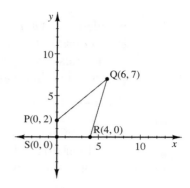

When you multiplied each coordinate of a shape by the same constant, you saw that sometimes the shape became smaller and sometimes it became larger. In Chapter 2, you moved shapes on a graph without changing their size or shape by rotating, reflecting and translating them. What other ways can you change a shape?

Your task: Work with your team to predict what you could do to the coordinates of the shape above to make it look stretched or squished, and what actions will keep the shape the same. Use the questions below to guide your discussion.

Discussion Points

What do you think will change if both the *x*- and *y*-coordinates of the points *P, Q, R,* and *S* are multiplied by the same number, such as 4?

What do you think will happen if only the *x*-coordinates are multiplied by 3?

What do you think will happen if just the *y*-coordinates are multiplied by 2?

What do you think will happen if the *x*- and *y*-coordinates are multiplied by different numbers, like 2 for *x* and 3 for *y*?

4-73.   Test the predictions your team made in problem 4-72. On the Lesson 4.3.1B Resource Page, graph each of the shapes described below.

a.   Dilate each coordinate of shape *PQRS* by multiplying each *x*-coordinate and each *y*-coordinate by 4. Graph the dilated shape on the same graph using a color other than black.

b.   Go back to the original shape and this time multiply only the *x*-coordinates by 3. Leave the *y*-coordinates the same. Find, graph, and connect the new coordinates.

c.   What happened to the shape? Why did this happen?

d.   Look at the predictions your team made in problem 4-72. Do you still agree with your predictions? Revise your predictions if necessary, based on your work so far. What do you think will happen if you multiply only the *y*-coordinates of the vertices by a number? Be ready to explain your **reasoning**.

4-74.   **Similar figures** are figures that have the same shape, but not necessarily the same size. One characteristic of similar shapes is that the sides of one shape are each the same number of times bigger than the corresponding sides of the smaller shape.

Which pairs of shapes that you have worked with in this lesson are similar and which are not? **Justify** your answer using specific examples.

METHODS AND MEANINGS

MATH NOTES

Corresponding Parts of Similar Shapes

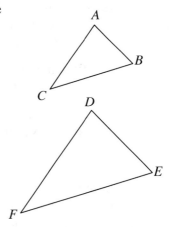

Two figures are **similar** if they have the same shape but not necessarily the same size. For example, all semi-circles are similar as are all squares, no matter how they are oriented.

In order to check whether figures are similar, you need to decide which parts of one figure **correspond** (match up) to which parts of the other. For example, in the triangles at right, triangle *DEF* is a dilation of triangle *ABC* where side *AB* is dilated to get side *DE*, side *AC* is dilated to get side *DF* and side *BC* is dilated to get side *EF*. We say that side *AB* **corresponds** to side *DE* or that they are **corresponding sides**. Notice that vertex *A* corresponds to vertex *D*, *C* to *F*, and *B* to *E*.

Not all correspondences are so easily seen. Sometimes you have to rotate or reflect the shapes in your mind so that you can tell which parts are the corresponding sides, angles, or vertices. For example, the two triangles at right are similar with *R* corresponding to *X*, *S* to *Y*, and *T* to *Z*. We can get triangle *XYZ* from triangle *RST* by a dilation of $\frac{1}{2}$ followed by a 90° counter-clockwise (↺) turn.

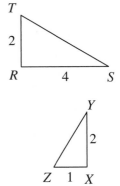

Shapes that are similar and have the same size are called **congruent**. Congruent shapes have corresponding sides of equal length and corresponding angles that have equal measure.

Chapter 4: Proportional Reasoning and Statistics   235

4-75. Create a large coordinate grid on graph paper and graph the triangle at right. Multiply the *y*-coordinate of each point by 4. Then graph the new shape. Make sure you connect your points. List the points for the new shape. Are the two figures similar? Why or why not?

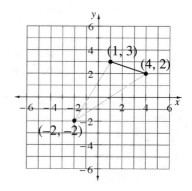

4-76. Kris said, "The Rawlings Rockets basketball team does not have any really tall players." These are the player's heights in inches: 70, 77, 75, 68, 88, 70, and 72.

a. Which number does not seem to fit this set of data?

b. Do you agree or disagree with Kris? Explain.

4-77. Dante is ordering wood flooring for his bedroom, which is shaped like a trapezoid (shown at right). If the flooring materials will cost $5 per square foot, how much should he expect to pay for the materials?

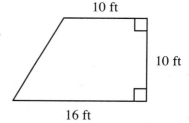

4-78. Copy and complete each of the Diamond Problems below. The pattern used in the Diamond Problems is shown at right.

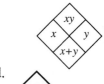

a.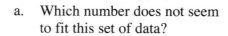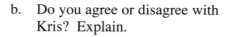

b.

c.

d.

4-79.   Darnell is designing a new game. He will
          have 110 different colored blocks in a bag.
          While a person is blindfolded, they will reach
          in and pull out a block. The color of the
          block determines the prize according to
          Darnell's sign at right.

blue → small toy
purple → hat
green → large stuffed animal

     a.   If he wants players to have a 60% probability of winning a small toy, how
          many blue blocks should her have?

     b.   If he wants players to have a 10% probability of winning a large stuffed
          animal, how many green blocks should he have?

$4.3.2$ Are they similar?

Identifying Similar Shapes

Have you ever noticed how many different kinds of cell phones there are? Sometimes you
might have a cell phone that is similar to one of your friends' cell phones because it is the
same brand, but it might be a different model or color. Occasionally, two people will have
the exact same cell phone, including brand, model and color. Sorting objects into groups
based on their sameness is also done in math. As you work with your team to sort shapes,
ask the following questions:

                    How do the shapes grow or shrink?

                    What parts can we compare?

                    How can we write the comparison?

4-80.   WHICH SHAPES ARE SIMILAR?

If two shapes appear to have the same
general relationship between sides,
how can you decide for sure if those
shapes are similar? Work with your
team to:

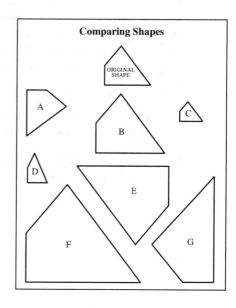

- Carefully cut out the
  original shape and shapes
  A-G from one Lesson
  4.3.2 Resource Page.

- Decide how each shape is
  related to the original
  shape. (Each person
  should use an uncut copy
  of the resource page and
  the team's cut out shapes
  to help.)

- Compare the angles and the sides of shapes A-G to the original
  shape.

a. Which shapes are similar to the original shape? Give specific reasons to
    justify your conclusions.

b. Look only at the shapes that are similar to the original shape. What do
    these shapes have in common? What is different about them? Be specific.

c. When two shapes are similar, the **scale factor** is the number you multiply
    the length of the side of one shape by to get the length of the corresponding
    side of the new shape. What is the scale factor between the original shape
    and shape E? Is each side of the shape enlarged the same number of times?
    Use a ruler to help you decide.

d. What is the scale factor between the original shape and shape C? Why is it
    less than 1?

Making Connections: Course 2

4-81.   Which shape from problem 4-80 is exactly equal to the original shape in every way? Shapes like this that are similar but do not grow or shrink are called **congruent** shapes.

   a.   Record the pairs of shapes below that appear to be congruent to each other.

   b.   Get a piece of tracing paper from your teacher and use it to check that the shapes you identified as congruent have exactly the same size and shape. Were you correct? If not, why not? Write your answers in complete sentences.

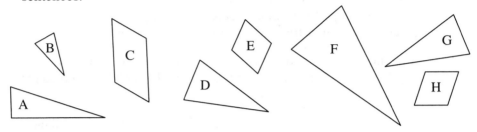

4-82.   Quan enlarged shape Q to make shape P, below. Are his shapes similar? If they are similar, identify the scale factor (multiplier). If they are not, demonstrate that at least one pair of sides does not share the scale factor.

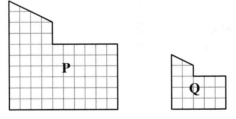

4-83.   Draw each of the shapes in problem 4-82 on graph paper. Color code the corresponding sides on each shape using the colors suggested by your teacher.

   a.   Compare the green sides of each shape. What do you notice about those sides?

   b.   Compare each of the other five sides of shape P with their corresponding sides on shape Q. What do you notice about those pairs of sides?

   c.   Imagine enlarging shape P to make a new shape R that has a base that is 25 units long. If shape R is similar to P, predict the length of the blue side of shape R *without drawing the shape*.

4-84. Using the triangle shown at right as the
original figure, *predict* which of the scale
factors below would enlarge (make bigger)
or reduce (make smaller) the shape. (Do
not actually make a new shape.)

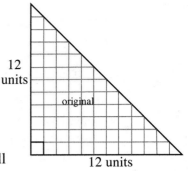

12
units

original

12 units

$$\frac{5}{3} \quad \frac{3}{4} \quad \frac{7}{6} \quad \frac{2}{3}$$

After you write down your prediction, decide
which scale factor each member of your team will
use. Then copy the original figure on graph paper
and draw a similar triangle using your scale factor.

a. Show your new triangle to your teammates and check your predictions.
    Which scale factors made the triangle larger? Which made the triangle
    smaller? Is there a pattern?

b. Which parts of the new triangles remained the same as the original triangle?
    Which parts changed? How do you know?

c. Each of the new triangles is similar to the original triangle used to create it.
    Compare the corresponding (matching) sides and angles to each other.
    Describe the relationship or explain why you think there is no relationship.

d. What scale factor could you use to create a triangle that is congruent
    (identical) to the original? Explain.

e. **Additional Challenge:** Find a scale factor that is less than 2 that will make
    a similar shape that is larger than the original.

4-85. LEARNING LOG

In your Learning Log, explain how to determine when shapes
are similar. In order to decide if two shapes are similar, what
do you need to know about the side length? The angles? Title
your entry "Finding Similar Shapes" and include today's date.

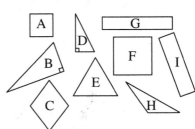

4-86. Which of the shapes at right appear to be similar? Explain how you know.

4-87. Mt. Rose Middle School collected canned food to donate to a local charity. Each classroom kept track of how many cans it collected. The number of cans in each room were: 107, 55, 39, 79, 86, 62, 65, 70, 80, and 77. The principal displayed the data in the box-and-whisker plot below.

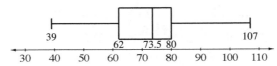

a. What is the range of the data? Are there any outliers?

b. The main office staff collected 55 cans, the counseling staff collected 74 cans, and the custodial staff collected 67 cans.

On grid paper, make a new box-and-whisker plot that includes this data. Clearly label the median and the upper and lower quartiles.

4-88. For the end of year party, Mt. Rose Middle School ordered 134 pizzas. There were eight fewer combo pizzas than there were pepperoni pizzas. There were three times as many combo pizzas as cheese pizzas. Use the 5-D Process to determine how many of each kind of pizza were ordered.

4-89. Copy each part below on your paper, then use the number line to help you fill in < (less than) or > (greater than) on the blank line.

$$-15\ -10\ -5\ \ 0\ \ 5\ \ 10\ \ 15$$

a. −5 __ −2   b. 8 __ −1   c. −5 __ 0   d. −15 __ −14

4-90. Simplify the following expressions using the order of operations.

a. $7 \cdot 8 - 4(6-2) + 18$

b. $6^2 - (8 \cdot 3) + 2^2(7 \cdot 3)$

c. $\frac{14}{2} - 3(8-6) + 7^2$

d. $-9 - 3(7-2) + \frac{24}{3}$

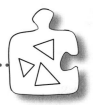

4.3.3 What do similar shapes tell us?

Working With Corresponding Sides

Sometimes graphic artists have a shape that they need to make larger to use for a sign or make smaller to use for a bumper sticker. They have to be sure that the shapes look the same no matter what size they are. How do artists know what the side length of a similar shape should be, if it needs to be larger or smaller than the original?

4-91. With your team, find the **scale factor** between each pair of similar shapes. That is, what are the sides of each original shape multiplied by to get the new shape? Assume shapes are drawn to scale.

a.

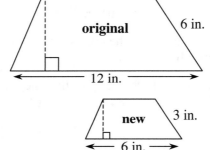

b.

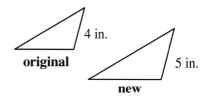

4-92. It may have been easier to recognize the scale factor between the two shapes in part (a) of problem 4-91 than it was to determine the scale factor between the two shapes in part (b). When sides are not even multiples of each other (like the sides labeled 4 in. and 5 in. in part (b)), it is useful to have another **strategy** for finding the scale factor.

Your task: Work with your team to describe a **strategy** for finding the scale factor between any two shapes. Refer to the questions below to begin your discussion.

Discussion Points

How can we use pairs of corresponding sides to write the scale factor?

Will the scale factor between the shapes be more or less than one?

Does it matter which pair of corresponding sides we use?

4-93. A study team was working together to find the scale factor for the two similar triangles at right.

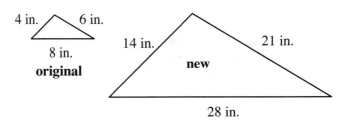

- Claudia set up the ratio $\frac{14}{4}$ to find the scale factor.

- Issac set up the ratio $\frac{28}{8}$ to find the scale factor.

- Paula set up the ratio $\frac{21}{6}$ to find the scale factor.

a. What did the students do differently when they found their scale factors?

b. Do the triangles have more than one scale factor? If not, show how they are the same.

c. Why does it make sense that the ratios are equal?

d. The different scale factors for this triangle form a **family of fractions**. In a fraction family, each of the fractions is equivalent to the others and can be related to the others using a Giant One. The fraction with the smallest numerator and denominator (that are still integers) in this family is the **root fraction**. For example, in the fraction family that includes $\frac{3}{6}$ and $\frac{5}{10}$, the root fraction is $\frac{1}{2}$. You have probably worked with root fractions before when you were reducing fractions to their lowest terms.

Are any of the scale factors the team wrote a root fraction for this family? If so, give **reasons** to explain how you know. If not, find the root fraction.

4-94.   Alex was working with the two triangles from problem 4-91, but he now has a few more pieces of information about the sides. He has represented the new information and his scale factor in the diagram reprinted at right. Sketch his diagram on your own paper.

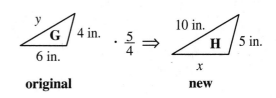

original   **new**

a.   Use the scale factor to find the length of the side labeled x. Show your work.

b.   Since Alex multiplied the side lengths of triangle G to get triangle H, he needs to undo the enlargement to find the side labeled y. What math operation would he use to undo the enlargement? Write an expression and be prepared to explain your **reasoning**. If you are able, simplify the expression to find y.

c.   If triangle H had been the original triangle and triangle G had been the new triangle, how would the scale factor change? What would the new scale factor be? Explain.

4-95.   Alex and Maria were trying to find the side labeled y in problem 4-94. Their work is below.

Maria: *"I made H the original triangle, then multiplied H by $\frac{4}{5}$. The side marked 10 inches became only 8 inches."*	**Alex:** *"To undo the change, I divided 10 inches by the scale factor ($\frac{5}{4}$), and that side of the triangle got shorter."*

Maria: original $\cdot \frac{4}{5} \Rightarrow$ new

$10 \text{ in.} \cdot \frac{4}{5} = 8 \text{ in.}$

Alex: original $\cdot \frac{5}{4} \Rightarrow$ new

$10 \text{ in.} \div \frac{5}{4} = 8 \text{ in.}$

a.   Compare the way Alex and Maria solved for y. Why did Alex divide and Maria multiply?

b.   Compare their scale factors. Why did Maria multiply by $\frac{4}{5}$?

Problem continues on next page. →

Making Connections: Course 2

4-95.   *Problem continued from previous page.*

c.   Consider the pair of similar
parallelograms below. For these
shapes, Alex found the scale factor
$\frac{\text{new}}{\text{original}} = \frac{6}{9}$ and used it to write the
expression $15 \div \frac{6}{9}$ to find x.

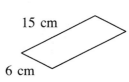

Use Maria's strategy to rewrite
the problem to find x.

- Which shape would she label "new" and
  which would she label "original"?

- What scale factor would she use?

- What does x equal?

4-96.   For the pairs of similar shapes below, find the lengths of the missing sides. Be
sure to show your calculation. You can choose which shape is "new" and
which is "original" in each pair. Assume the shapes are all drawn to scale. The
shapes in part (b) are parallelograms.

a.

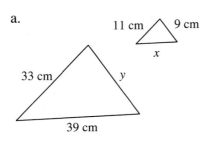

b.

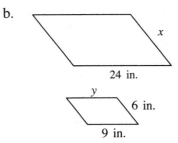

c.

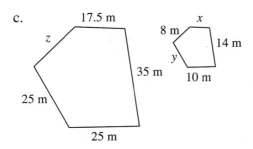

d.

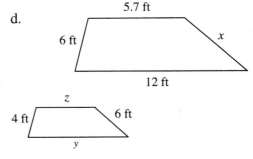

4-97. **Additional Challenge:** Copy the figure shown at right on graph paper.

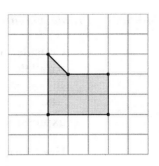

a. Find the area of the shape.

b. Enlarge the shape by a scale factor of 2, and draw the new shape. Find the area.

4-98. Sketch the two similar triangles at right on your own paper. Find the scale factor and the missing side lengths.

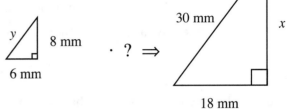

4-99. Alex and Maria were trying to find the side labeled x in problem 4-98. Their work is shown below.

Alex: *"I noticed that when I multiplied by 3, the sides of the triangle got longer."*

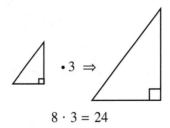

$8 \cdot 3 = 24$

Maria: *"I remember that when we were dilating shapes in Lesson 4.3.1, my shape got bigger when I divided by $\frac{1}{3}$."*

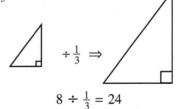

$8 \div \frac{1}{3} = 24$

a. Look at each student's work. Why do both multiplying by 3 and dividing by $\frac{1}{3}$ make the triangles larger?

b. Use Alex and Maria's **strategy** to write two expressions to find the value of y in problem 4-98.

4-100. Find the missing lengths or values on the diagram below. Assume that the line is evenly divided.

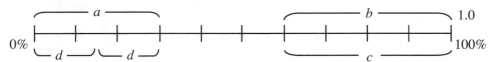

4-101. Use graph paper to solve the following problem.

a. Draw an *xy*-coordinate graph and label each axis. Plot the following ordered pairs: $(2, 3), (-2, 3), (-2, -3), (2, -3)$. Connect the points in the order given as you plot them, then connect the fourth point to the first one.

b. Describe the shape on your graph. What is its area? What is its perimeter?

c. Change only two points so that the shape has an area of 32 square units. List your points. Is there more than one answer?

4-102. Sketch the algebra tile shape at right on your paper. Write an expression for the perimeter, then find the perimeter for each of the given values of *x*.

a. $x = 7$ cm

b. $x = 5.5$ cm

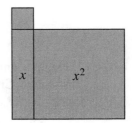

$4.3.4$ How do I find a missing side?

Solving Problems Involving Similar Shapes

Architects create scaled plans for building houses, artists use sketches to plan murals for the sides of buildings, and companies create smaller sizes of their products for display in stores. Each of these models is created to show all of the information about the "real" object, without being the actual size of the object. Today you will work with your team to find **strategies** that you can use when you are missing some of the information about a set of similar shapes. As you work, look for more than one way to solve the problem.

4-103. MODEL TRAINS

Kenen loves trains, especially those that
run on narrow gauge tracks (the gauge of
a track measures how far apart the rails
are). He has decided to build a model
train of the Rio Grande, a popular narrow
gauge train.

Use the following information to help
him know how big his model should be:

- The real track has a gauge of 3 feet (36 inches).

- His model railroad track has a gauge of $\frac{3}{4}$ inches.

- The Rio Grande train he wants to model has driving wheels that
  measure 44 inches high.

Your task: With your team, discuss what you know about the model train
Kenen will build. What scale factor should he use? What will be the height
of the driving wheels of his model? Be prepared to share your **strategies** with
the class.

4-104. Heather and Cindy are playing "Guess My Shape." Heather has to describe a
shape to Cindy accurately enough so that Cindy can draw it without ever seeing
the shape. Heather gives Cindy these clues:

Clue #1: The shape is similar to a rectangle with a base of 7 cm and a
height of 4 cm.

Clue #2: The shape is five times larger than the shape it is similar to.

a. Has Heather given Cindy enough information to draw the shape? If so,
sketch the shape on your paper. If not, write a question to ask Heather to
get the additional information you need.

b. Use what you know about similar shapes to write a set of "Guess My
Shape" clues to describe each of the mystery shapes below. Your clues
should be complete enough that someone in another class could read them
and draw the shape. Be sure to include at least one clue about the
relationship between the mystery shape and a similar shape.

i.   SHAPE A: Triangle

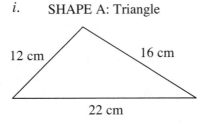

12 cm   16 cm

22 cm

ii.   SHAPE B: Parallelogram

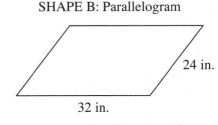

24 in.

32 in.

4-105. Nick enlarged figure A at right so that it became the similar figure B. His diagrams are shown at right.

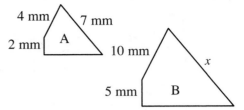

a. Write all the ratios that compare the corresponding sides of figure B to figure A.

b. What is the relationship between these ratios? How do you know?

c. Find two different ways to find the value of x in this quadrilateral. Does your solution seem reasonable? Be ready to share your **strategies** with the class.

4-106. Fatima solved for p in the diagram of similar triangles below and got $p = 30$. Looking at her answer, she knows she made a mistake. What would make Fatima think that her answer is wrong?

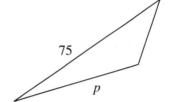

4-107. **LEARNING LOG**

In your Learning Log, write a description about how to find the missing side of a similar shape. Be specific about your **strategy** and include a picture with labels. Put today's date on your entry and title it "Finding Missing Sides of Similar Shapes."

MATH NOTES

METHODS AND MEANINGS

Scale Factor

A **scale factor** is a ratio that describes how two quantities or lengths are related. A scale factor that describes how two similar shapes are related can be found by writing a ratio between any pair of corresponding sides as $\frac{new}{original}$.

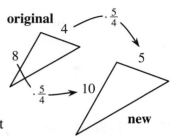

For example, the two similar triangles at right are related by a scale factor of $\frac{5}{4}$ because the side lengths of the new triangle can be found by multiplying the corresponding side lengths of the original triangle by $\frac{5}{4}$.

A scale factor greater than one **enlarges** a shape (makes it larger). A scale factor between zero and one **reduces** a shape (makes it smaller). If a scale factor is equal to one, the two similar shapes are identical and are called **congruent**.

4-108.   The electronics department is having a No Sales Tax Sale! In addition, all of the items in the department are on sale for 25% off. Wyatt is looking at a music player that normally costs $120. He has $95 to spend, and he is wondering if he has enough money to buy it.

a.   Wyatt sketched the diagram at right. Use the work he started to find 25% of $120. Is this the price he will pay?

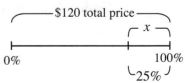

b.   Does Wyatt have enough money?

c.   Would he have enough money if he had to pay the 5.5% sales tax on the sale price?

Making Connections: Course 2

4-109.   For each expression below:

- Sketch and label a pair of similar shapes (like those at right, or in problem 4-94) that would result in this calculation.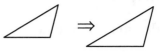

- Rewrite the expression so that the operation is multiplication.

- Calculate the value of the expression.

a. $6 \div \frac{1}{2}$ b. $4 \div \frac{2}{3}$

4-110.   A biologist was sitting near a pond and noticed a large number of dragonflies. He also saw both frogs and fish trying to eat the dragonflies. He counted a total of 89 fish, frogs, and dragonflies. He noticed that there were four times as many dragonflies as fish and that the frogs were five more than twice the number of fish.

Use the 5-D Process to determine how many fish, frogs, and dragonflies the biologist counted.

4-111.   Sketch the triangle, then redraw it with sides that are $\frac{1}{3}$ as long as the original.

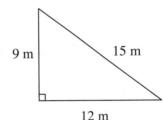

a.   Calculate the perimeters of both triangles.

b.   Calculate the areas of both triangles.

c.   What is the relationship between the perimeters of the triangles?

4-112.   Copy the following problems, then use the number line to help you fill in < (less than) or > (greater than) on the blank line.

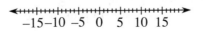

a.   −4 __ −8   b.   7 __ −7   c.   −6 __ −5   d.   −1 __ 0

Chapter 4 Closure   What have I learned?

Reflection and Synthesis

The activities below offer you a chance to reflect about what you have learned during this chapter. As you work, look for concepts that you feel very comfortable with, ideas that you would like to learn more about, and topics you need more help with. Look for connections between ideas as well as connections with material you learned previously.

①   SUMMARIZING MY UNDERSTANDING

Data is used every day in the world around us to help people make decisions. Oftentimes when people are trying to make a convincing argument or market a product, graphical displays and measures of center are chosen based on how they can help to make a strong, convincing argument.

Today you will use the skills you learned in this chapter to analyze the talents of two frogs. Look at the data provided about Frog A and Frog B and analyze the information.

- Work with your team to display the data in a box-and-whisker plot, a histogram, and a stem-and-leaf plot. Calculate any measures of central tendency that might help you decide which frog is a better jumper.

Seven best jumps (inches)	
Frog A	Frog B
177	177
221	201
224	203
230	230
239	236
240	236
239	257

- After you learn as much as you can about these two frogs, decide which frog you think is the best jumper. Obtain a Summarizing My Understanding Graphic Organizer, choose a data display, and present the statistics that you believe will support your claim.

- Write a convincing argument for why the frog you chose is the best jumper. Make sure to refer to your graphs and measures of central tendency in your argument.

②   **WHAT HAVE I LEARNED?**

Working the problems in this section will help you to evaluate which types of problems you feel comfortable with and which ones you need more help with.

Solve each problem as completely as you can. The table at the end of this closure section provides answers to these problems. It also tells you where you can find additional help and practice on problems like them.

CL 4-113. Evan is trying to save $60 to buy new parts for his bike. He has saved 45% of what he needs so far.

    a.   Draw a diagram to represent this situation.

    b.   How much has Evan saved so far?

    c.   How much does Evan still need to save? Write your answer as a dollar amount and as a percent.

CL 4-114. Mrs. Chen has two brothers. Mark is 7 years older than Mrs. Chen and Eric is 11 years younger than Mrs. Chen. The sum of all three of their ages is 149. Use the 5-D Process to determine the age of Mrs. Chen.

CL 4-115. Sketch the algebra tile shape at right on your paper.

    a.   Write and simplify an expression for the perimeter of the shape.

    b.   Evaluate your expression if $x = 5.5$.

    c.   What is x if the perimeter is 34?

CL 4-116. Find the area of the trapezoid and the triangle at right. Which figure has the larger area? Explain how you know.

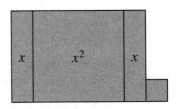

CL 4-117. Copy and complete each of the Diamond Problems below. The pattern used in the Diamond Problems is shown at right.

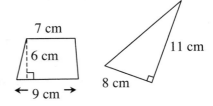

    a.   b.   c.   d.

CL 4-118. Copy the following expressions on your paper and simplify them by combining like terms. Using algebra tiles may be helpful.

a. $4x + 2 + 2x + x^2 + x$

b. $10x + 4 - 3 + 8x + 2$

c. $4 + x^2 + 3x + 2x^2 + 4$

d. $x + 4 + (x - 1) + 3 + 2x$

CL 4-119. The shapes at right are similar.

a. What is the scale factor?

b. Find the sides labeled x and y.

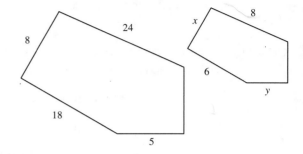

CL 4-120. Over the summer, Gabriel read books that had 192, 202, 175, 219, and 197 pages. What was the average number of pages in the books he read? Show your work.

CL 4-121. For each of the problems above, do the following:

- Draw a bar or number line that represents 0 to 10.

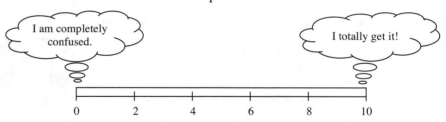

- Color or shade in a portion of the bar that represents your level of understanding and comfort with completing that problem on your own.

If any of your bars are less than a 5, choose *one* of those problems and do one of the following tasks:

- Write two questions that you would like to ask about that problem.
- Brainstorm two things that you DO know about that type of problem.

If all of your bars are a 5 or above, choose one of those problems and do one of these tasks:

- Write two questions you might ask or hints you might give to a student who was stuck on the problem.
- Make a new problem that is similar and more challenging than that problem and solve it.

③ WHAT TOOLS CAN I USE?

You have several tools and references available to help support your learning – your teacher, your study team, your math book, and your Toolkit, to name only a few. At the end of each chapter you will have an opportunity to review your Toolkit for completeness as well as to revise or update it to better reflect your current understanding of big ideas.

The main elements of your Toolkit should be your Learning Log, Math Notes, and the vocabulary used in this chapter. Math words that are new to this chapter appear in bold in the text. Refer to the lists provided below and follow your teacher's instructions to revise your Toolkit, which will help make it a useful reference for you as you complete this chapter and prepare to begin the next one.

Learning Log Entries

- Lesson 4.2.1 – Measures of Central Tendency
- Lesson 4.2.3 – Box-and-Whisker Plot
- Lesson 4.3.2 – Finding Similar Shapes
- Lesson 4.3.4 – Finding Missing Sides of Similar Shapes

Math Notes

- Lesson 4.1.1 – Equivalent Ratios
- Lesson 4.1.2 – Part to Whole Relationships
- Lesson 4.2.2 – Histograms and Bar Graphs
- Lesson 4.2.3 – Quartiles
- Lesson 4.2.4 – Box-and-Whisker Plots
- Lesson 4.3.1 – Corresponding Parts of Similar Shapes
- Lesson 4.3.4 – Scale Factor

Mathematical Vocabulary

The following is a list of vocabulary found in this chapter. Some of the words have been seen in the previous chapter. The words in bold are the words new to this chapter. Make sure that you are familiar with the terms below and know what they mean. For the words you do not know, refer to the glossary or index. You might also want to add these words to your Toolkit for a way to reference them in the future.

bin	**box-and-whisker plot**	**congruent**
corresponding	histogram	**lower quartile**
median	mode	**partition**
range	**ratio**	**scale factor**
similar figure	**stem-and-leaf plot**	**upper quartile**

Process Words

The list of words below are problem solving strategies and processes that you have been involved in throughout the course of this chapter. Make sure you know what it means to do each of the following. If you are not sure, look through your book for problems when you were asked to think in the following ways.

brainstorm	choose a strategy	describe
explain your reasoning	justify	predict
rearrange	reverse your thinking	test your prediction
visualize		

Answers and Support for Closure Activity #2
What Have I Learned?

Problem	Solution	Need Help?	More Practice
CL 4-113.	a. b. $27 c. $33 dollars, or 55% of $60	Lessons 4.1.1 and 4.1.2 Math Notes box in Lesson 4.1.2	Problems 4-2 through 4-10, 4-20, 4-43, 4-67, 4-79, and 4-108
CL 4-114.	Mrs. Chen is 51 years old.	Lessons 3.2.2, through 3.2.5 Math Notes box in Lesson 3.2.3 Learning Log (problem 3-98)	Problems CL 3-113, 4-88, and 4-110
CL 4-115.	a. $P = 4x + 6$ b. 28 units c. $x = 7$	Lessons 3.1.1, 3.1.2, 3.1.3, and 3.1.5 Math Notes boxes in Lessons 3.1.1, 3.1.2, and 3.1.3 Learning Logs (problems 3-28 and 3-37)	Problems CL 3-112, 4-32, 4-60, and 4-102
CL 4-116.	Area of the trapezoid = 48 sq. un. Area of the triangle = 44 sq. un. The trapezoid has the greater area.	Lessons 2.3.4 and 2.3.5 Math Notes box in Lesson 2.3.5 Learning Logs (problems 2-126 and 2-150)	Problems CL 2-163 and CL 3-111
CL 4-117.	a. $\frac{2}{15}, \frac{13}{15}$ b. $\frac{2}{12}$ or $\frac{1}{6}, \frac{11}{12}$ c. $\frac{4}{20}$ or $\frac{1}{5}, \frac{1}{4}$ d. $\frac{9}{32}, \frac{3}{8}$	Lessons 1.2.4 and 1.2.5 Math Notes box in Lesson 1.2.4 Learning Log (problem 1-107)	Problems 2-46, 2-57, 2-87, 2-118, 3-63, 4-48, and 4-78

Problem	Solution	Need Help?	More Practice
CL 4-118.	a. $x^2 + 7x + 2$ b. $18x + 3$ c. $3x^2 + 3x + 8$ d. $4x + 6$	Lesson 3.1.3 Math Notes box in Lesson 3.1.3 Learning Log (problem 3-28)	Problems 3-32, 3-101, and 4-66
CL 4-119.	a. Divide by 3 or multiply by $\frac{1}{3}$ b. $x = \frac{8}{3}$ or $2\frac{2}{3}$ $y = \frac{5}{3}$ or $1\frac{2}{3}$	Lessons 4.3.1, through 4.3.4 Math Notes boxes in Lessons 4.3.1 and 4.3.4 Learning Logs (problems 4-85 and 4-107)	Problems 4-82, 4-83, 4-84, 4-91 through 4-99, 4-105, and 4-106
CL 4-120.	197 pages	Lessons 1.1.3, 1.1.4, and 4.2.1 Math Notes box in Lesson 1.1.3 Learning Log (problem 4-29)	Problems CL 1-144 and CL 2-157

Puzzle Investigator Problems

PI-7. MAKING TRACKS!

Vu got a new bicycle for her birthday and
cannot wait to ride it all around her favorite
park. To find out which paths are best, she
wants to ride each of them exactly once,
without repeating any path and without missing
any. When she can do this, it is called an
"Euler" (pronounced "oy-ler") path after a
mathematician who investigated similar paths.

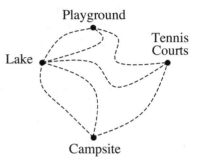

The map of the park is shown at right. Vu needs to decide
where her mother should drop her off to begin her ride.

a. Is it possible for Vu to ride each trail exactly once without repeating any
path and without missing any?

- If it is possible, show all the possible ways for her to do this.

- If none exist, find a new path you could add to the park to create an Euler
path.

b. The park manager is planning to add a parking lot as a new point on the
map. It will need to be connected to at least one of the other locations in
the park with a path. Propose a location of a parking lot and at least one
other path so that the park will have an Euler path. Remember that to be an
Euler path, it must use all the paths exactly once.

c. Vu is thinking about going to one of the parks shown below. Which of
them have Euler paths? Which do not? If an Euler path exists, show where
Vu could start and stop her ride, and use arrows to show the direction she
should travel. Look for reasons why some parks have Euler paths and
others do not.

    i.   *ii.* 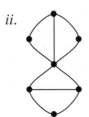   *iii.* 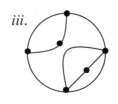   *iv.*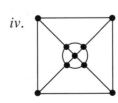

d. Draw two new parks that have Euler paths and two that do not.

e. Why do some parks have Euler paths and others do not?

PI-8.   TILING THE LAUNDRY ROOM

Travis is planning to tile his
laundry room with large L-shaped
tiles made with 3 squares. (See an
example at right.) According to
his floor plan, the room is a
4 ft. × 4 ft. square. There is a drain
in the floor that cannot be covered
and is shaded in the diagram.

Tile

**Laundry
Room Floor**

a. Show one way that Travis could tile his floor using his L-shaped tiles
   without breaking tiles and so that no tiles overlap or cover the drain. Use
   colors to help distinguish the tiles in your diagram. Is there more than one
   way to tile his floor?

b. While at the store, Travis suddenly worried that his diagram is wrong and
   he cannot remember where the drain is located. Does it matter? Can the
   floor be tiled no matter where the drain is located? Test the different
   possible locations of the drain (listed below) and write a short note to
   Travis about what you discovered.

   i. Drain is located in the middle   *ii.* Drain is located in the corner

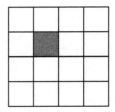

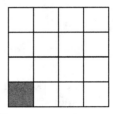

c. Uh oh! Travis came home with his tiles and found out that his floor is
   actually a 5 ft. × 5 ft. square and the drain is in the corner. (This is why
   measurements should always be checked twice!) Luckily, he bought extra
   tiles. However, can this floor be tiled? Using graph paper, draw a diagram
   of Travis' laundry room floor and find a way he can tile his floor with the
   same L-shaped tiles.

d. Given that his laundry room is a 5 ft. × 5 ft. square, does it matter where the
   drain is located? Find at least one more location (not in the corner) for the
   drain that would allow Travis to tile the floor. Also find at least one
   location for the drain that would not allow the floor to be tiled without
   breaking a tile.

Inequalities and Descriptive Geometry

5

CHAPTER 5   Inequalities and Descriptive Geometry

In Chapter 1 your teacher asked you to think of a number and then do several mathematical operations with it to find a specific answer. In Section 5.1, you will be using mathematical operations to do mathematical "magic" tricks. You will also learn how the tricks work and be able to create your own tricks using variables and algebra tiles.

In Section 5.2, you will compare two expressions using algebra tiles on Expression Comparison Mats, discovering the legal moves that allow you to simplify expressions. Then you will determine which expression is greater (or if they are equal) and learn how to record solutions to inequalities using number lines with boundary points. Then your class will study the amazing number zero.

Guiding Questions

Think about these questions throughout this chapter:

How can I build it?

What's the relationship?

Are they equivalent?

Is there more than one way?

How can I measure it?

Section 5.3 has you explore different geometric shapes using a compass, a straightedge, and a protractor. You will do a circle walk and learn how to find the area of a circle.

In this chapter, you will learn how to:

> ➤ Rewrite expressions by combining like terms and using the Distributive Property.

> ➤ Simplify and compare two algebraic expressions.

> ➤ Write and solve algebraic inequalities.

> ➤ Construct geometric shapes.

> ➤ Find the circumference and area of a circle.

Chapter Outline

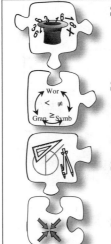

Section 5.1   As you play math tricks, you will learn symbolic manipulation skills such as simplifying, combining like terms, distributing multiplication across addition, and making zeros.

Section 5.2   In order to compare expressions, you will build additional strategies to maintain equivalence and relationships between expressions. You will solve inequalities and represent their solutions on a number line.

Section 5.3   You will use a straightedge and a compass as tools to create geometric shapes. You will also investigate how to find the area and circumference of a circle.

Section 5.4   This section offers several problems to use what you have learned in the first five chapters of this course.

Making Connections: Course 2

5.1.1 Why does it work?

Inverse Operations

Variables are useful tools to represent an unknown number. In some situations they represent a specific number, and in other situations they represent a collection of possible values. In previous chapters you have used variables to describe patterns in rules, to write lengths in perimeter expressions, and to define unknown quantities in word problems. In this chapter you will continue your work with variables and explore new ways to use them to identify specific values.

As you work in this chapter, you will often be called upon to **reverse** a process or operation in order to rewrite an expression or relationship. Applying this Way of Thinking by considering how to work in a different direction will help you understand several of the tools you will learn about in this chapter.

5-1.   THE MATHEMATICAL MAGIC TRICK

Have you ever seen a magician perform a seemingly impossible feat and wondered how the trick works? Follow the steps below to participate in a math magic trick.

Think of a number and write it down.
Add five to it.
Double the result.
Subtract four.
Divide by two.
Take away your original number.

What did you get?

a. Check with others in your study team and compare answers. What was the result?

b. Does this trick work no matter what number you pick? Have each member of your team test it with a different number. Consider numbers that you think might lead to different answers, including zero, fractions, decimals and integers.

c. Which steps made the number you chose increase? When did the number decrease? What connections do you see between the steps in which the number got larger and the steps in which it got smaller?

d. How could this trick be represented with math symbols? To get started, think about different ways to represent just the first step, "Think of a Number."

5-2.   Why does the magic trick from problem 5-1 work? Will the result always be the same?

To answer this question, Shakar decided to represent the steps with algebra tiles. Since he could start the trick with any number, he let an *x*-tile represent the "pick a number" step. With your team, analyze his work with the tiles. Then answer the questions below.

Steps	Trial 1	Trial 2	Trial 3	Algebra Tile Picture
1. Pick a number				
2. Add 5				
3. Double it				
4. Subtract 4				
5. Divide by 2				
6. Subtract the original number				

a.   For the step "Add 5," what did Shakar do with the tiles?

b.   What did Shakar do with his tiles to "double it?" Explain why that works.

c.   How can you tell from his table that this trick will always end with 3? Explain why the original number does not matter.

Making Connections: Course 2

5-3.   The table below has the steps for a new "magic trick." Use the Lesson 5.1.1
        Resource Page to complete parts (a) through (d) below.

Steps	Trial 1	Trial 2	Trial 3	Algebra Tile Picture
1. Pick a number				
2. Add 2				
3. Multiply by 3				
4. Take away 3				
5. Divide by 3				
6. Subtract the original number				

a.   Pick a number and place it in the top row of the "Trial 1" column. Then
     follow each of the steps for that number. What was the end result?

b.   Now repeat this process for two new numbers in the "Trial 2" and "Trial 3"
     columns. What do you notice about the end result?

c.   Now use algebra tiles to see why your observation from part (b) works. Let
     an x-tile represent the number chosen in Step 1 (just like Shakar did in
     problem 5-2). Then follow the instructions with the tiles. Be sure to draw
     diagrams on your resource page to show how you built each step.

d.   Explain how the algebra tiles help show that your conclusion in part (b) will
     always be true no matter what number you originally selected.

5-4. Now **reverse your thinking** to figure out a new "magic trick." Locate the table below on the Lesson 5.1.1 Resource Page and complete parts (a) through (c) below.

Steps	Trial 1	Trial 2	Trial 3	Algebra Tile Picture
Pick a number				[x]
1.				[x] [			]
2.				[x] [			] / [x] [			]
3.				[x] [		⊠] / [x] [		⊠]
4.				[x] [		]
5.				[x]

a. Use words to fill in the steps of the trick like those in the previous tables.

b. Use your own numbers in the trials, again considering fractions, decimals, and integers. What do you notice about the result?

c. Why did this result happen? Use the algebra tiles to help explain this result.

5-5. In the previous math "magic tricks," did you notice how *multiplication* by a number was later followed by *division* by the same number? These are known as **inverse operations** (operations which "undo" each other).

a. What is the inverse operation for addition?

b. What is the inverse operation for multiplication?

c. What is the inverse operation for "divide by 2?"

d. What is the inverse operation for "subtract −9?"

Making Connections: Course 2

5-6.   How does a trick (like the one from problem 5-1) work? You will answer this
         question by examining one more trick. In this last trick:

- Complete three trials using different numbers. Use at least one fraction
  or decimal.

- Use algebra tiles to help you analyze the trick, as you did in problem 5-3.
  Draw the tiles in the table on the resource page.

- Find at least two pairs of inverse operations in the process that are
  "undoing" each other.

Steps	Trial 1	Trial 2	Trial 3	Algebra Tile Picture
1. Pick a number				
2. Double it				
3. Add 4				
4. Multiply by 2				
5. Divide by 4				
6. Subtract the original number				

Review & Preview

5-7.   Write the inverse operations, that is, operations that "undo" one another for each
         situation below.

a.   What is the inverse operation for "add $\frac{3}{4}$?"

b.   What is the inverse operation for "subtract $1\frac{2}{3}$?"

c.   What is the inverse operation for "divide by 8?"

d.   What is the inverse operation for "multiply by 12?"

5-8.   Simplify the following expressions.

a. $1\frac{1}{2} + 2\frac{1}{8}$ b. $\frac{4}{5} - \frac{2}{3} + \frac{1}{6}$ c. $5\frac{3}{5} - 1\frac{4}{5}$

5-9.   Draw the table below on your paper and look carefully at the algebra tiles in order to fill in each of the "Steps." Use your own numbers in the trials, again considering fractions, decimals, and integers.

Steps	Trial 1	Trial 2	Trial 3	Algebra Tile Picture
1. Pick a number				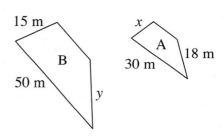
2. Add ____				
3. Multiply by ____				
4. Subtract ____				
5. Divide by ____				
6. Subtract the original number				

5-10.   The trapezoids at right are similar shapes.

a. What is the scale factor between shapes A and shape B?

b. Find the lengths of the missing sides.

5-11.   The Aloha Stadium in Honolulu, Hawaii, has seats for 50,000 people. At an upcoming football game, a company is planning to give away free hats to people based on where they are sitting.

a. The seats are divided into 40 different sections. If hats are given in only 5 sections, what is the probability of a guest sitting in a section that gets a hat?

b. The company is going to choose three rows in each section to win the hats. There are 46 rows in a section. If you are sitting in a winning section, what is the probability that you are not sitting in a winning row?

c. The company plans to give away 750 hats. If you buy a ticket to the game, what is the probability you will receive a hat?

5-12.   **Additional Challenge:** Robert found an old game in a closet and wanted to play it. However, a portion of the spinner shown at right could not be read. Find the missing portion of the spinner for Robert.

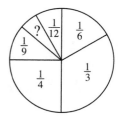

5.1.2   How can I represent it?

. . . .

Translating Situations into Algebraic Expressions

In Lesson 5.1.1, you looked at how mathematical "magic tricks" work by using inverse operations. In this lesson, we will connect the algebra tile picture to another representation of the situation: the variable expression. Consider the following questions today:

How can I **visualize** it?

How can I write it?

How can I express this situation efficiently?

5-13.   Today you will consider a more complex math magic trick. Today the table you use to record your steps will have only two trials, but it will add a new column to represent the algebra tiles with a variable expression. Get a Lesson 5.1.2 Resource Page from your teacher.

   - Work with your team to choose different numbers for the trials.

   - Decide how to write variable expressions that represent what is happening in each step.

Steps	Trial 1	Trial 2	Algebra Tile Picture	Variable Expression
1. Pick a number				
2. Add 7				
3. Triple the result				
4. Add nine				
5. Divide by 3				
6. Subtract the original number				

5-14.   For this number trick, the steps and trials are left for you to complete by using the variable expressions. To start, copy the table below on your paper and build each step with algebra tiles. Describe Steps 1, 2, and 3 in words.

Steps	Trial 1	Trial 2	Variable Expression
1.			x
2.			$x + 4$
3.			$2(x + 4)$
4.			$2x + 20$
5.			$x + 10$
6.			10

a.   Look at the algebra tiles you used to build Step 3. Write a different expression to represent those tiles.

b.   What tiles do you have to add to build Step 4? Complete steps 4, 5, and 6 in the chart.

c.   Complete two trials and record them in the chart.

5-15.   In Step 3 of the last magic trick (problem 5-14) you rewrote the expression $2(x + 4)$ as $2x + 8$. Can all expressions like $2(x + 4)$ be rewritten without parentheses? For example, can $3(x + 5)$ be rewritten without parentheses? Build it with tiles and write another expression to represent it. Does this work for all expressions?

5-16.   Diana, Sam, and Elliot were working on two different mathematical magic tricks shown below. Compare the steps in their magic tricks. You may want to build the steps with algebra tiles.

Magic Trick A

1. Think of a number.

2. Add three.

3. Multiply by two.

Magic Trick B

1. Think of a number.

2. Multiply by two.

3. Add three.

a.   Each student had completed one of the tricks. After the third step, Diana had written $2x + 6$, Sam had written $2(x + 3)$ and Elliot had written $2x + 3$. Which expression(s) are valid for Magic Trick A? Which one(s) are valid for Magic Trick B? How do you know? Use tiles, sketches, numbers, and **reasons** to explain your thinking.

b.   How are the two magic tricks different? How does this difference show in the expression used to represent each trick?

5-17.   Parentheses allow us to consider the number of groups of tiles that are present. For example, when the group of tiles $x + 3$ in problem 5-16 is doubled in Magic Trick A, the result can be written $2(x + 3)$. However, sometimes it is more efficient to write the result as $2x + 6$ instead of $2(x + 3)$.

a.   Show at least two ways to write the result of these steps:

1. Think of a number.

2. Add five.

3. Multiply by three.

b.   Write three steps that will result in $5(x - 2)$.

c.   How can the result from part (b) be written so that there are no parentheses?

5-18.   At right is an algebra tile drawing showing the result of the first three steps of a number trick.

a.   What could have been the three steps that led to this drawing?

b.   Use a variable to write at least two expressions to represent the tiles in this problem, one of which contains parentheses.

c.   If the next step in the trick is "Divide by 2," what should the simplified drawing and variable expression look like?

5-19.   You have been writing expressions in different ways to mean the same thing. These expressions depend on whether you see tiles grouped by rows (like four sets of $x + 3$ in problem 5-18) or whether you see separate groups (like $4x$ and 12). The **Distributive Property** is the formal name for linking these two equivalent expressions.

Write the following descriptions in two ways, one with parentheses and one without. For example, $4(x + 3)$ can also be written $4x + 12$.

a.   1. Think of a number.   b.   1. Think of a number.

2. Add 5.   2. Add 7.

3. Double it.   3. Multiply by 3.

5-20.   **Additional Challenge:** Mrs. Baker demonstrated an interesting math magic trick to her class. She said,

"Think of a two digit number and write it down without showing me."

"Add the 'magic number' of 90 to your number."

"Take whatever digit is now in the hundreds place, cross it out and add it to the ones place. Now tell me the result."

As each student told Mrs. Baker their result, she quickly told them their original number. Why does this trick work? Consider the following questions as you unravel this trick:

a.   Could you represent the original number with a variable? What is the algebraic expression after they add 90?

b.   What is the largest number the students could have now? The smallest?

Problem continues on next page. →

5-20.   *Problem continued from previous page.*

   c.   When the students cross off the 1 in the hundreds place (was any other number possible?), what have they subtracted from the expression? What is the new expression?

   d.   When the students add the 1 to the ones place, what is the simplified version of the expression they have created? What does Mrs. Baker mentally add to their result to reveal their original number?

METHODS AND **M**EANINGS

Algebraic Expressions

An **algebraic expression** consists of one or more variables, or a combination of numbers and variables possibly connected by mathematical operations. Each part of the expression separated by an addition or multiplication sign is called a **term**. A numerical term in an algebraic expression (like the 7 and 9 below) is called a **constant**. Expressions do not contain an equal sign (=). Four examples of algebraic expressions are:

$$4x, \ 4x - 3y + 7, \ \frac{3x^2}{2x+5} - 9, \ 3x - 5(x^2 + 2) + 1$$

In the examples above, the expressions have one term, three terms, two terms, and three terms, respectively. Algebraic expressions may be simplified or, if the values of the variables are known, expressions may be evaluated. See the examples below.

Simplify this expression:

$$4x + 5 - 2x + 1$$
becomes
$$2x + 6$$

Evaluate the expression $3y + y^2$ for $y = -2$.

$$3(-2) + (-2)^2$$
$$-6 + 4$$
$$-2$$

5-21.   Copy the chart on your paper, then complete two trials by reading the variable expressions. Write in the steps as well.

Steps	Trial 1	Trial 2	Variable Expression
1.			x
2.			$6x$
3.			$6x + 24$
4.			$6x + 18$
5.			$x + 3$
6.			3

5-22.   Translate each of these situations into a variable expression such as those found in a magic number chart.

   a.   Think of a number and multiply it by seven.

   b.   Think of a number and divide it by eight.

   c.   Think of a number and reduce it by ten.

   d.   Think of a number, add two, then multiply by five.

5-23.   Ms. Poppy has finished grading her students' tests. The scores were: 62, 65, 93, 51, 55, 76, 79, 85, 55, 72, 78, 83, 91, and 82.

   a.   Find the median.   b.   Find the range.

   c.   Find the mode.   d.   Find the quartiles.

   e.   Find the mean.

5-24.   The scale drawing at right shows the first
         floor of a house. The actual dimensions of
         the garage are 20 feet by 25 feet. All angles
         are right angles.

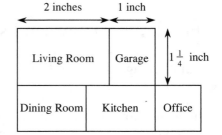

a.   How many feet does each inch represent?

b.   What is the length and width of the living
     room in inches?

c.   What is the length and width of the living room in feet?

d.   What is the area of the living room (in square feet)?

e.   What is the perimeter of the garage (in feet)?

5-25.   Graph the following points on a coordinate grid: $A(1,1)$, $B(2,3)$, $C(5,3)$, $D(5,1)$.
         Connect the points, including the last one to the first point.

a.   What shape have you created?

b.   What point can you move to create a rectangle? What would be the new
     coordinate?

c.   Reflect trapezoid *ABCD* across the *y*-axis. What are the new coordinate
     points of the trapezoids vertices?

5.1.3 How can I simplify it?

•••

Simplifying Algebraic Expressions

In the previous lesson, you represented more complex mathematical tricks with variable expressions instead of algebra tiles because the expressions were more efficient. In this lesson, you will explore various ways to make expressions simpler by making parts of them zero.

Zero is a relative newcomer to the number system. Its first appearance was as a placeholder around 400 B.C. in Babylon. The Ancient Greeks philosophized about whether zero was even a number: "How can nothing be something?" East Indian mathematicians are generally recognized as the first culture to represent the quantity zero as a numeral and number in its own right about 600 A.D.

Zero now holds an important place in mathematics both as a numeral representing the absence of quantity as well as a placeholder. Did you know there is no year 0 in the Gregorian calendar system (our current calendar system of 365 days in a year)? Until the creation of zero, number systems began at one. Consider the following questions as you work today:

How can I create a zero?

How can I rewrite this expression in the most efficient way?

5-26.   CONCEPTS OF ZERO

Zero is a special and unusual number. As you read above, it has an interesting history. What do you know about zero mathematically? The questions below will test your knowledge of zero.

a.   If two quantities are added and the sum is zero, what do we know about the quantities?

b.   If we add zero to a number, how does the number change?

c.   If we multiply a number by zero, what do we know about the product?

d.   What is the opposite of zero?

e.   If three numbers have a product of zero, what do we know about at least one of the numbers?

f.   Is zero even or odd?

276   *Making Connections*: Course 2

5-27.   As you know, +1 is represented with algebra tiles as a shaded small square and is always a positive unit. The opposite of 1, written –1, is an open small square and is always negative. Is this true with the variable x-tiles too?

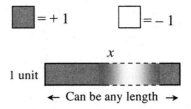

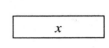

a.   The variable x-tile is shaded, but is the number represented by a variable such as x always positive? Why or why not?

b.   The opposite of the variable x, written $-x$, looks like it might be negative, but since the value of a variable can be any number (the opposite of –2 is 2), what can you say about the opposite of the variable x?

c.   Is it possible to determine which is greater: x or $-x$? Explain.

d.   What is true about $6 + (-6)$? What is true about $x + (-x)$ (the sum of a variable and its opposite)?

5-28.   Get a Lesson 5.1.3 Resource Page, from your teacher, which is called "Expression Mat." This will help you so you can tell the difference between the expression you are working on and everything else on your desk.

Expression Mat

$\blacksquare = +1$

$\square = -1$

From your work in problem 5-27, we can say that situations like $6 + (-6)$ and $x + (-x)$ create "zeros," that is, when we add an equal number of tiles and their opposites, the result is zero. The pairs of unit tiles and x tiles shown in that problem are examples of "zero pairs" of tiles.

Build each collection of tiles represented below on the mat. Name the collection using a simpler algebraic expression (one that has fewer terms) by finding and removing zero pairs and combining like terms.

a. $2 + 2x + x + (-3) + (-3x)$

b. $-2 + 2x + 1 - x + (-5) + 2x$

5-29. An **equivalent expression** refers to the same amount with a different name.

Build the expression mats shown in the pictures below. Write the expression shown on the expression mat, then write its simplified equivalent expression by making zeros (zero pairs) and combining like terms.

a.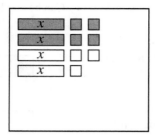

b.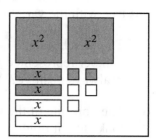

5-30. Build what is described in words below on your expression mat. Then write two different equivalent expressions to describe what is represented. One of the two representations should include parentheses.

a. The area of a rectangle with a width of 3 units and a length of $x + 5$.

b. Two equal groups of $3x - 2$.

c. Four rows of $2x + 1$.

d. A number increased by one, then tripled.

5-31. Copy and rewrite the following expressions by combining like terms and making zeros. Using algebra tiles may be helpful.

a. $(-1) + (-4x) + 2 + 2x + x$

b. $2x + 4 + (-3) + 3x$

c. $3x^2 + (-2x^2) + 5x + (-4x)$

d. $x - 6 + 4x + 5$

5-32. **Additional Challenge:** Division by zero is an interesting concept. Some students believe that when you divide by zero, the result is zero. Consider how the numerical equation $30 \div 6 = 5$ can be **reversed** to make the multiplication equation $5 \cdot 6 = 30$.

a. **Reverse** the division equation $24 \div 4 = 6$ into a multiplication equation.

b. Now take the equation $24 \div 0 = x$ and **reverse** it into a multiplication equation. What value of x can make this equation true? Explain.

c. Why do you think the solution to a number divided by zero is called "undefined?"

d. Is $0 \div 24$ also "undefined?" Why or why not?

5-33.   LEARNING LOG

In your Learning Log, explain how to simplify expressions
in your own words. Include an example of different ways
to write the expression $3(x+4)$ by drawing pictures and
writing equivalent expressions. Title this entry
"Simplifying Expressions" and include today's date.

METHODS AND **M**EANINGS

Distributive Property

The **Distributive Property** states that multiplication can be
"distributed" as a multiplier of each term in a sum or difference. It is a
method to separate or group quantities in multiplication problems. For
example, $3(2+4) = 3 \cdot 2 + 3 \cdot 4$. Symbolically it is written:

$$a(b+c) = ab + ac \quad \text{and} \quad a(b-c) = ab - ac$$

For example, the collection of tiles at   4 sets
right can be represented as 4 sets of $x+3$,   of $x+3$
written as $4(x+3)$. It can also be
represented by 4 x-tiles and 12 unit tiles,
written as $4x + 12$.

$$4(x+3) = 4x + 12$$

5-34.   Sketch each collection of tiles below. Name the collection using a simpler
algebraic expression, if possible. If it is not possible to simplify the expression,
explain why not.

a. $(-x) + 7 + 4x + x + (-3) + (-3x)$

b.   Seven plus three times a number, plus three minus three times the number.

c.   Two groups of a number plus three.

d. $7 + 4x^2 + 5x$

e. $x^2 + x^2 + (-5) + 2$

5-35.   What number do you get with this number magic trick? Support your answer
          with at least three trials.

                          1. Think of a number
                          2. Add the next higher number
                          3. Add nine
                          4. Divide by two
                          5. Subtract your original number

5-36.   Alden found a partially completed 5-D chart:

	Define			Do	Decide
					Target 74
Trial 1: 15	2(15) = 30	15 + 2 = 17		15 + 30 + 17 =	62 too small
Trial 2: 18	2(18) = 36	18 + 2 = 20		18 + 36 + 20 =	74 just right

          a.   Create a word problem that could have been solved using this chart.

          b.   What words would you put above the numbers in the three empty sections
               in the "Trial" and "Define" parts of the chart?

          c.   What word(s) would you put above the "Do" column?

5-37.   Rachel is collecting donations for the local animal shelter. So far she has
          collected $245, which is 70% of what she hopes to collect. How much money
          does Rachel plan to collect for the shelter? Show your work.

5-38.   Simplify each expression.

          a. $1.2 - 0.8$ b. $-4 - (-2)$ c. $-\frac{6}{11} - (-\frac{1}{4})$

          d. $\frac{2}{3} \cdot \frac{2}{5}$ e. $0.6 \cdot 8$ f. $-\frac{5}{4} \cdot \frac{8}{13}$

5-39.   Alex is trying to simplify the expression $-1\frac{1}{4}+(2\frac{1}{2})+(3\frac{1}{4})$. He started by rewriting it like this:

$$-1+(-\tfrac{1}{4})+2+\tfrac{1}{2}+3+\tfrac{1}{4}$$
$$(-1+2+3)+(-\tfrac{1}{4}+\tfrac{1}{4}+\tfrac{1}{2})$$

a.   Why might he have regrouped the expression in this way?

b.   Simplify the expression. What is the result?

c.   What property was Alex using when he rewrote the problem?

d.   Use this strategy to regroup the expression $\frac{3}{10}+2\frac{1}{10}+(-1\frac{2}{5})$ and find the result.

5.2.1 How do these compare?

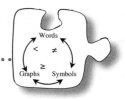

Comparing Expressions

You have been working with writing and simplifying expressions that represent the steps of a number trick. As you wrote these expressions you learned that it was helpful to simplify them by combining like terms and removing zeros. In this lesson you and your teammates will use a tool for comparing expressions to determine if one expression is greater than the other or if they are equal, that is, equivalent ways of writing the same thing.

Remember that to represent expressions with algebra tiles, you will need to be very careful about how positive and negative are distinguished. To help understand the diagrams in the text, the legend showing the shading for +1 and −1 at right will be placed on every page. This model also represents a zero pair.

5-40. COMPARING EXPRESSIONS

Ignacio and Olivia were playing a game. Each of them grabbed a handful of algebra tiles. They wanted to see whose expression had the greater value.

Two expressions can be compared by dividing the expression mat in half to change it into an **Expression Comparison Mat**. Then the two expressions can be built side by side and compared to see which one is greater.

- Olivia put her tiles on Mat A in the picture above and described it as $5 + (-3)$.

- Ignacio put his tiles on Mat B and said it was $(-5) + 2$.

With your team, find two different methods to simplify the two expressions in order to compare them. Which side of the mat is larger?

282   *Making Connections*: Course 2

5-41. Using your Expression Comparison Mat, build the two expressions at right. Find a way to determine which side is greater, if possible. Show your work by sketching it on the Lesson 5.2.1B Resource Page. Be ready to share your conclusion and your **justification**.

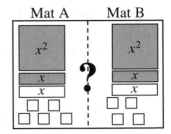

5-42. MORE COMPARING EXPRESSIONS – Is one expression greater?

Consider how you were able to compare the expressions in the previous problems. When is it possible to remove tiles to compare the expressions on the mats? In this problem you will work with your team to identify two different "legal moves" for simplifying expressions.

Build the mat at right using tiles and simplify the expressions. Record your work by drawing circles around the zeros or the balanced sets of tiles that you remove in each step on the Lesson 5.2.1B Resource Page. Which expression is greater?

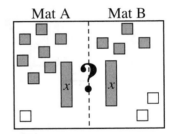

5-43. There are two kinds of moves you could use in problem 5-42 to simplify expressions with algebra tiles. They are removing zeros and removing matching (or balanced) sets of tiles from both sides of the mat as shown in the figures below. **Justify** why each of these moves can be used to simplify expressions.

Removing Balanced Sets

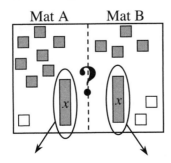

Removing Zeros

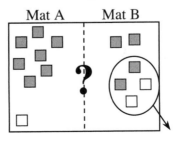

5-44.   WHICH SIDE IS GREATER?

For each of the problems below, use the Lesson 5.2.1 Resource Page and:

- Build the two expressions on your mat.

- Write an expression for each side below the mats for parts (a) through (d).

- Draw the tiles in the space given on the resource page for parts (e) and (f).

- Use legal moves to determine which mat is greater, if possible. Record your work by drawing circles around the zeros or the balanced (matching) sets of tiles that you remove in each problem.

a.

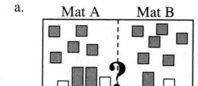

b.

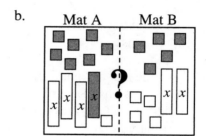

c.

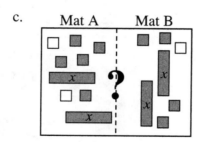

d.

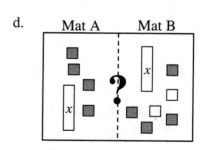

e.   Mat A: $3x - 4 - 2$

Mat B: $3(x - 1)$

f.   Mat A: $5 + (-3x) + 5x$

Mat B: $x^2 + 2x + 1 - x^2$

METHODS AND MEANINGS

Inequality Symbols

Just as the symbol "=" is used to represent that two quantities are equal in mathematics, the **inequality symbols** at right are used when describing the relationships between quantities that are not necessarily equal. Examples: $3 < 7$, $14 \le 14$, $7 > 3$, $19 \ge 14$.

< less than
≤ less than or equal to
> greater than
≥ greater than or equal

MATH NOTES

5-45. Write the expression shown on each of the Expression Mats below, then simplify them by making zeros and combining like terms.

a.

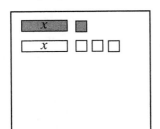

b.

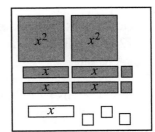

5-46. Copy and rewrite the following expressions by combining like terms, making zeros, and using the Distributive Property. **Visualizing** the expressions by using algebra tiles may be helpful.

a. $(-3) + 4x + 2 + 2x + 2x$

b. $-8x + 4 + (-3)$

c. $7x^2 + 3x + 4 + 7x^2 + 3x + 4$

d. $5(x - 4)$

5-47.   Simplify the following expressions.

   a. $-\frac{3}{4} - \frac{2}{5}$

   b. $\frac{7}{8} - \frac{2}{3}$

   c. $\frac{1}{3} - \frac{5}{6}$

   d. $1\frac{2}{3} + (-\frac{2}{5})$

   e. $\frac{4}{7} - (-\frac{3}{8})$

   f. $-4\frac{1}{2} + 3\frac{1}{9}$

5-48.   Figures A and B at right are similar. Assuming that figure A is the original figure, find the scale factor and find the lengths of the missing sides of figure B.

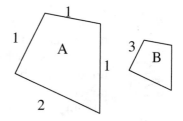

5-49.   Desmond is rolling a standard six-sided number cube. He plans to roll it 72 times.

   a.   About how many times would you expect Desmond to roll a 4? Why?

   b.   About how many times would you expect him to roll an even number? Why?

   c.   Desmond kept track of his results for all 72 rolls. The chart at right shows some of his results.

   Based on his partial results, how many times did he roll a 5 or a 6?

Result	Number of outcomes
1	9
2	14
3	11
4	8

5.2.2 What if I can't tell?

. . . .

Comparing Quantities with Variables

Have you ever tried to make a decision when the information you have is uncertain? Perhaps you have tried to make plans on a summer day only to learn that it *might* rain. In that case, your decision might have been based on the weather, such as, "I will go swimming if it doesn't rain, or stay home and play video games if it does rain." Sometimes in mathematics solutions might depend on something you do not know, like the value of the variable. Today you will study this kind of situation.

5-50. For each of the problems below, build the given expressions on your Expression Comparison Mat. Then use the simplification **strategies** of removing zeros and simplifying by removing matching pairs of tiles to determine which side is greater, if possible. Record your steps on the Lesson 5.2.2 Resource Page.

a.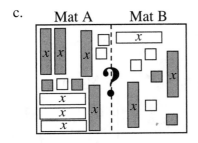

b. Mat A: $2(x+3)-4$

Mat B: $3x+(-1)-x+4$

c.

d.

5-51.   WHAT HAPPENED?

When Ignacio and Olivia compared the expressions in part (d) of
problem 5-50, they could not figure out which side was greater.

a. Is it always possible to determine which
    side of the Expression Comparison Mat is
    greater (has the larger value)? Why or why
    not? Be prepared to share your **reasoning**.

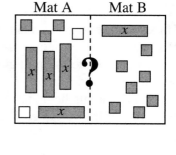

b. How is it possible for Mat A to have the
    greater value?

c. How is it possible for Mat B to have the
    greater value?

d. What other way can Mat A and B be related? Explain.

5-52.   Ignacio and Olivia are playing another game
with the algebra tiles. After they simplify
two new expressions, they are left with the
expressions on their mats shown at right.
Can you tell by looking which part of the mat
is greater?

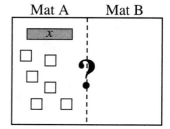

a. One way to compare is to separate the
    x-tiles and the unit tiles on different sides
    of the mat. Work with your team to find
    a way to have only x-tiles on Mat A.
    Make sure that you are able to **justify**
    that your moves are legal.

b. Using the same **reasoning** from part (a),
    what would you do to have only
    variables on Mat B in the Expression
    Comparison Mat at right?

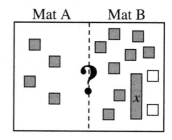

c. Write a short note to Ignacio and Olivia
    explaining this new **strategy**. Feel free
    to give it a name so it is easier for them
    to remember.

5-53.   Ignacio and Olivia are trying to decide if there are other ways to change expressions on the Expression Comparison Mat without affecting which side is greater. They have invented some new **strategies** and described them below.

$$\boxed{\begin{array}{l}\blacksquare = +1 \\ \square = -1\end{array}}$$

Your task: For each of the moves below:

- Build the Expression Comparison Mats on your paper.

- Follow each set of directions for the mat shown in each **strategy** below.

- Determine if the move in the **strategy** is valid for maintaining the relationship between the two expressions. Be prepared to **justify** your response.

Strategy #1

"If you have a mat like the one drawn below, you can add the same number of tiles to both sides. In this case, I added 3 negative tiles to both sides."

Strategy #2

"On a mat like the one below, I added +3 to Mat A and added −3 to Mat B."

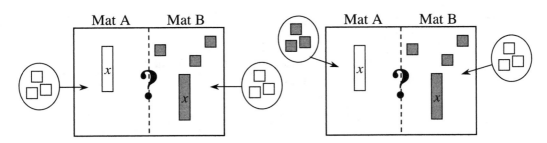

Strategy #3

"To simplify, I removed a positive x-tile from one side and a negative x-tile from the other side."

Strategy #4

"On a mat like the one below, I would add three zero pairs to Mat B."

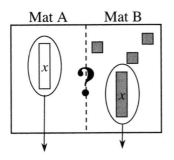

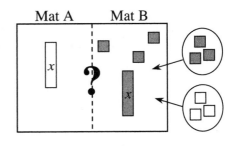

5-54.   LEARNING LOG

In your Learning Log, summarize the methods that your
team and class developed to simplify expressions on the
Expression Comparison Mat. Label your Learning Log
entry "Simplifying Expressions (Legal Moves)" and
include today's date.

(M)ETHODS AND MEANINGS

Additive Identity and Additive Inverse

Formal properties that state some of the legal moves that you
have been using are listed below.

Additive Identity: The number 0 is the additive identity because zero
added to any number is equal to that number. The value is unchanged.
For example, $5.2 + 0 = 5.2$ and $x + 0 = x$.

Additive Inverse: The sum of a number and its opposite is equal to 0.
That is, the additive inverse of a number is what needs to be added to
the number to get a sum of 0.

Examples: For 2, –2 is the additive inverse and $2 + (-2) = 0$.

For –5, 5 is the additive inverse and $-5 + 5 = 0$.

For x, $x + (-x) = 0$.

5-55.   Simplify the expressions below.

a. $5^2 \cdot (-3) - 4 \cdot 6 + 7$ b. $-3 \cdot (6 + 4 \cdot 2)$ c. $9 + 8 \div (-4) - 12$

d. $2^3 - 3 \cdot 4 + 6(-1 + 2)$ e. $4 + (3 + 4)^2$ f. $\frac{8-13}{10}$

5-56.   Write the following expressions in two ways, one with parentheses and one without. For example, $4(x-3)$ can be written $4x-12$.

   a.   A number reduced by 3, then multiplied by 2.

   b.   A number increased by 7, then multiplied by 5.

   c.   Ten times a number, then add twenty.

5-57.   Graph these points on a coordinate grid: $A(-2,0)$, $B(0,4)$, $C(4,1)$, $D(2,-3)$. Connect the points in order, with point D connected to point A. What shape have you created?

5-58.   Alan was paying a dinner check, but he was not sure how much he should tip for his bill of $27.38. If a 15% tip is standard, about how much should Alan leave for the server?

5-59.   Consider what you know about circles as you answer the questions below.

   a.   What do you know about the lengths of the spokes of a bicycle wheel? Draw a picture of a bicycle wheel with spokes and explain what you mean.

   b.   As a bicycle travels on flat ground, how does the center of its wheels (the hub) move? Explain and draw a picture showing what you mean.

5-60.   Elvin found the box-and-whisker plot below in the school newspaper.

Number of hours spent watching TV each week

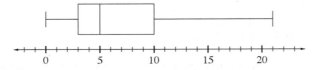

   a.   Based on the plot, what percent of students watch more than 10 hours of television each week?

   b.   Based on the plot, what percent of students watch less than 5 hours of television each week?

   c.   Can Elvin use the box-and-whisker plot to find the mean (average) number of hours of television students watch each week? If so, what is it? Explain your **reasoning**.

   d.   Can he use the plot to find the median? If so, what is it? Explain your **reasoning**.

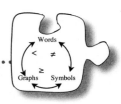

One Variable Inequalities

You have used Expression Comparison Mats to compare two expressions and found that sometimes it is possible to determine which expression is greater. You will again compare expressions, this time finding the values for the variable that make one expression greater than the other.

5-61.   Maria has been recording her work to see which side of an Expression Comparison Mat is greater, but she has been called away. Garth looked at her work, but he cannot figure out what Maria did to get from one step to another.

Mat A	Mat B
$5x + 2 + (-6)$	$2x + 2 + (-8)$
$5x + (-4)$	$2x + (-6)$
$3x + (-4)$	-6
$3x$	-2

Look at Maria's work above and help Garth by building the expressions on your mat and simplifying them. Write him a note explaining what Maria did to get from one step to another.

5-62.   Use Maria's method of recording to show your steps while you compare the expressions $2 + 2x + (-3)$ and $2x + (-4) + 1$ using algebra tiles. Make sure you record each step so that your teacher can see what you did on your Expression Comparison Mat.

a.   Which mat is greater?

b.   Use symbols (such as <, =, or >) to show the relationship of the final expressions on Mat A and Mat B.

5-63.   Maria and Garth were playing a game with the algebra tiles. They each grabbed a handful of tiles and put them on the Expression Comparison Mat at right to see whose side had greater value.

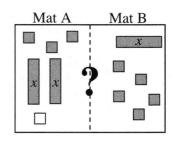

Maria said, *"I have Mat A and my side has more value."* Garth, who had Mat B, disagreed with her.

a.   Write expressions for Mat A and Mat B.

b.   Work with your team to simplify the expressions on the Expression Comparison Mat while carefully recording your work for each step on your paper. Can you tell whose side is greater? Why or why not?

c.   With your team, find at least four values for x that would make the expression on Maria's side (Mat A) greater than the expression on Garth's side (Mat B). Be prepared to share your values with the class.

d.   Any value for x that makes Mat A greater than Mat B is a solution to the inequality $2x + 3 + (-1) > x + 5$. This is read, *"Two x plus three plus negative one is greater than x plus five."*

Share your solutions with another team and see if you have the same solutions that they do.

5-64.   Karla had a hard time keeping track of all of the solutions to the inequality in problem 5-63 in her head. She decided to try to organize her answers. First she needed to know more about the problem.

a.   Is there a greatest number that is a solution? Discuss this question with your team and be prepared to share your ideas with the class.

b.   Is there a smallest number that is a solution? Again, be prepared to share your team's thinking with the class.

Problem continues on next page. →

5-64. *Problem continued from previous page.*

    c. What is special about the point where the solutions end? (This number is called the **boundary point**.) In other words, what relationship does this number have to the two expressions being compared?

    d. Karla was tired of listing so many solutions and wanted a way to show all of the solutions to this inequality quickly. She decided to draw a number line like the one below.

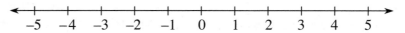

    On your own paper, draw a number line such as the one above then follow your teacher's directions to represent the answer to this question on your number line.

5-65. Now consider the inequality $2x + 5 < 3$, which can be read *"Two x plus five is <u>less</u> than 3."*

Build the inequality on your Expression Comparison Mat and record each step using variables on your paper. Work with your team to describe the least and greatest solutions to the inequality and draw your solution on a number line. Be prepared to **justify** your ideas.

5-66. Jerry and Ken were solving the inequality $6 > 2x + 2$. They set up the inequality on their Expression Comparison Mat and simplified it.

    a. Write a sentence in words to represent the original inequality.

    b. What did they get on each side of the mat when they simplified? Record your work on your paper.

    c. Graph all the solutions to this inequality on a number line.

5-67.   Write an algebraic expression for each mat below. Then use the legal moves that you have developed to simplify each mat and, if possible, decide which expression is greater.

a.
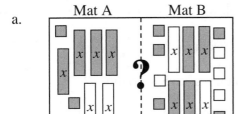

b.
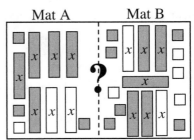

5-68.   Graph these inequalities on a number line.

a. $x > 3$ b. $x \leq 5$ c. $x \geq -4$

5-69.   Lynn was shopping and found a purse that was marked with a discount of "$\frac{1}{3}$ off." If the original cost of the purse was $80, how much will Lynn pay?

5-70.   The girls' basketball team weighed each player. Their weights in pounds were 120, 122, 126, 130, 133, 147, 115, 106, 120, 112, and 142.

a.   Make a stem-and-leaf plot of the teams' weights.

b.   What is the median weight of girls on the team?

c.   What is the range of the data?

d.   What are the mean and mode?

5-71.   Simplify each expression.

a. $\frac{2}{3}(0.8)$ b. $\frac{4}{3} \cdot \frac{3}{7}$ c. $-\frac{5}{6} \cdot \frac{4}{7}$ d. $-\frac{4}{5} \cdot (-1\frac{1}{3})$

5.2.4 How can I find all solutions?

Solving One Variable Inequalities

In this lesson, you will work with your team to develop and describe a process for solving linear inequalities. As you work, use the following questions to focus your discussion.

What is a solution?

What do all of the solutions have in common?

What is the greatest solution? What is the smallest solution?

5-72. Jerry and Ken were working on solving the inequality $3x - 1 \le 2x$. They found the boundary point and Ken made the number line graph shown at right.

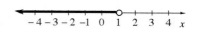

Jerry noticed a problem. *"Doesn't the line at the bottom of the $\le$ symbol mean the equal part? That means that $x = 1$ is also a solution. How could we show that?"*

"Hmmm," Jerry said. *"Well, the solution $x = 1$ would look like this on a number line. Is there a way that we can combine the two number lines?"*

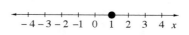

Discuss this idea with your team and be prepared to share your ideas with the class.

5-73. The diagram at right shows three possible ways to represent inequality statements. Review the meanings of the inequality symbols >, <, ≥, and ≤ with your team. Then, generate the two missing representations from each inequality described in parts (a) through (c) below.

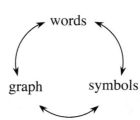

a. $x < -1\frac{1}{2}$

b. *x* is greater than or equal to two.

c.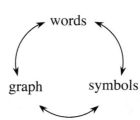

Making Connections: Course 2

5-74. WHEN IS THE BOUNDARY POINT INCLUDED?

Represent the solution for each of the variables described below as an inequality on a number line graph and with symbols.

a. The speed limit on certain freeways is 65 miles per hour. Let x represent any speed that could get a speeding ticket.

b. You brought $10 to the mall. Let y represent any amount of money you can spend.

c. In order to ride your favorite roller coaster, you must be at least five feet tall but less than seven feet tall. Let h represent any height that is allowed to ride the roller coaster.

5-75. Jordyn, Geri, and Morgan are going to have a kite-flying contest. Jordyn and Geri each have one roll of kite string. Together they also have 90 yards of extra string. Morgan has three rolls of kite string plus 10 yards of extra string. All of the rolls of string are the same length. The girls want to see who can fly their kite the highest.

a. Since Jordyn and Geri have fewer rolls of kite string, they decide to tie their string together so their kite can fly higher. Write at least two expressions to show how much kite string Jordyn and Geri have. Let x represent the number of yards of string on one roll.

b. Write an expression to show how much kite string Morgan has. x is the number of yards of string on one roll.

c. How long does a roll of string have to be for Jordyn and Geri to be able to fly their kite higher than Morgan's kite? Show your answer as an inequality and on a number line.

d. How long does a roll of string have to be for Morgan to be able to fly her kite higher than Jordyn and Geri's kite? Show your answer as an inequality and on a number line.

e. What length would the roll of string have to be for the girls' kites to fly at the same height?

5-76. **Additional Challenge:** Travis loves trains! Today he is beginning a train ride from Madison, Wisconsin all the way to Seattle, Washington.

Shortly after the train left the station in Madison, Travis fell asleep. When he woke up, it was dark outside and he had no idea how long he had been asleep. A fellow passenger told him they had already passed La Crosse, which is 135 miles from Madison. If the train travels at an average speed of 50 miles per hour, at least how long has Travis been asleep? Work with your team to represent this problem with an inequality and to solve it. Be prepared to share your ideas with the class.

5-77. LEARNING LOG

Work with your team to describe each step of your process for finding boundary points and deciding what part of the number line to shade. Then write down each step in your Learning Log. Be sure to illustrate your ideas with examples. Title this entry "Finding Boundary Points" and label it with today's date.

5-78. Solve each of the following inequalities. Represent the solutions algebraically (with symbols) and graphically (on a number line).

a. $3x - 4 < 3 - 2x$

b. $\frac{4}{5}x \geq 7$

5-79. Kindra would like to have more than $1500 in her savings account.

a. If she starts with $61 in her savings account, write an inequality to show how much she wants to have.

b. How much does Kindra need to save?

5-80. Reflect quadrilateral ABCD across the line $y = -2$. Write the new coordinate points.

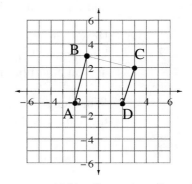

5-81.   Copy and complete each of the Diamond Problems below. The pattern used in the Diamond Problems is shown at right.

a.

b.

c.

d.

5-82.   Find the perimeter and area of each triangle below.

a.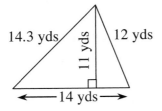

b.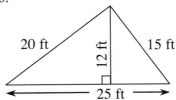

5.3.1 What can I build?

Introduction to Constructions

Architects and drafters make careful drawings before buildings are built. The drawings represent how the building should be constructed. They show the thickness of the walls and where doors, windows, and pipes will be. To make these precise diagrams, professionals often use special computer software. However, some architects prefer to draw the diagrams by hand. They use special drawing tools that look something like those in the drawing at right, including a right triangle tool and a device for measuring angles called a protractor.

Building plans are just one example of a precise geometric drawing. Mathematicians have used these basic tools to draw accurate diagrams for other reasons. The process of **constructing**, or building, shapes that meet different guidelines can help you understand many of the specific characteristics of those shapes.

In this lesson, you will be introduced to some ideas of mathematical construction and will construct your own shapes. As you work today, use the questions below to start mathematical discussions:

What is the relationship?

How can we describe it?

How do we know for sure?

5-83.   TRANSLATING THE LINE SEGMENT

One of the most basic drafting tools used is called a
T-square, a long straightedge that has a "T" at one
end. This tool slides along an edge of a table to allow
a person to draw several lines that go in exactly the
same direction, as if they were translated on the page.
An example of a T-square is shown at right.

Using tracing paper provided by your teacher, explore how a T-square works.

- Trace the line segment *AB* on the Lesson 5.3.1A Resource Page on
  tracing paper along with the "grid marker," an ∟ shape that can help
  you keep the tracing paper lined up with the grid as you move it.

- Use the tracing paper to translate the segment *AB* on the tracing paper
  vertically ($\updownarrow$) and horizontally ($\leftrightarrow$) on the graph any distance you
  choose. Be careful not to rotate the tracing paper or the resource
  page! One way to make sure that they stay lined up is to make sure
  that the ∟ shape matches up with two intersecting gridlines.

- How did the new translated segment compare to the original?

- Translate the segment to different positions on the grid. Pay attention
  to how the translated segment and the original segment compare.

Based on the translations you have made, what
is the relationship between two line segments
when one is a translation of the other? On the
resource page, sketch and describe the **general**
relationship you see.

Making Connections: Course 2

5-84.   ROTATING THE LINE SEGMENT

You have seen how line segments are related when one is a translation of the other. How does the relationship change if the segment is rotated? Trace segment *CD* and the grid marker from the Lesson 5.3.1A Resource Page to begin investigating.

- With the traced segment matched up on top of the original line segment, rotate the line segment 90° counter-clockwise (↺) about point *C*. Your grid marker will look like ⌐ when you have rotated a complete 90°. Pay attention to how the rotated segments compare to the original line. Sketch your line segment on the graph and label the endpoint *E*.

- Use a straightedge to extend segments *CD* and *CE* by starting at point C and moving out along each segment. Place an arrow at the end of each segment. The 90° angle formed by this rotation is a special angle called a **right angle**.

- Line your traced segment up with segment *CD* again. Choose another point on the segment and rotate the segment 90° clockwise or counter-clockwise about that point. Sketch where the new segment lands.

a.   What relationships do you notice between the rotated line segments and the original segment *CD*?

b.   When lines meet and form 90° angles they are called **perpendicular** lines. Are the rotated line segments you drew **perpendicular** to segment *CD*? Explain why or why not.

c.   How many total times would you need to rotate your line segment by 90° around the endpoint so that the rotated segment forms a straight line segment with the original segment? The new segment should be twice the original length. How many degrees of rotation is that?

d.   How many times would you rotate the segment by 90° to complete a full turn and end up back where you started?

5-85.   MEASURING ANGLES

Different angles are created when lines are rotated by different amounts around a point of intersection.

   a.   On the Lesson 5.3.1B Resource Page, locate the segment with endpoints at points *A* and *B*.

   • Trace segment *AB* on tracing paper and rotate it more than 90° (a $\frac{1}{4}$ turn) and less than 180° (a $\frac{1}{2}$ turn) about point *A*.

   • Copy this segment onto the resource page using a straightedge.

   • Label the new endpoint as point *C*.

   Estimate how many degrees you have rotated the line segment. What kind of angle is this?

   b.   Find segment *GH* on your resource page.

   • Use your tracing paper to rotate the segment around point *G* less than 90° (a $\frac{1}{4}$ turn).

   • Copy the rotated segment onto the resource page using a straightedge.

   • Label the new endpoint as point *K*.

   Estimate how many degrees you have rotated the line segment. Be prepared to explain your thinking. What kind of angle is this?

5-86.   A **protractor** is a tool for measuring angles. With a protractor you can measure the number of degrees of rotation that create an angle. Cliff used the protractor pictured here to measure the acute angle he created.

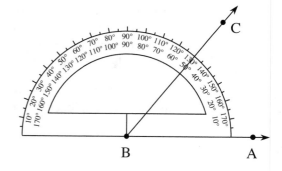

   a.   What is the measure of his angle? Make sure that your answer makes sense based on the size of the angle.

   b.   Obtain a protractor from your teacher and measure each of the angles you created in problem 5-85. How close were your estimates to the actual measurements?

   c.   Draw a new angle on your paper using a straightedge. Determine if it is obtuse, acute, or right, and estimate its measure in degrees. Then use your protractor to measure the angle. How close was your estimate? Use the Math Notes box at the end of this lesson if you need help with the names of the angle types.

5-87.   Architects and contractors often need to create angles that measure 45° or 60° as
         they build. Their measurements must be accurate in order for the buildings they
         design to fit together when they are built.

    a.   On your paper, create a 45° angle by following the steps below.

         • Use a straightedge to draw a line at least 4 inches long.

         • Mark a point on one end of the line and label it X.

         • Position the center point of your protractor on the point you marked X
           and the zero degree mark on the line.

         • From the line, read around the edge of the protractor to find the 45°
           mark. Make a point at 45°.

         • Draw a line connecting point X to your new point to create the angle
           with a measure of 45°.

         Label the angle with the measure 45°. Is your drawing **reasonable**?

    b.   Draw three new angles with the measures below. Label each one with its
         measure.

         i.   30°   ii.   75°   iii.   135°

5-88.   **Additional Challenge:** If you make four 90° rotations in the same
         direction, one after the other around the same point, you will complete
         a full circular angle.

    a.   How many 45° rotations does it take to make a circular angle?

    b.   Suppose you want to divide a circular angle into 3 angles of equal measure.
         What would the degree measure of each angle be? Draw and label a figure
         using a protractor.

    c.   Suppose you want to divide a circular angle into 5 angles of equal measure.
         What would the degree measure of each angle be? Draw and label a figure
         using a protractor.

    d.   Suppose you want to divide a circular angle into 24 angles of equal
         measure. What would the degree of each angle be?

METHODS AND MEANINGS

Angles and Their Measures

An **angle** is formed by two rays that start at a single point (called an **endpoint**), as shown in the diagram at right. A **ray** is part of a line that starts at an endpoint and extends without stopping in one direction. The **measure** of an angle is how much you rotate the starting ray to get to the ray that forms the other side of the angle. In this course, angles will be measured in degrees.

When trying to describe shapes, it is convenient to classify them by types of angles. This course will use the following terms to refer to angles:

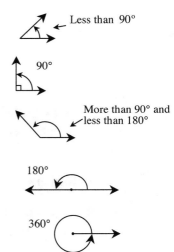

Acute: Any angle with measure *between* (but not including) 0° and 90°.

Right: Any angle that measures 90°.

Obtuse: Any angle with measure *between* (but not including) 90° and 180°.

Straight: Straight angles have a measure of 180° and the two rays of the angle form a straight line.

Circular: Any angle that measures 360°.

Review & Preview

5-89.   Look at the shapes below. Determine if they include a parallel set of line segments, a perpendicular set of line segments, both, or neither one.

a.   trapezoid   b.   c.   d.   rectangle

5-90.   Decide if these angles are acute, obtuse, or right angles. All diagrams are drawn to scale.

a.   b.   c.   d.

5-91.   Edwin's friends guessed how many jelly beans were in a jar at his birthday party. Here are their guesses: 75, 80, 95, 92, 100, 72, 71, 60, 65, 88, 60.

a.   Make a stem-and-leaf plot to display the data.

b.   Make a box-and-whisker plot to display the data.

c.   Which data display most clearly shows the median of the data? What is the median?

d.   Based on the box-and-whisker plot, estimate what percent of students guessed more than 65 jellybeans.

e.   Use the stem-and-leaf plot to determine the actual percent of students who guessed more than 65 jellybeans.

5-92.   Copy each problem, then find the sum, difference, product, or quotient. Remember to show all your steps.

a. $23.6 + 12$ b. $16.5 + 52.43$

c. $46.21 - 31.2$ d. $27.5 - 13.11$

e. $4.5(6)$ f. $55 \div 2$

5-93.   Mr. Crow, the head groundskeeper at High Tech Middle School, mows the lawn along the side of the gym. The lawn is rectangular, and the length is 5 feet more than twice the width. The perimeter of the lawn is 250 feet.

a.   Use the 5-D Process to find the dimensions of the lawn.

b.   Use the dimensions you calculated in part (a) to find the area of the lawn.

5.3.2 What is the relationship?

Compass Constructions

A compass is a simple tool that allows circles to be drawn quickly and accurately. Using this simple tool along with a ruler allows one to make precise drawings. In this lesson you will use a compass and ruler to build shapes, construct perpendicular lines, and partition segments.

5-94. Benjamin was drawing angles with a broken protractor and the largest angle he could measure was a 47° angle. Benjamin wanted to draw a 90° angle as well as a 180° angle.

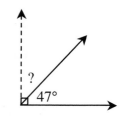

   a. Suppose Benjamin started by drawing a 47° angle. What angle would he need to measure to complete his right angle?

   b. When the sum of the measures of two angles is 90°, they are called **complementary angles**. What angle would be complementary to an 83° angle? Sketch a right angle showing this relationship.

   c. Angles that sum to make a 180° angle are called **supplementary angles**. What angle would you need to add to the angles below to create a 180° angle?

       i.   32°   ii. 90°   iii. 75°

5-95. DESIGNS WITH CIRCLES

   Celeste was playing with her compass and created the figure at right. When a compass and/or a straightedge is used to create a figure, the process is called **constructing**. Use a straightedge to draw a horizontal segment on your paper that is two inches long, label the endpoints *A* and *B*, then follow the directions below to recreate her **construction**.

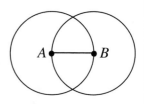

   • Use your compass to construct a circle that has a center at point *A* and passes through point *B*.

   • Construct a second circle that has a center at point *B* and passes through point *A*. Label the points where the circles **intersect** (cross) as points *C* and *D*.

Problem continues on next page. →

5-95.   *Problem continued from previous page.*

- Use a straightedge to draw segments from the center of each circle to point *C* and point *D*. Each of these line segments is a **radius** of the circle. A **radius** measures the distance from the center of the circle to any point on the circle itself.

a.   How are the four segments related? Is there another pair of points in the figure that create a segment that is the same as the ones you drew?

b.   What shapes do you see in the construction? Describe them and **justify** your descriptions.

5-96.   In part (a) of problem 5-95 you found that the segment that connects point *A* to point *B* is also a radius. Now connect point *C* to point *D*.

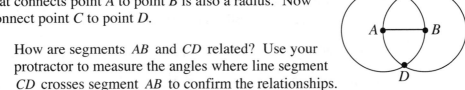

a.   How are segments *AB* and *CD* related? Use your protractor to measure the angles where line segment *CD* crosses segment *AB* to confirm the relationships.

b.   The word **bisect** means to cut into two equal pieces. Use a ruler to check that the segment connecting *C* and *D* goes through the **midpoint** (exact middle) of segment *AB*. Segment *CD* is called a **perpendicular bisector** of the segment connecting point *A* and point *B*.

c.   On a new piece of paper, use a straight edge to draw a line segment. Label the endpoints *E* and *F*. Use the construction process you used to construct segment *CD* (problems 5-95 and 5-96) to construct a perpendicular bisector for segment *EF*.

5-97.   SPECIAL TRIANGLES

Two of the triangles you created on the intersecting circles in problem 5-95 have special properties.

a.   Based on your work in the previous problems, how are the lengths of the sides of triangle *ABC* related?

b.   Examine triangle *ABD*. How is it related to triangle *ABC*?

c.   Use your protractor to measure each of the angles in triangle *ABC*. What do you notice about the angles?

Triangles like triangle *ABC* and *ABD* are called **equilateral** (all sides equal) and **equiangular** (all angles equal) because of the special relationships between their sides and angles.

5-98.   **Additional Challenge:** FLOWER PETALS

Using the idea of overlapping circles, Samantha constructed the picture at right. Follow the directions below to construct her pattern on your paper. Then answer the questions that follow.

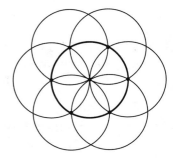

- In the middle of a large blank piece of paper, construct a circle. Be sure to mark the center of the circle. This point will be the center of the pattern.

- Pick and label a point (*A*) on the circle. Then use your compass to construct a circle with the same radius as the original circle, but with its center at point *A*. This new circle should intersect your original circle twice. Call these points *B* and *C*.

- Now draw new circles with centers at points *B* and *C* so that each circle has the same radius as the original circle. Each circle should intersect the original circle in two new points. Label these points *D* and *E*.

- Finally, draw two new circles with centers *D* and *E* so that they have the same radius as the original circle. They should intersect the original circle at the same point. Label this point *F*.

a.   Find a "flower petal" pattern in your diagram (you may see more than one). You may want to color the petals so that they are easy to find.

b.   If you connect the intersection points (*A*, *B*, *C*, …) in order around the original circle, what shape appears? Describe it.

Making Connections: Course 2

METHODS AND MEANINGS

Circle Vocabulary

MATH NOTES

The **radius** of a circle is a line segment from its center to any point on the circle. The term is also used for the length of these segments. More than one radius are called **radii**.

A **chord** of a circle is a line segment joining any two points on a circle.

A **diameter** of a circle is a chord that goes through its center. The term is also used for the length of these chords. The length of a diameter is twice the length of a radius.

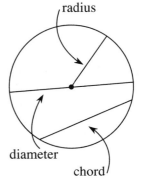

The **circumference** of a circle is its perimeter, or the "distance around" the circle.

5-99. The angle at right measures 90°. Estimate the measure (in degrees) of each angle below. Note: The angles are drawn to scale.

a. 　　b. 　　c. 　　d.

e. If the angle in part (a) measures 65°, what would be the measure of its supplementary angle? **Justify** your answer.

5-100. What number do you get with this number "magic trick"? Use at least two different original numbers for step #1 to confirm your solution.

        1. Think of a number.

        2. Add the next higher number.

        3. Add nine.

        4. Divide by two.

        5. Subtract your original number.

5-101. Write the expression as shown on the expression mats, then simplify by making zeros and combining like terms.

a.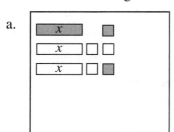

b.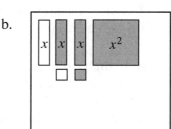

5-102. Draw an isosceles trapezoid. Label the top base 6 cm and the height 4 cm. If the area of this trapezoid is 36 square cm, what is the length of the other base? You may find it helpful to use the 5-D Process.

5-103. Look at the algebra tile shape at right.

    a. Write an algebraic expression for the perimeter of the shape in two ways, first by finding the length of each of the sides and adding them all together and then by writing an equivalent, simplified expression.

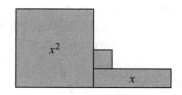

    b. Write an algebraic expression for the area of the shape.

5-104. The average annual rainfall in Tucson, Arizona is 12 inches. Between January and April, 2.4 inches of rain fell. What percentage of the annual rainfall fell after April (May through December)? You may want to draw a diagram to organize information.

5.3.3 What is the relationship?

Circumference and Diameter Ratios

The ability to measure objects without standard measuring tools is often very convenient. Have you ever seen anyone estimate the time until the sun sets by extending their arms and seeing how many fists there are from the horizon to the sun? Others use the distance from the tip of their thumb to their knuckle as an approximate inch. Today you will use your own foot as a unit of measure to look at another mathematical relationship.

5-105.   WALKING CIRCLES

Manny was walking around the edge of the circle painted on one of the basketball courts on the playground. He was carefully placing his feet heel-to-toe and counting as he walked. After he went all the way around the circle, he started to walk along the line across the middle of the circle.

His friend Jose was watching Manny walk this way and thought it was unusual. Jose asked, *"Why are you walking like that?"*

"I found a pattern in the number of steps I have to take around the circle and the number of steps across the circle. I'm testing to see if the relationship is true on different circles," Manny answered.

What relationship did Manny find? Today you and your team will walk around and across circles to see if you can find a pattern. You will need a Lesson 5.3.3A Resource Page to record your measurements (available at www.cpm.org/students).

a.   Your teacher will direct your team to a circle to measure. Measure the distance around the circle, called the **circumference**, using Manny's walking method. How many heel-to-toe steps does it take to trace the full circle? Record your result on the resource page.

b.   Measure the **diameter**, or distance across the circle through the center, once again using heel-to-toe units. Make sure you carefully count your steps and record your measurement.

c.   When each person in your team has made measurements using their own heel-to-toe units, look at your results. As a team, discuss the patterns you see. What relationship did Manny find? Write your observations and be prepared to explain your ideas.

5-106.   You may have noticed that the circumference measurement, C, was always larger than the diameter measurement, d, for the circles you measured. Could you determine how much larger?

    a.   Divide each circumference measurement by the diameter measurement. Record your results in the last column of your team chart, and label the column "$\frac{C}{d}$."

    b.   What relationship do you see in the results? Discuss with your team and then write a sentence summarizing the relationship between circumference and diameter.

5-107.   Looking at large amounts of data can help to confirm patterns that you identify in smaller data sets. To share your team data with the class, find the mean of your team's data in each column of the chart on your resource page and add your results to the class chart. Record the class results on your own resource page.

    a.   Are the class results similar to what your team found when it measured? Explain any differences you see, and what may have caused them.

    b.   Do the class results confirm the patterns you saw in problems 5-105 and 5-106? Describe any new patterns that you see and, if you are revising the patterns you found, explain why you are doing so.

    c.   With your team, go back to the sentence you wrote in part (b) of problem 5-106, summarizing the relationship between circumference and diameter. Add to or change your summary as needed.

5-108.   Use the relationships you have found to approximate the missing circumference and diameter measurements.

    a.   circumference = ?   b.   diameter = ?   c.   circumference =?
                                                                                diameter = ?

$d = 5$ cm

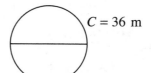

$C = 36$ m

$r = 5$ ft

5-109. Mathematicians have studied circles and the challenge of measuring them accurately for many years. Through their studies, mathematicians identified the ratio between the circumference and diameter of a circle as a special number. No matter how large or small a circle is, and no matter what units of measure are used, the circumference divided by the diameter is always equal to a little more than three. The Greek letter π (pi) is used to represent this number:

$$\pi = \frac{C}{d} \approx 3.14159265358979....$$

a. The relationship between circumference and diameter is often written as $\pi \cdot d = C$. Is this the same as writing $\frac{C}{d} = \pi$? Discuss this question with your team, and be prepared to share your **reasoning** with the class.

b. If the diameter of a circle is 100 inches, what is the circumference?

c. If the circumference of a circle measures 96 feet, what is the diameter?

M ETHODS AND MEANINGS

Angle Relationships

MATH NOTES

If two angles have measures whose sum is 90°, they are called **complementary angles**. For example, in the diagram at right, the 40° and 50° angles are complementary because together they form a right angle.

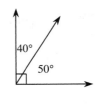

If two angles have measures whose sum is 180°, they are called **supplementary angles**. For example, in the diagram at right, the 60° and the 120° angles are supplementary because together they form a straight angle.

Two angles do not have to share a vertex to be complementary or supplementary. The first pair of angles at right are supplementary; the second pair of angles are complementary.

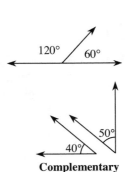

Supplementary

Complementary

5-110.   Remember that the circumference of a circle is equal to π times the diameter. Find the circumference of a circle with:

    a.   diameter = 10   b.   radius = 10   c.   diameter = 15

5-111.   Alexa is looking at the shape at right. She needs to make several different figures that are similar to it.

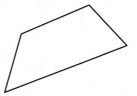

    a.   If she uses the scale factor $\frac{8}{5}$, will the new shape that she creates be larger or smaller than the original? **Justify** your answer.

    b.   List two different scale factors Alexa could use to make a smaller shape.

    c.   List two different scale factors Alexa could use to make a larger shape.

5-112.   Simplify each numerical expression.

    a. $\frac{1}{2}(5+13)-4\cdot5$ b. $(5+11)-(24-15)\cdot(3)$ c. $6^2+3\cdot7-9\div3$

5-113.   Simplify the following variable expressions.

    a. $2x+5+x-6+3x$ b. $x-8+x-5+x+1$

5-114.   Rewrite each fraction below as an equivalent fraction, a decimal, and a percent.

    a. $\frac{6}{18}$ b. $\frac{7}{20}$ c. $\frac{9}{10}$ d. $\frac{4}{25}$

5-115.   A radio station is giving away free t-shirts to students in local schools. It plans to give away 40 shirts at Big Sky Middle School and 75 shirts at High Peaks High School. Three hundred and fifty students attend Big Sky Middle School and 800 students attend High Peaks High School.

    a.   What is the probability of getting a t-shirt if you are a student at the middle school?

    b.   What is the probability of getting a t-shirt if you are a student at the high school?

    c.   Are you more likely to get a t-shirt if you are a student at the high school, or at the middle school?

Circle Area

The ratio known as π (read, "pi") was first discovered by the Babylonians nearly 4000 years ago. Over the years, Egyptian, Chinese, and Greek mathematicians also found the constant ratio between the circumference and diameter of a circle by using measurement. The Greek letter π has been used to represent this ratio since the 1700s when it was made popular by the Swiss mathematician Euler (pronounced "oy-ler"). Even though this ratio has been known for many years, the value commonly used for π is still only an approximation.

5-116.   ESTIMATING CIRCLE AREA

A circle is different from any shape we have studied so far because it has no sides or corners. This makes it difficult to apply the **strategy** of decomposing it into rectangles and triangles. In this situation, estimating its area can be a useful technique. Obtain a Lesson 5.3.4A Resource Page from your teacher.

a.   Using the first circle with a radius of 5 units on the resource page, estimate the area of the circle by counting whole and part squares. When each person in your team has finished their own estimate, share your results.

b.   Are all of the estimates in your team identical? How can you combine your data as a team to get a new estimate that may be more accurate?

5-117.   THE INSIDE OUTSIDE AVERAGE METHOD

While it is convenient to estimate area when shapes are drawn on grid paper, often shapes are not presented in that way. How can other shapes be used to help estimate area? Look carefully at the shape at right.

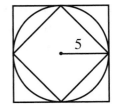

a.   What is the area of the larger square (also shown on the resource page)?

b.   What is the area of the smaller square (also shown on the resource page)?

c.   How does the area of each square compare to the area of the circle? Is either a good estimate of the circle's area? Why?

d.   Discuss with your team how to use the areas of both the squares to estimate the area of the circle. You might consider using what you have learned about analyzing data. Explain your thinking.

5-118.   Julia needs to estimate the area of a circle with a radius of 6. She is planning to use the Inside Outside Average method to make her estimate.

    a.   On the Lesson 5.3.4A Resource Page, estimate the area of the circle with a radius of 6 by counting whole squares and parts of squares. Share your results with your team.

    b.   When Julia was calculating the area of the outside square, she started by dividing the large square into four smaller ones. Her picture is at right.

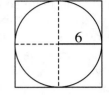

        To find the area of each small square, Julia multiplied the length times the width:

$$\text{Area} = 6^2 = 36$$

        How are the length, width, and area of each small square related to the radius of the circle? How is the area of the outside square related to the radius?

    c.   Julia divided the inside square into triangles. How is each triangle related to the radius? How is the area of the inside square related to the radius?

    d.   If the area of the two squares is related to the radius of the circle, Julia wonders if she can relate her circle estimate back to the radius as well. With your team, look at the estimate for area you have from part (a). How is that area estimate related to the radius of the circle?

5-119.   Julia is looking at a new square with a radius of 10. So far on her paper, she has written the work at right. What expression should she write to estimate the area of the circle?

Outside area $= 4(10)^2$

Inside area $= 2(10)^2$

5-120.   A FORMULA FOR CIRCLE AREA

By using the Inside Outside Average method for estimating, you discovered that the area of a circle is approximately three times the radius squared. There is another way to decompose and rearrange a circle in order to find a formula for its area. As you go through this process, think about these questions:

- *If a circle is cut up and rearranged into a new shape, is the area of the new shape the same as the area of the circle?*

- *How are the dimensions (base and height) of the new shape related to the circle?*

- *Would this process work for any circle? Does it matter how large the circle is?*

Take a circle and cut it into 8 equal parts and arrange them like this:

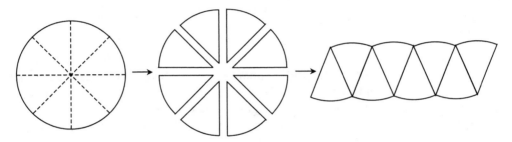

This rearrangement of the circle would look even more like a parallelogram or rectangle if we cut the circle into more pieces:

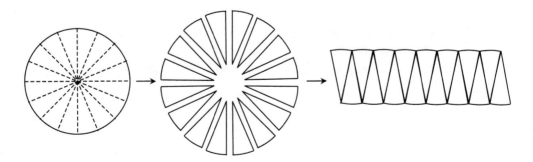

Problem continues on next page. →

5-120.   *Problem continued from previous page.*

The measurements of this parallelogram are actually related to the original measurements of the circle. The height of the parallelogram is the same as the radius of the circle:

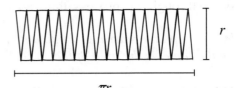

The length of the parallelogram is approximately half of the circumference of the circle. Since the circumference is equal to πd, half of the circumference is equal to:

$$\frac{\pi d}{2} = \frac{\pi(2r)}{2} = \pi r .$$

Substituting these values into the formula for the area of a parallelogram, you get:

$$A = hb = r(\pi r) = r^2\pi .$$

5-121.   Calculate the area for the circles with a radius of 5 and 6 using this new method (the formula $A = r^2\pi$) and compare your answers to your team's estimates in problems 5-117 and 5-118. How are the areas using this new method different from the estimates in the Inside Outside Average Method?

5-122.   How does the area that you found in problem 5-116 (counting estimate) compare to the calculating the area of a circle with a radius of 5 using the formula $A = r^2\pi$?

5-123.   **Additional Challenge:** A circle with radius 6 inches is cut into four quarters. Those pieces are rearranged into the shape at right. Find the area and the perimeter of the shape.

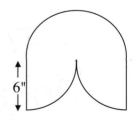

6"

5-124.   LEARNING LOG

Write a Learning Log entry that explains how to use the formula for the area of a circle. Include a solved example problem. Title this entry "Area of Circles" and include today's date.

MATH NOTES

Ⓜ️ETHODS AND MEANINGS

Circumference and Area of Circles

The **circumference** (C) of a circle is its perimeter, that is, the "distance around" the circle.

The number π (read "pi") is the ratio of the circumference of a circle to its diameter. That is, $\pi = \frac{circumference}{diameter}$. This definition is also used as a way of computing the circumference of a circle if you know the diameter as in the formula $C = \pi d$ where C is the circumference and d is the diameter. Since the diameter is twice the radius (that is, $d = 2r$) the formula for the circumference of a circle using its radius is $C = \pi(2r)$ or $C = 2\pi \cdot r$.

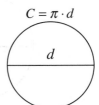

$$C = \pi \cdot d$$

The first few digits of π are 3.141592.

To find the **area** (A) of a circle when given its radius (r), square the radius and multiply by π. This formula can be written as $A = r^2 \cdot \pi$. Another way the area formula is often written is $A = \pi \cdot r^2$.

Review & Preview

5-125. The circle shown at right has a diameter of 20 cm.

    a. What measurement do you need to find in order to calculate the area inside the circle?

    b. Find the area inside the circle using the formula $A = r^2\pi$. Write your answer as a product of r^2 and π, and as an approximation using $\pi \approx 3.14$.

5-126.   Quintrell was writing a "Guess My Number" game. He decided to write the
          clues in a different way. He wrote, *"When 35 is added to my number, the
          answer is 4 times my original number plus 8. What is my number?"* Use the
          5-D Process to find Quintrell's number.

5-127.   Find the area and circumference of the following circles. You may want to
          refer to the Math Notes box in this lesson.

a.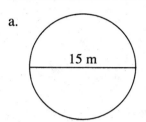

b.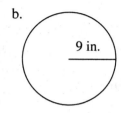

c.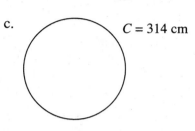

5-128.   One student rewrote the expression $17 \cdot 102$ as $17(100 + 2)$, and then simplified
          to get the expression $1700 + 34$.

          a.   Are the three expressions equal? **Justify** your answer.

          b.   What property of numbers does this demonstrate?

5-129.   Find the area of each of these trapezoids. Show all of your steps.

a.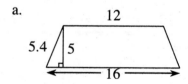

b.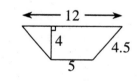

Making Connections: Course 2

5.4 How are they related?

Mid-Course Reflection Activities

The activities in this section review several major ideas you have studied so far. As you work, think about the topics you have studied and the activities that you have done during the first half of this course and how they connect to each other. Also think about which concepts you are comfortable using and those with which you need more practice.

As you work on this activity, keep in mind the following questions:

What mathematical concepts have you studied in this course so far?

What do you still want to know more about?

What connections did you find?

5-130. MEMORY LANE

Have you ever heard someone
talk about "taking a trip down
memory lane"? People use this
phrase to mean taking time to
remember things that have
happened in the past, especially
things that a group of people have
in common.

As you follow your teacher's directions to visit your mathematical "memory
lane," think about all the activities you have done and what you have learned in
this class so far this year. Your Toolkit should be a useful resource to help you
with this activity.

Focus your memories in six areas:

- Probability
- Data and Statistics
- Algebraic Thinking

- Geometry
- Representing and Working with Numbers
- Graphing

5-131.   SCAVENGER HUNT

Today your teacher will give you several clues
about different mathematical situations.
(These clues can be found on a resource page
at www.cpm.org/students.) For each clue,
work with your team to find all of the
situations (posted around the classroom or
provided on a resource page) that match each
clue. Remember that more than one situation
— up to five — may match each clue. Once
you have decided which situation(s) match a
clue, defend your decision to your teacher and
receive the next clue. Be sure to record your
matches on paper.

Your goal is to
find the match (or
more than one
match) for each
different clue.

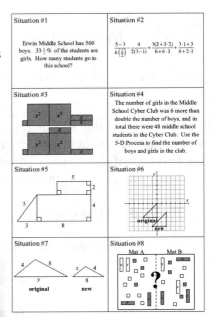

5-132.   WAYS OF THINKING

This course focuses on five different **Ways of Thinking**: generalizing,
reasoning and justifying, reversing thinking, choosing a strategy, and
visualizing. These are some of the ways in which you think while trying to
make sense of a concept or while solving a problem (even outside of math
class). During this course, you have probably used each Way of Thinking
multiple times without even realizing it!

The following problems will focus on the Ways of Thinking. As you work
them, refer to the description of the Ways of Thinking found at the end of this
lesson, and think about which Ways of Thinking you are using for each
problem.

Making Connections: Course 2

1. DESIGN YOUR OWN TRICK

   In this question, you will be designing your own number trick. Use these questions to guide your thinking.

   a. If your trick includes a subtraction step, what step will likely follow later? Why?

   b. If you "multiply by five" in your trick, what inverse operation will likely follow later?

   c. It is helpful to **visualize** how the expressions are being built up and reduced back down so that the original number does not matter. Do you prefer to use variable expressions or algebra tiles when you **visualize** how a variable can represent any number? Why?

   d. Individually or with your team design a new number trick that always results in the same integer answer no matter what number you start with. Organize your trick in a table that lists the steps, include three trials to show it works with specific numbers, and include the algebra tile drawings or expressions to show it works with any number.

2. Use the 5-D Process and table below to find a solution. Write a possible word problem that would fit the table.

Describe/Draw: [ ]

	Define and Predict		Do	Decide
	Length	Width	Perimeter	Target Perimeter = 88 ft
Trial 1:	10	$2 \cdot 10 + 5 = 25$	$10 + 25 + 10 + 25 = 70$	70 Too small

3. Each of the following shapes is missing either the height and/or the perimeter. Find the missing value for each problem. Explain your **strategy** for solving each problem.

a. Area = 24 sq. inches
Perimeter ≈ 26.4 inches
Height = ?

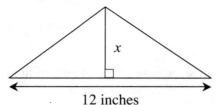

12 inches

b. Area = 42 sq. inches
Height = ?
Perimeter = ?

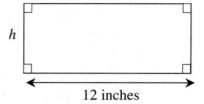

12 inches

c. Area = $4x + 12$
Perimeter = ?
Height = ?

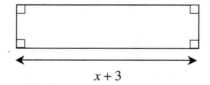

$x + 3$

d. Area = 198 sq. inches
Perimeter = ?
Top Base = ?

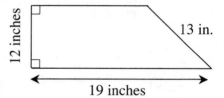

12 inches

19 inches

13 in.

4. Design a data set that satisfies the requirement listed each time.

a. Write six ages that would have modes of 12 and 13.

b. Write five heights that would have a median of 63 inches.

c. Write four different quiz scores that would have a mean of 75%.

d. Write 11 test scores that would be represented with the following box-and-whisker plot.

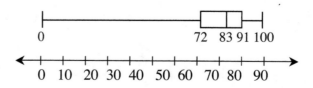

0   72 83 91 100

0 10 20 30 40 50 60 70 80 90

5. Use the triangle at right to answer the questions below.

a. Enlarge the triangle to create a similar triangle with side lengths that are twice as long as in the diagram. Label the new triangle B and be sure to label the lengths that you can determine.

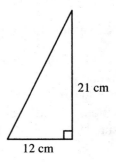

21 cm

12 cm

b. Reduce the original triangle to create a similar triangle with side lengths that are one-third as long as in the diagram. Label it triangle C and be sure to label the lengths that you know.

c. Find the area of each triangle.

d. How do the areas of the enlarged and reduced triangles compare to the original? Be as specific as you can.

e. If triangle B were dilated to become triangle C, what would the scale factor be? How do you know?

Ways of Thinking

Reasoning and Justifying:

To use logical reasoning means to organize information in order to draw a conclusion. When you explain why you think an idea is true, you are justifying. You often think this way when you try to convince yourself or someone else that an idea or solution is correct. Often, a justification is the answer to the questions, "Why?" or, "How do you know for sure?" When you think or say, *"I think this is true because…"*, you are justifying.

Choosing a Strategy:

To choose a strategy means to think about what you know about a problem and match that information with methods and processes for solving problems. As you develop this way of thinking you learn how to choose ways of solving problems based on given information. You think this way when you ask/answer questions like, "What strategy might work for…?" or , "How can I use this information to answer…?" When you are looking for a method to answer a question or solve a problem, you are choosing a strategy/tool.

Generalizing:

To generalize means to make a statement or conclusion, like a rule stating common properties, from a collection of evidence. You think this way when you describe patterns, because you are looking for a general statement that describes each term in the pattern. Often, a generalization is the answer to the question, "What is in common?" When you think or say, *"I think this is always true…"*, you are generalizing.

Reversing Thinking:

To reverse your thinking can be described as "thinking backward." You think this way when you want to understand a concept in a new direction. Often, it requires you to try to undo a process. When you think or say, *"What if I try to go backwards?"*, you are reversing your thinking.

Visualizing:

To visualize means to make a picture in your mind that represents a situation or description. As you develop this Way of Thinking, you learn how to turn a variety of situations into mental pictures. You think this way when you ask or answer questions like, "What does it look like when…?" or "How can I draw…?" When you wonder what something might look like and work to create an image of it, you are visualizing.

Chapter 5 Closure   What have I learned?

Reflection and Synthesis

The activities below offer you a chance to reflect about what you have learned during this chapter. As you work, look for concepts that you feel very comfortable with, ideas that you would like to learn more about, and topics you need more help with. Look for connections between ideas as well as connections with material you learned previously.

①   WHAT HAVE I LEARNED?

Working the problems in this section will help you to evaluate which types of problems you feel comfortable with and which ones you need more help with.

Solve each problem as completely as you can. The table at the end of this closure section has answers to these problems. It also tells you where you can find additional help and practice on problems like them.

CL 5-133. Copy the chart on your paper. Complete two trials by reading the variable expressions. Write in the steps as well.

Steps	Trial 1	Trial 2	Variable Expression
			x
			$3x$
			$3x + 27$
			$3x + 21$
			$x + 7$
			7

CL 5-134. When algebra tiles are grouped in sets, as shown below, they can be written in two different ways. Write two equivalent expressions that represent these collections of algebra tiles.

a.
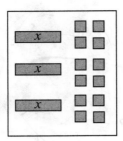

b.
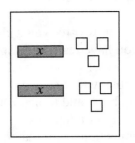

CL 5-135. Use the 5-D Process to help you solve the following problem.

Lillian and Isabella went shopping for school supplies. Lillian found her favorite notebook on sale so she bought three of the exact same notebook. Isabella also wanted a notebook. She bought one of the same notebooks that Lillian bought. Both girls started shopping with the same amount of money. If Lillian spent all of her money and Isabella had $5 left, then how much money did each girl have when she arrived at the store?

CL 5-136. Adriel and Gustavo were playing a game with algebra tiles. As they compared them, they were left with the following expressions on their mats. Use legal moves to simplify what is on the mats. Be sure to record your work in a way that others can understand.

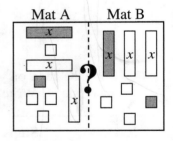

Can you determine which side has the greater value? If so, show why. If not, for what values of x is Mat A larger?

CL 5-137. Use graph paper to solve the following problem.

a. Draw an xy-coordinate graph and label each axis. Plot the following ordered pairs: $(3, 4)$, $(3, -5)$, $(-1, -2)$, and $(-1, 3)$. Connect the points in the order given as you plot them, then connect the fourth point to the first one.

b. Describe your shape. Where do you see the base(s) and height of your shape?

c. What is the area of your shape?

Making Connections: Course 2

CL 5-138. Alejandra has been practicing her free-throw shots as she gets ready for basketball season. At her last practice, she made 70% of her shots from the free-throw line. If she shot the ball 130 times,

 a.   How many times did she make a free-throw?

 b.   How many times did she miss? What percentage of her shots did she miss?

CL 5-139. Copy and complete each of the Diamond Problems below. The pattern used in the Diamond Problems is shown at right.

 a.   b.   c.   d.

CL 5-140. Build each collection of tiles represented below on a mat. Name the collection using a simpler algebraic expression, if possible. If it is not possible to simplify the expression, explain why not.

 a. $(-x) + 5 - 4x + x - (-3) + (-3x)$

 b.   Nine plus four times a number, plus three minus seven times the number

 c. $3 - 7x^2 + 9x$

 d. $2x + 3x^2 - 7 + (-x^2)$

CL 5-141. For each of the problems in this section of closure, do the following:

a. Draw a bar or number line like the one below that represents 0 to 10.

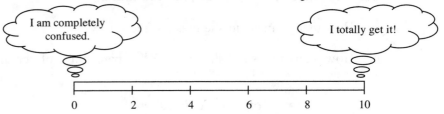

b. Color or shade in a portion of the bar that represents your current level of understanding and comfort with completing that problem on your own.

c. If any of your bars are less than a 5, choose *one* of those problems and do one of the following tasks:

  • Write two questions that you would like to ask about that problem.

  • Brainstorm two things that you DO know about that type of problem.

d. If all of your bars are a 5 or above, choose one of those problems and do one of these tasks:

  • Write two questions you might ask or hints you might give to a student who was stuck on the problem.

  • Make a new problem that is similar and more challenging than that problem and solve it.

WHAT TOOLS CAN I USE?

You have several tools and references available to help support your learning – your teacher, your study team, your math book, and your Toolkit to name only a few. At the end of each chapter you will have an opportunity to review your Toolkit for completeness as well as to revise or update it to better reflect your current understanding of big ideas.

The main elements of your Toolkit should be your Learning Log, Math Notes, and the vocabulary used in this chapter. Math words that are new to this chapter appear in bold in the text. Refer to the lists provided below and follow your teacher's instructions to revise your Toolkit, which will help make it useful for you as you complete this chapter and as you work in future chapters.

Learning Log Entries

- Lesson 5.1.3 – Simplifying Expressions
- Lesson 5.2.2 – Simplifying Expressions (Legal Moves)
- Lesson 5.2.4 – Finding Boundary Points
- Lesson 5.3.4 – Area of Circles

Math Notes

- Lesson 5.1.2 – Algebraic Expressions
- Lesson 5.1.3 – Distributive Property
- Lesson 5.2.1 – Inequality Symbols
- Lesson 5.2.2 – Additive Identity and Additive Inverse
- Lesson 5.3.1 – Angles and Their Measures
- Lesson 5.3.2 – Circle Vocabulary
- Lesson 5.3.3 – Angle Relationships
- Lesson 5.3.4 – Circumference and Area of Circles

Mathematical Vocabulary

The following is a list of vocabulary found in this chapter. The words in bold are the words new to this chapter. It is a good idea to make sure that you are familiar with these words and know what they mean. For the words you do not know, refer to the glossary or index. You might also want to add these words to your Toolkit for a way to reference them in the future.

acute angle	**boundary point**	**circumference**
complementary angle	**diameter**	**Distributive Property**
equilateral triangles	equivalent expressions	**inequality**
line segment	**midpoint**	obtuse angle
parallel	perpendicular	**perpendicular bisector**
pi (π)	**radius**	right angle
supplementary angle		

Process Words

These words describe problem solving strategies and processes that you have been involved in as you worked in this chapter. Make sure you know what each of these words means. If you are not sure, you can talk with your teacher or other students or look through your book for problems in which you were asked to do these things.

analyze	construct	estimate
explain	express	generate
justify	organize	record
represent	reverse	simplify expressions

Answers and Support for Closure Activity #1
What Have I Learned?

Problem	Solution	Need Help?	More Practice
CL 5-133.	Pick a number Multiply by 3 Add 27 Subtract 6 Divide by 3 Subtract the original number.	Lessons 5.1.1 and 5.1.2 Math Notes box in Lesson 5.1.2	Problems 5-2 through 5-4, 5-6, 5-9, 5-14, and 5-20
CL 5-134.	a. $3(x+4)$ and $3x+12$ b. $2(x-3)$ and $2x-6$	Lessons 5.1.2 and 5.1.3 Math Notes box in Lesson 5.1.3 Learning Log (problem 5-33)	Problems 5-15, 5-19, 5-29, and 5-45
CL 5-135.	Each girl started with $7.50.	Lessons 3.2.2 through 3.2.5 Math Notes box in Lesson 3.2.3 Learning Log (problem 3-98)	Problems CL 3-113, CL 4-113, 5-93, 5-102, and 5-126
CL 5-136.	Mat A has -3 and Mat B has -2, so Mat B is greater.	Lessons 5.2.1 and 5.2.2 Math Notes box in Lesson 5.2.1 Learning Log (problem 5-54)	Problems 5-40 through 5-44, 5-50 through 5-53, 5-61, 5-62, 5-63, and 5-67

Problem	Solution	Need Help?	More Practice
CL 5-137.	a. b. There is a trapezoid with two vertical bases: $(3, 4)$ to $(3, -5)$ and $(-1, -2)$ to $(-1, 3)$. The height can be seen on any horizontal line segment between $x = 3$ and $x = -1$. c. 28 square units	Lesson 2.3.5 Math Notes box in Lesson 2.2.2 Learning Log (problem 2-150)	Problems 2-135, 2-137, 2-151, 4-21, 5-24, 5-57, and 5-129
CL 5-138.	a. 91 b. 39 shots, 30%	Lessons 4.1.1 and 4.1.2 Math Notes box in Lesson 4.1.2	Problems CL 4-112, 5-37, 5-58, and 5-104
CL 5-139.	a. $\frac{15}{8}$ and $\frac{37}{12}$ b. 3 and $\frac{13}{2}$ c. -12 and 2 d. 16 and -3	Lessons 1.2.4, 1.2.5, and 2.3.1 Math Notes box in Lesson 1.2.4 Learning Log (problem 1-107)	Problems CL 4-116, and 5-81
CL 5-140.	a. $-7x + 8$ b. $x + 2$ c. Fully simplified. d. $2x^2 + 2x - 7$	Lessons 3.1.3 and 5.1.2 Math Notes boxes in Lessons 3.1.3 and 5.1.2 Learning Log (problem 3-28)	Problems CL 4-117, 5-31, 5-3, 5-46, and 5-113

Puzzle Investigator Problems

PI-9.   WHAT'S MY NUMBER?

Francesca has a game for you. She decided to show the rules of the game using a flowchart, at right.

a.   Show that if you start with the number 60, you will lose.

b.   How many starting numbers less than 100 will win? List the possible winning numbers and show how you know they will win.

c.   What if Francesca changed the rules so that you win if you end up with the number 1? What numbers would win?

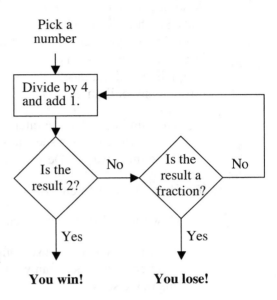

PI-10.   WAY TO GO!

The map at right shows the streets in Old Town. Assume Jacqueline is standing at the corner of A and 1st Streets. Assume Jacqueline will only walk South or East. The shaded rectangles represent large buildings. Assume Jacqueline will not pass through any buildings.

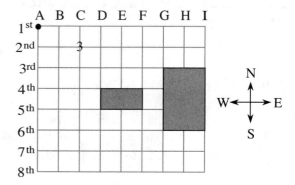

a.   The number "3" at the intersection of C and 2nd Streets means that there are three different ways she can get there from her starting position. What are those three ways? Describe them in words.

b.   How many different ways can she walk to the corner of F and 4th Streets?

c.   How many different ways can she walk to the corner of D and 5th Streets?

d.   Explain how you can use your answers to parts (b) and (c) to find the number of ways she can walk to the corner of F and 5th Streets. Why does this make sense?

e.   Find the number of different ways she can walk to the corner of I and 8th Streets.

f.   How could you change the map so that Jacqueline has only 7 ways to get to the corner of D and 3rd streets? You can remove blocks or add them.

Graphing and Solving Equations

CHAPTER 6 Graphing and Solving Equations

In earlier chapters, you used histograms and box-and-whisker plots to answer questions such as *"Are this year's frogs better jumpers than last year's?"* In this chapter, you will develop a way to see if there is a relationship between two different measures for a set of objects. For example, to answer the question, *"If a frog has longer legs, can it jump farther?"* you will use a new tool, called a scatterplot.

In this chapter, you will also extend what you know about comparing expressions to include those cases when expressions are equal. You will build equations on equation mats with algebra tiles as well as write equations with variables and solve them without tiles. This skill will provide a new way to solve word problems without completing a 5-D table. By the end of the chapter you will learn some efficient ways to justify the steps used to solve equations.

Guiding Questions

Think about these questions throughout this chapter:

What would a graph of this data look like?

Can I make a prediction?

Is there a relationship?

How can I represent it?

How can I solve it?

How can I check my answer?

In this chapter, you will learn how to:

➢ Create scatterplots that show relationships among two-variable data.

➢ Identify correlations between sets of data and represent the relationship with a trend line.

➢ Solve for a variable when two expressions are equal.

➢ Write and solve an equation to solve a word problem.

➢ Recognize when an equation has no solution or infinite solutions.

Chapter Outline

Section 6.1 In this section you will create and interpret circle graphs. You will also learn to make graphs that compare two sets of data. Then, you will use scatterplots and linear graphs to make observations and predictions about the data based on correlations.

Section 6.2 Using algebra tiles, you will explore what you can learn when expressions are equal. Solving equations will also provide you an opportunity to develop efficient simplification strategies and learn how to know that your solution is correct. You will also consider special cases, such as when an equation has no solution.

Making Connections: Course 2

6.1.1 How can I represent the data?

Circle Graphs

Data can be found everywhere in the world. When scientists conduct experiments, they collect data. Advertising agencies collect data to learn which products consumers prefer. In Chapter 4 you developed histograms and box-and-whisker plots to represent measures (such as lengths of frog jumps). However, how can you represent data that is non-numerical or that cannot be represented on a number line? Today you will look at a data display that is used for data that comes in categories or groups. As you work, keep these questions in mind:

What portion is represented?

Should I use a fraction or a percent?

Am I measuring in percents or degrees?

6-1. HUMAN CIRCLE GRAPH

Get a shape card from your teacher. Look at your shape and decide if your shape is a parallelogram, another form of quadrilateral, a triangle, or some other shape. Follow your teacher's directions to create a linear model and circle graph. Then answer the questions below.

a. Your class built a circle graph with your bodies. How can this model be drawn on paper? Work with your team to sketch a picture of your class circle graph showing the portion of your class that held parallelograms, other quadrilaterals, triangles, and other polygons. Be sure to label each section with the category of shape it represents and with an estimated percentage or angle measure.

b. Approximately what portion of the class held triangles? Write your answer as a percent. Then estimate the measure of the central angle on the graph for that portion. A **central angle** is an angle with its vertex at the center of a circle. Its sides are formed by two radii and its measure is a portion of 360°.

c. Was there a section of the circle that had a central angle that was approximately 90°? If so, what type of figure is represented in that section?

6-2.   Nate and Nick are interested in buying a car. According to an ad in the paper, they found that there were 12 cars, 9 pickup trucks, 6 SUVs, and 3 minivans for sale in their price range.

a.   How many vehicles were in Nate and Nick's price range?

b.   What portion of the total does each type of vehicle represent?

c.   On the Lesson 6.1.1B Resource Page, create a circle graph of the vehicles in Nate and Nick's price range. Label each section of the graph with the type of vehicle along with the fraction or percent of the circle it represents.

d.   Calculate the central angle created by each section in the circle graph.

e.   Is there another way to represent this data? Are a box-and-whisker plot, stem-and-leaf plot, histogram, or bar graph an appropriate way to display this data? Why or why not?

6-3.   Circle graphs can be used to compare data at different points in time. Analyze the two circle graphs below.

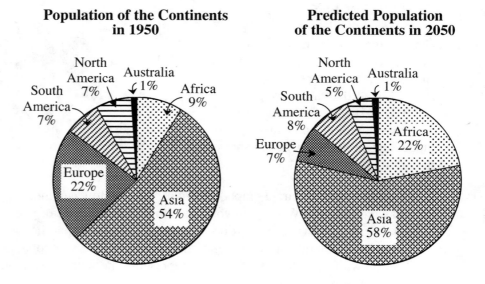

a.   According to the circle graphs, which continent had the largest population in 1950? Which has the largest predicted population in 2050? Do they represent the same percent of the world's population in both graphs?

b.   Which continent is predicted to have its percentage of world population increase the most between 1950 and 2050? By how much is its percentage expected to increase?

Problem continues on next page. →

6-3.   *Problem continued from previous page.*

c.   Which continent is expected to have its portion of the total population shrink the most between 1950 and 2050? By how much will its percentage of world population change?

d.   Is it reasonable to say that continents with a small percentage of the world population in 1950 will have small percentage of the populatation in 2050? What evidence from the graphs can you provide to **justify** your answer?

6-4.   The world's landmasses are divided into seven continents. The largest continent in terms of landmass is Asia, representing almost 30% of the Earth's land. In contrast, the smallest continent is Australia at about 6% of the Earth's land. Use the circle graph at right to help you make the following comparisons.

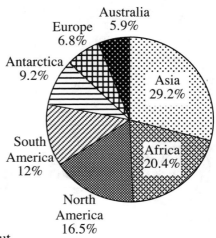

Landmass of Continents

a.   Which continents are approximately the same size?

b.   Which continent is about one-half the size of Asia?

c.   Which continents together make up about half of the world's land mass?

6-5.   The population of the world's people is not evenly divided over the Earth's surface. In 2009, only 0.0002% of the people in the world lived in Antarctica, while 60% of people lived in Asia.

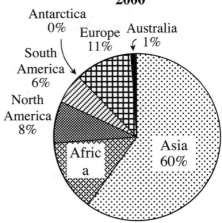

Population of Continents 2000

a.   Where is the portion representing Antarctica's population? Explain.

b.   What similarities and differences do you notice about the landmass and population circle graphs in problem 6-4 and this problem?

c.   Is it reasonable to say that larger continents have larger populations? Why or why not?

6-6. **Additional Challenge:** Take another look at the population graphs from problems 6-3 and 6-5.

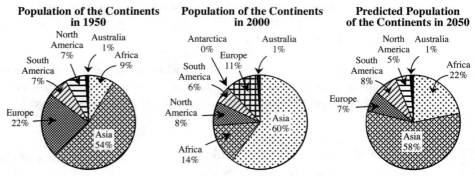

a. Note that Asia's population percentage goes from 54% to 60% to 58%. Does this mean the population of Asia is expected to shrink between 2000 and 2050? Why or why not?

b. What kind of graph could be used so that this misunderstanding would not occur?

Methods and Meanings

Special Quadrilaterals

MATH NOTES

Every rectangle is a parallelogram because opposite pairs of sides are parallel, but a rectangle is a special kind of parallelogram because it has four right angles. So every rectangle is a parallelogram, but not every parallelogram is a rectangle.

In the same way, every rhombus is a parallelogram and every square is a rhombus, a rectangle and a parallelogram.

The diagram below shows the relationships between some kinds of quadrilaterals and some of their properties. The arrows indicate that the properties of the previous figure(s) are also properties of that figure.

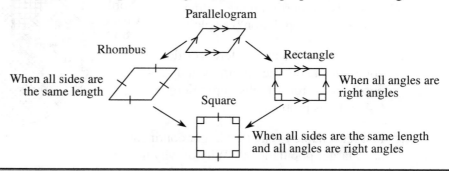

Energy Sources in the U.S.

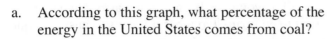

6-7.   Answer the following questions about the graph at right.

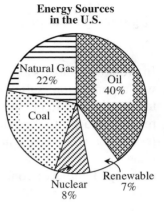

a.   According to this graph, what percentage of the energy in the United States comes from coal?

b.   Which two sources of energy equal about one-third of the total energy for the United States?

c.   What combination of energy sources provide about half of the total energy for the United States?

6-8.   If you can travel 156 miles on 4 gallons of gasoline, how far can you travel on 12 gallons? How many miles on 6 gallons? A diagram may help you with your **reasoning**. Show your work and explain your thinking.

6-9.   Use the Distributive Property to simplify the following expressions.

a. $4(x+2)$ b. $-5(9+x)$ c. $7(x-3)$

6-10.   In 2009, the federal government budget was $3.1 trillion ($3,100,000,000,000). The government was looking to cut costs.

a.   If it decided to cut 1%, how much did it cut?

b.   If the government reduced the budget by 7%, how much did it cut?

c.   If the government eliminated $93 billion ($93,000,000) from the budget, what percentage did it cut?

6-11.   The diameter of the large circle is 18 cm.

a.   What is the area of the shaded circle?

b.   What steps did you do need to do to find the answer?

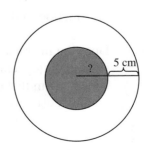

Chapter 6: Graphing and Solving Equations   343

6.1.2 Is there a relationship?

Organizing Data in a Scatterplot

In previous chapters and Lesson 6.1.1, you have been looking at single data sets, such as world population. Often we need to compare two measurements to answer a question or to see a connection between two types of data. For example, comparing the odometer reading of a car to the price of a car can help determine if these factors are related. In this lesson you will study scatterplots, a new tool for visually presenting data, as a way to relate two sets of measurements. You will be asked to analyze the data to see if you can make predictions or come to any conclusion about the relationships that you find.

As you work with your team today, use these focus questions to help direct your discussion:

How can I organize data?

Can I use this data to make a prediction?

What does a point represent?

Is there a connection between the two factors?

6-12.   HOW MUCH IS THAT CAR?

Nate and Nick were discussing cars. Nate claimed that cars with lower odometer readings were more expensive than cars with higher odometer readings. His evidence was that his car with 23,000 miles was worth more than Nick's car with 31,000 miles. To investigate Nate's claim, the boys researched several car ads and found the information in the table at right.

Does the information in the table support Nate's claim? That is, do you believe Nate's claim that cars with a lower odometer reading cost more money?

Nate's Data from Car Ads

Odometer Reading (thousands of mi)	Price (thousands of $)
35	$38
55	$16
6	$50
28	$30
50	$26
31	$35
15	$28
99	$10
99	$13

6-13.   Melissa looked at the data from problem 6-12 and said, *"I need to be able to see the data as a picture. I can't tell if there is a relationship from the lists of numbers."* She decided to use a box-and-whisker plot. Her box-and-whisker plots for odometer reading and price are shown below. Do these pictures help you decide if Nate is correct? Why or why not?

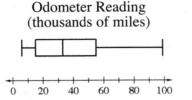

Odometer Reading
(thousands of miles)

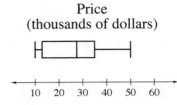

Price
(thousands of dollars)

6-14.   Melissa wondered if a coordinate graph could help determine if there was a relationship in Nate's data from problem 6-12.

   a.   Follow your teacher's directions to create a scatterplot of the data for Melissa.

   - Set up a graph showing Odometer Reading on the *x*-axis and Price on the *y*-axis.

   - Label equal intervals on each axis so that all of the data will fit on the graph.

   - Plot the data points from problem 6-12.

   b.   Describe the scatterplot you just created. What do you notice about how the points are placed on the graph? Do you see any patterns?

   c.   Place an additional point on your graph for Nate's car that has an odometer reading of 23,000 miles. Explain your **strategy** for deciding where to put the point.

   d.   When a relationship exists, one way to help show a trend in the data is to place a line or curve that in general represents where the data falls. This line (sometimes called a **trend line**) does not need to touch any of the actual data points, but instead shows where the data generally falls. The line is the set of points that represents your predictions for all cars no matter what their mileage or price.

   With your team, decide where a trend line could be placed that would best represent the data points. Are there any limits to when the trend line makes sense?

Problem continues on next page. →

6-14.   *Problem continued from previous page.*

    e.   Using the trend line, can you predict the price of a car with an odometer reading of 80,000 miles? If so, explain how the trend line helps. If not, explain why it is not helpful.

    f.   Based on the scatterplot, would you agree with Nate's claim that cars with a higher odometer reading cost less? Use the scatterplot to **justify** your answer.

6-15.   Sometimes what you know about relationships can help you predict what data will look like when it is graphed. For each situation below:

- Look at the scatterplots and use your experience to decide which statement fits each scatterplot.

- Decide if there is a relationship between the data, that is, as one quantity changes, does the other change in a predictable way?

- If there is a relationship, describe it in a sentence.

- If there is no relationship, explain why you think so.

i.   *ii.*   *iii.* 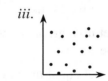   *iv.*

    a.   How fast a dog can run and the length of the dog's fur.

    b.   A person's age and their body temperature.

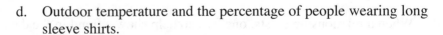

    c.   The child's age and the size of his or her feet.

    d.   Outdoor temperature and the percentage of people wearing long sleeve shirts.

METHODS AND MEANINGS

Circle Graphs

MATH NOTES

A **circle graph** (sometimes called a **pie chart**) is like a bar graph because it deals with categorical data (such as make of car or grade in school) and not continuous data, such as age or height.

Each category of data is put into its own sector of the circle. The measure of the central angle bounding the sector is proportional to the percentage of elements of that type of the whole. For example, if Central Schools has 40% of its students in elementary school, 35% in middle school, and 25% in high school, then its circle graph would have a central angle of 144° (0.4 times 360°) for the sector showing the elementary school, 126° for the sector showing the elementary school, and 90° for the sector showing the high school.

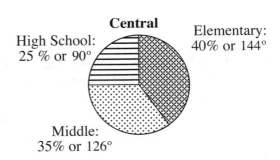

Central

High School: 25 % or 90°

Elementary: 40% or 144°

Middle: 35% or 126°

Review & Preview

6-16.   A class surveyed how students at their school travel to school. The results of the survey are shown in the table at right. Make a circle graph showing the results of the survey using percentages.

Mode of Transportation	Number of Students
Bus	90
Ride Bike	30
Ride in Car	75
Walk	45

6-17.   Simplify the following expressions.

  a. $-5 + 2(8 - 12)$ b. $(-5 + 2)(8 - 12)$ c. $-5 + 2 \cdot 8 - 12$

  d. $\frac{1}{2}(-6)(4 + 10)$ e. $-\frac{2}{3} \cdot 6 + 15 \div (-3)$ f. $(7 - 2)^2 - 5 \div 5$

6-18.   A triangle has a base that is two more than three times the length of its height. The area of the triangle is 400 square cm. What are the base and height of the triangle?

6-19.   Alan wants to convince his parents that he is doing well in math. His test scores are 83, 90, 58, 71, 82, 91, 82, and 64. Should he use the mean, median, or mode to convince them? Explain your **reasoning** and show your work.

6-20.   Find the lengths of the missing sides on the similar shapes at right.

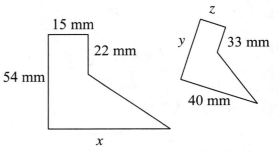

Making Connections: Course 2

6.1.3 What is the relationship?

Identifying Correlation

When is it reasonable to make a prediction? For example, when you know the height of a tree, can you predict the size of its leaves? Or if you know the outdoor temperature for the day, can you predict the number of glasses of water you will drink during the day?

In Lesson 6.1.2 you found that some data sets were related and others were not. In this lesson you will look at different situations and decide if they show a relationship, and if that relationship allows you to make a prediction. As you work with your team today, use these focus questions to help direct your discussion:

When one value goes up, what happens to the other one?

Is there a relationship between one thing changing and the other changing?

Can I make a prediction?

6-21.   Students in a science class have been experimenting with different factors that they think may affect how tall a plant will grow. Each team planted seeds in several pots using different experimental conditions.

With your team, read the questions that the students investigated. Write a team prediction (hypothesis) for the results for each experiment. Assume that all other variables are controlled (meaning that they will not affect the experimental outcome).

a.   Does the amount of fertilizer affect the plant height?

b.   Does how deep the seed is planted in each pot affect the plant height?

c.   Does the number of seeds in each pot affect plant height?

d.   Does the size of the pot affect plant height?

e.   Does the hours of sunlight per day affect the plant height?

6-22.   After three weeks, the teams measured the heights
of their plants and recorded the data. The Team 1
data chart and the question they investigated are
included below. On graph paper, make a
scatterplot for the data gathered. Be sure that you:

- Clearly label your axes

- Mark the scale at equal intervals

- Title your graph appropriately (such
  as with the experimental question)

Team 1: Does the amount of fertilizer affect the plant height?

Amount of fertilizer over 3 week period (ml)	5	10	15	20	25
Height of plant (cm)	9	12	18	24	30

6-23.   Your teacher will assign your team one of the remaining sets of data and will
provide you with poster material. Prepare a scatterplot poster for your assigned
set of data. Be sure your graph has a title and that the axes are correctly labeled.
Also make sure that the points on your graph will be easily seen from across the
room.

Team 2: Does the depth of seed in each pot affect the plant height?

Depth of seed in pot (cm)	3	6	9	12	15
Height of plant (cm)	24	21	18	12	6

Team 3: Does the number of seeds in each pot affect the plant height?

Number of seeds planted in pot	1	2	3	4	5
Height of plant (cm)	21	24	27	21	24

Team 4: Does the size of the pot affect plant height?

Diameter of pot (cm)	6	9	12	15	18
Height of plant (cm)	21	20	19	21	18

Team 5: Do the hours of sunlight per day affect the plant height?

Amount of light per day (hours)	1	3	5	7	9
Height of plant (cm)	3	9	12	24	27

6-24.   Examine your scatterplot for Team 1 (from problem 6-22) and the scatterplot posters created by your class. Then answer the following questions.

    a.   For each of the graphs of data, does there appear to be a relationship? If so, describe it by completing the sentence:

        As _____ gets larger, then _____ gets _____.

    b.   In a scatterplot, if there appears to be no relationship between the variables, then the points in the scatterplot have **no correlation**. But if one variable generally increases as the other variable increases, there is said to be a **positive correlation**. If one variable generally decreases as the other variable increases, there is said to be a **negative correlation**. See some examples below.

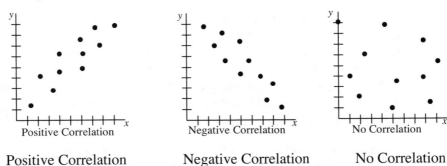

Positive Correlation   Negative Correlation   No Correlation

        Review each of the graphs of the plant experiment data and decide if there is a positive correlation, a negative correlation, or no correlation.

    c.   An **outlier** is a piece of data that does not seem to fit into the pattern. Do there appear to be any outliers in any of the scatterplots?

    d.   Now go back and look at your team predictions for each question (problem 6-21). Were your predictions accurate? Explain your **reasoning**.

6-25.   When there is a correlation, predictions can be made. One way to help make predictions is to draw a trend line or curve for the data.

    a.   Find your graph of Team 1's data (from problem 6-22). Work with your team to draw a straight line that represents the trend of the data on this graph. Remember that the line does not need to intersect each of the points.

    b.   Now use your trend line to predict the height of the plant when 12 milliliters of fertilizer is given to the plant over a 3-week period.

    c.   How much fertilizer would you predict is needed (over the 3-week period) to have the plant grow 26 cm?

6-26.   LEARNING LOG

In your Learning Log, describe how a graph can help you
tell if there is a relationship between two sets of data. That
is, what does it look like if there is a correlation? What
does it look like if there is no correlation? Title this entry,
"Correlations," and label it with today's date.

6-27.   HOW MUCH IS THAT CAR?

Nate and Nick were talking about cars. Nate claimed
that cars with more horsepower were more expensive
than cars with less horsepower. His reason was that his
300 horsepower sports car was worth more than Nick's
120 horsepower small economy car. To investigate
Nate's claim, the boys looked up information about their
friends' cars. The table at right shows their results.

a.   Does the information in the table support Nate's
     claim that cars with more horsepower cost more?
     Is there a relationship between horsepower and the
     price of a car?

b.   Set up a graph and plot the points from the table.
     Now do you believe Nick's claim? Explain your
     reasoning.

Nick and Nate's Data

Horsepower	Price (Thousands)
500	$38
160	$16
453	$23
505	$23
228	$30
311	$26
335	$15
197	$40

6-28.   Evaluate the inequality $x + 4 < 2x - 3$ for the following values of x. Decide if
the given value of x makes the statement true or false. Show all of your work.

a. $x = 4$ b. $x = -2$ c. $x = 7$ d. $x = 9$

6-29.   Evaluate the following expressions.

a. $7x + 8$ when $x = 9$ b. $6(y - 11)$ when $y = -6$

c. $45 - 5m + 7$ when $m = -4$ d. $-2t + 9$ when $t = -20$

6-30. Simplify each expression.

a. $-\frac{4}{5}+\frac{7}{12}$ b. $\frac{5}{9}+(-\frac{1}{4})$ c. $-\frac{3}{7}\cdot\frac{11}{12}$ d. $-1\frac{2}{3}\cdot\frac{4}{5}$

6-31. Here are the heights (in inches) of hollyhocks (tall, slender flowering plants) that are growing in the park: 10, 39, 43, 45, 46, 47, 48, 48, 49, 50, and 52.

a. Find the median.

b. Find the quartiles.

c. Make a box-and-whisker plot of the data.

6.1.4 What is the relationship?

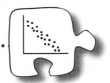

Introduction to Linear Rules

In Lessons 6.1.2 and 6.1.3, you made scatterplots and examined at how data was related. With your team, you will now explore how some kinds of correlations in scatterplots can be used to help make predictions. So far, the data you have graphed has been a collection of points that you have gathered from the world around you. Today we will begin to collect data from a mathematical situation and attempt to use this data to make predictions. This data, when displayed on a graph, will be like a scatterplot in some ways and different in other ways.

6-32. COLLECTING DATA

You and a partner will be given a short time to generate a list of number pairs that add to ten. For example, 3 plus 7 equals 10, so the number pair would be $(3, 7)$. Use a table like the one below to record your number pairs.

Number 1																
Number 2																

As you generate your list, think about kinds of numbers you can use.

- Do the numbers have to be positive?
- Do they have to be integers?
- What is the largest number you can use? What is the smallest?
- How many number pairs are possible?

6-33.   ANALYZING THE DATA

Follow the directions from your teacher to create a graph of the data. Then, with your team, discuss the questions below and record your answers.

a.   What do all of the number pairs have in common?

b.   Explain the **strategy** you used to find your number pairs.

c.   How many points could there be on the graph?

d.   How is this relationship different than the scatterplots that you have made in Lessons 6.1.2 and 6.1.3? How is this relationship the same?

6-34.   Now you will play what are known as Silent Board Games. Your teacher will put an incomplete $x \rightarrow y$ table on the overhead or board. For each:

- Copy the table, study the input and output values, and look for a relationship.

- Once you know the relationship between x and y, use the relationship to add the missing values to your chart.

- Finally, write the rule in words and symbols that finds each y-value from its x-value.

6-35.   In Chapter 1, your team looked for characteristics that sets of objects had in common. The points below were one of those sets of objects. Use what you learned about finding relationships during the Silent Board Game to describe the relationship between x and y in the points below. Then write a rule of the form $y =$ _____ .

(3, 5)   (98, 100)   (−6, −4)   (11, 13)

6-36. Look for a relationship between the numbers in each table below. Complete the last two entries for each table. Describe any relationships you notice.

a.
Number 1	2	12	6	8	24	−4	1	
Number 2	3	18	9	12	36	−6		30

b.
Number 1	2	−5	7	4	0	−1	3	
Number 2	5	−9	15	9	1	−1		11

c.
Number 1	−3	5	−5	0	2	−2		6
Number 2	1	−7	3	−2	−4	0	2	

METHODS AND MEANINGS

Correlation and Trend Lines

In a scatterplot, if one variable increases as the other variable increases, there is said to be a **positive correlation**. If one variable increases as the other variable decreases, there is said to be a **negative correlation**. If there is no relationship between the variables, then the points in the scatterplot have **no correlation**. An example of each situation is illustrated below.

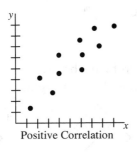
Positive Correlation

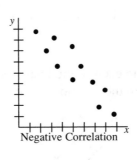
Negative Correlation

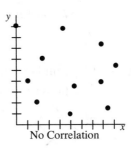
No Correlation

A **trend line** is a line that represents the general tendency of a set of data. It does not need to intersect each data point. Rather, it needs to approximate the data. A trend line looks and "behaves" like the data, as shown in the example at right.

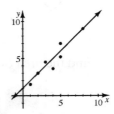

6-37.   Consider the following table.

x	−3	0.5	0	2	4
y	−1	2.5	2	4	6

a.   What is the rule for the table?

b.   Explain your **strategy** for finding the rule for this table.

6-38.   Write an expression for each mat at right.

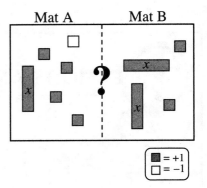

a.   Simplify each mat to determine which expression is greater, if possible.

b.   If $x = 3$, would your answer to part (a) change? Explain.

c.   If $x = -2$, would your answer change? Explain.

6-39.   **Multiple Choice:** Which of the following expressions could be used to find the average (mean) of the numbers k, m, and n?

A. $k + m + n$ B. $3(k + m + n)$ C. $\frac{k+m+n}{3}$ D. $3k + m + n$

6-40.   Copy and complete each of the Diamond Problems below. The pattern used in the Diamond Problems is shown at right.

a.   b.   c.   d.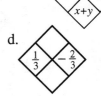

6-41.   Find the area of the shaded portion of each circle.

a.      b.

6.1.5   What is the pattern?

Intercepts

In past lessons you looked at data from several situations. Sometimes the data appeared to be random and sometimes it had a predictable pattern. When data has a rule-based pattern, we can make predictions by finding other data points that fit the pattern.

6-42.   SILENT BOARD GAME

Today you will continue to play the Silent Board Game. Your teacher will put an incomplete $x \to y$ table on the overhead or board. Study the input and output values and look for a pattern. Then write the rule in words and symbols that finds each y-value from its x-value.

6-43.   CLEANING THE TANK, Part One

Roland and Alli work at the Seattle Aquarium. Part of their job is to empty the tank that holds a Giant Pacific Octopus in order to clean the glass and rocks. It is quite a job!

On one cleaning day, Roland carefully transferred the octopus to another tank. He then opened the drain to remove the water. As the water drained, the water level (its height in the tank) lowered at a rate of 2 feet per hour.

When Alli arrived at work that afternoon, she noted that there was still 10 feet of water in the tank.

a.   Alli started a table to record the height, as shown below. Copy her table on your paper and complete the missing values. Then graph the data on graph paper.

x (hours after Alli arrived)	−5	−1	0	1	2	3	5	x
y (height in feet)		12	10					$y =$

b.   What do the x-values in Alli's table represent? For example, what does $x = 3$ represent? What does $x = -1$ represent?

c.   How does the graph tell you what is happening between 2 and 3 hours after Alli got to work? Use the graph to find the water level 2.5 hours after she got to work.

Problem continues on next page. →

6-43.   *Problem continued from previous page.*

d.   Does it make sense to connect the points? Why or why not? e. What will the height of the water be two hours after Alli gets to work? What was the height of the water two hours before she got to work?

f.   If the water level is 20 feet when the tank is full, how many hours did it take to drain it? How many hours before Alli got to work did Roland open the drain? Explain how you found your answer.

6-44.   INTERPRETING INTERCEPTS

The point where a line crosses the *x*- or *y*-axis on a graph often gives useful information about a situation. Examine your graph from problem 6-43.

a.   The point where the line crosses the *x*-axis is called the **x-intercept**. What are the coordinates of this point on your graph? What does that point tell you about the water in the tank?

b.   The point where the line crosses the *y*-axis is called the **y-intercept**. What are the coordinates of this point? What information does it give about the water in the tank?

6-45.   After Alli graphed the data (shown at right), she became concerned because her graph no longer made a straight line.

a.   At what *x*-value did Alli make her mistake? What *y*-value should she have?

b.   Explain to Alli how she could have recognized her mistake.

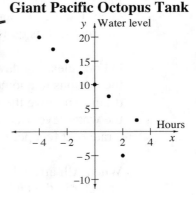

Giant Pacific Octopus Tank

6-46.   **Additional Challenge:** Alli's data table from problem 6-43 was based on when she arrived at work. However, if Roland had made the data table instead, starting with when he opened the drain, his table would have been slightly different. Assume that the tank originally was filled to a height of 20 feet.

a.   On your paper, create a new table that records the height of the water for the number of hours after the drain was opened. Start with *x* = 0 hours and include each hour until the tank was empty.

b.   If you graphed Roland's data from part (a), how would this graph be the same or different than Alli's graph from problem 6-43? **Visualize.**

c.   Graph Roland's data from part (a). Compare Roland's graph with Alli's graph. Write down your observations.

Making Connections: Course 2

6-47.   LEARNING LOG

In your Learning Log, explain how you can make predictions with scatterplots and linear graphs. Is one kind of graph easier to use to make predictions? Can you always make a prediction with a graph? Label this entry with today's date and title it "Scatterplot and Linear Graph Predictions."

METHODS AND **M**EANINGS

MATH NOTES

Making a Complete Graph

A complete graph has the following components:

- x-axis and y-axis labeled, clearly showing the scale.
- Equation of the graph near the line or curve as a label.
- Line or curve extended as far as possible on the graph.
- Coordinates of special points stated in (x, y) format.

x	−1	0	1	2	3
y	6	4	2	0	−2

Tables can be formatted horizontally, like the one above, or vertically, as shown below.

x	y
−1	6
0	4
1	2
2	0
3	−2
4	−4

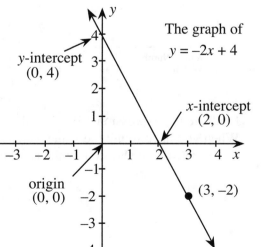

The graph of $y = -2x + 4$

y-intercept $(0, 4)$

x-intercept $(2, 0)$

origin $(0, 0)$

$(3, -2)$

Throughout this course, you will continue to graph lines and other curves. Be sure to label your graphs completely.

6-48.   Use the graph at right to add points to the table below.

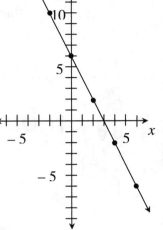

x							
y							

a.   Write the rule in words.

b.   Explain how to use the table to predict the value of y when x is –8.

6-49.   For each scatterplot below:

- Determine if there is a "trend" or correlation in the points. If there is, describe it.

- Label each graph as showing a positive correlation, negative correlation, or no correlation.

a.

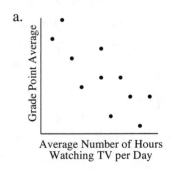

Average Number of Hours
Watching TV per Day

b.

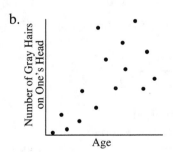

Age

c.

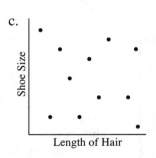

Length of Hair

6-50.   Evaluate the expressions $3x - 2$ and $4x + 4$ for the following values of x. When you have found the value for each expression, write a statement using $<$, $>$, or $=$ that shows how the two values are related.

a. $x = 0$ b. $x = -6$ c. $x = 5$ d. $x = -2$

6-51.   Draw a trapezoid. Label the top base 6 cm and the height 4 cm. If the area of this trapezoid is 36 square cm, what is the length of the other base? You may find it helpful to use the 5-D Process.

6-52.   Find the area of each shaded portion, called a **sector**, in the circles below.

a.   The diameter is 3 feet.

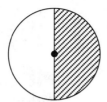

b.   The radius is 12 ft.

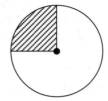

6.1.6   When does a graph make a straight line?

Tables, Linear Graphs, and Rules

In the previous lesson you made a graph showing how the water level in a tank changed as it was being drained at a constant rate. You noticed that the graph made a straight line. Today you will complete a table and graph what happens as the Giant Pacific Octopus tank is being filled. As you work with your team, think about the following questions:

How is the line changing?

What information can we get from a rule?

When does a graph form a straight line? When does it not?

6-53.   SILENT BOARD GAME

Today you will continue to play the Silent Board Game. Your teacher will put an incomplete $x \to y$ table on the overhead or board. Study the input and output values and look for a pattern. Then write the rule in words and symbols that finds each y-value from its x-value.

6-54.   CLEANING THE TANK, Part Two

Today Roland and Alli are filling the 20-
foot deep octopus tank from problem 6-43.
The tank started empty and began filling
earlier in the day. When Alli got to work
the water level was up to 8 feet. It is being
filled at a constant rate of four feet per hour.
Alli created the table below. She wants to
use a data table to predict when the tank
will be full so that she will know when to
shut off the water.

x (hours after Alli arrived)	−2	−1	0	1	2	3	x
y (height in feet)			8				y =

a.   Copy and complete Alli's table on your own paper. Then graph the data
      on graph paper. Be sure you have a complete graph.

b.   What will the height of the water be two hours after Alli gets to work?

c.   How long before Alli got to work did the tank begin to be filled? How do
      you know?

d.   How many hours after she got to work did Alli need to turn the water off
      because the tank was full?

e.   The table is set up like a Silent Board Game. What is the rule that describes
      the data in this table?

6-55.   Looking at the x-intercept and the y-intercept on a graph can help you tell the
         story of the data.

a.   What are the coordinates of the x-intercept and what information does that
      point tell you about the water in the tank?

b.   What are the coordinates of the y-intercept and what information does that
      point tell you about the water in the tank?

6-56.   CLEANING THE TANK, Part Three

The next day Alli started her day's work at the
jellyfish tank that had been cleaned the day before
and was now being refilled. There, she found a
30-foot deep tank that had four feet of water in it.
Alli started filling the tank so that after x hours,
the water level was $y = 3x + 4$ feet high. Alli knew
she could only work for seven hours that day.
After four hours she began to worry that the tank
would not be full before she had to leave.

a.   Using the rule, complete the table and then graph the height of the water in
the tank for the first four hours that Alli was at work.

x (hours)	0	1	2	3	4	x
y (height)						$y = 3x + 4$

b.   Based on your graph, will the tank be full when Alli has to leave work? If
not, how many feet of water still will be needed to fill the tank?

c.   What is the y-intercept and what does this point tell you about this
situation?

6-57.   Look at the following graphs and tell what is happening at each tank. Think
about whether the tank is filling or draining and what the x- and y-intercepts tell
you. Be specific about the water level in the tank.

a.   Sea Bass Tank
(height)

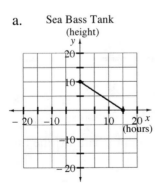

b.   Shark Tank
(height)

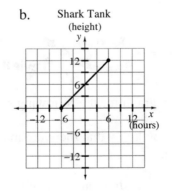

c.   Tidewater Tank
(height)

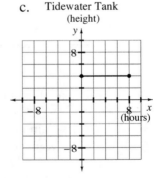

6-58.   Complete the table below and draw a graph of the rule $y = -3x + 18$. Check that
your points form a straight line and correct any errors.

x	−3	0.5	−1	6	1	0	3	−2	5
y			21		15				

METHODS AND MEANINGS

When is a Point on the Graph of a Rule?

MATH NOTES

So far you have drawn several graphs by starting with a rule, substituting x-values, computing y-values, and plotting the points on a set of axes. What if you have the coordinates of a point and want to know if it also belongs on the graph? Use the rule and determine whether the point makes the equation true or false. If the point makes the equation true, it is also on the graph; if it is false, it does not belong on the graph. Here are two examples:

Is $(10, 25)$ on the graph of
$y = 2x + 5$?

Is $(5, -3)$ on the graph of
$y = -2x - 7$?

Replace x with 10 and y with 25 and determine if the equation is true or false.

Replace x with 5 and y with -3 and determine if the equation is true or false.

Is $25 = 2 \cdot 10 + 5$?

Is $-3 = -2 \cdot 5 - 7$?

$25 = 25$ so yes, the point is on the graph.

$-3 \neq -17$ so no, the point is not on the graph.

Review & Preview

6-59.   Make a table and a graph for the following rule: $y = 2x - 4$.

   a.   Explain how you know that there are more points than just the ones shown on your graph.

   b.   Where would the additional points go on the graph?

6-60.   Determine if each of the numbers below is a solution to the inequality $3x - 2 < 2 - 2x$. Show all of your work.

   a.   2   b. $\frac{1}{2}$ c. -3 d. $\frac{2}{3}$

Making Connections: Course 2

6-61.   The school library has 6500 titles in its collection of books, magazines, and reference materials. The librarian is presenting information about the library to the parent association, and she made the graph at right.

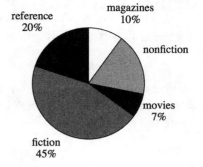

a.   According to the graph, what percentage of the collection are nonfiction books?

b.   Could the librarian have presented this information in a histogram? Why or why not?

c.   How many of the books in the library are fiction?

6-62.   Hector has a part-time job at a garage. He gets a paycheck of $820 every four weeks.

a.   Hector has to pay 15% of his income in taxes. How much money does he pay in taxes each paycheck? Show your thinking with a diagram and calculations.

b.   Hector took a 1-week vacation, so his next paycheck will only be for 3 weeks of work. What percentage of his regular pay should he expect to receive? How much is that?

c.   The garage owner is impressed with Hector's work, and is giving him a 10% raise. How much will Hector be paid when he receives his next 4-week paycheck?

6-63.   An NBA basketball hoop has an inside diameter of 18 inches. The official NBA basketball has a maximum circumference of 30 inches. What is the difference between the hoop diameter and the diameter of the ball? Show all of your work.

6-64.   Red apples cost $1.20 per pound and green apples cost $1.50 per pound.

a.   Write an expression to represent the total cost of x pounds of red apples and y pounds of green apples.

b.   What is the total cost if you buy 3 pounds of red apples and 2 pounds of green apples?

Extension Activity   What is the relationship?

Finding and Describing Relationships

Today you will become a point on a life-size, human graph. Your teacher will give the class instructions for how to form human graphs. Then you will work in study teams to complete the problems below.

6-65.   HUMAN DATA POINTS

Can you imagine what it is like to be a point on a graph? Today is your chance to find out. Your teacher will direct you to a set of axes and explain how to stand on the graph. As you are doing this problem, think about the different patterns you see. Is there a relationship between them?

6-66.   Your teacher will post the graphs for the points that you and your classmates used to form "human graphs."

a.   Compare the graphs. How are they the same and how are they different?

b.   Look at the graphs that formed scatterplots. Which graphs show a positive correlation? Negative correlation? Did any graph show no correlation?

c.   Were any graphs straight lines? If so, copy the table with all the points next to the graph you made on your resource page. Use the table to find a rule that finds each *y*-value from its *x*-value.

6-67.   LEARNING LOG

Write a paragraph in your Learning Log that describes what you did and what you observed in today's class work. How were the scatterplots different from the linear graphs? How did you identify which kind of graph you had? Put today's date on your entry and title it, "Human Data Points."

6-68.   Simplify each expression.

    a. $\frac{73}{100} \cdot (-\frac{2}{7})$

    b. $0.4 \cdot 0.3$

    c. $-\frac{63}{80} + \frac{7}{10}$

    d. $5\frac{1}{9} + 8\frac{2}{5}$

    e. $-\frac{9}{17} - \frac{1}{2}$

    f. $-1.2 + (-\frac{3}{5})$

6-69.   Graph the following points on a coordinate grid and connect them to make a triangle: $(0, 1), (3, 2), (2, 4)$. Then:

- Dilate the shape by multiplying each coordinate by two.

- List the coordinates of the new vertices.

What do you notice about the sides of the two shapes?

6-70.   Sketch the parallelogram shown at right, and then redraw it with sides that are half as long.

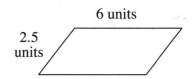

    a.   Find the perimeters of both the original and smaller parallelograms.

    b.   If the height of the original parallelogram (drawn to the side that is 6 units) is 2 units, find the areas of both parallelograms.

6-71.   Simplify each of the following expressions.

    a. $32 \div 2 \cdot 4$

    b. $3 \cdot 6 \div 2 + 6$

    c. $3^2 + 7$

6-72.   Use the 5-D Process to solve the following problem.

Jen, Carrie, and Fran are each thinking of a number. When you add their numbers together you get 207. Jen's number is 9 more than Carrie's, and Fran's number is 3 less than Jen's number. What is Fran's number?

6.2.1 What values make expressions equal?

. . . .

Solving Equations

In Chapter 5, you figured out how to determine what values of x make one expression greater than another. In this lesson you will study what can be learned about x when two expressions are equal. As you work today, focus on these questions:

> What if both sides are equal?

> Is there more than one way to simplify?

> What value(s) of x will make the expressions equal?

6-73.   CHOOSING A PRICE PLAN

Sandeep works at a bowling alley that currently charges a player $3 to rent shoes and $4 per game. However, his boss is thinking about charging $11 to rent shoes and $2 per game.

a.   If a customer rents shoes and plays two games, will he or she pay more with the original price plan or the new price plan? Show how you know.

b.   If the customer bowls 7 games, which price plan is cheaper?

6-74. **WILL THEY EVER BE EQUAL?**

Sandeep decided to represent the two price plans (from problem 6-73) with expressions, where x represents the number of games bowled:

Original price: $4x + 3$ New price: $2x + 11$

a. Do his new expressions find the same prices? Find both the original and new prices when $x = 2$ and then again when $x = 7$ games. Did you get the same prices as you found in problem 6-73?

b. Sandeep decided to place his expressions on an Expression Comparison Mat. What steps did Sandeep take to simplify the mat to this point?

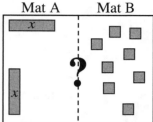

c. Sandeep noticed that for one number of games, a customer would pay the same amount no matter which price plan his boss used. That is, he found a value of x that will make $4x + 3 = 2x + 11$. How many games did that customer bowl? What was the price he paid? Explain.

d. The value of x you found in part (c) is called a **solution** to the equation $4x + 3 = 2x + 11$ because it makes the equation true. That is, it makes both expressions have the same value.

Is $x = 6$ also a solution? How can you tell?

6-75. **SOLVING FOR X**

When the expressions on each side of the comparison mat are equal, they can be represented on a mat called an **Equation Mat**. Obtain a Lesson 6.2.1 Resource Page from your teacher. Now the "=" symbol on the central line indicates that the expressions on each side of the mat are "equal."

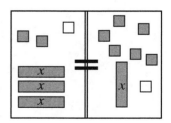

a. Build the equation represented by the Equation Mat above on your own mat using algebra tiles.

b. Record the original equation represented on your Equation Mat on your paper.

c. Simplify the tiles on the mat as much as possible. Record what is on the mat after each legal move as you simplify each expression. What value of x will make the expressions equal?

6-76.   Amelia wants to solve the equation shown on the
         Equation Mat at right. After she simplified each
         expression as much as possible, she was confused
         by the tiles that were left on the mat.

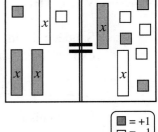

         a.   What was Amelia's original equation?

         b.   Remove any zero pairs that you find on each
              side of the Equation Mat. What happens?

         c.   What is the solution to this equation? That is, what value of x makes this
              equation true? Explain your **reasoning**.

6-77.   Amelia now wants to solve the equation $2x + 2 + (-3) = 5x + 8$. Help her find the
         value of x that makes these expressions equal. Be sure to:

         •   Build the expressions using algebra tiles on your Equation Mat.

         •   Draw the mat on your paper.

         •   Simplify the mat to help you figure out what value of x makes this
             equation true.

METHODS AND **M**EANINGS

MATH NOTES

Using an Equation Mat

An **Equation Mat** can help you visually represent an equation with algebra tiles and also assist with its solution.

For example, the equation $2(x-3)+x+4=9-2x+1+x$ can be represented as shown on the first equation mat and then solved using legal moves to show that the solution is $x=3$.

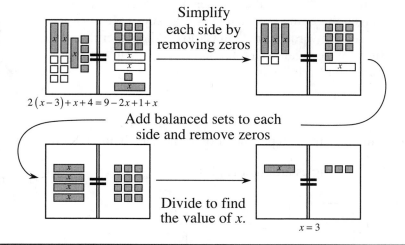

Simplify each side by removing zeros

$2(x-3)+x+4=9-2x+1+x$

Add balanced sets to each side and remove zeros

Divide to find the value of x.

$x=3$

Review & Preview

6-78.   Use the legal moves that you have developed to simplify each mat and, if possible, decide which expression is greater.

= +1
= −1

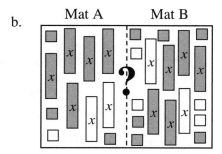

a.

Mat A   Mat B

b.

Mat A   Mat B

6-79.   Victor wants to play "Guess My Number." Use the clues below to figure out his number. Each part is a new game.

a.   *"When you double my number and subtract 9, you get my original number. What's my number?"*

b.   *"When you double my number and add 5, you get 17. What's my number?"*

6-80.   To solve the following problem, use the 5-D Process. Define a variable and write an expression for each column of your chart.

In the first three football games of the season, Carlos gained three times as many yards as Alden. Travis gained ten yards more than Carlos. Altogether the three players gained a total of 430 yards. How many yards did Carlos gain?

6-81.   Find the area and perimeter of each shape below. Show your steps and work.

a.   All angles are right angles.

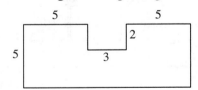

b.

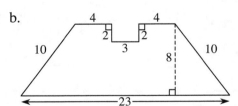

6-82.   Copy and complete the table. What is the rule for the table?

x	−2	4	$\frac{1}{2}$	0	7	−4
y	−7			−3	11	

6.2.2 How do I know that it is correct?

Checking Solutions and the Distributive Property

Sometimes a person's life can depend on the solution of a problem. For example, when skydiving teams jump from airplanes and aim for specific targets on the ground they need to carefully plan their speed and timing. If they are trying to land in a sports stadium as entertainment before a baseball game and they open their parachutes too soon, they may miss the landing area and crash into a building or a tree. If they jump out of the plane too soon, they may run into another skydiver. Even a small miscalculation could be dangerous.

Solving a problem is one challenge. However, once solved, it is important to have ways to know if the solution you found is correct. In this lesson you will be solving equations and finding ways to determine if your solution makes the equation true.

6-83. Chen's sister was making a riddle for him to solve, *"I am thinking of a number. If you add two to the number then triple it, you get 9."*

a. Build the equation on an Equation Mat. What are *two* ways that Chen could write this equation?

b. Solve the equation and show your work by writing the equation on your paper after each legal move.

c. When Chen told his sister the mystery number in the riddle she said he was wrong. Chen was sure that he had figured out the correct number. Find a way to **justify** that you have the correct solution in part (c).

6-84. Now solve the equation $4(x+3) = 8$. Remember to:

- Build the equation on your Equation Mat with algebra tiles.

- Simplify the equation using your legal moves.

- Record your work on your paper.

- Solve for x. That is, find the value of x that makes the equation true.

6-85.   CHECKING YOUR SOLUTION

When you solve an equation that has one solution, you get a value of the variable. But how do you know that you have done the steps correctly and that your answer "works"?

a.   Look at your answer for problem 6-84. How could you verify that your solution is correct and convince someone else? Discuss your ideas with your team.

b.   When Kelly and Madison compared their solutions for the equation $2x - 7 = -2x + 1$, Kelly got a solution of $x = 2$ and Madison got a solution of $x = -1$. To decide if the solutions were correct, the girls decided to check their answers to see if they made the expressions equal.

Finish their work below to determine if either girl has the correct solution.

Kelly's Work	Madison's Work
$2x - 7 \overset{?}{=} -2x + 1$	$2x - 7 \overset{?}{=} -2x + 1$
$2(2) - 7 \overset{?}{=} -2(2) + 1$	$2(-1) - 7 \overset{?}{=} -2(-1) + 1$

c.   When checking, Kelly ended up with $-3 = -3$. Does this mean that her answer is correct or incorrect? And if it is correct, does this mean the solution is $x = -3$ or $x = 2$? Explain.

d.   Go back to problem 6-84 and show how to check your solution for that problem.

6-86.   Kelly solved the equation $4(x + 3) = 8$ from problem 6-84. Her work is shown at right.

$$4(x + 3) = 8$$
$$x + 3 = 2$$
$$x + 3 + (-3) = 2 + (-3)$$
$$x = -1$$

a.   If $4(x + 3) = 8$, does $x + 3$ have to equal 2? Why?

b.   What did Kelly do to remove the 3 unit tiles from the left side of the equation? Does this move affect the equality?

c.   If Kelly were solving the equation $3(x - 5) = 9$, what might her first step be? You may want to build this equation on an Equation Mat to help make sense of her **strategy**.

Making Connections: Course 2

6-87.   Now practice this new solving skill by building the equation with tiles, solving for *x*, and checking your solution for each equation. Record your work.

   a. $4(x+1)+1+(-x)=10+x$

   b. $-1+2x-x=x-8+(-x)$

   c. $5+2(x-4)=4x+7$

   d. $9-3x=1+x$

   e. $3x+3-x+2=x+5$

   f. $4=3(2x+1)-11$

6-88.   Show the check for each of these problems and decide if the solution is correct or incorrect.

   a. $5x+8=3x-2$ Solution: $x=-5$

   b. $2(x+1)+6=20-3x$ Solution: $x=4$

6-89.   Consider the Equation Mat at right.

   a.   Write the original equation represented.

   b.   Simplify the tiles on the mat as much as possible. What value of *x* will make the two expressions equal?

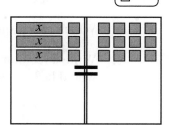

6-90.   When Lakeesha solved the equation $3(x+1)=12$ from problem 6-89, she **reasoned** this way:

   "Since 3 groups of (x+1) equals 3 groups of 4, then I know that each group of (x+1) must equal 4."

   a.   Do you agree with her **reasoning**? Explain.

   b.   How can the result of Lakeesha's **reasoning** be written?

   c.   Verify that your answer from problem 6-89 will make the equation you wrote in part (b) true.

6-91.   During this chapter, you will use your new solving skills to solve word
         problems. Think about and use the **strategies** you already have to answer the
         questions below.

   a.   Andy is 4 years older than Eduardo.
         If Andy is x years old, write an
         expression to represent Eduardo's
         age.

   b.   In Eduardo's collection, the number of
         butterflies is 12 more than twice the
         number of moths. If there are x moths,
         write an expression to represent the
         number of butterflies he has.

6-92.   The class advisor was helping students plan an
         end-of-the-year trip. The students were surveyed
         regarding their choices. The results are in the circle
         graph at right.

   a.   What percentage of the students chose the
         water park?

   b.   Which two results are very close?

   c.   Write a recommendation to the class advisor regarding what the next step
         would be?

6.2.3 How can I record it?

Solving Equations and Recording Work

In this lesson, you will continue to improve your skills at simplifying and solving more complex equations. You will develop ways to record your solving **strategies** so that another student can understand your steps without seeing your Equation Mat. Consider the following questions as you work today.

How can I record the steps I use to solve?

How can I record what is on the Equation Mat after each step?

6-93. Gene and Aidan were using the algebra tiles to solve equations. Aidan was in the middle of a problem when he was called away. Gene picked up Aidan's paper, but he had a hard time figuring out what he should do next.

Help Gene by completing his table on the Lesson 6.2.3 Resource Page.

Mat A	Mat B	Steps taken
$2x + 2(2x+1) + (-3x) + (-6)$	$4x + 3 + (-3) + x + 8$	Original Equation
		1. Distributive Property
$3x + (-4)$	$5x + 8$	2.
		3. Subtract $3x$ from both sides
-12	$2x$	4.
		5. Divide both sides by 2

6-94. Aidan was frustrated that he needed to write so much when solving an equation. He decided to come up with a shortcut for recording his work to solve a new equation.

As you look at Aidan's recording of how he solved $2x + 4 = -12$ below, **visualize** an Equation Mat with algebra tiles. Then answer the questions for each step below.

a. What legal move does writing -4 twice represent?

b. What legal move does circling the $+4$ and the -4 represent?

c. What does the box around the $\frac{2}{2}$ represent?

d. Why did Aidan divide both sides by 2?

e. Check Aidan's solution in the original equation. Is his solution correct?

6-95. The method of recording the steps in the solution of an equation is useful only if you understand what operations are being used and how they relate to the legal moves on your Equation Mat.

Find the work shown at right on your resource page for this lesson.

a. For each step in the solution, add the missing work below each line that shows what legal moves were used. You may want to build the equation on an Equation Mat.

b. Check that the solution is correct.

$$x + (-4) + 6x = 3x - 1 + 5$$

$$-4 + 7x = 3x + 4$$

$$7x = 3x + 8$$

$$4x = 8$$

$$x = 2$$

6-96. Gene is confused. He simplified an equation and ended up with the mat shown at right. What is the value of x?

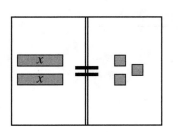

6-97.   For each equation below, solve for x. You may build the equation on your
         Equation Mat. Record your work in symbols using Aidan's method (problem
         6-94). Remember to check your solution.

   a. $-2x + 5 + 2x - 5 = -1 + (-1) + 6x + 2$ b. $3(4 + x) = x + 6$

   c. $5x + (-x) - 1 = 11 - 2x$ d. $3(-x + 2) + x - 1 = -x - 3$

6-98.   LEARNING LOG

         In your Learning Log, explain what it means to solve an
         equation. What is a solution? Be sure to give an example.
         Title this entry "Solving Equations and Finding Solutions"
         and include today's date.

METHODS AND MEANINGS

Checking a Solution

To check a solution to an equation, substitute the solution into the
equation and verify that it makes the two sides of the equation equal.

For example, to verify that $x = 10$ is a solution to the equation
$3(x - 5) = 15$, substitute 10 into the equation for x and then verify
that the two sides of the equation are equal.

As shown at right, $x = 10$ is a solution
to the equation $3(x - 5) = 15$.

$$3(10 - 5) \overset{?}{=} 15$$
$$3(5) \overset{?}{=} 15$$
$$15 = 15 \quad \checkmark \quad \textit{True, so x = 10 is a solution.}$$

What happens when you do this
check if your answer is incorrect?
For example, try substituting $x = 2$
into the same equation. The result
shows that $x = 2$ is not a solution to
this equation.

$$3(2 - 5) \overset{?}{=} 15$$
$$3(-3) \overset{?}{=} 15$$
$$-9 \neq 15 \quad X \quad \textit{Not true, so x = 2 is not a solution.}$$

6-99. Solve each equation below for x. Check your final answer.

a. $4x = 6x - 14$ b. $3x + 5 = 50$

6-100. Examine the table below.

x	0.5	0	2	4	5
y	−0.5	−2	4	10	13

a. What is the rule for the table?

b. Explain the **strategy** you used to find the rule.

6-101. Find the area of each shaded **sector** (region) in the circles below. Note that the smaller angles in parts (a) and (c) are 90° angles.

a. 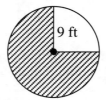   b. 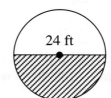   c.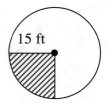

6-102. Copy and complete each of the Diamond Problems below. The pattern used in the Diamond Problems is shown at right.

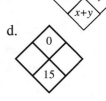

a.   b.   c.   d.

6-103. A cattle rancher gave $\frac{1}{3}$ of his land to his son and kept the remaining $\frac{2}{3}$ for himself. He kept 34 acres of land. How much land did he have to begin with?

Making Connections: Course 2

6.2.4 How can I represent it?

- -

Using a Table to Write Equations from Word Problems

In the last few lessons you used algebra tiles and Equation Mats to solve problems where variables represented specific numbers. Those tools are related to the processes you have used to solve word problems where a specific value is unknown. Today you will connect these two tools and the expressions you wrote using a part of the 5-D Process to extend your repertoire for solving problems.

6-104.   THE 5-D PROCESS REVISITED

Use the 5-D Process to set up the following problem. Complete only *three* trials. Even if you do not yet know the solution, wait for your teacher's instructions.

The Great Lakes contain the largest amount of fresh water on the surface of the planet. Combined, the five lakes (Superior, Michigan, Huron, Erie, and Ontario) contain 84% of North America's and 21% of the world's surface fresh water!

The amount of water in Lake Superior is 1720 cubic miles more than the amount of water in Lake Michigan. Lake Huron has 330 cubic miles of water less than Lake Michigan. If the total amount of water in the three lakes is 4,930 cubic miles, how much water is in Lakes Huron, Michigan, and Superior?

6-105.   GO FOR THE GOLD

As you saw in problem 6-104, sometimes organizing your thinking using the 5-D Process to solve a word problem involves a lot of work. Sometimes the tables are very complicated or the numbers require many trials to find the answer. How can your new equation solving skills help you solve word problems? Read the following word problem and then answer the questions below.

While looking at the country of Jamaica's results from the 2008 Beijing Olympics, Gemma noticed that the number of gold medals Jamaica received was twice the number of silver medals. She also realized that Jamaica received 1 fewer bronze medal than silver medals. Altogether, Jamaica received 11 medals.

a.   Gemma started by setting up the 5-D Process table below. What did she define x to represent?

Define			Do	Decide
# Gold	# Silver	# Bronze	Total Number of Medals	11?
$2x$	x	$x-1$		

b.   How did she represent the number of gold and bronze medals?

c.   Write an equation for the total number of medals.

d.   Solve your equation in part (c). What is the value of x? What does this represent?

e.   How many gold medals did Jamaica earn? Explain how you know.

6-106.   Solve the following word problems by writing and solving an equation. You may choose to use the 5-D Process and create a table to help you build your equation. It may be helpful to first do one or two trials with numbers to help establish a pattern. Whatever **strategy** you use, do not forget to define the variable. Check your answer.

   a.   A person's height is positively correlated to their arm span (the distance between the ends of your fingertips as your arms are held out on each side of your body). One of the tallest men in history had an arm span that measured 7 inches more than his height. The combined total of his arm span and height was 221 inches. How tall was this man?

   b.   Have you ever tried to hold your breath? Humans can only hold their breath an average of one minute. However, other animals can hold their breath for much longer.

         A Greenland whale can hold its breath three times as long as a beaver and a hippopotamus can hold its breath five minutes less than a beaver. If you added the time a Greenland whale, beaver, and hippopotamus can hold their breath, you would get 95 minutes! How long can a beaver hold its breath?

6-107.   LEARNING LOG

   In Chapter 3 you learned about variables and using the 5-D Process to solve problems. In Chapter 5 you simplified expressions using algebra tiles and in this chapter you focused on solving equations.

   In your Learning Log describe how variables and equations can be used to solve word problems. Use an example problem to help make your explanation clear. Title this entry, "Using the 5-D Process to Write and Solve Equations," and label it with today's date.

METHODS AND MEANINGS

Defining a Variable

When you write an equation, it is important to define your variable carefully. You need to be clear about what you are talking about so that someone else looking at your work understands what the variable represents. This step is an important habit to develop because it is an important step in solving many different math problems.

Suppose you have the problem:

> At the neighborhood grocery store, grapes cost $3 a pound. If Belinda spent $5.40 on grapes, how many pounds of grapes did she buy?

One equation you could write would be $3x = 5.4$, if you know what x stands for. The variable x should be clearly defined, such as $x =$ pounds of grapes, rather than just $x =$ grapes. You could also write $g =$ pounds of grapes, since any letter may be used as a variable.

Review & Preview

6-108.   Consider the equation $7 = 3x - 5$.

    a.   Stanley wants to start solving the equation by adding five to both sides, while Terrence wants to first subtract seven from both sides. Will both **strategies** work? Is one **strategy** more efficient than the other?

    b.   Solve $7 = 3x - 5$. Show your steps.

6-109.   The two triangles at right are similar shapes.

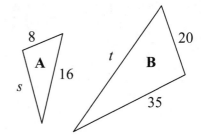

    a.   What is the scale factor between shape A and shape B?

    b.   Find the missing sides.

    c.   If you wanted to make shape A smaller instead of bigger, what is a scale factor you could use?

6-110.　Find the area and perimeter of the following figures.

a.

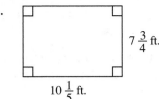

$7\frac{3}{4}$ ft.

$10\frac{1}{5}$ ft.

b.　square

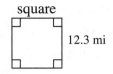

12.3 mi

c.

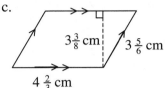

$3\frac{3}{8}$ cm　$3\frac{5}{6}$ cm

$4\frac{2}{3}$ cm

d.

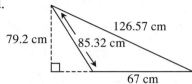

79.2 cm　85.32 cm　126.57 cm

67 cm

6-111.　Graph the following points on a coordinate grid: $(1,1)$, $(4,1)$, and $(3,4)$.

Connect the points, then translate the points three units right and three units up. What are the coordinates of the vertices of the new triangle?

6-112.　Find the value of the expression $2x+6$ for the given values of x.

a.　$x=6$　　b.　$x=-2$　　c.　$x=0$　　d.　$x=5$

6.2.5 How can I model it?

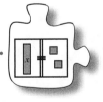

Writing and Solving Equations

Engineers investigate practical problems to improve people's quality of life. To investigate solutions to problems they often build models. These models can take various forms. For example, a structural engineer designing a bridge might build a small replica of the bridge. Civil engineers studying the traffic patterns in a city might create equations that model traffic flows into and out of a city at different times.

In this lesson you will be building equations to model and solve problems based on known information. As you work today keep the following questions in mind:

What does x represent in the equation?

How does the equation show the same information as the problem?

Have I answered the question?

6-113.   Today your team will be responsible for solving a problem and sharing your solution with the class. It is important that your poster communicates your thinking and **reasoning** so that people who look at your poster understand how you solved the problem. Your poster should include:

- Connections between the words in the problem and the relationships in your chart and/or equation. Connections can be made with arrows, colors, symbols, and labels.

- Variables that are defined completely.

- An equation to represent the problem.

- Your solution to the problem.

- The answer declared in a sentence.

Begin by solving one of the problems below and writing an equation. Make sure to define the variable you use and answer the question(s) being asked. Using the 5-D Process, including numerical trials, may be helpful.

a.   Hong Kong's tallest building, Two International Finance Center, is 88 stories tall. The former Sears Tower in Chicago is eight stories taller than the Empire State Building in New York City. If all of the buildings were stacked on top of each other, the combined heights would have 300 stories. How many stories does the Sears Tower have?

b.   Have you ever driven or walked across a suspension bridge? There are many suspension bridges in the world of different lengths that allow people to travel across rivers, bays and lakes.

The Mackinac Bridge in Michigan is 1158 meters long. The Tsing Ma Bridge in Hong Kong is 97 meters longer than the Golden Gate Bridge in California. Together, all three bridges have a length of 3815 meters. How long is the Tsing Ma Bridge?

Problem continues on next page. →

Making Connections: Course 2

6-113.   *Problem continued from previous page.*

c.   Elevations found in the United States range from California's Death Valley at 282 feet below sea level to Alaska's Mount McKinley at 20,320 feet above sea level.

The highest elevation in Delaware is 106 feet higher than the highest elevation in Florida. Louisiana's highest elevation is 190 feet higher than Florida's highest elevation. If you climbed from sea level to the highest points in Delaware, Florida, and Louisiana, you would only climb 1331 feet. How high is the highest elevation in each of the three states?

d.   Most states in the United States are divided into counties. Some counties are very large and some are very small, and different states have different numbers of counties. Pennsylvania has five less than twice as many counties as Oregon. Florida has one less county than Pennsylvania. All together, the three states have 169 counties. How many counties does Florida have?

e.   A train from Washington, D.C. to Chicago first stops in Pittsburg and then in Cleveland. The distance from Washington, D.C. to Pittsburg is 30 miles less than twice the distance from Pittsburg to Cleveland. The distance from Cleveland to

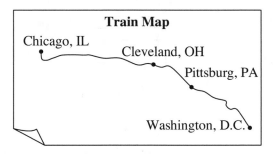

Chicago is 220 miles more than the distance between Pittsburg and Cleveland. If the entire train ride is 710 miles, how far is the train ride from Cleveland to Chicago?

6-114. On graph paper, graph the rule $y = 4x - 6$. Determine the value of y when $x = \frac{1}{2}$.

6-115. Solve the following equations using any method. Show your work and check your solution.

a. $2x + 16 = 5x + 4$ b. $3x - 5 = 2x + 14$ c. $5x - 5 = x + 15$

6-116. Janet lit a 12-inch candle. She noticed that it was getting an inch shorter every 30 minutes.

a. Is the correlation between the time the candle is lit and the height of the candle positive or negative?

b. In how many hours will the candle burn out? Support your answer with a **reason**.

6-117. Write the expression as shown on the expression mats, then simplify by making zeros and combining like terms.

a.
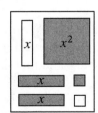

b.

6-118. Whole pizzas are described by the length of their diameters. For example, a 12-inch pizza has a diameter of 12 inches.

Stan the Pizza Man told a customer that a 12" medium pizza costs $10 and an 18" large pizza costs $16. Which pizza is the better deal for the customer (that is, which one costs less per square inch)? You may use a calculator, but you must show your work.

Making Connections: Course 2

6.2.6 Is there always a solution?

Cases With Infinite or No Solutions

Are all equations solvable? Are all solutions a single number? Think about this: Annika was born first and her brother William was born 4 years later. How old will William be when Annika is twice his age? How old will William be when Annika is exactly the same as his age?

In this lesson you will continue to practice your **strategies** of combining like terms, removing zeros and balancing to simplify and compare two expressions, but you will encounter unusual situations where the solution may be unexpected. As you work today, focus with your team on these questions:

What if both sides are not equal?

Are there many values of x that will make the expressions equal?

Is there always a solution?

6-119. Many students believe that every equation has only one solution. However, in the introduction to this lesson you might have noticed that if Annika was four years older than her brother, William, they could never be the same age. There are sometimes situations that have "one solution," or, "no solution," or "all numbers" as solutions.

For each of the following equations, **reason** with your team to decide if there is "One solution," "No solution," or "All numbers are solutions." If there is a single number solution, write it down. If you are not sure how many solutions there are, have each member of your team try a number to see if you can find a value that makes the equation work.

a. $x = x$

b. $x + 1 = x$

c. $x = 2x$

d. $x + x = 2 + x$

e. $x + x = x - x$

f. $x + x = 2x$

g. $x \cdot x = x^2$

h. $x - 1 = x$

6-120.   Use the 5-D Process to write an equation for the problem below. Then, answer the question.

Kelly is 6 years younger than her twin brothers Bailey and Larry. How old will Kelly be when the sum of their ages is 12 more than three times Kelly's?

6-121.   SPECIAL CASES – Part One

Use the equation $8 + x + (-5) = (-4) + x + 7$ to complete parts (a) through (c).

a.   Build the equation on your Equation Mat and simplify it as much as possible. Record your steps and what you see when you have simplified the equation fully. Draw a picture of your final mat.

b.   Have each member of your team test a different value for x in the original equation, such as $x = 0$, $x = 1$, $x = -5$, $x = 10$, etc. What happens in each case?

c.   Are there any solutions to this equation? If so, how many?

6-122.   SPECIAL CASES – Part Two

Use the equation $x + x + 2 = 2x$ to complete parts (a) through (c).

a.   Build the equation on your Equation Mat and simplify it as much as possible. Record your steps and what you see when you have simplified the equation fully. Draw a picture of your final mat.

b.   Have each member of your team test a different value for x in the equation, such as $x = 0$, $x = 1$, $x = -5$, $x = 10$, etc. What happens? Is there a pattern to the results you get from the equation?

c.   Did you find any values for x that satisfied the equation in part (a)? When there is an imbalance of units left on the mat (such as $2 = 0$), what does this mean? Is $x = 0$ a solution to the equation?

6-123.   Keeping these special cases in mind, continue to develop your equation solving
         strategies by visualizing and solving each equation below. Remember to build
         each equation on your mat, simplify as much as possible, and solve for x.
         Identify whether one number is the solution, any number is the solution, or there
         is no solution. Record your steps.

    a. $-x + 2 = 4$ b. $-3 + x = 2(x + 3)$

    c. $5x + 3 + (-x) = 2x + 1 + 2x + 3$ d. $3x + 7 + (-x) + -2 = 2x + 5$

    e. $4 + -3x = 2$ f. $3x + 3 = 4 + x + (-1)$

METHODS AND **M**EANINGS

Solutions to an Equation With One Variable

A **solution** to an equation gives the
value(s) of the variable that makes the equation
true. For example, when 5 is substituted for x in
the equation at right, both sides of the equation
are equal. So $x = 5$ is a solution to this equation.
Some equations have several solutions, such as
$x^2 = 25$, where $x = 5$ or -5.

$$4x - 1 = 2x + 9$$
$$4(5) - 1 = 2(5) + 9$$
$$19 = 19$$

Equations may also have no solution or an infinite
(unlimited) number of solutions.

Notice that no matter what the value of x is, the
left side of the first equation will never equal the
right side. Therefore, we say that $x + 2 = x + 3$ has
no solution.

Equation with no
solution:
$$x + 2 = x + 3$$
$$2 \neq 3$$

However, in the equation $x - 2 = x - 2$, no matter
what value x has, the equation will always be
true. So all numbers can make $x - 2 = x - 2$ true.
Therefore, we say the solution for the equation
$x - 2 = x - 2$ is **all numbers**.

Equation with
infinitely many
solutions:
$$x - 2 = x - 2$$

MATH NOTES

6-124. Copy and simplify the following expressions by combining like terms, making zeros, and using the Distributive Property. Using algebra tiles may be helpful.

a. $(-1) + 4x + 2 + 2x + x$

b. $-8x + 4 + (-3) + 10x$

c. $(-4) + 1x^2 + 3x + 4$

d. $2(3x - 2)$

6-125. Simplify and solve each equation below for x. Show your work and record your final answer.

a. $24 = 3x + 3$

b. $12 + x = 2x - 2$

6-126. Consider the following table.

x	-3	0.5	0	2	4
y	9	2	3	-1	-5

a. What is the rule for the table?

b. Explain your **strategy** for finding the rule for this table.

6-127. Show the "check" for each of these problems and write whether the solution is correct or incorrect.

a. For $3x + 2 = x - 2$, does $x = 0$?

b. For $3(x - 2) = 30 + x - 2 - x + 2$, does $x = 12$?

6-128. Some steps in solving an equation are more efficient than others. Complete parts (a) through (d) to determine the most efficient first step to solve the equation $34 = 5x - 21$.

a. If both sides of the equation were divided by 5, then the equation would be $\frac{34}{5} = x - \frac{21}{5}$. Does this make the problem simpler? Why or why not?

b. If we subtract 34 from both sides, the equation becomes $0 = 5x - 55$. Does this make the equation simpler to solve? Why or why not?

c. If we add 21 to both sides, the equation becomes $55 = 5x$. Does this suggestion make this a problem you can solve more easily? Why or why not?

d. All three suggestions are legal moves, but which method will lead to the most efficient solution? Why?

Making Connections: Course 2

6.2.7 Which method should I use?

Choosing a Solving Strategy

The 5-D Process and algebra tiles are useful tools for solving problems. Today you will practice writing equations from word problems and solving them using any of the tools you know. We are developing an efficient set of tools to solve any word problem. Having a variety of methods will allow you to choose the one that makes sense to you and ultimately makes you a more powerful mathematician.

6-129. Nick tried to use the symbolic **visualization** shortcut for $3x - 6 = 27$, but may have made a mistake. His work is shown at right. If he did, on which step did he first make a mistake and what was his mistake? If he did not make a mistake, check his solution and write "all correct."

$$3x \boxed{-6} = 27$$
$$\boxed{+6} = +6$$
$$\frac{3x}{3} = \frac{33}{3}$$
$$x = 11$$

6-130. Nick represented the equation $3(2x + 4) = -6$ on the Equation Mat at right.

a. Choose a strategy to solve for x. You may continue to use algebra tiles or may use numbers and variables.

b. Check your answer. If your answer does not make the equation true, try solving the equation using a different strategy.

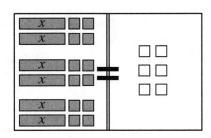

Chapter 6: Graphing and Solving Equations

6-131.   Read the problem below, then answer the questions
         in parts (a) and (b).

Cisco and Misty need to construct a chicken coop
for their famous egg-laying hens. The hens need at
least 108 square feet of living space. The space
available allows Cisco and Misty to make the
length of the coop 3 feet longer than the width and
to create exactly 108 square feet of area. What are
the dimensions of the coop?

   a.   Laura tried to use an Equation Mat for this problem but got stuck and
        decided to use a different **strategy**. Why do you think she decided not to
        use the Equation Mat?

   b.   Choose a different method, such as the 5-D Process or writing and solving
        an equation to solve this problem. Even if you solve an equation and do
        not use the chart from the 5-D Process, you still need to define how you
        are using variables and remember to write a sentence answer. Check your
        answer.

6-132.   Here is a problem started in a 5-D table.

         Describe/Draw:

         We want to find the side lengths so the perimeter is 35.

	Define			Do	Decide
	Side 1	Side 2	Side 3	Perimeter	Target: 35 ft
Trial 1	5	$5+2=7$	$7+4=11$	$5+7+11=23$	23 *Too small*
	x	$x+2$	$(x+2)+4$	$x+(x+2)+(x+2+4)=35$	

   a.   Write the word problem that could have accompanied this 5-D table.

   b.   What is your preferred method to solve this problem: algebra tiles, an
        equation, or the 5-D Process?

   c.   Decide on a method to solve this problem, use your method to find your
        answer, and write a Declare statement for your answer.

Making Connections: Course 2

6-133.   Apiologists (scientists who study bees) have
          found that the number and types of bees in a
          hive is based on the amount of nectar and
          pollen available. Within a hive there are
          three types of bees that help the queen.
          They are workers, drones, and nurses.

          In a recent study of a hive it was found that,
          not including the queen, there were a total of
          4,109 bees. There were thirty-three more
          nurses than drones. The number of workers
          was twelve more than six times the number
          of drones. How many of each type of bee
          was in the hive?

          Choose a method to solve this problem such as the 5-D Process or writing and
          solving an equation. Even if you solve an equation and do not use the chart
          from the 5-D Process, you still need to define how you are using variables and
          remember to Declare your answer in a sentence.

6-134.   Use any method to solve the following equations. Show your work.

          a. $3x + 4 = -5$ b. $3(x + 4) = -3$

          c. $3(x + 4) = x + 2(x + 6)$ d. $3x + 4 = 3x - 4$

Review & Preview

6-135.   Beth is filling a small backyard pool with a garden
          hose. The pool holds 300 gallons of water. After
          15 minutes the pool is about one-fourth full.

          a.   Assuming that the water is flowing at a
               constant rate, about how much water is going
               into the pool each minute?

          b.   About how long will it take to fill the pool?

6-136.   One way of thinking about solving equations is to work to get the variable terms on one side of the equation and the constants on the other side. Consider the equation $71 = 9x - 37$.

    a.   As a first step you could subtract 71 from both sides, or divide both sides by 9, or add 37 to both sides of the equation. Does one of these steps get all of the variable terms on one side of the equation and the constants on the other?

    b.   Solve $71 = 9x - 37$ for x. Show your steps.

6-137.   Make a table and a graph for the following rule: $y = 3x - 2$.

    a.   Explain how you know that there are more points than just the ones shown on your graph.

    b.   Where would the additional points go on the graph?

6-138.   For each equation below, solve for x. Sometimes the easiest **strategy** is to use mental math.

    a. $x - \frac{2}{3} = \frac{1}{3}$ b. $4x = 6$ c. $x + 4.6 = 12.96$ d. $\frac{x}{7} = \frac{3}{7}$

6-139.   Explain what the following graphs would look like. You may write your answer in words or sketch a graph.

    a.   Scatterplot with a negative correlation.

    b.   Scatterplot with no correlation.

    c.   Scatterplot with a positive correlation.

Chapter 6 Closure   What have I learned?

Reflection and Synthesis

The activities below offer you a chance to reflect about what you have learned during this chapter. As you work, look for concepts that you feel very comfortable with, ideas that you would like to learn more about, and topics with which you need more help. Look for connections between ideas as well as connections with material you learned previously.

①   SUMMARIZING MY UNDERSTANDING

In this chapter you have used algebra tiles and an equation mat as tools for solving equations, and you have represented your solution steps on an equation mat and with algebraic symbols. Today you will use what you have learned about equations in this chapter to show connections between all of these methods. To start, consider this problem:

Jamee is working to solve an equation. She did the work shown below. With your team, answer the following questions:

Jamee's work: Original problem: $3(2x-4) = 2(2x+5)$

                              Step 1: $6x-12 = 4x+10$

                              Step 2: $2x = -2$

- Explain what Jamee did at each step.

- What is her solution?

- Was her solution correct? **Justify** your answer. If it was not, find her error and the correct answer.

Problem continues on next page. →

①   *Problem continued from previous page.*

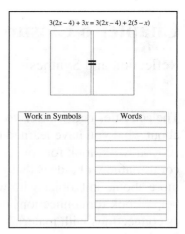

Obtain a Chapter 6 Closure Resource Page (shown at right) from your teacher. Follow the directions below to demonstrate your understanding of solving equations with an equation mat, algebraically (with numbers and symbols), and in words.

Part 1:   Sketch the equation on the mat on the resource page. You might also want to build it with algebra tiles.

Part 2:   Complete each step to solve the equation. Represent each step on the mat, in symbols, and in words. As you work, ask questions to clarify your thinking and understanding. Make sure you can give reasons for each step.

Part 3:   Color code the matching steps in each representation. For example, if your second step is to combine like terms, label this step with green in the symbols, on the mat, and in words. Use a new color to code each step.

②   WHAT HAVE I LEARNED?

Working the problems in this section will help you to evaluate which types of problems you feel comfortable with and which ones you need more help with.

Solve each problem as completely as you can. The table at the end of this closure section has answers to these problems. It also directs you to additional help and other similar practice problems.

CL 6-140. Ruthie did a survey among her classmates comparing the time spent playing video games to the time spent studying. The scatterplot of her data is shown at right.

a.   What correlation can you make from her data?

b.   Use an ordered pair (x, y) to identify any outliers.

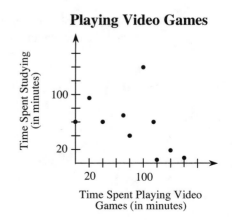

Playing Video Games

CL 6-141. Consider the equation mat at right.

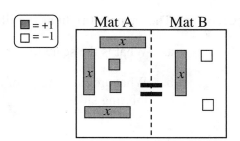

a. Write the original equation represented.

b. Simplify as needed. Record all steps of your work. What value of x will make the two sides equal?

c. Check your solution.

CL 6-142. Make a table with at least 6 entries and a graph for the following rule: $y = 3x - 5$.

a. If you added four more entries to your table and plotted the points, where would the points be on the graph?

b. Is there a limit to the number of points you could put in your table? Explain how you know.

CL 6-143. Find the area and perimeter or circumference of the following figures. Approximate π as 3.14.

a.

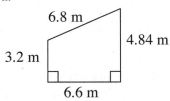

6.8 m

4.84 m

3.2 m

6.6 m

b.

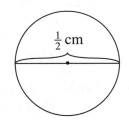

$\frac{1}{2}$ cm

CL 6-144. Write the expressions for the expression mats on the right.

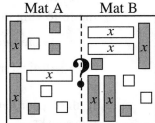

a. Simplify each mat to determine which side is greater.

b. If $x = 4$, would your answer to part (a) change? Explain.

CL 6-145. Serena found the spinner at the right. Help her find the value of the missing portion.

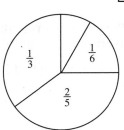

$\frac{1}{3}$

$\frac{1}{6}$

$\frac{2}{5}$

CL 6-146. The shapes at right are similar.

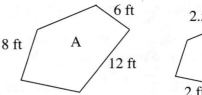

a. What is the scale factor?

b. What are the lengths of the missing sides?

CL 6-147. Solve this problem using the 5-D Process or writing and solving an equation. No matter which you method you use, be sure to define your variable and write an equation to represent the relationship.

A rectangle has a perimeter of 30 inches. Its length is one less than three times its width. What are the length and width of the rectangle?

CL 6-148. For each of the problems above, do the following:

- Draw a bar or number line that represents 0 to 10.

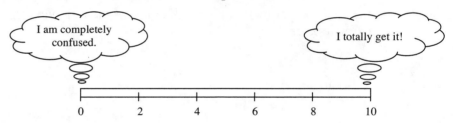

- Color or shade in a portion of the bar that represents your level of understanding and comfort with completing that problem on your own.

If any of your bars are less than a 5, choose *one* of those problems and do one of the following tasks:

- Write two questions that you would like to ask about that problem.

- Brainstorm two things that you DO know about that type of problem.

If all of your bars are a 5 or above, choose one of those problems and do one of these tasks:

- Write two questions you might ask or hints you might give to a student who was stuck on the problem.

- Make a new problem that is similar and more challenging than that problem and solve it.

③ WHAT TOOLS CAN I USE?

You have several tools and references available to help support your learning – your teacher, your study team, your math book, and your Toolkit, to name only a few. At the end of each chapter you will have an opportunity to review your Toolkit for completeness as well as to revise or update your Toolkit to better reflect your current understanding of big ideas.

The main elements of your Toolkit should be your Learning Log, Math Notes, and the vocabulary used in this chapter. Math words that are new appear in bold in the text. Refer to the lists provided below and follow your teacher's instructions to revise your Toolkit, which will help make it useful for you as you complete this chapter and as you work in future chapters.

Learning Log Entries
- Lesson 6.1.3 – Correlations
- Lesson 6.1.5 – Scatterplot and Linear Graph Predictions
- Extension Activity – Human Data Points
- Lesson 6.2.3 – Solving Equations and Finding Solutions
- Lesson 6.2.4 – Using the 5-D Process to Write and Solve Equations

Math Notes
- Lesson 6.1.1 – Special Quadrilaterals
- Lesson 6.1.2 – Circle Graphs
- Lesson 6.1.4 – Correlation and Trend Lines
- Lesson 6.1.5 – Making a Complete Graph
- Lesson 6.1.6 – When Is a Point on the Graph of a Rule?
- Lesson 6.2.1 – Using an Equation Mat
- Lesson 6.2.3 – Checking a Solution
- Lesson 6.2.4 – Defining a Variable
- Lesson 6.2.6 – Solutions to an Equation With One Variable

Mathematical Vocabulary

The following is a list of vocabulary found in this chapter. Some of the words have been seen in the previous chapter. The words in bold are the words new to this chapter. Make sure that you are familiar with the terms below and know what they mean. For the words you do not know, refer to the glossary or index. You might also want to add these words to your Toolkit for a way to reference them in the future.

circle graph	**Equation Mat**	**negative correlation**
no correlation	**outlier**	**positive correlation**
solution	scatterplot	**trend line**
x-intercept	*y*-intercept	

Process Words

The list of words below are problem solving strategies and processes that you have been involved in throughout the course of this chapter. Make sure you know what it means to use each of them. If you are not sure, look through your book for problems when you were asked to think in the following ways.

choose a strategy	compare	describe
explain your reasoning	generalize	justify
predict	reason	simplify
solve	test your prediction	visualize

Making Connections: Course 2

Answers and Support for Closure Activity #2
What Have I Learned?

Problem	Solution	Need Help?	More Practice
CL 6-140.	a. Negative: when the time playing video games increases, the time spent studying decreases. b. (100, 140)	Lessons 6.1.2, 6.1.3, and 6.1.4 Math Notes box in Lesson 6.1.4 Learning Logs (problems 6-26 and 6-47)	Problems 6-14, 6-15, 6-24, 6-25, 6-26, and 6-49
CL 6-141.	a. $3x + 2 = x - 2$ b. $x = -2$ c. $3(-2) + 2 = -2 - 2$ $-6 + 2 = -4$ $-2 = -2$	Lessons 6.2.1, 6.2.2, and 6.2.3 Math Notes boxes in Lessons 6.2.1, 6.2.3, and 6.2.6 Learning Log (problem 6-98)	Problems 6-75, 6-76, 6-77, 6-87, 6-89, 6-97, 6-99, 6-115, 6-125, 6-130, and 6-134
CL 6-142.	$\begin{array}{c\|c\|c\|c\|c\|c} x & 4 & -3 & 0.5 & 0 & 2 \\ \hline y & 7 & -14 & -3.5 & -5 & 1 \end{array}$ a. The points would follow the rule $y = 3x - 5$ and would fall on the same line. b. There are an infinite number of points possible, because we can choose any value for x.	Lessons 6.1.2, through 6.1.6 Math Notes boxes in Lessons 6.1.5 and 6.1.6 Learning Log (problem 6-47)	Problems 6-37, 6-43, 6-48, 6-56, 6-59, 6-114, and 6-137
CL 6-143.	a. $A = 26.532 \text{ m}^2$, $P = 21.44 \text{ m}$ b. $A \approx 0.196 \text{ cm}^2$, $C \approx 1.571 \text{ cm}$	Lessons 2.3.2, 2.3.5, 5.3.3, and 5.3.4 Math Notes box in Lesson 5.3.4 Learning Logs (problems 2-150 and 5-124)	Problems CL 2-163, CL 3-111, CL 4-116, 5-127, 5-129, and 6-11

Problem	Solution	Need Help?	More Practice
CL 6-144.	a. $x = x$, The mats are equal in value. b. No, the mats will be equal for any value of x.	Lessons 5.2.1, 5.2.2, and 6.2.1 through 6.2.6 Math Notes boxes in Lessons 5.1.2, 6.2.1, 6.2.3, and 6.2.6 Learning Log (problem 5-54)	Problems CL 5-134, CL 5-136, 6-38, 6-74, 6-75, 6-76, 6-78, and 6-117
CL 6-145.	$\frac{1}{10}$	Lessons 1.2.4 and 1.2.5 Math Notes box in Lesson 1.2.4 Learning Log (problem 1-107)	Problems CL 1-140, CL 2-160, CL 3-114, 4-45, and 5-12
CL 6-146.	a. Multiply by $\frac{1}{4}$ (or you can divide by 4 moving from shape A to shape B or multiply by 4 moving from shape B to shape A). b. On Shape A, the missing sides are 10 and 8 units; on shape B, the missing sides are 2 and 1.5 units.	Lessons 4.3.1 through 4.3.4 Math Notes boxes in Lessons 4.3.1 and 4.3.4 Learning Log (problem 4-76)	Problems CL 4-119, 5-10, 5-48, and 6-109
CL 6-147.	The length is 4 in and the width is 11 in. If x = width, one possible equation would be $x + (3x - 1) + x + (3x - 1) = 30$.	Lessons 3.2.3, 3.2.4, 3.2.5, 5.1.2, 5.1.3, 6.2.5, and 6.2.7 Math Notes boxes in Lessons 3.2.3 and 5.1.2 Learning Log (problems 5-32 and 6-107)	Problems CL 5-135, 6-97, 6-105, 6-113, 6-131, 6-132, and 6-133

404

Making Connections: Course 2

Puzzle Investigator Problems

PI-11. GRAPHING MADNESS

On graph paper starting at (0, 0), carry out the following moves:

Move Number	Directions
1	Right 1 unit
2	Up 2 units
3	Left 3 units
4	Down 4 units
5	Right 5 units

Continue moving counter clockwise using this pattern, increasing the length 1 unit each move.

a. What patterns can you find in the figure on the graph? For example, find the coordinates of each point in the design. How are the coordinates changing? How is the quadrant where each point is located changing with the addition of each new point?

b. In which quadrant will the 79th move land? What will be the coordinates` of this point? Explain how you can find your answer without listing 79 moves.

c. For **any** move, name which quadrant it will be in and what its coordinates will be. Explain the method you are using.

PI-12.   CONSECUTIVE SUMS

A consecutive sum is an addition sequence of consecutive whole numbers.

Examples: $2 + 3$

$8 + 9 + 10 + 11 + 12 + 13$

$7 + 8 + 9 + 10$

a.   Write the first 35 counting numbers (1 through 35) with as many consecutive sums as possible. The number 15 can be written as $7 + 8$ or $4 + 5 + 6$ or $1 + 2 + 3 + 4 + 5$. Make sure you organize your work in order to find patterns.

b.   Describe as many patterns as you find. For example, are there any numbers that have no consecutive sums? Which numbers can be written as a sum of two consecutive numbers? Which can be written as a sum of three consecutive numbers?

c.   Ernie noticed a pattern with the numbers that can be written as a sum of three consecutive numbers. He wants to understand why the pattern works. He thinks it might help to represent the consecutive numbers as x, $x + 1$, and $x + 2$.

   i.   Why do these expressions represent consecutive numbers?

   ii.   Find the sum of x, $x + 1$, and $x + 2$. How does this sum help make sense of the pattern?

Slopes and Rates of Change

CHAPTER 7   Slopes and Rates of Change

In Japan, speed limit signs on the highway say, "Speed Limit 100." Does this mean people in Japan are allowed to drive faster than people in the United States? In Section 7.1, you will explore questions involving rate, as well as look at how to find unit rates in order to make comparisons. You will examine races called "triathlons" to discover when rates are be the same and also different. You will also explore rate through the concept of slope, a measure of the steepness of lines, and examine multiple representations of slope such as situations, tables, and graphs.

In Section 7.2, you will explore new situations to consider when expressions are the same, called systems of equations. You will use some of the events at a county fair to practice working with systems of equations and use what you have learned about expressions to help solve them.

In this chapter, you will learn how to:

➢ Calculate rates, including unit rates.

➢ Compare ratios and rates with different units.

➢ Measure the steepness of a line using slope.

➢ Compare equations to determine when they have the same solution.

Guiding Questions

Think about these questions throughout this chapter:

What is being compared?

What does the comparison tell me?

How else can I represent it?

How can I find the solutions?

When are the solutions the same?

Chapter Outline

Section 7.1 You will compare ratios and rates using different representations including numbers, tables, and graphs. You will learn ways to rewrite ratios so that they can be compared more easily, and you will find out how to measure the steepness of a line on a graph.

Section 7.2 You will evaluate information from different expressions on graphs, in tables, and in words. You will learn how to compare and solve equations to determine when the solution is the same for more than one equation.

7.1.1 How can I compare rates?

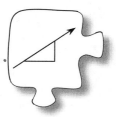

Comparing Rates

Whenever you are trying to describe how fast or slow something occurs, you are describing a **rate**. However, to describe a rate, you need to provide two pieces of information. For example, if two people each walk 10 miles, it may seem like they are doing the same thing. But if you find out that one person walked the whole distance in 3 hours, while another person took 8 hours, then it becomes clear that they were traveling at different speeds. In this lesson you will be describing how things change in comparison to each other.

7-1. The seventh graders at Shasta Middle School are planning a class trip to Washington, D.C. They need to raise enough money for all 140 seventh graders to travel, so they have a lot of work to do! The class officers have collected the data below about different kinds of fundraisers. They want your help in choosing a fundraising activity.

Type of Fundraiser	Time	Expected Profit
Cookie sales	3 weeks	$500
Car washes	4 weeks	$700
Recycling	$\frac{3}{5}$ week	$85
Yardwork	2 weeks	$320

a. How much will the class earn if they spend 6 weeks doing yardwork? How much will they earn if they spend six weeks having car washes? Be prepared to explain your **reasoning**.

b. How much money would the class earn if it recycled bottles and cans during the next 3 weeks of school?

7-2.   MAKING MONEY

The class president has decided that
the students will either sell cookies
or hold car washes. The rest of the
officers need your help to compare
the profit from cookie sales to the
profit from car washes.

Your task: Discuss with your team ways that you could compare the two
fundraising **strategies** to recommend which one to use. Use the data in problem
7-1 and the questions below to start your discussion. Then write a note to the
class officers recommending which fundraising activity they should do. Be sure
to **justify** your recommendation with details about rates.

Discussion Points

What can we compare?

Which fundraising activity raises money faster? Which raises money slower?

Further Guidance

7-3.   Isabelle decided to see how long it would take to earn $5000 with each kind of
fundraiser.

  a.   For how many weeks would the class need to sell cookies in order to earn
       $5000?

  b.   For how many weeks would the class need to have car washes to earn
       $5000?

  c.   How can this help Isabelle decide which way will earn more money?

7-4.   Liam thinks that the class could earn $175 each week by washing cars.

  a.   Is this **reasonable**? How could he have figured out this amount? Discuss
       his claim with your team and record your ideas.

  b.   How much could the class earn during one week of cookie sales? Show
       your work.

7-5.   Nicolette decided to see what the class could earn from each activity in the same number of weeks. She decided to see how much they could earn in 12 weeks.

    a.   Why do you think Nicolette chose 12 weeks?

    b.   How much could they earn from each activity in 12 weeks?

    c.   Write a pair of equivalent ratios for each of the relationships in parts (a) and (b) above.

7-6.   Which fundraising activity raises money the fastest: selling cookies or washing cars? Write a note to the class officers recommending the fastest fundraising activity. Be sure to **justify** your recommendation with how you know it will raise money the fastest.

Further Guidance section ends here.

7-7.   The eighth grade class was also looking at the data from problem 7-1. They had information about another fundraiser: they could earn $65 every two days selling lemonade. Assume all of the fundraising activities happen only on school days, and that there are 5 days in a school week.

    a.   Which activity will raise money faster: selling lemonade or selling cookies? The rate for selling cookies was $500 every 3 weeks. Be sure to **justify** your answer.

    b.   Trinh described the profit from lemonade sales as earning at a **rate** of "$325 in two weeks." A **rate** is a measure of how one quantity changes in comparison to another.

    Is Trinh's rate of $\frac{\$325}{2 \text{ weeks}}$ the same as earning money at a rate of $\frac{\$65}{2 \text{ days}}$? Why or why not?

7-8.   Eliza is saving her allowance to buy a new computer so she can email her pen
        pals around the world. She currently saves $45 every 4 weeks.

   a.   If her brother saves $39 every 3 weeks, who saves at a faster rate? Explain
        your **reasoning**.

   b.   Instead of using dollars and cents, money in Armenia is called "drams."
        One American dollar is worth the same as 360 drams. Eliza's pen pal in
        Armenia saves 2880 drams from her allowance every week. Work with
        your team to determine who is saving money faster, Eliza or her pen pal.
        Explain your **reasoning**.

   c.   Eliza's pen pal in Laos is also saving money. He is saving 17000 kips
        (Laotian money) per week. Can you determine who is saving at a faster
        rate? Determine the rate or write a question that you would need answered
        in order to determine it.

Review & Preview

7-9.   Solve the equations below for the variable. Be sure to check your answer.

   a. $3(2x-1)+2=5x$ b. $600x+200=500x$

7-10.   Adam earns $36 for every four hours of work. If he continues to be paid at the
        same rate:

   a.   How long will it take him to earn $144? Show and explain your **reasoning**.

   b.   How long will it take him to earn $222? Show and explain your **reasoning**.

   c.   How could you describe his rate for a 40-hour work week? For an 8-hour
        day? Show and explain your **reasoning**.

7-11.   A college has a 2:3 ratio of men to women in its
        student body.

   a.   What is the ratio of women to men?

   b.   What is the ratio of women to total students?

   c.   What percent of the college is men?

   d.   What fraction of the college is women?

7-12.   Complete the table below by following the rule $y = 10 - 2x$. Then graph the relationship on graph paper.

x	−3	−2	−1	0	1	2	3	4
y								

7-13.   Use $<$, $>$, or $=$ to compare the number pairs below.

a.   0.183 _____ 0.18

b.   −13 _____ −17

c.   0.125 _____ $\frac{1}{8}$

d.   −6 _____ −4

e.   72% _____ $\frac{35}{30}$

f.   −0.25 _____ −0.05

7.1.2   How can I find the rate?

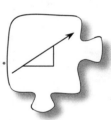

Comparing Rates with Graphs and Tables

Rates are used in many situations to describe and compare information. When purchasing a car you might compare the gas mileage of vehicles, that is, how many miles each car can travel per gallon of gas. When determining the print quality of a printer the number of dots per square inch is important. The percent of interest earned per dollar, or interest rate, is important when saving money in a bank.

Today you will focus on different ways to display rates in tables and graphs as a way to compare information. As you work with your team, ask each other these questions:

Which quantities can we compare?

Are the ratios equivalent?

How else can the ratio be expressed?

7-14.   The local news station is selecting this week's female student for "Athlete of the Week." Wendy and Yoshie, sprinters on the track team, are both finalists and they are trying to decide who is fastest based on recent race data. Wendy's times are represented in the table at right.

Yoshie can run 70 meters in 11 seconds, which can be expressed by the rate $\frac{70 \text{ meters}}{11 \text{ seconds}}$.

Wendy's Data

Time (seconds)	Distance (meters)
5	30
10	60
15	90
25	
35	210
45	
55	330
x	

a.   Copy the table and use the relationship to complete the table for Wendy. How can you use the table to find Wendy's running rate?

b.   Based on the information in the table, are the two runners traveling at the same speed? How can you tell? Explain your **reasoning**.

c.   To compare the two runners, the news station made a graph of the two runners' rates. Identify points (time, distance) on the graph at right and determine which line represents each runner. Based on the graph, who is running faster? **Justify** your answer.

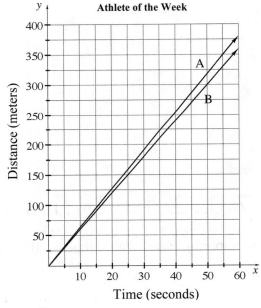

d.   Use the same graph to find two additional data points (time, distance) for each runner.

e.   The graph at right shows information for Vanessa, last week's Athlete of the Week. What is Vanessa's rate? If she were to race Yoshie and Wendy, who would win?

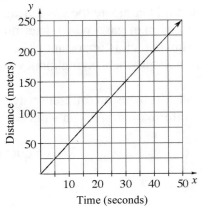

7-15.   TRAINING FOR THE TRIATHLON

A triathlon is a race where participants swim, bike, and run specific distances. Participants start by swimming, then jump out of the water, get dressed as fast as they can, and ride a bicycle. After they complete the biking section, the participants finish the race by running several miles.

Diane has been taking swimming lessons, riding her bike, and running to prepare for her first triathlon. She used the graph at right to analyze one of her practice sessions. Use the graph on the Lesson 7.1.2 Resource Page to help you answer the questions below.

a.   During which segment of the race (a, b, or c) did Diane go the fastest? Explain your **reasoning**.

b.   Use the graph to determine the distance traveled during each segment of the race.

c.   How much time did it take Diane to complete each segment of the race?

d.   Write a rate (in miles per minute) for each segment of the race.

e.   How can you show a rate on a graph? Work with your team to find a way to show the rates from part (d) on the resource page.

7-16.   Edgar is training to be on the high school cross-country running team. Edgar has training runs that are two different lengths. One trail is 4 miles, and he usually completes that run in 0.5 hours (30 minutes). If he runs the 10 mile trail, it usually takes him 1.25 hours (75 minutes).

a.   Graph points for the length and time of Edgar's run on a graph. Does it make sense to connect the points? Where could you add a point to show how far he has traveled after 0 minutes?

b.   Helena is a long-distance runner. Once a week she does a 16-mile training run that usually takes her 2 hours. Does she run slower or faster than Edgar? How do you know?

7-17.   Match each situation in parts (a) through (d) with its graph below, and state the rate in miles per minute.

   a.   Family A travels 30 miles in 25 minutes.

   b.   Family B travels 60 miles in an hour.

   c.   Family C travels 50 miles in an hour.

   d.   Family D travels 60 miles in $1\frac{1}{2}$ hours.

   e.   One graph below was not matched with a situation from parts (a) through (d). Describe the rate of travel for Family E if they are represented by the unmatched graph.

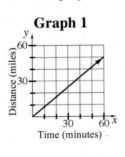

Graph 1

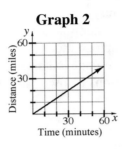

Graph 2

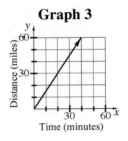

Graph 3

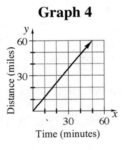

Graph 4

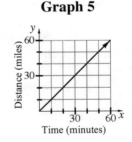

Graph 5

Review & Preview

7-18.   Beth and Amy are racing to see who can ride a tricycle the fastest.

   a.   Graph the data about Beth's travel that is recorded in the table at right.

Time (sec)	5	10	15	20
Distance (ft)	11	22	33	44

   b.   What is Beth's rate of travel?

   c.   If Amy travels at a rate of 75 feet per 30 seconds, would the line representing her distance and time be steeper or less steep than the graph of Beth's rate? Explain your **reasoning**.

Making Connections: Course 2

7-19.   Write an equation to represent the situation below and answer the question. You may use the 5-D Process to help you.

Andrew just opened a new office supply store. He has been keeping track of how many customers visit his store. During his second week, he had 18 more customers than he did the first week. The third week, he had four less than twice as many customers as he had during the second week. In his fourth week of business he had 92 customers. If he had 382 customers in total during his first four weeks of business, how many customers did he have during the second week?

7-20.   For each equation below, solve for x. Sometimes the easiest **strategy** is to use mental math.

a. $x - \frac{3}{5} = 1\frac{2}{5}$

b. $5.2 + x = 10.95$

c. $2x - 3.25 = 7.15$

d. $\frac{x}{16} = \frac{3}{8}$

7-21.   Simplify each expression.

a. $-\frac{9}{5} \cdot \frac{8}{15}$

b. $\frac{1}{5} + (-\frac{2}{15}) - (-\frac{4}{9})$

c. $-\frac{4}{8} \cdot \frac{3}{7} \cdot (-\frac{2}{5})$

d. $\frac{3}{5} \cdot (-\frac{2}{7}) + (-\frac{5}{7})(\frac{3}{10})$

e. $-8\frac{1}{9} + 3\frac{5}{6}$

f. $2\frac{1}{2} \cdot 4\frac{1}{5}$

7-22.   In one week the museum had attendance as shown in the table at right.

a.   Find the mean, the median, and mode for the daily attendance.

b.   The museum management needs to tell the staff their work schedule a week in advance. The museum wants to have approximately one staff member for every 150 visitors. How many staff members should be scheduled to work each week? Explain your **reasoning**.

Day	Attendance
1	870
2	940
3	731
4	400
5	861
6	680
7	593

7.1.3 How can I find the rate?

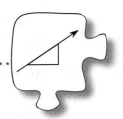

Unit Rates

News reports use rates to provide important information. For example, when there is a sudden heavy rain, reporting the rate at which the local river is rising gives people a sense of how quickly it might flood. Sometimes rates are reported in words, such as *"The pitcher struck out the batter after throwing the ball 92 miles per hour."* Other times the rate is provided in a graph or a table, such as the price of food over time or how rapidly a disease is spreading.

Today your team will develop **strategies** to find a rate in new contexts using tables and graphs.

7-23.   MAXIMUM MILES

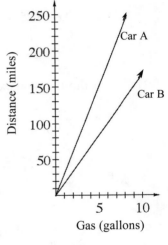

The graph at right compares how many miles are traveled to how many gallons of gas are used for two different cars. Use the Lesson 7.1.3 Resource Page or copy the graph at right on graph paper and answer the following questions.

a.   Which car can travel the farthest on 5 gallons of gas? Which one travels the shortest distance using 5 gallons of gas? How is this found on the graph?

b.   Does car A travel the same number of miles with every gallon of gas? How can you tell?

c.   A third car (Car C) uses 6 gallons of gas to travel 120 miles. Make a table for the car listing at least four equivalent ratios of gallons and miles, and add those points to the graph.

d.   Manufacturers often advertise the miles per gallon, or mpg, for the cars they make. This measurement is a **unit rate**, because it is the mileage for one gallon (unit) of gasoline. Calculate the unit rate (mpg) for each car. List cars in order from highest mpg to lowest.

e.   How can the graph help us compare the miles per gallon of the different cars? List the cars in order from the one with the steepest line to the one with the least steep line. Which car goes farthest for each gallon of gas it uses?

f.   How can you use the graph to figure out which car has the best gas mileage (the highest number of miles per gallon)?

Making Connections: Course 2

7-24. Tamika and Lois like to knit and have decided to knit a scarf using the same pattern. Tamika started knitting the scarf last week, but Lois is just starting now. The tables at right show information about the number of inches of scarf knitted per hour after Lois joins Tamika.

Tamika		Lois	
Time (in hours)	Length (in inches)	Time (in hours)	Length (in inches)
0	5	0	
1	7	1	
2	9	2	
3		3	
x		x	$3x$

a. Copy and complete each table to show the amount of time each girl has been knitting and the number of inches that have been knitted.

b. At what rate does Tamika knit? How can you use the table to find her rate?

c. At what rate does Lois knit? Explain how you found your answer.

d. If you graphed the data (so that x is the number of hours and y is the number of inches) for both Tamika and Lois on the same graph, which line would appear steeper? Explain why it would be steeper.

7-25. Olivia was curious about how fast she knits. She decided to measure how much she could knit in 10 hours. She already had a scarf started and recorded her data in the table at right.

Olivia	
Time (in hours)	Length (in inches)
0	12
10	67

If Olivia knits at a constant rate, what is Olivia's knitting speed in inches per hour? Discuss with your team and be prepared to explain your **reasoning**.

7-26. A wheel for a Wheel of Winning game makes one revolution in 4 seconds. What is the unit rate in terms of revolutions per minute? Use diagrams or words to explain your **reasoning**.

7-27.   LEARNING LOG

Think about what you have learned so far about rate.
Write a Learning Log entry that explains how to find a
rate from a table. How can you compare rates using a
graph? Be sure to include an example. Title this entry
"Rates, Tables, and Graphs" and include today's date.

MᴇTHODS AND MᴇANINGS

MATH NOTES

Rate of Change and Unit Rates

In Lesson 7.1.1, you learned that a **rate of change** is a ratio that
compares the amount one quantity changes as another quantity changes
by division.

$$\text{rate of change} = \frac{\text{change in one quantity}}{\text{change in another quantity}}$$

A **unit rate** is a rate that compares the change in one quantity to a
1-unit change in another quantity. For example, *miles per hour* is a
unit rate, because it compares the change in miles to a change of
1 hour. If an airplane flies 3000 miles in 5 hours and uses 6000
gallons of fuel, we can compute several unit rates.

It uses $\frac{6000 \text{ gallons}}{5 \text{ hours}} = 1200 \frac{\text{gallons}}{\text{hour}}$ or $\frac{6000 \text{ gallons}}{3000 \text{ miles}} = 2 \frac{\text{gallons}}{\text{mile}}$ and it travels at

$\frac{3000 \text{ miles}}{5 \text{ hours}} = 600 \frac{\text{miles}}{\text{hour}}$.

Review & Preview

7-28.   Which company offers the lowest unit rate per minute? Show how you decided.

Company	Price	# of minutes
AB & C	$19.95	100
Berizon	$24.95	150
Cinguling	$9.95	60
DWest	$14.75	100

Making Connections: Course 2

7-29.   The graph at right shows the cost per pound
         of strawberries at four different stores.

         a.   At which store are strawberries about
              $2 per pound?

         b.   What is the rate of cost of strawberries
              at store B?

         c.   Which store has the most expensive
              strawberries? How can you tell?

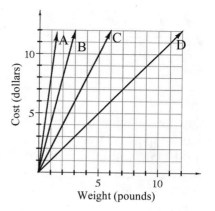

7-30.   Solve the following equations using any method. Show your work and check
         your solution.

         a. $2x + 16 = 5x + 4$ b. $3x - 5 = 2x + 14$ c. $5x - 5 = x + 15$

7-31.   Felipe knew that he was 60 inches tall
         and that his sister Maria was 5 feet tall.

         Felipe said, *"Hey, I'm 12 times as tall
         as you, since 5 times 12 equals 60."* At
         first, Maria was puzzled, but then she
         said, *"That's not true, and I know why."*

         Explain in a complete sentence what Maria realized.

7-32.   Look at the similar shapes shown at right.

         a.   What is the scale factor from shape A
              to shape B?

         b.   Find the lengths of the missing sides.

         c.   Sketch a new shape C that is similar to shape A and has a scale factor of 1.
              What do you know about the measures of the angles and sides on this new
              shape? Label them on your picture.

         d.   When two shapes are similar and have a scale factor of one, what are they
              called?

7.1.4 How does y change with respect to x?

Slope

Can you imagine swimming 1.5 km (just less than a mile), getting dressed as fast as you can, hopping on a bicycle to race 40 km (almost 25 miles), then getting off your bike to run 10 km (just more than 6 miles)? Athletes who compete in Olympic distance triathlons do exactly that! In the 2008 Summer Olympic Games, Jan Frodeno of Germany won the gold medal by finishing the triathlon in 1 hour, 48 minutes and 53.28 seconds. Frodeno did not finish the swimming section in first place, though. In fact, he was not even one of the first ten people to finish that part of the race. While Frodeno may not have been the fastest swimmer, what mattered most was his overall rate.

As you compare rates today, you will learn a new way to describe the rate of change of a line called **slope**. As you investigate rates of change, use the following questions to focus mathematical discussions with your team:

How can I use the graph to figure out which racer is faster?

How can we find the unit rate for each racer?

What if the line does not pass through $(0,0)$?

7-33.   BIKING THE TRIATHLON

The second part of the triathlon is a bicycle race. Since participants do not start the bicycle race until they complete the swimming portion, the bicyclists have varying starting times.

The graph at right shows information about four bicyclists during a 20-minute portion of a race.

a.   Based on the graph, list the bicyclists from slowest to fastest. How can you tell?

Problem continues on next page. →

422

Making Connections: Course 2

7-33.   *Problem continued from previous page.*

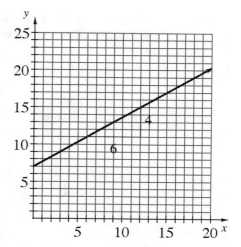

b. Lydia wants to describe each bicyclist's rate as a number of kilometers per minute for an article in the school paper. To do this, she sketched triangles like the one for line A on the graph at right.

Where do the 4 and 6 come from on Racer A's triangle? What do they represent?

c. These numbers can be written as a rate to describe the distance the bicyclist rides as time passes. The fraction $\frac{4}{6}$ represents how the graph of the line goes up 4 units for every 6 units that it moves to the right. The number $\frac{4}{6}$ is called the **slope** of the line.

On the Lesson 7.1.3 Resource Page, find the slope of each of the other three lines.

d. Did the slopes in part (c) confirm your ranking from slowest to fastest in part (a)? If not, review your slopes and your comparison of rates based on the graph to find any mistakes.

7-34.   While comparing the rates from problem 7-33, a study team is struggling to decide how to tell which athlete is moving faster.

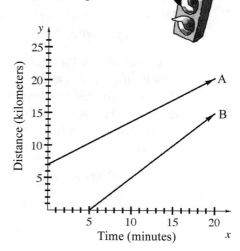

• Leo thinks that because athlete A's line is highest on the graph, he is traveling faster.

• Linda disagrees. *"He starts first, but racer B is moving faster."*

Which person do you agree with? Look at the graph of bicyclists A and B at right and discuss this with your team. Be prepared to explain your **reasoning** to the class.

7-35.   Mr. Regnier's class has been struck with hiccups! Three of the students track
         their number of hiccups over time. Assume each student hiccups at a constant
         rate.

Student I

Time (in min)	Number of Hiccups
2	8
4	16
7	28

Student II

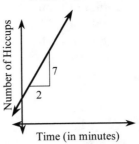

Student III

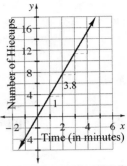

a.   Which student has the most hiccups per minute?
     Justify your answer.

b.   Find the slope that describes the rate of hiccups
     for each student. What does the slope tell you
     about each student?

c.   If you graphed a line for the student who hiccups 4 times per minute, would
     the line be steeper, less steep, or the same steepness as the line in the graph
     for Student II? Explain your **reasoning**.

7-36.   **Additional Challenge:** CHANGING LINES

         Lupe is a manager of an assembly line at a
         manufacturing company that makes cars.
         The speed at which the cars are usually
         built is represented by the graph at right.

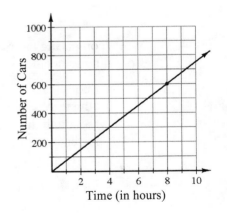

         Lupe has decided to increase the number of
         cars built each day and has written
         directions for her employees. Which of her
         directions below would increase the
         number of cars built each day? Explain
         how you know.

a.   Build 200 cars every 4 hours.

b.   Build 75 cars every hour.

c.   Build 500 cars every 5 hours.

d.   Decrease the time it takes to make each car.

Making Connections: Course 2

7-37. Compare the graphs of lines A, B, and C at right.

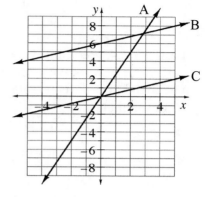

a. Which line has the greatest slope? **Justify** your answer.

b. What is the *y*-value of line A when $x = 2$?

c. Compare the slopes of lines B and C.

7-38. Lydia drew a graph of four athletes in the final part of the triathlon, the 10 km run. She found the slope of each runner's line. Her results are listed below.

Runner A: slope $= \frac{2}{6}$ Runner B: slope $= \frac{3}{7}$

Runner C: slope $= \frac{5}{12}$ Runner D: slope $= \frac{4}{10}$

List the runners from slowest to fastest.

7-39. If a car is parked on the side of the road and not moving, what is its speed? What would it look like on a graph of time and distance?

7-40. Find the missing measure(s) of each circle.

a. diameter = ?
    circumference = ?

$r = 12$ cm

b. diameter = ?
    radius = ?

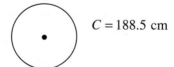

$C = 188.5$ cm

7-41. Write an equation to represent this problem and find the unknown side lengths. You may use the 5-D Process to help you organize your thinking and to define your variables.

A trapezoid has a perimeter of 117 cm. The two shortest sides have the same length. The third side is 12 cm longer than one short side. The final side is 9 cm less than three times one short side. How long is each side of the trapezoid?

7.1.5 How can I find the slope ratio?

Slope in Different Representations

In Lesson 7.1.4, you learned about how to describe the steepness of a line with a number. Today, you will work with different representations of lines and look for how the slope can be found in each representation. As you work with your study team today, keep these questions in mind:

What is being compared to find the slope ratio?

What would it look like in another representation?

7-42. A planting manual printed the graphs below so that gardeners could predict the height of trees after planting. Jill wants to figure out how fast each tree will grow. She remembers that **slope** is a ratio of the vertical change to the horizontal change between any two points on a line. Finding the slope for each graph will allow her to compare the change in height to the change in time.

a. On a Lesson 7.1.5 Resource Page, draw and label a slope triangle on the line in graph (*i*). Then write the slope ratio. How fast does tree *i* grow?

b. Can you find the slope on graph (*ii*) just by looking at the line? Why or why not? When it is difficult to read the slope on a graph, look for points where the line appears to pass through **lattice points** (where the grid lines intersect). Then use those points to create a slope triangle and find the slope.

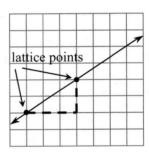

Slope Triangle

c. On the resource page, draw a slope triangle for lines (*iii*) and (*iv*) using lattice points. Then label each slope triangle with its dimensions and calculate the slope ratio.

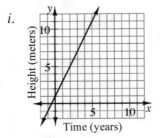

i.

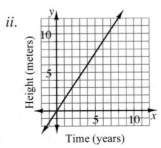

ii.

Problem continues on next page. →

Making Connections: Course 2

7-42. *Problem continued from previous page.*

iii.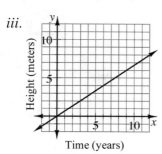

iv.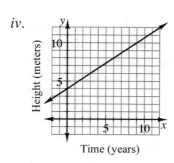

7-43. Three different students looked at the line graphed at right and each drew a different slope triangle as shown.

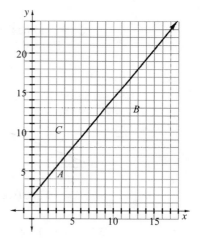

   a. Find each slope using the slope triangles on the Lesson 7.1.5 Resource Page.

   b. The numbers in the slope ratios found by the students are all different. Does this mean that the slope of the line changes depending on which points you pick? Discuss this with your team and be ready to share your **reasoning** with the rest of the class.

   c. Another student said her slope triangle goes up 20 units for every 16 units to the right. Where could her slope triangle be? Draw a possible slope triangle for this student.

   d. Simplify each of the four slope ratios and compare them. Describe what you find.

7-44.   IS SEEING BELIEVING?

Did you know that a bank will pay you
money (called **interest**) when you place
your money in a savings account? The
amount you receive is a portion of the
amount you deposit and the interest rate
often varies with each bank.

Thomas and Ryan have each invested the same amount of money in different
bank accounts that earn **simple interest**, which means the same amount of
interest is added each week. They decided to compare their earnings by
graphing how much interest each of them has earned over time, shown below.

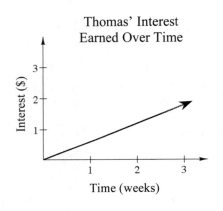

Thomas' Interest
Earned Over Time

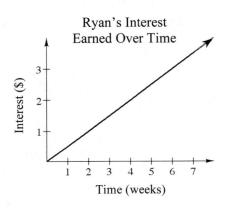

Ryan's Interest
Earned Over Time

a.   When you look at the graphs, which investment seems to be growing
      fastest? Explain how you decided.

b.   The tables for
      Thomas and Ryan's
      accounts are shown
      at right. Which
      table reflects
      Thomas' interest?
      Which one reflects
      Ryan's interest?
      How do you know?

Time (in weeks)	Interest Earned ($)	Time (in weeks)	Interest Earned ($)
1	0.60	2	1.00
4	2.40	3	1.50
7	4.20	6	3.00
10	6.00	12	6.00

c.   Use the tables to find the rate of *interest earned (in dollars)* to *time (in
      weeks)* for each of them. Whose money is growing faster?

d.   Did your answers from parts (a) and (c) agree? If not, compare the tables
      and graphs with your team to find out why the line that is less steep actually
      represents the bank account that grows faster. Be ready to share your ideas
      about why the graphs look the way they do.

Making Connections: Course 2

7-45.   The students in a study team are now arguing about who has graphed the steepest line. Assume that they set up their axes with the same scale. Here is some information about their lines:

Lucy: slope = $\frac{7}{5}$ Bree: slope = $\frac{5}{7}$

Cliff: slope = $\frac{14}{10}$ Geetha: slope = $\frac{12}{10}$

Can you use the slopes of their lines to **visualize** how each of them would look on a graph? Discuss their lines with your team, and then settle their argument without graphing. Explain completely who has the steepest line and who has the least steep line.

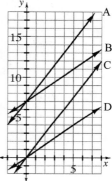

7-46.   Which lines on the graph at right and on your resource page appear to have the same slope? Which line or lines are steepest? Make a prediction, then check your prediction by finding the slope of each line in the graph on the Lesson 7.1.5 Resource Page.

7-47.   LEARNING LOG

What is slope? How is it calculated? In your Learning Log, sketch a graph of a line and explain how to find its slope. How would the slope be different if the line was steeper? Explain as completely as you can. Title this entry "Slope and Steepness" and include today's date.

7-48.   There are 36 green gumballs, 18 red gumballs, 22 white gumballs, 30 purple gumballs, and 14 blue gumballs in the gumball machine. Find the probability for each of the following outcomes and write it as a percent. Assume that the gumball machine is always full and that gumballs are released from the machine randomly. Show work to support your answer.

a.   Getting a purple gumball.

b.   Getting either a purple or a green gumball.

c.   *Not* getting a green gumball.

d.   Getting either a purple or a white gumball.

7-49. Graph the points in the table at right and draw a line. Then, find three different ratios to describe the slope of this line.

x	y
0	1
2	6
5	13.5
−2	−4
−4	−9

7-50. Find the slope of each line below.

a.
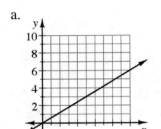

b.
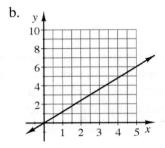

c.
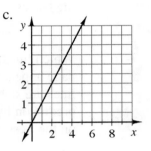

7-51. For each equation below, solve for x. Show the process you use to check your answer.

a. $2\frac{1}{2} = x - 1\frac{1}{4}$

b. $5x = 2x + 12$

c. $x - 14.6 = 8.02$

7-52. Use the hundredths grids at right to answer the following questions.

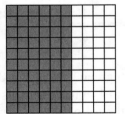
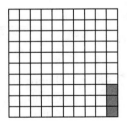

a. Give three names for the largest shaded area.

b. Give three names for the smallest shaded area.

c. What are two other names for 120%? Can you show 120% on a single hundreds grid? Explain your thinking.

7.1.6 What else can slope tell us?

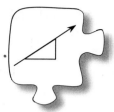

More about Slope

In recent lessons you have learned to find the slope of a line and how slope describes the rate of change and the steepness of a line on a graph. In this lesson you will learn about other information that slope can tell you.

7-53.   Will a line with a slope of $\frac{2}{5}$ or $\frac{5}{2}$ be steeper? How do you know? Explain.

7-54.   Compare the two lines in the graph at right.

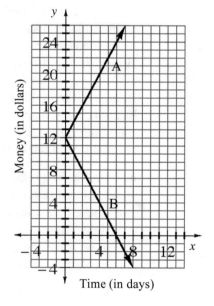

a.   How are the two lines the same? How are they different?

b.   Each line on this graph describes how much money a person has in her wallet over time (in days). Explain what is happening to the amount of money each person has. Be specific.

c.   To describe how person A's amount of money is changing, the unit rate (slope) represents the amount that is added each day. Since the value of money is increasing, the slope is positive. But what should we do when the value is decreasing? How should the decrease be reflected in the rate (slope)? Discuss this with your team.

d.   Remember that the slope ratio compares how the change on the *y*-axis compares to the change on the *x*-axis. Lines that go up from left to right show positive rates of change, or **positive slopes**, while lines that go down from left to right show negative rates of change, or **negative slopes**.

Find the slope of each line in the graph.

7-55. WHAT IF IT DOESN'T GROW?

The graph at right shows 3 different lines.

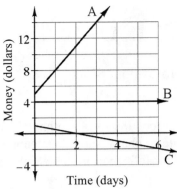

a. Describe each line in words. Is it increasing or decreasing? Quickly or slowly?

b. Line B is different from the other two lines. As the x-value increases, what happens to y?

c. Slope is a comparison of $\frac{\text{change in } y}{\text{change in } x}$. Pick two points on line B. How can you represent the change in y between these two points with a number? Use this number or the change in y to write a slope ratio for line B.

7-56. PERSONAL TRAINER

To prepare for biking long distances, Antoine has been trying to keep a steady pace as he bikes. However, since his hometown has many hills, he ends up biking faster and slower during different parts of his ride.

In order to track his distance and time when he trains for the triathlon, Antoine has purchased a special watch that tells him how far he has traveled at specific time intervals. He can set it to record data whenever he decides to push a button and then get a list of the data at the end of his workout.

a. On his first bike ride around town, he recorded several times and distances. These measures are shown in the table at right. Based on the table, does he appear to be traveling at a constant rate? Explain your **reasoning**.

b. Draw and label a graph that extends to 40 minutes on the x-axis and at least to 15 miles on the y-axis. Plot Antoine's distance and time data on the graph. What type of graph is this?

Antoine's Data

Time (minutes)	Distance (miles)
3	0.5
5	1
8	2
12	3
16	4.5
19	6

c. Draw a trend line that best represents Antoine's data. Then extend it to predict about how long it will take him to bike 10 miles (his normal long distance workout).

d. What is Antoine's **general** rate during his bike ride? Find the slope (rate of change) of the trend line you drew in part (c) to determine his **general** rate.

MATH NOTES

METHODS AND **M**EANINGS

Slope of a Line

The **slope of a line** is the ratio of the change in y to the change in x between any two points on the line. We compute the *ratio* that indicates how y-values are changing with respect to x-values. In essence, slope is the **unit rate of change** because it measures how much y increases or decreases as x changes by one unit. If the slope is positive (+), the y-values are increasing, and if it is negative (–), the y-values are decreasing. The graph of a line goes up for positive slopes and down for negatives slopes as the line moves across the graph from left to right.

$$\text{slope} = \frac{\text{vertical change}}{\text{horizontal change}} = \frac{\text{change in } y\text{-values}}{\text{change in } x\text{-values}}$$

Some textbooks write this ratio as $\frac{\text{rise}}{\text{run}}$.

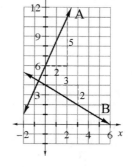

In the graph at right, the slope of line A is $\frac{5}{2}$ because for every 2 units the line increases horizontally, the line increases 5 units vertically, so y increases by $\frac{5}{2}$ units when x increases by 1 unit.

To find the slope of line B, notice that when x increases by 3, y *decreases* by 2, so the vertical change is –2 and the slope is written as $-\frac{2}{3}$.

It is important to notice that horizontal lines do not increase or decrease vertically, and so are described with a slope of 0. The slope of a vertical line is undefined because the horizontal change is 0, which would result in a slope of $\frac{y}{0}$, which is undefined.

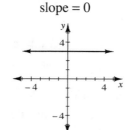

slope = 0

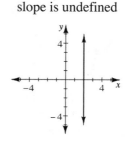

slope is undefined

7-57.   For each pair of slope ratios, decide if they are equivalent (=), or if one slope is greater. If the slopes are not equal, use the greater than (>) or less than (<) symbol to show which is greater.

   a. $\frac{6}{7}$, $\frac{5}{6}$ b. $\frac{3}{2}$, $\frac{15}{10}$ c. $\frac{12}{10}$, $\frac{7}{5}$

7-58.   Make a table and graph for the rule $y = -3x + 1$.

7-59.   Lynne took a taxicab from her office to the airport. She had to pay $3 per mile plus a $5 flat fee.

   a.   How much would she need to pay to go a distance of 2 miles? How much to travel 8 miles?

   b.   Her total cost was $23. Represent the cost of her trip with an equation. How far did she travel? Show your work.

7-60.   Forty percent of the students at Pinecrest Middle School have a school sweatshirt. There are 560 students at the school. Draw a diagram to help you solve each problem below.

   a.   How many students have a school sweatshirt?

   b.   If 280 students have school t-shirts instead of sweatshirts, what percentage of the school has a t-shirt?

   c.   What percentage of the school does not have a t-shirt or a sweatshirt?

7-61.   Ella and her study team are arguing about the slope of the line in the graph at right. They have come up with four different answers: $\frac{3}{4}$, $-\frac{4}{3}$, $-\frac{3}{4}$, and $\frac{4}{3}$. Which slope is correct? **Justify** your answer.

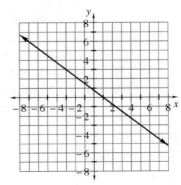

7.2.1 When are they the same?

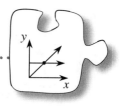

Systems of Equations

During the summer, county fairs are held all over the country. People from around the county attend the fairs to play carnival games and listen to music. Some people raise animals (such as pigs) that they take to the fair to show and be judged. Today you will use several of the skills you have learned in this course to solve problems in which two factors in a relationship are compared.

7-62.   It is almost time for the county fair! Juanita is looking forward to seeing the animals and enjoying the rides at the carnival on the fairgrounds. She lives near three different county fairs and has to decide which fair she will attend.

The Morgan County Fair charges ten dollars to get in the gate. There is also an additional charge of three dollars per ride at the carnival. The Larimer County Fair charges fifteen dollars to get in the gate, but only two dollars per ride.

Juanita cannot decide which of the two fairs would be cheaper. Help her answer this question by completing the tables on the Lesson 7.2.1 Resource Page and drawing a graph of the cost for each fair.

Morgan County Fair

Gate fee: ___

# of rides	Total cost

Larimer County Fair

Gate fee: ___

# of rides	Total cost

7-63.   Once Juanita estimated the number of rides she wanted to take, she realized that it did not matter which county fair she attended because the cost would be the same.

a.   How many rides does she plan to ride? How is this shown on the graph?

b.   How much should Juanita plan to pay? How is this shown on the graph?

7-64. While trying to decide which fair would be cheapest, Juanita considered another fair, the Weld County Fair. She made a table, shown at right, to figure out the costs for this fair.

a. Use the information in the table to add a line for the Weld County Fair on the resource page.

b. What is the cost to get in the entrance gate at the Weld County Fair? What is the cost per ride?

Weld County Fair

# of rides	Total Cost (\$)
0	6
1	6 + 5
2	6 + 5 + 5
3	6 + 5 + 5 + 5

7-65. How do the costs at the three county fairs compare? Look at the graph and tables on your Lesson 7.2.1 Resource Page to answer the following questions.

a. Which county fair costs most per ride? How is this shown on the graph?

b. Which county fair has the highest entry fee? How is this shown on the graph?

c. For how many rides do the Morgan County Fair and the Larimer County Fair cost the same total amount of money? How can you see that on the graph? How can you see that in the table?

d. Is there any amount of rides for which all three county fairs have the same cost? Explain.

7-66. Graphs are ways to tell stories without using many words. If you look at them carefully you can get a lot of information. Use the graphs to answer the following questions.

a. The graph below shows Mica and Joel's progress as they are walking. How can you tell when Joel and Mica will pass each other? When and where will that happen?

b. The graph below shows Mica and Joel walking for 15 minutes on a different day. If they both continue at the same rate, will they ever be the same distance from school at the same time? How do you know?

Distance from School

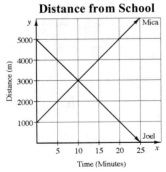

Time (Minutes)

Distance from School

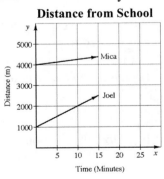

Time (Minutes)

436

Making Connections: Course 2

7-67. For each equation below, solve for x. Show the process you use to check your answer.

a. $x - \frac{2}{5} = 1\frac{3}{5}$

b. $5x = 0$

c. $x - 14.6 = 2.96$

7-68. Use the graph shown at right to enter the ordered pairs in the table below.

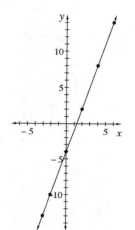

a. Write the rule in words.

b. Explain how to use the table to predict the value of y when x is -7.

7-69. Evaluate the inequality for the listed values of x. Decide if the value makes the statement true or false. Show your work.

$$3x - 3 \geq 2x + 3$$

a. $x = -3$

b. $x = 9$

c. $x = 6$

d. $x = 10\frac{1}{2}$

7-70. Mr. Takaya can eat three slices of pizza in five minutes. If he continues to eat at the same rate, how long will it take him to eat the whole pizza (twelve slices)? How many slices could he eat in half of an hour?

7-71. Use the similar shapes at right to answer the questions below.

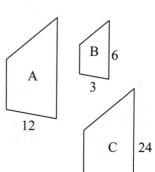

a. What is the scale factor from shape A to shape B?

b. What is the scale factor from shape B to shape C?

c. How are these scale factors related?

d. What do you know about shape A and shape C?

7.2.2   Where is the solution found?

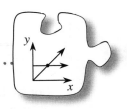

Solving Systems of Equations

In the previous lesson, you looked at tables and graphs to compare several relationships. Today, you will learn a new method of comparing to help you figure out when two relationships are the same.

7-72.   In problem 7-64, Juanita made a table like the one at right to figure out the cost to attend the Weld County Fair. Find the table you made on the Lesson 7.2.1 Resource Page. Add Juanita's expressions for total cost to your table and add the next two entries.

Weld County Fair	
# of Rides	Total Cost ($)
0	6
1	6 + 5
2	6 + 5 + 5
3	6 + 5 + 5 + 5
x	

a.   Is there a shorter way to write the expression for total cost? For example, for 10 rides, how could you calculate the total cost without adding $5 ten times?

b.   Add one more entry in the table by writing a variable expression for the cost of x rides.

7-73.   In Lesson 7.2.1, you used a graph to find out when two of the county fairs cost the same amount of money for the same number of rides. Another way to find out this information is to use expressions for each county fair.

a.   A table for the total costs to attend the Morgan County Fair is shown at right. Find the table you made on the Lesson 7.2.1 Resource Page. If you have not done so already, add the entries shown at right, as well as two more entries. Then write a variable expression for the total cost for x rides at the Morgan County Fair.

Morgan County Fair	
# of Rides	Total Cost ($)
0	10
1	10 + 3
2	10 + 3 + 3

Problem continues on next page. →

438   *Making Connections*: Course 2

7-73.   *Problem continued from previous page.*

    b.   Since the Larimer County Fair has a $15 entry fee and charges $2 for a ride, what would its table look like? Add to your table on the resource page and write a variable expression for the Larimer County Fair.

    c.   How can you use what you know about comparing expressions to find the number of rides for which the Larimer and Morgan County Fairs will cost the same amount? What is that cost?

    d.   Look at the graph on the Lesson 7.2.1 Resource Page. Where is your answer from part (c) found on the graph? What does the answer represent?

7-74.   When will the Weld County Fair and Larimer County Fair cost the same amount? Set up an equation using the expressions from the Weld County Fair and the Larimer County Fair. Make sure your answer includes both the number of rides and the total cost. Verify that this shared point is the same on your graph.

7-75.   Emilie and her sister Robin are excited because they have both been raising pigs to show at the county fair. When they first got their pigs, Emilie was worried because her pig was 5.5 pounds lighter than Robin's pig. Emilie knew weight was not the only factor on which her pig would be judged, but it was one of the more important factors.

As the pigs began to grow, Emilie decided to keep track of both pigs' weight so she could see when her pig would weigh as much as Robin's pig. Emilie recorded her data in the tables at right.

Emilie's Pig		Robin's Pig	
Time (weeks)	Weight (lbs)	Time (weeks)	Weight (lbs)
0	49.5	0	55
1	60	1	65.5
2	70.5	2	76
3	81	3	86.5
4	91.5	4	97

    a.   Write a variable expression for the weight of each pig in which x represents the number of weeks.

    b.   When will Emilie's pig weigh as much as Robin's pig? Explain your answer.

7-76. The graph at right shows the results of the weight for Emilie and Robin's pigs from problem 7-75. Does the graph **justify** your answer from that problem? Why or why not?

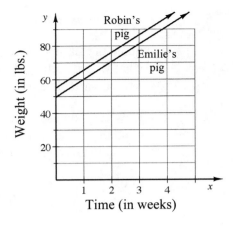

M|ETHODS AND MEANINGS

MATH NOTES

Systems of Linear Equations

You know how to solve equations like $3x - 4 = 14$. The solution is $x = 6$, since $3(6) - 4$ is $18 - 4$, which is 14. You also know that for the equation $y = 3x - 4$, you can create a table of xy-coordinates and represent the equation with a straight line on a graph.

A **system of linear equations** is a set of two or more linear equations in two variables that are considered together (simultaneously). In problem 7-73, you represented the cost of admission and x rides for Larimer County as $3x + 10$ dollars and Morgan County as $2x + 15$ dollars. If y represents the cost, we can write $y = 3x + 10$ and $y = 2x + 15$. The graphs of these two equations are shown at right.

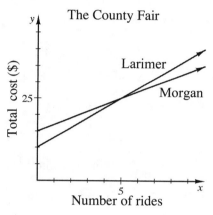

One way to **solve a system of linear equations** is to find the **point of intersection** (that is, where they cross – if they do) for the graph. The lines intersect at $(5, 25)$, which means that the cost, $25, is the same at both county fairs when you go on 5 rides.

A second way to find the point of intersection is to use what you know about comparing expressions. Since we want to know how many rides cost the same, y must have the same value in both equations, so we can set the two expressions in x equal to each other and solve the resulting equation.

$y = 3x + 10$ (Larimer)
$y = 2x + 15$ (Morgan)
$\qquad 3x + 10 = 2x + 15 \qquad x = 5$ rides

Then you can replace x with 5 in either equation to find the cost for 5 rides: $3(5) + 10 = \$25$ or $2(5) + 15 = \$25$, so the **solution** is 5 rides that cost $25.

7-77.   Pierre was walking toward school at a rate of two miles per hour. He started six miles from school. Dom left school and walked toward Pierre at a rate of four miles per hour. When and how far from school will the boys pass each other?

7-78.   Graph the rule $y = -6x + 4$. Use the graph to predict the value of y when $x = \frac{1}{3}$. Use the rule to check your prediction.

7-79.   Sketch each angle below on your paper, and label each one with its measure in degrees.

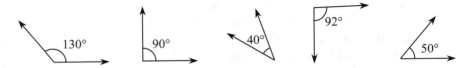

a.   Identify whether each angle is an acute, obtuse, or right angle.

b.   Which angles could form a complementary pair?

c.   Which angles could form a supplementary pair?

7-80.   Simplify each expression.

a. $\dfrac{2(5+3)}{4}$

b. $\frac{1}{2}(15+3) - 10 \div 2$

c. $5\frac{1}{2} - 2\frac{1}{4} + \frac{3}{8}$

d. $3 + \frac{3}{5} \cdot \frac{1}{4}$

e. $-2 + (-5 + 6)^2$

f. $\frac{3}{4} \cdot \frac{1}{4} + \frac{5}{8} \cdot (-\frac{3}{2})$

7-81.   Alex has a job delivering newspapers. He puts 20% of his earnings each week into his college savings account. Each week he puts $16 into the account.

a.   Draw a diagram to represent this situation. How much money does Alex earn each week?

b.   Alex spends 10% of his earnings on snacks each week. How much does he spend?

c.   When Alex has worked for one year, he will get a raise that is equal to 15% of his current earnings. How much more money will he earn each week?

Making Connections: Course 2

7.2.3 Is there always a solution?

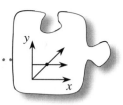

More Solving Systems of Equations

One of the most common events at the county fair is showing animals to a group of judges to win a "Best of Show" award. Many people compete with animals such as cows, pigs, sheep, goats, and even chickens! There are also many displays so that people can learn about these animals.

7-82. Emilie was looking at two tables that recorded the weekly weights of two lambs. She thinks she sees a way to tell where two lines on the graph will intersect without having to draw the graph.

She told her friend, Sterling, that the answer was nineteen because that number was in both tables, shown at right.

Sterling looked at what Emilie had done and said, *"I don't think 19 is the answer."*

x	y		x	y
0	3		0	10
1	7		1	13
2	11		2	16
3	15		3	(19)
4	(19)		4	22
5	23		5	25

a. Did Emilie make a mistake? Explain.

b. If both tables represent lines, when will the lines intersect? Write the intersection as a point in the form (x, y) and state what it tells you about the lambs.

7-83. Juanita is enjoying the Morgan County Fair. However, she noticed that the temperature is getting colder. When she arrived at the fair (when the fair opened), the temperature was 81°. However, due to an approaching storm, the temperature has dropped 3° per hour.

Meanwhile, the fair in Larimer County has had better luck with the weather. It opened at the same time and the temperature was 72°. It has only dropped 1° per hour.

Problem continues on next page. →

7-83.   *Problem continued from previous page.*

When Juanita called her friend at the Larimer County fair, she found out that both counties had the same temperature. How long has Juanita been at the fair?

a.   Discuss which representation your team would like to use to find the solution. Think about these questions as you discuss your ideas:

  • Are these numbers easy to graph accurately?

  • Is a table convenient?

  • Would an equation be faster?

  Be ready to share your **reasoning** with the class.

b.   Solve the problem using the representation your team chose in part (a). What does the solution represent?

7-84.   Answer the questions below based on the graph at right.

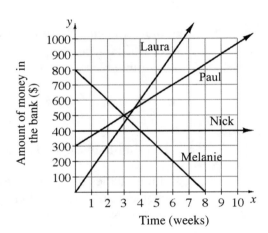

a.   Who is saving money the fastest and how can you tell?

b.   Who is not spending or saving? How can you tell?

c.   When did Paul and Melanie have the same amount of money?

d.   Will anyone run out of money? How can you tell?

7-85.   LEARNING LOG

In your Learning Log, explain how to find the intersection between two lines using graphs, tables, and equations. Use pictures, symbols, or words and give specific examples. Title this entry, "Systems of Equations," and label it with today's date.

Making Connections: Course 2

7-86.   Mimi is saving money. She already has $30 and earns an additional $10 per week. Alexis already has $80, but she is not spending or saving any additional money. When will the girls have the same amount of money and how much money will they have?

7-87.   Four pieces of taffy cost 25 cents. Complete the table below.

Taffy (# of pieces)	4	16	8	80	24	32	40
Cost (in dollars)							

7-88.   Simplify each expression below.

a. $2\frac{3}{10} - 1\frac{2}{5}$

b. $\frac{9}{3} \cdot \frac{4}{5}$

c. $\frac{3}{4} + 5\frac{7}{8}$

d. $\frac{2}{9} \cdot (-\frac{3}{7}) \cdot (\frac{14}{5})$

e. $-\frac{9}{15} - (-\frac{26}{45})$

f. $5\frac{1}{6} \cdot (-\frac{7}{9})$

7-89.   Richard's **strategy** to change a percent to a decimal is to put the decimal point in front of the percent number. On the right is an example of his work. Do you agree with Richard's method? Explain your **reasoning**.

$8\% = 0.8$
$80\% = 0.80$
$800\% = 0.800$

7-90.   Find the area and perimeter of each shape below. Show your steps and work.

a.
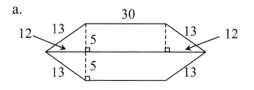

b.
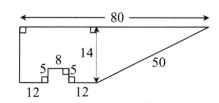

Chapter 7 Closure   What have I learned?

Reflection and Synthesis

The activities below offer you a chance to reflect about what you have learned during this chapter. As you work, look for concepts that you feel very comfortable with, ideas that you would like to learn more about, and topics you need more help with. Look for connections between ideas as well as connections with material you learned previously.

①   SUMMARIZING MY UNDERSTANDING

This section gives you an opportunity to show what you know about certain math topics or ideas.

Obtain both of the Chapter 7 Closure GO Resource Pages (the slope page is pictured at right) from your teacher. (GO is short for Graphic Organizer.) Follow the directions below to demonstrate your understanding of similar shapes and slope.

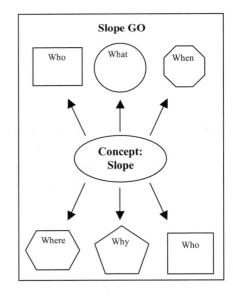

Part 1:   Answer the question provided in each section of the Similar Shapes GO. Be ready to share your ideas about similar shapes with your team.

Part 2:   Now, use the same format to create your own Slope GO. On the resource page, work with your team to write six "Who, What, When Where, Why, How?" questions about slope.

Part 3:   Follow your teacher's directions to pair up with students in another team and trade GO questions to answer.

Part 4:   Be ready to contribute your team's ideas to a class discussion. On your own paper, make note of new ideas about slope.

         Making Connections: Course 2

WHAT HAVE I LEARNED?

Working the problems in this section will help you to evaluate which types of problems you feel comfortable with and which ones you need more help with. This section will appear at the end of every chapter to help you check your understanding.

Solve each problem as completely as you can. The table at the end of this closure section has answers to these problems. It also tells you where you can find additional help and practice on problems like them.

CL 7-91. Annika is saving money for a trip. She is able to save $75 a week. Her friend from Iceland, Eva, is also saving money. Eva is able to save 9000 Kronas (Icelandic money) each week. If $4 is equal to 509 Kronas, who is saving at a greater rate?

CL 7-92. A breakfast cereal is made of oats, nuts, and raisins. The advertisements boast that 30% of the cereal in each box is raisins.

   a. What portion of each box is not raisins?

   b. If each box contains 8 cups of cereal, how many cups of raisins are in each box? Draw and label a diagram to represent the problem.

   c. If the box contains 2 cups of nuts, what percentage of each box is nuts?

CL 7-93. Clay and his friend Lacey are making cookies for the school dance. Clay started early and has already made 3-dozen cookies. He can make an additional two-dozen cookies an hour. Lacey has not started making cookies yet, but she has a bigger oven and can make four-dozen cookies an hour. If Lacey starts baking her cookies right away, how long will it take for her to have made as many cookies as Clay and how many cookies will they each have made?

CL 7-94. Complete the table and find the rule.

x	6	$\frac{1}{2}$	−6	8	−12	3	$\frac{2}{3}$
y				18		3	

CL 7-95. For the following examples, tell whether there is positive correlation, negative correlation, or no correlation.

    a.   The number of inches of rain per hour and the height of water in a reservoir.

    b.   Amount of food a person eats and how many pets they have.

    c.   The height of a tree and the amount of nutrients it gets.

    d.   Number of hours spent hiking in the mountains and the amount of water left in your water bottle.

CL 7-96. Use the following graph to complete the table and find the rule.

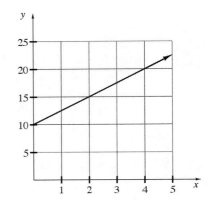

0	1	2	3	4	5	x
						$y =$

CL 7-97. Use the rule $y = 4x + 2$ to complete a table like the one in problem CL 7-96 and then draw a graph.

CL 7-98. Solve the following equations.

    a. $3x - 2 = 4x + 6$ b. $6x - 12 = -x + 2$

    c. $3(x + 2) - 3 = 3x - 2$ d. $5(x - 1) = 5(2x - 3)$

CL 7-99. For each of the problems above, do the following:

- Draw a bar or number line that represents 0 to 10.

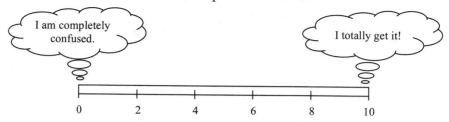

- Color or shade in a portion of the bar that represents your level of understanding and comfort with completing that problem on your own.

If any of your bars are less than a 5, choose *one* of those problems and do one of the following tasks:

- Write two questions that you would like to ask about that problem.

- Brainstorm two things that you DO know about that type of problem.

If all of your bars are a 5 or above, choose one of those problems and do one of these tasks:

- Write two questions you might ask or hints you might give to a student who was stuck on the problem.

- Make a new problem that is similar and more challenging than that problem and solve it.

③ WHAT TOOLS CAN I USE?

You have several tools and references available to help support your learning – your teacher, your study team, your math book, and your Toolkit, to name only a few. At the end of each chapter you will have an opportunity to review your Toolkit for completeness as well as to revise or update it to better reflect your current understanding of big ideas.

The main elements of your Toolkit should be your Learning Log, Math Notes, and the vocabulary used in this chapter. Math words that are new to this chapter appear in bold in the text. Refer to the lists provided below and follow your teacher's instructions to revise your Toolkit, which will help make it a useful reference for you as you complete this chapter and as you work in future chapters.

Learning Log Entries
- Lesson 7.1.3 – Rate, Tables, and Graphs
- Lesson 7.1.5 – Slope and Steepness
- Lesson 7.2.3 – Systems of Equations

Math Notes
- Lesson 7.1.3 – Rate of Change and Unit Rates
- Lesson 7.1.6 – Slope of a Line
- Lesson 7.2.2 – Systems of Linear Equations

Mathematical Vocabulary
The following is a list of vocabulary found in this chapter. Some of the words have been seen in the previous chapter. The words in bold are the words new to this chapter. Make sure that you are familiar with the terms below and know what they mean. For the words you do not know, refer to the glossary or index. You might also want to add these words to your Toolkit for a way to reference them in the future.

constant rate	**horizontal change**	**intersect**
negative slope	**positive slope**	**ratio**
rate	slope	**steep**
unit rate	variable expression	**vertical change**

Process Words
These words describe problem solving strategies and processes that you have been involved in throughout the course of this chapter. Make sure you know what each of these words means. If you are not sure, you can talk with your teacher or other students or look through your book for problems in which you were asked to do these things.

analyze	compare	explain
interpret	justify	predict
visualize		

Making Connections: Course 2

Answers and Support for Closure Activity #2
What Have I Learned?

Problem	Solution	Need Help?	More Practice
CL 7-91.	Annika is saving at a faster rate because she saves $75 a week and Eva saves about $71 a week.	Lessons 7.1.1, 7.1.2, and 7.1.3 Math Notes boxes in Lessons 4.1.1 and 7.1.3 Learning Log (problem 7-27)	Problems 7-8, 7-28, 7-35, 7-36, and 7-44
CL 7-92.	a. 70% is not raisins. b. 2.4 cups of raisins. $$\begin{array}{c}\text{0 cups} \qquad\qquad \overset{\text{2.4 cups}}{\underset{\text{raisins}}{}}\ \text{8 cups}\\ \vdash\!\!-\!\!-\!\!-\!\!-\!\!-\!\!-\!\!-\!\!-\!\!\dashv\\ 0\% \qquad\qquad\qquad 100\%\\ \quad\ 70\% \qquad\qquad 30\%\end{array}$$ c. 25% is nuts.	Lessons 4.1.1 and 4.1.2 Math Notes box in Lesson 4.1.2	Problem CL 4-112
CL 7-93.	In $1\frac{1}{2}$ hours they will each have made 72 cookies.	Lessons 7.1.3, 7.2.1, 7.2.2, and 7.2.3 Math Notes box in Lesson 7.2.2 Learning Log (problem 7-85)	Problems 7-73, 7-75, 7-77, 7-83, and 7-86
CL 7-94.	<table><tr><td>6</td><td>$\frac{1}{2}$</td><td>−6</td><td>8</td><td>−12</td><td>3</td><td>$\frac{2}{3}$</td></tr><tr><td>12</td><td>−4.5</td><td>−24</td><td>18</td><td>−42</td><td>3</td><td>−4</td></tr></table> $y = 3x - 6$	Lessons 6.1.4, 6.1.5, and 6.1.6	Problems 6-36, 6-37, 6-43, 6-54, 6-82, 6-100, 6-126, and 7-68

Problem	Solution	Need Help?	More Practice
CL 7-95.	a. positive correlation b. no correlation c. positive correlation d. negative correlation	Lessons 6.1.2 and 6.1.3 Math Notes box in Lesson 6.1.4 Learning Logs (problems 6-26 and 6-47)	Problems 6-15, 6-24, 6-49, 6-116, 6-139, and CL 6-140
CL 7-96.	<table><tr><td>0</td><td>1</td><td>2</td><td>3</td><td>4</td><td>5</td></tr><tr><td>10</td><td>12.5</td><td>15</td><td>17.5</td><td>20</td><td>22.5</td></tr></table> $y = 2.5x + 10$	Lessons 6.1.4, 6.1.5, and 6.1.6	Problems 6-48, 6-79, and 7-68
CL 7-97.	<table><tr><td>0</td><td>1</td><td>2</td><td>3</td><td>4</td><td>5</td></tr><tr><td>2</td><td>6</td><td>10</td><td>14</td><td>18</td><td>22</td></tr></table> $y = 4x + 2$	Lessons 6.1.4, 6.1.5, and 6.1.6	Problems CL 6-142, 7-12, and 7-58
CL 7-98.	a. $x = -8$ b. $x = 2$ c. no solution d. $x = 2$	Lessons 6.2.1, 6.2.2, and 6.2.3 Math Notes boxes in Lessons 6.2.1, 6.2.3, 6.2.4, and 6.2.6 Learning Log (problem 6-98)	Problems 6-87, 6-88, 6-97, 6-115, 6-125, 6-134, 7-9, and 7-30

Making Connections: Course 2

Puzzle Investigator Problems

PI-13.   GOING BANANAS!

This year's harvest from a small, remote banana plantation consists of 3000 bananas. The farmer's camel can carry up to 1000 bananas at a time. The market place where the bananas are sold is 1000 miles away. Unfortunately, the camel eats one banana each and every mile she walks.

Your task: Of the three thousand bananas harvested, what is the greatest number of bananas the farmer can get to market?

PI-14.   WITH OR WITHOUT FROSTING

Mr. Hamada baked a cake for his class that was in the shape of a big cube. As he carried the cake over to the frosting table, he slipped and the cake fell into a large tub of frosting!

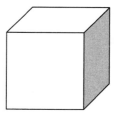

Amazingly, the cake stayed in one piece, but all 6 sides were now frosted. One student suggested the cake be cut into cube-shaped pieces, all the same size.

a.   There are 32 students in Mr. Hamada's class and he does not want more than 100 pieces of cake. If Mr. Hamada cuts the cake into cube-shaped pieces, all the same size, how many pieces of cake should he cut so that everyone could have a piece? (Note: You might want to use small blocks to explore this question.)

b.   A student noticed that some pieces have no frosting, while others have 1, 2, or 3 sides frosted. How many of each type of piece can Mr. Hamada offer?

c.   There were many students that wanted a piece with frosting on 3 sides, so Mr. Hamada changed his mind and decided to cut the cake into 125 cube-shaped pieces, all the same size. Did this increase the number of pieces with frosting on 3 sides? Why or why not?

Percents and More Solving Equations

CHAPTER **8** Percents and More Solving Equations

When traveling in a car, have you ever asked, *"When are we going to get there?"* Did you know that you could use mathematics to answer that question? In Section 8.1, you will use diagrams, like the ones you used for percents, to find the relationship between rate, time, and distance. You will also learn to compare quantities that are very different.

You will revisit scale factor in Section 8.2 and connect it to percents. You will learn to take difficult problems and make them simpler by rewriting equations to remove fractional and decimal coefficients. Finally, you will investigate how to find the percent increase, percent decrease, and simple interest.

Guiding Questions

Think about these questions throughout this chapter:

How is it changing?

What is the relationship?

What is the connection?

How can I represent it?

What strategy should I use?

In this chapter, you will learn how to:

 ➢ Solve problems involving distance, rate, and time.

 ➢ Convert units so that they are the same, then use them to compare rates.

 ➢ Solve equations that have fractional or decimal coefficients.

 ➢ Find the whole amount if you only know a percentage of it.

 ➢ Calculate simple interest.

Chapter Outline

Section 8.1 You will identify the relationship between distance, rate, and time and will use it to solve word problems. You will compare rates that do not involve the same units and determine when a unit conversion is necessary.

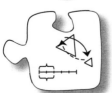

Section 8.2 You will connect your work involving percent and scale factors to solve new problems involving part-whole relationships. You will also develop multiple **strategies** to solve equations with fractional coefficients. Finally, you will explore percent change and examine how simple interest causes an account (such as a savings account or loan balance) to change over time.

Making Connections: Course 2

8.1.1 What is the relationship?

Distance, Rate, and Time

Throughout this course you have been developing skills for writing equations to describe relationships in tables, in graphs, and in situations. You have used the 5-D Process, diagrams of percentage problems, and geometric relationships to organize information for those equations. Today you will use your equation writing skills to represent the relationships between rate, time, and distance.

8-1. Axel is getting his pig ready for the pig races at the county fair. During the race, four juvenile pigs run around a track, trying to be the first pig to get to a cream-filled chocolate cookie. His pig, Hammy, can run at a rate of 11 feet per second.

   a. At this speed, how far will Hammy run in 3 seconds? In 5 seconds? In 1 minute (that is, in 60 seconds)?

   b. Write an expression that represents how far Hammy will run in x seconds.

   c. The race track at the fair is 150 feet long.

   • Draw a diagram that shows how long it will take Hammy to finish the race.

   • Write an equation to represent this situation.

   d. About how long it will take Hammy to finish the race?

8-2. A.J. and her sister are entering a 200-mile bike race on their bicycle built for two. On a training ride, they traveled 60 miles in 2.5 hours. They want to use this information to find out how long it will take them to finish the bike race. Draw a diagram for this situation and be ready to explain how you found your solutions to the questions below.

   a. What is their bicycling rate? What is their unit rate (per hour)?

   b. How far can they go in three hours? In six hours? Explain how you can use the rate of travel and the time to find the distance.

Problem continues on next page. →

8-2.   *Problem continued from previous page.*

    c. If they bicycle ten miles, how long will it take them? Explain how the distance and rate helped you find the time.

    d. If they bike at this same rate for the entire race, how long will it take them to finish the 200 mile race?

    e. Summarize in words the relationship between the distance the girls travel, their rate of travel, and how long they ride (the time).

8-3.   A new high-speed train travels 300 miles in 1.2 hours. Luis and Omar are trying to figure out how they can find the distance the train has traveled after any number of hours. Omar decided to draw a diagram to help figure out the problem. He drew the diagram below.

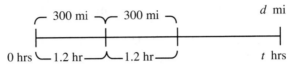

    a. Find a unit rate (in miles per hour) for the train. Then copy and change Omar's diagram to show the unit rate.

    b. How far will the train travel in 5 hours? Write an equation to represent how to use the picture to find out how far the train will go in miles (d miles) after t hours.

    c. Work with your team to write an equation to show the relationship between distance (d), rate (r), and time (t). Is there more than one way to represent this relationship in an equation? Explain.

8-4.   In problem 8-3 you wrote an equation to relate distance to rate of travel and time traveled. What if the rate does not involve distance? Use the situation below to investigate this question.

Fred was filling bags of food for families in need at the neighborhood food pantry. Fred could fill 6 bags in 15 minutes. Draw a diagram for this situation and be ready to explain how you found your solutions.

    a. How many bags could Fred fill in two hours?

    b. How many bags can Fred fill in $\frac{5}{6}$ of an hour? What **strategy** did you use to find this answer?

Problem continues on next page. →

8-4.   *Problem continued from previous page.*

    c.   Write a rule to **generalize** the relationship between the number of bags Fred can fill and the amount of time that he works. Be sure to define your variables.

    d.   Use your equation from part (c) to find the number of bags Fred will fill during a week (assuming he fills bags at a constant rate and that Fred works 36 hours in a week).

8-5.   Claudia and her cousin Brian often ride their bikes to meet each other. They live 16 miles apart. Claudia can bike at a speed of 8.5 mph, and Brian can ride 11 mph. If they leave their homes at the same time and bike towards each other for half an hour, will they meet?

Methods and Meanings

Distance, Rate, and Time

Distance (*d*) equals the product of the **rate of speed** (*r*) and the **time** (*t*). This is usually written as $d = r \cdot t$. We use the units of distance (such as feet or miles) and units of time (such as seconds or hours) to write the units of rate (feet per second or miles per hour).

One way to make sense of this relationship is to treat rate as a unit rate that equals the distance covered in one hour (or minute) of travel. Then $r \cdot t$ is *t* sets of *r* lengths, which is *rt* long. For example, if someone travels for 3 hours at 5 miles per hour, we could represent this situation by the following diagram.

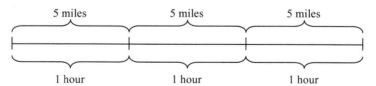

We can also use the same equation to find either rate or time if we know the other two variables. For example, if you need to travel 200 miles and need to be there in 4 hours, you have the equation $200 \text{ mi.} = r \frac{\text{mi.}}{\text{hr.}} \cdot 4 \text{ hrs.}$, so $r = 50 \frac{\text{mi.}}{\text{hr.}}$.

8-6.   If a train travels at an average rate of 40 miles per hour, how long will it take the train to travel 110 miles? Be sure to show all of your work.

8-7.   The graph at right represents this situation: Cara jogs every morning. After 30 minutes, Cara has run 3.5 miles.

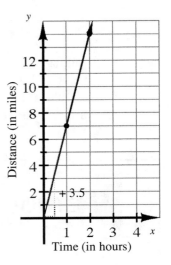

   a.   How is Cara's speed represented on the graph?

   b.   Write a rule for Cara's distance if t represents the number of hours.

   c.   If Cara continues to run at this rate, predict how far she will run in 4 hours.

8-8.   Solve each equation.

   a. $3(x+4) = -42$ b. $90 = 5 - (2x+1)$

   c. $5(3+x) = 3x$

8-9.   Consider the three similar shapes at right.

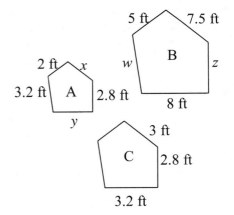

   a.   Find the lengths of the sides labeled with variables.

   b.   What is the scale factor between shapes A and B?

   c.   What do you know about shapes A and C? **Justify**.

8-10.   Find the area of each shaded **sector** (region) in the circles below. Write an exact answer in terms of π and an approximate answer as a decimal.

   a.   b.   Each sector has equal area.

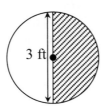

3 ft

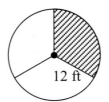

12 ft

Making Connections: Course 2

8.1.2 How can I compare them?

Comparing Rates

Have you ever heard someone use the expression, "They are like apples and oranges"? Usually the person talking means that the two things they are talking about are so different that they are hard to relate to each other. For example, it is very hard to decide which is heavier, a million feathers or 1000 bricks. The information you have does not describe their weight, and the two kinds of objects are so different that trying to **reason** about which is heavier is very difficult.

In order to compare two things, it is useful to find ways to relate them to each other. Often, quantities cannot be compared without doing some calculations or rewriting them in equivalent forms. As you work today, think about the quantities that you are comparing and what you need to do to be able to make a good comparison.

8-11.   Rob and Marla are going for a run. They typically run an average of five miles in one hour, as represented in the diagram at right. Today, they plan to run for 40 minutes.

5 miles

1 hour

a.   Estimate how far Rob and Marla run in 40 minutes. Remember that an estimate can be done with only simple mental calculations, and does not need to be an exact answer. Be ready to share your **reasoning**.

b.   Marla said, *"I know that in order to find distance, I need to multiply rate times time. Multiplying five by 40 gives me the answer 200 miles."* Do you agree with how she organized the problem? If not, explain what you think she did wrong, and what you think the actual distance should be.

8-12. Wei and Jinfai like to let their pet gerbils run on a small track. Wei thinks her gerbil can run faster than Jinfai's gerbil, but Jinfai disagrees. They decide to take some measurements and compare them. Wei's gerbil runs two yards in 20 seconds. Jinfai's gerbil runs 20 feet in one minute.

Your task: Work with your team to determine whose gerbil is fastest. Use a diagram to **justify** your answer and record your calculations carefully so that they are clear enough for someone else to understand.

Discussion Points

How can you represent the situation for each gerbil with a diagram?

How can you compare the rates?

How can you compare measures that are in different units?

Further Guidance

8-13. Why is it that Wei and Jinfai cannot compare the rates for their gerbils directly from the measurements that they took? That is, what makes it difficult to compare two yards per 20 seconds and 20 feet per minute to find out which gerbil is faster?

8-14. One way to begin changing the rates so that they can be compared is to make the time measurements have the same units. The times for the gerbils are given in minutes or seconds. Knowing that there are 60 seconds in a minute, decide if you want to use minutes or seconds and convert both measurements to the same units.

8-15. Jinfai has decided to change both of the time measurements into minutes. He started the diagram at right to find the rate for Wei's gerbil.

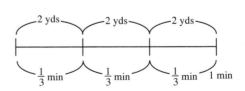

a. Why did Jinfai label the diagram with $\frac{1}{3}$ of a minute?

b. Can you use the diagram to figure out Wei's gerbil's rate and compare it to Jinfai's gerbil to decide which is fastest? If not, what do you still need to do?

Making Connections: Course 2

8-16.   If you have not done so already, use the fact that three feet are equal to one yard to modify the diagram in problem 8-15 to show how many feet Wei's gerbil travels in one minute. Then decide whose gerbil travels faster.

Further Guidance
section ends here.

8-17.   Use your understanding of the relationship between distance, rate, and time to find the following:

   a.   Jinfai and Wei let their gerbils run for 90 seconds. How far does each gerbil run?

   b.   If Jinfai and Wei let their gerbils run for 30 seconds, how far apart will they be and whose gerbil will be in the lead?

   c.   If Jinfai and Wei race their gerbils across a room that is 12 feet long, by how much time will the faster gerbil win?

8-18.   A professional speed walker who is training for the Olympics can walk two miles in 16 minutes. Calculate the following rates. Refer to the Math Notes box following this lesson if you need help with unit conversions.

   a.   What is the athlete's minutes per mile rate?

   b.   What is the athlete's miles per minute rate?

   c.   What is the athlete's feet per minute rate?

   d.   What is the athlete's feet per second rate?

8-19.   Use the relationship between distance, rate, and time to write an equation for the following problem. Then solve the equation to find the missing information.

Henry knows it takes approximately 4 hours to drive from Madison to Des Moines, a distance of about 275 miles. What must his average speed be to drive the distance in 4 hours? If the highway speed limit is 65 miles per hour, can he make it in this amount of time without breaking the law?

METHODS AND MEANINGS

MATH NOTES

Equivalent Measures

When you need to compare quantities, it is often helpful to write them using the same units. Here are some common units of measurement and their relationships:

Length	Volume	Weight
12 inches = 1 foot	8 ounces = 1 cup	16 ounces = 1 pound
36 inches = 1 yard	16 ounces = 1 pint	2,000 pounds = 1 ton
3 feet = 1 yard	2 pints = 1 quart	
5,280 feet = 1 mile	4 quarts = 1 gallon	

Time

60 seconds = 1 minute	24 hours = 1 day
60 minutes = 1 hour	7 days = 1 week

One year is closely approximated as 365.25 days, or a bit more than 52 weeks and 1 day. Two commonly used approximations based on these figures are:

$$365 \text{ days} \approx 1 \text{ year} \qquad 52 \text{ weeks} \approx 1 \text{ year}$$

Review & Preview

8-20. Mr. Benesh is in charge of facilities at Walt Clark Middle School. He is organizing a project to paint all 36 classrooms during the school's summer break. He estimates that it will take one person five hours to paint each classroom.

a. How many total hours would it take for one person to paint all of the classrooms?

b. Mr. Benesh has a team of four workers he is planning to assign to the job. Assuming they all paint at the same rate of five hours per classroom, how many hours would it take the team to do the painting?

c. Mr. Benesh realized that he needs the painting to be finished in nine hours so that a different team can come in to wax the floors before school starts. How many people will he need to assign to do the painting in order to do this?

Making Connections: Course 2

8-21.   Convert the following data and write equivalent measurements. Use the information in the Math Notes box to help you.

   a.   How many inches are in 6 feet?

   b.   How many inches are in 5 feet, 2 inches?

   c.   How many minutes are in 7.5 hours?

   d.   How many hours are in 2 days?

   e.   How many days are in 3168 minutes?

8-22.   Maia was serving five pizzas at the weekly meeting of the student council. She wanted to divide the pizzas into slices that were each $\frac{1}{8}$ of a whole pizza.

   a.   How many slices will she have?

   b.   Represent this problem using a mathematical sentence. Can you find more than one way to do this?

8-23.   Think of a standard deck of playing cards that has four suits in two colors: diamonds and hearts are red; clubs and spades are black. Each suit has 13 cards: an ace, the numbers two through ten, a jack, a queen and a king (the last three are called "face" cards). What is the probability of drawing:

   a.   A black 9 or 10?   b.   A red face card?   c.   A card less than 5?

8-24.   Copy the diagram below on your paper. Use the given information to fill in all of the missing labels.

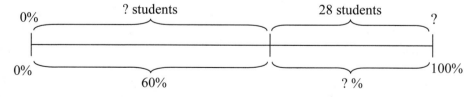

8-25.   Use the graph at right to answer the questions below.

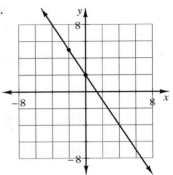

a.   Create a table of values for the line on the graph such as the one started below. Include at least 5 entries.

x	−2	
y	5	

b.   What is the slope of the line?

c.   Write an equation (rule) for the line.

8.2.1   How can I make it smaller or bigger?

Scaling Quantities

In Chapter 4 you learned how to find the percent of a number by making a diagram to relate the part to the whole and find the desired portion. This calculation is fairly straightforward if the percent is a multiple of 10, like 40%, or can be thought of as a fraction, like $\frac{1}{4} = 25\%$. However, it can be more challenging if the percent is something like 6.2% or 87.5%.

Today you will connect what you have learned previously about:

- The relationship between distance, rate, and time.

- How to use a scale factor to find the corresponding lengths of similar figures.

You will use these connections to develop a new method for calculating percents. They will add a powerful new tool to your collection of problem solving **strategies**.

8-26.   Dana is training for a bicycle race. He can ride his bike 25 miles per hour.

One day, when he had been riding for $\frac{3}{5}$ of an hour, he had to stop and fix a flat tire. How many miles had he ridden when he stopped? The diagram below may be useful.

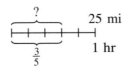

Making Connections: Course 2

8-27.   Matt thought about problem 8-26 and drew the diagram at right. Look at Matt's drawing and decide how he is thinking about this problem.

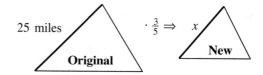

a.   Write an equation that uses the scale factor to find x.

b.   What connection is Matt making between finding a distance using the rate and time (as you did in problem 8-26) and using a scale factor with similar figures? How are the situations alike and how are they different?

8-28.   In the two previous problems, $\frac{3}{5}$ is used in two ways – as *time* in the rate problem $\frac{25 \text{ miles}}{1 \text{ hr}} \cdot \frac{3}{5}$ hrs and as the *scale factor* in the similar triangle problem used to find three-fifths of 25 miles. Both of these situations resulted in an equivalent calculation: $25 \cdot \frac{3}{5} = 15$. How else could this be written?

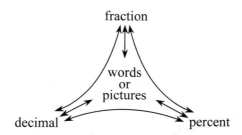

Representations of a Portion

a.   Using the Portions Web (shown at right), work with your team to find two other ways to write the equation $25 \cdot \frac{3}{5} = 15$. For example, one way might be $25 \cdot \frac{6}{10} = 15$.

b.   If you did not already find it, what percent would be equivalent to $\frac{3}{5}$? Use this percent to write a statement in words and symbols that is equivalent to $25 \cdot \frac{3}{5} = 15$.

c.   Use the idea of scaling to find the following values. Write an expression using either a fraction or a percent, then find the result.

    i.   90% of 25 miles   *ii.*   8% of $75   *iii.*   25% of 144

8-29.   Josea went out to dinner at an Indian restaurant. The total bill was $38. She wanted to leave a 15% tip.

a.   If we use the idea of scaling to find the tip amount, what would she need to multiply by? As you talk about this with your team, consider:

- How could you represent this multiplier as a fraction?
- How could you represent it as a decimal?
- Does it make a difference which representation, fraction or decimal, you use to solve this problem?
- Which do you think will be easier?

b.   How much should Josea leave for the tip? Show your calculations.

c.   If Josea changes her mind and wants to leave a 20% tip instead, how much will this be?

8-30.   While shopping for a computer game,
          Isaiah found one that was on sale for
          35% off. He was wondering if he
          could use $\frac{35}{100}$ as a multiplier to scale
          down the price to find out how much
          he would have to pay for the game.

   a.   If Isaiah uses $\frac{35}{100}$ as a scale factor
        (multiplier), will he find the price
        that he will pay for the game?
        Why or why not?

   b.   There is scale factor (multiplier) other than 35% that can be used to find the
        sale price. What is it? Draw a diagram to show how this scale factor is
        related to 35%. Label the parts of your diagram "discount" and "sale price"
        along with the relevant percents.

   c.   How much will Isaiah have to pay for the game if the original price is $40?
        Show your **strategy**.

ETHODS AND MEANINGS

Scale Factor

One way to increase or decrease a quantity is to use a **scale
factor**, which can also be called a **multiplier**. A scale factor compares
the sizes of the part and whole in a proportional relationship. You
learned about scale factors when you dilated shapes in Chapter 2 and
compared similar shapes in Chapter 4. Scale factors can also be used
to increase and decrease quantities that are not side lengths.

For example, if you want to scale down (reduce) a recipe that makes
six servings so that it makes only two servings, you would need to
multiply the quantity of each ingredient by $\frac{1}{3}$. This could be written:

$$\text{scale factor (multiplier)} = \frac{(2 \text{ servings})}{(6 \text{ servings})} = \frac{1}{3}$$

Making Connections: Course 2

8-31.   Ameena's boat travels 35 miles per hour. The best fishing spot in the lake is
         27 miles away from her starting point.

    a.   If she drives her boat for $\frac{2}{3}$ of an hour will she make it to the best fishing
         spot on the lake?

    b.   How long will Ameena need to drive to get to the best fishing spot on the
         lake? Express your answer in both a portion of an hour and in minutes.

8-32.   Use the triangles at right to answer the questions
         that follow. You may want to reread the Math
         Notes box for this lesson before you begin.

    a.   What is the scale factor change from A to B?

    b.   What is the scale factor change from B to A?

    c.   What is the relationship of the scale factors?

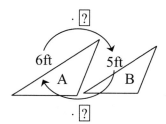

8-33.   Trina planted 43 plants in her garden last week. She planted twice as many
         cucumbers as zucchini and eight more tomatoes than cucumbers. Write and
         solve an equation to find the number of each kind of plant in her garden. Be
         sure to clearly identify your variable.

8-34.   Andre and Leticia plan to meet at the mall. Use
         the graph at right to answer these questions.

    a.   Who left first to go to the mall?

    b.   Who will arrive at the mall first?
         Explain how you know.

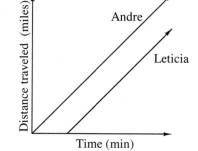

8-35.   Copy the diagram at right on your paper. Then
         use the diagram to answer the questions below.

    a.   Name two pairs of angles that are supplementary.

    b.   Name one pair of complementary angles.

    c.   Name two right angles.

    d.   Name one obtuse angle.

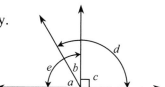

8.2.2 Which multiplier should I use?

Solving Problems Involving Percents

As you have seen many times in this course, there is usually more than one way to solve a problem. When a problem uses portions (fractions, decimals, or percents), there are different ways to write the numbers and different solving **strategies** to choose from. Today, you will look at the different multipliers that can scale a quantity and see what each of them will help you find. As you work with your team today, consider the questions:

What multiplier (scale factor) should I use?

How can I write an equation?

8-36. Hugo and his family were shopping and they purchased a new bed. The bed was a great deal at 60% off of the original cost. The bed originally cost $245.

a. Draw a diagram for this situation.

b. If Hugo scales (multiplies) the original price of the bed by 60%, what will his result represent?

c. What should Hugo scale (multiply) the original price by to find the new price of the bed?

d. Work with your team to find the sale price of the bed in two different ways, that is, using two different multipliers (scale factors). How do your answers from your two methods compare?

8-37.   Hugo's older sister, Sandra, had the same summer job for the past two years. Last year she worked the entire summer and was paid a salary of $3,000. This summer she is going to get a 6% raise in pay. In order to figure out how much she will make, Sandra drew the following diagram.

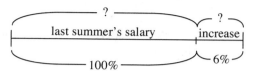

a.   Copy the diagram on your paper and fill in the missing information.

b.   Since Sandra's salary is increasing, does it make sense that her scale factor (multiplier) should be less than 1, equal to 1, or more than 1? Why?

c.   The diagram shows Sandra's original salary and the amount of the increase. What is the scale factor (multiplier) between her original salary and her new salary? That is, what number could Sandra multiply the original salary by to get the new salary?

d.   Show two ways that use different scale factors (multipliers) that Sandra can use to compute her new salary.

8-38.   Miranna teaches gymnastics lessons at summer camp. She is paid $12 per hour.

a.   If Miranna were offered a raise of 100% per hour, what would her new hourly rate be? What percent of her original pay would she be paid?

b.   Miranna is offered a raise of 75% of her hourly rate to teach a private lesson. How much per hour would she be paid for the private lesson? What percent of her original pay would she get?

c.   What is the relationship between the percent raise that Miranna gets and her new pay as a percent of her original pay? How is this related to the scale factor (multiplier) between her original pay and her new pay?

8-39.   Liam was working on a problem and drew a diagram like the one below. He then wrote the equation $(\$72)(0.14) = x$. Does his equation agree with his diagram?

- If you agree, then solve his equation for x.

- If you disagree, write and solve a new equation that will find x in his diagram.

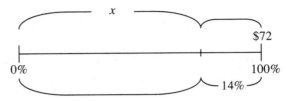

8-40.   **Additional Challenge:** Ramon went to the corner store and bought some more notebook paper to do his homework. The cost for the paper was $7.50 but he also had to pay the 8.2% sales tax. How much will the notebook paper cost Ramon? If Ramon gives the clerk $10 how much change should he receive?

8-41.   LEARNING LOG

In your Learning Log, describe how you scale a quantity. For example, how do you know what multiplier (scale factor) to use? How can you tell if your multiplier should be more than one? Title your entry "Scaling Quantities" and include today's date.

8-42.   A homeowner must reduce the use of the home's electricity. The home currently consumes 25 kwh (kilowatt hours) of electricity per day and the homeowner must reduce the use by 20%. Find the amount of electricity that will be used after the reduction in two different ways, using two different scale factors.

Making Connections: Course 2

8-43.   Copy the Diamond Problems below and complete each of them. The pattern used in the Diamond Problems is shown at right.

a.   b.   c.   d.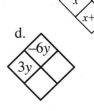

8-44.   Study the following division problems and the diagrams that represent them. Answer the question below each diagram.

a. $8 \div \frac{1}{3}$

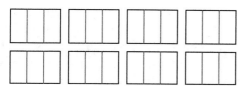

How many thirds?

b. $8 \div \frac{1}{4}$

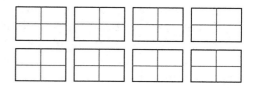

How many fourths?

8-45.   The table at right shows speed limits in some foreign countries in kilometers per hour. One kilometer is equal to 0.6 miles. What are these speed limits in miles per hour?

Speed Limits in km per hour

Country	Country Roads	Motorways
Australia	100	110
South Africa	100	120
Great Britain	96	112
Turkey	90	90

8-46.   Lue is rolling a random number cube. The cube has six sides, and each one is labeled with a different number one through six. What is the probability he will roll a 5 or a 3 on one roll?

8-47.   Simplify each expression.

a. $\left(-\frac{3}{4}+\frac{1}{8}\right)^2$

b. $\frac{2}{3}(9-6)+40$

c. $15 \div 5 + \frac{1}{2} \cdot \frac{-4}{7}$

d. $-\frac{7}{10}+\left(-\frac{5}{12}\right)-\left(\frac{1}{4}\right)$

e. $\frac{1}{4}\left(\frac{9}{14}-\frac{1}{7}\right)+\frac{2}{3}\cdot\left(-\frac{6}{8}\right)$

f. $\frac{7}{8}-\left(-\frac{1}{10}\right)+\left(-\frac{3}{5}\right)$

8.2.3 How can I solve it?

Equations with Fraction and Decimal Coefficients

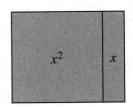

Throughout this course you have worked with quantities represented in multiple ways. You have seen that $\frac{12}{16}$, 0.75, 75%, and $\frac{3}{4}$ each represent the same portion even though they *look* different. In your work with algebra tiles you **visualized** and described perimeters in different ways. For example, the perimeter of the algebra tiles at right can be described by the expressions $3x+2+x$, $x+1+x+1+x+x$, or $4x+2x+2-2x$ units.

In this lesson, you will develop **strategies** to solve a new type of equation: equations with coefficients that are fractions. Recall that coefficients are the numerical part of a term, such as the 5 in $5x$ and the $\frac{2}{3}$ in $\frac{2}{3}x^2$. You will choose between different **strategies** based on how the problem is represented, what diagram you draw or whether you represent the situation with an equation. As you explore solving **strategies** today, keep the following questions in mind:

How can I represent it?

How are the representations related?

What is the best approach for this equation?

8-48.   ARE WE THERE YET?

The Sutton family took a trip to visit the mountains in Rocky Mountain National Park. Linda and her brother, Lee, kept asking, *"Are we there yet?"* At one point, their mother answered, *"No, but what I can tell you is that we have driven 100 miles and we are about $\frac{2}{5}$ of the way there."*

Linda turned to Lee and asked, *"How long is this trip, anyway?"* They each started thinking about whether they could determine the length of the trip from the information they were given.

Linda's Method

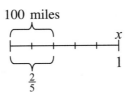

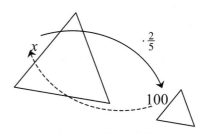

Lee's Method

Problem continues on next page. →

Making Connections: Course 2

8-48. *Problem continued from previous page.*

    a. Explain how both Linda's and Lee's work illustrate the situation described by their mother. What does x represent in each diagram?

    b. What equation could represent this situation? Use the scale factor (multiplier) to represent this situation in an equation. Let x represent the total distance in miles.

    c. Is the answer going to be more or less than 100 miles? Explain your thinking.

8-49. Linda had never seen an equation like this before. She wondered, *"When I look at my diagram I see that the total distance is two and a half times the distance we've driven."*

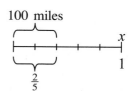

    a. Do you agree? How can you add labels to Linda's diagram to show $2\frac{1}{2}$ times the distance?

    b. How long is the trip? Show how you know.

8-50. Lee thinks what he knows about similar triangles can help.

    a. Review problem 8-32, which involved similar triangles. What was the relationship of the two scale factors?

    b. How can the relationship of the scale factors between similar shapes help Lee? Find the missing scale factor in his diagram at right. That is, what could he multiply 100 by to solve for x?

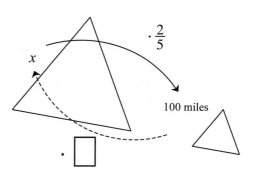

    c. Use the new scale factor to find x. Does your answer agree with the one you found in problem 8-49?

8-51.   As Linda and Lee were talking about the problem (from problem 8-48), their mother overheard and offered them another **strategy**. *"Here is how I would start solving the problem."* She showed them the work at right.

$$\frac{2}{5}x = 100$$

$$\frac{\frac{2}{5}x}{\frac{2}{5}} = \frac{100}{\frac{2}{5}}$$

a.   *"I see a Giant One!"* exclaimed Lee. Where is the Giant One? Help rewrite the left side of the equation.

b.   One way of making sense of $\dfrac{100}{\frac{2}{5}}$ is as $100 \div \frac{2}{5} = ?$. This could be read,

"How many two-fifths are in one-hundred wholes?" With your team, find one way to explain how you could figure out how many two-fifths are in 100.

8-52.   Lee began to wonder how his diagram could help him solve his mother's equation (from problem 8-51). He showed his work below.

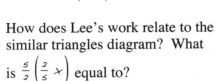

a.   How does Lee's work relate to the similar triangles diagram? What is $\frac{5}{2}\left(\frac{2}{5}x\right)$ equal to?

b.   Finish Lee's work to solve for x. Then check your solution.

8-53.   Linda and Lee wondered how these new equation-solving **strategies** would work with different equations. They made up more equations to try to solve. Copy the equations below on your paper and solve each one using either of the **strategies** from this lesson. How did you decide which **strategy** to use?

a. $\frac{9}{2}x = 27$ b. $12 = \frac{2}{7}x$ c. $-\frac{3}{4}x = 21$

Making Connections: Course 2

METHODS AND **M**EANINGS

MATH NOTES

Scaling

When a quantity is increased or decreased by a specific proportion of the original amount, it is changed by a specific scale factor (also called a multiplier). Quantities are **scaled up** when they are increased by multiplying by a number greater than one or **scaled down** when they are decreased by multiplying by a number less than one.

For example, if a music system is on sale for 25% off its original price of $500, the discount can be found by multiplying by 25%:

discount = 0.25(original price) = 0.25($500) = $125

The full price (100%) minus the discount (25%) would result in the sale price, which in this case is 75% of the original. The sale price can also be found by scaling:

sale price = 0.75(original price) = 0.75($500) = $375

Scaling can be used to enlarge and reduce side lengths of similar shapes, or to increase or decrease times, distances, and other related quantities.

8-54.   Mr. Anderson's doctor has advised him to go on a diet. He must reduce his caloric intake by 15%. He currently eats 2800 calories per day. Calculate his new daily caloric intake rate in two different ways, using two different multipliers.

8-55.   Last year a bonsai lemon tree grew half as much as a dwarf lemon tree. A full size lemon tree grew three times as much as the dwarf lemon. Together the three trees grew 9 inches. Write and solve an equation to determine how much each tree grew. Make sure you clearly identify your variable.

8-56.   Would you expect a scatter plot that compares "speed of a car" and "time it takes to drive 10 miles" to show a "positive correlation," a "negative correlation," or "no correlation?" Explain your thinking.

8-57.   Enrique is saving money to buy a graphing calculator. So far he has saved $30. His math teacher told him he has saved 40% of what he will need. How much does the calculator cost?

8-58.   Sao can text 1500 words per hour. He needs to text a message with 85 words. He only has 5 minutes between classes to complete the text. Can he do it in 5 minutes?

8-59.   Simplify each expression.

a. $3\frac{1}{4} + \frac{2}{5}$ b. $2\frac{3}{8} - 1\frac{5}{7}$ c. $4.25 - 7.06$ d. $18 \div \frac{3}{4}$

e. $-\frac{4}{7} \cdot (-\frac{2}{3})$ f. $10 \div \frac{1}{2}$ g. $-5\frac{1}{8} \cdot 1\frac{2}{3}$ h. $-\frac{3}{11} + \frac{1}{2} - \frac{3}{4}$

8.2.4 How can I eliminate the fractions?

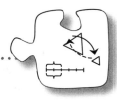

Creating Integer Coefficients

Often, one of the best ways to deal with a challenging task is to find a way to make the task easier. For example, lifting a heavy weight can often be made easier with a lever or pulley. Mathematical problems are very similar; often a challenging problem can be changed to create a new problem that is much easier to solve. In this lesson, you will develop **strategies** to rewrite a complicated equation into an equivalent equation that is more familiar and easier to solve.

8-60.   COMMUNITY SERVICE

The community service club at North Middle School is planning to paint apartments at the local senior citizen center next week. The club needs your help to determine how many apartments they should be able to paint in a day. Earlier in the year, when only $\frac{4}{7}$ of the students worked, they painted 9 apartments in one day. Next week all of the students are available.

a.   Assume that all of the workers contribute equally to the work. If x represents the number of apartments that can be painted by all of the students in the club, use a multiplier and your understanding of scaling to represent this situation as an equation.

b.   **Choose a strategy** to solve your equation in part (a). What does your answer represent? Be ready to share your **strategy**.

8-61.   HOW CAN I MAKE WHOLES?

Janice, the club's president, began to think about how she could **visualize** $\frac{4}{7}x$ to help her solve her equation (from problem 8-60). She recalled using algebra tiles to represent x. In her mind, she **visualized** the diagram at right.

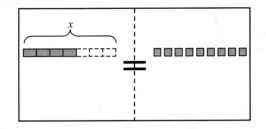

a.   Does this Equation Mat represent your equation from problem 8-60? Why or why not?

b.   Janice recognized that these numbers were not easy to work with, since she did not have whole tiles. After working on her paper for some time she said, *"Maybe I can make whole tiles using more than one set of partial tiles."* She drew the diagram shown at right.

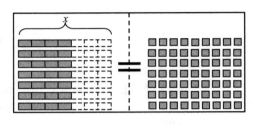

What is her new equation as represented in this picture?

c.   With your team or class, discuss Janice's **strategy** for solving this equation. During your discussion, answer the following questions (in any order):

•   What made Janice's **strategy** different than what you did in Lesson 8.2.3?

•   How many sets of $\frac{4}{7}x$ did Janice use to get a whole number of algebra tiles?

•   Why did the right hand side of the equation change?

•   How does the number of sets Janice used relate to the equation you wrote in part (a)?

8-62.   Will the **strategy** of turning fractions into integers from problem 8-61 work with other equations, such as $\frac{2}{3}x = 8$? Consider this question as you answer the questions below.

a.   How many sets of $\frac{2}{3}x$ would make a whole number of x-tiles?

b.   Solve for x using Janice's method from problem 8-61. How could you record your work on your paper?

c.   Show how your solution is also the number of two-thirds in 8 wholes (written $8 \div \frac{2}{3}$).

Making Connections: Course 2

8-63.   Janice wondered if the method of creating whole number x-terms would work with decimals. Suppose an item was marked 15% off and the sale cost was $36.21. Could this **strategy** help to find the original price? She wrote the equation below:

$$0.85x = 36.21$$

   a.   Is there a number she can multiply both sides of the equation by to get an integer coefficient (so there is no decimal)? If so, list at least one. If not, explain why not.

   b.   Use Janice's **strategy** to solve the equation. What was the original price of the item?

   c.   Does this method work for all equations with decimal coefficients? What if you wanted to solve the equation $1.2x = 14$? What about $0.999x = 71.2$? Discuss these equations with your team and write down your conclusion.

8-64.   Solve each equation below by changing the number that x is being multiplied by (the coefficient of x) to an integer. Check your answer.

   a. $\frac{5}{6}x = 4$ b. $0.8x = 19$ c. $\frac{5}{3}x = 12$ d. $0.12x = 1$

8-65.   LEARNING LOG

   In your Learning Log, summarize at least two **strategies** to solve an equation with fractional (or decimal) coefficients. Provide an example for each **strategy** and include a diagram. Title this entry, "Solving Equations with Fractional Coefficients" and include today's date.

8-66.   If $\frac{1}{4}$ of x is 16, what is $\frac{3}{4}$ of x? **Justify** your answer in more than one way.

8-67.   LuAnn talked on her cell phone for 180 minutes, using $\frac{3}{7}$ of her total monthly minutes. Find out how many total minutes LuAnn gets to talk in one month using at least two different methods.

8-68.   Jeffrey and Liz are each saving money for college.
         Their savings are shown in the graph at right.

         a.   Based on the graph, who is saving money
              fastest? **Justify** your answer.

         b.   What is the slope of each line? What does
              the slope tell you about this situation?

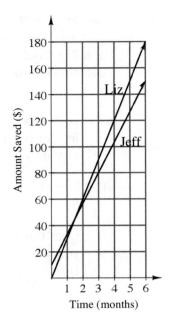

8-69.   Write the inequality represented by each graph.

         a.
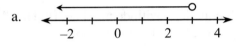

         b.
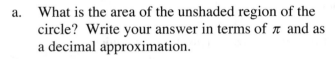

         c.
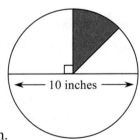

8-70.   In the circle at right, the shaded sector is $\frac{1}{8}$ of the circle.

         a.   What is the area of the unshaded region of the
              circle? Write your answer in terms of π and as
              a decimal approximation.

         b.   What is the area of the shaded region? Write your
              answer in terms of π and as a decimal approximation.

         c.   In a few sentences explain each of the steps you
              followed to answer parts (a) and (b).

8-71.   Daniella has $210 in the bank and her balance is growing at a rate of $3 each
         month. Lori has $187 in the bank but her balance is growing at a rate of $4.50
         each month. Choose a graph, a table, or an equation to find when the girls will
         have the same amount of money. Explain your solution choice and show all
         your work.

Making Connections: Course 2

8.2.5 Percent of what?

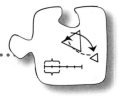

Percent Increase and Decrease

Perhaps you have heard an adult say something like, *"When I was growing up, it only cost a dime to go to the movies!"* The rate at which prices increase over a period of time, called **inflation**, is one of the many things that mathematics can help us to understand. In this lesson, you will be using diagrams and computations to calculate the way quantities (like cost or height) change.

As you work today, keep the following questions in mind:

Is it increasing or decreasing?

What is it changing from?

By how much did it change?

8-72.   **WHAT IS THE PERCENT INCREASE?**

Several years ago Joe started a lawn care business. Due to rising costs, he needs to raise his prices. He is concerned, however, because he has heard that if he raises his rates more than 33%, he might lose business. At right is a letter he sent to his clients.

Joe began to wonder about how the increase in his fees could be expressed in terms of a percent.

> *Dear Valued Customer,*
>
> *After several years of business, Mowcare is increasing its price for lawn service. Since the cost of gas and other supplies has increased, we need to raise our prices. Our prices will increase from $12.50 per hour to $15 per hour. We hope you continue to be happy with the quality of our work.*
>
> *Sincerely,*
> *Joe*

a.   Joe wants to determine the scale factor (multiplier) for the price increase and wrote the following equation:

$$12.50x = 15$$

Explain how this expression represents this situation. What does x represent?

b.   Solve the equation above to determine the scale factor for his change in fees. Represent this multiplier (scale factor) as a fraction, decimal, and percent.

Problem continues on next page. →

8-72.   *Problem continued from previous page.*

    c.   How could this situation be represented with a line diagram? With your team, copy and complete the diagram below.

- Which portion of the diagram corresponds to the original price? Circle and label this part "original."

- Which portion of the diagram corresponds to the change in price? Circle and label this part "change."

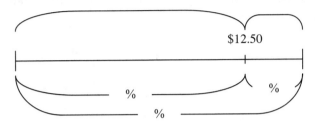

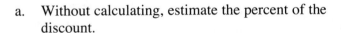

    d.   When Joe raised his rates, what was the **percent increase**? That is, what percent of the original price did the price change? Should Joe expect to lose business?

8-73.   Paige needs your help! She wants to convince her grandmother to let her sign up for a rock climbing class. The class normally costs $50, but the school is offering a special price of $34. Paige's grandmother wants to know what percent of the cost of the class she would save.

    a.   Without calculating, estimate the percent of the discount.

    b.   With your team, determine the percent change in the price of the class. Use the prompts below to help guide your team's discussion.

- Draw a diagram that represents the situation.

- What is the original (whole) value? Show this on your diagram.

- What is the percent of the change? Show this on your diagram.

- Does this situation represent an increase or decrease?

Making Connections: Course 2

8-74.   The **percent change** is a comparison of the amount of change to the original amount. If a number increases from the original amount it is called **percent increase**, while if the number decreases from the original it is called a **percent decrease**.

   a.   What is the percent change from $30 to $33? Is this a percent increase or decrease? To answer this question:

   • Draw a diagram to represent the problem.

   • Determine if it is a percent increase or decrease.

   • Calculate the percent change.

   b.   What is the percent change from $33 to $30? Is this a percent increase or decrease? To answer this question:

   • Draw a diagram to represent the problem.

   • Determine if it is a percent increase or decrease.

   • Calculate the percent change.

   c.   If both parts (a) and (b) above have a change of $3, why are the percent changes different? Explain.

8-75.   To attract new customers, a shoe company called Shoe Fits will raise their prices 10% and then offer a 10% off coupon.

   a.   Without doing any calculations, consider the following question: If a coupon is used, do you think the final price will be more than, less than, or the same as the original price? Discuss this with your team and be ready to share your thinking with the class.

   b.   Akari wants to use a coupon to buy a pair of shoes that originally cost $46. What will the increased price be? What will be the price after the 10% coupon is used? Show all calculations. Does this result confirm your answer to part (a)?

   c.   Akari had assumed that after the price increased 10%, and then he received a 10% discount, it would return to the original price. Explain why this did not happen.

METHODS AND **M**EANINGS

Percent Increase or Decrease

A **percent increase** is the amount that a quantity has increased represented as a percent of the original amount. A **percent decrease** is the amount that a quantity has decreased written as a percent of the original amount. We can write an equation to represent a percent change that is an increase or decrease using a scale factor or multiplier:

amount of increase or decrease = (% change)(original amount)

Example 1: A loaf of bread increased in price from $0.29 to $2.89 in the past 50 years. What was the percent increase?

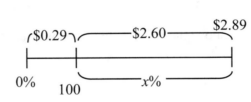

increase = $2.89 − $0.29
= $2.60

$2.60 = (x)($0.29)

$\frac{\$2.60}{\$0.29} = x$

$x \approx 8.97$ or 897%

Example 2: Calculator prices decreased from $59 to $9.95. What was the percent decrease?

decrease = $59 − $9.95
= $49.05

$49.05 = (y)($59)

$\frac{\$49.05}{\$59} = y$

$y \approx 0.83 = 83\%$

8-76.   Joe wanted to know more about how the cost of fertilizer for his lawn care business was changing. The cost of a bag of fertilizer just increased from $8 to $15. What is the percent increase of the price? Represent the change as a fraction, percent, and a decimal.

8-77.   Solve each equation. Show all work.

a. $0.85x = 200$

b. $\frac{7}{6}x = 140$

8-78.   Ellen is building a scale model of the space shuttle. A space shuttle is approximately 122 feet long and has a wingspan of 78 feet.

a.   How many inches long is the space shuttle?

b.   If Ellen builds her model so that 1 cm on the model represents 10 inches on the space shuttle, how many centimeters long will her model be?

c.   What will her model's wingspan be (in centimeters)?

d.   Remember that 1 inch is approximately equal to 2.54 cm. How many inches long will her model be?

8-79.   Graph the rule $y = 2x - 6$. Create a table if it will help.

8-80.   Use the drawing at right to answer the questions below. Assume the figure is drawn to scale.

a.   Identify three types of triangles in the drawing.

b.   What do you know about the angles labeled x and y?

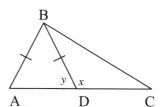

8.2.6 How does it change over time?

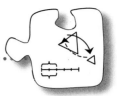

Simple Interest

When banks lend money, they charge **interest**, which is a fee for letting the borrower use the money. Interest is usually expressed as a percent of the amount borrowed, and is added to the amount that the borrower owes. For example, a bank might charge someone an 8% annual (yearly) interest rate for borrowing $500. In addition, if you have money in a savings account, banks generally pay interest to you on the money in the account. So by leaving your money in a bank you are earning more money.

There are different ways of calculating interest, and each one creates different patterns of growth. As you work with your team to investigate one kind of interest called **simple interest**, ask these questions to focus your discussion:

What patterns do you see?

How can you show the connection?

8-81.   RENTING THE HALL

The student council is planning a spring celebration. Unfortunately, to rent a hall for the event, they will need to pay a deposit in advance of the event. Since they have not started selling tickets yet, they asked the Parent-Teacher Association for a loan of $825 for the hall rental. The PTA agreed, but said they would charge 2% simple interest each week until the loan is paid back.

Ms. Becker, the student council advisor, explained to the students that the amount of the loan ($825) is called the **principal** amount. Until the loan is paid back, 2% (called the **weekly interest rate**) of the principal amount will be added to the amount owed each week.

a.   How much interest will the PTA charge each week?

b.   If the student council borrows $825, how much will it owe after 1 week? After 3 weeks? Show your calculations.

c.   How much would the student council owe two months (8 weeks) from now? Be prepared to **justify** your **strategy**.

8-82.   The Student Council members realized that they would also need funds before the event to pay the DJ and photographer a deposit. They will need a second loan of $1000 to pay for these two expenses.

   a.   If the PTA also charges them 2% weekly simple interest for this loan, how much will be added to this loan each week?

   b.   The PTA has decided that to cover its costs it only needs to earn $18 interest each week. What percent weekly interest should they charge the Student Council for this loan? Be prepared to share your **strategy**.

8-83.   A loan agreement between the Student Council and the PTA has finally been reached, but the PTA will not loan the full $1825 requested. To make sure everyone understands the agreement, the PTA created the table below.

Number of Weeks	Calculations	Total Loan Amount
0	$1250	$1250
1	$1250 + $18.75	$1268.75
2	$1250 + $18.75 + $18.75	$1287.50
3		
4		

   a.   Based on this table, how much will the Student Council borrow? What is the percent interest?

   b.   How much will the Student Council owe after 3 weeks? After 4 weeks? Show your calculations.

   c.   How is the amount of money that the Student Council owes changing each week? Show how this change can be found in your table.

   d.   The president wants to be able to quickly know how much the Student Council owes at any point. Use your table to write a variable expression that shows the amount of money the club owes the PTA after any number of weeks. Make sure to define your variable.

   e.   The president figured out that if the Student Council does not pay off the loan by the end of the school year, it would owe $1500. How many weeks of school are left? Use your expression from part (d) to write and solve an equation to answer this question.

8-84.   SHOPPING AROUND

The treasurer of the Student Council decided to look into some other funding options for the DJ and the photographer. With your team, examine how each loan would grow and find a way to compare them. (Assume that a month is 4 weeks). Then find answers to the questions below.

The local bank offered to loan the Student Council $955 for 1% weekly simple interest.

The Math Club offered to loan the Student Council $940 for 4.5% monthly simple interest.

The Booster Club offered to loan the Student Council $960 and would add $36 interest each month.

a.   Which loan would grow more quickly? That is, which has the most interest added each month?

b.   What is the monthly interest rate the Booster Club is offering? Show how you got your answer.

c.   For which loan would the Student Council owe the most money overall after 3 months? **Justify** your answer.

Making Connections: Course 2

METHODS AND MEANINGS

MATH NOTES

Simple Interest

Simple interest is interest paid only on the original amount of the principal at each specified interval (such as annually, or monthly). The formula to calculate simple interest is:

$$I = Prt \qquad \text{where} \qquad \begin{aligned} P &= \text{Principal} \\ I &= \text{Interest} \\ r &= \text{Rate} \\ t &= \text{Time} \end{aligned}$$

Example: Theresa invested $1425.00 in a savings account at her local bank. The bank pays a simple interest rate of 3.5% annually. How much money will Theresa have after 4 years?

$$I = Prt \quad \Rightarrow \quad I = 1425(0.035)(4) = \$199.50$$
$$\Rightarrow \quad P + I = \$1425 + \$199.50 = \$1624.50$$

Theresa will have $1624.50 after 4 years.

8-85. Ida wants to buy a car, but she does not currently have any money. The car she wants costs $2500. Consider her two options and decide which loan she should take.

a. She could borrow $2500 at a monthly interest rate of 4% simple interest and pay the total after 12 months. Write a simple interest expression and calculate what she would owe at the end of 12 months.

b. She could borrow $2500 at a weekly interest rate of 1% simple interest and pay the total after 12 months. Show calculations and a written explanation to **justify** your answer.

8-86.   The Jones family wants to remodel
         their kitchen. They have saved
         $23,000 in the last two years. Their
         contractor says the remodel will
         cost $40,000. They can borrow the
         difference at a monthly interest rate
         of 2% simple interest. If they pay
         the loan off in six months, how
         much will they have paid?

8-87.   Graph the following points on a coordinate grid: $A(-3,-3)$, $B(3,0)$, $C(3,6)$,
         $D(-3,6)$. Connect the points as you plot them. Then connect point A to
         point D.

         a.   Describe the shape you have created.

         b.   Identify the angles at points C and D.

         c.   Record the coordinates of the new points if you were to translate the
               original points three units left and five units up.

8-88.   Martha is saving money to buy a new laptop computer that costs $1800. She
         received $200 for her birthday and has a job where she makes $150 each week.

         a.   Make a table and a graph for this situation.

         b.   Explain how you can use the table or graph to predict how many weeks it
               will take Martha to earn enough money to pay for the new computer.

8-89.   Simplify each expression.

         a. $\frac{5}{4} \div \frac{7}{16}$ b. $-\frac{10}{13} \cdot \frac{5}{11}$ c. $\frac{9}{11} \div (-\frac{20}{21})$ d. $-\frac{8}{3} \div (-\frac{5}{18})$

Chapter 8 Closure   What have I learned?

Reflection and Synthesis

The activities below offer you a chance to reflect about what you have learned during this chapter. As you work, look for concepts that you feel very comfortable with, ideas that you would like to learn more about, and topics you need more help with. Look for connections between ideas as well as connections with material you learned previously.

①   SUMMARIZING MY UNDERSTANDING

This section gives you an opportunity to show what you know about certain math topics or ideas.

With a partner, obtain an envelope from your teacher. Follow the directions below to demonstrate your understanding of solving equations with rate, including those with fractional coefficients.

Part 1:   Decide which one of you is going to work a problem and which one of you is going to listen. (You will have to do both jobs before you are through with this lesson!) The partner working the problem should draw a problem out of the envelope.

Part 2:   **If you are working the problem**, clearly show all of your work on your paper, draw diagrams, and label them completely. Explain what you are thinking to your partner as you work.

            If you are the listener, pay attention to what your partner is saying as he or she solves the problem. When your partner is finished, you must tell him or her whether or not you agree with the solution and why or why not.

Part 3:   Trade jobs with your partner. The partner now working the problem should draw a new problem out of the envelope and explain the solution to the listener.

Two example problems are shown below. The problems are also available at www.cpm.org/students.

Problem A	Problem F
Omar has been riding his bicycle at a speed of 15 mph for 48 miles. How long has he been riding?	34% of the students at Maple Middle School are in the seventh grade. If there are 1300 students at the school, how many students are NOT in the seventh grade?

WHAT HAVE I LEARNED?

Working the problems in this section will help you to evaluate which types of problems you feel comfortable with and which ones you need more help with. This section will appear at the end of every chapter to help you check your understanding.

Solve each problem as completely as you can. The table at the end of this closure section has answers to these problems. It also tells you where you can find additional help and practice on problems like them.

CL 8-90. Aja and Emilie were riding their skateboards. They knew that they could ride 3 miles in 20 minutes. Use your problem solving **strategies** to find out how far the girls can ride in 45 minutes.

CL 8-91. Harley was eating pizza and had already eaten six pieces before his sister, Samantha, got home. Samantha was worried that she was not going to get a fair share of the pizza and wanted to know how many pieces were in the pizza originally. Harley told her, *"I have only eaten $\frac{3}{8}$ of the pizza."* Help Samantha figure out how many pieces of pizza there were to start with.

CL 8-92. Marcus has a summer job where he makes $45 a day. Yesterday, his boss told him that he was getting a raise to $63 a day because he was such a hard worker. What is the percent increase in Marcus' salary?

CL 8-93. Find the area and circumference of a circle with a diameter of 15 cm.

CL 8-94. Simplify and solve the following equations.

a. $5x + 2 = -3x - 14$ b. $2x + 3 = 3x - 12$

c. $2x - 2 = 3x + 4 - 4x$ d. $5x + 6 - 2x = 3x - 7$

CL 8-95. Joe is downloading songs from the Internet. He can download them at a rate of eight songs every 10 minutes. Jasmine, who is also downloading songs, can download at a rate of 12 songs every 15 minutes. Who is downloading songs faster?

CL 8-96. Graph a line that goes through the points $(0, 3)$ and $(2, -1)$. What is the slope of the line?

CL 8-97. Solve the inequality $8 + x \le 3$ and graph the solutions on a number line.

Making Connections: Course 2

CL 8-98. For each of the problems above, do the following:

- Draw a bar or number line that represents 0 to 10.

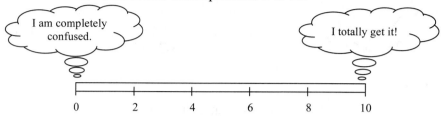

- Color or shade in a portion of the bar that represents your level of understanding and comfort with completing that problem on your own.

If any of your bars are less than a 5, choose *one* of those problems and do one of the following tasks:

- Write two questions that you would like to ask about that problem.
- Brainstorm two things that you DO know about that type of problem.

If all of your bars are a 5 or above, choose one of those problems and do one of these tasks:

- Write two questions you might ask or hints you might give to a student who was stuck on the problem.
- Make a new problem that is similar and more challenging than that problem and solve it.

③   WHAT TOOLS CAN I USE?

You have several tools and references available to help support your learning – your teacher, your study team, your math book, and your Toolkit, to name only a few. At the end of each chapter you will have an opportunity to review your Toolkit for completeness as well as to revise or update it to better reflect your current understanding of big ideas.

The main elements of your Toolkit should be your Learning Log, Math Notes, and the vocabulary used in this chapter. Math words that are new to this chapter appear in bold in the text. Refer to the lists provided below and follow your teacher's instructions to revise your Toolkit, which will help make it a useful reference for you as you complete this chapter and as you work in future chapters.

Learning Log Entries

- Lesson 8.2.2 – Scaling Quantities
- Lesson 8.2.4 – Solving Equations with Fractional Coefficients

Math Notes

- Lesson 8.1.1 – Distance, Rate, and Time
- Lesson 8.1.2 – Equivalent Measures
- Lesson 8.2.1 – Scale Factor
- Lesson 8.2.3 – Scaling
- Lesson 8.2.5 – Percent Increase or Decrease
- Lesson 8.2.6 – Simple Interest

Mathematical Vocabulary

The following is a list of vocabulary found in this chapter. Some of the words have been seen in the previous chapter. The words in bold are the words new to this chapter. Make sure that you are familiar with the terms below and know what they mean. For the words you do not know, refer to the glossary or index. You might also want to add these words to your Toolkit for a way to reference them in the future.

distance	equivalent measure	**interest**
multiplier	**percent decrease**	**percent increase**
principal	rate	scale factor
scaling	time	

Process Words

These words describe problem solving strategies and processes that you have been involved in throughout the course of this chapter. Make sure you know what each of these words means. If you are not sure, you can talk with your teacher or other students or look through your book for problems in which you were asked to do these things.

choose a strategy	compare	connect
describe	estimate	explain your reasoning
generalize	justify	predict
reason	represent	reverse your thinking
simplify	visualize	

Making Connections: Course 2

Answers and Support for Closure Activity #2
What Have I Learned?

Problem	Solution	Need Help?	More Practice
CL 8-90.	The girls can ride $6\frac{3}{4}$ miles in 45 minutes.	Lessons 8.1.1 and 8.1.2 Math Notes box in Lesson 8.1.1	Problems 8-1 through 8-7, 8-19, 8-20, and 8-31
CL 8-91.	There were 16 pieces in the pizza.	Lessons 8.2.3 and 8.2.4 Learning Log (problem 8-65)	Problems 8-48 through 8-53, 8-60, and 8-66
CL 8-92.	Marcus' salary increased by 40%.	Lesson 8.2.5 Math Notes box in Lesson 8.2.5	Problems 8-74 and 8-76
CL 8-93.	Area ≈ 176.7 square cm Circumference ≈ 47.1 cm	Lessons 5.3.3 and 5.3.4 Learning Log (problem 5-124) Math Notes boxes in Lessons 5.3.2 and 5.3.4	Problems 5-125, 5-127, CL 6-140, and 8-10
CL 8-94.	a. $x = -2$ b. $x = 15$ c. $x = 2$ d. no solution	Lessons 6.2.1, 6.2.2, and 6.2.3 Math Notes boxes in Lessons 6.2.1, 6.2.3, and 6.2.6 Learning Log (problem 6-98)	Problems CL 6-141, CL 7-98, and 8-8
CL 8-95.	They are downloading at the same rate.	Lessons 7.1.1, 7.1.2, 7.1.3, and 8.1.2 Math Notes boxes in Lessons 7.1.1 and 7.1.3	Problems CL 7-91 and 8-12

Problem	Solution	Need Help?	More Practice
CL 8-96.	Slope $= -2$	Lessons 7.1.4, 7.1.5, and 7.1.6 Math Notes box in Lesson 7.1.6 Learning Log (problem 7-47)	Problems 7-42, 7-43, and 8-25
CL 8-97.	$x \leq -5$ $-5 \quad -4 \quad -3 \quad -2 \quad -1 \quad 0$	Lessons 5.2.3 and 5.2.4 Math Notes box in Lesson 5.2.1 Learning Log (problem 5-76)	Problems 5-64, 5-65, 5-66, 5-72, 5-73, 5-74, 5-78, and 8-69

Puzzle Investigator Problems

PI-15.   HAPPY NUMBERS

Some numbers have special qualities that earn them a title, such as "square number" or "prime number." This problem will explore another type of number, called "happy numbers."

The number 23 is a happy number. To determine if a number is a happy number, square each of its digits and add.

$$2^2 + 3^2 = 13$$

Repeat this process several times until you get 1, or until you get the same sum twice (see below).

$$1^2 + 3^2 = 10$$

$$1^2 + 0^2 = 1$$

If the final answer is 1, the original number is called a **happy number**.

The number 34 is not happy number, as demonstrated below:

Step #1 $3^2 + 4^2 = 25$
Step #2 $2^2 + 5^2 = 29$
Step #3 $2^2 + 9^2 = 85$
Step #4 $8^2 + 5^2 = \mathbf{89}$
Step #5 $8^2 + 9^2 = 145$
Step #6 $1^2 + 4^2 + 5^2 = 42$
Step #7 $4^2 + 2^2 = 20$
Step #8 $2^2 + 0^2 = 4$
Step #9 $4^2 + 0^2 = 16$
Step #10 $1^2 + 6^2 = 37$
Step #11 $3^2 + 7^2 = 58$
Step #12 $5^2 + 8^2 = \mathbf{89}$

Since 89 is repeated, the final answer will be in a never-ending loop and, therefore, will never equal 1. This means that 34 is *not* a happy number.

a.   There are 17 two-digit happy numbers. Find as many as you can. Remember to keep all your work and ideas organized so you can refer back when writing up what you discovered.

b.   Find 5 three-digit happy numbers.

c.   Eve found out that 478 is a happy number. Based on this, what other numbers must be happy numbers? How do you know? Find at least 10 new happy numbers.

PI-16.   CANDY SALES

For a fundraiser, each math club member must
sell 30 candy bars each day for a week.
Although they all sold the same type of candy,
the members could choose their price to
compete for top sales member.

Alfredo decided to sell three candy bars for $1,
earning $10 per day, while June sold hers at
the rate of two for $1, earning her $15 per day.

One day, both Alfredo and June were on a field trip, so they asked Bomani to
sell their candy bars for them. Bomani agreed and promised he would not
change their prices. Bomani decided that instead of offering three for $1 and
two for $1, he would put them together and sell the 60 candy bars at the rate of
five for $2.

When Alfredo and June returned, Bomani handed them the money he had
earned for the day, $24. Alfredo and June were angry and demanded the dollar
they were sure Bomani stole! Bomani is now confused... what happened?

Your task: Discover what really happened to the extra dollar, and write a letter
to Alfredo and June before this scene turns really ugly.

Proportions and Pythagorean Theorem

CHAPTER 9 Proportions and Pythagorean Theorem

Maps, blueprints, and scale models all have one thing in common: they are proportional to what they represent. This is a concept that you will explore in Section 9.1 for similar figures, bank accounts, and gas mileage in cars. You will study proportional relationships using tables, graphs, and the Giant One.

In Section 9.2 you will broaden your work with similar shapes to include working with their areas and perimeters. You will solve puzzles by looking at how shapes can be fit together as their area and perimeter grow and shrink and learn short cuts for finding the area and perimeter of larger and smaller similar shapes.

Guiding Questions

Think about these questions throughout this chapter:

What's the relationship?

How else can I solve it?

What is being compared?

Which shapes are similar?

In Section 9.3, you will focus on the relationships between side lengths in individual triangles. You will learn how to decide if three different lengths will be able to form a triangle. You will use the unique relationship between the sides of right triangles to solve problems involving missing side lengths. You will also learn about a new mathematical operation, square root, and how it relates to squaring a number. Finally, you will look at some special numbers called irrationals and how they are different from other numbers you have dealt with.

In this chapter, you will learn how to:

> Set up and solve proportional equations.

> Identify and use the ratio between the areas of two similar shapes.

> Find missing side lengths of right triangles using the Pythagorean Theorem.

> Find the square root of a number and identify irrational numbers.

Chapter Outline

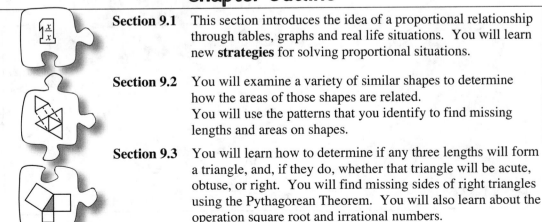

Section 9.1 This section introduces the idea of a proportional relationship through tables, graphs and real life situations. You will learn new **strategies** for solving proportional situations.

Section 9.2 You will examine a variety of similar shapes to determine how the areas of those shapes are related.
You will use the patterns that you identify to find missing lengths and areas on shapes.

Section 9.3 You will learn how to determine if any three lengths will form a triangle, and, if they do, whether that triangle will be acute, obtuse, or right. You will find missing sides of right triangles using the Pythagorean Theorem. You will also learn about the operation square root and irrational numbers.

Making Connections: Course 2

9.1.1 How does it grow?

Recognizing Proportional Relationships

Grocery stores often advertise special prices for fruits and vegetables that are in season. You might see a sign that says, "Special Today! Buy 2 pounds of apples for $1.29!" How would you use that information to predict how much you need to pay if you want to buy six pounds of apples? Or just 1 pound of apples? The way that the cost of apples grows (or shrinks) allows you to use a variety of different **strategies** to predict and estimate prices for different amounts (measured in pounds) of apples. In this section, you will explore different kinds of growth patterns and use those patterns to develop **strategies** for making predictions and deciding if answers are **reasonable**.

As you work in this section, ask yourself these questions to help you identify different patterns:

How are the entries in the table related?

Can I double the values?

What patterns can I see in a graph?

9-1.   COLLEGE FUND

Gustavo's grandmother put money in a college savings account for him on his birthday five years ago. The account pays simple interest, and now after five years the account is worth $500. Gustavo is planning ahead, and he predicts that if he does not deposit or withdraw any money then the account balance will be $1000 five years from now.

a.   How do you think Gustavo made his prediction?

b.   Do you agree with Gustavo's **reasoning**? Explain why or why not.

9-2.   When Gustavo got his bank statement in the mail, he was surprised to see a graph that showed that although his balance was growing at a steady rate, the bank predicted that in five years his account balance would be only $600. *"What is going on?"* he wondered. *"Why isn't my money growing the way I thought it would?"*

With your team, discuss how much Gustavo's account appears to be growing every year. Why might his account be growing in a different way than he expected? Be ready to share your ideas.

9-3. Gustavo decided to look more carefully at his balances for the last few years to see if the bank's prediction might be a mistake. He put together the table below:

Time since Original Deposit (in yrs)	2	3	4	5
Bank Balance (in dollars)	440	460	480	500

a. How has Gustavo's bank balance been growing?

b. Does Gustavo's money seem to doubling as time doubles? Explain your **reasoning**.

9-4. Once he saw the balances written in a table, Gustavo decided to take a closer look at the graph from the bank to see if he could figure out where he made the mistake in his prediction. Find the graph at right on the Lesson 9.1.1 Resource Page.

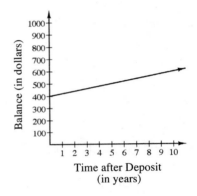

a. What additional information about Gustavo's account can you tell from the graph? For example, what was his starting balance? How much does it grow in 5 years?

b. Gustavo had assumed his money would double after 10 years. What graph would have resulted if that were true? Using a new color, add a line to the graph that represents what Gustavo was thinking.

c. How is the line for Gustavo's prediction similar to the bank's graph? How is it different?

d. Is it possible that Gustavo's account could have had $0 in it in Year 0? Why or why not?

e. Gustavo's mother looked at the graphs and his bank balance and said, *"Gustavo, you doubled the wrong amount when you made your prediction!"* What do you think his mother meant? What "doubles" in the graph? How else can you see this change?

Making Connections: Course 2

9-5.   FOR THE BIRDS

When filling her bird feeder, Sonja noticed
that she paid $24 for four pounds of
birdseed. *"Next time, I'm going to buy
8 pounds instead so I can make it through
the spring. That should cost $48."*

a. Does Sonja's assumption that doubling
the amount of birdseed would double
the price make sense? Is it
reasonable? Why or why not? How
much would you predict that 2 pounds
of birdseed would cost?

b. To check her assumption, she found a receipt for 1 pound of birdseed
(which cost $6). She decided to make a table, which is started below.
Copy and complete her table.

Pounds	0	1	2	3	4	5	6	8
Cost		$6			$24			

c. How do the amounts in the table grow?

d. Work with your team to describe two different **strategies** for finding the
cost of 6 pounds of birdseed.

e. Does the table confirm Sonja's doubling relationship? Give 2 examples
from the table that show how doubling the pounds will double the cost.

9-6.   What makes the Sonja's birdseed situation different from Gustavo's college
        fund? Why does doubling work for one situation but not in the other? Consider
        this as you examine the graphs below.

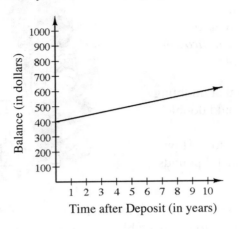

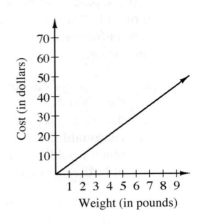

a. With your team:

    • Describe how each graph is the same.

    • Describe what makes each graph different.

b. How do the differences explain why doubling works in one situation and
    not the other? **Generalize** why doubling works in one situation and not in
    another.

c. The pattern of growth in Sonja's example of buying birdseed is an example
    of a **proportional relationship**. In a proportional relationship, if one
    quantity is multiplied by a scale factor, the other is scaled by the same
    amount. Gustavo's bank account is *not* proportional because it grows
    differently; when the number of years doubled, his balance did not.

    Work with your team to list other characteristics of proportional
    relationships, based on Sonja's and Gustavo's examples. Be as specific as
    possible.

Making Connections: Course 2

9-7.   IS IT PROPORTIONAL?

When making a prediction, it is important to be able to recognize whether a relationship is proportional or not.

Your task: Work with your team to read each new situation below. Decide whether you think the relationship described is **proportional** or **non-proportional** and **justify** your **reasoning**. Be prepared to share your decisions and **justifications** with the class.

a. Carlos wants to buy some new video games. Each game he buys costs him $36. Is the relationship between the number of games Carlos buys and the total price proportional?

b. Single tickets cost $56 while five tickets cost $250. Is the relationship between the number of tickets bought and the total price proportional?

c. Vu is four years older than his sister. Is the relationship between Vu and his sister's age proportional?

d. The triangles at right are similar. Is the relationship between the sides of one triangle and the corresponding sides of the other proportional?

e. Carl just bought a music player and plans to load 50 songs each week. Is the relationship between the number of weeks after Carl bought the music player and the number of songs on his player proportional?

f. Anna has a new video game. It takes her five hours of playing the game to master level one. After so much time, Anna better understands the game and it only takes her three hours of playing the game to master level two. Is the number of hours played and the game level proportional?

9-8.   LEARNING LOG

In your Learning Log, explain how you can tell if a relationship is proportional or not. Give several examples of a proportional relationship and at least one that is not proportional. Label this entry "Proportional Relationships" and include today's date.

9-9.   The lemonade stand at the county fair sells the lemonade at a price of two cups for $3.00. Complete the table below to find what Paula's family will pay to buy lemonade for all 8 members of the family.

# of Lemonades	Price (in dollars)
1	
2	3.00
3	
4	
5	
6	
7	
8	

9-10.   Carmen is downloading music for her piPod. It costs $1.75 for each song. Is this relationship proportional? Explain your **reasoning**.

9-11.   Graph the rule $y = \frac{3}{2}x + 2$. What is the slope? Explain what **strategies** you used to graph this rule.

9-12.   Samantha's parents are going to paint her room. Her color choices for the walls include three different shades of white, four shades of tan, two shades of blue, three shades of green, and four shades of pink. What is the probability that she will select any shade of blue or pink?

9-13.   The local sports shop has backpacks on sale for $28. The original price was $40. What is the percent of decrease for the backpack price?

9-14.   Simplify the expressions below.

a. $\frac{3}{4} - \frac{1}{3} + (-\frac{5}{24})$ b. $\frac{10}{12} \div \frac{1}{4}$ c. $3\frac{1}{2} \cdot 1\frac{3}{8}$ d. $-\frac{20}{7} \div \frac{1}{3}$

e. $-\frac{8}{25} \cdot (-\frac{15}{32})$ f. $\frac{9}{4} \div (-\frac{2}{3})$ g. $\frac{8}{21} + (-\frac{3}{7})$ h. $\frac{7}{4} \cdot (-\frac{2}{5}) \cdot \frac{3}{5}$

9.1.2   How can a graph help?

Proportional Equations

Proportional relationships can be identified in both tables and graphs. Today you will have
an opportunity to take a closer look at how graphs and slope triangles for proportional
relationships can help you organize your work to quickly find any missing value.

9-15.   Robert's new hybrid car has a gas tank that
          holds 12 gallons of gas. When the tank is
          full, he can drive 420 miles. Assume that his
          car uses gas at a steady rate.

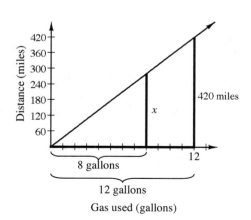

   a. Is the relationship between the number
       of gallons of gas used and the number
       of miles that can be driven
       proportional? For example, does it
       change like Sonja's birdseed prediction,
       or is it like Gustavo's college savings?
       Explain how you know.

   b. Show how much gas Robert's car will use at various distances by copying
       and completing the table below.

Distance driven (in miles)	0	3	6	12
Gas used (in gallons)				420

   c. Robert decided to graph the
       situation, as shown at right.
       Use Robert's graph to predict
       how far he can drive using
       eight gallons of gas.

   d. While a graph is a useful tool for
       estimating, it is often difficult to
       find an exact answer on a graph.
       Ian was looking at Robert's graph
       and noticed two slope triangles.
       Both triangles have a vertex at
       $(0,0)$. What does x represent?

Problem continues on next page. →

9-15.   *Problem continued from previous page.*

  e.   Using the triangles, he wrote the equation $\frac{420 \text{ miles}}{12 \text{ gallons}} = \frac{x \text{ miles}}{8 \text{ gallons}}$.

        How do the ratios he wrote relate to the triangles on the graph? Why are the ratios equal?

  f.   Work with your team to use the equation to find the exact number of miles Robert can drive with eight gallons of gas. Be prepared to share your **strategy**.

  g.   Use your graph and Ian's **strategy** to find out how far Robert can go on five gallons of gas.

9-16.   Lexie claims she can send 14 text messages in 22 minutes. Her teammates Kenny and Esther are trying to predict how many text messages Lexie can send in a 55 minute lunch period if she keeps going at the same rate.

  a.   Is the relationship between the number of text messages and time in minutes proportional? Why or why not?

  b.   Kenny represented the situation using similar triangles, while Esther wrote an equation. Their work is shown below.

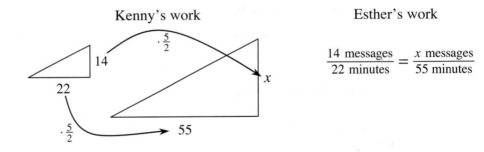

Kenny's work   Esther's work

$\frac{14 \text{ messages}}{22 \text{ minutes}} = \frac{x \text{ messages}}{55 \text{ minutes}}$

        Why do you think Kenny organized his information on triangles?

  c.   Why did Esther set up this equation? Does it make sense to compare these quantities?

Problem continues on next page. →

Making Connections: Course 2

9-16.   *Problem continued from previous page.*

d.   Kenny said, *"The scale factor I found can be written like a Giant One in your equation."* He wrote,

$$\frac{14 \text{ messages}}{22 \text{ minutes}} \cdot \frac{\frac{5}{2}}{\frac{5}{2}} = \frac{x \text{ messages}}{55 \text{ minutes}}$$

Does Kenny's work make sense? Simplify the expression. Is the answer the same as what you found in part (b)?

e.   Use what you know about proportional relationships to determine how many text messages Lexie could send in a different number of minutes. Show your work and your **reasoning**.

9-17.   THE YOGURT SHOP

Jell E. Bean owns the local frozen yogurt shop. At her store customers serve themselves a bowl of frozen yogurt and top it with chocolate chips, frozen raspberries, or any of the different treats available. Customers must then weigh their creation and are charged by the weight.

Jell E. Bean charges $32 for five pounds of dessert, but not many people buy that much frozen yogurt. She needs you to help her figure out how much to charge her customers. She has customers that are young children who buy only a small amount of yogurt as well as large groups that come in and pay for everyone's yogurt together.

a.   Is it **reasonable** to assume that the weight of the yogurt is proportional to its cost? How can you tell?

b.   Assuming it is proportional, make a table that lists the price for at least 10 different weights of yogurt that Jell E. Bean can enlarge to hang in her store. Be sure to include at least three weights that are not whole numbers.

c.   If Jell E. Bean decided to start charging $0.50 for each cup before her customers started filling it with yogurt and toppings, could you use the same **strategies** to find the new prices? If five pounds of yogurt still costs $32 (plus $0.50 for the cup), how much would half as much cost? How much would $\frac{1}{5}$ of a pound cost?

METHODS AND **M**EANINGS

Directly Proportional Relationships

A relationship is **directly proportional** if one quantity is a multiple of the other. Often in this course we will compare two quantities at the same time written as ratios and use a Giant One as the multiplier, as long as the ratio is always the same. For example, if 3 pounds of chicken costs $7, then 6 pounds of chicken costs $14. All other equivalent ratios can be found by multiplying by a Giant One.

Example: Three pounds of chicken costs $7.00. What is the cost for 12 pounds?

$$\frac{3 \text{ pounds}}{\$7} \cdot \left[\frac{4}{4}\right] = \frac{12 \text{ pounds}}{\$28}$$

Twelve pounds of chicken will cost $28.00. Other table values are shown and the values are plotted on the graph below.

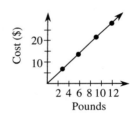

Pounds (x)	0	3	6	9	12
Cost (y)	0	7	14	21	28

The relationship between pounds and cost is directly proportional.

Example: The county fair costs $5.00 to enter and $1.00 per ride.

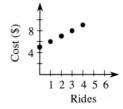

Rides (x)	0	1	2	3	4
Cost (y)	5	6	7	8	9

The relationship between rides and cost is not proportional because, for example, someone who goes on four rides ($9) does not pay twice as much as someone who went on two rides ($7). There is no multiplier for the relationship.

The general form of a **direct proportion**, also called **direct variation**, is $y = kx$, where k is the constant multiplier.

9-18.   Complete this proportion table and graph the results.

Pounds of Nails	2	3		6		10		x
Cost ($)			1.25	1.50	2.00		5.00	

   a.   What is the slope of the graph?

   b.   What does the slope tell you about the cost of nails?

9-19.   The choir is planning a trip to the water park.
          The cost to use a school bus is $350. Complete
          the table at right, graph your result, then answer
          parts (a) and (b).

   a.   Is this a proportional relationship?

   b.   Is there a correlation? How do you know?
        If so, what is it?

Number of students on the trip	Bus cost per student ($)
10	
15	
20	
35	

9-20.   Simplify and solve each equation below for x. Show your work and check your
          answer.

   a. $24 = 3x + 3$

   b. $2(x - 6) = x - 14$

   c. $3(2x - 3) = 4x - 5$

   d. $\frac{3}{4}x = 2x - 5$

9-21.   Joaquin has agreed to lend his younger brother $45 so that he can buy a new
          tank for his pet lizard. Joaquin is charging his brother 2% simple interest per
          month. If his brother pays him back in 6 months, how much will Joaquin get
          back?

9-22.   Tina's rectangular living room floor measures 15 feet by 18 feet.

   a.   How many square feet of carpet will Tina need to cover the entire floor?

   b.   The carpet Tina likes is sold by the square yard. How many square yards
        will she need?

9.1.3 How can I find the missing value?

Solving Proportions

You have examined several proportional contexts (such as the price of yogurt versus the number of pounds of yogurt) and non-proportional contexts (such as the value of a college fund over time). Today you will continue to develop **strategies** for solving proportional equations.

9-23.   J.R. reduced figure A at right so that it became the similar figure B.

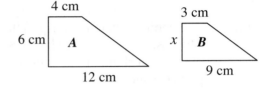

a.   Write all the ratios that compare the corresponding sides of figure B to figure A. What is the relationship between these ratios? How do you know?

b.   One of the relationships between the sides can be written as $\frac{3}{4} = \frac{x}{6}$. Find two different ways to find the value of x in this equation. Is your answer **reasonable**? Be ready to share your **strategies** with the class.

9-24.   MULTIPLE STRATEGIES

J.R.'s team is trying to find multiple ways to solve $\frac{3}{4} = \frac{x}{6}$ from problem 9-23. With your team, analyze each of the **strategies** below. Some of these **strategies** might be the same as what you came up with in problem 9-23. However, others may be new. Work to understand each **strategy** so that you can use it to solve a new problem.

a.   J.R. wants to use a **Giant One** to help find the value of x. Explain how he can find a value to use as a numerator and denominator in a Giant One, then find the value of x.

$$\frac{3}{4} \cdot \boxed{\frac{}{}} = \frac{x}{6}$$

Problem continues on next page. →

Making Connections: Course 2

9-24. *Problem continued from previous page.*

  b. Looking at J.R.'s work, Leticia said, *"I see it differently. We just need to find some number that when divided by 6 you get $\frac{3}{4}$. We can **undo the division** by multiplying each side of the proportion by 6 like this."*

$$\left(\tfrac{6}{1}\right)\tfrac{3}{4} = \tfrac{x}{6}\left(\tfrac{6}{1}\right)$$

  Work with your team to explain how Leticia's idea works. Are the two ratios still equal? Why did she choose to multiply by 6? Simplify each side of the equation.

  c. Avner asked, *"But if multiplying both sides by 6 gets rid of the denominator of the x, then can we use the same **strategy** to get rid of the 4 in the other denominator?"* Discuss Avner's question and decide if **undoing both denominators** is a **reasonable strategy**. Does this help solve the equation?

$$\frac{3}{4} = \frac{x}{6}$$
$$\frac{4 \cdot 6}{1}\left(\frac{3}{4}\right) = \left(\frac{x}{6}\right)\frac{4 \cdot 6}{1}$$
$$(6)(3) = (x)(4)$$

  Avner's work

9-25. Use the **strategies** from problem 9-24 to solve the problems below.

  a. Use Leticia's method of **undoing** division to solve this proportion: $\frac{p}{22.5} = \frac{7}{5}$. When you find p, replace the value in the original proportion to confirm that the two ratios are equal.

  b. Write and solve a proportional equation for x for the similar triangles at right. Then use Avner's method of **undoing** both denominators to solve for x.

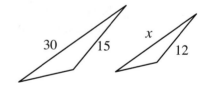

  c. An apple juice container has a tiny hole in it so it is slowly leaking. If the container leaks three ounces every 19 minutes, how long will it take for the 16 ounces of juice in the container to leak out? Write a proportional equation and solve with J.R.'s **strategy** of using a Giant One.

9-26.   For each problem below, decide if the situation is proportional. If the problem is proportional, solve the problem using any **strategy you choose**. If the problem is not proportional explain why it is not proportional and then solve the problem.

   a.   Steve drove 130 miles from Portland to Tacoma in 2 hours. If he continues to drive at the same speed, how long will it take him to drive 390 miles?

   b.   At an amusement park you pay a $15 entrance fee and then $4 for each ride you go on. How much will it cost you to go on seven rides?

   c.   Armando has collected 39 bottle caps in the past three months. At this rate, how many bottle caps will he have in five months?

   d.   The grocery store sells 3 limes for 99 cents. At this rate, how much will a dozen limes cost?

   e.   Margarit drove her friends to a movie. She drove for 30 minutes at 10 miles per hour in heavy traffic, then drove for 15 minutes at 40 miles per hour. How far did she travel in those 45 minutes?

9-27.   After Ramona had solved several proportional equations, she noticed a pattern. *"It looks like we just multiplied diagonally."*

$$\frac{10}{4} = \frac{x}{7}$$
$$(7)(10) = (x)(4)$$

   a.   What does she mean? For each of the proportions below, apply Ramona's diagonal multiplying pattern and determine whether the result is a true mathematical equation. Will her pattern always work?

$$\frac{8}{10} = \frac{12}{15}, \quad \frac{6}{4} = \frac{9}{6}, \text{ and } \frac{15}{3} = \frac{20}{4}$$

   b.   Then use her pattern to solve the equation $\frac{2}{5} = \frac{11}{x}$ for x.

METHODS AND MEANINGS

MATH NOTES

Solving Proportions

An equation stating that two ratios are equal is called a **proportion**. Some examples of proportions are shown at right:

$$\frac{6\text{ mi}}{2\text{ hr}} = \frac{9\text{ mi}}{3\text{ hr}} \qquad \frac{5}{7} = \frac{50}{70}$$

When two ratios are known to be equal, setting up a proportion is one strategy for solving for an unknown part of one ratio. For example, if the ratios $\frac{9}{2}$ and $\frac{x}{16}$ are equal, setting up the proportion $\frac{x}{16} = \frac{9}{2}$ allows you to solve for x.

Strategy 1: One way to solve this proportion is by using a **Giant One** to find the equivalent ratio. In this case, since the scale factor between 2 and 16 is 8, we create the Giant One below,

$$\frac{x}{16} = \frac{9}{2} \cdot \boxed{\frac{8}{8}} = \frac{9 \cdot 8}{2 \cdot 8} = \frac{72}{16} \quad \text{which shows that} \quad \frac{x}{16} = \frac{72}{16} \quad \text{so} \quad x = 72$$

Strategy 2: Use the inverse to undo. Another way to solve the proportion is to think of the ratio $\frac{x}{16}$ as, "x divided by 16." To solve for x, use the inverse operation of division, which is multiplication. Multiplying both sides of the proportional equation by 16 "undoes" the division.

$$\frac{x}{16} = \frac{9}{2}$$

$$\left(\frac{16}{1}\right)\frac{x}{16} = \frac{9}{2}\left(\frac{16}{1}\right)$$

$$x = \frac{144}{2} = 72$$

Strategy 3: Use Cross Multiplication. This is a solving strategy for proportions that is based on the process of multiplying each side of the equation by the denominators of each ratio and setting the two sides equal.

Complete Algebraic Solution

$$\frac{x}{16} = \frac{9}{2}$$
$$2 \cdot 16 \cdot \frac{x}{16} = \frac{9}{2} \cdot 2 \cdot 16$$
$$2 \cdot x = 9 \cdot 16$$
$$2x = 144$$
$$x = 72$$

Cross Multiplication

$$\frac{x}{16} = \frac{9}{2}$$
$$\frac{x}{16} \diagup\!\!\!\!\diagdown \frac{9}{2}$$
$$2 \cdot x = 9 \cdot 16$$
$$2x = 144$$
$$x = 72$$

9-28.   Solve the proportions using any **strategy you choose** and show all of your steps.

   a. $\frac{35}{70} = \frac{x}{100}$ b. $\frac{12}{33} = \frac{m}{11}$ c. $\frac{x}{15} = \frac{12}{75}$ d. $\frac{4}{32} = \frac{10.5}{x}$

9-29.   Triangle *ABC* is similar to triangle *DEF*.

   a. Find the scale factor
       from triangle *ABC* to
       triangle *DEF*.

   b. Find *x*.

   c. Find *y*.

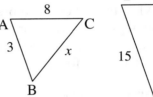

9-30.   Complete the table.

x	-6	3	6	0		1
y		4		2	-4	

   a. Find the rule.   b. What is the slope?

9-31.   Find the area and circumference of a circle that has a diameter of 17 mm. Write
         your answers in terms of π and as a decimal approximation.

9-32.   A ten-speed bicycle was originally priced at $1100. It is on sale for $500.
         What is the percent of decrease?

9-33.   Louis recorded how many times he could jump rope without stopping.
         Here is his data:

                   50 15 102 64 29 55 100 97 48 81 61

         Find the median, upper quartile, and lower quartile of his data.

9.2.1 How are the areas and perimeters related?

Area and Perimeter of Similar Shapes

As you have discovered in recent lessons, the sides of similar shapes can be compared in several different ways. In Chapter 4, you used scale factors to enlarge and reduce the size of similar figures and examined the side lengths of those figures as they changed. You also looked at perimeter and area using toothpicks and tiles. In this lesson, you will investigate whether there is a pattern to how the perimeters and areas of similar shapes grow.

9-34.   Jenna and Greg own a lawn care service. Jenna mows the lawns and charges $25 an hour. She has one customer (Mr. Dunlap) whose rectangular lawn is 18 yards by 30 yards (which takes one hour to mow). Mr. Dunlap mentions that his neighbor, Mrs. Toliver, wants to hire Jenna and that her rectangular lawn is "3 times as big" as Mr. Dunlap's. Jenna expects this job to take 3 hours.

a.   Draw a sketch of Mr. Dunlap's lawn. What is the area of Mr. Dunlap's lawn?

b.   According to Jenna's estimate, what is she assuming the area of Mrs. Toliver's lawn to be?

9-35.   Jenna gets the job at Mrs. Toliver's (see problem 9-34). On her first day, she is worried because after 3 hours, she has not completed even half of the job! She measures the rectangular lawn and finds out it has side lengths that are three times the length of Mr. Dunlap's.

   a.   What are the lengths of the sides of Mrs. Toliver's lawn? What is the area of her lawn?

   b.   Mr. Dunlap was describing the scale factor of the side lengths, not the area. What is the scale factor of the areas? That is, what would you multiply the area of Mr. Dunlap's lawn by to get the area of Mrs. Toliver's lawn?

   c.   Greg trims around the outside of each lawn while Jenna mows. If it usually takes him an hour to trim Mr. Dunlap's lawn, how long will it take him to trim Mrs. Toliver's lawn? Discuss the questions below with your team, and then explain your conclusion.

   •   What is the perimeter of each lawn?

   •   What is the scale factor of the two perimeters?

   •   Is the new perimeter longer than Greg expected from Mr. Dunlap's description?

9-36.   Jenna now realizes that her similarity diagram, which shows only the scale factor of the side lengths, is as unclear as Mr. Dunlap's description. She decided she should add more information, as shown in the diagram at right.

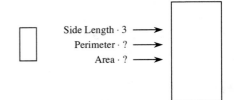

Use your results from the previous problem to copy the figures and complete the scale factors for the perimeter and area of the larger lawn.

9-37. Although the lawns that Jenna and Greg mowed were similar shapes, their areas and perimeters did not have the same scale factor. What exactly is the relationship of the scale factor between the sides of similar shapes and the area of those shapes? To investigate this question with your study team, get a set of pattern blocks and a copy of the Lesson 9.2.1A Resource Page from your teacher.

a. Take out a green triangle like the one at right. Using only other green triangles, build a similar shape with new side lengths that have a scale factor of two. Record the scale factors for the side lengths, perimeter, and area of the enlargement on the diagram provided on the resource page.

b. What if the shape is not doubled? Now use triangles to build a shape with a scale factor of 3 (so that its side lengths are three times as long as the small green triangle). Record the scale factors for the side length, perimeter, and area of the enlargement on your resource page. Repeat the process for a scale factor of 4.

c. What if the shape is not a triangle? Take out an orange square and follow the same process by building similar figures with scale factors of 2, 3, and 4 and finding the scale factors for the side length, perimeter, and area of the enlargements. Record your work on the resource page.

d. Do the patterns continue for other shapes? Take out a blue rhombus and follow the same process by building similar figures and finding the missing scale factors on the resource page. Record your work on the resource page.

e. **Additional Challenge:** Does this pattern of growth work for an isosceles trapezoid when the longer base of the trapezoid pattern block is twice the length of the shorter base? Repeat the process that you have done with other shapes for a scale factor of 2 and 3. Record your work on your resource page. If you can complete the resource page for a scale factor of 4, do so. If not, build the trapezoid shape with a scale factor of 4 and record your work.

9-38. Look carefully at the data on your scale factor resource page. How is the scale factor for side length related to the scale factor for perimeter of each enlarged shape? How is the scale factor for side length related to the scale factor for area? Be prepared to share your team's ideas with the class.

9-39.   A parallelogram with an area of 60 square units is enlarged to make a similar parallelogram with sides that are 10 times the length of the original. What is the area of the enlarged parallelogram?

9-40.   LEARNING LOG

What patterns do you see between the area of a shape and the scale factor of its side? If you know how a side of a shape is enlarged or reduced, can you use that information to make a prediction about the area? Write a Learning Log entry summarizing what you understand so far about the connection between scale factor and area in similar shapes. Title this entry, "Area Relationships in Similar Shapes," and label it with today's date.

9-41.   The two triangles at right are similar.

a. Find x.

b. Find the area of the smaller triangle.

c. Based on ratios of similarity, find the area of the large triangle.

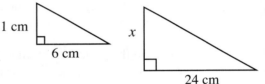

d. Find the area of the larger triangle by using the formula for the area of a triangle.

e. Verify that your answers to (c) and (d) are the same.

Making Connections: Course 2

9-42. In the polygons at right, all corresponding angles are the same and the side lengths are as shown.

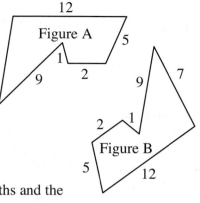

a. Find the ratios of the corresponding sides.

b. Are the two figures similar?

c. What is the special name for similar figures with a scale factor of $\frac{1}{1}$?

d. What does this tell you about the side lengths and the angles of the two shapes?

9-43. Find the numbers that belong in the Giant One in each problem to create an equivalent fraction. Copy each problem, and show the values you used within the Giant One.

a. $\frac{7}{12} \cdot \boxed{} = \frac{56}{m}$

b. $\frac{8}{3} \cdot \boxed{} = \frac{n}{48}$

c. $\frac{20}{26} \cdot \boxed{} = \frac{k}{39}$

d. $\frac{20}{42} \cdot \boxed{} = \frac{50}{h}$

9-44. Roger has a bag of marbles. There are 6 red, 4 blue, 3 white, and 7 green marbles in the bag. If he draws one marble and replaces it, find the following probabilities:

a. P(red)

b. P(not white or green)

c. P(blue or white)

9-45. Michaela is swimming at a rate of 25 feet in 4 minutes. At this rate, how far will she swim in 15 minutes?

9.2.2 Is the area relationship proportional?

Growth Patterns in Area

You have seen that when two figures are similar, their areas do not grow at the same rate as their sides. Is the area relationship still a proportion? Can proportions be set up to solve problems involving area of similar shapes? In today's lesson, you will investigate how to extend what you know about proportional relationships to work with the areas of similar figures.

9-46.   Ryan and Julia are working to find the area of a shape that is similar to the 2 cm by 3 cm rectangle at right. All they are told about the new shape is that it is similar and has a shorter side that is 80 cm long.

3 cm

2 cm

Julia made a sketch of the new shape, and wants to find the length of the longer side so that she can find its area. But Ryan is impatient, and he thinks he has a shortcut. *"The shapes are similar, so I think that there is a constant ratio. I am going to set up a proportion."* Here is Ryan's equation:

$$\frac{\text{side length}}{\text{area}} = \frac{2 \text{ cm}}{6 \text{ cm}^2} = \frac{80 \text{ cm}}{x \text{ cm}^2}$$

When Julia finished her calculations, she looked at Ryan's work and his answer. *"That's really different from what I found, Ryan,"* she said. *"I'm not sure that we can use a proportion here."* What is Julia talking about?

a.   Solve Ryan's equation to find his answer for area. Follow Julia's process to find the missing side, then calculate the area she found for the enlarged shape.

b.   Which answer is more **reasonable**? Why? Work with your team to **justify** your conclusion.

Making Connections: Course 2

9-47.   In Lesson 9.2.1, you noticed that the area and perimeter of shapes did not grow at the same rate. Which relationships between similar shapes are proportional, and which are not? Work with your team to investigate.

a.   On graph paper, draw rectangles similar to the 2 cm by 3 cm rectangle in problem 9-46. Use scale factors of 2, 3, 4, 5, and 6. Record your data in a table like the one below.

scale factor (side)	Original (1)	2	3	4	5	6
Length (cm)	3	6				
Width (cm)	2	4				
Perimeter (cm)	10					
Area (cm²)	6					

b.   Is the ratio between the length and width of similar rectangles proportional? How can you tell?

c.   Is the relationship between a rectangle's area and length proportional? **Justify** your conclusion.

d.   If a new similar shape has a scale factor of 10 for its length and width, how could you predict its area *without* calculating the new shape's length and width? Work with your study team to describe a **general** process.

9-48.   Jenna thinks she understands how scale factor relates to perimeter and area, but she has now been asked to mow lawns that are smaller than Mr. Dunlap's 18 yard by 30 yard lawn. She is trying to give a price quote for the smaller lawns and wonders if she can use the same patterns she found for scale factor when the similar lawns were bigger.

a.   Work with your team to draw diagrams for lawns so that the scale factors for the side lengths are $\frac{1}{2}$, $\frac{1}{3}$, and $\frac{1}{6}$. Use graph paper so you can accurately find the perimeter and area of the new lawns. Then complete similarity diagrams for each scale factor.

b.   Explain to Jenna how she can use the patterns she has found for scale factors to figure out how much to charge for mowing any size lawn.

9-49.   Use the patterns you identified between the scale factor for sides of similar
          shapes and their areas to find the missing scale factors and areas below.

    a.   If the area of rectangle A is
        14 cm², what is the area of
        rectangle B?

    b.   If the area of triangle C is
        125 in², what is the area of
        triangle D?

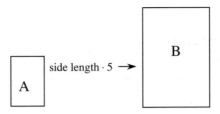

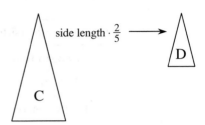

9-50.   **Additional Challenge:** Use what you know about ratios between similar figures
          to draw similarity diagrams and answer the following questions:

    a.   If you start with a 4 by 4 square and enlarge each side by a factor of $\frac{5}{4}$,
        calculate the perimeter and area using the scale factors.

    b.   Sketch the 4 by 4 square and its $\frac{5}{4}$ enlargement on graph paper. Was your
        answer from part (a) correct? Explain in complete sentences.

    c.   Begin with a 6 by 9 rectangle and create a new smaller rectangle using a
        scale factor of $\frac{1}{3}$. Calculate perimeter and area of the new rectangle.

    d.   A 3 by 5 rectangle is enlarged by a scale factor of $\frac{3}{1}$. Calculate the
        perimeter and area of the enlargement.

METHODS AND **M**EANINGS

MATH NOTES

Ratios of Similarity

When figures are similar, the ratio of their perimeters or diagonals is the same as the scale factor of the side lengths, while the ratio of the areas is the square of the scale factor of the sides. For the new and original figures:

The **perimeter ratio** is $\left(\frac{\text{new perimeter}}{\text{original perimeter}}\right) = \text{scale factor}$.

The **area ratio** is $\left(\frac{\text{new area}}{\text{original area}}\right) = (\text{scale factor})^2$.

For example, suppose you know that the two rectangles below are similar with a scale factor of $\frac{3}{2}$. Since the perimeter of the smaller rectangle is 20 m, the perimeter of the larger one is $\frac{3}{2} \cdot 20$ m $= 30$ m. Since the area of the smaller rectangle is 24 m^2, the area of the larger rectangle is $(\frac{3}{2})^2 \cdot 24$ m$^2 = (\frac{9}{4}) \cdot 24$ m$^2 = 54$ m^2.

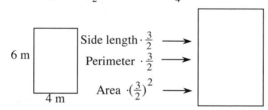

perimeter

$\frac{3}{2} = \frac{\text{new perimeter}}{20}$, P = 30 m

area

$(\frac{3}{2})^2 = \frac{\text{new area}}{24}$, $\frac{9}{4} = \frac{\text{new area}}{24}$,

A = 54 m^2

Review & Preview

9-51.   The area of a rectangle is 42 cm^2. If the length and width each grow four times longer, what will the new area be?

9-52. $\triangle ABC$ and $\triangle DEF$ are similar.

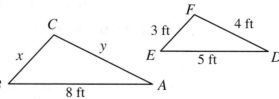

a.   Find x.

b.   Find y.

c.   Find the ratio of the perimeters of the two triangles.

d.   Can you predict the ratio of the areas of the two triangles? If so, state it. If not, write the information you would need or the question you would need to answer first.

Problem continues on next page. →

Chapter 9: Proportions and Pythagorean Theorem

9-52.   *Problem continued from previous page.*

e. Triangle *RST* is congruent to triangle *DEF*.
    Based on this, what are the side lengths of
    triangle *RST*? What is the measure of angle *E*?

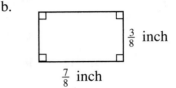

9-53.   Find the perimeter and area of each figure.

a.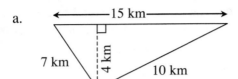

b.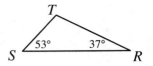

9-54.   If each triangle below is drawn accurately, identify whether it is an obtuse,
         acute, or right triangle. Name the angle or angles that helped you to decide.

a.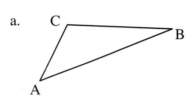

b.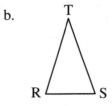

c.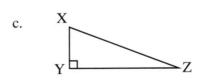

d.

9-55.   A candy store's specialty is taffy. Customers can fill a bag with taffy and the
         price is based on how much the candy weighs. The store charges $2 for 10
         ounces of taffy.

a. Copy the table below and fill in the missing values. Add three more entries.

Amount of taffy (ounces)	2	5	10	12	15	20
Price ($)			$2			$4

b. Graph the values in the table. Let *x* represent the number of ounces and
    y represent the price in dollars.

c. Is this situation proportional? Explain your **reasoning**.

d. What is the slope of the line you graphed? What information does the slope
    tell you?

Making Connections: Course 2

9.2.3 How can I use the area ratio?

Applying the Ratio of Areas

The ratios between similar shapes allow you to solve a variety of problems. Identifying the ratios that are equivalent can be challenging. It is often helpful to be able to **visualize** shapes in different ways and to develop multiple ways of seeing and representing relationships. As you work today, ask these questions in your team to focus discussion:

What is the relationship?

How can we solve the problem?

Is the answer **reasonable**?

9-56. The scale factor of two similar figures is $\frac{5}{3}$. Based on this information, answer each of the following questions.

   a. If the perimeter of the smaller figure is 15 cm, what is the perimeter of the larger figure?

   b. If the area of the larger figure is 50 cm², what is the area of the smaller figure?

9-57. The two parallelograms at right are similar.

   a. Find the missing length x.

   b. What is the ratio of the areas of these shapes?

   c. Find the area of each shape to check your ratio, or explain why you cannot.

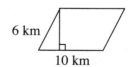

6 km · 10 km

30 km · x

9-58.   Jonas has built a scale model of a basketball
         court for his NBA player action figures. His
         model is built in the ratio $\frac{6 \text{ ft.}}{1 \text{ cm}}$.

   a.   If the real basketball court is 94 feet long,
        how long is his scale model?

   b.   The hoop on Jonas' model is $1\frac{2}{3}$ cm above
        the court floor. If he has constructed his
        model correctly, how high does this make
        the real-life hoop?

   c.   A real backboard is 72 inches wide. Jonas has made a model that is 8 cm
        wide. Did he scale his model correctly?

   d.   The area of an NBA court is 4700 square feet. What should the area of
        Jonas' model be?

9-59.   Tatiana set up these equations for the
         similar trapezoids at right:

         $$\frac{10}{16} = \frac{y}{5} \qquad\qquad \frac{x}{10} = \frac{16}{12}$$

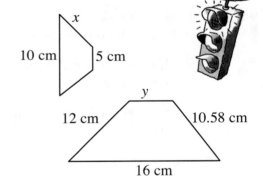

   a.   Are her equations correct?
        Explain completely.

   b.   Make any necessary corrections
        to her equations, then find the
        lengths of the missing sides.

9-60.   If one shape has area of 10 square units, and another similar shape has area of
         250 square units, how can you find the scale factor between the sides?

9-61.   Find each missing area.

   a.   One linear foot is equal to 12 inches. How many square inches cover the
        same area as one square foot?

   b.   One inch is approximately equal to 2.54 centimeters. How many square
        centimeters are in 15 square inches?

   c.   There are 3 feet in one yard. How many square feet cover the same area as
        4 square yards?

Making Connections: Course 2

9-62.   Ms. Murray and her class are looking at a series of similar triangles, and they are wondering if comparing the base of each triangle to its area is proportional. Find the base of the last two triangles and the area of all four triangles. Graph the base length compared to the area for each triangle. Does the graph show a proportional relationship? Why or why not?

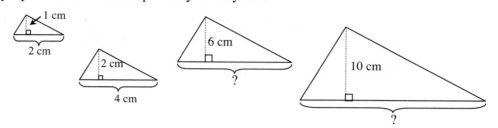

9-63.   LEARNING LOG

Reread your Learning Log entry titled, "Area Relationships in Similar Shapes" (from Lesson 9.2.1). What new information can you add? Explain how the ratio of the sides of similar shapes is related to the ratio of their areas. Give an example of how can you use the area of a shape to predict the area of another, similar shape if you know the scale factor for the sides. Add today's date to your entry.

9-64.   The perimeter of one shape is 5.5 times larger than the perimeter of a similar shape.

a.   How many times larger are the sides of the large shape than the corresponding sides of the smaller shape?

b.   How many times larger is the area?

9-65.   If each triangle below is drawn accurately, identify whether it is most likely an obtuse, acute, or right triangle. Label the angle or angles that helped you to decide.

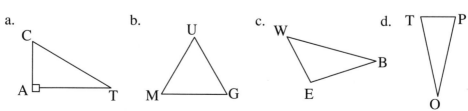

9-66.   Calculate the percent change in each problem below.

    a.   Robert wanted to buy a computer game that cost $25 last week. This week when he went back to buy the game, the price was $35. What was the percent of increase in the price?

    b.   Susan bought a jacket on sale. The original price of $35 was marked down to $25. What was the percent discount because of the sale?

    c.   Why were your answers to parts (a) and (b) different?

9-67.   Simplify each expression.

    a. $\frac{12}{5} \div \frac{7}{10}$ b. $\frac{9}{4} \div (-\frac{1}{3})$ c. $-\frac{3}{5} \div (-\frac{1}{6})$

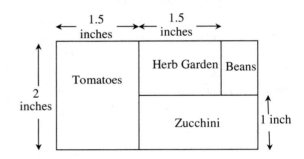

9-68.   Hank is planning his vegetable garden. He has created the scale drawing at right. He is planning for the actual area for the tomatoes to be 12 feet by 9 feet. All angles are right angles.

    a.   How many feet in the garden does each inch on the drawing represent?

    b.   What are the length and width of the herb garden on the drawing in inches?

    c.   What are the length and width of the real herb garden in feet?

    d.   What is the area of the real herb garden (in square feet)?

    e.   Remember that there are 12 inches in one foot. If Hank measures the real herb garden in square inches instead of square feet, what will its area be?

9.3.1 What kind of triangle can I make?

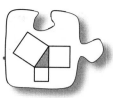

Side Lengths and Triangles

Triangles are made of three sides. But can any three lengths make a triangle? Is it possible to predict what kind of triangle – obtuse, acute, or right – three side lengths will make? Today, you will investigate these questions with your team.

9-69.   IS IT A TRIANGLE?

When do three lengths form a triangle? Are there special patterns in lengths that always make obtuse triangles or combinations of lengths that make right or acute triangles? To investigate these questions, you and your study team will build triangles and look for patterns that will allow you to predict what kind of triangle three lengths will make.

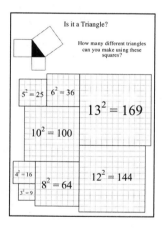

Your task: Obtain the Lesson 9.3.1A, B, and C Resource Pages. Cut out each square on the Lesson 9.3.1A Resource Page (shown at right). Using different combinations of three squares, decide if a triangle can be made by connecting the corners of the squares. If you can make a triangle, what kind of triangle is it? (The angle on the Lesson 9.3.1B Resource Page can help you determine if an angle is a right (90°) angle.) Record the side lengths and areas for each combination of squares you try on the Lesson 9.3.1C Resource Page. If you can make a triangle, complete the other columns of the chart. If you cannot make a triangle, write "No Triangle" across the other columns. The headings for the columns on that page appear below.

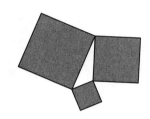

Side Length			Area of Small Square	Area of Medium Square	Area of Large Square	Small Area + Medium Area	Equal (=) Greater than (>) Less than (<)	Large Area	Acute △ Obtuse △ Right △
Sm	Med	Lg							

Discussion Points

How can we organize our data?

What other combinations can we make?

What do we expect will happen?

9-70.   Look at your data for the combinations that did *not* form triangles.

> - What do you notice about how the three side lengths compare to each other?
> - How are the sets that did not form triangles different from the sets of side lengths that *did* form triangles? Be as specific as you can.

When your team has reached a conclusion, copy and complete the two statements below on your paper.

> *Three side lengths WILL NOT make a triangle if...*
>
> *Three side lengths WILL make a triangle if...*

9-71.   Now look at the data that you collected for the acute, obtuse, and right triangles. What patterns do you see between the sum of the areas of the two smaller squares and the area of the larger square that formed the triangles in each row? Copy and complete the sentence starters below to summarize the patterns that you see.

> *If three squares have sides that make an* acute triangle, *then the area of the two small squares...*
>
> *If three squares have sides that make an* obtuse triangle, *then the area of the two small squares...*
>
> *If three squares have sides that make a* right triangle, *then the area of the two small squares...*

9-72.   Use the patterns you found to predict whether each set of lengths below will form a triangle. If a set will form a triangle, state whether the triangle will be acute, obtuse, or right. **Justify** your conclusion.

>   a.   5 cm, 6 cm, and 7 cm   b.   2 cm, 11 cm, 15 cm
>
>   c.   10 cm, 15 cm, 20 cm   d.   10 cm, 24 cm, 26 cm
>
>   e.   1 cm, 3 cm, 9 cm   f.   2 cm, 10 cm, 11 cm

9-73.   **Additional Challenge:** Lewis wants to build an obtuse triangle. He has already decided to use a square with an area of 81 square units and a square with an area of 25 square units.

   a.   What area of square could he use to form the third side of his triangle? Explain your **reasoning**.

   b.   If he makes an acute triangle instead, what size square should he use? Explain your **reasoning**.

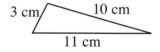
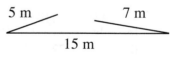

Review & Preview

9-74.   The two triangles at right are similar.

   a.   Find x. Show your **strategy**.

   b.   What is the scale factor ($\frac{\text{big}}{\text{small}}$)?

   c.   Find the area of each triangle.

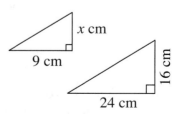

9-75.   Sasha saved $850 from her summer job last summer. She put it in an account
         that earns simple interest each month. After 9 months, her account is worth
         $1003. What percent interest did she earn each month?

9-76.   Anthony has added a trend line to the
         scatterplot at right. Do you agree with where
         he put the line? Explain your **reasoning**.

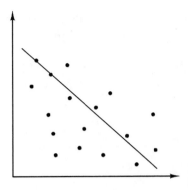

9-77.   A rental car company allows a customer to select any car available on the lot.
         Currently there are three blue sedans, two tan trucks, two black trucks, four red
         convertibles, four blue minivans, two black SUVs, and three tan hybrids. What
         is the probability a customer will select a black vehicle?

9-78.   Find the area and circumference of a circle with a radius of 7 cm.

9-79.   Elyse, Paul and J'Marcus were
         looking at the graph at right.
         Based on the graph, Elyse wrote
         the rule $y = 3x + 22$. Paul wrote
         the rule $y = 22x + 3$. J'Marcus
         wrote the rule $y = 22 + 3x$.

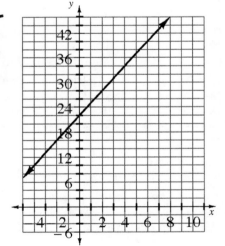

   a.   Are the three equations
         equivalent, or are they different?
         Explain your conclusion.

   b.   Which equation (or equations)
         match the line on the graph?
         Justify your answer.

9-80.   Jenna is working with three squares with areas of 16 cm², 9 cm², and 36 cm².
         She thinks they will make an obtuse triangle. Do you agree? Explain your
         reasoning.

Making Connections: Course 2

9-81.   Find the missing side lengths of each rectangle (a and c) or square (b and d).

a.
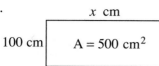
100 cm   A = 500 cm²

b.
y cm
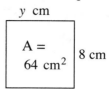
A = 64 cm²   8 cm

c.
5 cm
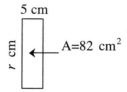
r cm   A=82 cm²

d.
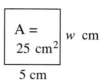
A = 25 cm²   *w* cm
5 cm

9-82.   Copy and complete the following table.

x	5		4		-2	3
y	-17	-5		-2	4	-11

a.   What is the rule?

b.   What is the slope?

9-83.   Simplify each expression.

a. $\frac{5}{12}+(-\frac{7}{8})-(-\frac{1}{6})$

b. $-\frac{11}{15}-\frac{4}{5}-(-\frac{57}{60})$

c. $4\frac{1}{12}+(-1\frac{5}{6})$

d. $-\frac{7}{11}\cdot\frac{8}{9}$

e. $\frac{1}{3}\cdot\frac{1}{2}+\frac{5}{6}$

f. $-\frac{4}{6}\cdot(-\frac{9}{2})$

9-84.   Use the graph below to answer the following questions.

a.   What is this graph describing? Write an appropriate title for the graph.

b.   How far from home is the person when the graph starts?

c.   How fast is the person traveling? Explain how you can use the graph to determine the rate of travel.

d.   Write an equation to represent the line on the graph.

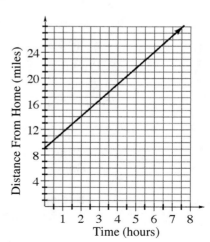

9.3.2 What is special about a right triangle?

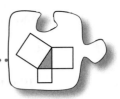

Pythagorean Theorem

In Lesson 9.3.1, you saw that in order for three lengths to form a triangle they must be related to each other in a special way. Today, you will investigate a special relationship between the side lengths of right triangles. This relationship will allow you to find the length of a missing side.

9-85. Use your patterns from Lesson 9.3.1 to decide if the squares listed below will form a right triangle.

    a. Squares with side lengths 6, 8, and 10 meters

    b. Squares with areas 64 in^2, 100 in^2, 144 in^2

    c. Two squares with side length 5 feet and a square with area 50 square feet

    d. Explain how you know whether three squares will join at their corners to form a right triangle.

9-86. THE PYTHAGOREAN RELATIONSHIP

Based on your work so far, if you know the area of three squares you can tell if they will connect at their corners to form a right triangle. But what if you know that a triangle has a right angle? Will the squares of the side lengths be related in this way? Work with your team to look more closely at side lengths of some right triangles.

    a. On centimeter graph paper, form a right angle by drawing one 5 cm length and one 12 cm length as shown at right. (If you do not have centimeter graph paper then use any graph paper to draw and measure these lengths with a ruler.) Then create a right triangle by connecting the ends of the two lengths with a third side.

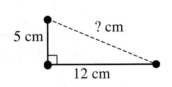

    b. With a ruler, measure the longest side of the triangle in centimeters and label the side length.

Problem continues on next page. →

                                                              Making Connections: Course 2

9-86.   *Problem continued from previous page.*

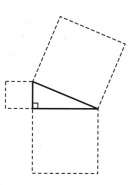

c.   **Visualize** a square connected to each side of the right triangle. Sketch a picture like the one at right on your paper. What is the area of each square? Is the area of the square connected to the longest side equal the sum of the areas of the other two squares?

d.   Check this pattern with a new example.

   • Draw a new right angle on the centimeter paper using 9 cm and 12 cm lengths.

   • Connect the endpoints to create a triangle and measure the third side.

   • Create a sketch for this triangle like the one you created in part (c) and find the areas of the squares.

   Is the area of the square connected to the longest side equal to the sum of the other two areas?

e.   The two shorter sides of a right triangle are called the **legs**, and the longest side is called the **hypotenuse**.

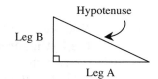

   Use words to describe the relationship between the lengths of the legs and the length of the hypotenuse.

9-87.   The relationship you described in part (e) of problem 9-86 is called the
         Pythagorean Theorem. It states that in a right triangle, the length of one leg
         squared plus the length of the other leg squared is equal to the length of the
         hypotenuse squared, and can be written as an equation like this:

$$(\text{leg A})^2 + (\text{leg B})^2 = (\text{hypotenuse})^2$$

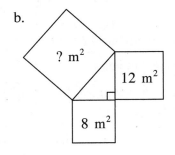

         Use the Pythagorean Theorem to write an equation
         for each diagram below. Find each missing area.

a.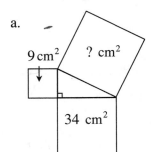

b.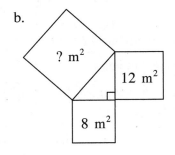

c.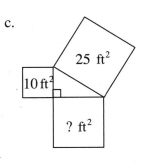

9-88.   Your earlier work with squares that formed right triangles used the **converse of
         the Pythagorean Theorem**. That is, you found that if the sum of the squares of
         the two shortest sides in a triangle equals the square of the length of the longest
         side, then the triangle is a right triangle. Use this idea to determine whether the
         lengths listed below form a right triangle. Explain your **reasoning**.

a.   15 feet, 36 feet, and 39 feet   b.   20 in., 21 in., and 29 in.

c.   8 yards, 9 yards, and 12 yards   d.   4 meters, 7 meters, and 8 meters

9-89.   Find the area of the square in each picture below.

a.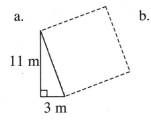

b.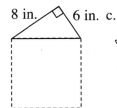

c.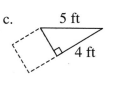

d.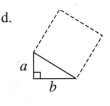

9-90.   How long is the missing side of each triangle in parts (b) and (c) of problem
         9-89? Be prepared to explain your **reasoning**.

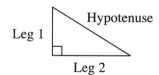 ETHODS AND MEANINGS

MATH NOTES

Right Triangles and the Pythagorean Theorem

A **right triangle** is a triangle in which the two shorter sides form a right (90°) angle. The shorter sides are called **legs**. The third and longest side, called the **hypotenuse**, is opposite the right angle.

The **Pythagorean Theorem** states that for any right triangle, the sum of the squares of the lengths of the legs is equal to the square of the length of the hypotenuse.

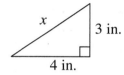

$$(\text{leg } 1)^2 + (\text{leg } 2)^2 = (\text{hypotenuse})^2$$

Example:

$$3^2 + 4^2 = x^2$$
$$9 + 16 = x^2$$
$$25 = x^2$$
$$5 = x$$

The **converse of the Pythagorean Theorem** states that if the sum of the squares of the lengths of the two shorter sides of a triangle equals the square of the length of the longest side, then the triangle is a right triangle. For example:

Do the lengths 6, 9, and 11 form a right triangle?

$$6^2 + 9^2 \overset{?}{=} 11^2$$

$$36 + 81 \overset{?}{=} 121$$

$117 \neq 121$ No, these lengths do not form a right triangle.

Do the lengths 9, 40, and 41 form a right triangle?

$$9^2 + 40^2 \overset{?}{=} 41^2$$

$$81 + 1600 \overset{?}{=} 1681$$

$1681 = 1681$ Yes, these lengths form a right triangle.

9-91. If you have 24 square tiles, how many different rectangles can you make? Each rectangle must use all of the tiles. Sketch each rectangle on graph paper and label its length and width. Can you make a square with 24 tiles?

9-92. Lydia has four straws of different lengths, and she is trying to form a right triangle. The lengths are 8, 9, 15, and 17 units. Which three lengths should she use? **Justify** your answer.

9-93. What kind of triangle will the edges of these squares form? What will the side lengths be?

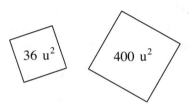 

9-94. Find the missing dimension on each rectangle or square.

a.
8 ft | A=100 ft^2

b.
12 mm
A= 144 mm^2

c.
10 cm
A= 144 cm^2

d.
7 in.
A= 49 in.^{2}

e.
6 km | A=144 km^2

9-95. Eric set up this ratio for two similar triangles:

$$\frac{x}{12} = \frac{5}{9}$$

He solved the problem and found $x \approx 6.67$. What was his mistake?

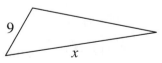

9-96. Write an equation to represent this situation and answer the question. You may choose to use the 5-D Process to help you organize your thinking.

Ella is trying to determine the side lengths of a triangle. She knows that the longest side is three times longer than the shortest side. The medium side is ten more than twice the longest side. If the perimeter is 142 cm, how long is each side?

Making Connections: Course 2

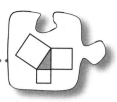

9.3.3 How can I find the side length?

Understanding Square Root

You have developed a way to decide if a triangle is a right triangle by looking at the squares of the side lengths of the triangle. If you already know a triangle is a right triangle, how can the Pythagorean Theorem help you determine the length of a leg or the hypotenuse? Today you and your team will develop new ways to find missing lengths of right triangles.

9-97. Nikita wants to use the area of the squares in the figure at right to help him find the lengths of the sides of a right triangle.

a. Find the missing area.

b. What are the lengths of the legs of the right triangle in Nikita's diagram? How do you know?

c. About how long is the hypotenuse? Are you able to find the length exactly? Explain your **reasoning**.

9-98. The numbers 36, 64, 4, 16, 100, 144, 121, and 225 are all examples of **perfect squares**.

a. If each of these numbers represents the number of square units in a square, what is the side length of each square?

b. Why do you think these numbers are called perfect squares?

9-99. To find the side length of a square with a particular area, we use a process called the **square root**. The square root symbol looks like $\sqrt{}$, and is also called a **radical sign**.

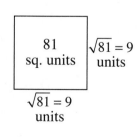

To find the side length of a square with an area of 81 square units, for example, we would write $\sqrt{81}$ (read, "the square root of 81"). Since $9 \cdot 9 = 81$, then $\sqrt{81} = 9$.

Copy each square root expression below. If the expression is the side length of a square, what does it tell you about the area of the square? Rewrite each square root as an equivalent expression without the radical sign. Explain your method for finding the square root of these numbers.

a. $\sqrt{49}$ b. $\sqrt{121}$ c. $\sqrt{9}$ d. $\sqrt{169}$

9-100.   Look back at problem 9-91, when you tried to make a perfect
          square with 24 tiles and could not. Why was it impossible?

   a.   Estimate the length of a side of a square with an area
         of 24 square units. What two whole numbers is the
         length between?

   b.   Is $\sqrt{24}$ closer to one of the whole numbers or to the other? If you did not
         already do so, make your estimate to the nearest tenth.

   c.   Multiply your estimate by itself. How close to 24 is your answer? If you
         revised your estimate, how would you change it?

9-101.   Between which two whole numbers is each of the following square roots? To
          which whole number do you think it is closer? Estimate the value of the square
          root to the nearest tenth (0.1). You may find it helpful to create a list of the
          whole numbers from one to 17 and their squares to use with this kind of
          problem.

   a. $\sqrt{40}$ b. $\sqrt{95}$ c. $\sqrt{3}$

   d. $\sqrt{59}$ e. $\sqrt{200}$ f. $\sqrt{154}$

   g.   Describe your method for estimating the approximate value of a square root
         when the number is not a perfect square. Check each estimate for parts (a)
         through (f) on a calculator.

9-102.   ESTIMATING WITH A GRAPH

          In Chapters 6, 7, and 8, you examined the graphs of various relationships. What
          would the relationship between the side length of a square and the area of a
          square look like on a graph?

   a.   On the Lesson 9.3.3 Resource Page, complete the table for the side lengths
         and areas. Graph the points. Does it make sense to connect them? If so,
         connect them with a smooth curve.

   b.   Describe the relationship between the side length of a square and the area of
         the square. How is it the same or different than other relationships you
         have graphed?

   c.   How can you use the graph to estimate the side length for a square with
         an area of 24 square units? Does this estimate match your estimate in
         problem 9-100?

   d.   Use your graph to estimate these square roots:

         i. $\sqrt{10}$ ii. $\sqrt{15}$ iii. $\sqrt{5}$ iv. $\sqrt{33}$

Making Connections: Course 2

9-103.   In Chapter 1, you worked with decimals that repeated and terminated. All of these numbers are called **rational** because they can be written as a ratio, like $\frac{2}{3}$ and $\frac{5}{1} = 5$. Because $\sqrt{9} = 3$, $\sqrt{9}$ is also a rational number.

However, there are some numbers that, when written as a decimal, do not repeat or terminate. $\sqrt{2}$ is one example of a number like this. These numbers are called **irrational**, and they cannot be written as a ratio of any two integers (in other words, as a fraction).

$\sqrt{2} = 1.41421356237...$

Use your calculator to find the square root of the following numbers. Decide whether the decimals are rational (those that have decimals that terminate or repeat) or irrational.

a. $\sqrt{6.25}$ b. $\sqrt{100}$ c. $\sqrt{7}$

9-104.   **Additional Challenge:** Nikita wonders, "*What can we say about the square root of a negative number?*" Discuss this question with your team. For example, can you find $\sqrt{-16}$? Write an explanation of your thinking. Be ready to share your ideas with the class.

9-105.   LEARNING LOG

How can you estimate a square root? Write directions for a fifth grader to follow, explaining how to estimate a square root to the nearest tenth. Include examples of perfect squares and non-perfect squares. Title this entry in your Learning Log, "Estimating Square Roots," and label it with today's date.

MⒺTHODS AND MⒺANINGS

Squaring and Square Root

When a number or variable is multiplied by itself, it is said to be **squared**. **Squaring** a number is like finding the area of the square with that number or variable as its side length. For example,

$6 \cdot 6 = 6^2 = 36$ and $\boxed{36 \text{ cm}^2}$ 6 cm $\quad a \cdot a = a^2$ and $\boxed{a^2}$ a

6 cm $\qquad\qquad\qquad\qquad a$

The **square root** of a number or variable is the positive factor that, when multiplied by itself, results in the given number. Use a **radical sign**, $\sqrt{}$, to show this operation. If you know the area of a square, then the square root of the numerical value of the area is the side length of that square.

For example, $\sqrt{49}$ is read as, "the square root of 49," and means, "Find the positive number that multiplied by itself equals 49." $\sqrt{49} = 7$, since $7 \cdot 7 = 49$.

By definition, -7 is not the square root of 49 even though $(-7) \cdot (-7) = 49$, since we only consider positive numbers to be square roots. No real square region could have a negative side length.

9-106.   Find the missing length or area.

a.
x
x | 225 cm^2

b.
11 cm
| 11 cm

c.
5 m | 100 m^2
w

d.
y
y | 150 ft^2

Making Connections: Course 2

9-107.   A triangle is enlarged by a scale factor of $\frac{10}{3}$.

        a.   If the perimeter of the enlargement is 36 m, find the perimeter of the original triangle.

        b.   If the area of the enlarged triangle is 25 square meters, what is the area of the original triangle?

9-108.   Cisco was looking at a table of values from a silent board game of $y = x^2$. She said, "This table contains $(0,0)$ so I think it shows a proportional relationship." Is Cisco correct? Why or why not?

9-109.   The hypotenuse and one leg of a right triangle are 65 and 60 meters. What is the length of the third side?

9-110.   Solve these equations for x. Check your answers.

        a. $2(x+4.5)=32$ b. $6+2.5x=21$ c. $\frac{x}{9}=\frac{5}{16}$

9-111.   A box contains 15 yellow, 15 orange, and 15 green tennis balls. If Izzy draws a tennis ball at random out of the box, what is the probability that he drew either a green or an orange tennis ball? Show your work and express your answer as a percent.

9-112.   Find the area and circumference of a circle with a diameter of 14.4 inches. Round your answer to the nearest hundredth.

9-113.   One of the triangles at right is a reduction of the other. Find each of the missing parts listed below.

        a.   Find the length of side BC.

        b.   Find the length of side AB.

        c.   Find the ratio of the areas of the two triangles.

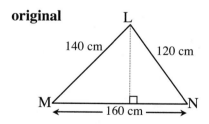

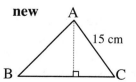

9-114.   Determine the positive value that makes each equation true. If the answer is not a whole number, write it as a square root, then approximate it as a decimal rounded to the nearest tenth.

a.   If $x^2 = 36$, $x = ?$ b.   If $x^2 = 65$, $x = ?$

c.   If $x^2 = 84$, $x = ?$ d.   If $x^2 = 13$, $x = ?$

9-115.   Copy the following table on your paper.

x	4	$\frac{1}{2}$	−2		−1	7
y	−11		1	−3	−1	

a.   Complete the table.   b.   Write the rule.   c.   What is the slope?

9.3.4   How can I find missing parts?

Applications of the Pythagorean Theorem

In this section you have studied different properties of triangles and have used the Pythagorean Theorem to describe the special relationship between the sides of a right triangle. In this lesson, you will use these ideas to solve a variety of different problems.

9-116.   Ann is measuring some fabric pieces for a quilt. Use the Pythagorean Theorem and your calculator to help her find each of the missing lengths below. Decide whether each answer is rational or irrational. If it is rational, explain whether the decimal repeats or terminates.

a.
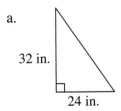
32 in.

24 in.

b.
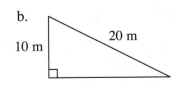
10 m

20 m

c.
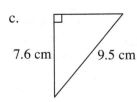
7.6 cm

9.5 cm

9-117.   Coach Kelly's third period P.E. class is playing baseball. The distance between each base on the baseball diamond is 90 feet. Lisa, at third base, throws the ball to Dano, at first base. How far did she throw the ball? State whether or not your answer is rational or irrational.

Making Connections: Course 2

9-118.   As the city planner of Right City, you are responsible to report information to help the Board of Supervisors make decisions about the budgets for the fire and police departments. The board has asked for a report with answers to the following questions. Each grid unit in the figure at right represents 1 mile.

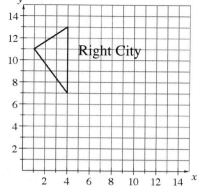

a.   For fire safety, bushes will be cleared along the perimeter of the city. What is the length of the perimeter? Please include all of your calculations in your report.

b.   Some people say that Right City got its name from its shape. Is the shape of the city a right triangle? Show how you can tell.

9-119.   Clem and Clyde have a farm with three different crops: a square field of corn, a rectangular field of artichokes, and a right triangle grove of walnut trees (as shown at right). A fence totally surrounds the farm. Find the total area of their land in square miles and tell them how much fencing they need to enclose the outside of their farm.

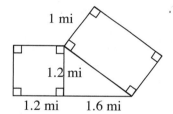

9-120.   Scott and Mark are rock climbing. Scott is at the top of a 75-foot cliff, when he throws a 96-foot rope down to Mark, who is on the ground below. If the rope is stretched tightly from Mark's feet to Scott's feet, how far from the base of the cliff (directly below Scott) is Mark standing? Draw a diagram and label it. Then, find the missing length. Is the length irrational?

9-121.   Nicole has three long logs. She wants to place them in a triangle around a campfire to allow people to sit around the fire. The logs have lengths 19, 11, and 21 feet.

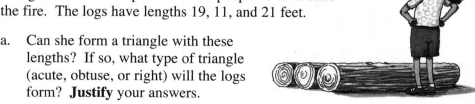

a.   Can she form a triangle with these lengths? If so, what type of triangle (acute, obtuse, or right) will the logs form? **Justify** your answers.

b.   Nicole realized she wrote the numbers down incorrectly. Her logs are actually 9, 11, and 21 feet. Will she still be able to surround her campfire with a triangular seating area? If so, will the shape be a right triangle? **Justify**.

9-122. LEARNING LOG

The Pythagorean Theorem describes the special
relationship that exists between the side lengths of a
right triangle. In your Learning Log, describe how the
Pythagorean Theorem can be used to find a missing side
length on a right triangle. Make up examples where the
hypotenuse length is missing or a leg length. Be sure to
include pictures, and to describe how you would find
each missing length. Title this entry, "Pythagorean
Theorem," and label it with today's date.

METHODS AND MEANINGS

Side Length Patterns in Triangles

The Triangle Inequality (Lesson 9.3.1 Math Note) establishes
the required relationships for three lengths to form a triangle. You can
also use these lengths to determine the type of triangle they form —
acute, obtuse, or right — by comparing the squares of the lengths of
the sides as follows:

Acute triangle: The sum of the
squares of the lengths of the two
shorter sides is greater than the
square of the length of the longest
side.

$x^2 + y^2 > z^2$

Obtuse triangle: The sum of the
squares of the lengths of the two
shorter sides is less than the square
of the length of the longest side.

$p^2 + q^2 < r^2$

Right triangle: The sum of the
squares of the lengths of the two
shorter sides is equal to the square of
the length of the longest side.

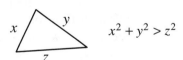

$a^2 + b^2 = c^2$

Making Connections: Course 2

9-123. The figure shown at right is made up of a right triangle and a rectangle.

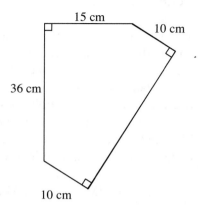

15 cm

10 cm

36 cm

10 cm

    a.   Copy the shape on your paper. Then draw a line to help divide the figure into two separate shapes.

    b.   Use the dimensions given to find the area of the triangle, the rectangle, and the whole figure. Be sure to show all of your subproblems.

9-124. On a coordinate grid, draw a triangle with vertices at $(2, 6)$, $(2, 2)$, and $(5, 6)$.

    a.   Find the lengths of each side of the triangle. What is the perimeter?

    b.   What type of triangle is formed by these points? **Justify** your answer.

9-125. Graph the rule $y = -2x + 5$.

    a.   What is the slope of the line?

    b.   Where does the line cross the y-axis?

9-126. Stephanie is earning simple interest of 3.5% on her money each month. She currently has $1325 in her account. What will her balance be in 5 months?

9-127. Ann lives on the shoreline of a large lake. A market is located 24 km south and 32 km west of her home on the other side of the lake. If she takes a boat across the lake directly toward the market, how far is her home from the market?

Chapter 9 Closure   What have I learned?

Reflection and Synthesis

The activities below offer you a chance to reflect about what you have learned during this chapter. As you work, look for concepts that you feel comfortable with, ideas that you would like to learn more about, and topics with which you need more help. Look for understanding of the ideas in this chapter as well as connections with material you learned previously.

① SUMMARIZING MY UNDERSTANDING

This section gives you an opportunity to show what you know about certain math topics or ideas.

Jasmine and Jason are spending the summer with their Uncle Simon. He lives in an old castle that has many interesting doors, not all of them rectangles. One day, while looking through the books in the castle library, Jasmine found an unusual piece of paper in a book.

"Look, Jason! This looks like some kind of a treasure map," she exclaimed. Jason looked at the paper and read, *"A valuable secret is hidden inside. But beware – danger lurks behind the other doors. Only those who can follow the clues will succeed in the search."*

He also saw that it had a series of clues and pictures of triangular doors. Read the clues below and, with your team, help Jasmine and Jason find the secret door and the treasure.

- My sides are not congruent.

- My angles are not congruent.

- I am similar to another door.

- One of my sides is $\sqrt{41}$ units long.

a.   Look at the doors on the Closure Resource Page A, available at www.cpm.org/students.

b.   Using what you have learned in this chapter, decide which door is the secret door.

c.   **Justify** your answer.

Problem continues on next page. →

Making Connections: Course 2

① *Problem continued from previous page.*

d.   List the triangles which were not the secret door and **justify** why each one did not fit the clues.

When you have solved the problem and found the treasure, answer the following questions:

- What skills learned in this chapter did I use to solve this problem?

- What knowledge from earlier chapters helped solve the problem?

② WHAT HAVE I LEARNED?

This section will help you determine which kinds of problems you feel comfortable with and those with which you need more help, based on the kinds of problems you have seen so far. Even if your teacher does not assign this section, it is a good idea to try these problems and find out for yourself what you know and what you need to work on.

To help you determine how well you understand the concepts in this chapter, solve each problem as completely as you can. The table at the end of this closure section has answers to these problems. It also directs you to additional help and other similar practice problems.

CL 9-128. Solve the proportion $\frac{22}{7} = \frac{5}{x}$ in two different ways. Show your work.

CL 9-129. The triangles at right are similar.

a.   Find x.

b.   Find y.

c.   Find the ratio of the perimeters of the two triangles.

d.   Find the ratio of the areas of the two triangles.

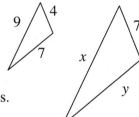

CL 9-130. The hypotenuse and one leg of a right triangle are 85 and 51 feet long. What is the length of the third side?

CL 9-131. The rent for Sonja's Haircuts shop has just been raised, so Sonja decided to increase the cost of a haircut from $8.50 to $10. What is the percent increase for a haircut?

CL 9-132. At a family reunion, each family member recorded their age and their height.

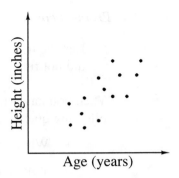

a. What kind of correlation does the scatter plot have?

b. Copy the scatterplot and draw the trend line.

CL 9-133. At the farmer's market Laura bought three pounds of heirloom tomatoes. If the tomatoes are priced at $8 per five pounds, what did Laura pay for her tomatoes?

CL 9-134. Find the area and circumference of a circle with a radius of 6.5 cm.

CL 9-135. Juana has three red belts, four black belts, two purple belts, and five navy belts in her drawer. It is still dark and her sister is sleeping so she does not want to turn on the light. What is the probability that she will select a red or a black belt?

CL 9-136. For each of the problems above, do the following:
- Draw a bar or number line that represents 0 to 10.

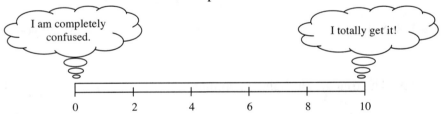

- Color or shade in a portion of the bar that represents your level of understanding and comfort with completing that problem on your own.

If any of your bars are less than a 5, choose *one* of those problems and do one of the following tasks:
- Write two questions that you would like to ask about that problem.
- Brainstorm two things that you DO know about that type of problem.

If all of your bars are a 5 or above, choose one of those problems and do one of these tasks:
- Write two questions you might ask or hints you might give to a student who was stuck on the problem.
- Make a new problem that is similar and more challenging than that problem and solve it.

③ WHAT TOOLS CAN I USE?

You have created or have available to you several tools and references that help support your learning – your teacher, your study team, your math book and your Toolkit to name a few. At the end of each chapter you will have an opportunity to review your Toolkit for completeness as well as to revise or update your Toolkit to better reflect your current understanding of big ideas.

Listed below are the main elements of your Toolkit, Learning Log Entries, Methods and Meanings Boxes, and vocabulary used in this chapter. The words that appear in bold are new to this chapter. Use these lists and follow your teacher's instructions to ensure that your Toolkit is a useful tool as well as a complete reference for you as you complete this chapter and prepare to begin the next one.

Learning Log Entries
- Lesson 9.1.1 – Proportional Relationships
- Lesson 9.2.1 – Area Relationships in Similar Shapes
- Lesson 9.3.3 – Estimating Square Roots
- Lesson 9.3.4 – Pythagorean Theorem

Math Notes
- Lesson 9.1.2 – Directly Proportional Relationships
- Lesson 9.1.3 – Solving Proportions
- Lesson 9.2.2 – Ratios of Similarity
- Lesson 9.3.1 – Triangle Inequality
- Lesson 9.3.2 – Right Triangles and the Pythagorean Theorem
- Lesson 9.3.3 – Squaring and Square Root
- Lesson 9.3.4 – Side Length Patterns in Triangles

Mathematical Vocabulary

The following is a list of vocabulary found in this chapter. Some of the words have been seen in the previous chapter. The words in bold are the words new to this chapter. Make sure that you are familiar with the terms below and know what they mean. For the words you do not know, refer to the glossary or index. You might also want to add these words to your Toolkit for a way to reference them in the future.

hypotenuse	inverse	**irrational**
legs	**non-proportional**	**perfect squares**
proportional	**proportional relationship**	**proportions**
Pythagorean Theorem	**radical sign**	**rational**
square root		

Process Words

The list of words below are problem solving strategies and processes that you have been involved in throughout the course of this chapter. Make sure you know what it means to use each of the following strategies. If you are not sure, look through your book for problems when you were asked to think in the following ways.

brainstorm	choose a strategy	describe
explain your reasoning	generalize	justify
predict	reason	reverse your thinking
test your prediction	visualize	

Answers and Support for Closure Activity #2
What Have I Learned?

Problem	Solution	Need Help?	More Practice
CL 9-128.	$x = \frac{35}{22} \approx 1.59$	Lesson 9.1.3 Math Notes box in Lesson 9.1.3	Problems 9-23, 9-27, and 9-28
CL 9-129.	a. $\frac{63}{4}$ b. $\frac{49}{4}$ c. $\frac{35}{20} = \frac{7}{4}$ d. $\left(\frac{7}{4}\right)^2 = \frac{49}{16}$	Lessons 9.1.3, and 9.2.1 Math Notes box in Lesson 9.2.2 Learning Log (problem 9-40)	Problems 9-23, 9-25, 9-29, 9-41, 9-52, 9-74, and 9-113
CL 9-130.	68 feet	Lessons 9.3.2, 9.3.3, and 9.3.4 Math Notes boxes in Lessons 9.3.2 and 9.3.3 Learning Log (problem 9-122)	Problems 9-87, 9-89, 9-109, and 9-120
CL 9-131.	17.6%	Lesson 8.2.5 Math Notes box in Lesson 8.2.5	Problems CL 8-92, 9-13, 9-32, and 9-66
CL 9-132.	a. positive correlation b.	Lessons 6.1.2 and 6.1.3 Math Notes box in Lesson 6.1.4 Learning Logs (problems 6-26 and 6-47)	Problems CL 6-140, CL 7-95, and 9-76

Problem	Solution	Need Help?	More Practice
CL 9-133.	$5.25	Lessons 9.1.1, 9.1.2, and 9.1.3 Math Notes boxes in Lessons 9.1.2 and 9.1.3 Learning Log (problem 9-8)	Problems 9-5, 9-9, 9-26, 9-45, and 9-55
CL 9-134.	$A \approx 327.7$ cm^2 $C \approx 40.8$ cm	Lessons 5.3.3 and 5.3.4 Math Notes box in Lesson 5.3.4 Learning Log (problem 5-124)	Problems CL 6-143, CL 8-93, 9-31, 9-78, and 9-112
CL 9-135.	$P = \frac{7}{14}$ or $\frac{1}{2}$ or 50%	Lessons 1.2.1 and 1.2.2 Math Notes boxes in Lessons 1.2.1 and 1.2.2	Problems CL 2-162, 9-12, 9-44, 9-77, and 9-111

Puzzle Investigator Problems

PI-17.　ROMAN NUMERALS

Perhaps you learned to count by counting on your fingers! The fact that we have 10 fingers might explain why we count in the base 10 system. This means that as we count, we group objects in sets of 10 (and sets of 100, which are each 10 sets of 10). We also write our numbers in a way to quickly represent the number of sets of 10. For example, when we want to count 21 objects, the digit 2 represents the number of 10s and the digit 1 represents 1.

However, throughout history, there were other number systems, as well as other ways of writing numbers. Romans counted in base 10, but used a different symbol system. The letter I is used for the digit "1," V is used for "5," X is used for "10," and L is used for "50." Then other numbers up to 98 are created by placing combinations of these letters together.

Study the examples at right to figure out the Roman Number system of writing.

a.　Based on these examples, describe the process for writing a Roman Numeral. For example, why does "XL" represent 40 while "L" represents 50?

b.　Based on your patterns, how would Romans write the number 87? 55? 98?

c.　What is the smallest number you can create with one of each letter? What is the largest?

Sample Roman Numerals

I	=	1	XI	=	11
II	=	2	XVI	=	16
III	=	3	XVIII	=	18
IV	=	4	XIX	=	19
V	=	5	XXIII	=	23
VI	=	6	XXIX	=	29
VII	=	7	XL	=	40
VIII	=	8	XLIX	=	49
IX	=	9	LXIV	=	64
X	=	10	LXXI	=	71

d.　Katrina thinks that adding Roman Numerals is similar to collecting like terms, so that XIX + XL = LXXXI. Explain to her why this is not correct and give her another counterexample. Does her **strategy** ever work? If so, what are the conditions that will enable her to use this **strategy**?

PI-18.   TO TELL THE TRUTH

Alicia, Ben, Cassie, and Daryl shared some birthday cake before going into the living room to work on their homework. During the rest of the afternoon, each one of them left the room by themselves for a few minutes.

When they finished their homework, they went into the kitchen and discovered that the rest of the cake was missing. Below are their statements:

Alicia: *"Ben ate it!"*

Cassie: *"I didn't eat it!"*

Ben: *"Daryl must have eaten it."*

Daryl: *"Ben is lying."*

a.   If only one of these statements is a lie, who ate the rest of the cake? Explain how you know which statement is false.

b.   If only one of the above statements is the truth, who ate the rest of the cake? Explain how you know which statement is true.

c.   While sorting out this mess, Ben's dad said, "What I am saying is not true." Is this statement true or false? Explain.

Exponents and Three Dimensions

10

CHAPTER 10 Exponents and Three Dimensions

In previous chapters you have investigated relationships that have a constant rate and can be represented as lines on a graph. Other relationships do not change at the same rate all of the time. For example, the height of the tide on a beach increases and decreases over the course of a day, and the number of cells in a sample gets larger very quickly as each cell divides and makes a new cell. In Section 10.1, you will work with percentages and interest to investigate one kind of non-linear growth called exponential growth. You will look for patterns to identify the characteristics of this kind of growth in tables, graphs, and expressions.

In Section 10.2, you will explore how to measure the surface area and volume of three-dimensional solids by designing and building cereal boxes. You will practice **visualizing** flattened shapes, called nets, to think about how their parts fit together to make different three-dimensional solids. Finally, you will experiment with the surface area and volume of shapes that cannot be sliced into equal layers.

In this chapter, you will learn how to:

➢ Calculate compound interest.

➢ Determine whether a relationship grows linearly or exponentially.

➢ Rewrite expressions using exponents and scientific notation.

➢ Find the surface area and volume of rectangular prisms.

➢ Find the surface area and volume of non-rectangular shapes including pyramids, cylinders, and cones.

Guiding Questions

Think about these questions throughout this chapter:

How is it changing?

What patterns can I see?

How much will it hold?

Am I measuring in one, two or three dimensions?

How are they related?

Chapter Outline

Section 10.1 You will learn about compound interest, and use patterns of growth to write expressions. You will analyze the patterns in tables, graphs, and expressions to compare linear and exponential growth. You will also learn new ways to rewrite numbers and expressions.

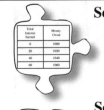

Section 10.2 You will compare how surface area and volume are related by building three-dimensional rectangular prisms. Then you will **visualize** shapes using nets. Finally you will learn to find both the surface area and volume of cylinders, pyramids, and cones.

Making Connections: Course 2

10.1.1 Is the graph linear?

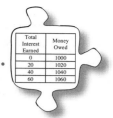

Total Interest Earned	Money Owed
0	1000
20	1020
40	1040
60	1060

Patterns of Growth in Tables and Graphs

Have you ever noticed that the sun rises earlier and sets later in the summer than it does in the winter? If you live north of the equator, you may have noticed that in December you often wake up for school while it is still dark, but if you wake up at the same time of day in May the sun is shining. The number of hours of sunlight in any one place changes during the year (unless you live directly at the equator). This is because the earth's tilt changes in comparison to the sun. The number of hours of daylight is approximately equal to the number of hours of darkness at just two times of year – the fall equinox and the spring equinox.

If you compared the average number of hours of daylight to the time of year on a graph, you would be able to see a pattern in how the number of hours of daylight changes. Today you will explore situations, tables and graphs that change in different ways and build **strategies** for **visualizing** different patterns of growth. As you work with your team, ask each other these questions:

> How does this grow?

> What happens when one measurement changes?

> How can we see the pattern of growth in the table?

10-1.   With your team, discuss each of the comparisons described below. Consider how the measurements are related and **visualize** what each relationship would look like on a graph. Sketch your prediction after you discuss your ideas with your team.

a.   The month of the year compared to the average daily hours of sunlight.

b.   The number of months money has been invested compared to the total balance for a bank account earning simple interest.

c.   The cost of an item that has had its price repeatedly increased by 50%.

d.   The length of the base of a rectangle that has an area of 24 square centimeters compared to its height.

10-2.   Now that you have predicted what different graphs will look like, investigate how some of the measures are related. To start, consider this situation:

Oscar puts $1000 of principal in a bank account that earns 2% simple interest each month. He wants to track how his money is growing over time.

a.   On the Lesson 10.1.1A Resource Page, complete the table to show the interest Omar has earned after 1, 2, 3, 4, and 5 months. How do you find his new balance each month?

Months	Total Interest Earned	Bank Balance
0	$0	$1000
1		

b.   Make a graph comparing months and interest on the resource page.

c.   What patterns do you notice in the table and the graph? How can you see each pattern in the other representations (situation, table, graph)?

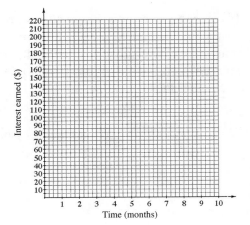

d.   Use the patterns you have found to predict how long it will take before Oscar has $1800 in the bank. **Justify** your prediction.

e.   Compare your graph from part (b) to the sketch you made in part (b) of problem 10-1. Did you predict that the graph would be a straight line? Explain why your prediction was correct, or any changes you would make and why.

10-3.   PROFIT, PROFIT, PROFIT

Anita bought a special baseball card for $8.00. Later, she decided to sell it but she wanted to make a profit. She added 50% to the price she paid and sold the card to Brandon. When he decided to sell it, he also wanted to make a profit, so he added 50% to the price he paid for the card and sold it to Casey. Casey increased the price by 50% and sold the card to Eli, who increased the price another 50% when he sold it to Fernanda.

a.   On the Lesson 10.1.1B Resource Page, make a table and graph of the new price after 1, 2, 3, 4, and 5 exchanges. How do you find the new price at each exchange?

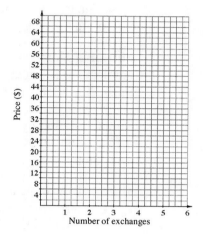

Exchanges	Increase in Price	New Price
0	$0	$8
1		

b.   What patterns do you notice in the table and the graph? Is the graph a straight line? How can you **justify** your conclusion based on the table or the graph?

c.   How does the graph you made compare to your sketch from part (c) of problem 10-1? Did you predict that the graph would curve?

d.   How much did Fernanda pay for the baseball card?

10-4.   In problems 10-2 and 10-3, one graph made a straight line while the other curved.

a.   How was the situation that created a straight line changing (growing)?

b.   Growth that creates a straight line shows constant change, and is called **linear growth**. What made the graph in problem 10-3 curve? How did the growth show in the table and the graph?

10-5. Guillermo was studying the two different situations below. He knows that one is represented by a line on a graph but that the other is represented by a curve.

The Basketball Tournament: The first round of a basketball tournament starts with 16 teams that each play one game. The eight winning teams move on to Round 2 and the other teams are done competing. The tournament continues in this way until Round 4, the finals, where the last two teams play to determine the champion.

The Basketball Tournament	
Round	Number of teams left
1	16
2	8
3	4
4	2

Finishing Homework: You have 16 problems to finish at home tonight. You can finish 4 problems in 10 minutes.

Finishing Homework	
Time spent working	Problems left to complete
0	16
10	12
20	8
30	4

Help Guillermo by explaining how you see the situations above changing over time. For each situation:

a. Copy the table and describe to Guillermo how you see the values in the table changing.

b. Explain whether the change is constant from one row to the next.

10-6. Guillermo graphed the points for each table and sketched a trend line for each graph to show the pattern in the points. He forgot to label his axes. Decide which graph matches the basketball data and which graph matches the homework data. Explain how you know that they match.

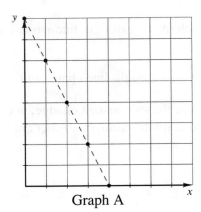

Graph A

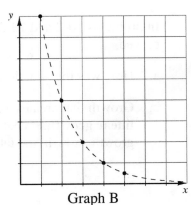

Graph B

10-7. Cassandra is calculating how much interest she will earn on investments that are earning simple interest using the formula at right. She knows that simple interest is paid only on the original amount that was deposited (the principal). For one amount of money that was invested for four years, she wrote the equation below.

Simple Interest Formula
$I = Prt$ where
P = Principal
I = Interest
r = Rate
t = Time

$$I = 500(0.025)(3) = \$37.50$$

Use what you know about simple interest to answer the questions below. Refer to the Math Notes in Lesson 8.2.6 if you need additional information.

a. In Cassandra's equation, identify the principal, interest, rate, and time.

b. Use this formula to calculate how much interest you would earn if you deposit $200 for 5 years at an annual (yearly) simple interest rate of 4%.

10-8. Mighty Max started the wrestling season weighing 135 pounds. By the time the season ended, he weighed 128 pounds. What was the percent decrease in his weight?

10-9. Which is a better deal? Sabrina wants to buy a new digital camera. The one she wants is currently on sale for $300. She could borrow the money at a monthly interest rate of 4% simple interest and pay it off after 6 months. Her other option is to work for 6 months and then pay cash, but the camera will no longer be on sale and will cost $350.

Which option will cost her the least money? Include calculations to **justify** your advice.

10-10.   Scooter and Kayla are building a chicken coop in their back yard. The coop
will be in the shape of a right triangle. One of the sides will be the wall of the
garage. They have 11 feet of fencing, and one leg will be 4 feet long.

a.   If the garage forms the hypotenuse of the triangle, how long will the other
leg be? How long will the hypotenuse be?

b.   If the garage wall is one leg of the triangle, how long will the hypotenuse
be? How long will the leg along the garage be?

c.   What is the area of each chicken coop in parts (a) and (b)?

10-11.   The two pentagons at right are similar.

a.   What is the scale factor between their side lengths?

b.   What is the scale factor between their areas?

c.   If the original shape has an area of
60 square centimeters, what is the
area of the new shape?

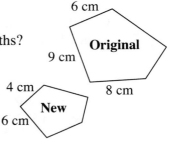

10.1.2 How can I describe the growth?

. . . .

Compound Interest

So far in this course you have studied simple interest, which only pays interest on the
amount invested. It might be used for informal loan arrangements made between parents
and children. However, banks and other financial institutions calculate interest in a
different way. They commonly use **compound interest**.

In the last lesson you explored how simple interest increases a bank balance and how that
growth can be seen in a table and a graph. You also saw that in another situation, where
prices grow by 50% each time they increase, the amount added is not constant. In this
lesson you will learn about **compound interest** and how to create an expression to
describe this non-linear growth. Continue to ask these focus questions in your team:

What patterns do we see?

How can we show the connection?

Making Connections: Course 2

10-12. Ms. Hartley won $20,000 in the lottery! She decided to spend half of it right away, and invest the other half of the money for her retirement.

The interest rate on the account Ms. Hartley chose is 5%. She calculated that after 10 years, based on simple interest her account balance should be $15,000. But the banker told her that after 10 years the account balance would be $16,289.

A financial adviser explained to her that the bank is paying her **compound interest**. That means that the bank is calculating the interest each year on the total of the principal and any interest she has earned so far, rather than just the $10,000. If Ms. Hartley leaves the money in the account for 30 years, her $10,000 will grow to more than $40,000.

To help Ms. Hartley see the difference between simple interest and compound interest, her adviser made the following tables for her.

Simple Interest	
Years of Teaching	Account Balance
0	$10,000
5	$12,500
10	$15,000
15	$17,500
20	$20,000
25	$22,500
30	$25,000

Compound Interest	
Years of Teaching	Account Balance
0	$10,000
5	$12,763
10	$16,289
15	$20,789
20	$26,533
25	$33,864
30	$43,219

a. Explain how you see the interest growing in the simple interest chart.

b. Explain how the interest grows in the compound interest chart.

c. After 30 years, how does the simple interest balance compare to the balance in the compound interest table?

10-13. Compound interest is calculated on all of the money in an account at specific points in time. Each time interest is calculated it is based on both the principal amount and any interest that was earned before. This is similar to how the price of the baseball card grew in problem 10-3. In that situation each price increase was based on what the seller paid, not on what the card originally cost.

Mariana's grandfather invested $500 for her college tuition in a savings account when she was born. The account pays 5% compound interest every year. How could you figure out how much money was in Mariana's account at the end of one year? How much will be there on her 8th birthday?

a. On the Lesson 10.1.2 Resource Page, complete the middle column of the table to show the account balance each year after the money was deposited. How do you find the new balance each year?

Time (years)	Balance ($)
0	500
1	525
2	551.25
3	
4	
5	
6	

·1.05

·1.05

b. Use the information in this column to fill in the "Total Interest Earned" column in the table (on the resource page) to show the total interest earned after any number of years. How can you calculate the total interest earned?

c. Make a graph of the years and total interest earned on the resource page. Work with your team to show the growth in both the table and the graph.

- What patterns do you see on the graph and in the table?

- How does the interest increase?

10-14.   Mariana is curious how much money will be in her account when she is 18 and graduates from high school. She went back to the table she had created. As she looked at the numbers in the first two columns (years and balance), she noticed a pattern that she thought she could rewrite into a shortcut. Study the table and her work:

Time (years)	Balance ($)	
0	500	
1	525	$= 500 \cdot 1.05$
2	551.25	$= (500 \cdot 1.05) \cdot 1.05$
3	578.81	$= (500 \cdot 1.05 \cdot 1.05) \cdot 1.05$
4		

$\cdot 1.05$
$\cdot 1.05$
$\cdot 1.05$
$\cdot 1.05$

a.   What changes in Mariana's calculations as she works down the table to fill in entries? What patterns do you see in her work?

b.   In her calculation for 2 years, what does $(500 \cdot 1.05)$ represent? What is $(500 \cdot 1.05)$ equal to?

c.   How could you rewrite Mariana's balance at the end of any year in terms of the principal, $500? **Generalize** the pattern you see in the table in words.

d.   Based on this pattern, describe how you would find Mariana's balance after 18 years *without* first finding her balance at 17 years. Then, use your calculator to find out her balance in year 18.

10-15.   The pattern you described in words in part (c) of problem 10-14 can be rewritten in symbols using an exponent. For example, $4 \cdot 4 \cdot 4 \cdot 4 \cdot 4$ can be rewritten using an exponent like this:

$$4 \cdot 4 \cdot 4 \cdot 4 \cdot 4 = 4^5$$

Here, 4 is the **base** and 5 is the **exponent** (sometimes called a power). 4^5 is read, *"Four raised to the fifth power"* or *"Four multiplied by itself 5 times."*

a.   Write the numbers you multiplied in part (c) of problem 10-14 as an expression using an exponent.

b.   Write an expression to represent this situation:

A comic book is purchased for $6. It is resold 7 times, and each time it is resold the seller charges 15% more than she paid for it.

10-16.   Simplify each expression.

    a. 5^3 b. 3^5 c. $\left(\frac{2}{3}\right)^4$ d. $(0.8)^3$

(M)ETHODS AND MEANINGS

Exponents

Bases and exponents can be used to rewrite expressions that involve repeated multiplication by the same number or variable. The expression a^n is written in **exponential form**. The **base**, a, is a factor that is raised to a power. The **exponent**, n, is sometimes called the power. It shows how many times the base is used as a factor.

In general, a^n means a multiplied by itself n times. For example,

$$2^4 \text{ means } 2 \cdot 2 \cdot 2 \cdot 2.$$

The base is 2 and the exponent is 4.

10-17.   Rachel has been given $1000 to put into a savings account. She earns 2% simple interest every month. Rachel hopes to buy a car in two years. Help Rachel determine whether she will have enough money if the car will cost $1500.

10-18.   Jack noticed there was a sale on his favorite model of All-Terrain Vehicle (ATV). The salesperson said the company was cutting the price for that weekend, so Jack got an 8% discount.

    a.   If the usual price of the ATV was $4298, estimate how much the discount will be. Explain your **reasoning**.

    b.   Calculate the amount Jack did pay with the 8% discount.

    c.   If the store sold three of the ATVs that weekend, how much money was saved by the three customers combined?

10-19.   Copy and complete the table at right for powers of 10.

a.   Use the pattern in the completed table to decide how many zeros 10^7 will have. How many zeros will 10^{23} have?

b.   How would you tell someone to write 10^{50}? Do not actually write the number; just write a sentence telling someone how s/he would write it.

Powers of 10	Standard Form
10^0	
10^1	10
10^2	100
10^3	
10^4	
10^5	

10-20.   Multiply each pair of numbers below.

a. $68 \cdot 100$ b. $0.68 \cdot 100$ c. $6.8 \cdot 1000$

d.   Describe in words what is happening to the decimal point in each problem.

10-21.   Rewrite each decimal as a fraction or fraction as a decimal.

a. 0.007 b. 0.103 c. 1.21

d. $\frac{505}{1000}$ e. $\frac{505}{100}$ f. $\frac{2}{100000}$

10-22.   There are 18 chocolate chip cookies, 12 oatmeal cookies, and 10 raisin cookies in a cookie jar. If Miguel takes a cookie from the jar without looking, what is the probability that he does *not* get a chocolate chip cookie? Show your work to support your answer.

10.1.3 What patterns can I see?

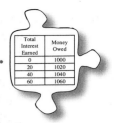

Total Interest Earned	Money Owed
0	1000
20	1020
40	1040
60	1060

. . . .

Linear and Exponential Growth

Patterns in tables, graphs, and expressions give clues about the kind of growth that is being represented. Today, you will work with your team to identify whether a table, graph, or situation represents simple interest or compound interest based on the kind of growth that is shown. You will also compare the different kinds of interest in situations to see which one is a better deal. By the end of this lesson, you should be able to answer these questions:

> What are the patterns in the tables, graphs, and
> expressions for each kind of interest?
>
> What are the differences between the two kinds of interest?
>
> How does the pattern relate to how the amounts are growing?

10-23.   John needs to borrow $250. Moneybags Municipal Bank will charge him 8% simple interest each week to borrow the money. Scrooge Savings will charge him 6% compound interest each week. With your team, help John decide which loan is the better choice.

   a.   Make a table for each bank showing the amount John owes after each week. Graph both tables on the same set of axes.

   b.   Which bank will charge him more if he pays the loan back in 12 weeks? Should he choose the same bank if he plans to pay back the loan in just 4 weeks?

   c.   Simple interest is an example of **linear growth**, and compound interest is an example of **exponential growth**. Talk with your team about how you could explain the difference between the two kinds of growth to someone else.

574   *Making Connections*: Course 2

10-24. The table at right represents the balance in Devin's bank account for the last five months. Has Devin been earning simple interest or compound interest? How do you know?

Time (months)	Balance ($)
0	257.50
1	263.25
2	269.00
3	274.75
4	280.50
5	286.25

10-25. Imari borrowed money from her uncle to buy a new bicycle. She made the graph at right to show how much interest she will need to pay him if she pays back the loan at different points in time.

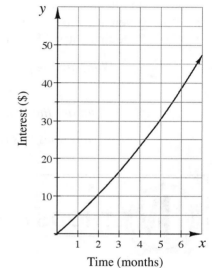

a. About how much interest will Imari owe him if she pays him back in 3 months? When will she owe him $40 in interest?

b. Is her uncle charging her simple or compound interest? **Justify** your answer. How would the graph be different if he was charging her the other type of interest (simple or compound)?

10-26. Tom has the option of borrowing $250 from his grandmother, who will charge him simple interest, or the bank, which will charge him compound interest at the same percentage rate. He plans to pay off the loan in 8 months. He wrote the two equations below to figure out how much he would owe for both of these options:

$$250(1.02)^8 \qquad\qquad 250 + 8(5.00)$$

a. What percent interest will he be charged? Where can you see the rate (percent) in each expression?

b. Which expression represents the amount he would owe his grandmother? Which one represents what he would owe the bank? **Justify** your conclusion.

c. Evaluate each expression. From whom should he borrow the money?

10-27.   **Additional Challenge:** Four years ago, Spencer borrowed $50 from his cousin, who charged him a simple interest rate each year. If he pays him back $62 today, what annual interest rate did his cousin charge? Could you figure this out if he had been charged compound interest instead?

10-28.   LEARNING LOG

How can you describe the differences between simple and compound interest? In your Learning Log, write down what each kind of interest looks like in a table, on a graph, and in an expression. Be sure to answer the questions given at the beginning of the lesson (reprinted below). Title this entry, "Simple and Compound Interest" and include today's date.

What are the patterns in the tables, graphs, and expressions for each kind of interest?

What are the differences between the two kinds of interest?

How does this relate to how the amounts are growing?

METHODS AND MEANINGS

MATH NOTES

Compound Interest

Compound interest is interest paid on both the original principal (amount of money at the start) and the interest earned previously.

The formula for compound interest is: $A = P(1 + r)^n$

where A = total amount including previous interest earned,
P = principal,
r = interest rate for each compounding period, and
n = number of time periods

Example: Theresa has a student loan that charges a 1.5% monthly compound interest rate. If she currently owes $1425.00 and does not make a payment for a year, how much will she owe at the end of the year (12 months)?

$$A = P(1 + r)^n \implies A = 1425(1 + 0.015)^{12}$$
$$\implies 1425(1.015)^{12} = 1425 \cdot 1.1956 = \$1703.73$$

Theresa will owe $1703.73 after 12 months (1 year).

Making Connections: Course 2

10-29. Read the Math Notes box about compound interest in this lesson, then answer the questions below.

    a.   What does the $(1+r)$ represent in the formula? Why are the two quantities added together?

    b.   If Melanie invests $2500 at a 3% interest rate compounded annually, how much will she have at the end of four years?

10-30. Simplify each exponential expression.

    a. 2^4 b. 3^6 c. 25^3

    d. 4^2 e. 9^3 f. 5^6

    g.   What patterns do you see between the expressions in parts (a) through (f) whose simplified forms are equal?

10-31. Copy and complete the chart at right.

10-32. Divide each pair of numbers below.

    a. $75 \div 10$

    b. $75 \div 100$

    c. $75 \div 1000$

    d.   Describe in words what happens to the decimal point in each problem.

Exponent Form	Factored Form	Standard Form
2^3	$2 \cdot 2 \cdot 2$	8
3^3		
	$4 \cdot 4 \cdot 4$	
		125
6^3		
7^3		
	$8 \cdot 8 \cdot 8$	
9^3		

10-33. Write and solve a proportion for the following problem.

In a recent survey for the student council, Dominique found that 150 students out of a total of 800 students on campus did *not* like soda. If half of the student body was going to attend a dance, how many students could she expect would want soda?

10-34. The art club has made a scale drawing of the new mural they will paint on the wall of the school. The area of the actual mural is 36 times larger than the area of the drawing. What is the scale factor between the side length of the drawing and the side length of the mural?

10.1.4 How can I rewrite it?

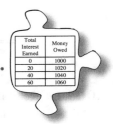

Total Interest Earned	Money Owed
0	1000
20	1020
40	1040
60	1060

Exponents and Scientific Notation

Earlier in this chapter you worked with expressions for interest problems. You could rewrite them in simpler ways using multiplication in place of repeated addition, and use exponents in place of repeated multiplication. Rewriting expressions in different forms can be a powerful tool for simplifying expressions and for seeing patterns. In this lesson, you will develop new ways of rewriting expressions using exponents.

10-35. Is 3^5 the same as $3 \cdot 5$? Explain.

10-36. Exponents allow you to rewrite some multiplication problems in a simpler form. Can exponent expressions also be simplified? Complete the table below on the Lesson 10.1.4 Resource Page, or copy and complete it on your own paper.

Original Form	Factored Form	Simplified Form
$5^2 \cdot 5^5$	$(5 \cdot 5) \cdot (5 \cdot 5 \cdot 5 \cdot 5 \cdot 5)$	5^7
$2^2 \cdot 2^4$		
$3^7 \cdot 3^2$		
$x^3 \cdot x^5$		
$x^3 y^2 \cdot x y^2$		
$7^2 \cdot x^3 \cdot 7 \cdot x^2$		
$2 \cdot x^4 \cdot 3 \cdot x y^2$		

a. Work with your team to compare the bases and exponents of the original form to the base and exponent of the simplified form. Write a statement to describe the relationships you see.

b. **Visualize** how you would expand $20^{12} \cdot 20^{51}$ in your mind. What would this expression be in a simplified form? Describe your **reasoning**.

c. One study team rewrote the expression $10^3 \cdot 5^4$ as 50^7. Is their simplification correct? Explain your **reasoning**.

Making Connections: Course 2

10-37.   When you multiply, the order of the factors does not matter. That means that you will get the same answer if you multiply $3 \cdot 2 \cdot 3$ and if you multiply $2 \cdot 3 \cdot 3$. This is the **Commutative Property of Multiplication**.

   a.   Check that $2 \cdot 10$ is equal to $10 \cdot 2$. Is it also true that $2 \div 10$ is equal to $10 \div 2$?

   b.   Write the expression $5^2 \cdot x^4 \cdot 5x$ in factored form. Explain how the Commutative Property helps you to simplify the expression to equal $5^3 \cdot x^5$.

10-38.   Multiplying a number by 10 changes the number in a special way. Simplify each expression below without using a calculator. As you work, pay attention to how the number changes when you multiply it by powers of 10.

   a. $9.23 \cdot 10$

   b. $9.23 \cdot 10^2$

   c. $9.23 \cdot 10^3$

   d. $9.23 \cdot 10^4$

10-39.   Talk with your team about any patterns you see in your answers in problem 10-38. Based on those patterns, what do you think $9.23 \cdot 10^7$ would be? Why?

   a.   Use the patterns you have found to predict the product for each expression without calculating it.

   i. 78.659×10^2

   ii. 346.38×10^5

   b.   With your team, write a statement describing **in general** how you can quickly multiply by powers of 10. You may want to include information about where the decimal point moves after multiplying the number by a power of 10 or why you have to add zeros. Work with your team to write a clear explanation for why this pattern works.

10-40.   When astronomers describe distances in space, often the numbers are so large
          that they are difficult to write. For example, the diameter of the sun is
          approximately one million, three hundred ninety thousand kilometers, or
          1,390,000 km. To make these numbers easier to write, astronomers use
          scientific notation. Using scientific notation, the diameter of the sun is:

$$1.39 \times 10^6 \text{ km}$$

   a.   Rewrite 10^6 as a single number without an exponent. What happens when
        you multiply 1.39 by this number?

   b.   In scientific notation, the mass of the sun is approximately 1.99×10^{30} kg.
        What does this number mean? Discuss with your team how to rewrite this
        number without scientific notation, then write it.

10-41.   Scientific notation requires that one factor is a power of 10, and the other
          factor is a number greater than or equal to 1 but less than 10. For example,
          2.56×10^5 is written in scientific notation, but 25.6×10^4 is not. Scientific
          notation also uses the symbol " $\times$ " for multiplication instead of " $\cdot$ " or
          parentheses. None of the numbers below are correctly written in scientific
          notation. Explain why each one does not meet the criteria for scientific
          notation, then write it using correct scientific notation.

   a. 25.6×10^4 b. $5.46 \cdot 100$ c. 0.93×10^8

10-42.   Scientific notation makes large
          numbers easier to write, but it
          also provides you with quick
          information about the size of
          the numbers. For example,
          Pluto and Haumea are both
          dwarf planets. Pluto has a
          mass of 1.305×10^{22} kilograms
          and Haumea has a mass of
          4.006×10^{21} kilograms.

Without rewriting the mass of each planet, can you tell which of these dwarf
planets is larger? Explain your **reasoning**.

10-43.   **Reverse** your thinking. Write each number below in scientific notation.

   a.   370,000,000   b.   48,710,000,000

METHODS AND MEANINGS

Commutative and Associative Properties of Multiplication

When two numbers or variables are combined together using multiplication, the order in which they are multiplied does not matter. This fact is known as the **Commutative Property of Multiplication**, so $5 \cdot 10 = 10 \cdot 5$. This result may be generalized using variables as:

$$a \cdot b = b \cdot a$$

Note that division does not satisfy the Commutative Property of Multiplication since $10 \div 5 \neq 5 \div 10$.

When three factors are multiplied together, we usually multiply the first two of them together and then multiply that product by the third factor. However, we could also multiply the last two together and then multiply the first with that product. The **Associative Property of Multiplication** tells us that the order in which three or more numbers are multiplied together does not matter. The answer to the problem $(5 \cdot (-6)) \cdot 10$ is equal to $5 \cdot (-6 \cdot 10)$. This is generalized using variables as:

$$(a \cdot b) \cdot c = a \cdot (b \cdot c)$$

Note that division is not associative since $(10 \div 2) \div 5 \neq 10 \div (2 \div 5)$
$$5 \div 5 \neq 10 \div 0.4$$

10-44.   Which number is greater, 3.56×10^4 or 1.9×10^6. Explain how you know.

10-45.   Rewrite each of the expressions below in a simpler form using exponents.

   a. $4 \cdot 4 \cdot 5 \cdot 5 \cdot 5$

   b. $3 \cdot 3 \cdot 3 \cdot 3 \cdot 3 \cdot y \cdot y$

   c. $(6x)(6x)(6x)(6x)$

10-46.   Maria and Jorge were trying to simplify the expression $1\frac{2}{5} \cdot (-\frac{3}{4}) \cdot (-\frac{4}{3})$. Maria started by rewriting $1\frac{2}{5}$ as $\frac{7}{5}$. Her work is below.

$$1\frac{2}{5} \cdot (-\frac{3}{4}) \cdot (-\frac{4}{3})$$

$$\frac{7}{5} \cdot (-\frac{3}{4}) \cdot (-\frac{4}{3})$$

$$(-\frac{21}{20}) \cdot (-\frac{4}{3})$$

$$\frac{84}{60} = 1\frac{24}{60} = 1\frac{2}{5}$$

Jorge had a different idea. He multiplied $(-\frac{3}{4}) \cdot (-\frac{4}{3})$ first.

a.   Simplify the expression $1\frac{2}{5} \cdot (-\frac{3}{4}) \cdot (-\frac{4}{3})$ using Jorge's method. Is your answer equal to Maria's?

b.   Why might Jorge have decided to multiply $(-\frac{3}{4}) \cdot (-\frac{4}{3})$ first?

c.   In a multiplication problem, the factors can be grouped together in different ways. This is called the **Associative Property of Multiplication**. Read the Math Notes box for this lesson, then show that $(\frac{3}{4} \cdot \frac{2}{5}) \cdot (-2) = \frac{3}{4} \cdot (\frac{2}{5} \cdot (-2))$.

d.   Simplify each expression. First, decide if you want to group some factors together.

    i. $(-9) \cdot (\frac{1}{9}) \cdot (\frac{3}{8})$ ii. $-\frac{5}{12} \cdot \frac{3}{7} \cdot \frac{4}{9}$ iii. $-8.1 \cdot 5 \cdot 2$

10-47.   Calculate the following products.

Factors	Product
6.5901×10^2	
0.6893×10^7	
5.86×10^4	
0.092×10^3	

10-48.   Simplify each expression.

    a. 6^5 b. $\left(\frac{2}{3}\right)^3$ c. $(2+3)^4$ d. $2(-\frac{1}{2}+\frac{3}{4})^3$

10-49.   Determine the compound interest earned on $220 invested at 3.25% compounded annually for 6 years.

Exponent Rules

In the previous lesson you expanded expressions written with exponents into factored form and then rewrote them in simpler form (problem 10-36). You also looked at ways to rewrite very large numbers in order to compare them easily.

In this lesson you will continue to develop ways to rewrite expressions using exponents. Use the questions below to focus discussion in your study team:

What part of the expression is being raised to a power?

What are the factors?

How can we rewrite the expression to have fewer terms?

10-50.　Rewrite each expression below in a simpler form.

　　a.　$10^2 \cdot x^3 \cdot 10 \cdot y$　　　　b.　$20^3 \cdot 20^8$　　　　c.　$x^2 y^2 z^2 \cdot x^3 z^5$

10-51.　Erin wants to rewrite the expression $5^2 x^2 \cdot 5^4 x^3$ in simpler form. She started by expanding the expression like this:

$$5 \cdot 5 + x \cdot x + 5 \cdot 5 \cdot 5 \cdot 5 + x \cdot x \cdot x$$
$$25 + x^2 + 625 + x^3$$

Do you agree with her work so far? Work with your team to complete the problem or, if you do not agree, to write Erin a note explaining how to correct her work.

10-52.   When a number is raised to a power, and then raised to a power again, the result follows a consistent pattern. Copy the table below or find it on the Lesson 10.1.5 Resource Page. Complete the table by expanding each expression into factored form and then rewriting it with new exponents.

Original Form	Factored Form	Simplified Form
$(5^2)^5$	$(5 \cdot 5)(5 \cdot 5)(5 \cdot 5)(5 \cdot 5)(5 \cdot 5)$	5^{10}
$(2^2)^4$		
$(3^7)^2$		
$(x^3)^5$		
$(x^3 y^2)^2$		

a.   Work with your team to describe the pattern between the exponents in the original form and the exponent(s) in the simplified form.

b.   **Visualize** $(20^3)^8$ written in factored form. What is multiplied, that is, what is the base? How many times is it multiplied? Use the expression you **visualized** to help you rewrite the expression in simplified form. Describe in detail how you figured out what exponent to use in the simplified form.

10-53.   In problem 10-50 you simplified the expression $20^3 \cdot 20^8$. Compare the factored form you wrote for that expression to the expression you **visualized** in part (b) of problem 10-52. How are the two expressions different?

10-54.   Heidi is trying to rewrite the two expressions below.

$$(2x)^3 \qquad 2x^3$$

"Are these two ways of writing the same thing? Or do they mean something different?" Heidi wonders.

a.   Rewrite $(2x)^3$ by expanding and then simplifying. What part is being raised to the third power? What is the result?

b.   Heidi thinks $2x^3$ is the same as $2 \cdot x^3$. Do you agree? If so, how would you expand the expression?

c.   Are $(2x)^3$ and $2x^3$ equivalent? Explain why or why not.

10-55.   Alex was trying to simplify the exponent expression $\frac{5^7}{5^3}$, and started by writing out the factored form. Once he saw the factors he recognized a Giant One in his work.

a.   Copy Alex's expression on your paper and write out the factored form. Where did he see a Giant One?

b.   Work with your study team to use the Giant One to simplify and rewrite the expression. What is the result?

10-56.   Expand each expression below into factored form, then rewrite it in simplified form.

a. $\frac{2^4}{2^2}$ b. $\frac{3^4}{3^5}$ c. $\frac{y^7}{y^4}$ d. $\frac{x^3 y^2}{xy^2}$

10-57.   Two of the problems below are correct, and four contain errors. Expand each original expression to verify that it is correct. If it is not, identify the mistake and simplify to find the correct answer.

a. $x^3 y^2 x^4 \overset{?}{=} x^7 y^2$ b. $2^3 \cdot 2^4 \overset{?}{=} 2^{12}$

c. $\frac{7^2 \cdot 8^3}{7^3 \cdot 8^2} \overset{?}{=} \frac{8}{7}$ d. $3^5 \cdot 3^2 \overset{?}{=} 9^7$

e. $\frac{6^2}{6^5} \overset{?}{=} 6^3$ f. $\frac{z^3}{z^3} \overset{?}{=} 0$

10-58.   LEARNING LOG

You have worked with your team to describe ways to
rewrite and simplify exponent expressions involving
multiplication and division. In your Learning Log, give
examples of each kind of expression. Describe in words
how to rewrite each one. Include factored and simplified
expressions to go with your descriptions. Title this entry,
"Simplifying Exponent Expressions," and label it with
today's date.

10-59.   Rewrite each expression in a simpler form using the patterns you have found for
rewriting expressions with exponents. If it is reasonable, write out the factored
form to help you.

a. $2^3 \cdot 2^4$ b. $\dfrac{2^8}{2^5}$ c. $(5x^2)^3$ d. $(4x)^2(5x^2)$

10-60.   **Additional Challenge:** Alice was simplifying the
expressions at right when she noticed a pattern.
Each exponent under the radical (square root) sign
was two times the exponent of the final answer.
She wanted to know more about why this was
happening.

$\sqrt{3^4} = \sqrt{81} = 9 = 3^2$

$\sqrt{6^2} = \sqrt{36} = 6 = 6^1$

$\sqrt{5^4} = \sqrt{625} = 25 = 5^2$

$\sqrt{2^6} = \sqrt{64} = 8 = 2^3$

a.   Confirm Alice's pattern by simplifying the expression $\sqrt{5^6}$ on your
calculator. Can you rewrite your answer as five raised to a power?

b.   What does the operation "square root" do to an expression? What operation
does it "**undo**"?

c.   Investigate this pattern using the expression $\sqrt{4^6}$.

•   Expand the expression.

•   Rewrite 4^6 as an expression raised to the second power.

•   Use the square root to "**undo**" the squaring.

•   Write your final answer, and check it on your calculator.

d.   Use that thinking to rewrite each expression below.

i. $\sqrt{7^4}$ ii. $\sqrt{9^8}$ iii. $\sqrt{3^{14}}$

METHODS AND MEANINGS

Scientific Notation

Scientific notation is a way of writing very large and very small numbers compactly. A number is said to be in scientific notation when it is written as a product of two factors as described below.

- The first factor is less than 10 and greater than or equal to 1.
- The second factor has a base of 10 and an integer exponent.
- The factors are separated by a multiplication sign.

Scientific Notation	Standard Form
5.32×10^6	5,320,000
3.07×10^{-4}	0.000307
2.61×10^{-15}	0.00000000000000261

Review & Preview

10-61. Simplify each expression.

a. $\frac{3^2 \cdot 5^3 \cdot 8}{3 \cdot 5^3 \cdot 8}$
b. $(3x)^4$
c. $3^3 \cdot 3^5 \cdot (\frac{1}{3})^2$
d. $\frac{7^4 \cdot 9^2}{9^3 \cdot 7^2}$

10-62. Gail bought a new baseball cap for $7.50, which was $\frac{1}{3}$ off the original price. What was the original price?

10-63. Find the missing side on this right triangle.

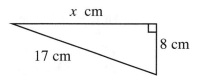

x cm

17 cm

8 cm

10-64. Simplify each expression.

a. $\frac{9}{15} \div \frac{4}{3}$ b. $-\frac{19}{20} + \frac{4}{5}$ c. $-\frac{8}{9} \div (-\frac{2}{5})$ d. $3\frac{1}{2} \div 1\frac{1}{7}$

e. $-\frac{3}{4} - (-\frac{11}{16})$ f. $\frac{2}{9} \cdot \frac{14}{15} \cdot (-\frac{9}{10})$ g. $-10\frac{4}{5} + (-\frac{3}{8})$ h. $\frac{12}{5} \div (-\frac{1}{10})$

10-65. The Wild West Frontier Park now offers an unlimited day pass. For $29.00, visitors can go on as many rides as they want. The original plan charged visitors $8.75 to enter the park plus $2.25 for each ride. Write an equation to determine the number of rides that would make the total cost equal for the two plans. Solve the equation.

10.1.6 What happens if it is negative?

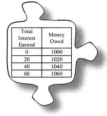

Negative Exponents

Earlier in this chapter you learned how to write large numbers in scientific notation. Those large numbers are used by astronomers to measure the great distances in space. Not all scientists work with such a large scale. Some scientists use very small numbers to describe what they measure under a microscope. In this lesson you will learn about how scientific notation can be used to represent small numbers.

10-66. Salvador was studying microscopic pond animals in science class. He read that amoebas were 0.3 millimeters to 0.6 millimeters in length. He saw that euglenas are as small as $8.0 \cdot 10^{-2}$ millimeters, but he did not know how big or small a measurement that was. He decided to try to figure out what a negative exponent could mean.

a. Copy and complete Salvador's calculations at right. Use the pattern of dividing by 10 to fill in the missing values.

b. How is 10^2 related to 10^{-2}?

c. What type of numbers did the negative exponents create? Did negative exponents create negative numbers?

$10^3 = 1000$ ⟍ $\div 10$
$10^2 = 100$ ⟍ $\div 10$
$10^1 = 10$ ⟍ $\div 10$
$10^0 =$
$10^{-1} =$
$10^{-2} =$
$10^{-3} =$

10-67. Ngoc was curious about what Salvador was doing and began exploring patterns himself. He completed the calculations at right.

$$2^5 = 32$$
$$2^4 = 16$$
$$2^3 = 8$$
$$\cdots$$
$$\cdots$$
$$2^{-1} = \frac{1}{2}$$
$$2^{-2} =$$
$$2^{-3} =$$

   a.   Copy and complete his calculations. Be sure to include all of the integer exponents from 5 to −3.

   b.   Look for patterns in his list. How are the values to the right of the equal sign changing? Is there a constant multiplier between each value?

10-68. In problems 10-66 and 10-67 you saw that 10^0 and 2^0 both simplify to the same value. What is it? Do you think that any number to the zero power would have the same answer? Explain.

10-69. Both Ngoc and Salvador are looking for ways to calculate values with negative exponents without extending a pattern. Looking at the expression 5^{-2}, they each started to simplify differently.

Salvador thinks that 5^2 is 25, so 5^{-2} must be $\frac{1}{25}$. Ngoc thinks 5^{-2} is $\frac{1}{5} \cdot \frac{1}{5}$. Which student is correct?

10-70. **Reverse** your thinking. If negative exponents can create fractions, then can fractions be written as expressions including negative exponents? Simplify the expressions below. Write your answer in two different forms: as a fraction and as an expression with a negative exponent.

   a. $\dfrac{6^3}{6^5}$ b. $\dfrac{3^2}{3^6}$ c. $\dfrac{m^5}{m^6}$ d. $\dfrac{b^2}{b^5}$

10-71. Salvador's first questions about negative exponents came from science class where he had learned that euglenas measured 8.0×10^{-2} millimeters. Use your understanding of negative exponents to rewrite 8.0×10^{-2} in standard form.

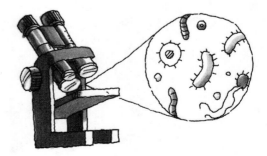

10-72.   The list below contains a star, a river and a type of bacteria. Which one is which? Use your understanding of scientific notation to put the three items listed below in order from largest to smallest. Which of these items is very small? Explain how you know.

   a.   Yangtze measures 6.3×10^5 meters

   b.   Staphylococcus measures 6×10^{-7} meters

   c.   Eta Carinae measures 7.1×10^{17} meters

10-73.   Which of the numbers below are written in scientific notation? For each that is not, rewrite it correctly.

   a. 4.51×10^{-2} b. 0.789×10^5 c. 31.5×10^2 d. 3.008×10^{-8}

10-74.   Rewrite each expression in a simpler form. **Visualize** the factored form to help you, or write it out if it is reasonable to do so.

   a. $2^3 \cdot 2^4$ b. $\dfrac{2^8}{2^5}$ c. $(5x^2)^3$ d. $(4x)^2(5x^2)$

10-75.   **Additional Challenge:** Lamar has a list of 600 words to learn for the upcoming spelling bee. His goal is to learn half of the words left on his list each day.

   a.   How many words will Lamar have to learn the first day? How many will he have left to learn after 3 days?

   b.   How many words will he need to learn on day 8? With your team, write two different expressions to show how you found your answer.

METHODS AND MEANINGS

Laws of Exponents

Expressions that include exponents can be expanded into factored form and then rewritten in simplified form.

Expression	Factored Form	Simplified Form
$(5x)^3(2y)(x^2)y$	$5 \cdot x \cdot 5 \cdot x \cdot 5 \cdot x \cdot 2 \cdot y \cdot x \cdot x \cdot y$	$250x^5y^2$

The **Laws of Exponents** summarize several rules for simplifying expressions that have exponents. The rules below are true if $x \neq 0$ and $y \neq 0$.

$$x^a \cdot x^b = x^{(a+b)} \qquad (x^a)^b = x^{ab} \qquad \frac{x^a}{x^b} = x^{(a-b)}$$

$$x^0 = 1 \qquad (x^a y^b)^c = x^{ac} y^{bc} \qquad x^{-a} = \frac{1}{x^a}$$

Review & Preview

10-76.   Decide which numbers below are correctly written in scientific notation. If they are not, rewrite them.

a. 92.5×10^{-2} b. 6.875×10^2 c. 2.8×10 d. 0.83×100^2

10-77.   In the table at right, write each power of 10 as a decimal and as a fraction.

a.   Describe how the decimals and fractions change as you progress down the table.

b.   How would you tell someone how to write 10^{-12} as a fraction? You do not have to write the actual fraction.

Power of 10	Decimal Form	Fraction Form
1		
10^{-1}	0.1	$\frac{1}{10}$
10^{-2}		$\frac{1}{100}$
10^{-3}		
10^{-4}		
10^{-5}		

10-78.   The probability of being struck by lightening in the United States is 0.000032%, while the probability of winning the grand prize in a certain lottery is 6.278×10^{-7} percent. Which event is more likely to happen? Explain your **reasoning**, including how you rewrote the numbers to compare them.

10-79.   Mary wants to have $8500 to travel to South America when she is 21. She currently has $6439 in a savings account earning 4% annual compound interest. Mary is 13 now.

    a.   If Mary does not take out or deposit any money, how much money will Mary have when she is 15?

    b.   Will Mary have enough money for her trip when she is 21?

10-80.   Daniel needed to paint his patio, so he made a scale drawing of it. He knows the width of the patio is 10 feet, but the scale drawing is in inches.

    a.   Find the length of the patio in feet.

    b.   Find the area of the patio so Daniel knows how much paint to buy.

    c.   One can of paint covers 125 square feet. How many cans of paint will Daniel need to buy?

10.2.1 Does surface area affect volume?

Surface Area and Volume

In your work with two-dimensional (flat) shapes you have described their dimensions, their perimeters, and their areas. For three-dimensional shapes — shapes that have length, width, *and* depth — you can measure the lengths of their edges and calculate the areas of their faces (sides). Three-dimensional shapes can also be described by their volume, that is, how much space they enclose. Today you will work with rectangle-based prisms. As you work, keep these questions in mind:

How many cubes would it take to fill it?

How many squares would it take to cover the outside of it?

Making Connections: Course 2

10-81.   PERFECT PACKAGING

Cereal boxes come in different shapes and sizes. Some are tall and skinny, others are shorter or deeper. The Bravo Breakfast cereal company is considering changing the size of its box, and the staff need some data to help them make the best choice.

The company currently packages its Morning Math Crunch cereal in a box that is 2" deep by 4" wide by 8" tall, as pictured at right. This shape is called a **right rectangular prism** because the top and bottom faces are rectangles that are congruent and parallel to each other. These are called the **bases**. The other faces (sides of the box) are also rectangles that are perpendicular to the bases. Use a set of cubes to build a model of this box. Assume that the edge of one cube represents 1" of length on the real cereal box.

a.   Describe the box as completely as you can.

- What shapes do you see when you look at the faces of the box?

- What lengths or other measurements can you describe?

- Sketch each shape on your paper, and label it completely.

b.   The cardboard sides of the box are called its **faces**. How much cardboard is needed to create all of the faces of the box? Work with your team to develop a method for calculating this amount. Discuss the kind of units to use. Be ready to explain your method to the class.

c.   The square units that it takes to cover the outside of an object, like the amount of cardboard you found in part (b), is called the object's **surface area**. The **volume** of a shape is the measure of how much it will hold. Volume is measured in cubic units.

How many cubes did you use to make this model of the cereal box? How many cubic inches of cereal will the box hold?

10-82.   The waste management division at Bravo Breakfast is worried that the box for Morning Math Crunch uses too much cardboard. They want to make a box that holds the same amount of cereal but uses less cardboard.

   a.   What measurement of the box is the waste management division interested in **minimizing** (making as small as possible)? What measurement does the company want to keep the same? What could change?

   b.   With your team, use the cubes to build different rectangular prisms that will hold 64 cubic inches of cereal. Each box must be a rectangular prism with exactly six faces. For each prism you create:

   • Sketch the prism.

   • Label the dimensions on your sketch.

   • Find the surface area.

   How many different prisms can you make?

   c.   Do all of the prisms you built have the same volume? How do you know?

   d.   Which box will use the smallest amount of cardboard?

10-83.   Use cubes to build each prism below. Find the surface area and volume of each shape.

   a.   b.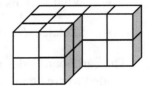

   c.   Use at least 15 cubes to build a prism of your own design. Sketch the prism and find its surface area and volume.

   d.   Write step-by-step directions explaining to another student how to find the surface area of a prism. You may want to use one of the prisms above as an example. Give **reasons** for each step.

Making Connections: Course 2

ETHODS AND MEANINGS

Polygons, Prisms, and Pyramids

A **polygon** is a two-dimensional closed figure made of straight-line segments connected end to end. The segments may not cross. The point where two sides meet is called a **vertex** (plural: vertices). Polygons are named by the number of sides they have. Polygons with three through 10 sides are named and illustrated below:

Triangle: Hexagon: Nonagon:

Quadrilateral: Septagon: Decagon:

Pentagon: Octagon:

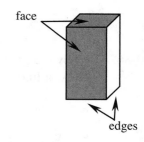

Three-dimensional figures are those that have length, width, and height. If a three-dimensional figure is completely bounded by polygons and their interiors, it is a **polyhedron**. The polygons are called **faces**, and an **edge** is where two faces meet. A cube and a pyramid are each an example of a polyhedron.

A **prism** is a special kind of polyhedron that has two congruent, parallel faces called **bases**. The other faces (called **lateral faces**) are parallelograms (or rectangles). No holes are permitted in the solid.

A prism is named for the shape of its base. For example:

triangular prism   pentagonal prism

A **pyramid** is a three-dimensional figure with a base that is a polygon. The lateral faces are formed by connecting each vertex of the base to a single point (the vertex of the pyramid) that is above or below the surface that contains the base.

10-84. Read the Math Notes box in this lesson. Use the information to determine whether each shape below is a polygon.

a.   b.   c.   d.

10-85. Find the volume and surface area of each shape below. Assume that the edge of each cube measures 1".

a.   b.   c.

10-86. Copy the graph at right on graph paper. Draw a line through the two points.

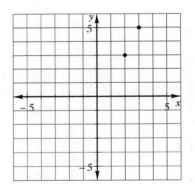

a. What is the slope of the line?

b. What is the rule for all points on the line?

10-87. Simplify each of the following expressions.

a. $8^2 + 7^2$

b. $7^2 \cdot 7 \cdot 7$

c. $(\frac{1}{2})^2 + (\frac{2}{3})^2$

d. $(2^2 + 6)^2$

e. $-4 \cdot 3^2 - 2$

f. $x - x$

g. $3 \cdot 3 \div 3$

h. $4x + x - 2x$

i. $-2 \cdot 4 \div 4$

10-88. Juan found that 20 new pencils weigh 12 ounces. How much will 50 new pencils weigh? Show your **reasoning**.

10-89. A principal made the histogram at right to analyze how many years teachers had been teaching at her school.

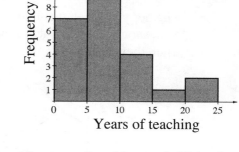

a. How many teachers work at her school?

b. If the principal randomly chose one teacher to represent the school at a conference, what is the probability that the teacher would have been teaching at the school for more than 10 years? Write the probability in two different ways.

c. What is the probability that a teacher on the staff has been there for fewer than 5 years?

10.2.2 How can I visualize it?

· ·

Visualizing Three-Dimensional Shapes

Can you picture what something will look like, even before you see it built? Are you able to look at leftovers after a meal and decide what size container you will need in order to hold them, or do you often choose a container that is too big or too small? Being able to **visualize** what something will look like in a different form or shape is a useful skill that can be developed with practice. Today you will work with your team to **visualize** different three-dimensional shapes.

10-90. Your teacher will show you a cardboard box. What will this box look like when it is unfolded and flattened out? Look carefully at the box and discuss possibilities with your team. Draw a picture or write a description of the unfolded box.

10-91. Picture in your mind each figure below as a three-dimensional object. What would each shape look like if it were unfolded so that each face was flat on the table? A flat picture that can be folded up to form a three-dimensional solid is called a **net**. Work with your team to draw a net for each of the shapes below. Listen carefully to your teammates' ideas, because there is more than one way to unfold each shape.

a.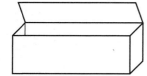

b.

10-92.   Mark and Thomas are looking at the two nets shown below. They have decided
that each one will form a pyramid, but they disagree about whether the
pyramids will be identical or not. Look carefully at the two nets, and decide
whether you agree that they will each form a pyramid. Then, explain what the
boys should compare about the two nets to decide if the shapes will be identical
when they are built.

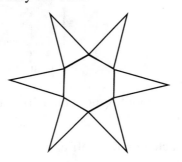 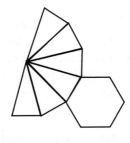

10-93.   SHAPE VISUALIZATION CHALLENGE

How much can you tell about a shape from its net? In this challenge, each
member of your study team will receive a different net for a three-dimensional
solid. Together, you must describe each shape completely *without building it*.
Use the questions below to help you make a complete description.

Will the shape be a pyramid or a prism?

What shape is the base?

Will the shape be tall or short?

Will the shape be narrow or wide?

How many different faces will it have?

When you are satisfied that you have described as much as you can, call your
teacher over to check that your description is complete. If it is, cut out the net
and fold it into the shape to check your work.

Net A   Net B   Net C   Net D

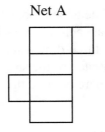  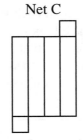 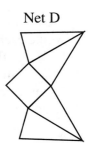

Making Connections: Course 2

10-94.   When the nets in problem 10-93 are cut and folded to create solids, which solid
has the greatest surface area? Write down a prediction along with your
justification. Then test your prediction by measuring the dimensions of your
shape in centimeters, calculating the surface area and sharing your data with
your team. Was your prediction correct?

METHODS AND MEANINGS

Surface Area

The **surface area** of a prism or pyramid is the sum of the areas
of each of the faces, including the bases. Surface area is expressed in
square units.

A **net** is a drawing of each of the faces of a prism, or pyramid, as if it
was cut along its edges and flattened out. A net can be helpful to see
the different area subproblems that need to be solved in order to find
the total surface area. There are usually several ways to make a net of
a prism or pyramid. One example for each solid is shown below.

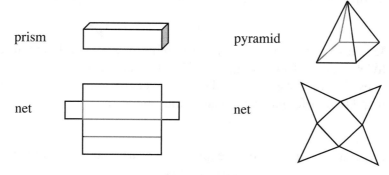

prism

net

pyramid

net

10-95.   Which net(s) below will fold up to make a complete prism? If a net will not
          form a prism, explain what is wrong.

          a. 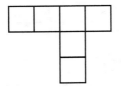   b.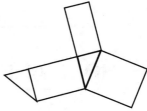

          c. 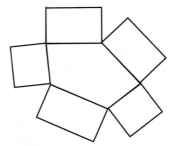   d.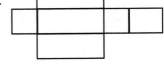

10-96.   Find the surface area and volume of the rectangular
          prism at right.

10-97.   Jeenie's solar hybrid car gets 35% more miles per gallon than Karla's traditional
          hybrid car. If Jeenie's car gets 60 miles per gallon, how many miles per gallon
          does Karla's car get? Calculate Karla's car's mileage in two different ways,
          using two different scale factors (multipliers).

10-98.   Expand and simplify each expression, or use the exponent patterns you
          identified in Section 10.1 to simplify.

          a. $\dfrac{x^4}{x^3}$ b. $(x^3)^4$ c. $(2y^2)^2$ d. $(x^2)^4$

          e. $x^2 x^{-3}$ f. $(xy^2)^2$ g. $(x^2y^2)^4$ h. $(2x)^3$

10-99.   Josue called his father to say that he was almost home. He had traveled 61.5
          miles, which was $\frac{3}{4}$ of the way home. Write and solve an equation to calculate
          the total distance he will travel to get home.

10.2.3 How much will fill it?

- -
Volume of a Prism

You have had a lot of practice with finding the area of flat, two-dimensional shapes. Today you will begin using those skills to help you understand shapes with a third dimension. As you work on the problem, consider the following questions:

How can I see the shape in layers?

How can I slice the shape so that the layers are identical?

10-100.   BIRTHDAY SWEETS

Laverne is making a birthday dessert for her cousin Leslie. She wants to incorporate Leslie's favorite ingredients, cookies and chocolate mousse. She will make the dessert in a special L-shaped pan that is 9.5 cm deep.

First, Laverne is going to make a cookie crust as the bottom layer. The crust will be 1 cm thick so that it is nice and crunchy. She is going to add chocolate mousse on top of the crust until the mousse is 7 cm thick. Finally, she will add a 1.5 cm layer of whipped cream on the mousse and top it with chocolate sprinkles.

a.   What area will the dessert cover (in square centimeters) on the pan?

b.   Laverne needs to know what quantity of cookies to buy to make the crust layer of the dessert. Does the measurement she needs describe length, area, or volume? Discuss this with your team, and then write down your explanation.

c.   One cookie will crush into about 5 cubic centimeters of cookie crumbs. Show Laverne how to find out how many cookies she will need to make the crust layer. Be sure to explain your **reasoning**. How many cookies should she buy?

10-101. Laverne wants the mousse on top of the crust to be seven cm thick. Use your answer from part (c) of problem 10-100 to help you figure out how many cubic centimeters of mousse Laverne will need. Explain your **reasoning**.

10-102. Laverne has 1200 cubic centimeters of whipped cream ready to spread on top of the mousse. Erika looked at Laverne's notes about how much cream she would need and exclaimed, *"You have too much! You will overflow the pan!"*

How could Erika know that Laverne has too much whipped cream? Be prepared to share your ideas with the class.

10-103. Laverne needs to be sure that her finished dessert will be enough to serve everyone.

a. What is the total volume of dessert that Laverne is planning to make? Be ready to share your study team's **strategy** with the class.

b. If one serving is 285 cm³, how many people will the dessert serve?

10-104. For the prism at right, find the volume of a one cm high layer. Then, find the total volume of the prism. Every face is a rectangle.

10-105. When finding the volume of the shape below, Audrey found the volume of the shaded layer first. Her work is shown below:

$$5 + 20 = 25 \text{, so } 25 \cdot 8 = 200 \text{ ft}^3$$

Then she said, *"The shape is 22 feet high, so there are 22 one-foot-high layers."* She then multiplied and got this answer:

$$22 \cdot 200 = 4400 \text{ ft}^3$$

a. What was Audrey's mistake?

b. What is the actual volume of the shape? Explain how you found it.

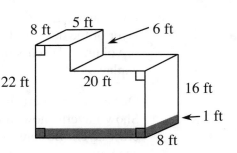

METHODS AND MEANINGS

Measurement in Different Dimensions

Measurements of **length** are measurements in **one dimension**. They are labeled as cm, ft, km, etc.

Measurements of **area** are measurements in **two dimensions**. They are labeled as cm^2, ft^2, m^2, etc.

Measurements of **volume** are measurements **in three dimensions**. They are labeled as cm^3, ft^3, m^3, etc.

1 centimeter

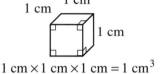

$1 \text{ cm} \times 1\text{cm} = 1 \text{ cm}^2$

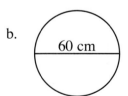

$1 \text{ cm} \times 1 \text{ cm} \times 1 \text{ cm} = 1 \text{ cm}^3$

Review & Preview

10-106. Find the surface area and volume of the prism shown at right.

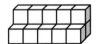

10-107. Find the area of each circle below.

a. radius = 8 cm

b. 60 cm

10-108. Write each number in scientific notation.

a. 5467.8   b. 0.0032   c. 8,007,020

10-109.   Find the missing length on this right triangle.

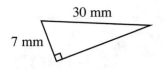

10-110.   Graph the rule $y = -3x + 2$.

    a.   What is the slope?   b.   What is the y-intercept?

10-111.   Simplify each of the following expressions.

    a. $3\frac{1}{5} \cdot \frac{7}{4}$ b. $5^3 \cdot (-\frac{4}{5})$ c. $2^4 \cdot \frac{5}{8}$ d. $-\frac{1}{2} \cdot 3^2$

    e. $-\frac{5}{6} + (\frac{1}{2})^2$ f. $(-\frac{4}{5})^2 - \frac{3}{50}$ g. $(\frac{3}{10})^2 - (-\frac{2}{5})^2$ h. $8^2(-\frac{7}{8}) - \frac{1}{2}$

10.2.4 How much will it hold?

···

Volume of Non-Rectangular Prisms

In this lesson you will investigate different **strategies** for finding the volume of non-rectangular prisms. The problems require you to describe how you **visualize** each shape. As you work with your team, ask each other these questions to focus your discussion:

> How can the shape be broken down into simpler shapes?

> Can we break the shape into equal layers or slices?

10-112. THE SHELL BOX

Laurel keeps her seashell collection in a small box that is shaped like a rectangular prism with a base of 4" x 3" and height of 5" (see diagram at right). She wants to make a bigger box for her shells, and she has found a pattern that she likes. The pattern has two sides that are pentagons and the finished box will look like a miniature house (see picture at right). Use the net on the Lesson 10.2.4 Resource Page to construct a paper model of Laurel's new box.

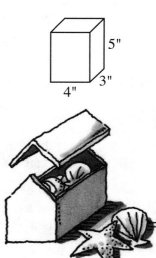

a.   Calculate the volume of Laurel's original small box. What method did you use?

b.   Laurel was trying to figure out the volume of the new box.

One of her friends said, *"Why don't you find the volume of one layer and then figure out how many layers there would be?"*

Another friend said, *"What if you separated the pentagon into two parts, so that you have a rectangular prism and a prism with a triangle base? Then you could find the volume of the two parts separately and put them back together."*

Talk about each of these **strategies** with your team. Could Laurel use these ideas to find the volume of her new box?

c.   Work with your team to calculate the volume of Laurel's new box. Show your thinking clearly and be prepared to share your method with the class.

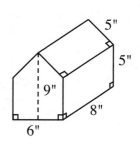

10-113.   Locate the two nets for prisms you cut out in Lesson 10.2.2. Decide which face is the base on each shape and which edge is the height. Then:

- Mark each base with one color.

- Mark each height with another color.

- Write down which color signifies the bases and which signifies the heights.

- Find the volume of each prism.

10-114.   Find the volume of the prism at right using any method you choose. Be prepared to explain your **reasoning**.

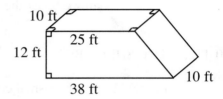

10-115.   Bryan was looking at the prism in problem 10-114 with his team. He wondered how they could slice the prism into layers horizontally that would all be the same size.

a.   If the team slices the shape so that the bottom layer has the 10 m by 38 m rectangle as its base, will each layer be equal in size?

b.   How could the team turn or tip the shape so that if the shape is sitting on a table and is cut horizontally, each layer will be the same size and shape? Which face will rest on the table?

c.   When does it make sense to tip the shape in order to see the layers? Discuss this question with your team and summarize your conclusion on your paper.

10-116.   LEARNING LOG

The method for finding the volume of a prism is commonly described as "finding the area of the base, then multiplying by the height." Discuss with your study team how this **strategy** works. How does the area of the base help to find the volume? Does it matter which face is the base? Why do you multiply by the height? Record your conclusions in your Learning Log. Title the entry, "Volume of a Prism," and label it with today's date.

METHODS AND MEANINGS

MATH NOTES

Volume of a Prism

The **volume** of a prism can be calculated by dividing the prism into layers that are each one unit high. To calculate the total volume, multiply the volume of one layer by the number of layers it takes to fill the shape. Since the volume of one layer is the area of the base (B) multiplied by 1 (the height of that layer), we can use the formula below to compute the volume of a prism.

If h = height of the prism, V = (area of base) · (height)
$V = Bh$

Example:

Area of base = (2 in.)(3 in.) = 6 in.^{2}

(Area of base)(height) = (6 in.^{2})(4 in.) = 24 in.^{3}

Volume = 24 in.^{3}

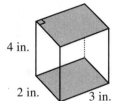

4 in.

2 in.   3 in.

Review & Preview

10-117. Is each shape below a prism? If so, identify the shape that is the base. If not, explain why not.

a.   b.   c.   d.

10-118. Find the volume of a 1-unit-high layer of each prism below. Then find the total volume and the surface area of each figure.

a. A rectangular prism

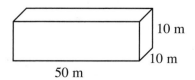

10 m

10 m

50 m

b. A triangle-based prism

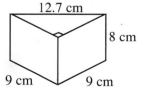

12.7 cm

8 cm

9 cm   9 cm

10-119.   Sketch a circle with a radius of 4 cm. Find the area and circumference of the circle.

10-120.   If the area of this triangle is 132 cm², what is the height?

16 cm

10-121.   Leonard has purchased packages of grid paper for $2.25. If he wants to make a 40% profit on each package he sells to his classmates, by how much should he increase the price? What will the new price be?

10-122.   Simplify each expression.

a. $(3x)^4 x^3$

b. $\dfrac{2^4 \cdot 3}{2^3 \cdot 3^2}$

c. $4^{-3} \cdot 4^2$

$\mathbf{10.2.5}$ What if the base is not a polygon?

Surface Area and Volume of Cylinders

Soup cans and rolls of paper towels are each examples of **cylinders**. Cylinders are like prisms in many ways, except that, unlike prisms that have polygons as bases, cylinders have circles as bases. In this lesson you will compare the surface area and volume of prisms and cylinders.

10-123.　COMPARING THE GYM BAGS

The CPM Sports Company is planning a new product line of gym bags. They have decided that the outside of the bag (without the ends) will be made with a rectangular piece of cloth that is 40 inches by 52 inches. They are trying to decide whether the end pieces will be squares or circles. They will decide by comparing the surface area and volume of each bag and considering their advantages and disadvantages. Your team will provide data for their decision.

40 inches

40 inches

52 inches

40 inches

40 inches

Use a standard piece of paper that measures 8.5" on one edge and 11" on the other to create a model of each gym bag. To model the square-based prism:

- Fold the paper in half so that the 8.5" edges match up, then unfold.

- Fold each 8.5" edge in to the center crease, then unfold.

- Tape the 8.5" edges together to form the **lateral face** of a square-based prism. The open squares at either end are the bases.

Use a new piece of paper to model the cylinder:

- Roll the paper so that one 8.5" edge matches up with the other.

- Tape the edges together to form the **lateral face** of a cylinder. The open circles formed at each end are the bases.

Your task: Using the models for reference, find the surface area and volume of each gym bag. How much fabric will it take to make each bag? How much will each bag hold? Remember that the shorter length on the paper (8.5") models the 40" dimension of the cloth, and the longer length (11") models the 52" dimension of the cloth. The model you have created is *not* to scale.

Discussion Points

What dimensions will we need to find?

How can we organize our work?

What shape is each surface?

How are prisms and cylinders alike? How are they different?

10-124.   Focus first on the square-based prism. Sketch
the prism on your paper, and then use the
dimensions given for the cloth to answer the
questions below.

    a.   What is the perimeter of the square base?
How long is each side of the square base?

    b.   What is the surface area of the prism?

    c.   Calculate the volume of the prism.

10-125.   Sketch the cylinder on your paper.

    a.   Label all of the lengths that you know on your sketch. What shape is the
lateral face (the face formed by the original piece of cloth)? Find the area
of the lateral face and the area of each base. If you do not have enough
information to find the area, list the measurements that you need.

    b.   Melissa is looking at the base of the cylinder, and realizes that the only
measurement she knows is the circumference of the circle. She thinks she
can use the circumference to find out other measurements. What is the
circumference of this circle? What other lengths can Melissa find using this
measurement?

    c.   Find the area of each base of the cylinder and then calculate the total
surface area.

10-126.   To find the volume of the cylinder, Melissa started by comparing it to a prism.
*"To find the volume of a prism, I slice it into equal layers. I wonder if the same
method will work for a cylinder?"* she asks. Work with your team to answer
Melissa's question. How could a cylinder be sliced into layers? What shape
would each layer be? Find the volume of the cylinder.

*Further Guidance
section ends here.*

10-127.   How does the amount of fabric required to make the cylindrical bag compare to
the amount of fabric required to make the square-based prism bag? How much
will each bag hold? Based on this information, which bag style do you think the
CPM sports company should make? Explain your **reasoning**.

10-128.   Find the surface area and volume of this cylinder. Show your work clearly.

diameter = 10 cm

10 cm

10-129.   **LEARNING LOG**

With your team, look carefully at how you found the surface area of the cylindrical bag. What measurements did you use to find the area of the base of a cylinder? What measurements did you use to find the lateral area? What measurement is important for both calculations? After your team has discussed these questions, record your ideas in your Learning Log. Title this entry, "Surface Area and Volume of a Cylinder," and label it with today's date.

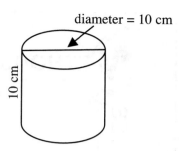

10-130.   **Additional Challenge:** Louise calculated the volume of the prism at right to be 702 m³. She is trying to find the surface area, but needs help.

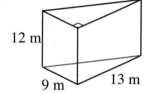

12 m

9 m   13 m

a.   Sketch the shape on your paper and label any lengths that you know. How can you find the lengths of the unlabeled edges?

b.   What are the length and width of each rectangle?

c.   What is the total surface area of the shape?

METHODS AND **M**EANINGS

MATH NOTES

Volume of a Cylinder

The **volume of a cylinder** can be calculated in exactly the same way as the volume of a prism. That is, the volume can be calculated by dividing the cylinder into layers that are each one unit high. To calculate the total volume, multiply the volume of one layer by the number of layers it takes to fill the shape.

The volume of a cylinder can also be calculated by multiplying the area of the base (B) by the height (h).

Volume = (area of base)(height)

$$V = Bh = (r^2\pi)(h)$$

For example, for the cylinder at right,

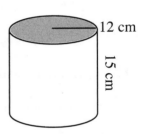

Area of the base: $B = (12)^2\pi = 144\pi$

Volume: $V = 144\pi(15) = 2160\pi \approx 6785.84$ cm^3

10-131. Find the area of the base of each cylinder below, and then calculate the volume of each cylinder. Show your steps.

a.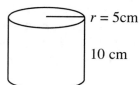
$r = 5$cm

10 cm

b.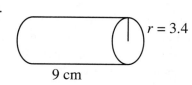
$r = 3.4$

9 cm

10-132. What is the volume of a hexagonal-based prism with a height of 12 in. and a base area of 62 in.²? Would the volume be different if the base were a pentagon with an area of 62 in.²? Explain.

10-133. Find the length of the side labeled x in each of the right triangles pictured below.

a.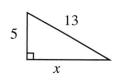
5   13

x

b.
x   3

6

c.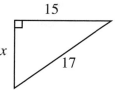
15

x

17

10-134. Solve these equations for x.

a. $(x + 3.5)2 = 16$

b. $23 + 5x = 7 + 2.5x$

c. $3x + 4.4 = -(6.6 + x)$

10-135. Two employees of Frontier Fence Company can install 100 feet of fence in three days. At the same rate, how many employees are needed to install 150 feet of fence in one day?

10-136. Simplify each expression.

a. $\dfrac{3^5}{3^{10}}$

b. $10x^4(10x)^{-2}$

c. $(\tfrac{1}{4})^3 \cdot (4)^2$

d. $\dfrac{(xy)^3}{xy^3}$

10.2.6 What if the layers are not the same?

Volume of Cones and Pyramids

Cones and **pyramids** are three-dimensional objects that have only one base, and come to a point opposite their base. A **cone** has a circular base, while a **pyramid** has a base that is a polygon and lateral faces that are triangles. Today you will be investigating how to use what you know about cylinders and prisms to find the volume of a cone and a pyramid. Questions to keep in mind as you work are:

What is the shape of the base?

How does the shape compare to a cylinder or a prism?

10-137. HOW MUCH SHOULD IT COST?

You have a choice of purchasing a small or a large serving of popcorn at the movies. A small popcorn comes in a cone and costs $1.50, and a large popcorn comes in a cylinder that costs $3.50. Both containers have the same height and bases with the same circular area. Based on their prices, discuss with your team which container of popcorn you think is a better deal. Be prepared to share your **reasons** with the class.

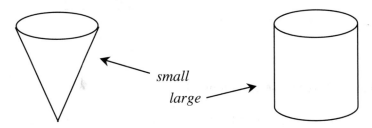

small

large

10-138. Your teacher will lead you through a demonstration about the volume of cones.

a. How are the radius and height of each cone related to the radius and height of each corresponding cylinder?

b. Sketch each cone and cylinder on your paper, and estimate which cone will have a greater volume.

c. How many cones full of rice were needed to fill each corresponding cylinder?

d. Based on the demonstration, describe how the volume of a cone compares to the volume of a cylinder when their heights and base areas are equal.

Making Connections: Course 2

10-139. Based on the relationship you found in problem 10-138, if a cone of popcorn costs $1.50 what would a fair price be for the cylinder of popcorn? At the advertised prices (problem 10-137), which popcorn is the better deal?

10-140. A different movie theater sells popcorn in the containers shown below. This time the small container is a pyramid priced at $2.50. The large container is a prism with the same height and base as the pyramid and is priced at $5.50. At this theater, which popcorn do you think is a better deal? Be prepared to give **reasons** for your prediction.

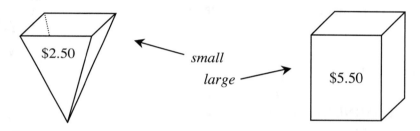

10-141. Your teacher will now lead you through another demonstration to help you decide if you need to adjust your thinking about the relationship between the volume of a pyramid and a prism that have the same base and the same height. After you have seen the demonstration with the pyramid and the prism, which container of popcorn is a better deal? **Justify** your answer.

10-142. Ann and Dan were trying to find the volume of the cone at right. Ann thinks that the cone is 8 inches tall and Dan thinks that the cone is 10 inches tall. Write them a note explaining who is correct.

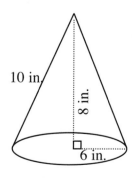

10-143.   Ann, Dan, and Jan calculated the volume of some shapes and got different answers. Look at their work shown below and make a sketch of the shape that each set of calculations might represent. Why do Dan and Jan's calculations have the same result even though they look different?

Dan's work: $V = \frac{(4^2\pi)(9)}{3} = 150.8$ cm^3

Ann's work: $V = (4^2\pi)(9) = 452.4$ cm^3

Jan's work: $V = \frac{1}{3}(4^2\pi)(9) = 150.8$ cm^3

10-144.   Find the volume of the pyramid at right. The hexagonal base has an area of 128 cm^2.

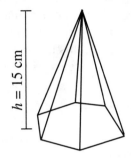

$h = 15$ cm

10-145.   LEARNING LOG

If you know the volume of any prism, how can you find the volume of a pyramid that has the same base area and height as the prism? If you know the volume of any cylinder, how can you find the volume of a cone that has the same base area and height as the cylinder? Answer these questions in your Learning Log. Label this entry with today's date, and title it "Volume of Cones and Pyramids."

ETHODS AND MEANINGS

MATH NOTES

Surface Area of a Cylinder

A **cylinder** has two congruent, circular bases. The **lateral surface** of the cylinder, when opened flat, forms a rectangle with a height equal to the height of the cylinder and a width equal to the circumference of the cylinder's base.

The **surface area of a cylinder** is the sum of the two base areas and the lateral surface area. The formula for the surface area is:

$$S.A. = 2r^2\pi + \pi dh$$
$$= 2r^2\pi + 2\pi rh$$

where r = radius, d = diameter, and h = height of the cylinder.

circumference

lateral face
rectangle

For example, to find the surface area of the cylinder below:

Area of the two circular bases:

$$2(28 \text{ cm})^2 \pi = 1568\pi \text{ cm}^2$$

Area of the lateral face:

$$\pi(56)(25) = 1400 \text{ cm}^2$$

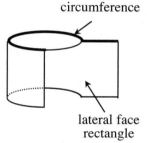

25 cm

28 cm

Total Surface Area = $1568\pi \text{ cm}^2 + 1400\pi \text{ cm}^2 = 2968 \text{ cm}^2$

$$\approx 9324.25 \text{ cm}^2$$

Review & Preview

10-146.   Find the volume of the cone shown in problem 10-142.

10-147.   The pyramid at right has a volume of 312 cubic feet. If the prism next to it has the same base area and height, what is its volume? Explain how you know.

10-148.　Complete the table.

x	−5	1	3	0	8	−2	−1
y	7			2		4	

　　　a.　Find the rule.

　　　b.　What is the slope?

10-149.　Jack has a tree in his backyard that he wants to cut down to ground level. He needs to know how tall the tree is because when he cuts it, it will fall towards his fence. Jack measured the tree's shadow and it is 20 feet long. At the same time, Jack's shadow was 12 feet long. Jack is five feet tall.

　　　a.　How tall is the tree?

　　　b.　Will the tree hit the fence if the fence is nine feet away?

10-150.　The Shones' family orchard produces 130 pounds of fruit per tree using traditional farming techniques. They would like to change to biodynamic farming techniques that will increase their crop by 20%. Changing techniques will cost money, but the fruit crop will be larger. Help them decide if they should change by calculating how much they will be able to grow two different ways, using two different scale factors (one multiplier will be greater than one). How many more pounds of fruit per tree will they get?

10-151.　A box of candy holds 36 pieces. Sixteen pieces in the box are caramels, three pieces are marshmallow chews, five pieces are fruit centers, eight pieces are nut clusters, and the rest are white chocolate.

　　　a.　What is the probability of randomly choosing a caramel out of the box?

　　　b.　What is the probability that you will not choose a fruit center or a nut cluster?

　　　c.　In a different box, there is a $\frac{1}{6}$ chance that you will choose a fruit center. From which box is it more likely that you will choose a fruit center?

Chapter 10 Closure What have I learned?

Reflection and Synthesis

The activities below offer you a chance to reflect
about what you have learned during this chapter.
As you work, look for concepts that you feel
very comfortable with, ideas that you would like
to learn more about, and topics you need more
help with. Look for connections between ideas
as well as connections with material you learned
previously.

① SUMMARIZING MY UNDERSTANDING

This section gives you an opportunity to show what you know about certain
math topics or ideas.

THE INTEREST GAME

Today you are going to play a game with your teacher. Your team task is to
have more money in your account than any other team at the end of the game.
You will start with an account balance of $1000. You will record your work
and your balances throughout the game on Closure Resource Page A. Your
team will also need an envelope containing interest rate cards.

To start the game, your teacher will select a card that gives you a time. Record
the starting balance and time in the first section on your resource page. Then, as
a team, pull a card from the envelope and compute the interest on your account
based on the card and the time given to you by your teacher. When you have
finished with a card, you will leave it on the desk. Transfer your new account
balance to the starting amount in a new section on the resource page. Your
teacher will then give you a new time and you will draw another card from your
envelope. Your teacher will tell you how many cards to select during the course
of the game. While playing the game, ask your teammates the following
questions.

- How do we determine compound interest?

- How do we find simple interest?

- How is the interest growing? How can we see this in the interest
  expression?

Problem continues on next page. →

①   *Problem continued from previous page.*

When playing the Interest Game, you were trying to get the most amount of money in your team account.

     a.   What was your final amount?

     b.   Did you do more compound interest or simple interest problems?

     c.   What do you think made the most difference in the amount of money you made, the interest rate or the kind of interest earned (simple or compound)?

②   **WHAT HAVE I LEARNED?**

Working the problems in this section will help you to evaluate which types of problems you feel comfortable with and which ones you need more help with. This section will appear at the end of every chapter to help you check your understanding.

Solve each problem as completely as you can. The table at the end of this closure section has answers to these problems. It also tells you where you can find additional help and practice on problems like them.

CL 10-152.   Find the surface area and volume of each solid below.

     a.   All angles are right angles.   b.   Right prism with base area = 48 cm²

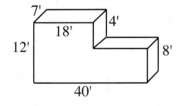 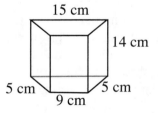

CL 10-153.   Rewrite each expression in a simpler form. If it is reasonable, write out the factored form to help you.

     a. $3^2 \cdot 3^5$ b. $\frac{4^5}{4^3}$ c. $(3x^2)^4$ d. $(3x^3)(7x^5)$

CL 10-154.   Daniel has $1200 in the bank. He is earning 3.5% compound interest each month. How much money will he have in the bank in one year?

CL 10-155.   Find the surface area and volume of a prism with a square base with sides of eight inches and a height of 12 inches.

CL 10-156.   Jamie bought a music player on sale for $65. The original price was $80. What percent discount did she receive?

CL 10-157.   Copy and complete the table.

x	−1	4	2	0	−4	−2
y	7		−2			10

a.   What is the rule for the table?

b.   What is the slope of the line through the points?

CL 10-158.   Find the area and circumference of a circle with a radius of 6.25 cm.

CL 10-159.   Shawn's science class has a ratio of 4:5, girls to boys.

a.   What is the ratio of boys to girls?

b.   What is the ratio of boys to total students?

c.   What percent of the class is boys?

d.   What fraction of the class is girls?

CL 10-160.   Sara walks ten blocks north from her house, turns a corner, and walks five blocks west. She wants to know how far she is from her house, that is, the direct distance from where she is standing (not how far she walked). How far is it?

CL 10-161.   For each of the problems above, do the following:

- Draw a bar or number line that represents 0 to 10.

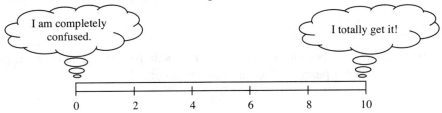

- Color or shade in a portion of the bar that represents your level of understanding and comfort with completing that problem on your own.

If any of your bars are less than a 5, choose *one* of those problems and do one of the following tasks:

- Write two questions that you would like to ask about that problem.

- Brainstorm two things that you DO know about that type of problem.

If all of your bars are a 5 or above, choose one of those problems and do one of these tasks:

- Write two questions you might ask or hints you might give to a student who was stuck on the problem.

- Make a new problem that is similar and more challenging than that problem and solve it.

WHAT TOOLS CAN I USE?

You have several tools and references available to help support your learning – your teacher, your study team, your math book, and your Toolkit, to name only a few. At the end of each chapter you will have an opportunity to review your Toolkit for completeness as well as to revise or update it to better reflect your current understanding of big ideas.

The main elements of your Toolkit should be your Learning Log, Math Notes, and the vocabulary used in this chapter. Math words that are new to this chapter appear in bold in the text. Refer to the lists provided below and follow your teacher's instructions to revise your Toolkit, which will help make it a useful reference for you as you complete this chapter and as you work in future chapters.

Learning Log Entries

- Lesson 10.1.3 – Simple and Compound Interest
- Lesson 10.1.5 – Simplifying Exponent Expressions
- Lesson 10.2.4 – Volume of a Prism
- Lesson 10.2.5 – Surface Area and Volume of a Cylinder
- Lesson 10.2.6 – Volume of Cones and Pyramids

Math Notes

- Lesson 10.1.2 – Exponents
- Lesson 10.1.3 – Compound Interest
- Lesson 10.1.4 – Commutative and Associative Properties of Multiplication
- Lesson 10.1.5 – Scientific Notation
- Lesson 10.1.6 – Laws of Exponents
- Lesson 10.2.1 – Polygons, Prisms, and Pyramids
- Lesson 10.2.2 – Surface Area
- Lesson 10.2.3 – Measurement in Different Dimensions
- Lesson 10.2.4 – Volume of a Prism
- Lesson 10.2.5 – Volume of a Cylinder
- Lesson 10.2.6 – Surface Area of a Cylinder

Mathematical Vocabulary

The following is a list of vocabulary found in this chapter. Some of the words have been seen in a previous chapter. The words in bold are the words new to this chapter. Make sure that you are familiar with the terms below and know what they mean. For the words you do not know, refer to the glossary or index. You might also want to add these words to your Toolkit for a way to reference them in the future.

area	base	base of a polygon
compound interest	**cone**	**cylinder**
edge	**exponent**	**faces**
interest rate	lateral faces	length
linear growth	**net**	one dimension
polygon	**power**	principal
prism	**pyramid**	right rectangular prism
scientific notation	simple interest	**surface area**
three dimensions	two dimensions	volume

Process Words

These words describe problem solving strategies and processes that you have been involved in throughout the course of this chapter. Make sure you know what each of these words means. If you are not sure, you can talk with your teacher or other students or look through your book for problems in which you were asked to do these things.

brainstorm	calculate	choose a strategy
compare	describe	explain your reasoning
generalize	justify	measure
predict	reason	reverse your thinking
simplify	test your prediction	visualize

Answers and Support for Closure Activity #2
What Have I Learned?

Problem	Solution	Need Help?	More Practice
CL 10-152.	a. SA = 1512 ft^2 V = 2744 ft^3 b. SA = 572 cm^2 V = 672 m^3	Lessons 10.2.1, 10.2.2, 10.2.3, and 10.2.4 Math Notes boxes in Lessons 10.2.2 and 10.2.4 Learning Log (problem 10-116)	Problems 10-85, 10-96, 10-104, 10-106, 10-114, 10-118, and 10-132
CL 10-153.	a. 3^7 b. 4^2 c. $81x^8$ d. $21x^8$	Lessons 10.1.2, 10.1.4, and 10.1.5 Math Notes boxes in Lessons 10.1.2 and 10.1.6 Learning Log (problem 10-58)	Problems 10-15, 10-36, 10-45, 10-50, 10-51, 10-52, 10-57, 10-59, 10-61, 10-74, and 10-98
CL 10-154.	$1242	Lessons 10.1.2 and 10.1.3 Math Notes box in Lesson 10.1.3 Learning Log (problem 10-28)	Problems 10-12 through 10-14, 10-26, 10-29, 10-49, and 10-79
CL 10-155.	Surface area = 512 in^2 Volume = 768 in^3	Lessons 10.2.1, 10.2.2, and 10.2.3 Math Notes boxes in Lessons 10.2.2 and 10.2.4 Learning Log (problem 10-116)	Problems 10-85, 10-96, 10-104, 10-106, 10-114, 10-118, and 10-132
CL 10-156.	About 19%	Lesson 8.2.5 Math Notes box in Lesson 8.2.5	Problems CL 8-92, CL 9-134, and 10-8

Problem	Solution	Need Help?	More Practice
CL 10-157.	$\begin{array}{c\|c\|c\|c\|c\|c\|c} x & -1 & 4 & 2 & 0 & -4 & -2 \\ \hline y & 7 & -8 & -2 & 4 & 16 & 10 \end{array}$ $y = -3x + 4$ slope $= -3$	Lessons 6.1.6, 7.1.4, and 7.1.5 Math Notes box in Lesson 7.1.6 Learning Log (problem 7-47)	Problems CL 7-94, 10-86, 10-110, and 10-148
CL 10-158.	$A \approx 122.7$ cm^2 $C \approx 39.27$ cm	Lessons 5.3.3 and 5.3.4 Math Notes box in Lesson 5.3.4 Learning Log (problem 5-124)	Problems CL 6-143, CL 8-93, CL 9-134, and 10-119
CL 10-159.	a. 5:4 b, 5:9 c. about 56% d. $\frac{4}{9}$	Lesson 7.1.1 Math Notes box in Lesson 7.1.1	Problems 7-11, and 8-18
CL 10-160.	Distance $= \sqrt{125} \approx 11.18$, or about 11 blocks	Lessons 9.3.2, 9.3.3, and 9.3.4 Math Notes boxes in Lessons 9.3.2 and 9.3.3 Learning Logs (problems 9-105 and 9-122)	Problems CL 9-130, 10-10, 10-63, and 10-133

Puzzle Investigator Problems

PI-19.   GEOMETRIC GIFTWRAP

Rowena is wrapping presents for the
Geometry club party. The gifts are
geometric blocks of various shapes, and
she is cutting the wrapping paper in "nets"
that can be folded to perfectly cover each
object, without any overlap or uncovered
parts. Two of the many nets that she can
use to cover a cube are shown at right.

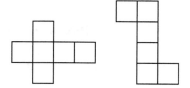

a.   Study the two nets above and try to **visualize** how they could each be
folded to cover a cube completely. Then find three new arrangements of
6 squares that will fold to cover a cube. Assume that if a design can be
turned or flipped to look like another then they are the same.

b.   After wrapping a cube box, Rowena decided to reinforce the edges with
tape. If she places tape on all edge lengths (leaving no part of the edge
without tape), how much tape is needed? Assume the cube has side lengths
of 5 inches.

c.   Below are some gifts Rowena still needs to wrap. Help her by creating a
net that would wrap each box. Draw your designs accurately on graph
paper and use arrows and/or colors to help show which squares of the paper
would lie on top of which faces of the box. Assume each small block
below is a unit cube and that no cubes are floating or otherwise hidden.

i.   ii.   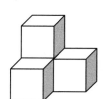   iii.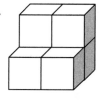

PI-20.   MAKING DECISIONS

Carlos wanted to get a part-time job to have extra money for the holidays. After reading the advertisement at right, he applied. His interview went well, and he was offered the job. He had to choose between the following two pay scales:

HELP WANTED
CABANA'S
DEPT. STORE
Nov. 25 – Dec. 24
Wrapping Gifts
6pm – 9pm daily

Pay Scale # 1

He would earn $10 per hour.

Pay Scale # 2

On day # 1, he would earn a total of 1¢.
On day # 2, he would make a total of 2¢.
On day # 3, he would make a total of 4¢.

Each day, his salary rate would double from the day before.

a.   Before starting the problem, guess which pay scale Carlos chose. Explain why you think this.

b.   If the store is closed on Thanksgiving (November 27th), and Carlos works every day that the store is open through December 24th, make a table that shows how much he makes each day using both pay scales.

c.   If you had a job offer like this one, which pay scale would you choose? Why?

Growth, Probablility, and Volume

CHAPTER 11   Growth, Probability, and Volume

What kind of equation makes a graph that is not a line? In the first section of this chapter, you and your team will investigate non-linear graphs and identify patterns of growth for these graphs in different representations.

In Section 11.2, your team will return to probability and investigate whether different games are fair. You will calculate the probability of more than one event taking place, such as drawing a two out of a deck of cards and then a queen. You will also learn new ways to organize the possible outcomes to help you determine different probabilities, and explore situations where one outcome is more likely than another.

Finally, you will work with your team to look more closely at the volume of prisms. You will build cubes and investigate how the volumes of similar solids are related.

Guiding Questions

Think about these questions throughout this chapter:

What shape will the graph be?

How does it grow?

Which is more likely?

Is it fair?

How many cubes fit inside?

In this chapter, you will learn how to:

> ➤ Identify patterns of growth for non-linear equations in graphs and tables.
> ➤ Determine which of two events will be more likely.
> ➤ Calculate probability of compound (multiple) events.
> ➤ Use the scale factor to find the volume of a similar solid.

Chapter Outline

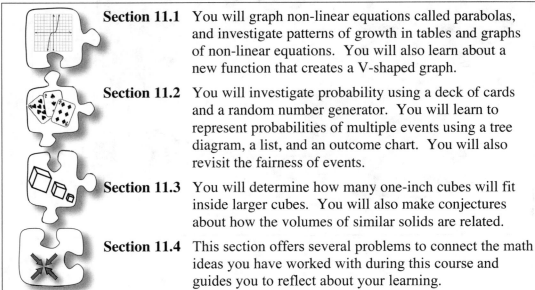

Section 11.1   You will graph non-linear equations called parabolas, and investigate patterns of growth in tables and graphs of non-linear equations. You will also learn about a new function that creates a V-shaped graph.

Section 11.2   You will investigate probability using a deck of cards and a random number generator. You will learn to represent probabilities of multiple events using a tree diagram, a list, and an outcome chart. You will also revisit the fairness of events.

Section 11.3   You will determine how many one-inch cubes will fit inside larger cubes. You will also make conjectures about how the volumes of similar solids are related.

Section 11.4   This section offers several problems to connect the math ideas you have worked with during this course and guides you to reflect about your learning.

Making Connections: Course 2

11.1.1 How does it grow?

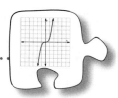

Non-Linear Growth

In this course, you have looked at several situations that model linear growth. Other curves can also be described mathematically. When engineers design satellite dishes or headlights for cars, it is critical that the curves they design are smooth and evenly shaped. If the curve is not correct, satellite dishes will not receive a clear signal and a car's headlights will not focus light on the road so the driver can see. In this section, you are going to explore several situations that are not linear. As you work with patterns, think about how these new patterns are growing.

11-1.   CHANGING BASES

In previous lessons you determined that simple interest grows at a constant (linear) rate, that is, by adding the same amount each time the x-value increases. Compound interest grows by multiplying by the same amount (exponential) each time the x-value increases. Work with your team to analyze the patterns created by the equation $y = x^2$.

a.   What is changing in this equation? What stays the same? Predict what the graph will look like and explain your **reasoning**.

b.   Create and complete a table like the one at right for the rule $y = x^2$. What patterns can you identify in the table? Use arrows, labels, and color to show them.

c.   Based on these patterns (and without graphing), do you predict that this equation is linear (makes a line)? Why or why not?

d.   Graph the equation. Use arrows, labels, and color to show how each of the patterns you found in the table shows in the graph. If you see new patterns, add them to the graph and then find them in the table.

x	y
-5	
-4	
-3	
$\vdots$	
3	
4	
5	

11-2.   A.J. noticed some interesting patterns in her table from problem 11-1.

> *"Even if the x-value I use is negative, my y-value comes out positive."*

> *"Each y-value seems to show up in my table twice – one time with a*
> *positive x-value and one time with a negative x-value."*

With your team, discuss these patterns. What happens in the equation that
causes the pattern? How does it affect the shape of the graph? Analyze any
other patterns you found in problem 11-1 as well. Be as specific as you can. Be
prepared to share your **reasoning** with the class.

11-3.   Colin noticed that when he folded his graph down the center of the U-shape, both
sides matched up perfectly. This characteristic is called **symmetry**. Colin
wondered if other graphs with similar equations would make this same U-shape
(called a **parabola**) and have the same symmetry patterns. He created the three
graphs below:

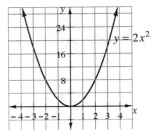 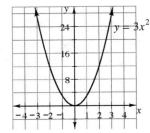 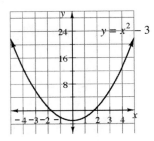

What do these graphs appear to have in common with the equation $y = x^2$?
What is different about each graph?

11-4.   Do all equations that have a variable as a base raised to a power show these
same patterns? Investigate the equation $y = x^3$ with your team.

Your task: On the Lesson 11.1.1 Resource Page, make a new table and graph
for the equation. Work with your team to find as many patterns in the table,
rule, and graph as you can. Be ready to share your patterns with the class.

Discussion Points

How do the values in the table grow? How does it show on the graph?

What happens when x is negative? What if x is positive, or equals zero?

Is there symmetry in the graph or table? Why or why not?

Making Connections: Course 2

11-5.   With your team, examine the patterns you found in the graphs of $y = x^2$ and $y = x^3$. How are the two kinds of growth similar? How are they different? Summarize your conclusions in a short paragraph.

Review & Preview

11-6.   Anna kept track of the height of her fast-growing corn. Her records are shown in the table below.

Day	0	2	4	6	8	x
Height (cm)	2	7.5	13	18.5	24	

a.   What is the growth rate of Anna's corn? Is this number always the same?

b.   If you graph the points in this table, will they form a line or a curve? Explain how you know.

c.   How would the growth rate show in the graph?

d.   If Anna harvests the corn when it reaches 3 meters, when will she harvest it?

11-7.   Howie and Steve are making cookies for themselves and some friends. The recipe they are using will make 48 cookies, but they only want to make 16 cookies. They have no trouble reducing the amounts of flour and sugar, but the original recipe calls for $1\frac{3}{4}$ cups of butter. Help Howie and Steve determine how much butter they will need.

11-8.   Find the area of the figure. Copy the figure on your paper, and show your work for each of the different pieces you use to find the total area.

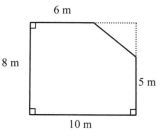

11-9.   Find the volume of each shape below.

   a.   Rectangle-based prism

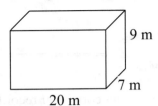

   b.   Rectangle-based pyramid

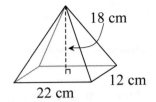

11-10.   Use the laws of exponents to simplify the following expressions.

   a. $(x^2)(x^5)$ b. $\dfrac{y^7}{y^4}$ c. $x^3 \cdot x^4$

11-11.   Write the following numbers in scientific notation.

   a.   370,000,000   b.   0.0000000000076

11.1.2 How can growth be described?

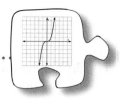

Absolute Value

In Lesson 11.1.1 you used equations to generate tables and graphs, and then analyzed the patterns that you found. Today, you and your team will **reverse** this process; you will analyze graphs to see what they can tell you about new kinds of equations.

11-12.   AN UNUSUAL GRAPH

Lauren was flipping through her sister's algebra book when she noticed an unusual graph. She copied it into her notebook to show her study team. The graph she drew is shown at right.

Lauren wondered what the equation for such an unusual graph could be. *"It's not a parabola, but it's not a line either! It doesn't look like compound interest. What do you think?"* Lauren asked her team. *"Clearly there are lots of patterns..."*

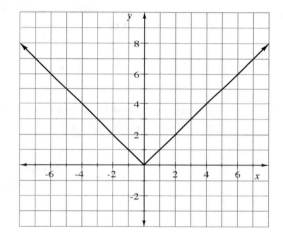

Your task: Obtain a copy of the graph on the Lesson 11.1.2 Resource Page. Work with your team to identify patterns in the graph and use them to describe the math operations that would create these patterns. Use the questions below to help you get started.

Discussion Points

How does the graph grow?

How is the new graph similar to a parabola or a line? How is it different?

What would a table of values tell us?

11-13.   Lars focused on the graph to see what he could learn. *"This graph is kind of like a line, and kind of like a parabola,"* he said. What do you think Lars means? What does the graph have in common with a line? With a parabola? How is it different? Be specific.

x	y
−4	4
−3	3
−2	2
−1	1
0	0
1	1
2	2
3	3
4	4

11-14.   *"I see patterns better with numbers than pictures,"* Mackenzie said. She used information from the graph to create the table at right. Copy the table and find as many patterns as you can.

11-15.   Based on the patterns you have found, describe in words what happens to each input value as it becomes an output.

—————————— *Further Guidance* ——————————
section ends here.

11-16.   Lauren went back to her sister to ask what she knew about the graph. She learned that the V-shape showed that this was an **absolute value** graph, and the equation for it is $y = |x|$. *"From the patterns I've found, I know that this seems to take any inputs and turn them into positive outputs,"* Lauren said. Her sister explained that when you find the **absolute value** of a number, you actually find the distance between that number and zero on a number line. She used this example:

If $x = -7$, then the distance between −7 and 0 on the number line is 7 units, so $|-7| = 7$. The distance from +7 to zero is the same number of units, so $|7| = 7$. Because we are counting a number of units, the absolute value is always positive.

Find each absolute value below:

a. $|-20|$ b. $|25|$ c. $|-8 + 4|$ d. $2 \cdot |-500|$

11-17.   Create a table to represent the equation $y = |-2x|$.

   a.   What shape do you predict the graph will be? Explain your **reasoning**.

   b.   Can y ever have a negative value in this expression? Why or why not?

11-18.   Lars was curious about other graphs.
          He found the strange graph at right and
          brought it to the team:

   a.   Describe the graph as completely
         as you can.

   b.   Predict what the equation for this
         line looks like. Be ready to **justify**
         your team prediction.

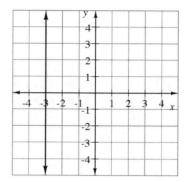

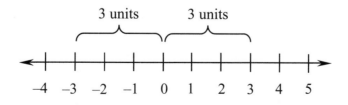

(M)ETHODS AND MEANINGS

MATH NOTES

Absolute Value

   Absolute value is the distance a number is from zero on the
number line in either direction. We use the symbol $|x|$ to indicate the
absolute value of any number x. For example:

$$|-3| = 3 \quad \text{and} \quad |3| = 3$$

3 units   3 units

$$
\begin{array}{ccccccccccc}
& -4 & -3 & -2 & -1 & 0 & 1 & 2 & 3 & 4 & 5
\end{array}
$$

11-19. Read the Math Notes box for this lesson. Then simplify each of the following expressions.

  a. $|-15|+|-26|$

  b. $-|-40|$

  c. $|0.5|+|-1\frac{1}{2}|$

11-20. Find the area of the shape at right. Show your steps.

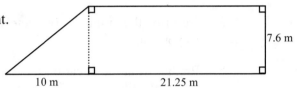

10 m   21.25 m   7.6 m

11-21. Marcus subscribes to several different magazines. On his bookshelf now he has 32 magazines about cars, 14 news magazines, 17 magazines about the outdoors, and 7 magazines about sports. If Marcus randomly pulls a magazine off of the shelf, what is the probability that he will not choose one about the outdoors?

11-22. Answer the comparison questions below.

  a. How many times larger is $3 \cdot 3 \cdot 3$ than $3+3+3$?

  b. How many times larger is $\frac{1}{3}+\frac{1}{3}+\frac{1}{3}$ than $\frac{1}{3} \cdot \frac{1}{3} \cdot \frac{1}{3}$?

Age of car (years)	Avg. miles per gallon
7	28
2	36
5	29
1	42
4	32
10	16
2	39
3	35
8	18

11-23. Graph the data in the table at right on graph paper. Is there a correlation?

11-24. Simplify each expression.

  a. $\frac{3}{8}+(-\frac{4}{6})-\frac{1}{3}$

  b. $-\frac{5}{7}+\frac{4}{9}-(-\frac{2}{3})$

  c. $\frac{2}{5} \cdot \frac{3}{8}-\frac{3}{4}$

  d. $-\frac{6}{11}+(-\frac{2}{3})-\frac{5}{6}$

  e. $-\frac{2}{3} \cdot 2\frac{1}{4} \cdot \frac{3}{4}$

  f. $\frac{5}{7}+(-\frac{1}{3})-(-\frac{1}{2})$

11.2.1 How likely is it?

· ·

Revisiting Probability

Have you ever had someone do a card trick with you by asking you to *"pick a card, any card"*? How do you determine the chances of getting a particular card? In Chapter 1, you learned about theoretical and experimental probabilities. In this lesson, you will continue to investigate probability by looking at a standard deck of playing cards.

As you work with your team, ask the following questions:

How many outcomes are there?

How likely is the outcome?

How do I represent it?

11-25.   PICK A CARD, ANY CARD

A standard deck of playing cards has four suits in two colors: diamonds and hearts are red; clubs and spades are black. Each suit has 13 cards: an ace, the numbers two through ten, a jack, a queen, and a king. What is the probability of picking the following cards from the deck?

a. What is P(black)?   b. What is P(ace)?   c. What is P(club)?

d. If you drew a card from the deck and then replaced it, and repeated this 100 times, about how many times would you expect to draw a face card (king, queen, or jack)?

e. What would happen to the probability of getting an ace on a second draw if you draw an ace on the first draw and do not return it to the deck? **Justify** your answer.

11-26. Get a deck of playing cards from your teacher. Make sure that you have removed the directions and the Jokers. Shuffle the cards at least six times before drawing the first card. You do not need to shuffle the deck between draws. With your team, take turns removing a card, recording the value of the card, and returning the card to the deck somewhere in the middle. Record the number of the card you drew, or whether it was a king, queen, or jack. You do not need to record the suit or color of the card. Do this 50 times.

    a. Compare your results with the rest of the class. Which card(s) were selected the most?

    b. How close were the experimental probabilities to the theoretical probabilities?

11-27. Rob decided to play a card game with his friend, Travis. He told Travis that, if he picked a black card with a value of nine or greater, Travis would win. (Jack, Queen, and King are considered to be greater than nine.) If Rob picked a red card of less than nine, Rob would win. (Ace is considered to have the value of one.)

    a. What is the probability that Travis will win?

    b. What is the probability that Rob will win?

    c. Is this a fair game?

11-28. The state has created a new contest to raise funds for a big Fourth of July fireworks celebration. People buy tickets and scratch off a special section on the ticket to reveal if they have won a prize. One out of every five people who play get a free entry in a raffle. Two out of every fifteen people who play win a small cash prize.

    a. If you buy a scratch off ticket, is it more likely that you will win a free raffle ticket, or a cash prize?

    b. How can you use the probabilities you have already calculated to write an expression for the probability that you will win anything?

    c. What is the probability that you will win nothing at all? Write an expression and find the result, and **justify** your thinking.

11-29.   **Additional Challenge:** Alicia's favorite candy is Fruiti Tutti Chews, which come in three flavors: Killer Kiwi, Crazy Coconut, and Ridiculous Raspberry. This year will be the 50th year that the candy has been made. To celebrate, the company that makes Fruiti Tutti Chews is running new advertisements and introducing a fourth flavor: Perfect Peach.

   a.   One of the new ads states that if you reach into any bag of Fruiti Tutti Chews, you have a $\frac{2}{3}$ probability of pulling out a Killer Kiwi candy. Another ad says that $\frac{3}{5}$ of each bag is Ridiculous Raspberry. Are the ads telling the truth?

   b.   Alicia learns that when she opens a new bag of candy, she has a $\frac{2}{5}$ chance of pulling out a piece of Ridiculous Raspberry and a $\frac{1}{3}$ chance of pulling out a piece of Killer Kiwi. Could she have a $\frac{4}{15}$ chance of pulling out a piece of Perfect Peach? Explain your **reasoning**.

   c.   When they introduce the new flavor, the company plans to make Perfect Peach $\frac{3}{10}$ of the candy in each bag. If there is an equal amount of the remaining three flavors, what is the probability that the first piece you pull out of the bag will be Crazy Coconut? **Justify** your answer.

11-30.   Find the probability of each event. Write your answer as a fraction and as a percent.

   a.   Drawing a diamond from a standard deck of cards.

   b.   Rolling a number less than five on a standard number cube.

   c.   Drawing a blue marble from a bag of 18 marbles, three of which are blue.

11-31.   Imagine a standard deck of cards with all of the aces and twos removed. Find each probability below.

   a.   P(heart)

   b.   P(black)

   c.   P(face card)

   d.   How is the P(face card) different with this deck from the probability if the deck was not missing any cards? Which probability is greater? Why?

11-32.   Graph each of the pairs of points listed below and draw a line segment between
          them. Use the graph to help you find the length of each line segment.

          a. $(-3, 0)$ and $(0, -3)$ b. $(2, 3)$ and $(-1, 2)$ c. $(3, 2)$ and $(3, -3)$

11-33.   Johanna is planting tomatoes in the school garden
          this year. Tomato plants come in packs of six.
          She needs 80 plants in the garden and already has
          28. How many packs of plants will she need?

11-34.   Two mechanics can assemble 10 bicycles in 8 hours. At the same rate, how
          many mechanics would be needed to assemble 25 bicycles in 10 hours?

11-35.   Simplify each expression.

          a. $|-5 + -1|$ b. $|-2 \cdot 4|$ c. $3|-8|$

          d. $-3 \cdot |8|$ e. $5 - |-5 + 10|$ f. $|6 - 10|$

11.2.2   Which is more likely?

· ·

Comparing Probabilities

Have you ever played a game where everyone should have an equal chance of winning,
but one person seems to have all the luck? Did it make you wonder if the game was fair?
Sometimes random events just happen to work out in one player's favor, such as flipping a
coin that happens to come up heads four times in a row. But it is also possible that games
can be set up to give an advantage to one player over another. If it is not equally possible
for different players to win, a game is considered unfair. The game Rob and Travis played
in problem 11-27 is an example of an unfair game.

In this lesson you will find probabilities to determine whether different outcomes are
equally likely. Ask these questions in your study team as you work:

                        How likely is it?

                Is another outcome equally likely?

                Which player has a greater chance?

11-36.   RANDOM NUMBER GENERATOR

A random number generator produces numbers without using a pattern or rule. An example of this is a standard number cube, which will randomly generate a number from 1 to 6 when you roll it because each of the numbers is equally likely to show when the cube lands. Other tools can generate numbers with a wider range of values. Imagine a random number generator that produces numbers from 1 to 20. In each game below, if the stated outcome happens, Player X wins. If it does not, then Player Y wins.

> Game 1:   A prime number = Player X wins
>
> Game 2:   An even number = Player X wins
>
> Game 3:   A number not divisible by three = Player X wins

a.   In each case, what is the probability that Player X wins? That Player Y wins? Decide whether each game above is fair.

b.   In which of the three games is Player X most likely to win? Why?

c.   In Game 1, the prime number game, if you play 40 times, how many times would you expect Player X to win? What if you played 50 times?

d.   Obtain a random number generator from your teacher and set it up to generate integers from 1 to 20. Play the prime number game (Game 1) 10 times with a partner. Start by deciding who will be Player X and who will be Player Y. Record who wins each time you play.

e.   How did the experimental and theoretical probabilities of Player X winning from part (a) and part (d) compare?

11-37.   A BETTER CHANCE OF WINNING

Each of the problems below describes two different games you can play with a random number generator. In each case, you will win if the random number generator gives you the indicated kind of number. Find the probability that you win each game below. Decide and **justify** whether Game I or Game II in each part gives you a better chance of winning.

	Game I	**Game II**
a.	Picking a prime number from the integers between 1 and 20	Picking a prime number from the integers between 21 and 40
b.	Picking a multiple of 5 from the integers between 1 and 20	Picking a multiple of 5 from the integers between 1 and 40
c.	Picking a multiple of 7 from the integers between 1 and 40	Picking a multiple of 6 from the integers between 1 and 25

11-38.   Using a random number generator for the numbers from 1 through 20, what is the probability of getting each of these outcomes?

    a.   A multiple of three *or* a multiple of 7, P(multiple of 3 or multiple of 7)

    b.   P(even or odd)

    c.   P(prime or 1)

    d.   How did you find the probabilities of these events? Be ready to share your ideas with the class.

11-39.   LEARNING LOG

So far you have calculated probabilities of different events and have compared them to decide if events are equally likely to happen. You have also found the probability of one or another event taking place (such as drawing a king or a queen from a deck of cards).

In your Learning Log, create an example and explain how you would calculate the probability when two different outcomes are asked for (such as the example of drawing a king or queen from a deck of cards). Then, record any questions you have about probability. Your questions might relate to things that you have already worked on or may be about situations you have not yet studied. Title this entry "Multiple Outcomes and Questions," and label it with today's date.

11-40.   Marissa is drawing erasers from a bag containing 6 pink erasers, 2 yellow erasers, 5 green erasers, and 3 purple erasers.

    a.   What is the probability that she will draw a pink eraser?

    b.   If one yellow, two green, and one purple eraser are added to the bag, what is the new probability that she will draw a pink eraser?

    c.   In which situation is it more likely that she will draw a pink eraser?

11-41.   For each of the experimental results described, write the indicated probability.

   a.   A coin is flipped 80 times. It lands tails 47 times. What is P(heads)?

   b.   A bag contains purple and orange marbles. Sam randomly takes out one marble then returns it to the bag. He does this 18 times, and 12 of those times an orange marble is pulled out. What is P(green)?

   c.   Sarah pulls a card from a standard deck and then replaces it. She does this 30 times, and 40% of the time it is hearts. What is P(~hearts)? Recall that ~ means "not hearts."

11-42.   Simplify each of the following expressions.

   a. $4x^3y \cdot 3xy^2$ b. $6a^5b^2 \cdot 3ab^2$ c. $m^2n \cdot 9mn$

   d. $\dfrac{3^5 \cdot 8 \cdot 5^3}{3^2 \cdot 2^3 \cdot 5^3 \cdot 3^3}$ e. $\dfrac{m^4 \cdot n}{n^3}$ f. $\dfrac{9a^4b^2}{15b}$

11-43.   Solve the following equations.

   a. $12 = \frac{6}{7}x$ b. $3x + (-4) = 2x + 9$ c. $3x - 8 = 4x + (-2)$

   d. $2x - 6 = 1 - 3x$ e. $\frac{38}{6} = \frac{x}{18}$ f. $\frac{9}{x} = \frac{85}{10}$

11-44.   Which table or tables below show a proportional relationship? **Justify** your answers.

   a.

x	5	7	9	-8	0	11	15
y	9	13	17	-17	-19	21	29

   b.

x	7	14	91	9	-12	-36	81
y	$2\frac{1}{3}$	$4\frac{2}{3}$	$30\frac{1}{3}$	3	-4	-12	27

   c.

x	-3	-10	0	10	5	4	$\frac{1}{2}$	$-\frac{3}{2}$
y	-27	-1000	0	1000	125	48	$\frac{1}{8}$	$-\frac{27}{4}$

11-45. Find the volume of the prism at right.
All angles are right angles.

9 mm

3 mm

3 mm

3 mm

7 mm

7 mm

5 mm

15 mm

11.2.3   What if there is more than one event?

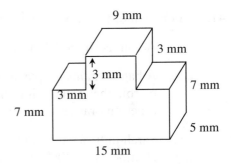

Modeling Probabilities of Compound Events

In Chapter 1 and earlier in this chapter, you have investigated ways to find out how likely it is that single events will happen, such as drawing one card from a deck of playing cards, pulling one marble from a bag, or spinning a color on a wheel. How would the probabilities you find change if you draw two cards from a deck of cards or roll two number cubes? In this lesson you will work with different models for organizing outcomes of multiple events.

11-46. WALKING THE DOG

Marcus and his brother always argue about who will walk the dog. Their father wants to find a random way of deciding who will do the job. He invented a game to help them decide. Each boy will have a bag with three colored blocks in it: one yellow, one green, and one white. Each night before dinner, each boy draws a block out of his bag. If the colors match, Marcus walks the dog. If the two colors do not match, his brother walks the dog. Marcus' father wants to be sure that the game is fair. Help him decide.

a. Make a **systematic list** (organized list) or table of all of the possible combinations of draws that Marcus and his brother could make. How many possibilities are there?

b. What is the probability that the boys will draw matching blocks? Is the game fair? **Justify** your answer.

Making Connections: Course 2

11-47.   THE DOUBLE SPIN

In Chapter 1, you found probabilities for the Giant
Spin carnival game in which players spin a giant
wheel that is equally divided into 24 sections labeled
−2, −1, 0, 1, or 3. In that problem, players could spin
only one time. At the Double Spin, players spin the
smaller wheel shown at right two times. The sum of
their spins determines whether they win.

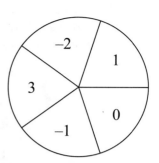

Work with your team to determine probabilities of
different outcomes by answering the questions below.

a.   Make a list of the possible sums you could get.

b.   Which sum do you think will be the most probable?

c.   Travis set up the chart at right, called an
      outcome chart, to find out which sum would
      occur the most often. He listed the possibilities
      for Spin 1 across the top and for Spin 2 down
      the left side.

	−2	−1	0	1	3
−2	−4	−3	−2	−1	1
−1	−3	−2	−1	0	2
0	−2	−1			
1	−1	0			
3	1	2	3	4	

      Copy the chart on your paper. Determine how
      Travis found the numbers inside the chart, and
      fill in the missing numbers.

d.   If Travis could choose the winning sum for the Double Spin game, what
      sum would you advise him to choose? What is the probability of getting
      that sum with two spins?

11-48.   Scott's job at Crazy Creations Ice Cream Shop is to design new ice cream
         flavors. The company has just received some new ingredients, and Scott wants
         to be sure to try all of the possible combinations. He needs to choose one item
         from each category to create the new flavor.

Base flavor	Chunky mix-in	Fruit swirl
Vanilla	Hazelnuts	Apricot
Chocolate	Sprinkles	Plum
	Toffee bits	Berry
		Grape

a.   Without talking with your teammates, list three different combinations
      Scott could try. Then, share your combinations with your study team. How
      many different combinations did you find? Do you think you found all of
      the possibilities?

b.   Creating a list of all of the possibilities would
      take time and require a lot of writing the same
      words over and over. Because there are more
      than two options, an outcome chart is also
      challenging. An alternative is creating a **tree
      diagram** to show the different combinations.
      A tree diagram, like the one started at right
      and on the Lesson 11.2.3 Resource Page,
      shows the different possibilities branching off
      each other. In this case, the two lines on the
      left show the base flavors. Each different
      mix-in choice branches off of the base flavor,
      and each fruit swirl branches off each mix-in
      choice. The first letter of each choice is used
      to label this diagram.

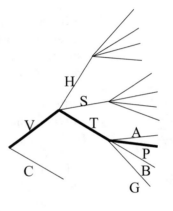

      The bold line in the diagram shows the combination vanilla, toffee, plum
      swirl. Complete the tree diagram to find all of the possible combinations.

c.   How many different flavor combinations are possible? Where do you look
      on the diagram to count the number of complete combinations?

d.   Use your tree diagram to help you find the probability that Scott's final
      combination will include plum swirl.

e.   What is the probability that his final combination will include hazelnuts?

11-49.   In a power outage, Rona has to reach into her closet in the dark to get dressed. She has three different pairs of pants hanging there: one black, one brown, and one plaid. She also has two different shirts: one white and one polka dot.

   a.   Draw a tree diagram to organize the different outfit combinations Rona might choose.

   b.   What is the probability that she will wear a polka dot shirt with plaid pants?

   c.   What is the probability that she will not wear the black pants?

11-50.   Find the indicated probability in each situation below. Represent all of the possible outcomes using a systematic list, an outcome chart, or a tree diagram.

   a.   You flip a coin three times in a row, and get heads exactly twice.

   b.   You spin the two spinners at right and exactly one spinner lands on 4.

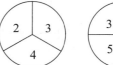

   c.   At the car rental agency you will either be given a truck or sedan. Each model comes in four colors: green, black, white, or tan. If there is one vehicle of each color for each model available, what is the probability you will get a green truck?

METHODS AND MEANINGS

Probability Models for Multiple Events

To determine all possible outcomes for multiple events, there are several different models you can use to help organize the information.

Consider spinning each spinner at right once.

If you are able to find the outcomes in an order, a **systematic list** can be helpful. For example, assume that you first spin B on spinner 1. Then, list all of the possible outcomes on spinner 2. Next, assume that your first spin is W on spinner 1 and complete the list.

Systematic List

BR	WR
BG	WG
BY	WY

A **probability outcome chart** can also organize information if there are only two events. The possibilities for each event are listed on the sides of the chart as shown, and the combinations of outcomes are listed inside the chart. In the example at right, the possible outcomes for spinner 1 are listed on the left side and the possible outcomes for spinner 2 are listed across the top. The possible outcomes of the two events are shown inside the rectangle. In this chart, the top and side are divided evenly because the outcomes are equally likely. Inside the table you can see the possible combinations of outcomes.

Outcome Chart

	R	G	Y
B	BR	BG	BY
W	WR	WG	WY

A **probability outcome tree** is another method for organizing information. The different outcomes are organized as branches of a tree. The first section has two branches because there are two possible outcomes of spinner 1, namely B and W. At the end of the first branches are three branches to represent the possible outcomes of the second spinner. These possible outcomes of the two events are shown as the six branch ends.

Outcome Tree

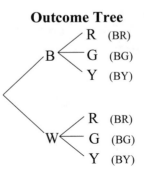

11-51.   Nicole has a random number generator that will produce the numbers from 1 through 50 when she pushes a button. If she pushes the button, what is:

   a.   P(multiple of 10)?

   b.   P(~100)?

   c.   P(~multiple of 4)?

   d.   P(one-digit number)?

11-52.   Graph the points $(-2, 4)$, $(2, 1)$, and $(-2, -2)$ and connect the points to create a triangle. What is the perimeter of the triangle?

11-53.   For the rule $y = 6 + (-3)x$:

   a.   What is the y-intercept?

   b.   What is the slope?

11-54.   Scooter rides his skateboard every day after school. He often stops to do tricks. On Monday, he rode for 2 hours and went 3 miles. By the end of the week, he had gone a total of 11 miles and it took him a total of 9 hours. Did he ride the same time and distance every day after school? **Justify** your answer.

11-55.   Find the volume of the cone.

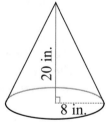

11-56.   Simplify each numerical expression.

   a. $|5 - 6 + 1|$

   b. $-2|-16|$

   c. $|6 - 2| + |-8 - 1|$

11.2.4 What if the events are not equally likely?

Compound Events

In Lesson 11.2.3, you used systematic lists, outcome charts, and tree diagrams to organize the outcomes of different probability situations. Today you will use an outcome chart to help organize events when one outcome is more likely than another.

11-57. Nina is buying a new pet fish. At the pet store, the fish tank has an equal number of two kinds of fish – tetras and guppies. Each kind of fish comes in four different colors: yellow, orange, blue, and silver. There is an equal number of each color of fish in the tank.

a. If Nina scoops out a fish at random, what is the probability that she will scoop out a silver tetra? Show how you decided.

b. Nina set up the chart below to organize the different possible outcomes. She represented the kind of fish on one side of her chart and the color possibilities on the other. What do the fractions inside her chart represent?

	Yellow	Orange	Blue	Silver
Tetra	$YT = \frac{1}{8}$	$OT = \frac{1}{8}$	$BT = \frac{1}{8}$	$ST = \frac{1}{8}$
Guppy	$YG = \frac{1}{8}$	$OG = \frac{1}{8}$	$BG = \frac{1}{8}$	$SG = \frac{1}{8}$

c. As Nina looked at her work, she noticed that her chart looked a lot like a rectangle with the area divided up into parts. *"Could that help me calculate the probabilities?"* she wondered. She used the length and width of the silver tetra section to set up this equation: $\frac{1}{4} \cdot \frac{1}{2} = \frac{1}{8}$.

How does this equation relate to the length, width, and area of this section of the rectangle? Does this match the probability you found in part (a)?

d. What is the area of the complete large rectangle?

Making Connections: Course 2

11-58.   TESTING THE AREA MODEL

Nina decided to see if finding area would help find other probabilities. She put three cubes in a bag – two blue cubes and one yellow cube. She pulled one cube out, put it back in the bag, and then drew another.

a.   Use a list or a tree diagram to organize the possible color combinations she could draw. How many are there? What is P(blue and blue)?

b.   This time Nina made the chart at right. Based on the chart, what is the probability of drawing two blue blocks? Is this the same probability you found in part (a)?

	B	B	Y
B	BB	BB	BY
B	BB	BB	BY
Y	YB	YB	YY

c.   Looking at her work, Luis said, "I think I can simplify this diagram." His rectangle is shown at right. What is the area of the section representing blue and blue? Does this match the probability that Nina found?

	B ($\frac{2}{3}$)	Y ($\frac{1}{3}$)
B ($\frac{2}{3}$)	BB	BY
Y ($\frac{1}{3}$)	YB	YY

11-59.   The pet store sells a lot of pet food. On a slow day at the pet store, three people buy cat food, two people by dog food, and one person buys food for a pet snake. If half of the customers pay with cash and half pay with credit card, what is the probability that a customer buying pet food will buy dog food with cash? Set up an outcome table to help you find the probability.

11-60.   SPINNING ODDS AND EVENS — PART 1

Your team is going to play against your teacher in a game with two hidden spinners. Spinner A has the numbers 2, 3, and 4 on it. Spinner B has the numbers 6, 7, and 8 on it. The rules are:

1.   Spin each spinner.

2.   Add the results.

3.   If the sum is even, one team gets a point. If the sum is odd, the other team gets a point.

4.   The first team to earn 10 points wins.

Should you choose the odd or even numbers in order to win? Discuss the choices with your team and decide which side to take. Be prepared to **justify** your choice with mathematics.

11-61.   Play the game at least three times with your teacher. Your teacher will spin the spinners and announce the results. Record the results of each spin and their sum. Is the result odd or even most often? Does this match with your prediction?

11-62.   SPINNING ODDS AND EVENS — PART 2

Now that you have played the game several times, obtain a Lesson 11.2.4 Resource Page from your teacher and take a close look at the hidden spinners.

a.   Are the spinners different from what you expected? How? Be as specific as you can. Do you still think you made the correct choice of odd or even numbers?

b.   What is the probability of spinning each outcome on Spinner A? On Spinner B?

11-63.   Raul had imagined that the spinners were divided into equal parts before he saw them. He created the chart at right to organize the outcomes. *"I thought there would be a $\frac{1}{3}$ chance of spinning a 3 on Spinner A. But now that I see the spinners, I know that is not true. I need to make a new rectangle in order to find the probability."*

	6	7	8
2	8	9	10
3	9	10	11
4	10	11	12

a.   Create a new rectangle. Label each side with the outcomes and their probabilities.

b.   Write a multiplication problem to show the probability of spinning a three and a seven. Calculate P(3 and 7).

c.   What is the probability of spinning an odd sum? What is the probability of spinning an even sum?

d.   Did you make the right choice of an odd or even number in problem 11-62? Explain your **reasoning**.

11-64. Elliot loves music, especially listening to his music player on shuffle. He has songs stored in four categories: country, blues, rock, and classical. Two-fifths of his songs are country songs, one sixth of his songs are classical, one third are blues, and the rest are rock.

    a.   What is the likelihood that the first two songs will be a country song and then a classical?

    b.   What is the likelihood that a blues song *or* a country song will come up first?

METHODS AND **M**EANINGS

MATH NOTES

Compound Probability

    Sometimes when you are finding a probability, you are interested in either of two outcomes taking place, but not both. For example, you may be interested in drawing a king or a queen from a deck of cards. At other times, you might be interested in one event followed by another event. For example, you might want to roll a one on a number cube and then roll a six. The probabilities of combinations of simple events are called **compound probabilities**. For an explanation of finding probability of simple events, see the Math Notes box on probability in Lesson 1.2.1.

To find the probability of one event *or* another event that has nothing in common with the first, you can find the probability of each event separately and then add their probabilities. Using the example above of drawing a king or a queen from a deck of cards:

$$P(\text{king}) = \tfrac{4}{52} \quad \text{and} \quad P(\text{queen}) = \tfrac{4}{52} \quad \text{so} \quad P(\text{king or queen}) = \tfrac{4}{52} + \tfrac{4}{52} = \tfrac{8}{52} = \tfrac{2}{13}$$

Two events are **independent** when the occurrence of one does not change the probability of the other one occurring. To find the probability of two independent events both occurring, you can find the probability of each event separately and then multiply their probabilities. Using the example of rolling a one followed by a six on a number cube:

$$P(1) = \tfrac{1}{6} \quad \text{and} \quad P(6) = \tfrac{1}{6} \quad \text{so} \quad P(1 \text{ then } 6) = \tfrac{1}{6} \cdot \tfrac{1}{6} = \tfrac{1}{36}$$

Note that you would carry out the same computation if you wanted to know the probability of rolling a one on a green cube and a six on a red cube if you rolled both of them at the same time.

11-65.   Alan is making a bouquet to take home to his grandmother. He needs to choose one kind of greenery and one kind of flower for his bouquet. He has a choice of ferns or leaves for his greenery. His flower choices are daisies, carnations, and sunflowers.

    a.   Draw a tree diagram to show the different bouquets he could make. How many are there?

    b.   What is the probability he will use ferns?

    c.   What is the probability he will not use sunflowers?

11-66.   Imagine spinning the spinner at right.

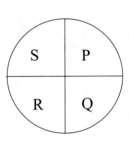

    a.   What is the probability you will spin a P or a Q on your first spin?

    b.   Find all of the possible outcomes of spinning the spinner twice. What is the probability you will spin a P on your first spin and then a Q on your second spin? Explain how you decided.

11-67.   Make a table for the rule $y = 2x^3$ that includes x-values from -3 to 3. Graph the rule on graph paper.

11-68.   Solve for x.

    a. $2(x+18) = 10$ b. $\frac{4}{3}x - 9 = -3$

    c. $24 = 2(2x+4)$ d. $2(x-4) = x - 7$

11-69.   Dawn drove 420 miles in 6 hours on a rural interstate highway. If she maintains the same speed, how far can she go in 7.5 hours?

11-70.   Lucas is having yogurt and an apple for a snack.
There are five containers of yogurt in the refrigerator:
three are raspberry, one is vanilla, and one is peach.
There are also two green apples and three red apples.

a.   If he reaches into the refrigerator to get a yogurt
without looking, what is the probability Lucas
will choose a raspberry yogurt?

b.   What is the probability he will choose a red apple if it is the first item he
selects?

c.   What is the probability Lucas will eat a raspberry yogurt and a red apple?

11-71.   Find the probability of each event, based on the given information.

a.   If $P(\text{getting clubs}) = \frac{1}{4}$, what is $P(\sim\text{getting clubs})$?

b.   If $P(A) = 0.4$, what is $P(\sim A)$?

c.   If $P(\text{win}) = x\%$, what is $P(\sim\text{win})$?

11-72.   Graph the points $(0, 2)$, $(6, 2)$, $(7, 4)$, and $(1, 4)$ and connect the points in order
to create a parallelogram. What is the perimeter of the parallelogram?

11-73.   Determine which nets below will form a prism. If a net will not form a prism,
explain why not.

a. 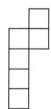   b.   c.   d.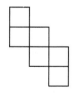

11-74.   Tim wants to invest some money that his grandmother gave him. He has $2000 and can put it in an account with simple interest or an account with compound interest.

   a.   The simple interest account is for 5 years with an interest rate of 10%. Use the formula $I = P \cdot rt$ to find the interest he earned at the end of five years. How can you use the interest to calculate the total amount in the account at the end of 5 years? What is the total?

   b.   The compound interest account is also for 5 years (compounded yearly) at an interest rate of 8%. Find the total in the account (A) using the formula $A = P(1+r)^t$. What is the total?

   c.   Which account is a better investment?

11.3.1 How many cubes fit inside of it?

Exploring Volume

Children often enjoy putting smaller toys into larger containers. A child might stack small blocks inside a wagon or put toys away in a toy box. But how do you know how much will fit inside a container? As you explore the concept of volume today, think about how many cubes can fit inside each shape.

11-75.   BUILDING CUBES

   How many one inch cubes will fit inside a larger cube with faces that measure two inches by two inches? What about a cube that measures six inches by six inches by six inches? Discuss your predictions with your teammates and copy and complete the second column of the table below for four different cube sizes.

Edge length of cube	Prediction of number of one-inch cubes that fit inside	Actual number of one-inch cubes that fit inside
1 inch		
6 inches		
9 inches		
12 inches		

11-76.   Today each member of your team will
construct a one-inch cube and then
together you will build one larger cube
that your teacher will assign you. The
one-inch cube will be your unit of
measure.

a.   Make a sketch of a net for your
one-inch cube. What should the
dimensions of each edge be? How
will the dimensions change for the
larger cube? Explain how you
will put each cube together. Check with your teacher and then get a sheet
of one-inch grid poster paper to create your cubes.

b.   Cut the paper and carefully make the one-inch cube. Then work together to
design and construct the larger cube. As you construct the larger cube,
leave one side open like a lid.

c.   When you have finished, use your smaller cubes to check your predictions
and complete the third column of the table from problem 11-75. You may
want to work with other teams who have different sized cubes to check your
predictions.

11-77.   The one-inch cube and the larger cube your team built are similar solids. That
is, they have the same shape and the same angle measures. Their edge lengths
are related by a common scale factor.

a.   What is the scale factor ($\frac{\text{large}}{\text{small}}$) between your small cube and the larger cube?

b.   Are the volumes of the two cubes related by the same scale factor? If not,
what is the scale factor between the volumes?

c.   Find the area of one face of each cube. Are those areas related by the same
scale factor as the edges? By the same scale factor as the volume?

11-78.   Find a team that has built a cube that has an edge twice as long or half as long
as the edge of your team's cube. For example, if your cube has an edge of 3
inches, find a team with a cube that has an edge of 6 inches.

a.   By what scale factor is the edge of the small cube multiplied to make the
edge of the large cube?

b.   Predict how many of the smaller cubes would fit inside the larger cube.
Then, use the cubes to check your prediction.

11-79.   There are several ways to describe parts of a cube. You have learned about volume, surface area, and dimensions, but now you will have a chance to look more closely at some of the special features of this three-dimensional shape. Record your work for this problem on the Lesson 11.3.1 Resource Page. You should carefully record your answers in words or drawings so you can understand the concepts if you do not have an actual cube in front of you.

   a.   Sketch two intersecting lines and mark the intersection. Name the geometric figure that marks the intersection of two lines.

   b.   Darken two different intersecting edges on the cube. Name the geometric figure that marks the intersection of two edges.

   c.   Find and darken a pair of parallel edges on the cube and shade the face that contains them.

   d.   Darken two parallel edges on the cube that are not part of the same face and sketch in the flat surface that contains them. This flat region is part of a **plane**, a flat surface that extends infinitely in all directions.

   e.   Darken a pair of edges on the cube that can be extended to create **skew lines** (lines in three-dimensional space that do not lie in the same flat surface, do not intersect, and are not parallel).

   f.   Shade a pair of intersecting faces on the cube and darken the edge that marks the intersection. Extend each edge with a dotted line and add arrows to show that the line is infinite. Name the geometric figure that is made by the intersection of the faces.

   g.   Shade three intersecting faces on the cube. Name the geometric figure that marks the intersection.

   h.   Darken a pair of opposite corners and draw the diagonal that connects them.

11-80.   Name the geometric figures formed by the intersection of:

   a.   Two distinct lines

   b.   Two distinct planes (flat surfaces)

   c.   Three distinct planes (flat surfaces)

11-81.   Imagine a cube that has edges that are each one foot long.

    a.   How long is each edge in inches?

    b.   What is the area of one face, measured in square feet? What is the area measured in square inches?

    c.   What is the volume of one cube, measured in cubic feet? What is the volume measured in cubic inches?

    d.   Do these results surprise you? Why or why not? Describe any patterns you notice in these numbers.

Review & Preview

11-82.   The two triangles at right are similar.

    a.   Find the area of each triangle.

    b.   What is the scale factor for the side lengths of the two triangles?

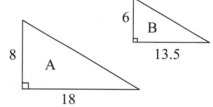

    c.   What is the ratio of the areas ($\frac{\text{Area B}}{\text{Area A}}$)? How is this ratio related to the ratio you found in part (b)?

11-83.   Skye's Ice Cream Shoppe is Mario's favorite place to get ice cream. Unfortunately, because he was late arriving there, his friends had already ordered. He did not know what they ordered for him. They told him that it was either a waffle cone or a sundae and that the ice cream flavor was either apricot, chocolate, or blackberry.

    a.   What is the probability that Mario will get something with apricot ice cream?

    b.   What is the probability that he will get a sundae?

    c.   What is the probability that he will get either something with chocolate or a waffle cone with blackberry?

    d.   What is the probability that he will get orange sherbet?

11-84.   Simplify each expression.

    a. $x^2 x^3 x^2$ b. $(xy^3 z)(xy)$ c. $5 \cdot t^2 \cdot 5^3 \cdot t$

11-85.   The area of the base in the prism at right is 96 square inches.

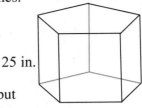

25 in.

a.   Find the volume of the prism.

b.   Find the volume of a pyramid with the same base and height.

c.   If another prism has the same volume as this prism, but its base area is 80 square inches, what is its height?

11-86.   Sixty-five percent of the 8th grade class is selling magazines for the class fundraiser. If 112 students are selling magazines, how many students are in the 8th grade class?

11-87.   Think about the different three-dimensional vocabulary you learned in this lesson.

a.   Name two sets of geometric figures that can intersect to form a point.

b.   Is the face of a cube an example of a point, a plane (flat surface), or skew lines? Explain why it cannot be either of the other two.

11-88.   **Multiple Choice:** Which of the cylinders matches the net? Explain how you know. Note that the length above each cylinder is the radius of the base.

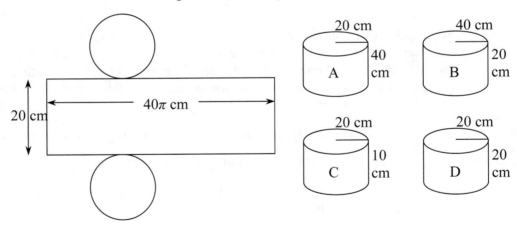

11-89.   Simplify each of the following expressions.

a. $(5x^3)^2$

b. $\dfrac{14a^3b^2}{21a^4b^3}$

c. $2m^3n^2 \cdot 3mn^4$

11-90.   Janet sells erasers at a price of 8 erasers for 60 cents. She started this table to
          show the price for different numbers of erasers. Complete her table.

Erasers	8	4	1	12	10	16	100
$	0.60						

11-91.   The attendance at the county fair was lowest on Thursday, the opening day. On
          Friday 5500 more people attended than attended Thursday. Saturday doubled
          Thursday's attendance, and Sunday had 3000 more people than Saturday. The
          total attendance was 36,700. Write and solve an equation to find how many
          people attended the fair each day.

11-92.   Make a table for the rule $y = -2x^2$ that includes x-values from −3 to 3.
          Graph the rule on graph paper.

11.3.2   How does the volume change?
··
Scale Factor and Volume

In Chapter 9 you investigated the relationship between the areas of two shapes that are
similar and their scale factor. If a box is enlarged so that each edge is three times longer
than the original, how will the surface area change? What will happen to the volume? In
this lesson you will answer these questions using different three-dimensional shapes.
With your team you will practice **visualizing** three-dimensional shapes, finding patterns,
and describing patterns.

11-93.   The city of Lakewood is building a new playground in the city park. The
          contractor will use sand to provide a soft landing area under the swings. On the
          architect's scale model, the sand is 1 cm deep by 15 cm long by 20 cm wide. On
          the actual playground, the length, width, and depth of the sand area will each be
          100 times larger.

          When the model was finished, the architect figured
          out how many cubic centimeters of sand she used
          for the model, and then ordered 100 times that
          volume. Work with your team to decide whether
          she ordered the right amount of sand *without making
          any calculations*.

11-94.   GROWING, GROWING, GROWING, …

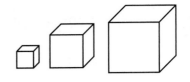

To investigate how the volume of a solid
changes as the edge length changes, obtain a
Lesson 11.3.2A Resource Page and a set of
cubes from your teacher.

   a. For this problem, the edge length of a single cube will be called one unit.
       Use your small cubes to build a larger cube with a scale factor of 2.

   b. Calculate the length of one edge, the area of one face, and the volume of the
       cube you built, then record your work in the table on the Lesson 11.3.2
       Resource Page.

   c. Repeat this process for cubes with scale factors of 3 and 4, and record your
       work on the resource page.

   d. With your team, discuss any patterns you can find in the data for different
       scale factors so far. Then complete the resource page for cubes with scale
       factors of 5, 6, 7, 8, 9, and $\frac{1}{2}$.

   e. Suppose that a cube had a scale factor of x units. What would the edge
       length, area of one face, and the volume be? Add these expressions to your
       table.

11-95.   Now that you know the area of one face for all of the cubes in problem 11-94,
          find the total surface area for each of the cubes, including a cube with a scale
          factor of x.

11-96.   Next, work with your team to use graphs to investigate the question: How is the
          volume changing? On the axes on the Lesson 11.3.2B Resource Page, make
          three graphs: one comparing scale factor and edge length, the second comparing
          scale factor and surface area, and the third comparing scale factor and volume.
          With your team, describe how each quantity (edge length, surface area, and
          volume) changes as the scale factor changes.

11-97.   Look again at the sand order the architect placed in problem 11-93. Calculate
          the volume of the sand in her scale model and in the actual playground. Did she
          order the correct amount of sand? How does your result make sense based on
          what you learned in problems 11-94 and 11-95?

11-98. Use the rectangular prism shown at right to complete parts (a) through (d) below.

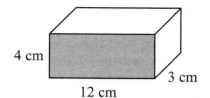

4 cm

12 cm

3 cm

    a. Calculate the surface area of the prism. Show all your subproblems.

    b. Explain why the exponent for area units is 2 (that is, cm²).

    c. Calculate the volume of the prism.

    d. Explain why the exponent for volume units is a 3 (that is, cm³).

11-99. Calculate the height and area of this triangle.

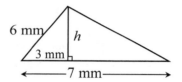

6 mm h 3 mm   7 mm

11-100. A bag contains 3 red, 5 yellow, and 7 purple marbles. Find the probability of drawing a purple marble followed by a red marble. The purple marble is put back in the bag between draws.

11-101. Estimate each square root below to the nearest tenth. Then check your estimate on your calculator. Be sure to write down your estimate before you check!

    a. $\sqrt{45}$ b. $\sqrt{260}$ c. $\sqrt{650}$ d. $\sqrt{57}$

11-102. Consider the expression $(56 \cdot 25) \cdot 4$.

    a. How can regrouping the numbers in this expression make it easier to simplify? Rewrite the expression and simplify it.

    b. What property did you use to rewrite the expression?

11.3.3 What if it is not a cube?

More Scale Factor and Volume

Today you will continue to explore how the volume of a three-dimensional shape changes as the sides are multiplied by a scale factor.

11-103. Bethany's study team just bought her an amazing Cube-o-saurus for her birthday. The package says, "Soak in water overnight and the Cube-o-saurus will get an amazing eight times larger." The cube-shaped dinosaur starts out about one centimeter on a side. Bethany and her study team members are looking forward to seeing the 8-centimeter long creature. Bethany went home and soaked the Cube-o-saurus in water. When she brought it to school the next day, her team was disappointed to see that the Cube-o-saurus was the same shape and only 2 centimeters long, 2 centimeters tall, and 2 centimeters wide. Was the Cube-o-saurus falsely advertised? Is the new shape eight times larger?

11-104. HOW DOES THE VOLUME CHANGE?

In Lesson 11.3.2, you worked with different sized cubes and saw that when cubes are enlarged by a scale factor, the surface area and volume grow, but in different ways than the edge lengths.

Use the data from the Lesson 11.3.2A Resource Page to complete the table on the Lesson 11.3.3 Resource Page or copy the table below on your paper and complete it.

Scale Factor	Edge Length	Face Area	Volume
1	1	1	1
2	2	4	8
3			
...			
9			
x			

Problem continues on next page. →

11-104.   *Problem continued from previous page.*

a.   Use the pattern in the table to explain how the area changes compared to the length of the edge in similar cubes. How is this change related to the scale factor?

b.   Use the pattern in the table to explain how the volume changes compared to the length of an edge in similar cubes. How is this change related to the scale factor?

c.   If the scale factor for a $1 \times 1 \times 1$ cube is 12, what is the face area of its enlargement? The volume?

11-105.   Does the pattern you found for length and volume with cubes apply to all similar solids? Answer the questions below with your team to decide.

a.   Use the original figures on the Lesson 11.3.3 Resource Page (at right) and the scale factors to find the dimensions of the enlarged shapes.

b.   Find the volumes of each original and enlarged shape.

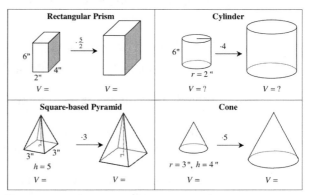

c.   Use your results from part (b) to complete the table on the Lesson 11.3.3 Resource Page (shown below).

Figure	Scale Factor	(scale factor)³	enlarged volume / original volume	Volume ratio reduced
Rectangular Prism				
Cylinder				
Square-based prism				
Cone				

d.   Compare each scale factor, its cube, and the reduced ratio of the two volumes. What pattern do you see?

e.   If two prisms are similar with a scale factor of 3 and the volume of the smaller prism is 21 cm³, what is the volume of the enlarged prism?

11-106. The graph at right shows how the height, base area, and volume of a cone change for different scale factors. Which graph represents the base area of the cone? Which graph represents the height? Which graph represents the volume? Explain how you determined your choices.

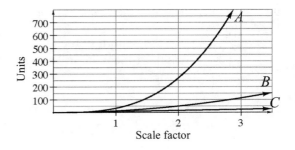

Scale factor

11-107. Back at the store, David sees a Prismasaur that is advertised to grow 64 times bigger. If this advertisement refers to the growth of the volume and the Prismasaur is shaped like a rectangular prism that starts out 2 cm wide by 4 cm long by 2 cm tall, will the Prismasaur be 8 cm long after it is soaked overnight? How many times longer will each side be?

11-108. Consider the square-based pyramid at right.

a. What is the volume of the pyramid?

b. Each triangular face has an area of 3.16 cm². What is the total surface area of the pyramid?

c. If each dimension of the pyramid is increased by a scale factor of 5, what will the new volume be? Make your prediction based on the patterns you found so far.

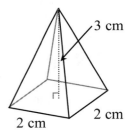

d. Calculate the volume of the new pyramid. Was your prediction correct?

11-109. LEARNING LOG

If the linear dimensions (edges) of a three-dimensional shape grow by a scale factor of 10, how will the volume grow? Show and explain your answer in your Learning Log. Title your entry "Volume in Similar Shapes," and label it with today's date.

MATH NOTES

METHODS AND MEANINGS

Ratios of Similarity — 3D

When a three-dimensional solid is enlarged proportionally, each dimension is multiplied by the same scale factor.

The ratio of the edges is the scale factor, $\left(\frac{a}{b}\right)$.

The **surface area ratio** is the square of the scale factor.

$$\left(\frac{\text{surface area of new}}{\text{surface area of original}}\right) = (\text{scale factor})^2 = \left(\frac{a}{b}\right)^2$$

The **volume ratio** is the cube of the scale factor.

$$\left(\frac{\text{volume of new}}{\text{volume of original}}\right) = (\text{scale factor})^3 = \left(\frac{a}{b}\right)^3$$

For example, comparing the rectangular prisms at right, for $\frac{\text{figure 2}}{\text{figure 1}}$:

The scale factor is $\frac{3}{1}$.

The surface area ratio is $\frac{360}{40} = \frac{9}{1} = \left(\frac{3}{1}\right)^2$.

The volume ratio is $\frac{432}{16} = \frac{27}{1} = \left(\frac{3}{1}\right)^3$.

Figure 1

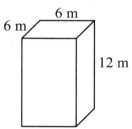

2 m   2 m

4 m

SA = 40 m^2
Vol = 16 m^3

Figure 2

6 m   6 m

12 m

SA = 360 m^2
Vol = 432

11-110.   Rick's favorite drink, Aloha Pineapple Juice, is packaged in a can like the one shown at right. It contains 350 ml of juice. Even after drinking it, he always feels thirsty. He wants the company to package the juice in a larger can.

   a.   If the company enlarges the dimensions of the can by a ratio of $\frac{4}{1}$, how much juice would the can hold? Show your work or explain how you got your answer.

   b.   Does it seem likely that the company will make a can that size? Explain.

11-111.   The label of the Aloha Pineapple Juice can is seven inches high and has an area of 140 square inches. What is the diameter of the can?

11-112.   On a piece of grid paper, plot the following points and connect them: $A(-3, -4)$, $B(2, 4)$, $C(5, -4)$.

   a.   What is the area of triangle ABC?

   b.   What is the perimeter of triangle ABC?

11-113.   Simplify each expression.

   a. $-\frac{11}{15} + \frac{3}{4}$ b. $5\frac{2}{9} + (-2\frac{1}{10})$ c. $-\frac{7}{8} + \frac{2}{3} - (-\frac{1}{4})$

11-114.   Sherice can fill lemonade cups at a rate of four cups per minute.

   a.   How many cups can she fill in 6 minutes?

   b.   How many cups can she fill in 10 minutes?

11.4.1 How can I find the measurement?

Indirect Measurement

When most people think of measurement, they think of using a ruler or tape measure to find a length. However, during this course you found the measures of objects using other types of information, a process called **indirect measurement**. Today's activity will provide you opportunities to connect several ways you know how to find measures. As you work with your team, ask the following questions:

How can we **visualize** it?

What information do we need?

Which **strategy** should we use?

11-115.   The beautiful young princess of Polygonia is very sad. A mean ogre has locked her into a tower of a castle. She could escape through the window, but it is 50 feet above the ground (a long distance to jump). A moat full of alligators surrounds the tower. Naturally, her prince charming wants to rescue her.

The prince has some rope. His plan is to use an arrow to shoot one end of the rope up to her window. The princess can then slide down the rope to the other side of the moat, and off they will ride into the sunset.

Help the prince save the princess by answering the questions below.

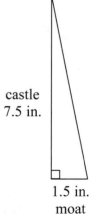

castle
7.5 in.

1.5 in.
moat

a.   The prince knows that the closer he is to the tower, the less rope he will need. However, he is not sure how wide the moat is around the castle.

In a book about the castle, the prince found a photograph of the tower and moat. Using his ruler, he found that the window in the photo is 7.5 inches above the moat, while the farthest edge of the moat is 1.5 inches from the base of the tower. How close to the tower can the prince get? Draw diagrams and show your work.

Problem continues on next page. →

11-115.   *Problem continued from previous page.*

    b.   Before he shoots the arrow, the prince wants to make sure he has enough rope. If he needs an extra 2 feet of rope for tying it to the window frame and holding it on the ground, how long does his rope need to be? Explain.

    c.   The princess thinks she might fall off the rope if the slope is steeper than $\frac{5}{4}$. The prince plans to attach the rope to the ground at the edge of the moat and the princess will attach the rope to the window frame 50 feet above the ground.

        i.   According to the prince's plan, what would be the slope of the rope? Would it be too steep? **Justify** your answer.

        ii.   Should the princess worry about the prince's plan? How steep would the prince's rope be? Find the angle the rope would make with the ground. Use a protractor to measure the angle.

    d.   If one end of the rope is attached to the window frame and the prince holds his end of the rope 2 feet above the ground, where would the prince need to stand so that the slope of the rope is only $\frac{5}{4}$? If he has a rope that is 62 feet long, will his rope be long enough? **Justify** your conclusion. Draw a picture and label it with all your measurements.

    e.   What if the prince holds his end of the rope 5 feet above the ground? Can he stand in some location so that the rope is not steeper than $\frac{5}{4}$? (The rope is still 62 feet long.) **Justify** your conclusion.

11-116.   MAKING CONNECTIONS

When you solved this problem, you needed to use what you learned about several different math ideas.

    a.   Discuss how you solved the problem with your team.

      •   Use colors to mark parts of your solution that used particular math ideas. (For example, did you compare portions? Did you solve equations?)

      •   Label each math idea with words in the margin of your paper.

    b.   Contribute your ideas to a class discussion. Did any other teams identify math ideas that you used but did not notice? If so, add them to your notes. Then write each math idea on an index card.

    c.   How are these different math ideas connected in this problem? Work with your team and follow your teacher's instructions to make a concept map. Work with your team to find ways to show or explain each of the connections you find.

11-117.   THINKING ABOUT THINKING

This course focuses on five different Ways of Thinking: generalizing, reasoning and justifying, reversing thinking, choosing a strategy and visualizing. Some of the Ways of Thinking you used in this lesson were **reasoning and justifying** and **choosing a strategy**.

a.   With others, read and discuss the descriptions of **reasoning and justifying** and **choosing a strategy** below.

Reasoning and justifying: When you **reason** and **justify** as you solve problems, you think about what makes sense and why. Often, reasoning and justifying helps you to answer the question, "Why?" You think this way when you say or ask, *"If this is true, then..."* and *"We know that..., because..."* and *"How can we be sure?"*

Choosing a strategy: To **choose a strategy** means to think about what you know about a problem and match that information with methods and processes for solving problems. You think this way when you ask/answer questions like, "What strategy might work for...?" or , "How can I use this information to answer...?"

b.   What questions did you ask yourself and your team that helped you to understand your thinking and the thinking of others, that is, to **reason** through problem 11-116? How did you decide what information was necessary to **justify** your conclusions? Be ready to explain your ideas.

c.   How did your team **choose a strategy** as you figured out how to solve the different parts of problem 11-116? Did you choose different strategies for different parts? Be ready to share your ideas with the class.

11.4.2   How does it grow?

. . . .

Representing and Predicting Patterns

You have often worked with teams to describe relationships between quantities. For example, you have used tables, graphs, and rules to show how pigs have grown, how runners have traveled, and how money has increased over time. In this lesson, you will revisit a game you may have played early in the course and apply your learning to analyze it. While you work, keep the following questions in mind:

Which representation should we use?

Is this like any other problem we have seen?

11-118.   TOOTHPICKS AND TILES RETURN!

Laurel and Sandra are playing a new version of the Toothpick and Tiles game from Chapter 1. In this game, each player takes turns building shapes that form a pattern.

They have taken three turns so far, shown below. A player will get an extra point if the number of tiles ever equals the number of toothpicks. Remember that the toothpicks create the border (perimeter) of the shape.

<table>
<tr><td>Turn 1</td><td>Turn 2</td><td>Turn 3</td></tr>
<tr><td>by Laurel</td><td>by Sandra</td><td>by Laurel</td></tr>
</table>

a.   Represent the number of toothpicks for each turn in a table and with a rule. Let x represent the turn number.

b.   Represent the number of tiles for each turn in a table and with a rule. Let x represent the turn number.

c.   Will anyone get the extra point? If so, on which turn and who will get the extra point? Use two different representations to **justify** your answer.

d.   Laurel is worried that they might run out of toothpicks and tiles. They only have 30 of each. How many tiles will they need to build the shape on the 10th turn? How many toothpicks?

Problem continues on next page. →

11-118.   *Problem continued from previous page.*

e.   Laurel won this game. That means she gets to choose the next pattern. She wants to create a pattern that will have its perimeter grow by 3 units each turn. Is this possible? Test this idea out and explain your thinking.

f.   Laurel wants your help to create a pattern so that the perimeter would be represented with the graph at right. Draw Turn #1, Turn #2, and Turn #3 of a pattern that would match this graph. Explain how your design is changing with each turn.

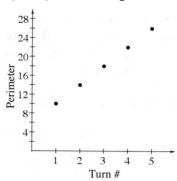

11-119.   THINKING ABOUT THINKING

This course focuses on five different Ways of Thinking: generalizing, reasoning and justifying, reversing, choosing a strategy and visualizing. Two of the Ways of Thinking you may have used in this lesson are **generalizing** and **reversing your thinking**.

a.   With others, read and discuss the descriptions of **generalizing** and **reversing your thinking** below.

Generalizing: When you **generalize**, you make a statement about a characteristic that a group of things shares, based on a collection of evidence. Often, a generalization is the answer to the question, "What is in common?" When you think or say, *"I think this is always true…"*, you are generalizing.

Reversing thinking: To **reverse your thinking** can be described as "thinking backward." You think this way when you want to understand a concept in a new direction. Often, it requires you to try to undo a process. When you think or say, *"What if I try to go backwards?"*, you are reversing your thinking.

b.   How did your algebra skills help you to **generalize** the pattern created in this game? How is generalizing important in problems such as this one?

c.   How did **reversing your thinking** help you solve problem 11-118? Be ready to explain your ideas.

d.   Work with your team to brainstorm other problems in this course in which you **generalized** and used **reversing your thinking**. Be ready to share your ideas with the class.

11.4.3   How much should it cost?

Volume and Scaling

Have you ever made choices about which size of an item (such as a pizza or bottle of juice) to buy? If so, you may have considered which size was priced to give you the most for your money. In this lesson, you will work with your team as you analyze pricing of popcorn at a popular movie theater.

11-120.   The Maverick Movie Theater sells a small tub of popcorn for $1.

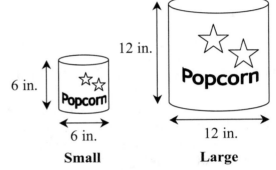

a. To keep their prices proportional to the amount of popcorn offered, what should they charge for the large tub shown at right? Show how you found your answer.

b. The medium size tub is a cylinder with diameter 9 inches and height 12 inches. It currently costs $6 and is not selling well. The owner wants you to decide if this price is fair. How much should it cost? Write a note to the owner that explains whether the medium-sized tub is priced correctly.

c. Customers have complained that the large tub is too wide to carry into the theater without spilling. The owner wants to change the diameter to be 10 inches instead. To keep the same volume, the owner thinks that the new tub will need to be 14 inches tall. She **reasons** that if the width gets two inches shorter, the height should grow by two inches.

Do you agree? If so, show how you know. If not, determine the new height of the tub.

d. The owner decided to create a new size that is 50% wider and 50% taller than the small tub. The owner plans to charge 50% more. Do you agree? If not, what should the owner charge and what percent increase is this price? **Justify** your answer.

e. The owner wants to offer a box of popcorn that would cost $6. She wants you to design the box. Assume that the price should be proportional with the amount of popcorn in the small tub of popcorn. While the box can have any length, width, and height, be sure to make it a reasonable design for someone to hold and for the employees to fill with popcorn.

Draw a diagram of your box with all measurements labeled.

Making Connections: Course 2

11-121. MAKING CONNECTIONS

When you solved this problem, you needed to use what you learned about several different math ideas.

a. Discuss how you solved the problem with your team.

- Use colors to mark parts of your solution that used particular math ideas. (For example, did you compare portions? Did you solve equations?)

- Label each math idea with words in the margin of your paper.

b. Contribute your ideas to a class discussion. Did any other teams identify math ideas that you used but did not notice? If so, add them to your notes. Then write each math idea on an index card.

c. How are these different math ideas connected in this problem? Work with your team and follow your teacher's instructions to make a concept map. Work with your team to find ways to show or explain each of the connections you find.

11-122. THINKING ABOUT THINKING

This course focuses on five different Ways of Thinking: generalizing, reasoning and justifying, reversing, choosing a strategy and visualizing. Two of the Ways of Thinking you used in this lesson are **choosing a strategy** and **visualizing**.

a. Read the descriptions of **choosing a strategy** and **visualizing** below.

Choosing a strategy: To **choose a strategy** means to think about what you know about a problem and match that information with methods and processes for solving problems. You think this way when you ask/answer questions like, "What strategy might work for…?" or , "How can I use this information to answer…?"

Visualizing: To **visualize** means to think about what something looks like or could look like in order to better understand the problem or situation. You think this way when you ask or answer questions like, *"What does it look like when…?"* or *"How can I draw…?"*

b. How did your team **choose a strategy** as you figured out how to solve the different parts of problem 11-120? Did you choose different strategies for different parts? Was there ever more than one strategy you could have used? Explain.

c. A lot of the **visualizing** you did in this lesson related to geometry and shapes. Find a different problem you did in this course that was *not* about a geometric shape, but for which **visualizing** the mathematical ideas helped you make sense of the problem or understand the problem more deeply. Describe what you **visualized** and explain how this helped you work through the problem.

11.4.4 How is it changing?

Analyzing Data to Identify a Trend

Have you ever tried to figure out whether you could earn enough money to be able to buy something that you want? In this lesson, you will consider the relationship between the time you work and your pay rate as you work with your team to analyze data and make predictions.

11-123. Devon hopes to get a job in the summer at an amusement park. He is hoping to earn enough money during the summer to buy a laptop for $875. He is not sure what pay rate he will be offered so he asked his friends who work at the same amusement park for information from their last paycheck. The information he gathered is in the table at right.

	Time (hours)	Pay (dollars)
Frieda	21	$200.00
Ben	25	$305.00
Emory	36	$252.00
Si Yun	50	$480.00
Jillian	55	$600.00
Malik	64	$512.00
Dazjon	72	$600.00
Grace	80	$700.00

a. On graph paper, set up a graph, carefully decide how to scale the axes, and graph Devon's data.

b. Find the hourly rate for each of Devon's friends.

c. What is the highest rate per hour one of Devon's friends is earning? What is the lowest rate per hour? Explain how you found your answer.

d. Draw a trend line that represents this data. Use your trend line to help Devon predict how much he will earn. Why does it make sense that the trend line should pass through the origin?

e. Devon hopes to work 4 hours each day. If he works Friday through Sunday for 10 weeks, how many hours would he work?

f. Based on your trend line, how much money can Devon expect to be paid per hour? Show how you found your answer.

g. Devon knows that he will need to pay 7.5% tax for his laptop. Will he make enough money? Explain how you know.

11-124. **MAKING CONNECTIONS**

When you solved this problem, you needed to use what you learned about several different math ideas.

a. Discuss how you solved the problem with your team.

   • Use colors to mark parts of your solution that used particular math ideas. (For example, did you calculate volume? Did you use transformations?)

   • Label each math idea with words in the margin of your paper.

b. Contribute your ideas to a class discussion. Did any other teams identify math ideas that you used but did not notice? If so, add them to your notes. Then write each math idea on an index card.

c. How are these different math ideas connected in this problem? Work with your team and follow your teacher's instructions to make a concept map. Work with your team to find ways to show or explain each of the connections you think of.

Chapter 11 Closure   What have I learned?

Reflection and Synthesis

The activities below offer you a chance to reflect about what you have learned during this chapter. As you work, look for concepts that you feel very comfortable with, ideas that you would like to learn more about, and topics you need more help with. Look for connections between ideas as well as connections with material you learned previously.

①   WHAT HAVE I LEARNED?

Working the problems in this section will help you to evaluate which types of problems you feel comfortable with and which ones you need more help with.

Solve each problem as completely as you can. The table at the end of this closure section has answers to these problems. It also tells you where you can find additional help and practice on problems like them.

CL 11-125.   Look at the graph at right. What type of equation does it represent? Explain how you know.

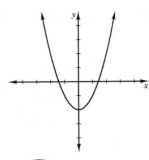

CL 11-126.   Erika is playing a game where the number of spaces she moves is determined by the spinner at right. Each half of the spinner — left and right — is divided into equal regions as shown.

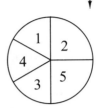

a.   What is the probability that Erika will spin an even number on her next spin?

b.   If Erika spins a four she will land on a space that says "Get an extra turn." If she then spins a five, she gets 50 bonus points and she will win the game. What is the probability that she can spin a four and then a five?

CL 11-127.   Find the volume of a pyramid with a square base with sides of eight inches and a height of 12 inches.

CL 11-128.   Ella's cat has climbed up on the roof of her house and cannot get down! The roof of the house is 24 feet above the ground. The fire department has set up a 28-foot ladder to climb to rescue the cat. The base of the ladder is resting on the ground, and the top of the ladder extends 2 feet beyond the edge of the roof. How far away from the base of the house is the base of the ladder? You may want to draw a diagram to help you solve the problem.

CL 11-129.   Simplify the following exponential expressions.

a. $4^3 \cdot 4^7$

b. $(5x^4)^3$

c. $\dfrac{3^7}{3^4}$

d. $(4x^5)(3x^8)$

CL 11-130.   **Visualize** a line through the two points on the graph at right.

a.   What is the slope of the line?

b.   What is the rule for the line?

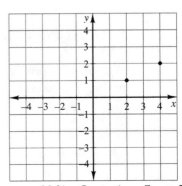

Making Connections: Course 2

CL 11-131.   Manuela found a great deal on pens at 3 for $0.99. It was such a good deal that she decided to buy 2 dozen. How much did she pay for all of the pens?

CL 11-132.   Casey was building a rectangular pen for his pigs. He has 62 feet of fencing. The length of his pen is 9 feet longer than the width. Write and solve an equation to find the dimensions of the pen.

CL 11-133.   For each of the problems in this section of closure, do the following:

Draw a bar or number line like the one below that represents 0 to 10.

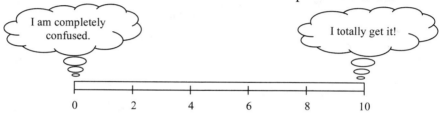

Color or shade in a portion of the bar that represents your current level of understanding and comfort with completing that problem on your own.

If any of your bars are less than a 5, choose *one* of those problems and do one of the following tasks:

- Write two questions that you would like to ask about that problem.

- Brainstorm two things that you DO know about that type of problem.

If all of your bars are a 5 or above, choose one of those problems and do one of these tasks:

- Write two questions you might ask or hints you might give to a student who was stuck on the problem.

- Make a new problem that is similar and more challenging than that problem and solve it.

You have several tools and references available to help support your learning – your teacher, your study team, your math book, and your Toolkit to name only a few. At the end of each chapter you will have an opportunity to review your Toolkit for completeness as well as to revise or update it to better reflect your current understanding of big ideas.

The main elements of your Toolkit should be your Learning Log, Math Notes, and the vocabulary used in this chapter. Math words that are new to this chapter appear in bold in the text. Refer to the lists provided below and follow your teacher's instructions to revise your Toolkit, which will help make it useful for you as you complete this chapter and as you work in future chapters.

Learning Log Entries

- Lesson 11.2.2 – Multiple Outcomes and Questions
- Lesson 11.3.3 – Volume in Similar Shapes

Math Notes

- Lesson 11.1.2 – Absolute Value
- Lesson 11.2.3 – Probability Models for Multiple Events
- Lesson 11.2.4 – Compound Probability
- Lesson 11.3.3 – Ratios of Similarity — 3D

Mathematical Vocabulary

The following is a list of vocabulary found in this chapter. Some of the words have been seen in a previous chapter. The words in bold are the words new to this chapter. It is a good idea to make sure that you are familiar with these words and know what they mean. For the words you do not know, refer to the glossary or index. You might also want to add these words to your Toolkit for a way to reference them in the future.

absolute value	**compound probability**	experimental probability
independent event	linear	**outcome chart**
parabola	**plane**	point
ratio	scale factor	**skew line**
symmetry	**systematic list**	theoretical probability
tree diagram	volume	

Process Words

These words describe problem solving strategies and processes that you have been involved in as you worked in this chapter. Make sure you know what each of these words means. If you are not sure, you can talk with your teacher or other students or look through your book for problems in which you were asked to do these things.

analyze	construct	describe
estimate	explain	express
justify	organize	reason
record	represent	reverse
scale		

Answers and Support for Closure Activity #1
What Have I Learned?

Problem	Solution	Need Help?	More Practice
CL 11-125.	It represents an equation of the form $y = x^2$.	Lesson 11.1.1	Problems 11-1 through 11-3, 11-92
CL 11-126.	a. $\frac{1}{4} + \frac{1}{6} = \frac{3}{12} + \frac{2}{12} = \frac{5}{12}$ b. $\frac{1}{6} \cdot \frac{1}{4} = \frac{1}{24}$	Lessons 11.2.3 and 11.2.4 Math Notes boxes in Lessons 11.2.3 and 11.2.4	Problems 11-46 through 11-51, 11-57 through 11-66, 11-70, 11-71, 11-83, and 11-100
CL 11-127.	Volume = 256 in^3	Lesson 10.2.6 Learning Log (problem 10-145)	Problems 10-144, 11-9, 11-85 (b), and 11-108

Problem	Solution	Need Help?	More Practice
CL 11-128.	The base of the ladder will be approximately 10 feet from the base of the house.	Lessons 9.3.2, 9.3.3, and 9.3.4 Math Notes boxes in Lessons 9.3.2 and 9.3.3 Learning Logs (problems 9-105 and 9-122)	Problem CL 10-160
CL 11-129.	a. 4^{10} b. $125x^{12}$ c. 3^3 d. $12x^{13}$	Lessons 10.1.2, 10.1.4, and 10.1.5 Math Notes boxes in Lessons 10.1.2 and 10.1.6 Learning Log (problem 10-58)	Problems CL 10-153, 11-10, 11-42, and 11-84
CL 11-130.	a. The slope is $\frac{1}{2}$. b. $y = \frac{1}{2}x$	Lessons 6.1.6, 7.1.4, and 7.1.5 Math Notes box in Lesson 7.1.6 Learning Log (problem 7-47)	Problems CL 7-94 and CL 10-147
CL 11-131.	$7.92	Lessons 9.1.1, 9.1.2, and 9.1.3 Math Notes boxes in Lessons 9.1.2 and 9.1.3 Learning Log (problem 9-8)	Problems CL 9-133, 11-69, and 11-90
CL 11-132.	$2x + 2(x+9) = 62$ OR $4x + 18 = 62$ The dimensions of the pen are 11 feet by 20 feet.	Lesson 6.2.4 Math Notes boxes in Lessons 6.2.4 and 6.2.6 Learning Log (problem 6-107)	Problems CL 6-147, 11-33, and 11-91

Puzzle Investigator Problems

• •

PI-21.   SECRET CODE

Arianna wants to send a secret code through her computer. By using a two-digit number for every letter, she can build secret words with numbers. For example, using her code below, "SECRET" becomes "180402170419."

A	B	C	D	E	F	G	H	I	J	K	L	M
00	01	02	03	04	05	06	07	08	09	10	11	12
N	O	P	Q	R	S	T	U	V	W	X	Y	Z
13	14	15	16	17	18	19	20	21	22	23	24	25

a.   To answer the question "who is your favorite mathematician," Arianna wrote 00170207081204030418. Decipher her message. Remember that every pair of numbers represents a letter.

b.   To send secret messages through computers, the numeric codes must be changed so that they only contain the digits 0 and 1. These are called **binary codes**, and use the base-2 number system. The base-2 number system counts in sets of 2 instead of sets of 10. The first 12 counting numbers in base-2 are shown in the table below. Based on this counting system, how would you write "12" in base-2? What about 15? 16?

Base 10:	00	01	02	03	04	05	06	07	08	09	10	11
Base 2:	00	01	10	11	100	101	110	111	1000	1001	1010	1011

c.   To make a computer code for the entire alphabet, plus a code for a space and a code for an exclamation point, you will need the base-2 equivalents for the numbers 0 through 27. The codes will have 5 digits so that every letter has the same number of digits. Copy and complete the table below.

A = 00	00000	H = 07		O = 14	01110	V = 21	
B = 01	00001	I = 08		P = 15		W= 22	10110
C = 02	00010	J = 09		Q = 16		X = 23	
D = 03	00011	K = 10		R= 17		Y = 24	
E = 04	00100	L = 11		S = 18	10010	Z = 25	
F = 05		M = 12		T = 19		= 26	
G = 06		N = 13	01101	U = 20		! = 27	11011

c.   To send the message "NOSE," Arianna's computer would change 13141804 to 01101011101001000100. What would be the computer code for "MATH"?

d.   Decipher Arianna's secret message below. Remember that every 5 digits is a letter.

   01111101001100111001010110010011010001011010001101111011

PI-22.   STAIRCASES

Study the following staircases.

  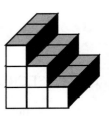

The first staircase is made of one cube. Its volume is 1 cubic unit and its surface area is 6 square units.

a.   Show that the second staircase has a volume of 6 cubic units and a surface area of 22 square units.

b.   Find the volume and surface area of the third staircase.

c.   Describe in words what the 50th staircase will look like. For example, how many steps will it have? How wide will it be?

d.   Use geometric patterns, tables, and sketches to find the volume and surface area of the 50th staircase. In your explanation, describe as many **patterns** as you can and explain how you arrived at your answers and why you think they are correct.

Glossary

5-D Process   An organized method to solve problems. The 5 D's stand for Describe/Draw, Define, Do, Decide, and Declare. This is a problem-solving strategy for which solving begins by making a prediction about the answer or one element of it (a trial), and then confirming whether the result of the trial is correct. If not, information is gained about how close the trial is to the correct value, so that adjustments to the trial value may be made. Being organized is extremely important to the success of this method, as well as writing a usable table. The 5-D process leads to writing equations to represent word problems. (p. 179)

absolute value   The absolute value of a number is the distance of the number from zero. Since the absolute value represents a distance, without regard to direction, absolute value is always non-negative. Thus, the absolute value of a negative number is its opposite, while the absolute value of a non-negative number is just the number itself. The absolute value of x is usually written "$|x|$." For example, $|-5| = 5$ and $|22| = 22$. (p. 637)

acute angle   An angle with a measure greater than 0° and less than 90°. An example is shown at right. (p. 304)

acute triangle   A triangle with all three angle measures less than 90°.

addition $(+)$ An operation that tells how many objects there are when two sets are combined. The result is the number of objects in the two sets together which is called a sum. In arithmetic, the word "object" usually means "number." (p. 90)

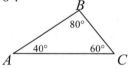

Additive Inverse Property   The Additive Inverse Property states that for every number a there is a number $-a$ such that $a + (-a) = 0$. For example, the number 5 has an additive inverse of -5; $5 + (-5) = 0$. The additive inverse of a number is often called its opposite. For example, 5 and -5 are opposites. (p. 290)

adjacent angles   For two angles to be adjacent, the angles must satisfy these three conditions: (1) the two angles must have a common side; (2) the two angles must have a common vertex; and (3) the two angles may have no interior points in common. Meeting these three conditions means that the common side must be between the two angles. No overlap between the angles is permitted. In the example at right, $\angle ABC$ and $\angle CBD$ are adjacent angles.

algebra   A branch of mathematics that uses variables to generalize the rules of numbers and numerical operations.

algebra tiles An algebra tile is a manipulative whose area represents a constant or variable quantity. The algebra tiles used in this course consist of large squares with dimensions *x*-by-*x* and *y*-by-*y*; rectangles with dimensions *x*-by-1, *y*-by-1, and *x*-by-*y*; and small squares with dimensions 1-by-1. These tiles are named by their areas: x^2, y^2, *x*, *y*, *xy*, and 1, respectively. The smallest squares are called "unit tiles." In this text, shaded tiles will represent positive quantities while unshaded tiles will represent negative quantities. (p. 156)

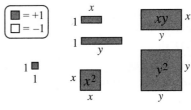
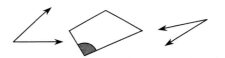

algebraic expression See *expression.*

algorithm A fixed rule for carrying out a mathematical procedure. For example, to find the average of a set of values, find the sum of the values and divide by the number of values.

altitude of a triangle The length of a segment that connects a vertex of the triangle to a line containing the opposite base (side) and is perpendicular to that line. (See *height.*)

angle Generally, an angle is formed by two rays that are joined at a common endpoint. Angles in geometric figures are usually formed by two segments that have a common endpoint (such as the angle shaded in the figure at right). (Also see *acute angle, obtuse angle,* and *right angle.*) (p. 304)

angle bisector A ray that divides an angle into two congruent parts.

arc A part of a circle or curve between two points on the circle.

area For this course, area is the number of square units needed to fill up a region on a flat surface. In later courses, the idea will be extended to cones, spheres, and more complex surfaces. (Also see *surface area.*) (p. 10, 603)

Area = 15 square units

area of a circle $A = \pi r^2$, where *r* is the length of the radius of the circle. (See "circle.") (p. 319)

area of a triangle To find the area of a triangle, multiply the length of the base *b* by the height *h* and divide by two: $A = \frac{1}{2}bh$. (Also see *altitude of a triangle.*) (p. 127)

Associative Property of Addition   The Associative Property of Addition states that if a sum contains terms that are grouped, then the sum may be grouped differently with no effect on the total, that is, $a + (b + c) = (a + b) + c$. For example, $3 + (4 + 5) = (3 + 4) + 5$. (p. 78)

Associative Property of Multiplication   The Associative Property of Multiplication states that if a product contains terms that are grouped, then the product may be grouped differently with no effect on the result, that is, $a(bc) = (ab)c$. For example, $2 \cdot (3 \cdot 4) = (2 \cdot 3) \cdot 4$. (p. 581)

average   The sum of given values divided by the number of values used in computing the sum. For example, the average of 1, 4, and 10 is $(1 + 4 + 10)/3$. (See *mean*.) (p. 13)

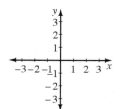

axis (plural: axes)   In a coordinate plane, two number lines that meet at right angles at the origin (0, 0). The x-axis runs horizontally and the y-axis runs vertically. (p. 85, 94)

bar graph   A bar graph is a set of rectangular bars that have height proportional to the number of data elements in each category. Each bar stands for all of the elements in a single distinguishable category (such as "red"). Usually all of the bars are the same width and separated from each other. (Also see *histogram*.) (p. 219)

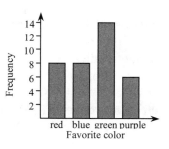

base of a geometric figure   (a) The base of a triangle: any side of a triangle to which a height is drawn. There are three possible bases in each triangle. (b) The base of a trapezoid: either of the two parallel sides. (c) The base of a parallelogram (including rectangle, rhombus, and square): any side to which a height is drawn. There are four possible bases. (d) The base of a solid: also see *cone*, *cylinder*, *prism*, and *pyramid*. (p. 115, 595)

base of an exponent   When working with an exponential expression in the form a^b, a is called the base. For example, 2 is the base in 2^5. (5 is the exponent, and 32 is the value.) (Also see *exponent*.) (p. 572)

bimodal   A set of numbers that has two modes.

boundary point   The endpoint or endpoints of a ray or segment on a number line where an inequality is true, marked with a solid dot. For strict inequalities (that is, inequalities involving < or >), the point is not part of the solution, and is marked with an open dot. Boundary points may be found by solving the equality associated with the given inequality. For example, the solution to the equation $2x + 5 = 11$ is $x = 3$, so the inequality $2x + 5 \geq 11$ has a boundary point at 3. A boundary point is also sometimes called a "dividing point." (p. 294)

box-and-whisker plot A graphic way of showing a summary of data using the median, quartiles, and extremes of the data. (p. 230)

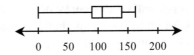

center (center point) Within a flat surface, the point that is the same distance from all points of a circle. (Also see *circle*.)

central angle An angle with its vertex at the center of a circle. (Also see *circle*.) (p. 339)

certainty When an event will definitely happen. The probability of a certain event is 1. (p. 33)

chord A line segment with its endpoints on a circle. A chord that passes through the center of a circle is called a "diameter." (Also see *circle*.) (p. 309)

circle The set of all points on a flat surface that are the same distance from a fixed point. If the fixed point (center) is O, then the symbol $\odot O$ represents a circle with center O. If r is the length of the radius of a circle and d is the length of its diameter, then the circumference of the circle is $C = 2\pi r$ or $C = \pi d$. (p. 309)

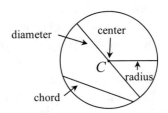

circumference The perimeter of (distance around) a circle. (Also see *circle*.) (p. 309, 319)

coefficient (numerical) A number multiplying a variable or product of variables. For example, -7 is the coefficient of $-7xy^2$. (p. 159)

combining like terms Combining two or more like terms simplifies an expression by summing constants and summing those variable terms in which the same variables are raised to the same power. For example, combining like terms in the expression $3x + 7 + 5x - 3 + 2x^2 + 3y^2$ gives $8x + 4 + 2x^2 + 3y^2$. When working with algebra tiles, combining like terms involves putting together tiles with the same dimensions. (p. 161)

common Shared.

common factor A common factor is a factor that is the same for two or more terms. For example, x^2 is a common factor for $3x^2$ and $-5x^2y$.

common multiple A number that is a multiple of the two or more numbers. For example, 24 and 48 are common multiples of 3 and 8.

Commutative Property of Addition The Commutative Property of Addition states that if two terms are added, then the order may be reversed with no effect on the total. That is, $a + b = b + a$. For example, $7 + 12 = 12 + 7$. (p. 78)

Commutative Property of Multiplication The Commutative Property of Multiplication states that if two expressions are multiplied, then the order may be reversed with no effect on the result. That is, $ab = ba$. For example, $5 \cdot 8 = 8 \cdot 5$. (p. 581)

complementary angles Two angles whose measures add up to 90°. Angles T and V are complementary because $m\angle T + m\angle V = 90°$. Complementary angles may also be adjacent, like $\angle ABC$ and $\angle CBD$ in the diagram at far right. (p. 313)

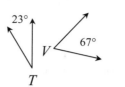

complementary probabilities Two probabilities are complementary if the sum of the probabilities is one.

complex fraction A fraction with a fraction in the numerator and/or denominator.

composite figure A shape made of several simpler figures.

composite number A number with more than two factors.

compound event A compound event in probability is an outcome that depends on two or more other events. For example, finding the probability that both a red ball and also a blue block are drawn from a bag in two draws. (p. 650, 655)

compound interest Interest that is paid on both the principal and the previous interest earned which grows over time. Compound interest may be calculated using the formula $B = p(1 + r)^t$, in which B is the balance, p is the principal, r is the annual rate, and t is the time in years that the account earns interest. (p. 576)

cone A three-dimensional figure that consists of a circular face, called the "base," a point called the "apex," that is not in the flat surface (plane) of the base, and the slant surface that connects the apex to each point on the circular edge of the base. (p. 614)

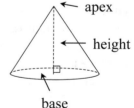

congruent Two shapes are congruent if they have exactly the same shape and size. Congruent shapes are similar and have a scale factor of 1. The symbol for congruence is $\cong$. (p. 235, 250)

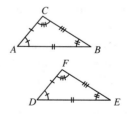

conjecture An educated guess that often results from noticing a pattern. Conjectures are also often written in conditional ("If..., then...") form. Once a conjecture is proven, then the conjecture becomes a theorem. (p. 103)

consecutive numbers Integers that are in order without skipping any integers. For example, 8, 9, and 10 are consecutive numbers. (p. 185)

constant A symbol representing a value that does not change. For example, in the equation $y = 2x + 5$, the number 5 is a constant. (p. 161, 273)

construction with a compass and straightedge The process of using a straightedge and compass to solve a problem and/or create a geometric diagram. (p. 299)

coordinate The number corresponding to a point on the number line or an ordered pair (x, y) that corresponds to a point in a two-dimensional coordinate system. In an ordered pair, the x-coordinate appears first and the y-coordinate appears second. For example, the point $(3, 5)$ has an x-coordinate of 3. (See *ordered pair*.) (p. 79)

coordinate grid (system) A system of graphing ordered pairs of numbers on a coordinate plane. An ordered pair represents a point, with the first number giving the horizontal position relative to the x-axis and the second number giving the vertical position relative to the y-axis. (Also see *ordered pair*.) (p. 92)

correlation A measure of the relationship between two sets of data. (p. 355)

corresponding parts Points, sides, edges, or angles in two or more figures that are images of each other with respect to a transformation. If two figures are congruent, then the corresponding parts of the figures are congruent to each other. (See *ratio of similarity* and *congruent*.) (p. 242)

cube A polyhedron of six faces, each of which is a square.

cubic unit A cube, each of whose edges measure 1 unit in length. Volume is measured in cubic units. (p. 603)

cylinder A three-dimensional figure that consists of two parallel congruent circular regions (called *bases*) and a vertical surface containing segments connecting each point on the circular boundary of one base to the corresponding point on the circular boundary of the other. (p. 617)

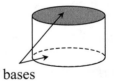
bases

decimal point The dot separating the whole number from the decimal portion, that is, the ones and tenths places in a decimal number. (p. 46)

decompose If a geometric figure is broken up into separate parts, then the figure is decomposed. Similarly, if a number is written as a sum or difference (such as $28 = 30 - 2$), then the number is decomposed. (Also see *recompose*.) (p. 123)

denominator The lower part of a fraction, which expresses into how many equal parts the whole is divided. (p. 37)

dependent events Two events are dependent if the outcome of one event affects the probability of the other event. For example, if one card is drawn out of a deck of cards, then the probability that the first card is red is $\frac{26}{52} = \frac{1}{2}$ because 26 of the 52 cards are red. However, the probability of the second card now depends on the result of the first selection. If the first card was red, then there are now 25 red cards remaining in a deck of 51 cards, and the probability that the second card is red is $\frac{25}{51}$. The second event (selecting the second card) is dependent on the first event (selecting the first card).

diagonal In a polygon, a diagonal is a line segment that connects two vertices of the polygon but is not a side of the polygon.

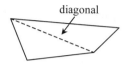
diagonal

diameter A line segment drawn through the center of a circle with both endpoints on the circle. The length of a diameter is usually denoted d. Note that the length of the diameter of a circle is twice the length of its radius. (Also see *circle*.) (p. 309)

difference The result of subtraction. (p. 90)

digit One of the ten numerals: 0, 1, 2, 3, 4, 5, 6, 7, 8, or 9.

dilation A transformation which produces a figure similar to the original by proportionally shrinking or stretching the figure. In a dilation, a shape is stretched (or compressed) proportionally from a point, called the point of dilation. (p. 102)

dimensions The dimensions of a figure that is a flat region or space tell how far that the figure extends in each direction. For example, the dimensions of a rectangle might be 16 cm wide by 7 cm high. (p. 603)

Distributive Property For any a, b, and c, $a(b+c) = ab + ac$. For example, $10(7+2) = 10 \cdot 7 + 10 \cdot 2$. (p. 279)

dividend A quantity to be divided. (See *divisor*.)

divisible A number is divisible by another if the remainder of the division is zero.

division ($\div$) The inverse operation to multiplication, or the operation that creates equal groups.

divisor The quantity by which another quantity is to be divided. dividend/divisor = quotient + remainder (if there is any).

edge In three dimensions, a line segment formed by the intersection of two faces of a polyhedron. (p. 595)

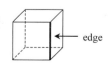
edge

endpoint Either of the two points that mark the ends of a line segment. (Also see *line segment*.) (p. 304)

enlargement ratio   The ratio of similarity comparing a figure to a similar larger figure is often called the enlargement ratio. This ratio shows by what factor the first figure is enlarged to get the second figure. (p. 250, 477)

equal (=)   Two quantities are equal when they have the same value. For example, when $x = 4$, the expression $x + 8$ is equal to the expression $3x$ because the values of the expressions are the same. (p. 285)

equal ratios   Two equivalent fractions, also called a proportion. For example, $\frac{40 \text{ miles}}{2 \text{ gallons}} = \frac{100 \text{ miles}}{50 \text{ gallons}}$. (p. 205)

equation   A mathematical sentence in which two expressions appear on either side of an "equals" sign (=), stating that the two expressions are equivalent. For example, the equation $7x + 4.2 = -8$ states that the expression $7x + 4.2$ has the value –8. In this course, an equation is often used to represent a rule relating two quantities. For example, a rule for finding the area y of a tile pattern with figure number x might be written $y = 4x - 3$. (p. 371)

equilateral   A polygon is equilateral if all of its sides have equal length. The word "equilateral" comes from "equi" (meaning "equal") and "lateral" (meaning "side"). Equilateral triangles not only have sides of equal length, but also angles of equal measure. However, a polygon with more than three sides may be equilateral without having congruent angles. For example, see the rhombus at right. (p. 308)

equivalent   Two expressions are equivalent if they have the same value. For example, $2 + 3$ is equivalent to $1 + 4$. Two equations are equivalent if they have all the same solutions. For example, $y = 3x$ is equivalent to $2y = 6x$. Equivalent equations also have the same graph. (p. 278)

equivalent fractions   Two fractions are equivalent if they have the same numerical value. For example, 3/6 and 5/10 are equivalent fractions. (p. 38, 46, 243)

evaluate (an expression)   To find the numerical value of. To evaluate an expression, substitute the value(s) given for the variable(s) and perform the operations according to the order of operations. For example, evaluating $2x + y - 10$ when $x = 4$ and $y = 3$ gives the value 1. (Also see *expression*.) (p. 273)

even number   A whole number that is divisible by two with no remainder. (p. 185)

event   One or more results of an experiment. (p. 33)

experimental probability   The probability based on data collected in experiments. The experimental probability of an event is defined to be $\frac{\text{number of successful outcomes in the experiment}}{\text{total number of outcomes in the experiment}}$. (p. 33)

Making Connections

exponent   In an expression of the form a^b, b is called the exponent. For example, in the expression 2^5, 5 is called the exponent (2 is the base, and 32 is the value). The exponent indicates how many times to use the base as a multiplier. For example, in 2^5, 2 is used 5 times: $2^5 = 2 \cdot 2 \cdot 2 \cdot 2 \cdot 2 = 32$. For exponents of zero, the rule is: for any number $x \neq 0$, $x^0 = 1$. (p. 572, 591)

expression   An expression is a combination of individual terms separated by plus or minus signs. Numerical expressions combine numbers and operation symbols; algebraic (variable) expressions include variables. For example, $4 + (5 - 3)$ is a numerical expression. In an algebraic expression, if each of the following terms, $6xy^2$, 24, and $\frac{y-3}{4+x}$, are combined, the result may be $6xy^2 + 24 - \frac{y-3}{4+x}$. An expression does not have an "equals" sign. (p. 273)

expression mat   An organizing tool used to visually represent an expression with algebra tiles. An expression mat has two regions, a positive region at the top and a negative region at the bottom. The tiles on the expression mat at right represent a value of –3. (p. 277)

Value: –3

face   One of the flat surfaces of a polyhedron, including the base(s). (p. 595)

factor   (1) In arithmetic: when two or more integers are multiplied, each of the integers is a factor of the product. For example, 4 is a factor of 24, because $4 \cdot 6 = 24$.
(2) In algebra: when two or more algebraic expressions are multiplied together, each of the expressions is a factor of the product. For example, x^2 is a factor of $-17x^2y^3$, because $(x^2)(-17y^3) = -17x^2y^3$. (3) To factor an expression is to write the expression as a product. For example, the factored form of $x^2 - 3x - 18$ is $(x - 6)(x + 3)$. (p. 44)

family of fractions   All fractions that are equivalent to each other form a family of fractions. (See *equivalent fractions*.) (p. 38, 243)

formula   An equation that shows a mathematical relationship. (p. 129)

fraction   A number expressed in the form $\frac{a}{b}$ for which a and b are integers and b is not equal to 0. A fraction is also called a rational number. (p. 22, 103)

frequency   The number of times that something occurs within an interval or data set. (p. 219)

generic rectangle   A type of diagram used to visualize multiplying expressions without algebra tiles. Each expression to be multiplied forms a side length of the rectangle, and the product is the sum of the areas of the sections of the rectangle. For example, the generic rectangle at right may be used to multiply $(2x + 5)$ by $(x + 3)$.

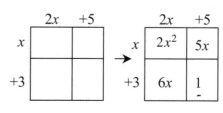

$$(2x + 5)(x + 3) = 2x^2 + 11x + 15$$

area as a product   area as a sum

graph   A graph represents numerical information in a visual form. The numbers may come from a table, situation (pattern), or rule (equation or inequality). Most of the graphs in this course show points, lines, and/or curves on a two-dimensional coordinate system like the one at right or on a single axis called a number line (see diagram below right). (p. 94, 359)

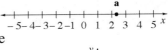

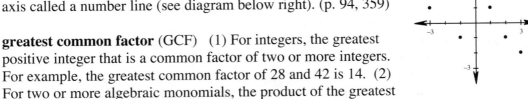

greatest common factor (GCF)   (1) For integers, the greatest positive integer that is a common factor of two or more integers. For example, the greatest common factor of 28 and 42 is 14. (2) For two or more algebraic monomials, the product of the greatest common integer factor of the coefficients of the monomials and the variable(s) in each algebraic term with the smallest degree of that variable in every term. For example, the greatest common factor of $12x^3y^2$ and $8xy^4$ is $4xy^2$. (3) For a polynomial, the greatest common monomial factor of its terms. For example, the greatest common factor of $16x^4 + 8x^3 + 12x$ is $4x$.

height   (a) Triangle: the length of a segment that connects a vertex of the triangle to a line containing the opposite base (side) and is perpendicular to that line. (b) Trapezoid: the length of any segment that connects a point on one base of the trapezoid to the line containing the opposite base and is perpendicular to that line. (c) Parallelogram (includes rectangle, rhombus, and square): the length of any segment that connects a point on one base of the parallelogram to the line containing the opposite base and is perpendicular to that line. (d) Pyramid and cone: the length of the segment that connects the apex to a point in the plane containing the base of a figure and is perpendicular to that plane. (e) Prism or cylinder: the length of a segment that connects one base of the figure to the plane containing the other base and is perpendicular to that plane. (See *altitude*.) (p. 115)

hexagon   A polygon with six sides. (p. 595)

histogram   A way of displaying data that is much like a bar graph in that the height of the bars is proportional to the number of elements. The difference is that each bar of a histogram represents the number of data elements in a range of values, such as the number of people who weigh from 100 pounds up to, but not including, 120 pounds. Each range of values should have the same width. (See *bar graph*.) (p. 219)

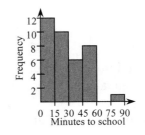

horizontal   Parallel to the horizon. The *x*-axis of a coordinate grid is the horizontal axis. (p. 93, 94)

hypotenuse   The longest side of a right triangle (the side that is opposite of the right angle). (See *Pythagorean Theorem* for a diagram.) (p. 541)

Making Connections

Identity Property of Addition   The Identity Property of Addition states that adding zero to any expression leaves the expression unchanged. That is, $a + 0 = a$. For example, $7 + 0 = 7$, and $-2y + 0 = -2y$. (p. 290)

Identity Property of Multiplication   The Identity Property of Multiplication states that multiplying any expression by 1 leaves the expression unchanged. That is, $a(1) = a$. For example, $437x \cdot 1 = 437x$. (p. 39)

impossibility   An event with a probability of zero. (p. 33)

independent events   If the outcome of a probabilistic event does not affect the probability of another event, then the events are independent. For example, assume that a normal six-sided die is being rolled twice to determine the probability of rolling a 1 twice. The result of the first roll does not affect the probability of rolling a 1 on the second roll. Since the probability of rolling a 1 on the first roll is $\frac{1}{6}$ and the probability of rolling a 1 on the second roll is also $\frac{1}{6}$, then the probability of rolling two 1s in a row is $\frac{1}{6} \cdot \frac{1}{6} = \frac{1}{36}$. (p. 655)

inequality   An inequality consists of two expressions on either side of an inequality symbol. For example, the inequality $7x + 4.2 < -8$ states that the expression $7x + 4.2$ has a value less than –8. (p. 285, 294)

inequality symbols   The symbol ≤ read from left to right means "less than or equal to," the symbol ≥ read from left to right means "greater than or equal to," and the symbols < and > mean "less than" and "greater than," respectively. For example, "$7 < 13$" means that 7 is less than 13. (p. 285)

integers   The set of numbers $\{\ldots, -3, -2, -1, 0, 1, 2, 3, \ldots\}$. (p. 86, 90)

intersect   To meet or cross. The x-axis intersects the y-axis at the origin. (See *axis*.) (p. 441)

interval   A set of numbers between two given numbers. (p. 51)

inverse operation   An operation that undoes another operation. For example, multiplication is the inverse operation for division. (p. 266)

irrational numbers   The set of numbers that cannot be expressed in the form $\frac{a}{b}$, where a and b are integers and $b \neq 0$. For example, π and $\sqrt{2}$ are irrational numbers. (p. 545)

isosceles triangle   A triangle with two sides of equal length.

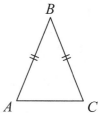

iterate   The process of repeating a measurement many times, such as the use of a one-foot ruler to measure a long room by placing the ruler end-to-end many times.

kite A quadrilateral with two distinct pairs of consecutive congruent sides.

least common multiple (LCM) (1) The smallest common multiple of a set of two or more integers. For example, the least common multiple of 4, 6, and 8 is 24. (2) For two or more algebraic monomials, the product of the least common integer multiples of the coefficients of the monomials and the variable(s) in each algebraic term with the greatest degree of that variable in every term. For example, the least common multiple of $12x^3y^2$ and $8xy^4$ is $24x^3y^4$.

leg of a right triangle Either of the two shorter sides of a right triangle that form the right angle. (See *Pythagorean Theorem* for a diagram.) (p. 539, 541)

less than (1) One expression is less than another if its value is not as large. This relationship is indicated with the less than symbol "$<$." For example, $1+1$ is less than $4+5$, so the comparison is written as $1+1<4+5$. (2) Sometimes the comparison is made that one amount is a certain quantity less than another amount. For example, a student movie ticket might cost two dollars *less than* an adult ticket. (p. 285)

like terms Two or more terms that contain the same variable(s), with corresponding variables raised to the same power. For example, $5x^2$ and $2x^2$ are like terms. (See *combining like terms*.) (p. 161)

line A line is an undefined term in geometry. A line is one-dimensional and continues without end in two directions. A line is made up of points and has no thickness. A line may be named with a letter (such as *l*), but also may be labeled using two points on the line, such as $\overleftrightarrow{AB}$ shown the right.

line segment The portion of a line between two points. A line segment is named using its endpoints. For example, the line segment at right may be named either $\overline{AB}$ or $\overline{BA}$.

linear equation An equation in two variables whose graph is a line. For example, $y=2.1x-8$ is a *linear equation*. The standard form for a linear equation is $ax+by=c$, where a, b, and c are constants and a and b are not both zero. Most linear equations may be written in $y=mx+b$ form, which is more useful for determining the slope and y-intercept of the line. (p. 359)

linear expression An expression in the form of $ax+b$ for which a and b are numbers.

lower quartile The median of the lower half of an ordered set of data is the lower quartile. (p. 226)

lowest common denominator (LCD) The smallest common multiple of the denominators of two or more fractions. For example, the LCD of $\frac{5}{12}$ and $\frac{3}{8}$ is 24. (p. 44)

mean The mean, or average, of several numbers is one way of defining the "middle" of the numbers. To find the average of a group of numbers, add the numbers together then divide by the number of numbers in the set. For example, the average of the numbers 1, 5, and 6 is $(1+5+6) \div 3 = 4$. (See *average*.) (p. 13)

measure of central tendency Mean, median, and mode are all measures of central tendency, reflecting special statistical information about a set of data. (p. 13, 18)

median The middle number of an ordered set of data. If there is no distinct middle, then the average of the two middle numbers is the median. (p. 18)

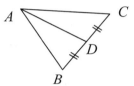

midpoint A point that divides a segment into two segments of equal length. For example, D is the midpoint of $\overline{BC}$ in $\triangle ABC$ at right. (p. 307)

mixed number (fraction) A number that consists of an integer and a fraction. For example, $3\frac{3}{8}$. (p. 103)

mode The number or numbers that occur the most often within a set of data. There may be more than one mode for a set of data. (p. 18)

multiple The product of a whole number and any other (nonzero) whole number. For example, 15 is a multiple of 5.

multiplication ($\cdot$) An operation that reflects repeated addition. For example, $3 \cdot 4 = 4 + 4 + 4$. (p. 44, 108)

Multiplicative Identity The Multiplicative Identity Property states that multiplying any expression by 1 leaves the expression unchanged. That is, $a(1) = a$. For example, $437x \cdot 1 = 437x$. (p. 39)

natural numbers The counting numbers beginning with 1. For example, 1, 2, 3….

negative correlation A relationship between two sets of variables in which one generally increases while the other decreases. (p. 355)

negative number A negative number is a number less than zero. Negative numbers are graphed on the negative side of a number line, which is to the left of the origin. (p. 83)

negative slope Lines are said to have negative slope if they slant downward from left to right. That is, as the x-values increases, the y-value decreases. (p. 433)

non-linear   A set of points that do not lie on a straight line when connected. (p. 631)

number line   A diagram representing all real numbers as points on a line. All real numbers are assigned to points. The numbers are called the coordinates of the points and the point for which the number 0 is assigned is called the origin. (Also see *boundary point*.) (p. 11)

numeral   A symbol that names a number. For example, each item of the following list is a numeral: 22.6, –19, 0.

numerator   The number above the bar in a fraction that tells the numbers of parts in relationship to the number of parts in the whole. (p. 37)

obtuse angle   Any angle that measures between (but not including) 90° and 180°. (p. 304)

obtuse triangle   A triangle with one obtuse angle. (p. 112)

octagon   A polygon with eight sides. (p. 595)

odd number   An integer that cannot be evenly divided by two. (p. 185)

operation   A mathematical process such as addition, subtraction, multiplication, division, raising to a power, or taking a root. (p. 130)

order of operations   The specific order in which certain operations are to be carried out to evaluate or simplify expressions: parentheses (or other grouping symbols), exponents (powers or roots), multiplication and division (from left to right), and addition and subtraction (from left to right). (p. 133)

ordered pair   Two numbers written in order as follows: (x, y). The primary use of ordered pairs in this course is to represent points in an xy-coordinate system. The first coordinate (x) represents the distance from the x-axis. The second coordinate (y) represents the distance from the y-axis. For example, the ordered pair $(3, 5)$ represents the point shown in bold at right. (p. 94)

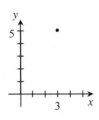

origin   The point on a coordinate plane where the x-axis and y-axis intersect is called the origin. This point has coordinates $(0, 0)$. The point assigned to zero on a number line is also called the origin. (See *axis*.) (p. 94)

outcome   Possible result in an experiment or consequence of an action. (p. 33, 650)

outlier   A number in a set of data that is much larger or much smaller than the other numbers in the set. (p. 13)

parallel   Two or more straight lines on a flat surface that do not intersect (no matter how far they are extended) are parallel. If two lines have the same slope and do not coincide, then they are parallel. For example, the graphs of $y = 2x + 3$ and $y = 2x - 2$ are parallel (see diagram at right). When two equations have parallel graphs, the equations have no solutions in common. (p. 119)

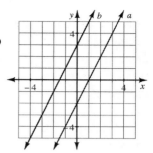

parallelogram   A quadrilateral with two pairs of parallel sides. (p. 119, 342)

pentagon   A polygon with five sides. (p. 595)

percent (%)   A ratio that compares a number to 100. Percents are often written using the "%" symbol. For example, 0.75 is equal to $\frac{75}{100}$ or 75%. (p. 22, 57)

perfect square   The product of an integer multiplied by itself gives a perfect square. For example, 1, 4, and 9 are perfect squares because $1 = 1 \cdot 1$, $4 = 2 \cdot 2$, and $9 = 3 \cdot 3$. (p. 543)

perimeter   The distance around a figure on a flat surface. (p. 10)

Perimeter =
$5 + 8 + 4 + 6 = 23$ units

perpendicular   Two rays, line segments, or lines that meet (intersect) to form a right angle (90°) are called perpendicular. A line and a flat surface may also be perpendicular if the line does not lie on the flat surface but intersects the surface and forms a right angle with every line on the flat surface passing through the point of intersection. A small square at the point of intersection of two lines or segments indicates that the lines form a right angle and are therefore perpendicular. (p. 119, 301)

perpendicular bisector   A line, ray, or segment that divides a segment into two congruent segments and is perpendicular to the segment. (p. 307)

pi (π)   The ratio of the circumference (C) of the circle to its diameter (d). For every circle, $\pi = \frac{\text{circumference}}{\text{diameter}} = \frac{C}{d}$. Numbers such as 3.14, 3.1416, or $\frac{22}{7}$ are approximations of π. (p. 313, 319)

place value   The number assigned to each place that a digit occupies. (p. 46)

plane.   A plane is a two-dimensional flat surface that extends without end. It is made up of points and has no thickness. (p. 660)

point   An exact location in space. In two dimensions, an ordered pair specifies a point on a coordinate plane. (See *ordered pair*.) (p. 94)

polygon A two-dimensional closed figure of three or more line segments (sides) connected end to end. Each segment is a side and only intersects the endpoints of its two adjacent sides. Each point of intersection is a vertex. At right are two examples of polygons. (p. 595)

polyhedron A three-dimensional figure with no holes for which all faces are polygons. (p. 595)

population A collection of objects or group of people about whom information is gathered.

portion A part of something; a part of a whole. (p. 22, 57)

portions web The web diagram at right illustrates that fractions, decimals, and percents are different ways to represent a portion of a number. Portions may also be represented in words, such as "four-fifths" or "seven-fourths," or as diagrams. (p. 57)

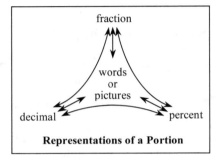

Representations of a Portion

positive correlation A relationship between two sets of variables in which one generally increases while the other also increases. (p. 355)

positive numbers Numbers that are greater than zero.

positive slope Lines are said to have positive slope if they slant upwards from left to right. That is, as the x-value increases, the y-value also increases. (p. 433)

power A number or variable raised to an exponent in the form x^n. (See *exponent*.) (p. 572)

prime factorization The expression of a number as the product of prime factors. (p. 45)

prime number A positive integer with exactly two factors. The only factors of a prime number are 1 and itself. For example, the numbers 2, 3, 17, and 31 are all prime. (p. 45)

prism A three-dimensional figure that consists of two parallel congruent polygons (called *bases*) and a vertical surface containing segments connecting each point on each side of one base to the corresponding point on the other base. The lateral surface of a prism consists of parallelograms. (p. 595)

probability   A number that represents how likely an event is to happen. When a event has a finite number of equally-likely outcomes, the probability that one of those outcomes, called A, will occur is expressed as a ratio and written as: $P(A) = \frac{\text{number of successful outcomes}}{\text{total number of possible outcomes}}$.
For example, when flipping a coin, the probability of getting tails, $P(\text{tails})$, is 1/2 because there is only one tail (successful outcome) out of the two possible equally likely outcomes (a head and a tail). Probability may be written as a ratio, decimal, or percent. A probability of 0 (or 0%) indicates that the occurrence of that outcome is impossible, while a probability of 1 (or 100%) indicates that the event must occur. Events that "might happen" will have values somewhere between 0 and 1 (or between 0% and 100%). (p. 27, 33, 650, 655)

product   The result of multiplying. For example, the product of 4 and 5 is 20. The product of $3a$ and $8b^2$ is $24ab^2$.

proportion   An equation stating that two ratios (fractions) are equal. For example, the equation at right is a proportion. A proportion is a useful type of equation to set up when solving problems involving proportional relationships. (p. 517)

$$\frac{68 \text{ votes for Mr. Mears}}{100 \text{ people surveyed}} = \frac{34 \text{ votes for Mr. Mears}}{50 \text{ people surveyed}}$$

proportional relationship   Two values are in a proportional relationship if a proportion may be set up that relates the values. (p. 512)

protractor   A geometric tool used for physically measuring the number of degrees in an angle. (p. 302)

pyramid   A polyhedron with a polygonal base formed by connecting each point of the base to a single given point (the apex) that is above or below the flat surface containing the base. Each triangular slant face of the pyramid is formed by the segments from the apex to the endpoints of a side of the base and the side itself. A tetrahedron is a special pyramid because any face may act as its base. (p. 614)

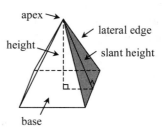

Pythagorean Theorem   The statement relating the lengths of the legs of a right triangle to the length of the hypotenuse: $(\text{leg \#1})^2 + (\text{leg \#2})^2 = \text{hypotenuse}^2$. The Pythagorean Theorem is powerful because if the lengths of any two sides of a right triangle are known, then this relationship may be used to find the length of the third side. (p. 541)

quadrants The coordinate plane is divided by its axes into four quadrants. The quadrants are numbered as shown in the first diagram at right. When graphing data that has no negative values, sometimes a graph that shows only the first quadrant is used. (p. 93)

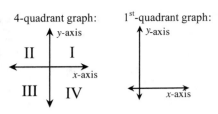

quadrilateral A polygon with four sides. The shape at right is a quadrilateral. (p. 342, 595)

quartile Along with the median, the quartiles divide a set of data into four groups of the same size. (p. 226)

quotient The result of a division problem.

radius (plural: radii) Of a circle: The line segment drawn from the center of a circle to a point on the circle. Of a regular polygon: A line segment that connects the center of a regular polygon with a vertex. The length of a radius is usually denoted r. (p. 309)

random sample A sample in which each item in the population or sample space has an equal chance of being selected.

range The range of a set of data is the difference between the highest and lowest values. (p. 211)

rate A ratio comparing two quantities, often a comparison of time. For example, miles per hour. (p. 420, 433, 459)

ratio A ratio compares two quantities by division. A ratio may be written using a colon, but is more often written as a fraction. For example, the comparison may be made of the ratio of female students in a particular school to the total number of students in the school. This ratio could be written as 1521:2906 or as the fraction shown at right. (p. 205, 250)

$$\frac{1521 \text{ female students}}{2906 \text{ total students}}$$

ratio of similarity The ratio of any pair of corresponding sides of two similar figures. This means that once it is determined that two figures are similar, all of the pairs of corresponding sides of the figures have the same ratio. For example, for the similar triangles $\triangle ABC$ and $\triangle DEF$ at right, the ratio of similarity is $\frac{5}{11}$. The ratio of similarity may also be called the linear scale factor. (p. 250)

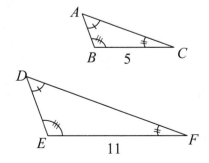

rational number   Numbers that may be expressed in the form $\frac{a}{b}$, where a and b are integers and $b \neq 0$.   For example, 0.75 is a rational number because 0.75 may be expressed in the form $\frac{3}{4}$. (p. 545)

ray   A ray is part of a line that starts at one point and extends without end in one direction.   In the example at right, ray $\overrightarrow{AB}$ is part of line $\overleftrightarrow{AB}$ that starts at A and contains all of the points of $\overrightarrow{AB}$ that are on the same side of A as point B, including A.   Point A is the endpoint of $\overrightarrow{AB}$. (p. 304)

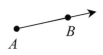

real numbers   Irrational numbers together with rational numbers form the set of the real numbers.   For example, the following are all real numbers: $2.78, -13267, 0, \frac{3}{7}, \pi, \sqrt{2}$.   All real numbers are represented on the number line.

reciprocals   The reciprocal of a nonzero number is its multiplicative inverse, that is, the reciprocal of x is $\frac{1}{x}$.   For a number in the form $\frac{a}{b}$, where a and b are non-zero, the reciprocal is $\frac{b}{a}$.   The product of a number and its reciprocal is 1.   For example, the reciprocal of 12 is $\frac{1}{12}$, because $12 \cdot \frac{1}{12} = 1$.

recompose   If a geometric figure is broken up into pieces and the pieces are put back together, possibly in a new way, then the figure is recomposed.   Similarly, if two or more numbers have been written as sums or differences in an expression and these numbers are put back together into sums or differences, then the expression is recomposed.   (Also see *decompose*.) (p. 123)

rectangle   A quadrilateral with four right angles. (p. 10, 342)

reduce   To put a fraction into simplest form. (p. 243)

reflection   A transformation across a line that produces a mirror image of the original (pre-image) shape.   The reflection is called the "image" of the original figure.   The line is called a "line of reflection."   Note that a reflection is also sometimes referred to as a "flip."   See the example at right above. (p. 99)

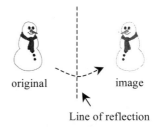

original   image

Line of reflection

regular polygon   A polygon is regular if the polygon is a convex polygon with congruent angles and congruent sides.   For example, the shape at right is a regular hexagon. (p. 94)

REGULAR HEXAGON

repeating decimal   A repeating decimal is a decimal that repeats the same sequence of digits forever from some point onward.   For example, 4.56073073073... is a decimal for which the three digits 073 continue to repeat forever.   Repeating decimals are always the decimal expansions of rational numbers. (p. 21)

representative sample   A subset (group) of a given population with the same characteristics as the whole population.

rhombus   A quadrilateral with four congruent sides. (Also see *equilateral*.) (p. 342)

right angle   An angle that measures 90°. A small square is used to note a right angle, as shown in the example at right. (p. 304)

right triangle   A triangle that has one right angle. The side of a right triangle opposite the right angle is called the "hypotenuse," and the two sides adjacent to the right angle are called "legs." (See *Pythagorean Theorem* for a diagram.) (p. 451)

rigid transformations   Movements of figures that preserve the shape and size of the figures. (p. 99)

root fraction   The member of a family of fractions with the smallest integer values, the most simplified form. For the fraction family $\frac{2}{3}, \frac{4}{6}, \frac{6}{9}$, etc., $\frac{2}{3}$ is the root fraction. (p. 243)

rotation   A transformation that rotates (or turns) all of the points in the original (pre-image) figure the same number of degrees around a fixed center point (such as the origin on a graph). The result is called the "image" of the original figure. The point that the shape is rotated about is called the "center of rotation." To define a rotation, the measure of turn (in degrees) must be stated, the direction in which the shape is turned (such as clockwise or counter-clockwise), and the center of rotation. See the example at right. Note that a rotation is also sometimes referred to as a "turn." (p. 99)

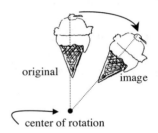

scale (scaling)   The ratio between a length of the representation (such as a map, model, or diagram) and the corresponding length of the actual object. For example, the map of a city may use one inch to represent one mile. (p. 250, 468)

scale factor   A ratio that compares the sizes of the parts of one figure or object to the sizes of the corresponding parts of a similar figure or object. (p. 250, 468)

scalene triangle   A triangle with no congruent sides. (p. 177)

scatterplot   Two related sets of data may have the corresponding values of the sets listed as ordered pairs. If these ordered pairs are graphed in the coordinate plane, then the result is a scatterplot. (Also see *negative correlation* and *positive correlation*.) (p. 346, 355)

scientific notation   A number is expressed in scientific notation when the number is in the form $a \times 10^n$, where $1 \le a < 10$ and n is an integer. For example, the number 31,000 may be expressed in scientific notation as 3.1×10^4. (p. 587)

Making Connections

sector   A region formed by two radii of a central angle and the arc
between the endpoints of the radii on the circle. The shaded portion of
the drawing at right is a sector. (p. 347, 460)

sector

semi-circle   In a circle, a semicircle is an arc with endpoints that are
endpoints of any diameter of the circle. A semi-circle is a half circle and has
a measure of 180°.

set   A collection of items.

similar figures   Similar figures have the same shape but are not
necessarily the same size. For example the two triangles at right
are similar. In similar figures, the measures of corresponding
angles are equal and the lengths of corresponding sides are
proportional. (p. 235)

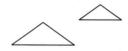

simple interest   Interest that is paid only on the principal (the amount originally
invested). Simple interest (I) is found by multiplying the principal (P), the rate (r), and the
amount of time (t): $I = Prt$. (p. 491)

simplest form of a fraction   A fraction for which the numerator and the denominator
have no common factor greater than one. (p. 243)

simplify   To simplify an expression is to write a less complicated expression with the
same value. A simplified expression has no parentheses and no like terms. For example,
the expression $3-(2x+7)-4x$ may be simplified to $-4-6x$. When working with algebra
tiles, a simplified expression uses the fewest possible tiles to represent the original
expression. (p. 273)

skew lines   Lines that do not lie in the same flat surface. (p. 660)

slope   A ratio that describes how steep (or flat) a line is.
Slope may be positive, negative, or even zero, but a straight
line has only one slope. Slope is the ratio $\frac{\text{vertical change}}{\text{horizontal change}}$ or
$\frac{\text{change in } y\text{-value}}{\text{change in } x\text{-value}}$, sometimes written $\frac{\Delta y}{\Delta x}$. When the equation of
a line is written in $y = mx + b$ form, m is the slope of the
line. A line has positive slope if the line slopes upward from
left to right on a graph, negative slope if the line slopes
downward from left to right, zero slope if the line is
horizontal, and undefined slope if the line is vertical.
Parallel lines have equal slopes, and the slopes of
perpendicular lines are opposite reciprocals of each other
(e.g., $\frac{3}{5}$ and $-\frac{5}{3}$). (p. 433)

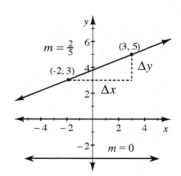

solution The number or numbers that when substituted into an equation or inequality make the equation or inequality true. For example, $x = 4$ is a solution to the equation $3x - 2 = 10$ because $3x - 2$ equals 10 when $x = 4$. A solution to a two-variable equation is sometimes written as an ordered pair (x, y). For example, $x = 3$ and $y = -2$ is a solution to the equation $y = x - 5$. This solution may be written as $(3, -2)$. (p. 379, 391, 441)

square A quadrilateral with four right angles and four congruent sides. (p. 342)

square

square measure The units used to describe the measure of an area in the form of 1×1 unit squares. (p. 10)

square number The numbers in the pattern 1, 4, 9, 16, 25, …. That is, the squares of the counting numbers 1, 2, 3, 4, 5, … are known as square numbers. (p. 543)

square root ($\sqrt{\ }$) A number a is the square root of b if $a^2 = b$ and $a \geq 0$. The square root of 9 ($\sqrt{9}$) is 3. A negative number has no real square root, a non-negative number has just one square root. (p. 543)

stem-and-leaf plot A frequency distribution that arranges data so that all digits except the last digit in each piece of data are in the stem, the last digit of each piece of data are the leaves, and both stems and leaves are arranged in order from least to greatest. The example at right displays the data: 49, 52, 54, 58, 61, 61, 67, 68, 72, 73, 73, 73, 78, 82, 83, 108, 112, and 117. (p. 213)

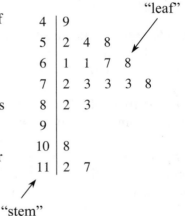

"leaf"

4	9
5	2 4 8
6	1 1 7 8
7	2 3 3 3 8
8	2 3
9	
10	8
11	2 7

"stem"

straight angle An angle that measures 180°. This occurs when the rays of the angle point in opposite directions, forming a line. (p. 304)

180°

subproblems A problem solving strategy that breaks a problem into smaller parts that must be solved in order to solve the original, more complex problem.

substitution Replacing one symbol with a number, a variable, or another algebraic expression of the same value. Substitution does not change the value of the overall expression. For example, suppose that the expression $13x - 6$ must be evaluated for $x = 4$. Since x has the value 4, 4 may be substituted into the expression wherever x appears, giving the equivalent expression $13(4) - 6$. (p. 130, 273)

subtraction (−) An operation that gives the difference between two numbers. (p. 90)

sum The result of adding two or more numbers. For example, the sum of 4 and 5 is 9. (p. 90)

Making Connections

supplementary angles Two angles A and B for which $A + B = 180°$. Each angle is called the supplement of the other. In the example at right, angles A and B are supplementary. Supplementary angles are often adjacent. For example, since $\angle LMN$ is a straight angle, then $\angle LMP$ and $\angle PMN$ are supplementary angles because $m\angle LMP + m\angle PMN = 180°$. (p. 313)

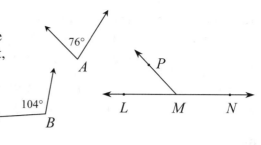

surface area The sum of all the area(s) of the surface(s) of a three-dimensional solid. For example, the surface area of a prism is the sum of the areas of its top and bottom bases, and its vertical surfaces (lateral faces). (p. 592, 599, 617)

term A term is a single number, variable, or the product of numbers and variables, such as –45, 1.2x, and 3xy^2. (p. 133, 273)

terminating decimal A terminating decimal is a decimal that has only a finite number of non-zero digits, such as 4.067. Terminating decimals are a particular kind of repeating decimal for which the repeating portion is zeros, so the example could be written 4.0670000000… but it is not necessary to write the zeros at the end. (p. 53)

tetrahedron A polyhedron with four faces.

theoretical probability A calculated probability based on the possible outcomes when each outcome has the same chance of occurring: (number of successful outcomes)/(total number of possible outcomes). (p. 33)

tick mark A symbol that shows that a number line has been divided into intervals of equal length. (See *number line*.)

translation A transformation that preserves the size, shape, and orientation of a figure while sliding (moving) it to a new location. The result is called the "image" of the original figure (pre-image). See the example at right. Note that a translation is sometimes referred to as a "slide." (p. 99)

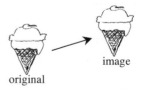

image

original

trapezoid A quadrilateral with at least one pair of parallel sides. (p. 125)

triangle A polygon with three sides. (p. 595)

unit of measure   A standard quantity (such as a centimeter, second, square foot, or gallon) that is used to measure and describe an object. A single object may be measured using different units of measure. For example, a pencil may be 80 mm long, meaning that the pencil is 80 times as long as a unit of 1 mm. However, the same pencil is 8 cm long, so that the pencil is the same length as 8 cm laid end-to-end. This is because 1 cm is the same length as 10 mm. (p. 10, 84, 464)

unit price   The cost of one item or one measure of an item. For example, cost for one pound or one gallon.

unit rate   A rate with a denominator of one when simplified. (p. 420)

units digit   The numeral in the ones place.

upper quartile   The median of the upper half of an ordered set of data. (p. 226)

variable   A symbol used to represent one or more numbers. In this course, letters of the English alphabet are used as variables. For example, in the expression $3x - (8.6xy + z)$, the variables are x, y, and z. (p. 156, 384)

Venn diagram   A type of diagram used to classify objects that is usually composed of two or more overlapping circles representing different conditions. An item is placed or represented in the Venn diagram in the appropriate position based on the conditions that the item meets. In the example of the Venn diagram at right, if an object meets one of two conditions, then the object is placed in region A or C but outside region B. If an object meets both conditions, then the object is placed in the intersection (B) of both circles. If an object does not meet either condition, then the object is placed outside of both circles (region D).

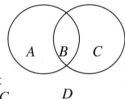

vertex (plural: vertices)   (a) For polygon, a vertex is the point at which two line segments meet to form a "corner." (See *regular polygon*.) (b) For an angle, the common endpoint of the defining rays. (See *vertical angles*.) (c) For a three-dimensional polyhedron, a vertex is a point where the edges of the solid meet. (See *edge*.) (p. 93, 595)

vertical   At right angles to the horizon. In a coordinate grid, the y-axis runs vertically. (p. 93, 94)

vertical angles   The two opposite (that is, non-adjacent) angles formed by two intersecting lines. "Vertical" is a relationship between pairs of angles, so one angle cannot be called vertical. Angles that form a vertical pair are always congruent.

volume   A measurement of the size of the three-dimensional region enclosed within an object. Volume is expressed as the number of $1 \times 1 \times 1$ unit cubes (or parts of cubes) that fit inside a solid. (p. 593, 603)

x-axis   The horizontal number line on a coordinate grid. (See *axis*.) (p. 94)

x-coordinate   In an ordered pair, (x, y), that represents a point in the coordinate plane, x is the value of the x-coordinate of the point. That is, the distance from the x-axis that is needed to plot the point. (p. 94)

x-intercept   The point(s) where a graph intersects the x-axis. A graph may have several x-intercepts, no x-intercepts, or just one. An x-intercept may be written as an ordered pair $(x, 0)$ or as a single number. For example, in the graph below for "y-intercept," the x-intercept may be written as $(-2, 0)$ or simply -2. (See *y-intercept*.) (p. 358, 359)

y-axis   The vertical number line on a coordinate grid. (See *axis*.) (p. 94)

y-coordinate   In an ordered pair, (x, y), that represents a point in the coordinate plane, y is the value of the y-coordinate of the point. That is, the distance from the y-axis that is needed to plot the point. (p. 94)

y-intercept   The point(s) where a graph intersects the y-axis. A function has at most one y-intercept while a relation may have several. The y-intercept of a graph is important because the y-intercept often represents the starting value of a quantity in a real-world situation. A y-intercept may be written as an ordered pair $(0, y)$ or as a single number. For example, it may be said that that the y-intercept of the graph at right is $(0, 2)$, or it may also be said that the y-intercept is 2. When a linear equation is written in $y = mx + b$ form, b is the y-intercept of the graph. For example, the equation of the graph at right is $y = x + 2$ and its y-intercept is 2. (p. 358, 359)

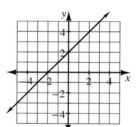

Index
Student Version

Many of the pages referenced here contain a definition or an example of the topic listed, often within the body of a Math Notes box. Others contain problems that develop or demonstrate the topic. It may be necessary to read the text on several pages to fully understand the topic. Also, some problems listed here are good examples of the topic and may not offer any explanation. The page numbers below reflect the pages in the Student Version. References to Math Notes boxes are bolded.

Making Connections: Course 2